WHITFIELD RECORDS

OF

UNITED STATES

1620 - 1995

Compiled by

VALLIE JO WHITFIELD

WHITFIELD RECORDS OF UNITED STATES

Copyright ©, Vallie Jo Whitfield, 1998

REFERENCE BOOK

WHITFIELD . WHITEFIELD . SURNAMES .

Assistance by many people

International Standard Book Number 0-930920-20-1

Library of Congress Catalog Card Number

Printed in the United States of America

Database on ISBN Numbers has addresses for book vendors.

Cast forth that faith forever for
the Lord almighty, the creator of
race of men and women who fall
successive, and must successive
rise; so generations are left in
the course of time.

Local history is the best history,
the history with more of ourselves
in it than other kinds. It is by
definition recent. It does not
have to be split up into categories
and kinds, economic, political,
military, social. It is the record
of human living in its daily
complexity, and the sense of place
is strong in it. Its actors are
our neighbors, our families,
ourselves. It is a history of a
handmade kind, homely and familiar,
human lives on their slow way into
memory and the tradition.

WHITFIELD

AND

WHITEFIELD

CONTENTS

CONTENTS

COLLECTIVES

CONTENTS

IX

CONTENTS

XI

CONTENTS

CONTENTS

XV

CONTENTS

APPENDIX

ILLUSTRATIONS

PARISH OF WHITFIELD
Northumberland, England

It was long ago that the Minister Robert Whitfield began in Scotland and received Whitefield land.

Province boundaries changed and the Parish began at Hexham, England.

During the Norman period of England, Whitfield belonged to the Saxon earls of Northumbia, England. one of the earls was called Waltheof or Siward, and was created Earl of Huntington and Northampton. His daughter was Natilda who was called Maud, and she married King David I of Scotland. Whitfield was listed among the possessions she brought to her husband prince ("Earl") Henry, their son married the Countess Ada by whom he had two sons who eventually succeeded to the Scottish throne, Malcolm III, 1153-1165, and William the Lion, 1165-1214.

Beginning of the Parish of Whitfield

Countess Ada resided at Eads Hall, which in 1550, stood near Ding Bell Bridge, a stone's throw from the old church. There is for certainty documentary evidence that Whitfield belonged to her and that with her sons' consent, she gave half of Whitfield to Robert, her chaplain, for "one soar hawk" and half to the ancient abbey of hexham for "a pound of pepper." In turn the Prior and canons, with her consent and that of her sons, leased their share, except for some six acres, to Robert, the chaplain's son, Matthew, for two hundred years, at a rent of one silver mark. The documents cover the years 1165-1174 in England.

The Parish Under the Whitfields

The reign of Henry II of England and Edward VI provided changes to authority of religious bishops and the crown favored the Anglican Church. This had an effect in England and later colonies in America. For six hundred years the Whitfields ruled there. There were warring groups in the area and center section formed the defensive system. 1453 to 1520 there was need for protection and security. In the outcome Oliver Cromwell made the property over outright in 1655 to Sir Matthew Whitfield and his successors appear to have been known as the Yearls or Earls of Whitfield until 1750. This property was brought 1750 by William Ord of Fenham, Newcastle upon the Tyne.

References: 1. Parish of Whitfield by A.F. Donnelly, publ. 1960.

2. History of Northumberland by John Hodgson. 3. Black Book of Hexham, pub., 1479.

The Old Parish Church

St. John's Church and churchyard lie between the road to Haltwhistle and the once seventy cottages there at "Town Green" and old Town farm. It is believed to be that St. John Church could be on the original church 1550. A guide published gives the details on the architecture of the building which was built before 1782 and other details beneath a hillock called "Chapel Hill" in the Hall grounds. The exact date is unknown.

The Church dedication to St. John seems to have originated at the time of the first rector, Robert de Quitfield. The Church building was of stone consisting of a nave forty-six feet long, lighted by three square-headed windows in the south wall and a chancel twenty feet in length with two small pointed windows in its south wall. Both were seventeen feet wide. Above the west wall was a bell turret. The Church had remodeling in 1782. St. John was a good, simple building and accommodated 230 persons.

The Parish Under the Ords

The old estate had fallen into disrepair. The Ords made demolition of old farms, cottages, buildings and adopted a policy of improvements of rebuilding and enlarging the remaining farms. Coal mines in Coanwood were added to the estate. The Hexham - Alston turnpike was built in 1778 and improved in 1824.

The present Trinity Church was the gift of Rev. and Mrs. Blackett-Ords in memory of wife's uncle who made her the heir of the whole estate.

TRINITY CHURCH
built in 1860.

WHITFIELD ST. JAMES
CHURCH
as it was about 1782
to 1860.
======
WHITFIELD HALL
WHITFIELD HEXHAM
NORTHUMBERLAND
John Blackett-Ord,
Owner

The building was dedicated Trinity Church. Stones from the old demolished tower and bays of the old church were kept. The new stone was quarried locally from Dyke Row and Morley Hill.

Once the Parish was established with families there were 220 people who were members of the church. After many years the local population increased and the diocese divisions became two. The first Bishop of Newcastle, the Right Reverend Ernest R. Witherforce, visited the church in 1883. The late J.R. Blackett-Ord, Esquire, patron of the living, was rector's warden from 1906 to a year before his death in 1967 - in that time he had known seven diocesan bishops and nine rectors. The Church of the Holy Cross, Fenham, was his benefaction to the diocese in 1936.

Time with the rotation of the earth, its light and darkness, and people of generations bring change. The Trinity Church has a commemorative plaque which speaks of it as the Church of the Divine Trinity of Father, Son and Holy Spirit. This has inspired memorials which have been added in the church. These include several windows and organ in 1865, a new organ in 1895, the brass Lectern in 1884, the fine reredos for the east window in 1891, the Tower Clock for Queen Victoria Jubilee in 1899, the pulpit and priest stall in 1934, the children's corner in 1943, the board with the list of rectors, new lighting installation and the provision and furnishing of the sanctuary at the nave crossing in 1971, the font canopy. All the memorials have modernized the interior of the church with its stone walls.

PARSONAGE OR RECTORY

A lasting Church building and Parish must have a pastor and religious leader. Along with this the building of the living person with this work is called a Parsonage or Rectory.

XXIII

The first reference to a parsonage is in 1332, when Robert Whitfield, owner of the Manor of Whitfield, obtained a license, "to give to Thomas de Whitfield, parson of the Church of Whitfield, and to his successors, a message and thirty-one acres of land in this parish, to maintain a chapel to do divine services every day, for his soul and the soul of his ancestors, in the church there."

In the beginning it was a two-story building, the lower part providing accommodation for cattle, while outside steps led to the dwelling quarters above. This is how a few people and the religious man live. This is one of the buildings remolded in 1765.

The stipend in 1825 for a religious man maintaining the church and saving souls were f 200 a year, with the house, garden, and churchyard, all the taxes paid and repairs of every kind kept up. A place of forty acres, all in grass, and sloping down prettily in front of the house was the landscaping. Rev. Anthony Hedley, fathered the "parochial school." He improved the highways of the Parish. Whitfieldee School is a new building.

Just after Canon Mason came the house was enlarged again, and it was reduced to many rooms which was manageable proportions for servants of the house and church and yards with planted gardens for the Mansion. By 1990 there were twelve servants needed to care for the buildings and gardens of manageable landscaping knowledge and applied to the yards. The Mansion and beautiful gardens are constantly cared for and maintained.

The Parsonage or Rectory is a mansion building. Antic frontier high stone walls provide security and protection from outsiders and any invading enemies. The enclosed structures make it a compound of people, houses and community.

FORWARD

I began writing for the public in 1960. Robert Edward Whitfield (b. 1922-d. 1990) provided encouragement, and presented <u>The Writer's Handbook</u> to me suggesting I practice writing for a skill.

This resulted in two years of freelance writing of short stories and articles. In 1962 I moved to book length writing and published in 1964 the book <u>Whitfield History and Genealogy of Tennessee</u>. The book had a second edition in 1979.

I began publishing books in the Whitfield Books business at Pleasant Hill, California, which is 30 miles northeast of San Francisco. Eventually I qualified as a publisher and joined an editors and publishers association.

I gathered much family history and state history. I confined the genealogies to the surname as many surnames are linked by marriages to the American Whitfields who came to colonial Virginia and the colonies along the Atlantic coast.

Readers of the books grew, and many letters flowed to Whitfield Books. There were inquiries for family trees and ancestral roots, and requests for information, usually on a woman named Whitfield who had married into other families. Surnames grew from many other names.

There were many letter writers who sent their family sketch on roots, and some offered more history about the Whitfields and sent census records they had researched. Some wanted a publishing office to know their family history. There were many who kindly offered records on the surname Whitfield. There were professional people checking what Vallie Jo Whitfield had written as historical facts; and they found some prints from old newspapers and sent along the information. From the letters, notes, papers of collective works and the thirty years of genealogical and historical work and research of the author, this book was made to pass along to all people. It is a collective work of many people. It is the last book written by the author. It has taken thirty years to gather this information.

Acknowledgments of private records used give names and states. All of these records are printed as received. If there is any discrepancy in materials or varied spellings, the reader will draw their own conclusion. The maker of this volume has no responsibility for the individual or family histories but all sources came from reliable individuals who are referenced here within.

If merit be worthy of note or selfless devotion deserves remembrances, then may this reference book claim "justification" in that it records the lives of countless men and women. They are worthy of remembrance.

                                        Vallie Jo Whitfield

WHITFIELD HEADS OF FAMILIES IN 1985

Initial	State	Count	Initial	State	Count
AL	Alabama	340	OH	Ohio	223
AK	Alaska	2	OK	Oklahoma	118
AZ	Arizona	31	OR	Oregon	29
AR	Arkansas	159	PA	Pennsylvania	166
CA	California	476	RI	Rhode Island	11
CO	Colorado	64	SC	South Carolina	276
CT	Connecticut	29	SD	South Dakota	0
DE	Delaware	11	TN	Tennessee	243
FL	Florida	503	TX	Texas	714
GA	Georgia	465	UT	Utah	10
HI	Hawaii	4	VT	Vermont	0
ID	Idaho	6	VA	Virginia	197
IL	Illinois	284	WA	Washington	59
IN	Indiana	126	WV	West Virginia	9
IA	Iowa	25	WI	Wisconsin	22
KS	Kansas	43	WY	Wyoming	8
KY	Kentucky	135			
LA	Louisiana	197			
ME	Maine	1		TOTAL WHITFIELD FAMILIES 7,025	
MD	Maryland	70			
MA	Massachusetts	43			
MI	Michigan	296			
MN	Minnesota	21			
MS	Mississippi	229			
MO	Missouri	187			
Mt	Montana	5			
NE	Nebraska	20			
NV	Nevada	7			
NH	New Hampshire	10			
NJ	New Jersey	83			
NM	New Mexico	26			
NY	New York	253			
NC	North Carolina	719			
N D	North Dakota	2			

International Business Machine Company had the Computer Project with the surname Whitfield first in 1980 and found the Total Whitfield Families to be 6,680.

There have been four computer print-outs on surname Whitfield.

Washington District of Columbia had sixty-seven Whitfield heads of families in 1985.

Whitfield and Whitefield residents 1722 to 1825 of South Carolina had 170 persons named by Vallie Jo Whitfield and five were WHITEFIELDS. Sixty-six heads of household or first individual to SC. Ninety-one Whitfield names. Children's names unknown on SC Census 24. Others' spouses unknown. Whitfields lived in 14 SC Counties, 2 Districts, 1 Island.

ABBEVILLE	COLLETON	MARION
Anderson	CRAVEN	Maralborough
BEAUFORT	GEORGETOWN	Ninety-Six District
BERKELEY	GRANVILLE	Pendleton District
CHARLESTON	JOHN'S ISLAND	Williamsburgh
CLARENDON	LAURENS	

Genealogy is the whole descent of families.
Lineage is the heritage descent of person or one family.
Family Group is a single family with parents and children.
Family Tree is children, parents, grandparents, uncles, aunts, and brothers, sisters and cousins.

Example for descent, generation, person, family group of a genealogical lineage. Member in a genealogy.

Number System: Number (469) number given person in line of descent from first known ancestor in Colonies and United States.

Name: Emma Morehead Whitfield

Line of Descent:

Father	Grandfather	Great Grandfather	G. G. Grandfather	G.G.G. Grandfather
(Theodore,	Benjamin,	William,	William,	William)
G5	G4	G3	G2	G1

Line of Generation: Begin with the first and downward in numbering the generation.

G for Generation.   G6 denotes the generation for Emma Morehead Whitfield.

Parent and children have different numbers. List of a parent children will have a child number which is carried forward to find that person and the family group.

Genealogy is the whole descent of families.

Lineage is the heritage descent of person or one family.

Family Group is a single family, parents, and children.

First Whitfield Men To America

There were the first English ships to Barbados and to the West Indies and these places were island lands. Barbados Island became a colony. This island has a history on the Whitfield families and a historic cemetery of the early settlers there.

Three records of Whitfields found that left Barbados and came to the Virginia Colony. Records of two white men and one black man. There were only eight men that likely came to Virginia. There are only names and no records.

White families did not stay at Barbados 100 years later. The African-American men and women populated the Barbados land and lived and worked on plantations.

ABBREVIATIONS SYMBOLS WITH WORD MEANINGS			
# - Number	$ - Money	& - and	* - mark of asterisk
= married	(1) first	(2) second	(numbers) - references

ABBREVIATIONS

A.B. - Bachelor of Arts. A degree given by a University or college to person who has completed a four-year course.
Adj. - Adjoining
Ala. - Alabama
Amt. - Amount
ARK. - Arkansas
At. - Amount
B. - Black
b. - born
Bapt. - Baptist
bk. - book
bro. - brother
bt. - bought
Brig. - Army Depot Brig.
c - copy or copied
ca. - Circa
CAI Cataloging Alphabetical Index
Calif. - California
capt. - captain
cem. - cemetery
cert. - certified
Co. - County
Col. - Colonel
ct. - Court
C S A - Civil Service Army
C.W. - Wentworth
D. - "dated" when Will was written
d. - died
D.A.R. - Daughters of American Revolution
dau. - daughter
D.C. - District of Columbus
dec. - deceased
Dr. - Doctor

D.V.C. - Diablo Valley College
Edge. - Edgecombe Co.
etc. - etcetera
f - female
F - farming
Fla. - Florida
G. or g. - great
3 g/f - Great-great-great grandfather
gen - General
gnd - grand
gr - grandson or granddaughter
Ill. - Illinois
Inf. - Infantry of Army
Jr. - Junior
Kty - Kentucky
L. - Location
Leg. - Legal
Ltrs - Letters
M. or m. - Married
Ma. - Married
md. - Married
M.D. - Medical Doctor
Mass. - Massachusetts
Miss. - Mississippi
Money - Shillings: equal to 5 pennies. Pound: equal to 20 shillings or 100 pennies. British.
Mr. - Mister
Mrs. - Mistress. A title used before name of married woman.
Mt. - Mountain
n.a. - passenger from vehicle. New arrival
N.C. - North Carolina

N.E.S.W. - North, East, South, West.
No. - number
p. - page
p.p. - pages
q.v. - Question. Query on print of Virkus publication print.
R. - Recorded after probate in a court
Rev. - Reverend
Rev. - Revolution
res. - resident
riv. - river
S - Ship
S.C. - South Carolina
SCMAR - South Carolina Magazine of Ancestral Research
sec. - section
Sgt. - Sergeant in Army
sis - sister
So. - South
Sr - Senior
St. - Saint
Tenn. - Tennessee
T.N. - U.C. of M.C. - Union Catalog of Manuscript Collection. Library of Congress.
Th.D. - Doctor of Theological Degree
twp. or T.-township
twns - townships
unmd - unmarried
U.S.A. - United States of America
Vol. - volume
W - white
Wm - William

South Carolina records

References:
1. Heitman Year Book. Roster of Soldiers, 1782. Provincial Troops.
2. Heitman Year Book. Revolution Provincial Soldiers, published 1897.
3. Historical Register of Officers of Continental Army During the War of the Revolution, April 1773 to December 1783.

IN THE BEGINNING

According to the Bible, God created the earth and all the things. God allowed the creation of a man and then a woman many centuries ago. The first names of Adam and Eve appear with a family. The Bible is the source for the early genealogy known that produced a Savior named Jesus Christ. This sets our calendar with terms of BC-before Christ and AD-after the death of Christ. (1)

However, in the beginning the earth was quiet and the animals lived. Two million years ago the earth's oceans and land areas had assumed a form. Large animals existed, and mammals were the most successful class of animals on earth. Among the animals there evolved a number of early forms of man, or "hominids."

Upright man of the Stone Age lived about half a million years ago and was widely distributed in Asia, Europe, and Africa. As long as 200,000 years this upright species replaced previous forms of man in various parts of the "globe."

PEOPLING THE GLOBE

For the last 30,000 years or so, Homosapiens have been the form of man on earth. It was probably during the last 20,000 or 30,000 years that mankind became divided into the four separate racial groups known today. The three main groups are the Caucasoids, Europeans and their descendants in former colonies, and the Indians. The Whitfield were natives of Europe. The Mongoloids were the Asians and America Indians. The Negroids. From this group comes the word Negro. The fourth group were old stock and the australoids Aborigines. (2)

The Asian groups moved across the Bering Strait, then a land bridge joining Asia to America 30,000 years ago. God allowed white, black, brown colors of skin and physical characteristics which held human genetic factors. God allowed many tongues and brought this on the mankind. The Bible is source for the many languages and what happened in history as to languages.

Studies indicate that ninety-five percent of all North and South American Indians descended from a small bank of hardy pioneers that included mostly men and only a few women. Their descendants spread out to become tribes as disparate as the Algonquins of the United States Northeast, the Maya of Central America and the Ticuna of South America. They shared common ancestors of Asia thousands of years ago.

It was the main tribe's scattered people forming on lands that brought six hundred extant Native American languages. Scientific scholars often ask, *Was there a single migration that accounts for the majority of American Indians?* The answer is clearly yes. These people were diggers and food gatherers for the earth's foods, on both land and water.

Virtually all researchers agree that Native Americans are descendants of Asians who migrated from what is now the Soviet Union to Alaska. The land bridge was strong long ago but the continents were formed and they had land movements. This bridge was Asia and Alaska land.

It is and was a travel of cold and frozen ice and one that few human beings have survived on.

There is a general agreement that two other waves of migration occurred relatively recently - 6,000 to 4,000 years ago. These waves brought the Native Americas who speak two language groups known as Nadene, spoken mainly by natives of Northwestern Canada, but also by the Apache and Navajo nations, and Eskimo-Aleut, spoken mainly by residents of Alaska and the northern rim of Canada.

Indians with 12,000 years of descendants on the land of North America did much settlement, and they were the first to help with the development of the southern portion of North America. They made the first colonies in America.

Early Caucasoids traveled in different directions. They were among the first men and families and in the desert in the area near the Black Sea which ran into the Mediterranean Sea. White people were members of the Mediterranean sea area coastal lands and became the Mediterranean division of the Caucasian race. They spread into northern Europe. It was in the northern land area that the name Whitfield first appears.

Early Negroids were sent into a direction, and they had a different direction. The Bible has the story of how this race began. The Bible does not define the languages and explain, but it tells the story of why there became many tongues.

It is the European Spaniards and their discovery of the earth being round and the ship travels of the early 1400's that the exploration of the earth's lands really began. In a short period of time migrations took place among people using ships on the waters of the earth.

The countries of Spain, Great Britain, France took an interest in North America, and the citizens of these countries brought the first settlers to America in the 1600's who were successful in making settlements in colonies. Among the settlers were several with the surname coming from Europe. The origin of the surname began about 1154 in Scotland. After a period of time the Whitfield families are in Northumberland, England. So begins the story of Whitfield in the 1200 century in Europe. At first it is seen Witefeld, then Whitfield. A Countess of Scotland grants land of Witefeld to Robert, a church chaplain and he is Robert Whitfield. Then seen later are Whitfield and in England varied spellings of the name by people who were beginning to write their names. These are also people of Whitfield origin. In America only Whitfield and very few are named Whitefield.

_____
References.
(1) Bible. Old Testament. King James Version.
(2) The Last Two Million Years. Pages 15-21. Book edited and designed by the Reader's Digest Association, London, England. Published 1973.
(3) Newspaper Article Study Traces Most Indians to Four Maternal Ancestors, by Thomas H. Maugh, II, Los Angeles Times, 1990. Reprint, Contra Costa Times, July 28, 1990, page 12D.

WHITFIELD

The history of a nation with the actions of its people and the kind of activities has a record of advancement or retrogression. In this people take pride as being part of history which their ancestors, although unknown have contributed.

There is a beginning with far-distant progenitors. So the story of Whitfield goes. So begins the family of Whitfield now being told. Scotland was independent and frequently at war with England. This country had wars starting with the Holy Crusades in the tenth century. Despite the enmity between England and Scotland kingdoms there was a marriage of David I, King of Scotland and Maud (1), heiress of the Earl Waltheof, Sr. David was King of Scotland from 1124 to 1153.

By the marriage of Maud a large part of England proper, being the northern half of Bernicia, became the inheritance of the kings of Scotland. Included I this portion of Bernicia was the ancient franchise of Tindale, the western part of the present County of Northumberland. This franchise contained the parish of Whitfield of some 12,157 acres or nearly twenty square miles.

David and Maud's son, Henry, Earl of Huntingdon, married the Countess Ada. She had for her chaplain Robert to whom she gave the lands of "Witefeld." Countess Ada jointly with a son Robert granted the lands of Witefeld to the Prior and Convent of Hexham by whom Robert the chaplain and his descendants were confirmed in their possession of Witefeld. This document long preserved was at Whitfield Hall, Northumberland. *A Grant of the Manor of Whitfield from the Prior and Convent of Hexham to Matthew, the son of Robert, the Chaplain of the Countess Ada.* Whitfield Manor was held by the annual payment of one silver mark to the convent.

Robert the chaplain becoming the Lord of Whitfield had less need of his living associated with his ecclesiastical functions. He gave this living to his nephew Robert between the years 1154 and 1194. The chaplain was permitted to have a coat of arms.

The History of Northumberland gives the lineage of the family and the descending families with the name Whitfield. From this time onward for several generations, the houses of Whitfield grew in importance at Northumberland to 1434.

The parent line of Whitfield of Whitfield Hall was divided into three branches about 1600. The senior line claims descent from the owners of the manor of Whitfield. The junior line descended from the holders of the living of the church at Whitfield. The third line is the people without known beginnings of its house.

The senior line is known but not with a house of influence today. Early records can be found in the Great Charter Convent of Hexham which mentions the owner and his holdings. In an Inspectimus granted by Edward I, 1280 ca., to the Prior and Convent of Hexham which mentions the owner and his holdings. In an Inspectimus of the Charter of Ivo de Veteriponte, granting lands at Alston (Cumberland), England, to the Prior and Convent of Hexham, 1307 ca.

Whitfield

CULPAM METUIT FIDES

WHITFIELD

Whitefield

Coat Of Arms with a shield, argent, upon which was a bend plain between two cottises, engrailed sable. A crest was added in the form of a pallisado, or radiated crown, silver, out of which sprang a stag's head.

Whitefield is flat on top. Shield has the bell pulls spread around. The same shield with crosses - 3 and 3 .

HERALDRY

In has been recorded that for many generations the heads of the House of Whitfield were styled "Yearls." It is now Earl of a House and land and district.

The junior line has descends from an owner of a House and land in 1540 who had a coat of arms. The name can be found at Oxforshire in early times and later in many country shires.

The parent line of Whitfield of Whitfield Hall was divided into three branches about the year 1600. The senior branch remained at Whitfield. The second branch settled in Durham and the third at Wadhurst, County Sussex.

The branches divide making new branches and the third with many branches and a variety of spellings of the name Whitfield. All branches have spread over the land of England.

The original village of Whitfield is situated on the north side of the river West Allen, eleven miles west/southwest from Hexham. The Church there was a plain structure. Whitfield Hall was there in 1750. There is a building there today on the site. To make connections with the oldest lines is not easy for a claim of the descendant who went to the colonies. English families have long family trees and charts. IT is easier for immigrants of the 1900's to make ancestral connections with the country of England than to observe the old records of England if you are an American with ancestry for two and three hundred years on land of the United States.

The English parliament had men who were interested in the British navies, and in expeditions, land discovery, and land companies for England. English men had an interest in the colonization of America. It began in 1608 and the first trips were to the West Indies. Servants went to foreign plantations 1654-1679.

Among the early Colonial records are several references to Whitfield in Barbados. There were Council Books called Tolzey Books. There are several ships records of sailings and the list of passengers.

WHITFIELD WENT TO WEST INDIES AT BARBADOS AND JAMAICA
WHITFIELD WENT TO VIRGINIA, CONNECTICUT, MASSACHUSETTS, AND NEW YORK IN THE 1600's. There were other colonies in the 1700's and Whitfields went to these colonies along the Atlantic Ocean shore.

The history of England's explorations and developments are in records of England. People have visited England to gather its records of the colonies. Immigration early records are in the shippers recordings. The genealogical ancestors at England existed there were not much in people records on names of England. At least the family links are almost impossible for the 1600's.

So begins our story, on the Atlantic Ocean shore, and its Whitfield people and related people.

(1) Maud is often written as Matilda for the name of King David's wife.
(2) There are some twenty names known who have worked on the work of native English people records who came to America. Other sources cite these people for their work and publication.

WHITEFIELD

Robert Whitfield, a chaplain, received the land of Witefield of many acres in part of Northumberland, England, before 1150. His heir and later the church received the land. The name Whitfield flourished for 150 years until a like name appeared on a record of Inspectimus involving a granting of land.

Whitfield has old Anglo Saxon spelling of the name in very old records and Whytfield is used. The name has always been Whitfield and pronounced as Witfield. Witefiled was the early land name.

The signature of Roberto de Whitefield and Johanne de Whitefield appeared on an Inspectimus of the Charter of Ivo de Veteriponts, granting land at Alston (Cumberland) to the Prior and Convent of Hexham, 1307 circa. This man and woman were part of the Whitfield clan.

Later a manor house of Whitefield did have some influence for it had a heraldic crest. Yet this house with families did not have a genealogy of the descendants.

England had a land system and the people saw several spellings of the name Whitfield. The names appear creative with alphabet letters arranged the way a person could write. Such changes did give identification to each such family. In the United States there are less than ten of these personalized spellings of names which came from the Whitfield name. They appear in American publication but not in the genealogical recordings.

Whitefield families appear in Person County, North Carolina, and in Tennessee. Person County, North Carolina, had five Whitfield Marriage Bonds with Whitfield 1978 to 1863. This county had thirty Marriage Bonds filed with Whitfield from 1793 to 1868. Fifteen were grooms and fifteen were brides. A study has not been done on the history of these families at Person County, NC.

The Tennessee censuses of 1850 and 1860 list seven Whitefield families with twenty-six children inclusive of fifteen sons.

On passengers ship records of England, there are four Whitefield names. Barbara in 1685 from Orkneys, Scotland. John arrived in 1850, an Irishman. Thomas arrived in 1851, and Irishman. Marie arrived in 1850, an Irishwoman. The first to arrive in the colony was George Whitefield, born 1715 in Gloucester, England, and who died 1770 in Massachusetts. He was the evangelist minister that influenced many to religion. He had no children of his own.

Baptisms in church parish sometimes had the minister writing Whitefield instead of Whitfield.

There are name changes from Whitfield to Whitefield. William Whitfield born 1751 resided at Goochland, Virginia, and moved to Alabama, and he changed his name to Whitefield in 1776. William and Mary Towler had twelve children and they became Whitefield. Their descendants are both Whitefield and Whitfield. Records written by other persons have often spelled Whitefield when it should be Whitfield for a name.

NATIONS EXPEDITIONS TO NORTH AMERICA
SPAIN

1492. Three ships of Spanish government led by Christopher Columbus discovered America. They left some of the sailors there with the natives but friction existed there and the village was destroyed.

Spain had a powerful navy and there were many ships on expeditions to the new world. In 1513 Spaniards discovered Mexico. Spain took an interest in Mexico. The first horses were brought from Europe to North America. In 1526 a Spanish ship left men as colonists in Georgia and the people were never found. All had perished. In 1565 Spanish men left at St. Augustine, Florida, for a colony. No survivors. The Spanish established a settlement at Santa Elena on the original site of Charlesfort. The Spanish built a fort called San Felipe atop the Charlesfort fortifications that features a moat and four bastions. Many years later half of this fort located about 200 yards from the site washed into Port Royal Sound.

Other nations had their ships on the oceans. Spain built a fleet of warships. The Spaniard fleet, consisting of 130 ships called the Spanish Armada, sent her fleet against English ships in the reign of Queen Elizabeth I, 1588. The English ships destoryed many ships in this sea battle. In 1610 Spaniards founded Santa Fe, New Mexico.

FRANCE

In 1587 colonists settled first at New Foundland. In 1608 the French settled at Quebec, Canada. The French people were traders. The French were interested in New Orleans Port and the land of Louisiana. The French and Indian War lasted for nine years. The French wanted the migration from the Atlantic Coast stopped to the seaport of New Orleans. The French moved into the St. Lawrence region. Then from the basin of the Great Lakes to the basin of the Mississippi River, the French pressed on to spread the faith and reap the profits of the fur trade. From 1673 to 1760 they held the vast land area. It took several explorers and about a century and a half to claim and confirm the French from Lake Michigan by way of the Chicago-Illinois portage to the Mississippi River and down to the Gulf. The French brought to America its culture of France. The first French colony was established in May 1562, a tiny outpost of 27 men called Charlesfort. The outpost was to serve refugee Huguenots fleeing religious persecution. This outpost lasted less than a year.

ENGLAND

In 1500 the English were more interested in building the English navy than exploration. This in time gave England an advantage in the struggle for colonization in America. The government did not finance any colonization but formed several joint-stock companies. Outstanding was the East India Company. In 1606 King James I granted the Virginia Charter. The London Company was successful but the Plymouth Company was not. In December 1606 three small ships commanded by Christopher Newport. The ships, Goodspeed, Discovery, and Sarah, carried 120 passengers. Sixteen died on the voyage. They were boys and men. They reached Virginia, sailed up the James River and in May 1607 made a settlement called Jamestown. They built a Fort for protection. The settlers suffered hardships and had attacks by the Indians.

In 1609 three more ships came with immigrants and animal stock. In 1612 it was discovered that tobacco could be successfully grown and cured. This became the commodity for England.

In 1620 a ship load of women were brought to Virginia to provide wives for the men. In 1620 the Pilgrims settled at Plymouth on the coast of Massachusetts. In 1644 the English took New York. There was war in 1689, the English had a thirteen year war with the French. England beat the French and gained all of Canada.

All during the 1700's England continued with land companies colonizing America with thirteen colonies on the lands along the Atlantic Ocean coast. In 1702 there was the Queen's Ann's War in the Huston Bay. King George's war in the 1700's was over the Saint Lawrence River passages. Virginia became a crown colony in 1624, and other lands on the Atlantic coast found England making treaties with the Indians, making and clearing space on land for the immigrants that kept coming to America.

126 YEARS – THE THIRTEEN COLONIES OF THE NEW WORLD

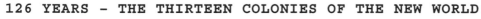

1607 - 1733

In 1788 they began with a new government to ratify the Constitution of the U.S.A.

10th state	1.	- 1607-VIRGINIA
6th state	2.	- 1620-MASSACHUSETTS
9th state	3.	- 1623-NEW HAMPSHIRE
11th state	4.	- 1624-NEW YORK
5th state	5.	- 1633-CONNECTICUT
7th state	6.	- 1634-MARYLAND
13th state	7.	- 1636-RHODE ISLAND
1st state	8.	- 1638-DELAWARE
2nd state	9.	- 1643-PENNSYLVANIA
12th state	10.	- 1653-NORTH CAROLINA
3rd state	11.	- 1660-NEW JERSEY
8th state	12.	- 1670-SOUTH CAROLINA
4th state	13.	- 1733-GEORGIA

West Indies
English ships went to the West Indies to Barbados and Jamaica. Barbados Island has a history on the Whitfield families and the historic cemetery of the early settlers.

How many pioneers finished their indentured servant work and time and left the Islands is unknown

.....Submitted by Frank T. Post, Professor, Fullerton College, Orange County, California, April 25, 1996.

VIRGINIA LAND SYSTEM AND COMPANY REORGANIZATIONS

In the Virginia Company reorganization of 1616 each of the settlers received 100 acres of land for his own use. Later the head-right system became the basis of the land system in Virginia. Each emigrant who paid his way across the Atlantic was promised a 50 acre tract. Each person was given an additional 50 acres for every new settler that he brought over. This made it possible for large estates called plantations. The population in the colony increased.

In 1612, the Company received a charter and was allowed self-government. In 1619, the Governor called on the free inhabitants of the colony to choose representatives who were called burgesses. Together Governor, Councilors, and Representatives passed laws. Eleven boroughs were formed. These did not last.

When the settlement became a crown colony, the King appointed the Governors and Councilors. In time the government of the colonies was modeled after the English Parliament. The burgesses and councilors reported and became two houses.

There is a story of the settlement and development of each new colony in America. Each is important and happened at different times and dates between 1606 and 1740. The Pilgrims were made up largely of farmers, laborers, and artisans in the group that came to Massachusetts Bay. There were few of that class.

The Massachusetts Company differed from the Plymouth group in that its members belonged to a somewhat wealthier class of English Society. During the year 1630 seventeen vessels came to America carrying about 2,000 people to Massachusetts Bay, where Boston was the first town settled. This was the beginning of the "Great Migration." In ten years 16,000 people went to Massachusetts. In New England colonies settled were Connecticut, Rhode Island, and New Hampshire.

New York was settled by the Dutch. The Dutch West India Company received from the Netherlands (often called Holland) a charter in 1621. Dutch attempted settlement at Delaware and failed. The colony was made by the Swedes. In 1638, fifty emigrants were brought over by a Swedish trading company. There were a few settlers in New Jersey of Dutch, Swedes, and Swiss. In March 1681, King Charles II gave a Pennsylvania Charter for a colony.

THE SOUTHERN PROPRIETARY COLONISTS

Maryland was settled in 1634 and was the first of the proprietary colonies. This was King Charles II's grant to George Calvert, Lord Baltimore. The King granted liberal charters to these colonies. These which were free of taxation.

1663, King Charles II gave the territory known as the Carolinas to eight of his courtiers who had aided in his restoration. In North Carolina, there was one settlement made on Albermarle Sound in 1653 by immigrants from Virginia. There was a settlement in 1670 made in South Carolina, and the settlers came directly from England. There was much friction between the colonists and the proprietors who were the absolute owners of land. In 1729 the region was divided into two royal provinces of North Carolina and South Carolina.

13

Georgia was the last of the original 13 colonies settled in 1733. This was 70 years after the grant of the Carolinas.

Puritans or Separatists were a group of people in England who wanted a greater reformation of the Church of England. In 1608, the people moved to Holland. Puritans wanted religion to fit their interests and ideas. In 1620, the people left Holland for Virginia. Winds of weather flew the Pilgrim's ship, Mayflower, to the north to Cape Cod Bay of Massachusetts. There were thirty-eight Pilgrims on the ship Mayflower. There were servants, strangers and hired hands. Some passengers did not survive the trip. All their clothing were Dutch garments.

MAYFLOWER PASSENGERS

Pilgrims
Isaac Allerton, tailor
Mary Allerton, wife
Bartholomew Allerton, son
Mary Allerton, daughter
Remember Allerton, daugther
William Bradford, silk weaver
Dorothy Bradford, wife
William Brewster, printer
Mary Brewster, wife
Love Brewster, son
Wrestling Brewster, son
John Carver, merchant
Catherine Carver, wife
Francis Cooke, wool comber
John Cooke, son
John Crackston
John Crackston, son
Moses Fletcher, blacksmith
Samuel Fuller, physician
John Goodman, linen weaver
Desire Minter, single woman
Degory Priest, hatter
Thomas Rogers, merchant
Joseph Rogers, son
Edward Tilley, cloth maker
Anne Tilley, wife
John Tilley, silk worker
Bridget Tilley, wife
Elizabeth Tilley, daughter
Thomas Tinker, wood sawyer
  Tinker, wife
  Tinker, son
John Turner, merchant
  Turner, son

Richard Clarke
Humility Cooper

  Elizabeth Winslow, wife

Servants
John Hooke
Richard More
  More, brother
Roger Wilder
William Latham
John Howland
William Butten, died at sea
Edward Dotey
Edward Leister
John Langemore
Robert Carter
William Holbeck
Edward Thompson
Ellen More
Elias Story
George Soule
  an unknown maid servant

Strangers
John Billington
Ellen Billington, wife
Francis Billington, son
Richard Britteridge
Peter Browne
James Chilton, tailor
  Chilton, wife
Mary Chilton, daughter
Richard Clarke
  Turner, son
William White, wood carver
Edward Winslow, printer

Francis Eaton, carpenter
Sarah Eaton, wife
Samuel Eaton, son
Edward Fuller
Ann Fuller, wife
Samuel Fuller, son
Richard Gardiner
Stephen Hopkins, merchant
Elizabeth Hopkins, wife
Giles Hopkins, son
Constance Hopkins, daughter
Damaris Hopkins, son
Oceanus Hopkins, born at sea
Edmund Margeson
Christopher Martin, died at sea
  Martin, wife
Solomon Prower, stepson
William Mullins, shopkeeper

Alice Mullins, wife
Priscilla Mullins, daughter
Joseph Mullins, son
John Rigdale
Alice Rigdale, wife
Henry Samson
Myles Standish, soldier
Rose Standish, wife
Richard Warren, merchant
Thomas Williams
Gilbert Winslow, brother

Hired hands
John Alden, cooper
John Allerton, mariner
Ellis, sailor
Thomas English, mariner
William Trevore, sailor

The Puritans obtained permission from the Virginia Land Company of England to make the first permanent settlement in New England, and finally they received the King's consent of England after they pledged their loyalty to the crown. People were friendly and the Indians taught them how to survive. The Massachusetts Bay Colony was formed in 1630. Then people came in hundreds and later created a Commonwealth form of government.

AFRICAN-AMERICANS

In the 15th century, the English mariners had taken a hand in the African slave-trade. The first introduction of Negro-slaves into Virginia came in 1619 when a Dutch man-of-war shipper sold 20 slaves. The Portuguese began the slave trade in 1400's.

A census taken in 1624 showed 22 Negroes in the colony. The increase in their numbers was at first very slow. It was the establishment of slave labor later for the tobacco plantations that produced 58,850 black people as immigrants in twelve colonies by 1715 in middle North America.

CENSUSES

Colony Governors sent out militia men at certain times to count the number of people in the districts. The count was to determine how many men, women, children and slaves were in the community. There was also a count of the agriculture crops and animals a property owner had.

Masters of plantations and property owners were names on old English records but not other people. Masters or widows were responsible for the taxes owed. Vestry Parishes handled these records. There was not identification by names on public records except for these two groups. Rarely were the first names taken of Negroes who were heads of families.

The new Congress in 1790 called for censuses of the states every ten years. The practice of counting and identifying people did continue for 250 years and will continue. Slow were the changes in census taking. It took a Civil War to change the economic basis of the South and the acceptances of industrial northern basis for economics. Only then did the censuses include all names of people.

The Civil War of the United States between Northern and Southern forces lasted from April 12, 1861 to May 26, 1865. The end of the War put an end to slavery. Reconstruction following the War meant many changes. The black people had to register for census counting and when they did, they reported the first name of their own and the former master's surname and plantation of work. Thus, many former slaves became owners of the surname of the masters. There were many in the South who were black native people reporting with a name of Whitfield in 1870 and the census taker marked B for black, W for white, M for Mulatoo, a mixture of black and white races. In 1850 only about 350,000 white families out of a total 1,800,000 held slaves.

In genealogical history a person must know if the race is white or black. It is called black history. It is assumed it is people of white race unless stated as other. Thus, the Whitfield records of United States in this text are white people.

Other nationalities and races later were listed on the censuses. A word is used denoting the country of birth for the race.

SHIPS of Spain to America 1492 and Later
and West Indies and Islands
SPANISH COLONY 1565

PEDRO MENENDEZ DE AVILES arrived in America in 1565 with many soldiers and settlers to found the Spanish colony he called St. Augustine decades before the English established the Virginia colony at Jamestown in 1607 and the Pilgrims on the Mayflower ship that landed at Plymouth Rock in 1620.

The landing site then was Spanish Florida. There a 16th century fort was built and later burned down. They came and they left. There were no survivors to continue a settlement in the new country.

However, there was Santa Elena, a Spanish colonial settlement founded a year later than St. Augustine at a site known today as Parris Island, South Carolina. The colony did not survive.

SHIPS that sailed the sea from England to Virginia, New England, Bermudas, Barbados, Nevis and other places from 1607 to 1660. List from Bristol, England of Bristol Record-Archives Office, and from Crown Documents, and Court Records.

SHIPS of England to America Colonies and West Indies Islands

AMITY of London 1640.
BONA NOVA 1619 and 1620.
BONNY BESS 1623.
CHARLES of Gloucester 1640.
DIANA 1618.
Eleanor 1621.
Elizabeth 1621, 1635, 1659
 and this ship went to
 Barbados, Nevis and Bermuda.
FELLOWSHIP 1640.
FLYING HART 1621.
GEORGE 1616 and 1623.
GIFT 1618.
GLOBE 1635.
GREAT HOPEWELL 1623.
GREEN LION 1640.

INCREASE 1635, Master was
 Richard Ellis.
JAMES 1622.
JOHN AND FRANCIS 1611.
LONDON MERCHANT 1620.
MARY AND JAMES 1610.
MARY MARGARET 1608.
MERCHANT ADVENTURER 1640.
NEPTUNE 1618.
PROVIDENCE 1623.
ROBERT BONADVENTURE 1634.
SAINT JOHN 1640.
STAR 1610.
SUSAN 1606 and 1616.
SWAN 1610 and 1624.
TIGER 1621.
WARWICK 1621.
A few of the ships that went to the new colonies.

These ships from English public records carried people to the Americas for political, religious, and economic reasons, and those persons deported for vagrancy, roguery, or nonconformity, and those persons who were sold to laborers in the new colonies.

WHITFIELD RECORDS OF ENGLAND AND THE PRESERVATIONS

There have been few men and women to handle these old records for preservation. There have been few business companies later to handle these records and publish compilations on residents of early United States and the British colonies. Almost nothing was done at the 13 colonies of North America to preserve any knowledge about those pioneers arriving here to start life anew along the Atlantic Ocean coast and the southern islands.

Records of sailings of ships and passengers were kept in Britain. Some of the early records of colonists were kept in British archives. England claimed the land of the 13 colonies. Many patriots of the American Revolution were of the third and fourth generations from their immigrant ancestors and possessed only a traditional knowledge of their European beginnings. They had only Bibles, diaries, and a few public records that had escaped the ravages of war.

About a hundred years after the War a Connecticut lawyer, John Camden Hotten, went to England to copy the original documents of port sailings: <u>The Original Lists of Persons of Quality, Emigrants, Religious Exiles, Political Rebels, Serving Men, Sold For a Term of Years, Apprentices, Children Stolen, Maidens Pressed, and Others Who Went West From Great Britain to The American Plantations</u>, etc. published by Hotten, long remained the most important source of information of this character in this country. This valuable work is far from complete for death cut Hotten off in the midst of his work.

There were 500,000 people who took ships to the Americas. Between 1614 and 1775 some 50,000 Englishmen were sentenced by legal process to be transported to the American colonies. Some of the people were deported for vagrancy, roguery, or non-conformity. Some were sold to labor in the new colonies. Some came because of political, religious, or economic reasons, and some came because of famines of the country they left. A few came indentured with a plan, and more were unindentured. Some came for a new life and adventure.

N. Dermott Harding, Keeper of the Bristol Archives, states: *In 1925, the top floor of the Council House of Bristol was being cleared for additions and alterations. Here was housed a great mass of records.* Among the records were two volumes: <u>Servants to Foreign Plantations, 1654-1679.</u> These were the <u>Tolzey Books</u> which mean Council Books. In these books were the names of 10,000 persons and attached to some the home address of the emigrant, destination abroad, and the name of the person to whom indentured. This meant that the person so named was indentured to service to another for a period of years for paying the captain the cost of transporting the "servant."

G. C. Greer and Mrs. Nell Nugent have also published immigrant lists. After 1845, the immigrants flooded the United States. There have been workers to make immigrant list compilations of the early times. Bibliography of books list some of the titles on immigration of early times.

George C. Greer was a resident of England. These men worked in England on the early records of people to the American colony. Lists of names, ships and information were written. This work lay in England. The Americans of the United States became interested and funding was provided for publishing houses to print these emigrants' lists. They were needed in the United States.

Peter Wilson Coldham was a resident of Surrey, England, and was a compiler of nine volumes. All lists of emigrants and passengers in bondage 1656 to 1775 were compiled from English public records of those who took ships to the Americas.

There were English ships to colony Barbados and to West Indies Islands, south of the Colonial England Colonies on the coast of the Atlantic Ocean.

Barbados Island has a history on the Whitfield families and the historic cemetery of the early settlers there. It is unknown who left the Islands and came to American Colonies.

The Whitfield men and women came from England.

EMIGRANTS

GREEN LION on June 9-11, 1640 carried cattle and goods to New England. Fellowship on June 1, 1640 carried cattle.

WHITFIELD ON SHIPS

From the above lists and public records of England was GILBERT WHITFIELD, age 23, to Virginia in the FLYING HART 1621. He was a servant of Mr. Daniell Gookin and appears in Virginia colonial records. Whitfield later returned to England.

JOHN WHITFIELD had a Probate of nuncupative will August 3, 1614, and John Whitfield was lying sick in BLESSING ship bound to Bermuda. This record is from Commissary Court of London.

September 19, 1659 on ship Thomas Bushell of Acton, Glos, yeoman, bound to John Whitfield, planter, to serve four years in Barbados.

October 24, 1660, Thomas Joy, yeoman, and ROBERT WHITFIELD, yeoman, bound to Charles Legg, planter, to serve eight years in Barbados.

There are a few more named Whitfield who came on ships from England that appear in the copied English ship records. They were mostly named William Whitfield or John Whitfield.

Ships with early Whitfield colonists sailed after 1669 to North Carolina to colonize the land. Land patents were issued in 1700.

Ships with Whitfield sailed after 1732 to begin the colony at Georgia. Settlements were slow because of the Indians. Ships went to South Carolina seaport for immigrants to Georgia. The first Whitfield appears to have arrived about 1765.

Abstracts of Virginia Land Patents and Grants 1623- 1666 are in the book <u>Cavaliers And Pioneers</u> by Nugent.

CAVALIERS AND PIONEERS

WILLIAM WOOLRITCH, 400 acs. Eliz. City Co. 17 June 1635, p. 309. lying in the woods Wly. upon land of Christopher Calthroppe, Ely. upon Samuell Bennett & Robert Thresher, N. upon Mr. Phettiplace Cloyse & Sly. into the maine woods. Trans. of 8 pers: Joane Woolrich, Humphrye Edwards, Margarett Clement, Mark Foster, Robt Reeves, Jon. Hunt, Robt. Reeves, Wm. Jening.

JOHN VASLER, 150 acs. Warresquioake Co., 18 Nov. 1635, p. 310. Being a necke of land lying up the maine Cr. of Warresquioake bay, next behind the land of Warresquioake & Nathaniell Loyd, a back Cr. parting them, which Cr. runs up W. N. W. neare the maine Cr. & the sd. maine Cr. S. W. on the other side. Trans. of himselfe, his wife Elizabeth Vasler & 1 servt. called William Baker.

WILLIAM CLARKE, 100 acs. Eliz. Citty Co., 18 Nov. 1635, p. 310. S. W. upon land of Mr. Georg White, Minister, E. into the woods, W. upon the New Pocoson Riv. & N. upon Clarkes Cr. Trans. of 2 pers: John Oker, Nich. Bennett.

CAPT. THOMAS WILLOWBYE, 300 acs. adj. land now in his possession, 19 Nov. 1635, p. 311. N. upon the maine river, Sly. into the woods, & E. upon his now dwelling howse. Trans. of 6 pers: John Draper, Giles Collins, Theod. Loyd, Jon. Scot, Wm. Palmer, Walter Howell. Note: Renewed in his name 19 Mar. 1643. Test: Sam. Abbott, Clr.

SAME. 300 acs. Eliz. Citty Co., 19 Nov. 1635, p. 312. Upon the "hither" Cr. between Francis Mason & his own land, S. upon the woods, W. upon the Cr., N. upon land formerly taken up by him. Trans. of 6 pers: Jon. Pinches, Howell Hayward, Jon. David, Weymouth Vensey, Jon. Wood, Rich. Jackson. Note: Renewed 19 Mar. 1643 in his name. Samll. Abbot, Cl.

SAME. 300 acs. in Eliz. Riv., being 2 or 3 small necks of land, W. upon a

br. of Eliz. Riv., S. E. upon the maine land & N. upon the Sly. br. of Eliz. Riv. Same date & page. Trans. of 6 pers: Tymothy Barloe, Nich. Fortescue, Jon. Farrow, Mary Wormewell, Robt. Barkwith, Demis (or Dennis) Reeve.

THOMAS KEELING, 100 acs. Eliz. Citty Co., 18 Nov. 1635, p. 313. Nly. upon land of Henry Southwell, Ely. up on the back river, Sly. upon land of William Morgan & Wly. on the maine land. Trans. of 2 pers.*

THOMAS WARREN, 300 acs., Chas. City Co., 20 Nov. 1635, p. 314. S. upon Bayliffs ——, E. upon the maine woods, W. upon the river, & N. upon 4 Mi. Cr. 150 acs. in right of his wife Susan Greeneleafe, the relict of Robert Greeneleafe; 50 acs. due for her per. adv. & 100 for sd. Robert her former husband, being an Ancient Planter in the time of Sir Thomas Dale; 50 acs. due sd. Warren for his own per. adv. & 100 acs. for the trans. of 2 servts: John Fouke, Rich. Whitfeild.

EDWARD SPARSHOTT, 100 acs. Chas. Citty Co., 20 Nov. 1635, p. 314. At Merchants Hope Cr. at the parting of same, S. up the Cr., W. upon the maine woods, E. upon the Cr. & on the N. side of the Indian feild. 50 acs. for the per. adv. of his wife Maudelin (or Mandelin) Canes (or Caves) & 50 acs. for trans. of 1 servt. called Robert Honyborne. Note: Renewed & 250 acs. added.

WILLIAM WILKINSON, Minister, 700 acs. in Linhaven, comonly called Chisopeian river, upon a Cr., W. on Thomas Keeling & Georg Downes, S. into the woods, Ely. along the Cr., being opposite to Capt. Thorrogoods plantation in Lynhaven & N. upon Chisopeian bay. 20 Nov. 1635, p. 315. 200 acs. due by assignment from Robert Newberke, 3 Oct. 1635, to whom it was due, viz: 50 acs. for his own per. adv. & 150 acs. for trans. of 3 servts, 500 acs. due sd. Wilkinson, viz: 100 acs. for the per. adv. of himselfe & wife Naomy Wilkinson & 400 acs. for trans. of 8 pers.

Other Whitfields

George C. Greer's *Early Virginia Immigrants*
Whitfield, Gilbert, 1637, by Daniel Gookins, New Norfolk County.
Whitfield, Wm., 1636, by John Chandler, Elizabeth Citie County.

Frank R. Holmes' *Directory of the Ancestral Heads of New England Families* 1620-1700
Whitfield, Edward, resident Reading, Mass. 1649.
Whitfield, John, resident Dorchester, Mass., 1634, removed to Windsor, Conn., 1635.

Nugent's *Cavaliers and Pioneers* (1934)
Whitfield: Elizabeth, Gilbert, Richard, and William.

Hotten's *The Original Lists of Persons . . . to the American Plantations 1600-1700* (1874)
Whitfield: Matthew, Roger, Gilbertt.
Whitfield, John (aged 20 in 1635).

1941 Supplement to the 1922 Index of Ancestors — General Society of Colonial Wars
Whitfield, William . . . c. 1770, North Carolina Captain, North Carolina Militia, 1754.

Index of Ancestors — National Society Daughters of Colonial Wars (1950-58)
Whitfield, William II 1715-1795. Bertie County and Wayne County, N.C. Capt. Militia 1754-55. Member of North Carolina Assembly 1761-62.

Cockrane & Wood's *History of Francestown*, New Hampshire 1758-1891
George Whitfield, born in Dunstable, resided in Hollis, and removed to Wilton, Maine, and then to Francestown in 1825. He married Lydia Tanger November 27, 1801.

Virkus' *Compendium of American Genealogy* — Immigrant Ancestors
Whitefield, William (1688-ca. 1770) from England in his own ship "The Providence," in early part of the 18th century, and settled at Nansemond, Va.; finally to Lenoir Co., North Carolina; married, 1713, Elizabeth Goodman (ca. 1697-1773) of Gates County, North Carolina.

John Chandler 1000 acres. Elizabeth City County, Point Comfort,, Virginia. July 6, 1636. Carried on ship William Whitfield

Daniel Gookins, Esquire. 2500 acres in Upper County of New Norfork. 29 Dec. 1637 transportation of 50 persons including Gilbert Whitfield.

Published by <u>Hobbies</u> magazine. Feb. 1968, page 118.

WHITFIELD EMIGRANTS FROM ENGLAND TO WEST INDIES, VIRGINIA, NEW ENGLAND, NEW YORK AND PENNSYLVANIA
AND
WHITFIELD IRISH EMIGRANTS OF IRELAND LEAVING FROM LIVERPOOL PORT

1621   Nov. 22, GILBERT WHITFIELD came in the ship Flying Hart to Elizabeth City County, Virginia. He returned to England, and came again in 1624. In 1628, Gilbert Whitfield was a guard at the Court of James City, Virginia.

1635   JOHN WHITFIELD came from England in the ship Globe Of London when he was age 20 and settled at Norfolk, Virginia.

1635   RICHARD WHITFIELD was a headright of Thomas Warren, whose patent of land was dated 1635. Richard lived in lower Norfolk County, Virginia.

1635   RUTH WHITFIELD was brought in by Thomas Warren during the same time. She settled at Norfolk County, Virginia.

1636   WILLIAM WHITFIELD settled at Point Comfort, Elizabeth City County, Virginia. He was a headright of John Chandler.

1639   HENRY WHITFIELD and DOROTHY SHEAFFE WHITFIELD, husband and wife with children. Henry was a clergyman. He came from Surrey, England. July 1639 this ship landed at Newhaven, Connecticut. The family settled at Guilford, Connecticut. In 1650, Henry Whitfield and sons returned to England. Wife Dorothy Whitfield and members of the family stayed to care for the plantation. Dorothy and family members later joined Henry Whitfield at Winchester, England.

1654-1663 In one of these years, ROBERT WHITFIELD came from Bristol, England, and his destination was Barbados. He was a servant to a foreign plantation.

1664   February 27-April 28. DANIEL WHITFIELD. Shippers by the Society, Mr. John Pearse, bound from London for New England, thirty-eight men including Daniel Whitfield, one woman Lucy Knight.

1664   NATHANIEL WHITFIELD, March 21-April 19. Shippers by the Supply, Mr. John Fairweather bound from London for New England. Nathaniel Whitfield and twelve other men.

1664   MATTHEW WHITFIELD, August 15. Apprenticed in Bristol, England to William Dale, four years at Virginia.

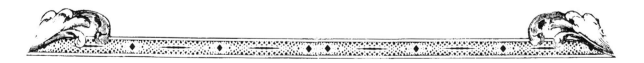

EMIGRANTS

1665   THOMAS WHITFIELD, May 2.   Newgate prisoners reprieved to transported to Barbados.   Thomas Whitfield and 18 other men, and 1 spinster, Frances Hulman.

1666   TOBIAS WHITFIELD came from Barnstaple, England.   He was a ship crew member with 16 other crew members.   He stayed with the ship which had an official pass and was a sea pirate vessel.   They delivered cargo supplies to Virginia.   A pass for the ship was recorded in a Royal Book account on Feb. 13, 1666 for Fellowship.

1670   ROGER WHITFIELD, Sept. 17.   Apprenticed in Bristol. Richard Martin to Roger Whitfield, four years, Virginia by William and Ann.

1671   WILLIAM WHITFIELD, Aug. 4.   Apprenticed in Bristol, England.   William Whitfield to William Smith, four years, Virginia by Trial ship.

1671   JOHN WHITFIELD early settler in Virginia had a plantation and was sponsor for men who came from England to work at his plantation.   Men to his place arrived 1671, 1675, 1676.

1671   November 17.   Apprenticed in Bristol.   PETER EDWARDS to JOHN WHITFIELD, four years, Virginia.   Arrived by Barbados Merchant ship.

1675   October 6.   Apprenticed in Bristol.   EDWARD ELLIS to JOHN WHITFIELD, four years, Virginia.

1676   Sept. 25.   Apprenticed in Bristol.   ELIZABETH AUSTIN to JOHN WHITFIELD, four years, Virginia by William And Ann Ship.

1676   Oct. 13.   Apprenticed in Bristol.   RACHELL SHELTON to JOHN WHITFIELD, four years, Virginia by William And Ann.

1676   Oct. 30.   Apprenticed in Bristol.   JOHN COLLINS to JOHN WHITFIELD, Seven years, Virginia by William And Ann ship.

1679   ROGER WHITFIELD, Sept. 19-Oct. 2.   By the Lisbon Merchant, Mr. Rodger Whitfield, from Barbados to New York; and George Blunt and Jane Jenkins.

1679   MATTHEW WHITFIELD, 2-13 days of May.   By the Prosperous, Mr. David Fogg, from Barbados to Virginia.   Mathew Whitfield and Katherine Arthur; Luke Rainy; Samuel Davies; John Pinke; Dennis Burne; Ann Box; Frances Southworth.

1680   May 3.   Apprenticed in Bristol.   WILLIAM BARTON to JOHN WHITFIELD, ten years, Jamaica by William And Mary.

1682   MATTHEW WHITFIELD and ship departure port of England.   He was a ship commander.   Matthew brought in 13 passengers to Virginia.   Matthew Whitfield received a land patent on Dec. 22, 1682 for the cove inlet land at the shoreline of Norfolk, Virginia.   A Matthew Whitfield also received 650 acres in Lower Norfolk, VA.

Whitfeild, Geo n.a.; Georgia, 1738
Whitfeild, Gilbert n.a.; Virginia, 1623
Whitfeild, John n.a.; Barbados, 1684
Whitfeild, Mathew n.a.; Virginia, 1663–1679
Whitfeild, Mathew n.a.; Virginia, 1679
Whitfeild, Robert n.a.; Barbados, 1654–1663
Whitfield, Barthia n.a.; America, 1746
Whitfield, Fredrick K n.a.; Philadelphia, Pa., 1852

Whitfield, George n.a.; New Castle County, Del., 1854

Whitfield, Gilbert n.a.; Virginia, 1623
Whitfield, Gilbert n.a.; Virginia, 1637
Whitfield, Henry n.a.; America, 1772
Whitfield, Henry n.a.; Connecticut, 1620–1650

Whitfield, Henry n.a.; New England, 1639
Whitfield, Henry n.a.; New England, 1639
Whitfield, John 20; Virginia, 1635
Whitfield, John 20; Virginia, 1635
Whitfield, John P Y n.a.; Philadelphia, Pa., 1848

Whitfield, Joseph n.a.; Philadelphia, Pa., 1844

Whitfield, Joshua n.a.; America, 1766
Whitfield, Mary n.a. *SEE* Whitfield, Richard

Whitfield, Richard n.a.; Philadelphia, Pa., 1683

Wife: Mary n.a.
Whitfield, Robert 25; Charleston, S.C., 1821
Whitfield, Thomas n.a.; America, 1765
Whitfield, Wm n.a.; Virginia, 1636
Whitfild, Gilbert 23; Virginia, 1621

Whitfild, Gilbert 23; Virginia, 1624

1981 compilation

Whitfield, Mrs. n.a.; San Francisco, Cal., 1851

Whitfield, Edward n.a.; Boston, Mass., 1707
Whitfield, George n.a.; Georgia, n.d.
Whitfield, Jane 21; Jamaica, 1684
Whitfield, Joshua n.a.; America, 1764
Whitfield, S n.a.; San Francisco, Cal., 1851
Whitfield, Susanna n.a.; Philadelphia, Pa., 1746

Whiftield, Thomas n.a.; Maryland, 1661
Whitfield, Wm n.a.; Maryland, 1668
Whitfild, Gilbert 23; Virginia, 1621

1982 compilation

n. a. means no age . n. d. means no date.

22

Whitfeild, Eliz n.a.; Virginia, 1664
Whitfeild, Eliza n.a.; Virginia, 1714
Whitfeild, Mary n.a.; Virginia, 1700
Whitfeild, Mary n.a.; Virginia, 1704
Whitfeild, Rich n.a.; Virginia, 1635
Whitfeild, Thomas n.a.; Virginia, 1700
Whitfeild, Wm n.a.; Virginia, 1636
Whitfeild, Wm n.a.; Virginia, 1714
Whitfield, George T n.a.; New York, 1834

Whitfield, Henry n.a.; New England, 1639

Whitfield, Jane 21; Jamaica, 1684
Whitfield, John 20; Virginia, 1635
Whitfild, Gilbert 23; Virginia, 1621

1984 compilation

Immigrants

1684   JANE   WHITFIELD came to America from Alston Moor
Cumberland. Spinister   age 21   X.

1684   HENRY   WHITFIELD came to America.   Married settler.
        Massereene.

1712 circa.WILLIAM   WHITFIELD came from Lancaster, England
        in his own ship The Providence , and settled at Nanse-
        mond, Virginia. In 1713 William Whitfield married
        Elizabeth Goodman.

1765   THOMAS T. WHITFIELD departed England April 1765.
        Anne M. Spelled Whittfield on passenger list and
        no destination given.

1664, 24, August. Passengers departed England including
        ELIZABETH WHITFIELD. Mr. Richard Webley , Robert Davis
        and Thomas Freshwater. 7221 acres in Rappahannock River
        area and North Cumberland County, Virginia.

1763   Joshua Whitfield came from Lincolnshire, England.

1738   George Whitfield born in Gloucester came from London,
        England.

EMIGRANTS

1680   April 6. Apprenticed in Bristol. JOHN GALLASTON to JOHN WHITFIELD, four years, Jamaica by William And Mary ship.

1683   RICHARD WHITFIELD, 3-31 days May. Shippers by the America, Mr. Joseph Wasey, bound from London for Pennsylvania. Richard Whitfield and seven other men.

1683   NATHANIEL WHITFIELD, March 12-April 17. Shippers by the Rebecca, Mr. Edward Clements, bound from London for New York. Nathaniel Whitfield and six other men.

1684   July 16. Apprenticed in Bristol. STEWARD HADDICK of North Molton, Devon, to JOHN WHITFIELD, four years, Jamaica by Dragon.

1684   JOHN WHITFIELD, August 2. Apprenticed in Bristol. JOHN WHITFIELD to William Stoakes, four years, Barbados by Diligence ship.
   JOHN WHITFIELD, settler at Jamaica, had a plantation and sponsor to men in 1680 and 1684 years.

1684   August 9. DANIEL MARLOW of Coventry, Waru, tailor, to JOHN WHITFIELD, four years, Jamaica by Dragon.

1684   August 16. Apprenticed in Bristol. SILVESTER STILLINGFLEET of Pontefract, Yorks to JOHN WHITFIELD, four years, Jamaica by Dragon.

1684   JANE WHITFIELD, March 26-28. Apprenticed in Middlesex to serve THOMAS RICHARDSON citizen and surgeon of London, for four years in Jamaica, Jane Whitfield of Alston Moor, Cumberland, spinster.

1685   BARBARA WHITFIELD, August 12. Apprenticed in London. Barbara Whitefield, widow without children, age 26. Daughter of Edward Scholler of the Orkneys in Scotland, husbandman deceased to Ernest Keckerbecke of Whitechapel, Middlesex, surgeon, four years, Virginia.

1686   JOHN WHITFIELD, February 6. Home Circuit prisoners to be transported to Barbados reprieved or Jamaica, Essex. Including JOHN WHITFIELD of Waltham Cross, and fourteen men and four women.

Whitfield, Barthia. S Feb-Apr 1746. M.
Whitfield, Charles. S s mare & R Summer 1775. Wa.
Whitfield, Daniel. S s sacks Lent 1768. Ca.
Whitfield, Henry. S Apr-Jun T Jly 1772 *Tayloe*. M.
Whitfield, John of Waltham Cross. R for Barbados or Jamaica Feb.
   1686. E.
Whitfield, John. S Lent 1758. La.
Whitfield, Joshua. S s sheep Summer 1763 R 14 yrs Lent 1764. Li.
Whitfield, Joshua. S Oct 1765 T Jan 1766 *Tryal*. L.
Whitfield, Richard. S s from bleaching croft at Whorlton & R 14 yrs
   Lent TB Aug 1770. Y.
Whitfield, Thomas. R for Barbados May 1665. X.

24

IRISH RESIDENTS OF IRELAND SAILING FROM LIVERPOOL ENGLAND
THE FAMINE IMMIGRANTS

SUSANNA WHITFIELD age 20 spinster. May 29, 1848. Ship Thomas-Bennett from Liverpool, England.

JAMES WHITFIELD, age 13 child. May 17, 1846.

GEORGE WHITFIELD age 30. Machinist. Wife, SARAH WHITFIELD age 30 mgt., Children: Robert Whitfield age 9, Sarah Whitfield age 5, Samuel Whitfield age 2. Sept. 11, 1846 ship Rochester from Liverpool, England arriving at the port of New York. Irish family immigrants.

CATHERINE WHITFIELD age 20, May 22, 1847 from Liverpool.

ELIZA WHITFIELD age 19, Servant, July 11, 1848 ship Centurion from Liverpool, England.

EDWARD WHITFIELD age 23, Saddler. Aug. 17, 1848 ship Waterlou from Liverpool, England.

JOHN WHITFIELD age 23, Shop Boy, Sept. 16, 1848 ship James-Foster from Liverpool, England.

ISABELLE WHITFIELD age 18, Sept. 11, 1848 from Liverpool in ship Caleb-Grimshaw.

WILLIAM WHITFIELD age 40, Farmer from London Wenham, May 5, 1849, arrived Port of New York.

JOHN WHITEFIELD age 23, Nov. 1, 1850, ship Nat. Kimbell from Liverpool, England.

MARIE WHITEFIELD age 21, Servant. March 20, 1850 ship Wm. H. Harbeck from Liverpool.

THOMAS WHITFIELD age 25, Laborer. May 1851 arrived New York Port from Liverpool, England. Ship Hope.

FAMINE YEARS OF IRELAND 1846-1851

Food crops and potato crops failed to grow with weather conditions and economic conditions of Ireland. Many Irish people left Ireland and went to New York and to Boston, Massachusetts and to other states.

The American Flag of the United States was created in 1779.

Paul Revere charged in expenses 14 pounds 2 shillings in English money for his ride to New York and Philadelphia to deliver news of the Boston Tea Party in December 1773, the first event of the Revolution of the Colonies. The trip took Revere eleven days on horseback. He bill was endorsed by John Hancock.

EMIGRANTS
SYDNEY, WALES TO SAN FRANCISCO, CALIFORNIA

Mrs. _____ WHITFIELD sailed in a British Bark type of ship named Maria from Sydney, N. S. Wales. Captain _____ Plank. Passage eighty-six days from Sydney, New South Wales and arrived on January 4, 1851 at San Francisco, California.

Ship Gulnare from Sydney, New South Wales. Captain Nosworthy. Passage ninety days. Ship arrived May 27, 1852 at San Francisco, California. From good field of Mount Alexander Mrs. _____ WHITFIELD and three daughters arrived 1852.

HISTORY

There were other ships at port of San Francisco from Wales in the days of the gold rush 1849, 1850, 1851 bringing men to mine gold. The diggers were men who found employment in digging for water, and digging of agricultural crops, and digging for minerals in the ground soils. The Welsh people and those emigrants who were men from Wales brought families to California, and their work of digging in the coal mines was a grand contribution to the development of the San Francisco, California area and the coal mines. For twenty years they created the towns of Nortonville and Sommerville near Pittsburg in Contra Costa County, California.

In 1896, Empire Coal Company installed a generator at Black Diamond mines to light its coal mines. The success was not permanent for the coal mines exhausted their supply of product and closed. The miners turned to farming in California.

EMIGRANT RECORDS

Gilbert Whitfield lived at Bass's Goise. Gilbert was age 23 when he came as a Servant in 1621 to Virginia Colony. Mr. Danniell Gookines, Muster.

August 7, 1635. John Whitfield age 20 and other people to be transported to Virginia in ship Globe of London. Mr. Jeremy Blackman was examined by Minister of Gravese for passengers comformitie, and took the oaths of allegiance and supremacy.

Charles Whitfield came from Warwickshire, England in 1775.
Henry Whitfield came from Ockley, Sussexshire, England 1639.
Joshua Whitfield came from Lincolnshire, England in 1763.

Daniel Whitfield came from Cambridgeshire, England in 1768.
Jane Whitfield came from Alston Moor Cumberland in 1684.
William Whitfield came from Lancaster, England circa 1712.

Richard Whitfield came from Whorlton, England in 1770.
There were Whitfields that came from London, England.
Whitfield came from Bristol, England.
Thomas R. Whitfield came from Newgate, England in 1665.

Virginia Record. 1870 VA Whitfield W for white person and B for black person. This census had 42 black persons, and 20 white persons and 3 mulatto persons. This year black persons had freedom and had to register on census. They took their master's surname.

THE STRUGGLE FOR CONTROL IN NORTH AMERICA

It took 126 years to develop thirteen colonies. There were four wars. The first war was between England and France in 1689, and was known as King William's War. In America there were French and Indian raids against the outlying settlements in New York, New Hampshire, and Maine. The English colonists with the support of the Iroquois Indians attacked the French in Canada, and an English expedition captured Port Royal. The War ended with the area returned to French in 1697.

In 1702, the War of the Spanish Succession began. This conflict was known in America as Queen Annie's War. The French attacks were Indian raids. The French and English had conflicts on land areas. The French continued to extend and tighten their grip on the interior of the continent. France created a province. However, the Indians and resentful Spanish prevented the French from securing all the fur trade along the Missouri River.

In 1739, Great Britain went to war again on a conflict with Spain, and France came in on the side of Spain. The latter half of the War was known in America as King George's War 1744-1748.

Causes of the French and Indian War were mainly France's effort in 1749 to claim the Ohio Valley in America. While France did this, King George II was chartering the Ohio Company. This Company was granted half a million acres of land in what is now West Virginia. A war began when the Virginians began a fort at the forks of the Ohio. This site was taken by the French.

The home government in the colonies now began to take more interest in the affairs of America. France sent an army to Canada. The British began to seize French ships bound for North America. The attempt of the colonists failed at fighting. War was declared in 1756 and lasted until 1763. The War was known in America as the French and Indian War. British men left their ships to fight. Finally the Peace of Paris was signed in February 1763. By it France surrendered to Great Britain her claims to Canada, Cape Breton, and all of Louisiana east of the Mississippi River except the Isle of Orleans, New Orleans, and the vast region between the Mississippi River and the Rocky Mountain which were ceded by France to Spain.

Spain had aided France in the Seven Year War, and in making peace with Great Britain, Spain was obliged to give up her possession of Florida. The British now held all of North America east of the Mississippi River.

The colonists bought most of their imports from England. The colonies had become valuable for supplies of fish, furs, naval stores, tobacco, dyestuff and sugar. The colonists sent these supplies to England. There were socio-economic differences and discontent. The First Continental Congress met September 5, 1774 for the purpose of discussing the conditions which had arisen. This Congress passed a series of resolutions known as the Declaration Of Rights.

As the British government tried to perfect its imperial organization by imposing new taxes on the American Colonists and by regulating their industries, the opposition to British rule became so bitter that it finally caused the Colonists to resist all British attempts to govern them and led to a complete separation.

INDEPENDENCE WAR

The Second Continental Congress was a continuous body holding sessions during the period from 1775 to 1781. Under the leadership of George Washington, the Americans organized armed forces which were able to defeat the British. The American Revolutionary War began with the battle of Lexington in 1775 at Massachusetts.

By the Declaration of Independence, written by Thomas Jefferson and adopted by the Continental Congress in 1776, the colonies declared themselves free and independent states. Following this declaration, the colonies adopted state constitutions and thereby were changed from dependent colonies to self-governing commonwealths. They united in their resistance to Great Britain through the Continental Congresses.

The American people did not act as a unit in opposing Great Britain. Each colony quarrel with the Mother Country took on several different aspects. It was a severe test for the colonies. The complex nature of the Revolutionary War is a story of its own. The battles continued and then ended victoriously for the Americans with the defeat of the British at Yorktown in 1781. The Independence War began April 19, 1775 at Lexington and Concord and ended at Yorktown on Oct. 19, 1781.

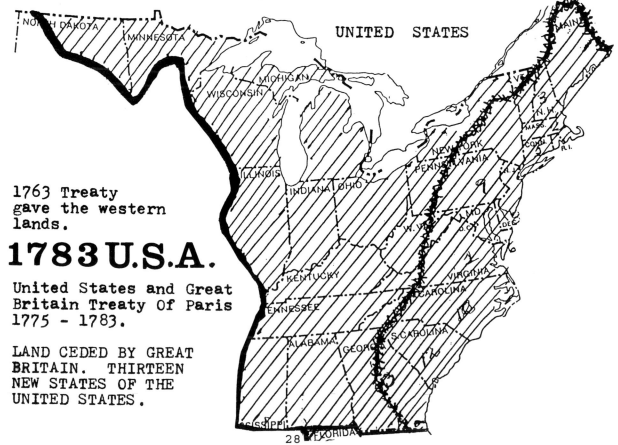

UNITED STATES

1763 Treaty
gave the western
lands.

1783 U.S.A.

United States and Great
Britain Treaty Of Paris
1775 - 1783.

LAND CEDED BY GREAT
BRITAIN. THIRTEEN
NEW STATES OF THE
UNITED STATES.

NEW NATION

The Land Act was made May 20, 1785 and opened the nation to expansion. Ohio Valley was called Northwest Territory and Northwest Ordinance was adopted July 13, 1787. This territory gave five new states: Ohio, Indiana, Illinois, Michigan, Wisconsin.

All states were made equal and had to be admitted in an orderly manner in the union of states. Surveyors were appointed and surveys began. A township was 36 square miles with six sections time six sections and one section was equal to one mile which had 640 acres. One mile of a square mile section was dedicated to education.

TAKING CARE OF THE CHILDREN

Children's care in early times was by one or two, or many persons. There were various methods adopted at different times by families, communities, churches, and government programs for seeing to the needs of children who, for whatever reasons of misfortune, could not be cared for by their families of origin.

The preschool programs can be found in 19th-century kindergartens which began for the education of impoverished immigrant children who were also in need of supervision while their parents worked.

While mothers were full-time home care givers on the farms, the health of family members was as important as the agriculture.

The early schools existed for education but school was only opened two or three months each year. Reading and writing often were not learned. This was the reason many people could not sign their signature and had to use "X" while a learned person spelled and wrote the name.

In ancient times only scribes of the king or the royal house did the writing and paper did not exist. With the colonial apprentice systems the men were the primary care givers and educators of their mostly male charges.

In early colonial times when the westward movement began in 1776, the orphan children joined the walkers and wagons as persons to help with development of the west and provide population. Regardless of the historical era, the real-life causes that had precipitated lengthy separations of children from their parents have tended to be the same - poverty, hardship and parental illness or death.

As for the rise of the orphanage in the 18th century, the idea of the family as the ideal place for children-any children-gave way to the idea of the orphanage as the most practical way to care for large numbers of them. Institutional solutions replaced personal ones.

The ways and accepted practices, policies or institution espoused by one generation have all too often been discarded by the next generation, only to be rediscovered and refitted to meet the social, or political, and ideas of yet another generation.

The single-parent family, far from being a modern problem, existed at close to today's level for much of this country's history. In 1930, there were more than three million female-headed households.

Of course, by the middle of this century, public attitudes and childcare policies had shifted. Experts reviled dormitory-like institutions and favored individualized foster care instead, with family preservation as the ultimate goal of any governmental intervention. This frames up public opinions on taking care of some children.

Why children in a record book? Adoptions have name changes, and genealogy cannot be done if information cannot be reached. Also court minutes give names of children that have guardians and provide a source of information.

Historically, the first orphan house in colonial America was established by George Whitefield who was born December 20, 1714 and died September 30, 1770. He was a Methodist clergyman. He sailed January 10, 1738 from England to Georgia arriving on May 18 in Savannah. He saw the need of the colony's people and especially for an orphan house. The trustees of Georgia presented him with living opportunity in Savannah and granted 500 acres of land as a site for the orphan house. In England and Wales he collected funds for his orphan house. Whitefield gathered forty children. In March 1740 the building of orphans' house began. The place was called Bethesda.

_____
Reference: "Appletons Cyclopaedia Of American Biography", pages 477, 478, Volume VI, 1889.

There was as much preaching as teaching in colonial American schools. But that's more than half the children of the period could have told you, they never set foot in a classroom.

From the outset, the primary goal of American education was support of revealed religion. Though secular sciences gained growing footholds in colonial curriculums after 1700, it was not until the Civil War that intellectual values superseded those of the Gospel.

The English shippers required passengers to America to be age twenty. There were a few Whitfield children that came as immigrants and those that came were with parents. The most remarkable colonizing in America were by the Spanish-Mexicans in 1775 with 118 children to upper California.

GOVERNMENT OF NEW STATES

The Second Continental Congress was retained, but they created a new Congress. A Senate with 26 members. A House Of Representatives with 64 (?). One Representative for 60,000 people. Soon after the Declaration Of Independence, the congress committee had a plan for central government called Articles Of Confederation, but the colonists got rid of the Articles. There were many changing conditions after the Revolutionary War. There were many problems to work out and to find solutions with the freedom of independence.

Most of the Colonies adopted State Constitutions which defined what powers belonged to the government. The principal idea was, *Government of the people, by the people, for the people.* A national Constitutional Convention began work in 1786, and the work was completed Sept. 27, 1787. The United States Constitution was written in four months. To obtain ratifications of the Constitution for the United States Of America, the Constitution had to be placed before the people of the different states for approval and adoption. For a colony to become a state it had to ratify the United States Constitution and meet the requirements for being a state.

The Congress saw that elections were held in the states. Senators and Representatives were chosen in March 1789 at the capitol in NY. On April 30, 1789 George Washington was inaugurated as the first President of the US. There was much work for the government people and workers to follow: Other elections, structural plan of government, development of departments, courts, army, and all entities needed for a government operation. The Bill of Rights was ratified Jan. 8, 1798. The Capitol was moved from NY to Washington, DC, in 1800.

Western lands were a problem with trade as well as the trade arrangements with European powers. Financial problems were many and slowly were solved. Spain held the claim to land west of the Mississippi River in America, although the frontier western territories were not under control of any nation. This need for future control of lands and trading resulted in the United States getting the land of middle America by the Louisiana Purchase of 1803. The government made payment for the land. It took sixty years to acquire the land. There was an Army of the West in expeditions and explorations but not much else except for the Indians. All the Indian Bureaus and territory districts had to be worked out with various tribes.

The Battle of Alamo at Texas in 1845 brought the Texas annexation of land to the US. The Mexican-American war took place in 1846 to 1848. The US acquired these western lands by Mexico's Treaty of Guadalupe Hidalgo in 1848. The Americans gained CA, AZ, NV, UT, and part of TX west of the Rocky Mountains.

The United States government had an Oregon Territory Treaty from Great Britain in 1846. The area included Oregon, Washington, and parts of states east of Oregon.

After 1912 the US had 48 stars on the flag. After 1942 Hawaii and Alaska became states of the US of America making 50 stars on the American flag.

Immigrants

They came to America for the opportunity for freedom and the opportunity for work. They felt they would be self-reliant immigrants. All they needed was work and food crops and the opportunity.

Forgotten in a haze of history and family lore are the nation's struggles near the turn of the century to accommodate the tidal wave of new arrivals from which so many of today's Americans are descended.

Life in the beginning in the colonies was hard for all working people whether immigrants or natives. Most people with the surname of Whitfield were natives. <u>Huddled masses yearning to breathe free</u> is a romantic phrase.

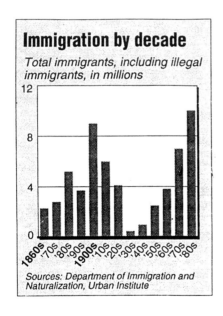

Immigration by decade

Total immigrants, including illegal immigrants, in millions

Sources: Department of Immigration and Naturalization, Urban Institute

Researched accumulated by a 1911 commission on immigration concluded that half of the welfare recipients nationwide in 1909 were immigrant families. According to calculations from the 1990 census, 9% of immigrant households received welfare payments, compared with 7.4% of households headed by natives.

Schooling has lifted succeeding generations of new Americans to better economic circumstances drained budgets everywhere.

During the early years of this century the 30 biggest cities had more than half of the students from immigrant families in public schools.

In reality, immigration was a temporary escape from a jobless and famine-ridden Europe.

Historians estimate that as many as a third of the nearly 30 million foreigners who arrived between the Civil War and World War I moved back to their native countries.

United States in 1908 and 1930's saw economic depression in the country. Nevertheless once this condition lifted, the flow of foreigners continued to the United States. American cultures and principles that were developed were constantly changing. The immigrant influx soared in the 19th century. Argument began to focus on economic and cultural reasons.

In the 20th century rules emerged requiring that new arrivals possess money, good health, skills, and eventually literacy.

In other respects everywhere immigrants have enriched and strengthened the fabric of American life.

New Americans: a sense of scale

Net immigrant arrivals as a percentage of population growth.

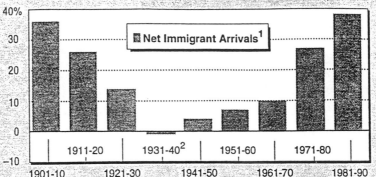

[1] New arrivals, legal and illegal, minus emigrants from the U.S.

[2] Net migration was negative in this decade, the only one in U.S. history, reflecting both little immigration and the Depression-encouraged emigration

Milestones in immigration legislation

CHINESE EXCLUSION ACT (1882); First major federal legislation, this act begins a long era of Asian exclusion.

IMMIGRATION ACT of 1917; Required literacy (reading of 40 words in immigrant's native language) for the first time.

NATIONAL ORIGINS ACT (1924 and later); Sharply reduced immigration and applied per-country limits on arrivals that strongly favored Northern Europe.

HART-CELLER ACT of 1965; Removed per-country limits on arrivals (though left overall limits); greatly eased immigration for all with relatives in the U.S.

IMMIGRATION REFORM AND CONTROL ACT (1986); Known as "IRCA," the act legalized more than 2.5 million previously illegal U.S. residents and applied sanctions on employers of illegal immigrants.

IMMIGRATION ACT of 1990; Opened up a worldwide limit of about 700,000 arrivals annually, but many aren't subject to this cap and, in 1993, legal admissions totaled 904,000, the highest since 1914.

Sources: Immigration and Naturalization Service, Census Bureau, Urban Institute

Steady Population Growth. In 1750, there were one million people. In 1775-2.5 million people. In 1800-5.3 million. In 1900-76 million. 1950-150 million.

The United States population increased more than 50 times since the first census counted 3,929,214 Americans (including 697,697 slaves). In 1970, the total population was expected between 205 and 210 million people.

Opposition to immigration came from organized labor. The Americanization process became almost impossible with people coming from all countries. It was in the 1880's that the movement to restrict immigration began. During the 1880's a change took place in the character of the immigration with people coming from southeastern Europe and the Near East.

Population Growth United States 1790 to 1960

Year	Population
1790	3,929,214
1800	5,308,483
1810	7,239,881
1820	9,638,453
1830	12,866,020
1840	17,069,453
1850	23,191,876
1860	31,443,321
1870	39,818,449
1880	50,155,783
1890	62,947,714
1900	75,994,575
1910	91,972,266
1920	105,710,620
1930	122,775,046
1940	131,669,275
1950	150,697,361
1960	179,323,175

Population of the twelve colonies in 1715. America Colonies by Chalmer.

	White	Black	Total
Massachusetts	94,000	2,000	96,000
Virginia	72,000	23,000	95,000
Maryland	40,700	9,500	50,200
Connecticut	46,000	1,500	47,500
Pennsylvania Delaware	43,300	2,500	45,800
New York	27,000	4,000	31,000
New Jersey	21,000	1,500	22,500
South Carolina	6,250	10,500	16,750
North Carolina	7,500	3,700	11,200
New Hampshire	9,500	150	9,650
Rhode Island	8,500	500	9,000
	375,750	58,850	434,600

Report of Contra Costa Times, Dec. 28, 1994.

Overtaking New York, Texas now is the nation's second most populous state, the Census Bureau reported Tuesday.

California remained No. 1 by a wide margin, gaining 214,000 residents to close the year ending July 1 at 31.4 million.

Texas and New York each trailed by 13 million — 18.4 million and 18.2 million, respectively.

Nevada, which grew by 5.4 percent, remained the fastest-growing state.

Texas gained 356,000 people in 1994 — Nevada had the highest rate of growth, but Texas had the largest number of new residents.

Population in the U.S.

Texas added 356,000 people in one year to surpass New York as the nation's second most populous state. Most and least populous states as of July 1 1994 (all figures are in millions):

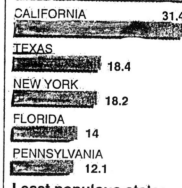

Most populous states

CALIFORNIA	31.4
TEXAS	18.4
NEW YORK	18.2
FLORIDA	14
PENNSYLVANIA	12.1

Least populous states

WYOMING	.48
VERMONT	.58
ALASKA	.61
NORTH DAKOTA	.64

Source: Census Bureau

WASHINGTON — U.S. residents who were born in another country made up 8.7 percent of the population last year, the highest proportion of immigrants since World War II, a new Census Bureau study shows.

That means 22.6 million people — nearly one in 11 U.S. residents — were foreign-born, and one-third of them lived in California, according to the study released 1996.

One-fifth of the immigrants, or 4.5 million people, arrived here in the last five years.

The 8.7 immigrant percentage of the population is up from 7.9 percent in 1990 and nearly double the 1970 level of 4.8 percent.

Early this century, the percent of foreign-born was far higher than now — 14.7 percent in 1910 — following 50 years of sustained immigration. But the flow declined sharply after Congress in 1924 enacted a system of racial and ethnic quotas. By 1970 the percent of foreign-born dropped to 4.8 percent of the population.

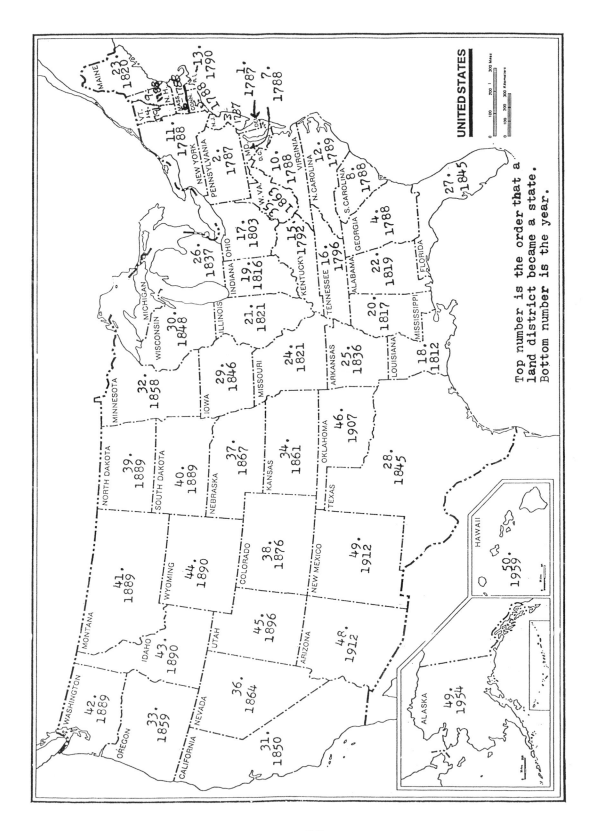

Top number is the order that a
land district became a state.
Bottom number is the year.

POPULATION

In 1783 the new nation had an area of 850,000 square miles and the people lived on or near the Atlantic Coast, a large part of the land remainder was occupied by the Indians.

Following the War of 1812 the most outstanding of all the western migrations took place. By 1820 the western movement had carried three million people across the Appalachian mountains. Settlers to the west were nearly half of the people of the United States. The steamboat and the traveling wagons on trails were the factors in this movement. Durimg the period from 1820 to 1860 more than 5,000,000 immigrants came to America in the hope of improving their conditions.

In the South in 1850 only about 350,000 white families, out of a total of 1,800,000, held slaves. The plantations of the south varied in size. Fully two thirds of the white population of the south had no direct connection with slavery.

The eighteen free-labor states of the North had a population in 1860 of about 19,000,000. The northern states had an advantage of man power and economic industrial resources. The population of the States which joined the Confederacy was slightly in excess of 9,000,000, over one-third of whom were slaves. The Civil War resolved the conflict from new changes in the country.

The expansion of industry began a shift from farms to towns. The population increased from 31,500,000 in 1860 to about 76,000,000 in 1900. Foreigners were welcomed by the government and by industry. The United States in 1930 had ninety-three metropolitan districts, each having an aggregate population of 100,000 or more. To the large towns these foreigners found work in the industries and on the rural farms.

In 1864, the Federal government set up the Immigration Bureau in Washington, D.C. for the purpose of assisting immigrants coming from other countries to America.

There was something that happened in the discovery of gold in California that no one had planned. In 1849 the people went for gold and homesteads. This brought the people westward and from other countries to mining and agriculture. It brought the population for California which became the fiftieth state to join the union of states in 1850.

The Chinese immigrants to California had done much to build the railroads and make water irrigation to land for agricultural pursuits. It was a historic day when the railroads of the east and west were to met linking the country from east to west and from west to east.

The Spanish-Mexicans did the colonization of California and the Missions of the Church were the centers for the people including the Indians.

WHITFIELD AND ALL THREE HUNDRED YEARS AND MORE

The following States in the reference text tell the history of Americans with the surname Whitfield from 1620 to a later 1900 time.

For three hundred years and more the Whitfield families and generations of Whitfield members were and continue to be a part of the history and development of the country.

ALABAMA

Restoration of Gaineswood, a 107-year-old Greek-revival mansion in Demopolis, Alabama, will be undertaken by the Alabama Historical Commission in order to return the structure to its nineteenth-century elegance. Perhaps the state's best known antebellum mansion, Gaineswood has suffered from many years of disrepair despite urgings from historic preservationists that the building be saved. The Alabama Historical Commission acquired the property late in 1971 and immediately initiated plans to restore the structure.

Gaineswood was built over an eighteen-year period by General Nathan B. Whitfield, who served as his own architect. The sixteen-room mansion, completed in 1860, features two domes, one over the parlor and one over the dining room, equipped with windows to provide lighting. Ornate chandeliers hang from long chains secured in the top of the ceiling. Many of the original furnishings in the house were imported from England.

The Alabama Department of Conservation purchased Gaineswood in 1966 when private individuals could no longer afford upkeep of the mansion. The state agency conducted tours of the property, though it attempted no systematic restoration to prevent further deterioration. Now that the Alabama Historical Commission has assumed responsibility for the landmark, research into the original plans, paint colors, and so on will begin in preparation for authentic restoration. When completed, the restored structure will be maintained as a house museum for an estimated 25,000 visitors annually.

Shortly before announcing the proposed restoration of Gaineswood, the Alabama Historical Commission reported that more than $14 million has been spent by public and private organizations in the state for historic preservation during the past five years. According to Commission chairman, Milo B. Howard, Jr., the largest sum of money for preservation, $4,366,408, was spent in 1971, more than twice the amount spent in 1967. Most of the major restorations were accomplished by local preservation societies and city and county governments. An estimated $5.5 million more in public and private funds would have been available for preservation projects had there been matching funds from state or federal governments.

Gaineswood

A National Historic Landmark
805 Whitfield Street East
Demopolis, Alabama 36732

Gaineswood Mansion

George S. Gaines, U.S. Indian Factor made his home among the forest of trees in the fertile region of Alabama. Gaines sold the property to General Nathan Bryan Whitfield who had moved his family from Lenoir County, North Carolina to Marengo County, Alabama in 1834. Whitfield began a plantation with fifty-six slaves on fifteen hundred acres and became the architect and builder of Gaineswood House about twelve miles south of Demopolis.

Three styles of Greek architecture were represented in the house. The outside had Doric order of lines. The interior was Ionic with the exception of the drawing room in the Corinthian style. The ceilings of the dining room and the parlor had flat domes, over large rooms, cupolas with stained glass which provided reflections of color. Chandeliers and Gothic designs of wood molds were part of a room. All wood boards of lumber in the building were "edgegrain" or "rift" and were made for durability in the house.

A portico, like a porch, was fifty-one feet square and flanked on the north by a terrace of equal length. Flower garden could be entered from the terrace. The poplar and oak trees were many and were a grove of random planting.

The kitchen with its great fireplace, equipped with cranes for handling pots, and ovens was apart from the house and some sixty feet away. Over the years the kitchen obtained a new place in the basement, and very late a space on the first floor of the building. The artesian well with water was east of the north terrace.

On the plantation there were servant houses, the barn, the stables, the shop, smoke house, and an office house, and other buildings. There were driveways and arches.

Cotton crops and corn crops were carried to market from the plantation. Steamboats traveled the Tombigby River and took the crops to market.

Gaineswood is the finest Greek Revival Mansion in the South

The travel was first by carriages, stagecoach or private conveyance. In the early 1800's the Memphis and Charleston Railroad passed through the northern part of Alabama. Travel later by railroad to Louisiana, Mississippi, and Alabama opened agriculture development and supplied a cotton and corn belt.

The people went southwest and among them were many named Whitfield. Many Whitfield families in North Carolina moved and in another generation to develop the southwest part of the United States.

ALABAMA AND MIGRATION

The first southwestern migration was for cotton and new land and good soil. Cotton succeeded tobacco as the staple crop of the South. The planters of the eastern coast had exhaused lands and streamed into Alabama with a large number of slaves. The inventions of the cotton gin in 1793 and the steamboat in 1807 did much to assist in this migration.

Alabama was formed and admitted to the Union on December 14, 1819. It was a territory before becoming a state. The land area was 51,998 square miles. Population 2,646,248. Montgomery was the capital. Nine representatives in the federal congress between 1933 and 1942. (1)

Cotton culture operations required planting, hoeing, picking and ginning and was simple and required very little training. Alabama, South Carolina, and Georgia had the nation's crops. Cotton gave the cultivators something to do in labor all year long. Southerners raised corn, wheat, hogs, and cattle but "Cotton was King." It was the greatest export of the nation and equal to wheat export.

There had been a migration in 1790 to the western part of the coastal new states. In 1820 this was the second migration westward in the southern and northern parts of the new land. This included Alabama, Georgia, Tennessee, Kentucky, West Virginia, Ohio, northern part of Pennsylvania, and western part of New York. This migration also included the southern coastal parts of Mississippi and Louisiana. (2)

Reference. 1. The Development Of America by Fremont P. Wirth, published 1956. 2. History of A Free People by Henry W. Bragdon and Samuel P. McCutchen, published editions 1954, 1956, 1958, 1960.

MARRIAGES

Alabama
1. Edith James Whitfield, b. Feb.4 , 1842 and d. 1904. On Oct. 24, 1865 she married Gen. Charles William Dustin (also Dustan).
2. Loudie Whitfield was born March 1856. On Dec. 15, 1882 she married Joseph A. Elliott. In 1933 they were residents of Moundville, Alabama.
3. Addie Whitfield was b. Jan. 2, 1857 in Tuscaloosa, AL. In 1876 Addie married Thomas J. Powers (b. 1846-d. 1928).
4. Leonie Sauvalle Whitfield was married Feb. 17, 1897 to Walter W. McDaniel. He was born Oct. 3, 1871. In 1927 the family resided in Sumter County, AL.
5. Gladys Whitfield, age 20, married George Elbert Barnett, age 31, of Birmingham, AL on July 28, 1920. Gladys Whitfield's parents were Nicholas Whitfield and Anna Whitfield from England.

....There are many other marriages in Alabama.

Georgia Record. Henry Hodges Whitfield (1826-1886) married Elizabeth Pipkin who died 1856.

Georgia Record. George W. Whitfield born 1853 married (1) K.C. Daniel and (2) Mary Wilcox Daniel born 1845.

PART II

Compiled for the purpose of showing the lineage of

Nathan Bryan Whitfield
Architect and Builder of "Gaineswood"

October 6, 1975 Bruce Whitfield Jr.

= Priscilla Lawrence

1713 = Elizabeth Goodman

1741 = Rachel Bryan b.1723

1798 = Winifred Bryan b.1774

1819 = Elizabeth Whitfield b.1801

1855 = Mary Alice Toscue b.1938

Constantine Whitfield b.1728 — 1754 = Barba. Williams b.1756

Sarah Jones Watkins b.1777 — 94 = Rachel Whitfield b.1740

Nathan Whitfield b.1758

Betsy Whitfield b.1825

John Whitfield 1778 — 18 27 = Mary Lewis Slade b.1853

Thomas Brigham Winn b.1938 = 1854 Nathalie Carr Whitfield b.1859

Luke Whitfield 17 89 = Louisa Forville

Samuel Slade — Mary Whitfield b.1825

(3) Three brothers William, Bryan and Needham were present at
the Battle of Moores Creek Bridge, Feb. 1776. Needham had
to Col. Caldwell who commanded the Wing. William was a Private
in the Light Horse. He and his brother-in-law Lewis Williams
took prisoners. Dr. McDonald commander B.A. Jones William
and Needham also captured Col. Farquard Campbell who after
the war married the widow of his captor who was then
the Widow Smith.

(4) Needham Bryan II
was on the Bryan side at the Battle of the
Alamance, 16th May, 1771, but then
took the part of the Revolt. He was a
member of the Johnston County of the
Provisional Congress which met at
New Bern the April 1776.

(5) Hon. Nathan Bryan was Grand father of
Jones County N.C. was Nathan Whitfield Jr. 1794 the
father of Nathan Bryan Whitfield. He married Ann
was elected to represent his county in the N.C.
District in Congress and relative of Philadelphia
He died while in Congress at Phila. His
1795 and was buried in the Baptist Meeting
house yard.

40

PART I

MARRIED

Sir Thomas Whitfield (1)
1st Ancestor from Roberts
Chaplain (etd) in (1154)

(1) Sir Thomas Whitfield
2nd Hon East India Co.
Incorporated by Q Elizabeth
31. Dec 1600.

Sir Robert Mudlam
D 1653

Lady Eliano Sutton
B 1665

Matthew Whitfield

Ria

Sir Charles Mudlam
B 1660

Bridgit Drury
B 1642

Matthew Whitfield

16 36

14 55

17

Sir Thomas Smith
1st Hon East India Co.

William Bryan
B 1654

Lady Alice Mudlam
B 1654

Matthew Whitfield

Eliz

Arthur Smith

Needham Bryan
B 1670

Ann Rawbau
B 1675

William Whitfield

13

John Smith

Needham Bryan
B 1726

Nancy Smith
B 1728

William Whitfield
B 1725

Kate
D 1772

(4) 17

14 89

11

(2) 17

17

John Smith
B 1673

Matthew Bryan
B 1754

Winifred Bryan
B 1755

Bryan Whitfield
B 1577

Wm

Hardy Bryan
B 1715 Q B 1740

(5) 17 75

(3) 17 75

41

17 08

17 48

Nathan Bryan Whitfield
B 1799

Eliz

Elizabeth Whitfield

Bryan Watkins Whitfield
B 1828

Mary
B 1838

Mrs Sarah (Bonnie) Worsley
B 1724

(2) William Whitfield II
Was a member of Gov. Caswells Council 1799
Appointed by the Council held in new Bern 1775
J.P. for Johnston County Member from Dobbs
to the Assembly held in Wilmington 1761-1762.

Whitfield Pedigree

ALABAMA – UNITED STATES CENSUS 1820 – 1850 WITH WHITFIELD

1820 Year

1820	Whitfield , Ansil	.....	Limestone County, Al
1820	Whitfield , Ansil	.....	Limestone County, Al
1820	Whitfield , Ansil	.....	Limestone County, Al
1820	Whitfield , Bynum	.....	Limestone County, Al
1820	Whitfield , Bynum	.....	Limestone County, Al
1820	Whitfield , Bynum	.....	Limestone County, Al
1820	Whitfield , Wright	.....	Limestone County, Al
1820	Whitfield , Wright	.....	Limestone County, Al

1830 Year

1830	Whitfield , David	.....	Shelby County, Al

1840 Year

1840	Whitfield , George W.		Limestone County, Al
1840	Whitfield , George W.		Sumter County, Al
1840	Whitfield , Henry	.....	Montgomery County, Al
1840	Whitfield , Nancy	.....	Sunter County, Al
1840	Whitfield , Sarah	.....	Loundes County, Al

1850 Year

1850	Whitfield , Allen	.....	Talladega County, Al
1850	Whitfield , Benjamin	....	Perry County, Al
1850	Whitfield , Benjamin	....	Tuscaloosa County, Al
1850	Whitfield , Betty	....	Greene County, Al
1850	Whitfield , David	.....	Shelby County, Al
1850	Whitfield , Calons	.....	Marengo County, Al
1850	Whitfield , George	.....	Shelby County, Al
1850	Whitfield , George W.	...	Marengo County, Al
1850	Whitfield , James	.....	Sumter County, Al
1850	Whitfield , John	.....	Limestone County, Al
1850	Whitfield , John	.....	Limestone County, Al
1850	Whitfield , John	.....	Clarke County, Al
1850	Whitfield , Margaret	...	Lawrence County, Al
1850	Whitfield , Martha	.....	Limestone County, Al
1850	Whitfield , N. S.	.....	Tuscaloosa County, Al
1850	Whitfield , Nathan B.	...	Marengo County, Al
1850	Whitfield , William	...	Jefferson County, Al

GENEALOGY GROUPS RECORDS

DESCENDANTS OF CHARLES P. N. WHITFIELD AND MARY ADELINE HICKS WHITFIELD OF GEORGIA.
....Submitted by Gene T. Bell of Orlando, Florida, April 13, 1994.

Gene T. Bell searches for the ancestors of Charles P. N. Whitfield born about 1823 in Georgia and for information on the family of Charles P. N. Whitfield, and the early history of the ancestors.

Gene T. Bell is in communication with the Church of Latter Day Saints Library Archives. He has compiled a listing of 16 men named Charles Whitfield from various sources of history and records.

The Genealogy pages are kept together and under Alabama for this state had the most birth and death records in the lineage kinship. Alabama with 46 records. Florida with 21 records. Georgia with 15 records. South Carolina with two records. North Carolina with one record.

FAMILY GROUP RECORD Page One
I.   Family of Charles P. N. Whitfield born 1823 and Mary Adeline Hicks Whitfield (b. 1827 SC-d. 1897). Residents of Georgia, Washington County.
....Note by Gene T. Bell-Page two.

FAMILY GROUP RECORD Page Two
II.   Family of REUBEN HENRY WHITFIELD (b. 1843 GA-d. 1935 FL) and Catherine Bethney Faulk Whitfield (b. 1844 AL-d. 1910 AL). Eight children with surname Whitfield. Residents of Georgia and Alabama.

FAMILY GROUP RECORD Page Three
III.   Family of WILLIAM J. HARDY (b. 1869 AL-d. 1944 AL) and Martha Jane Whitfield (b. 1881 AL-d. 1967 AL). Nine Hardy children. Residents of Alabama.

FAMILY GROUP RECORD Page Two
IV.   Family of CHARLES RANSOM WHITFIELD (b. 1871 GA-d. 1957 FL) and Emma Williams Whitfield (b. 1870-d. 1952 FL). Seven Whitfield children. Residents of Alabama.

FAMILY GROUP RECORD Page Four
V.   Family of JOHN HENRY KEMBO (b. 1875 GA-d. 1962 FL) and Mary Adeline Whitfield Kembro (b. 1885 AL-d. 1967 FL). Nine Kembro children. Residents of Alabama and Florida.

FAMILY GROUP RECORD Page Three
VI.   Family of RENEGER KEMBRO (b. 1873 GA-d. 1966 FL) and Georgia Ann Whitfield Kembro (b. 1878 AL-d. 1968 FL). Nine living Kembro children. Residents of Alabama and Florida.

FAMILY GROUP RECORD Page Four
VII.   Family of JOHN EDWARD HUDSON (b. 1869 AL-d. 1929 FL) and Amelia Alice Whitfield (b. 1869 GA-d. 1946 FL). Thirteen Hudson children. Residents of Georgia, Alabama, and Florida.

FAMILY GROUP RECORD. Pages Four.
VII. Family of JOHN EDWARD HUDSON (b.1869-d.1929 FL)
And Amelia Alice Whitfield (b.1869 GA-d.1946 FL).
Thirteen Hudson children. Residents of Georgia,
Alabama and Florida.

Family Group Record

Husband Given name(s)	CHARLES P. N.			Last name	WHITFIELD
Born (day month year) 1823	Place	GA		CKDI- LI	
Christened	Place				
Died	Place	CIVIL WAR, CONFEDERATE			
Buried	Place				
Married 18 FEB 1847	Place	WASHINGTON CO., GA.			
Husband's father Given name(s)				Last name	WHITFIELD
Husband's mother Given name(s)				Maiden name	

Wife Given name(s)	MARY ADELINE			Last name	HICKS
Born (day month year) 1827	Place	SC		CKDI- M 6	
Christened 1 MCH 1828	Place				
Died 9 NOV 1897	Place				
Buried	Place				
Wife's father Given name(s)				Last name	HICKS
Wife's mother Given name(s)				Maiden name	

Children List each child (whether living or dead) in order of birth.

1 Sex M	Given name(s)	RUBEN HENRY		Last name	WHITFIELD
Born (day month year) 20 OCT 1849	Place			GA.	
Christened	Place			Baptized 9 MAY 1954	
Died 7 DEC 1935	Place	PANAMA CITY, BAY, FL.		Endowed 12 MAY 1954	
Spouse Given name(s)	CATHERINE		Last name	FAULK	
Married 8 JAN 1897	Place			Sealed to spouse 8 FEB 1955	

Your name	GENE T. BELL
Address	ORLANDO, FL.,
	Date prepared 5 OCT 1992
Your relationship to the husband and wife on this form	
Husband G G GND SON	Wife G G GND SON

44

FAMILY GROUP RECORD – Georgia, Alabama, Florida

Husband   -RUBEN HENRY WHITFIELD.   Born-October 20, 1843.
Place   -Dooley County, Georgia. (Church of Latter Day Saints
           (LDS) Ordinance data. B. May 8,1954)
Died   -December 7, 1935. Place-Panama City, Bay, Florida.
           (LDS E. May 12, 1954)
Buried   -December 8, 1935. Place-Dundee, Geneva, Alabama
Married   -January 8, 1883 in dale County, Alabama. (LDS ss 8
           Feb. 1955 88)
Father   -CHARLES P. N. WHITFIELD, 1823
Mother   -Mary Adeline Hicks (Ruben for Reuben)
Other Wife - Bertha Mitchell, 1849
Wife   -Catherine Bethney Faulk, born March 18, 1844.   Place-
           Coosa County, Alabama. Died-August 2, 1910.   Place-
           Geneva County, Alabama.
Father   -John S. Faulk
Mother   -Mary Gilmore. Children eight.

1. Amelia Alice Whitfield, born December 3, 1869 in Georgia, and
    died March 3, 1946. Amelia Whitfield married John Hudson.
2. Charles Ransom Whitfield, born December 11, 1871 in Georgia,
    and died July 15, 1967. Charles R. Whitfield married Emma
    Williams on January 9, 1898.
3. Laurinda Whitfield, born March 21, 1874 in Georgia, and died
    March 8, 1942 in Hartford, Geneva County, Alabama. Buried-
    March 10, 1942 in Dundee, Geneva County, Alabama. Laurinda
    Whitfield married John B. Norwood on August 17, 1899 in
    Geneva County, Alabama.
4. John Marion Whitfield, born March 14, 1876 in Georgia, and
    August 16, 1943 he died. John M. Whitfield married Maggie E.
    Ward on April 28, 1905.
5. Georgia Ann Whitfield, born November 21, 1878 in Georgia, and
    died August 18, 1968. Georgia A. Whitfield married Reneger
    Kembro on April 11, 1901.
6. Martha Jane Whitfield, born October 18, 1881.   Place-
    Skipperville, Dale County, Alabama. She died December 28,
    1967. Martha J. Whitfield married William Hardy on January
    20, 1898.
7. Mary Adeline Whitfield, born July 18, 1885.   Place-
    Skipperville, Dale County, Alabama. She died November 7,
    1967, Mary A. Whitfield married John Henry Kembro on
    November 3, 1901.
8. Susan Agusta Whitfield, born July 18, 1888, Place Dundee,
    Geneva County, Alabama. She died September 22, 1901

LDS-B: May 8, 1954 E: May 14, 1954 SP: February 10, 1955.

Dallas County, TX Record. George Washington Whitfield, born
Feb. 12, 1806, in Sussex County, VA, and died after 1891 at
Garland Town, Dallas County, TX.

"Memorial and Biographical History of Dallas County, TX." pp
615, 616. Published 1892.
Marriage Records. "Williamson County, Tennessee Marriages" by
Bejach Wilena Roberts. pp 5, 48, 53, 63, 193, 203, 280.
"Old Cemeteries of Dallas County" by Willie Flowers Carlisle.
P 147.
"History of Dallas County, Texas." p 615.
This family appears in "Albemarle Parish Register 1739-1778."

Whitfield family notes by Gene T. Bell, the great grandson of this family:

Catherine (Katherine Faulk) burial place at Shiloh Baptist Cemetery.

Amelia A. Whitfield-Hudson died March 3, 1946 in Apopka, Orange County, Florida.

Charles Ransom may have died 15 July 1957 at Orlando, Orange County, Florida. After his first wife died, he married.

Laurinda Whitfield-Norwood is known to have these names-Laurinda Cordelia Ophelia Catherine Martha Ann Bethney Whitfield.

John Marion Whitfield died August 16, 1943 in Panama City, Bay Florida.

Martha Jane Whitfield-Hardy died December 28, 1967 in Phoenix City, Russell County, Alabama. After first husband died she married.

Mary Adeline Whitfield-Kembro died November 7, 1967 in Orange County, Florida.

Husband CHARLES RANSOM		name WHITFIELD	
Born (day month year) 11 DEC 1871	Place	GA.	
WIFE Lella Linda Kindell			
Died 15 JUL 1957	Place ORLANDO, ORANGE, FL.		
Buried 17 JUL 1957	Place ORLANDO, ORANGE, FL.		
Married **Charles Ransom Whitfield married second wife**			
Husband's father Given name(s) RUBEN HENRY		Last name	WHITFIELD
Husband's mother Given name(s) SUSAN BETHNEY CATHERINE		Maiden name	FAULK

Lella Linda Kindell-Whitfield died January 1, 1974. Gene T. Bell prepared the chart. Husband-Nephew. Wife-Nephew. Chart made November 27, 1992.

Church of The Latter Days Saints Heritage Collection Codes: AFN-ancestral File Number. B-Baptized. E-Endowed. SS-Sealed to Spouse. SP-Sealed to Parents

WHITES AND CHEROKEES

The whites were among the Cherokees Indians in Georgia 1828-1838. The Cherokee Nation occupied all of present Georgia counties of Bartow (formerly Cass), Catoosa, Chatooga, Cherokee, Cobbs, Dade, Dawson, Fannin, Floyd, Forsyth, Gilmer, Gordon, Lumpkin, Murray, Paulding, Pickens, Polk, Towns, Union, Walker, White, and Whitfield.

The land lotteries attracted whites to counties where there were not Indians. In 1832 there was Cherokee land lottery Revolutionary winners.

The immigrants to Georgia came mostly from North Carolina. And there were those people who came by ship by Europe.

NEWT WHEELER married first wife SAVANNA WHITFIELD, daughter of Charles P. N. Whitfield and Mary Adeline Hicks-Whitfield. They had no children. Newt Wheeler married second wife Lou Caraway.

RUBEN WHITFIELD born in North Carolina married RHODA-born in North Carolina. They had children: 1. Emily Whitfield, girl in Georgia. 2. Pinkney Whitfield, boy in Georgia. 3. Josephine Whitfield, girl in Georgia.
_____
Reference: 1850 Census, Washington County, Georgia, page 494, number 661.

SHELLMAN WHITFIELD, born in Georgia, and married Julian who was born in Georgia. They had daughter Martha Ann Whitfield born in Georgia.

Reference: 1850 Census, Washington County, Georgia, page 491, Number 627.

NAPOLEAN B. WHITFIELD born in Georgia, and married Martha born in South Carolina. They had daughter Amanda Whitfield.

Reference: 1850 Census, Washington County, Georgia, page 509, Number 775, and on the 1850 Census.

WILLIAM A. WHITFIELD may have been the brother. Napolean B. Whitfield married Martha Hicks, February 18, 1847 at Washington County, Georgia.

Gene T. Bell of Orlando, Florida who researched in 1993 on Charles P. N. Whitfield believes that Charles was the brother of Napolean Whitfield and Sheldon Whitfield on the 1850 Census of Washington County, Georgia. Two brothers with same marriage date, and wives with the same maiden name of Hicks.

SHELDON WHITFIELD married Julia Ann Begood, November 20, 1843, Washington County, Georgia.

Reference: 40,000 Georgia Marriages, Washington Co., GA. Page 316. Microfiche at FHC, LDS, Orlando, Florida.

GEORGIA MARRIAGES

George A. P. Whitfield to Sarah Stanford, August 31, 1834, Columbia, Georgia.

John Whitfield to Anna Jones September 15, 1824. Reg. Bulloch County, Georgia.

A. R. Whitfield to Smatha Braswell, May 12, 1882, Decatur County, Georgia.

Robert Whitfield to Anna Jones, December 1852. Reg. Decatur County, Georgia.

Charles Whitfield Private in Company E 6th Georgia Infanty in Civil War.
    Georgia Record. Caroline Matilda Smith married Benjamin S. Whitfield before 1818. Benjamin S. was born about 1785 to 1787 at Hancock Co., GA, and died after Oct. 18, 1831, in Putnam Co., FA.

Family Group Record

Husband Given name(s)	WILLIAM J.		Last name	HARDY

	Born (day month year) 28 DEC 1869	Place BLUE SPRINGS, BARBOUR, ALA.
	Christened	Place
	Died 3 MAY 1944	Place PHENIX CITY, RUSSEL, ALA
	Buried 4 MAY 1944	Place DUNDEE, GENEVA, ALA.
	Married 20 JAN 1898	Place DUNDEE, GENEVA, ALA.

Husband's father Given name(s)	WILLIAM ALLEN	Last name	HARDY
Husband's mother Given name(s)	ELIZABETH	Maiden name	HICKS

Wife Given name(s)	MARTHA JANE		Last name	WHITFIELD

	Born (day month year) 18 OCT 1881	Place SKIPPERVILLE, DALE, ALA
	Christened	Place
	Died 28 DEC 1967	Place COLUMBUS, MUSCOGEE, GA.
	Buried 29 DEC 1967	Place DUNDEE, GENEVA, ALA.

Wife's father Given name(s)	RUBEN HENRY	Last name	WHITFIELD
Wife's mother Given name(s)	CATHRINE	Maiden name	FAULK

Children List each child (whether living or dead) in order of birth.

1 Sex F

Given name(s)	LENIA EVEA		Last name	HARDY
Born (day month year) 18 OCT 1899	Place DUNDEE, GENEVA, ALA			
Christened	Place			
Died 16 MAY 1943	Place ALA.			
Spouse Given name(s)	CHARLIE O.		Last name	INGRAM
Married 29 APR 1917	Place			

2 Sex F

Given name(s)	MARY LESIE		Last name	HARDY
Born (day month year) 24 MCH 1901	Place DUNDEE, GENEVA, ALA.			
Christened	Place			
Died /0 9 APR 1939	Place			
Spouse Given name(s)	WILLIAM CARSWELL		Last name	BARNES
Married 29 DEC 1919	Place			

3 Sex F

Given name(s)	OZZIE LOUISE		Last name	HARDY
Born (day month year) 13 FEB 1903	Place SLOCOMB, GENEVA, ALA.			
Christened	Place			
Died 14 MAY 1959	Place			
Spouse Given name(s)	QUINN		Last name	CULVERHOUSE
Married 3 JAN 1931	Place			

Your name GENE T. BELL	Your relationship to the husband and wife on this form Husband GRT NEPHEW Wife GRT NEPHEW

| Husband Given name(s) | WILLIAM J. | Last name | HARDY |
| Wife Given name(s) | MARTHA JANE | Maiden name | WHITFIELD |

Children List each child (whether living or dead) in order of birth.

4 Sex F
Given name(s)	MAMMIE IDEL	Last name	HARDY
Born (day month year)	18 OCT 1904	Place	SLOCOMB, GENEVA, ALA.
Christened		Place	
Died	3 March 1979		
Spouse Given name(s)	JOHN OLIN	Last name	INGRAM
Married	1920	Place	

5 Sex F
Given name(s)	DOLLIE JANE	Last name	HARDY
Born (day month year)	26 JUL 1907	Place	SLOCOMB, GENEVA, ALA.
Christened		Place	
Died		Place	
Spouse Given name(s)	WALTER JOSEPH	Last name	JOHNSON
Married	8 June 1923		

6 Sex M
Given name(s)	WILLIAM ALLEN	Last name	HARDY
Born (day month year)	16 OCT 1910	Place	DUNDEE, GENEVA, ALA.
Christened		Place	
Died		Place	
Spouse Given name(s)	CORA EONIA	Last name	TINDELL
Married	11 JAN 1934	Place	

7 Sex M
Given name(s)	WALLACE GENE	Last name	HARDY
Born (day month year)	24 AUG 1914	Place	DUNDEE, GENEVA, ALA
Christened		Place	
Died		Place	
Spouse Given name(s)	VELMAR	Last name	SAMMONS
Married	18 NOV 1936	Place	

Other marriages List other marriages and sealings of the husband, wife, and children on this form. List any necessary explanations.
WIFE MARRIED 2ND HUSBAND, BROOM AFTER 1ST HUSBAND DIED.

Family Group Record

Husband Given name(s)	WILLIAM J.		Last name	HARDY

Born (day month year)	Place			
28 DEC 1869	BLUE SPRINGS, BARBOURK, ALA.			
Christened	Place			
Died	Place			
3 MAY 1944	PHENIX CITY, RUSSEL, ALA.			
Buried	Place			
4 MAY 1944	DUNDEE, GENEVA, ALA.			
Married	Place			
20 JAN 1898	DUNDEE, GENEVA, ALA.			

Husband's father Given name(s)	WILLIAM ALLEN		Last name	HARDY
Husband's mother Given name(s)	ELIZABETH		Maiden name	HICKS

Wife Given name(s)	MARTHA JANE		Last name	WHITFIELD

Born (day month year)	Place			
18 OCT 1881	SKIPPERVILLE, DALE, ALA.			
Christened	Place			
Died	Place			
Buried	Place			

Wife's father Given name(s)			Last name	
Wife's mother Given name(s)			Maiden name	

Children List each child (whether living or dead) in order of birth.

8 M

Given name(s)	LEONARD CALVIN		Last name	HARDY
Born (day month year)	Place			
16 NOV 1917/6	DUNDEE, GENEVA, ALA.			
Christened	Place			
Died	Place			
Spouse Given name(s)	HILDA EARLE		Last name	BROOM
Married 19 FEB 1937	Place			

9 M

Given name(s)	OLIN BILLY		Last name	HARDY
Born (day month year)	Place			
24 AUG 1919	DUNDEE, GENEVA, ALA.			
Christened	Place			
Died	Place			
Spouse Given name(s)	CARYLON		Last name	DYKES
Married 16 Oct.1940				

Number 9   OLIN   BILLY
Married   Betty   Sonders   ,   Elizabeth   Andrews.
Married   Evelen   Hines ,   Doris   3 July 1952.

By   Gene T.   Bell

Family Group Record

Husband Given name(s)	CHARLES RANSOM		Last name	WHITFIELD

	Born (day month year) 11 DEC 1871	Place		GA.
	Christened	Place		*4 DEC 1964*
9	Died 15 JULY 1957	Place ORLANDO, ORANGE, FLA.	*9 ✓*	*✓ LANGE*
	Buried 17 JULY 1957	Place ORLANDO, ORANGE, FLA.	*PRE*	*1970*
9	Married 8 JAN 1898	Place DUNDEE, GENEVA, ALA.		

Husband's father Given name(s)	RUBEN HENRY	Last name	WHITFIELD
Husband's mother Given name(s)	SUSAN BETHNEY CATHERINE	Maiden name	FAULK

Wife Given name(s)	EMMA	Last name	WILLIAMS

Born (day month year) 8 OCT 1870	Place NEWTON, DALE, ALA.	LDS ordinance dates
Christened	Place	Baptized 8 MAY 1954
Died 8 MAY 1952	Place ORLANDO, ORANGE, FLA.	Endowed 14 MAY 1954
Buried 10 MAY 1952	Place ORLANDO, ORANGE, FLA.	

Wife's father Given name(s)	BOB	Last name	WILLIAMS
Wife's mother Given name(s)	POLLY SARAH	Maiden name	

Children List each child (whether living or dead) in order of birth.

1	Sex F	Given name(s) ETHEL OWDER		Last name	WHITFIELD
		Born (day month year) 9 OCT 1898	Place Geneva CO., ALA.		
		Christened	Place		
		Died 11 NOV 1969	Place FORT PIERCE, ST LUCIE, FL.		
		Spouse Given name(s) M. AURB		Last name	PATRICK
		Married 5 APR 1918	Place		

2	Sex F	Given name(s) ELMA LOIS		Last name	WHITFIELD
		Born (day month year) 5 JAN 1900	Place GENEVA CO., ALA.		
		Christened	Place		
		Died	Place		
		Spouse Given name(s) JOHN		Last name	DUKE
		Married 25 JAN 1916	Place		

3	Sex M	Given name(s) EDGAR ROBERT "ED"		Last name	WHITFIELD
		Born (day month year) 28 MCH 1903	Place Geneva Co., ALA		
		Christened	Place		
		Died 17 AUG 1975	Place MONTGOMERY, MONTGOMERY, ALA.		
		Spouse Given name(s) LOUISE E.		Last name	POWELL
1		Married 15 MAR 1927	Place		

51

Husband Given name(s)	CHARLES RANSOM	Last name	WHITFIELD
Wife Given name(s)	EMMA	Maiden name	WILLIAMS

Children List each child (whether living or dead) in order of birth.

4 Sex F

Given name(s)	ELEANOR LULA "COOT"	Last name	WHITFIELD
Born (day month year) 11 JAN 1908	Place LAKELAND, POLK, FLA.		
Christened	Place		
Died 6 FEB 1968	Place ORLANDO, ORANGE, FLA.		
Spouse Given name(s) JOHN ELLIOTE		Last name	BEAN
Married 11 JUL 1925	Place		

5 Sex M

Given name(s)	JOHN MORGAN	Last name	WHITFIELD
Born (day month year) 3 JUL 1912	Place LAKELAND, POLK, FLA.		
Christened	Place		
Died 3 MAY 1985	Place ORLANDO, ORANGE, FLA.		
Spouse Given name(s) MAY		Last name	ANDERSON
Married	Place		

6 Sex F

Given name(s)	EVELENE	Last name	WHITFIELD
Born (day month year) 28 OCT 1909	Place LAKELAND, POLK, FLA.		
Christened	Place		
Died 23 NOV 1910	Place LAKELAND, POLK, FLA.		
Spouse Given name(s)		Last name	
Married	Place		

7 Sex F

Given name(s)	EDITH	Last name	WHITFIELD
Born (day month year) 1910	Place LAKELAND, POLK, FLA.		
Christened	Place		
Died 1910	Place LakeLAND, POLK, FLA.		
Spouse Given name(s)		Last name	
Married	Place		

Other marriages List other marriages and sealings of the husband, wife, and children on this form.
List any necessary explanations.

HUSBAND, CHARLES RANSOM WHITFIELD,
REMARRIED AFTER FIRST WIFE'S DEATH.
HE MARRIED, LELLA LINDA KINDELL,
SHE DIED 1 JAN 1974.

REFERENCES

[1]Info from Mary Hambrick Williams.

[2]Ida R. Whitfield Hambrick diary

William Edward Searcy Hambrick
4 b. 17 Aug 1890
* at Madison co, Ala
  d. 22 Jan 1974
  at Amarillo, Potter co TX
  m. 15 Aug 1909
  at Italy Ellis co, TX

Whit Windell Hambrick
1 b. 29 Apr 1938
* at Hillsboro, Hill co TX
  rs.
  at Johnson, Stanton co KS
  m. 20 Jul 1956
  at Faith Aztec NM

Eldridge Whitfield (Whit Eldridge) Hambrick
2 b. 24 May 1916
* at Atlanta, Cass co, TX
  rs.
  at San Juan co NM
  m. 20 Jun 1937
  at Hillsboro, Hill co TX

William Eldridge Hambrick
8

Mary Elizabeth Elmore
9

Alice Faye Caldwell
WIFE

Ida Rhoda Whitfield
5 b. 1 Jun 1892
* at Shelby co, AL
  d. 16 Aug 1973
  at Amarillo Potter, co TX

Jessie Collins Whitfield
1 b. 30 Jun 1860
  at
  d. 31 Jan 1925
  at
  m. 27 Apr 1880
  at

Wife: Mary Whitfield b. 1827 Ca. Alabama
                Parent of seven children.
1. Ruby Whitfield b. 1847 Alabama
2. David Whitfield b. 1850 ca. Alabama
 3. Lucinda Whitfield b. 1852 ca. Alabama
 4. John Whitfield b. 1853 ca Alabama.
5. Samuel Whitfield b. 1857 ca. Alabama
6. Jessie Collins Whitfield b. June 30, 1860
        Jessie married Mary Pamela Brown April 27 , 1880.
7.   He was a carpenter.
     Daniel Whitfield b. 1869 ca. Alabama
Prepared by Whit Windell Hambrick who was born 1938,Texas.
Relative to husband. Relative to wife: 2 g-Grandson.
  Whitfield Family on 1870 Census, Wilsonville,Shelby County.
..Submitted by Gene T. Bell, Orlando, Florida, April 1995.

Family   1870 Census of Mobile County, Alabama

James Whitfield ,age 45 , b. N.J.
Frances Whitfield, age 40,b. AL
Clara Whitfield ,age 15, b. AL
John Whitfield, age 13,b. AL
Aslet Whitfield , age 8
    female, b. AL.

Family
   Luke Whitfield, age 38, b. Miss.
     Occupation - Truckerman.
   Charlotte Whitfield, age 24,b.AL
   Sarra Whitfield , age 6 ,b. AL
   Sanford Whitfield, age 3, b. AL
   Silas Whitfield , age 1,b. AL

Family Group Record

Husband				
Given name(s) Jessie Collins			Last name	Whitfield

	Born (day month year) 30 June 1860	Place Wilsonville,Shelby,Alabama		
	Christened	Place		
	Died 31 Jan 1924	Place Malakoff,Henderson,Texas		
	Buried	Place Malakoff,Henderson,Texas		
	Married 27 Apr 1880	Place Malakoff,Henderson,Texas		
	Husband's father Given name(s)		Last name	
	Husband's mother Given name(s)		Maiden name	

Wife				
Given name(s) Mary Pamela			Last name	Brown

	Born (day month year) 28 May 1857	Place Fairburn,Fulton,Georgia		
	Christened	Place		
	Died 29 Mar 1942	Place Italy,Ellis,Texas		
	Buried	Place Malakoff,Henderson,Texas		
	Wife's father Given name(s) Robert Watson		Last name	Brown
	Wife's mother Given name(s) Theresa M.		Maiden name	Suddeth

Children

1. Pallie Marion Whitfield b. Feb. 4, 1881, Talladega, AL. She died Dec. 9, 1968.
2. Oscar Franklin Whitfield b. Aug. 24, 1882 , Talladega, Talladega Co.,Alabama . He died Sept. 1954.
3. Mary Ann Whitfield b. March 24, 1884 , Talladega, AL.
4. Sarah Jane Whitfield b. April 14, 1886 , Columbiana , Alabama.
5. John Robert Whitfield b. July 29 ,1888 , Columbiana, Shelby Co., Al.   John married Sue Honea on March 9, 1909. John died Sept. 9, 1974.
6. Jessie Ada Whitfield b. April 11, 1890 , Columbiana, Shelby Co., AL, and she died Sept. 16 , 1934.
7. Ida Rhoda Whitfield b. June 1, 1892 , Columbiana, Shelby Co., AL. Ida Whitfield married William Edward S. Hambrick on Aug. 15, 1909 at Italy, Ellis County, Texas. Ida Hambrick died Aug. 16, 1973 at Amarillo, Potter County, Texas.
8. Lola Armenta Whitfield b. May 24, 1894. She was born at Columbiana, Shelby Co., Alabama.
9. David Taylor Whitfield b. Dec. 24 , 1896 , Columbiana,AL. He died August 1954.
10. Ethel Essie Whitfield b. April 24, 1898, Columbiana, AL.
11. Texie Bell Whitfield b. March 19, 1900, Brushy Creek, Aderson, Texas. She died Sept. 1900 the same place.
12. Elsie Pearl Whitfield b. Jan 7, 1902 Brushy Creek, Texas and lived two weeks.

Family group by Nelda Coleman of Amarillo, Texas , 1995.
Submitted by Gene T. Bell of Orlando, Florida, April 1995.

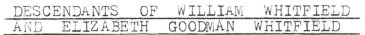

DESCENDANTS OF WILLIAM WHITFIELD AND ELIZABETH GOODMAN WHITFIELD

William and Elizabeth were married 1713 in an area of Gates County, North Carolina. To this union were born four boys and seven daughters. The boys later had families and the Whitfield names were carried forth for nine generations. At first the families at North Carolina stayed and some new generation people stayed for a century in the land area. Once the United States were formed these Whitfield families moved in search of new land, warmer weather, and opportunities. The descendants moved to Alabama, Tennessee, Mississippi, and other southwestern states.

With acknowledgement we glean the writings of Emma Morehead Whitfield and Theodore Marshall Whitfield, and many others in that collection.

The following are biographical sketches of a single family group. Location in the state, generation of descendants, head of family Whitfield name, and the brackets show the father, and grandfathers for the lineage.

Marengo County, Alabama
Fourth Generation

NATHAN BRYAN WHITFIELD

(Bryan, William, William)

Nathan Bryan Whitfield (Sept. 19, 1799—Dec. 27, 1868) was born in North Carolina. February 16, 1819, he married Elizabeth Watkins Whitfield. After the death of his first Elizabeth, Nathan married Elizabeth Whitfield.

Children:

1. Sarah Watkins Whitfield; b. 1819, d. 1822.
2. Winifred B. Whitfield; b. 1821, d. 1822.
3. Nathan Bryan Whitfield; b. 1824, drowned 1832.
4. Mary Elizabeth Whitfield; b. April 5, 1825, at Demopolis, d. Jan. 2, 1859, in Mobile, Ala. She married William Wiltshire Whitfield. She was buried in Mississippi.
5. Bryan Watkins Whitfield.
6. Needham George Whitfield; b. Aug. 21, 1830, d. Feb. 13, 1884. He enlisted in the Marengo Rifles, the first company to leave Demopolis, Ala., in the service of the Confederacy. He was an honor graduate of the University of North Carolina, 1849, and a law student in Cumberland University, Lebanon, Tenn., however, he never practiced law. Unmd.
7. Edith Winifred Whitfield; b. 1832, d. 1842.
8. Nathan Bryan Whitfield.
9. James Bryan Whitfield; b. 1837, d. 1842.
10. Sarah Elizabeth Whitfield; b. 1839, d. 1842.
11. Edith James Whitfield.
12. Bessie Winifred Whitfield; b. Nov. 24, 1843; m. Francis Eugene Whitfield (234). John Bryan Williams in his notes calls her Betsy and gives her birth as Nov. 29, 1843. Theodore Whitfield who knew her and visited her in 1889 in her home called her Bessie. She was living in Demopolis, in 1929.

Second marriage
13. Natalie Ashe Whitfield.

55

To this rich endowment of mind was added an exceptionally favored environment. Nathan Bryan Whitfield's father, Gen. Bryan Whitfield, was one of the foremost and most progressive men of his day in his State. Immediately following the Revolution, North Carolina resolved to establish a State army, the higher officers of which were drawn from the best of the citizenry. The master of "Pleasant Plains" was chosen Major General, which position was held successively in his family for many years. His first successor was Nathan Bryan Whitfield.

Nathan Bryan Whitfield moved to Marengo County, Al., thirteen miles south of Demopolis.

Alabama Fair Association, at Demopolis, was designed by him, and he was the prime promotor of the fairs held there. In politics he endorsed the principles of Yancey.

In 1841 Nathan Bryan Whitfield purchased from a good friend, George B. S. Gaines, an agent of the United States government, a property which he promptly named Gaineswood and adorned with a mansion famous for its beauty.

The house on the place at the time of the sale, two stories in height and formed of hewn logs, was made the nucleus of a better structure. As the work progressed a friend remarked that the old structure would rot and so ruin the whole. The master of Gaineswood caused the old logs to be replaced. It was wittily remarked that General Whitfield built the new house over the old one which he threw out the window.

Photographs of Gaineswood may be seen in U. B. Phillips, *Life and Labor In The Old South* and in *House and Garden*, November, 1939.

Gaineswood like many other fine homesteads suffered in the War for Southern Independence. In these days it was impossible to carry on in the earlier style, but later, 1896, it was bought by Edith James Whitfield and restored to its former beauty. During the war it was the headquarters of Gen. Leonidas Polk, C. S. A., when he and his staff were guests of Gen. Whitfield.

Data concerning children based on records of Bryan Watkins Whitfield.

Marengo County, Alabama
Fourth Generation

GAIUS WHITFIELD   (Needham, William, William)
Gaius Whitfield was born November 15, 1804, in North Carolina. He married July 15, 1834, Mary Ann Whitfield.
The Census of 1860 showed Gaius a prosperous planter of Marengo County, Alabama, whose property approached a million dollars in value. He was widely known as the richest man in the county.

Fearing the Federal troops approaching Mobile, Gaius Whitfield sent barrels of money to his plantation near Demopolis. Here he buried a quantity of gold that lay forgotten until his grandsons came across a map describing the location of the treasure in 1926.

Children:

1. Gaius Whitfield; b. Feb. 6, 1837, in North Carolina or Alabama, d. March 3, 1908. Served as a private in the C. S. A. Unmd.
2. Charles Boaz Whitfield.
3. Needham Bryan Whitfield; b. April 4, 1840, in Ala., d. unmd. Private in the C. S. A.
4. James Bryan Whitfield.
5. Bryan Whitfield; b. March 24, 1844, d. of camp fever Oct. 14, 1862. C. S. A.
6. George Nathan Whitfield; b. Feb. 4, 1848, d. Dec. 14, 1871, unmd. Private in Gen. Forrest's Cavalry, C. S. A.

Dayton, Summerfield , and Mobile, Alambama

Fourth Generation

JOHN WHITFIELD
(James, Constantine, William)

John Whitfield married Mary Lewis Slade, of New Bern, N. C. probably the daughter of Samuel and Sarah (Whitfield) Slade. He lived at Dayton, Summerfield, and Mobile, AL..
Marriage Bond Sept. 28, 1827.
Children:

1. Elizabeth Whitfield; m. Nathan Bryan Whitfield . Child under father.
2. Sarah Whitfield; m. Andrew Jackson Bryant; lived in Demopolis, Ala., until moving to Texas.
3. Caroline Whitfield; m. Abner McGehee and lived at Summerfield, Ala.
4. Rachel Whitfield; m. Thomas Ridgeway and lived in Ashley, Ill. until moving to Texas.
5. Mary Whitfield; died unmarried.
6. Martha (Matt) Whitfield; m. Abraham Adams and lived in Summerfield until moving to Dublin, Ga., where they finished their days.
7. Evelyn Whitfield; m. Dabney Sims and lived in Waxahatchie, Texas.
8. ——— (son) Whitfield; died in infancy.

Fifth Generation
JAMES KENAN WHITFIELD
(Edmund, William, William, William)

James Kenan Whitfield was born in 1826. He was a doctor. In 1847 he married ——— Buckner, of Mobile, Ala. They had twelve children, but only three lived to maturity. Of these only one is known.
Children:

1. William E. Whitfield. He attended the Academy at Annapolis and died while on duty in Washington, D. C.

Marengo County, Albama

Fifth Generation

BRYAN WATKINS WHITFIELD
(Nathan, Bryan, William, William)

Bryan Watkins Whitfield was born March 27, 1828, in Lenoir Co., N. C., at Rockford. While yet a child he was taken to Marengo Co., AL..

57

In 1849 Bryan Watkins Whitfield was graduated from the University of North Carolina with his A.B. From the University of Pennsylvania he received his M.D. in 1853 and three years later the honorary A.M. was conferred on him by the University of Alabama. He practiced medicine in Walker County, and died at Demopolis, Ala., Dec. 15, 1908.

February 13, 1855, Bryan Watkins Whitfield married Mary Alice Foscue .

During the war Bryan Watkins Whitfield was a surgeon in the Confederate Army.

Children:

1. Allen Wooten Whitfield; b. 1856, d. 1858.
2. *son* Whitfield; d. in infancy.
3. Bessie Alice Whitfield; b. April 25, 1858, d. 1909. She married James Bryan Whitfield ,

4. Jesse George Whitfield.
5. Augustus Foscue Whitfield.
6. Bryan Watkins Whitfield.
7. Nathan Bryan Whitfield.
8. Alice Hall Whitfield.
9. *son* Whitfield; d. in infancy.
10. Mehetable Hatch Whitfield.
11. *son* Whitfield; b. 1873, d. in infancy.
12. Mary Elizabeth Whitfield.
13. Edith Winifred Whitfield; b. 1881, d. 1881.

Demopolis , Alabama

Fifth Generation

CHARLES BOAZ WHITFIELD

(Gaius, Needham, William, William)

Charles Boaz Whitfield was born July 19, 1838. He married June 23, 1881, in Florence, Ala., Mary Whitfield Keyes.
He attended the University of North Carolina and received his A.B. and A.M. degrees from this institution in 1858 and 1861 respectively. War immediately called him and he took up duties as drill master in Tuscaloosa, Ala., in 1861. Next May 15th he enlisted in Company B, 40th Alabama Infantry, C. S. A. Promotions followed: sergeant-major July 1, 1862; aide-de-camp to Gen. A. W. Reynolds Aug. 14, 1863; later aide-de-camp to Gen. Stephen D. Lee. He served in the battles of Vicksburg, Chickamauga, Missionary Ridge, Rocky Face Bridge, and Kennesaw Mountain, Ga. After an illness in early 1865, Charles Boaz Whitfield attempted to return to the army, but the army surrendered before he could resume military service.

The return of peace brought Charles Boaz Whitfield opportunity to study medicine. In 1871 he was graduated by the College of Physicians and Surgeons in New York City. In time he became president of the Alabama Medical Society. In this profession he found many kinsmen of the same name. Tradition tells us that upon occasion a man drove up to a drug store in

Demopolis and called out, "Is Dr. Whitfield here?" The answer came back "Which one? There are just seven of them present".

For a time Dr. Whitfield made his home at Jefferson, in Marengo Co., AL. Later he moved to Demopolis, AL. He and his children were Episcopalians. He is buried at Demopolis. Children:

1. Gaius Whitfield.
2. Wade Keyes Whitfield; b. May 27, 1884, d. Jan. 1, 1894.
3. Winifred Bryan Whitfield; b. 1886; d. Jan. 22, 1946, unmd. She taught in the public schools of Demopolis.
4. Mary Alice Whitfield; b. June 4, 1888, d. Oct. 27, 1888.
5. Henry Jones Whitfield.
6. Nelley Keyes Whitfield; b. Dec. 19, 1893. In 1947 she was employed in the State Health Laboratory, Montgomery, Ala.

Demopolis, Alabama

Fifth Generation

JAMES BRYAN WHITFIELD

(Gaius, Needham, William, William)

James Bryan Whitfield (June 13, 1842-June 9, 1914), married June 7, 1882, at Demopolis, AL., Bessie Alice Whitfield.

He received his M.D. degree at University of Pennsylvania in 1867. He was a drill master and sergeant in the 40th Alabama Regiment, C.S.A. He died at Demopolis.

Children:

1. Marianna Bryan Whitfield; b. July 14, 1883, d. Dec. 26, 1900.
2. Bessie Eugenia Whitfield; b. Jan. 24, 1885.
3. Eleanor Foscue Whitfield; b. Oct. 19, 1886.
4. James Bryan Whitfield.
5. Grace Fonville Whitfield; b. Nov. 8, 1890.
6. Alice Mehetable Whitfield; b. July 17, 1893.
7. Edith D. Whitfield; b. Feb. 7, 1895.

Gainesville, Alabama

Fifth Generation

GEORGE WILLIAM WHITFIELD

(William, Lewis, William, William)

George William Whitfield was born in Johnston County, N. C. He died May 14, 1842, in Gainesville, AL. He was the only child of his parents. Feb. 7, 1828, he married in Edgecombe County, N. C., Catharine Diggs Hart. She was born Dec. 22, 1810, in Edgecombe. She died in Gainesville Nov. 7, 1840. She was the daughter of Richard and Catharine (Diggs) Hart. George William Whitfield made his home at Pine Level in Johnston County, N. C. Here all his children with the exception of the youngest were born. In the fall of 1836 or the next year George William Whitfield took his family to live in Alabama, but he was not long to enjoy his new home. Death soon made orphans of his children, but they were received by Nathan Bryan Whitfield into his home at Gaineswood.

Children:

1. George William Whitfield.
2. Richard Henry Whitfield.

JESSE GEORGE WHITFIELD
(Bryan, Nathan, Bryan, William, William)

Jesse George Whitfield was born November 25, 1859, in Alabama. He married June 7, 1882, Penelope Clinton Holmes.

Jesse Whitfield was a civil engineer and a man of high culture. He became interested in family history and was good enough to contribute a deal of material upon which part of this genealogy is based. He was living in Demopolis, AL., in 1947.

Children:

1. William Holmes Whitfield; b. April 13, 1885, at Demopolis, AL..; d. Oct. 14, 1891.
2. Foscue Bryan Whitfield; b. Sept. 4, 1888, in Demopolis; m. ———.
3. Thomas Holmes Whitfield; b. Nov. 22, 1890, in Aberdeen. Miss.

Alabama and Kentucky

Sixth Generation

AUGUSTUS FOSCUE WHITFIELD was born Dec. 1861 Marengo County, Alabama and lived there for some time. In 1909 he was living in Middles-boro, Kentucky in 1923. After a year in Harlan he moved to Kitts where he died Feb. 28, 1947.

BRYAN WATKINS WHITFIELD born in 1864 in the same county as his brother. He had similar interest as Augustus Foscue Whitfield. He moved to Kentucky with his brother. He was living 1948 in Brookside, Kentucky. Bryan W. died Jan . 4 , 1949.

Jefferson County, Ala. and Birmingham, Ala.

Sixth Generation

GEORGE WHITFIELD
(George, George, Bryan, William, William)

George Whitfield was born March 14, 1873. He married Oct. 15, 1896, in Saint Paul's Episcopal Church, Lowndesboro, AL ., Mary Clara Whitman. Following her death April 26, 1920, George Whitfield married, 1921, Mrs. Eva Purnell Mullen. George Whitfield served his county and state for twenty four years as clerk in attendance upon the Probate Court, Jefferson County, AL , and the Circuit Court for the 10th Judicial Circuit.

Res., 1947, Birmingham, AL..

Children:

1. Cecil George Whitfield; b. Nov. 10, 1897, d. July 24, 1898; bu. at Lowndesboro, Ala.
2. Dove Whitfield.
3. Virginia Dibrell Whitfield.

HENRY JONES WHITFIELD
(Charles, Gaius, Needham, William, William)

Henry Jones Whitfield was born Aug. 12, 1890, in Alabama. He married Libby Emma Bridgers Jan. 7, 1914. She was the daughter of Frank P. and Justa (Hatch) Bridgers, and lived in Laurel, Miss. Henry Jones Whitfield was graduated by the University of The South, Sewanee, Tenn. He also studied law at the University of Alabama.   1947, President of Robertson Banking Company, Demopolis.

_____Child , 1. Henry Jones Whitfield; b. Jan. 15, 1917.

Demopolis and Gainesville, Ala.

Sixth   Generation

FRANCES JANE WHITFIELD
(George, William, Lewis, William, William)

Frances Jane Whitfield (July 1, 1836-April 9, 1919) was born at Pine Level, Johnson County, N. C. After the death of her father she went to live with Nathan Bryan Whitfield,   but about 1849 she went with her brothers James and Robert to live with John A. Minniece in Gainesville, Ala. She graduated with her sister Charlotte at Judson Institute. For a while she lived with her brother George in North Carolina. It was perhaps while here she fell in love with George Lewis Wimberly, brother of her hostess. Oct. 8, 1857, she became the bride of George Wimberly in the home of her sister Charlotte Manly then living in Richmond, Va.

George Lewis Wimberly was born July 30. 1836. He was a graduate of the University of North Carolin .

_____

La Crange, Ga.&   Montgomery , Alabama

Sixth   Generation

LOUIS BROUGHTON WHITFIELD
(Mathew, Horatio, Benjamin, Luke, William)

Louis Broughton Whitfield (July 8, 1868—December 1, 1942) was born at Whitfield's Crossing on the West Point Road, in Troup County, Georgia. Shortly his family moved to LaGrange, Georgia. His father was killed in an accident when the boy was only six.

In 1906, he founded and developed, as owner, the Alabama-Georgia Syrup Company, located in Montgomery, Alabama, whose most widely known brand is "Alaga" and is well known to the public. The syrup factory is one of the largest syrup refineries in the South. The W & W Pickle & Canning Company was organized in 1942, with Mr. Whitfield as President. This business has made possibly even greater growth during the same number of years than was made by the Syrup Company.

Some years ago, Mr. Whitfield became interested in Florida real estate, and founded the Whitfield Estates, near Sarasota. This property he sold in the spring of 1925.

In addition to his own business interests, Mr. Whitfield was a director of the Alabama National Bank and Transportation Bureau, both of Montgomery, Alabama; the Manhattan Life Insurance Company, of New York; and National Councillor of the United States Chamber of Commerce. For thirty-five years he was a steward of the Methodist Church. He was active in civic affairs and a heavy contributor to charity organizations, and a colorful and well-known figure in the South in a business and social capacity.

Louis Broughton Whitfield married Nov. 8, 1893, Willie Vandiver. She was born Aug. 25, 1872, and died Nov. 30, 1933, in Baltimore, Md. She was the daughter of William F., and Sallie Vandiver, of Montgomery. Ala.

Children:
1. Katherine Whitfield.
2. Louis Broughton Whitfield.
Three others who died in infancy.

Birmingham , Alabama

Seventh Generation

DOVE WHITFIELD
(George, George, George, George, Bryan, William, William)

Dove Whitfield was born February 2, 1902, in Birmingham, Ala. She married Sept. 8, 1921, in the Church of the Advent, Birmingham, Ala., Malcolm David Pendleton, sometime of Charlottesville, Va. The officiating clergyman was the Rev. Noble C. Powell, later Episcopal bishop of Baltimore, Md.

Children:
1. Malcolm David Pendleton; b. Aug. 4, 1926, Birmingham, Ala.
2. Ann Whitman Pendleton; b. Oct. 28, 1928; student, 1947, at the University of Alabama, Tuskaloosa, Ala.

References . Whitfield , Bryan , Smith And Related Families . Book I . Compiled by Emma Whitfield from Collective works of many people. Whitfield . First names and pages.

Nathan , p.p. 99, 100, 101.   Gaius , p.105-106. John P. , p. 117 . James K. , p. 137. Bryan W. p.p. 144 , 145. Charles B., p.p. 153,154. James B., p. 154. George W. , p. 156,157. Jesse G., p. 210. George , p. 210. Nathan W., p. 214 . Henry J. , p. 217. Frances J., p.224. Louis B., p. 234. Dove , p. 257.

Fifteen Whitfield family groups residing in Alabama 1827to 1948, in biographical sketches.

NATHAN WILLIAM WHITFIELD
(William, William, Needham, William, William)

Nathan William Whitfield was born Nov. 23, 1848, or '49, in Alabama. June 23, 1869, he married Laura Eloise Pickett. She was born June 21, 1851, the daughter of the Rev. James Thomas and Elizabeth J. (Haughton) Pickett. Her birth place was Columbus, Miss.

Children:

1. Thomas Pickett Whitfield; b. Nov. 14, 1870, d. May 18, 1871.
2. Mary Elizabeth Whitfield; b. Apr. 19, 1872, d. Sept. 13, 1873.
3. Sarah Haughton Whitfield; m. April 21, 1897, Needham Whitfield Holmes
4. Eloise W. Whitfield; b. Sept. 17, 1876.
5. William James Whitfield.
6. Nathan Wilmer Whitfield.

LOUIS BROUGHTON WHITFIELD
(Louis, Mathew, Horatio, Benjamin, Luke, William)

Louis Broughton Whitfield was born March 21, 1899, in Montgomery, Ala. After graduation from the Barnes School, Montgomery, Ala., he entered the University of Alabama. His college education was interrupted by World War I, as he volunteered his services and was sent to the Officers' Training School at Camp Pike, Ark. After the Armistice and his discharge from the army on Dec. 2, 1918, he returned to the University and completed his college education, and was graduated in February, 1921, with the B. S. degree.

Louis Broughton Whitfield became actively engaged in his father's business, the Alabama-Georgia Syrup Company, as vice-president. In 1929 he followed his father in the office of president. In 1942 after the death of his father, he became president of the W. & W. Pickle and Canning Company of Montgomery, Ala., and Dallas, Tex.

Louis Broughton Whitfield married Virginia Lenora Goodwin, of Hot Springs, Ark., on Nov. 16, 1926. She was born Oct. 17, 1908.

They are Methodists. Res., 1948, Montgomery, Ala.

Children:

1. Louis Broughton Whitfield; b. Nov. 8, 1928, Montgomery, Ala.
2. Frank Goodwin Whitfield; b. Nov. 30, 1937, Montgomery, Ala.

NATHAN BRYAN WHITFIELD
(Nathan, Bryan, William, William)

Nathan Bryan Whitfield (July 7, 1835-1914, Calif.) married, July 10, 1862, Medora Shackleford (May 10, 1842-Dec., 1910), daughter of Richard Danford Shackleford, of Sumter County, Ala. He entered the University of North Carolina from Demopolis, Ala.; A.B., 1857; Engineer in C.S.A. In November, 1868, he moved with his family to Fresno, Calif., and from thence to Portland, Oregon. He surveyed the Thule Lands in Alaska, and lived for a time at Ketchikan, Alaska.

Child. 1. Richard Danford S. Whitfield.

WHITFIELD Residents 1981. Montgomery, Alabama.

Whitfield E R 1925 Captl Av — 262-8726
Whitfield Frank Goodwin
  2521 Hermitage Dr — 834-2522
Whitfield Frank Goodwin
  Ofc 1101 N Court — 263-2541
Whitfield Kindergarten 2673 Fisk Rd — 281-2470
Whitfield L B III ofc 1101 N Court — 263-2541
  Res 2080 Allendale Rd — 262-2377
Whitfield L M 1527 College Ct — 262-3450
Whitfield Memorial United Methodist
  Church 2673 Fisk Rd — 281-2467
  If No Answer Dial — 288-7035
Whitfield Mitchell Alms House Rd — 288-5120
Whitfield Mozell Alms House Rd — 288-5120
Whitfield Nelly K Miss 630 E Edgmnt Av — 263-6328
WHITFIELD PICKLE COMPANY
  DIVISION OF ALAGA WHITFIELD
  FOODS INC 1101 N Court — 263-2541
Whitfield Tommy 3512 Lehigh — 834-6690
WHITFIELD'S OF MONTGOMERY
  549 N Eastern Blvd — 277-8510

WHITFIELD Residents 1981. Birmingham, Alabama. Addresses and Telephone Numbers. Inclusive of white and black race. Post Office Zip Code Number.

Whitfield Albert J Lee's Apartments Helena — 663-7026
Whitfield Amye 3741 4th Pl W Hooper City — 328-7415 — _ 35207
Whitfield Anna 2038 Hollins Dr — 322-3922
Whitfield Arnold Vandvr — 672-7709
Whitfield Benny 1 Pea Ridge — 665-7530
Whitfield Beverly Ann
  3741 4th Pl W Hooper City — 328-7415
Whitfield Bill Jr 540 Valley Dr — 833-6935
Whitfield Bobbie 1621 20th Ensley — 785-6113 — _ 35218
Whitfield Bobby W 4707 40th Pl N — 841-2489
Whitfield Brisco 1312 N 20th — 324-0931
Whitfield Brown 664 Circle Av Besmr — 426-6134
Whitfield Calvin 117 Westbrook Rd Hueytown — 497-0908
Whitfield Carl B Sterrett — 672-2472
Whitfield Carl Eugene Vandvr — 672-7782
Whitfield Charles Jr Vandvr — 672-7566
Whitfield Charles D 4744 40th Pl N — 841-1900 — _ 35217
Whitfield Charles Edward 9th Siluria — 663-7007
Whitfield Charles M Alabstr — 663-6337
Whitfield Clay Vandvr — 672-7171
Whitfield Collins Siluria — 663-3232
Whitfield D L 1715 32nd Ensley — 787-4173
Whitfield David E 6412 Tennessee Av S — 595-7124
Whitfield Don 206 Shelby Montvlo — 665-4505
Whitfield Donald R 825 9th Av Plesnt Grv — 744-7828
Whitfield Donnis D 319 Cimmaron Dr — 798-2915
Whitfield Dorothy Harpersvle — 672-7072
Whitfield E G Dogwood — 665-2711
Whitfield E J Sr Minor Heights — 786-4854
Whitfield E N 1340 Five Mile Rd — 853-4702
Whitfield E W
  3127 Pine Tree Dr Cahaba Heights — 967-3508
Whitfield E W Westvr — 678-6966
Whitfield Edgar Maylene — 663-3493
Whitfield Edmond L Jr 2310 Patton — 979-7181 — _ 35226
Whitfield Ella 1308 21st Av N Bessmr — 424-4213
Whitfield Emma Mrs
  603-E Crumpton Dr SW Bessmr — 424-1767
Whitfield Emma Jean Vandvr — 672-2523
Whitfield Emmett O 3327 Avenue B Ensley — 788-5203
Whitfield Evelyn Siluria — 663-3013
Whitfield Everett L & Leesther B
  936 Cherrydale Cir S — 798-5631
Whitfield F E 1516 28th Ensley — 788-4737
Whitfield F E Jr 3228 Virginia Dr Hueytown — 491-7781 — _ 35209
Whitfield Faye 821 Park Ln Fultndale — 849-7844
Whitfield Fred D Vandvr — 672-7763
Whitfield G L 4340 Pinson Valley Pkwy — 856-0543
Whitfield George Calera — 668-2809
Whitfield Gladis 779 Railroad — 744-8279
Whitfield Glenn Wilsonvle — 669-6819

Whitfield Gordon L 2915 Pahokee Trace — 967-6953   35243
  Children's Telephone
  2915 Pahokee Trace — 967-3376
Whitfield Gorman Otis Dunnavant Rd — 967-6144
Whitfield H C 207 Vann Midfield — 923-7949   35215
Whitfield H L 100 Nekoma Dr — 853-5904
Whitfield H T Helena — 663-7614
Whitfield Henry J Jr 2144 30th Pl Ensley — 785-6684
Whitfield Henry L 1412 30th Ensley — 788-2900
Whitfield Homer Vandvr — 672-2687
Whitfield Hoy Sterrett — 672-9408
Whitfield Hubert F Vandvr — 672-2926
Whitfield Ida V 600 Osceola Cir — 785-1814
Whitfield J A Vincent — 672-7518
Whitfield James W Colmbna — 669-7162   35209
  Res Colmbna — 669-7182
Whitfield Jesse G 116 Lakevw Dr — 942-5208
Whitfield Jimmy Raye Vandvr — 672-7457
Whitfield Jo rl est 2711 Montgomery Hwy — 663-1011
Whitfield John A
  1754-A Woodbrook Tr Alabstr — 663-3561
Whitfield John C 1561 Druid Hill Dr — 252-1874
Whitfield John K Highway 25 Vincent — 672-9464
Whitfield Ken 2163 Highway 31 S — 988-3051   35244
Whitfield Kenneth Westvr — 678-6671
Whitfield Kenneth W
  2800 Clyburne Hueytown — 491-2237
Whitfield L D 4713 40th Pl N — 849-5512
Whitfield Lillian Harpersvle — 672-2356
Whitfield Loudella 3439 17th Av N — 324-0431   35234
Whitfield Louis Maylene — 663-0003
Whitfield M S 825-B Tyler Cir Hoover — 979-9947
Whitfield Mary Brantleyvile — 663-4735
Whitfield Mary Margaret
  2118 Greentree Dr — 987-8381
Whitfield Michael Pelham — 663-4485
Whitfield Mona 779 Railroad — 744-8279   35224
Whitfield N J Dunnavant Rd — 967-8874
Whitfield Nonnie Sterrtt — 672-2502
Whitfield O H Dunnavant Rd — 967-0639
Whitfield Olice 3632 43rd Av N — 841-4767
Whitfield Oliver Carl 1233 Steiner Av SW — 785-0069   35211
Whitfield P H 928 11th Terr Plesnt Grv — 744-6750
Whitfield Pete 905-C Beacon Parkway E — 942-6874
Whitfield R 1938-A Tree Top Ln — 979-7058   35216
Whitfield R C Jr 1848 Glendmere Dr — 822-1594
Whitfield R M 605 Osceola Cir Fairfld — 785-2416
Whitfield Raymond W 4217 Spanish Trace — 854-7858
Whitfield Richard Lee
  3015 Avenue H Ensley — 788-0946
Whitfield Robert Vandiver — 672-2911
Whitfield Robert C 1848 Glendmere Dr — 822-1594
  Res Riverwood — 436-3504
Whitfield Robert H 105 Beasley Dr Concord — 491-9027
Whitfield Robin 1247-A Beacon Parkway E — 871-0124
Whitfield Roy 7531 Division Av — 836-8159
Whitfield Ruel David
  540 Parkell Av Hueytown — 491-7303
Whitfield S K 2117 Whiting Rd Hoover — 979-6304
Whitfield Sanitation Services
  27 Monte Tierra Tr Alabstr — 663-4862
Whitfield Steve & Candy
  Terri Lynn Trailer Park — 663-4935
Whitfield Sylane Sterrtt — 672-2502
Whitfield T A Dunnavant Rd — 967-1199
Whitfield Terry Fungo Hollow Pelham — 663-6123
Whitfield Thomas 779 Railroad — 744-8279
Whitfield Tolbert Alabstr — 663-7927
Whitfield Tom 3141 Jeffrsn Av SW — 925-6953   35221
Whitfield Tommy D 2708 2nd NW — 853-6349
Whitfield Troy Pinson — 681-2256
Whitfield Valerie
  Belle Vista Trailer Park Pelham — 663-4141
Whitfield Velpoe 1016 Oakley Dr — 798-1518   35214
Whitfield W J 1709 32nd Ensley — 787-7416
Whitfield W T Mulga — 436-3718
Whitfield W T Vandvr — 672-2539   35210
Whitfield W W 217 Redwood Crestline Gardens — 956-4060
Whitfield Wayne 1253-A Beacon Parkway E — 879-5083
Whitfield Wayne 2173 Chapel Hill Rd — 822-8019
Whitfield William I 2345 Centr Pl S — 324-0493
Whitfield William J Dr 533 Lanewood Dr — 791-0183
Whitfield Willie 7317 Belgium Av — 788-9781
Whitfield Willie Guice   35208
  2636 Bush Blvd Ensley — 786-0837

GEORGE WHITFIELD

(George, Bryan, William, William)

George Whitfield was born June 14, 1831. He married Virginia Edwinella Dibrell of Richmond, Va., in that city on Dec. 3, 1863. In 1850 he was living with his father in Leon Co., Fla. He died in Alabama in 1909.

Children:

1. Alice Lee Whitfield; b. June 30, 1865; living unmarried 1947 in Demopolos, Ala.
2. Kate Whitfield; d. 1930 ca., unmd.
3. Virginia Whitfield; b. 1859 ca., d. 1879.
4. Richmond Whitfield b. March 26, 1871. Living unmarried in Demopolis, Ala., 1947.
5. George Whitfield.
6. Wade Keyes Whitfield; b. 1875 ca., d. Nov. 9, 1899.
7. Blackledge Whitfield; d. young; unmd.
8. William Skinner Whitfield; d. 1930 ca. He is buried in the U. S. National Cemetery, Biloxi, Miss.
9. Mary Dibrell Whitfield; living with her brother Richmond and sister Alice Lee at 711 E. Decatur St., Demopolis, Ala., 1947. Unmd.

ALABAMA RECORDS

Dictionary of Alabama is a published volume with about 1765 pages of biographies on Alabama residents. Biographies are fully written and include occupational work, and military and war service accounts.

HAMPTON S. WHITFIELD, Professor Mathematics, University of Tennessee, 1870-71, of Mathematics and Astronomy, 1872-76, and Mathematics, 1876-1878.

WHITEFIELD WILLIAM, *Soldier of the American Revolution*, aged 84, and a resident of St. Clair County; private Virginia Continental Line; enrolled on January 18, 1830, under act of Congress of March 18, 1818, payment to date from January 18, 1830; annual allowance $96; sums received to date of publication of list, $396.64.-*Revolutionary Pension Roll*, in vol. xiv, Sen. Doc. 514, 23rd Cong., 1st sess. 1833-34.

Newton L. Whitfield born 1818. He married Esther Witherspoon Friarson. They had one child, Addie Whitfield, born 1858. She married Thomas J. Powers. They resided in Moundville, Alabama in 1885. Newton L. Whitfield was a speaker at the Historical Society of Alabama at Tuscaloosa on July 13, 1858 at annual meeting.

C. B. Whitfield resided October 1879 at Marengo County, Alabama.

Julia Whitfield married Colonel Isham Harrison who died in the Civil War with Confederacy men. She was a daughter of a Governor Whitfield.

George Whitfield, 1829 was a physician at Spring Hill, Marengo County, Alabama.

Robert Allen Whitfield in 1839 at Gainesville, Alabama.

There were many black people of African-American descent who lived at Alabama. Their surnames are not on censuses until after 1860, and they take the last name of Whitfield because of the plantation they lived on.

1850 United States Census, Shelby County, Alabama.

        David Whitfield, age 58, Farmer, born North Carolina
        Hannah Whitfield, age 56, born North Carolina
        Mary, age 30, born South Carolina
        Caroline, age 24, born Alabama
        Margaret, age 23, born Alabama
        Abraham, age 21, born Alabama
        David, age 20, born Alabama

        George Whitfield, age 35, Farmer, born Alabama
        May Whitfield, age 26, born Alabama
        James, age 6, born Alabama
        Rhoda, age 3, born Alabama
        David, age 2

IN 1990, WHITFIELD HEADS OF FAMILIES WHO LIVED IN ALABAMA WERE
392 PERSONS

JOHN FREDERICK WHITFIELD born March 16, 1836 in Lowndes County
and died April 24, 1891 in Montgomery, AL. Son of George B. (b.
NC) and Sarah Vaner (b. VA). He married Florence C. Sanders
who died September 17, 1906.

John F. Whitfield joined the army in 1861 and fought in several
battles and was taken prisoner and released in 1864. John
contributed much during the Civil War.

John F. was Editor of Montgomery Daily Mail. He was made
foreman and purchased half interest in the newspaper plant
until 1870. Then he became a railroad agent serving Montgomery
and Eufaula and Lousville and Nashville Railroads. He studied
law and was a lawyer in 1874 until his death.

Reference: Dictionary of Alabama Biography.

California Record
On January 24, 1848, James Wilson Marshall discovered gold at
Colma, CA. Marshall found the original mill's tailrace on the
South Fork of the American River. They were just shining metal
flecks in the water he was panning with. He said, "I believe
I have found a gold mine." The tools, a spade, a pick, a
rifle, and a gold pan and a water stream, did not make Marshall
rich.

In 1848 only a few hundred pioneers were making their way to
California each year. The state had a non-Indian population of
just 20,000 which swelled to 230,000 just a few years after
Marshall's find. They found mostly farming and not gold.

ALASKA

A land of ice and snow north of Canada. This land became a
State of the United States.

Two named Whitfield have worked at Alaska.

ARIZONA

"My father was born in Maryport, England. One of my ancestral uncles was a ship's captain. I am engaged in work of Consulting and Licensing."
....Letter submitted November 9, 1983, by Marshall G. Whitfield of Sun City, AZ.

1864 Charles Whitfield lived in Arizona County, Arizona. 1880 Wilbert J. lived in Pima County, Arizona.

In 1990, 61 Whitfield heads of families lived in Arizona state.

ARKANSAS

FEDERAL CENSUS with WHITFIELD names

IZARD COUNTY, ARKANSAS, 1880 Census. Enumerated July 14, 1880 Assistant Marshal W. J. Cagle, Union Township. Post Office Benbrooks Mill.

Name-Description, Occupation, value of estate owned, place of birth, year married, attended school, over of school age.

Family Group:

J. W. G. WHITFIELD, age 36, M, Blacksmith, 100 value, birth in TN.
    Serena A. Whitfield, age 21, female, birth in Missouri.
    Lucinda Whitfield, age 7, female, birth in Arkansas.
    Jasper M. Whitfield, age half year, M, birth in Arkansas.

ALLEN WHITFIELD, age 34, M, Farmer-value 150 real estate and value personal property 800, birth in Tennessee.
    Margaret, age 19, female, birth in Arkansas.
    Jernesa (G), age 2, female, birth in Arkansas. Pernecia*
    Sophronia Whitfield, age 2½, female, birth in Georgia.

William B. Whitfield, age 26, M, Farmer, 1000 value of real estate, 1100 value of personal property, birth in Tennessee.
    Elizabeth Whitfield, age 24, female, birth in Arkansas.
    Henry Whitfield, age 10, M, birth in Arkansas.
    Alex Whitfield, age 1, M, birth in Arkansas.
    Michael Hivety, age 20, was farm laborer on this farm, value of real estate 130, value of personal property 100, he was born in Tennessee on Whitfield farm. Wife, Jane Hivety, age 16.

ELI WHITFIELD, age 55, M, Farmer, value of real estate 130, personal property value 1100, birth in Tennessee.
    Mary A. Whitfield, age 46, female, birth in Georgia.

W. W. WHITFIELD, age 26, M, Farmer, 550 value of real estate, 100 personal value property, birth in Tennessee.
    Elizabeth Whitfield, age 24, female birth in Arkansas.
    Rhoda Whitfield, age 2, female, birth in Arkansas.
    Mary B. Whitfield, age 6, female, birth in Arkansas.

DAVID WHITFIELD, age 26, M, Farm Laborer, birth in Tennessee.

*Name spelling change.

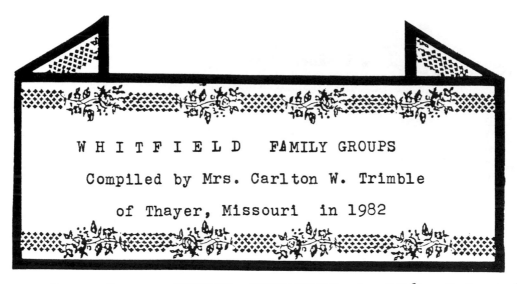

W H I T F I E L D   FAMILY GROUPS

Compiled by Mrs. Carlton W. Trimble

of Thayer, Missouri in 1982

Group One.   WILLIS WHITFIELD b. 1761 N C and
              d. 1836 Tennessee.

  Wife : RHODA W. ALLEN   b. 1761 N C   and
         d. after 1850 in Tennessee.

      Twelve children , six sons and six daughters.

Willis Whitfield (1761 - 1826) was on tour in the
Revolutionary War and received land bounty Tennessee
grant for the service.

Group Three.   JOHN G. WHITFIELD b. 1770 Georgia or
        North Carolina and d. 1850 Cannon County
        Tennessee.
Wife . KIZZIAH RUTLEDGE b. 1785 circa, Georgia state
        and died , Izard County, Arkansas.

      Eight children : six sons.

  Group Five.   MATTHEW WHITFIELD   b. 1772 N C and
           d. 1827 Rutherford County , Tennessee.
  Wife : LEVINA ROBINSON   b. 1776 and d. after 1850.

      Five children :   three sons and two daughters.

NERVA TRIMBLE , wife of Carlton , contributed all the
descendants of these three men in twenty groups records.

68

Family Group Sheet

Full Name of Husband ➤

		ID No.	WILLIS WHITFIELD

	Day / Month / Year	Address, Ward, Town or City, Township, Precinct, District, County, Territory.
Born	1761	NASH CO., N.C.
Marriage	1/11/1788	
Died	3/9/1836	RUTHERFORD CO., TENN.
Burial Date / Cemetery / Location:		
HUSBAND'S OTHER SPOUSE(S):	NONE	
OCCUPATION: FARMER		Church Affiliation:
Military / Misc. Remarks: TWO OR MORE TOURS IN THE REVOLUTION UNDER GEN. GREENE STATIONED NEAR CHARLESTON, S.C.		
HUSBAND'S FATHER: THOMAS WHITFIELD, JR	Born 1741 VA	Died 1799 NC
HUSBAND'S MOTHER: ELIZABETH YOUNG	Born	Died NC

Full Maiden Name of Wife ➤

		ID no.	RHODA W. ALLEN

	Day / Month / Year	Address, Ward, Town or City, Township, Precinct, District, County, Territory.
Born	1/12/1767	
Died	AFTER 1840	CANNON CO., TENNESSEE
Burial Date / Cemetery / Location:		
OTHER HUSBAND (s) NONE		
Remarks:		
WIFE'S FATHER: ARTHUR ALLEN		
WIFE'S MOTHER: ELIZABETH		

REFERENCES:
MRS. CARLTON W. TRIMBLE Sheet
RT 2 BOX 132
THAYER, MISSOURI

OCT. 16 1982

CHILDREN (Given Names)	BORN WHEN WHERE	DIED WHEN WHERE
1 ANSIL	25/8/1789 NASH CO. N.C.	
2 WRIGHT	20/3/1791 NASH CO. N.C.	
3 CHRISTINA	1/11/1793 SUMNER CO. TENN.	
4 SALLY	5/5/1795 TN.	
5 TEMPERANCE	26/2/1797 TN	
6 RHODH	27/12/1798 TN	
7 THOMAS YOUGH	5/2/1801 TN	
8 ARTHUR ALLEN	30/1/1803 TN	
9 WILLIS	30/1/1805 RUTHERFORD, TN	
10 ELI	2/5/1807 RUTHERFORD, TN	1860-1870 IZARD CO., ARK.
11 ELIZABETH EASTY	26/2/1810	
12 ALFRED	19/1/1812 RUTHERFORD TN	

Children living in Tennessee.

Birth name was Christian.

Rhodh and Eli with descendants in Arkansas.

Eli married Mary A. (Polly).

69

Family Group Sheet

Fam. Grp. No. 3

Name of Husband - JOHN G. WHITFIELD
  Born 1770 N.C. or GA.   Married in Georgia. Died 1850,
Cannon County, Tennessee.
Maiden Name of Wife -   KIZZIAH   RUTLEDGE.
  Born ca. 1785 , Georgia. Died between 1860-1864 , Izard
County, Arkansas. **Children.**
  1. Healey Whitfield b. Georgia. Md Cary Jarnagin. (2)
  2. Polly Whitfield.
  3. James Whitfield , b. Georgia.
  4. John Whitfield , b. 1820 , Tennessee.
  5. Allen Whitfield b. 2/2/1826 , Cannon County, Tenn.
     Died 6/ 13, 1906 , Pineville, Arkansas. Allen md
     Margaret Langeston 3/15/ 1842 Izard County, AR.
  6. George Whitfield.
  7. William B. Whitfield , b. 1830 Tennessee. William
     married Elizabeth Hively.
Submitted by Mrs. Carlton W. Trimble of Thayer, Missouri,
May 1995.

Family Group Sheet

Fam. Grp. No. 5

Name of Husband ▶ | MATTHEW WHITFIELD

	Day / Month / Year	Address, Ward, Town or City. Township.
Born	1772	N.C.
Marriage		
Died	1827	RUTHERFORD Co., TN.

Full Maiden Name of Wife ▶ ID no. | LEVINA ROBINSON

	Day / Month / Year
Born	1776
Died	after 1850

CHILDREN (Given Names)	BORN WHEN WHERE	DIED	MARRIAGE DATA TO WHOM WHEN WHERE
1 WILLIAM	1800 N.C.	ARK.	MATILDA TN.
2 BENJAMIN	14/5/1805 SUMNER Co, TN.	14/5/1900 STONE Co ARK.	ELIZABETH HERROD 5/5/18__ /RUTHERFOR c.TN.
3 MARY	RUTHERFORD Co. TN		
4 GIRL	RUTHERFORD Co. TN		
5 MATTHEW	1814 RUTHERFORD Co TN	TN	FANNY R. MONAHAN 30/7/1834 RUTHERFORD Co., TN.

70

JOHN GEORGE WHITFIELD AND KIZZIAH RUDLEDGE OF GEORGIA AND TENNESSEE AND DESCENDS

Kizziah Rutledge Whitfield was born near Wilkes County, Georgia and she had parents and ancestors there. Kizziah was born 1785 and she died between 1860 and 1864 in Arkansas. According to the Censuses study she had nine children. Five boys and four girls.

John G. Whitfield was born in Georgia or North Carolina, or he was an immigrant as a small child. His father may have been named John. John G. Whitfield married Kizziah between 1805 and 1812 in area near Wilkes County, Georgia. There were children born in Georgia and in Tennessee. John and family moved from Georgia crossing North Carolina to Tennessee in 1819. They lived at Cannon County, Tennessee. There John G. Whitfield died in 1850 after the Census was taken and he was age 80. They went for opportunity of land ownership in Tennessee. Daughters were named Kezihan, Healey, Polly and a fourth female.

After the farmer John G. died, Kizziah Whitfield took her sons Allen, James, and William and moved to Izard County, Arkansas. She had neighbors who moved there. The brothers Matthew and Willis Whitfield had children to move there. Two of Kizziah's children married children of Willis Whitfield's family. Matthew Whitfield sons went to Arkansas. Kizziah lived with her son Allen's family at Pineville, Arkansas. When Kizziah died she was buried there in Creswell Cemetery.
Kizziah had in her household Coleman Whitfield and grandchildren. She had many grandchildren and over fifty great-grandchildren.

John G. Whitfield and Kizziah Whitfield had children:
1. Healy Whitfield was born 1813 in Georgia. She married first Coleman Porter. She married second Cary Jarnagin in Dec. 1838.
2. Polly Whitfield b. 1814 in Georgia. Polly married Eli Whitfield. He was the son Willis Whitfield (1761-1836) and Rhoda of Rutherford Co., Tennessee.
3. James Whitfield b. 1818 in Georgia. James married Elizabeth b. 1821 in Tennessee.
4. John G. Whitfield, Jr. b. 1820 in Tennessee. John married first Marina McCloud. He married second, Malissa McCloud. Twin sisters.
5. George Whitfield b. about 1821 in Tennessee.
6. Allen Whitfield b. Feb. 2, 1823 Cannon County, Tennessee, and died 1806 in Pineville, Arkansas.
7. William Bradley Whitfield b. 1830 Cannon County, Tennessee. William married Elizabeth Jane Hively.

Searches have to be made in GA in counties around Wilkes County to locate Rutledge's records. There are two early men named John Whitfield in GA. One with date 1780 in Wilkes County fort area. One court document on property of Wilkes region and the Court hearing was in South Carolina Court. The second record is John Whitfield 1806 tax list Franklin County, GA.

DESCENDANTS OF JOHN G. WHITFIELD (1770 NC-1850 TN) AND KIZZIAH RUTLEDGE WHITFIELD (1785 ca.-d. after 1860 Arkansas)

The parentage of John G. Whitfield is not known, Kizziah Rutledge Whitfield's parents were living in Wilkes region of Georgia. The history of these families are of Georgia, Tennessee and Arkansas, and other states. Herein this book their records are in Georgia, Tennessee, and Arkansas. They have a lineage and 11 family groups are of residence in Arkansas.

1. Andrew B. Whitfield (1874-1923 AR), eighth child of Allen and Margaret Whitfield.
2. William Bradley Whitfield (1830 TN-1881), seventh child of Allen Whitfield.
3. Blake Sedgle Whitfield (1866 AR-d. OK), son of William Bradley Whitfield.
4. Coleman Porter-Whitfield (1832 TN-d 1870 AR), son of Healey Whitfield and Coleman Porter.
5. David Becton Porter-Whitfield (1833 TN-1895 OK), son of Healy Whitfield and Coleman Porter.
6. James Wortham Whitfield (1863 AR-d), son of David Becton Whitfield Porter-Whitfield.
7. Herron Thompson Whitfield (1914 AR-living 1995 AR), son of Young Whitfield (1876-1958 AR).
8. George Herman Whitfield (1900 AR-1977 AR), son of Young Whitfield (1876-1958).
9. Willie Jaden Whitfield (1908 AR-1983 AR), son of Young Whitfield (1876-1958).
10. Asas Dale Whitfield (1911 AR-), son of Young Whitfield (1876-1958).
11. Finis Howard Whitfield (1919 AR-1986 AR), son of Young Whitfield (1876-1958).
12. Carl Dean Whitfield (1938 AR-living 1995).
13. Noel Rex Whitfield (1947 AR-living 1995).
14. Gladys Fern Whitfield (1942 AR-living 1995 AR). She is Mrs. William Earl Estes. She is the daughter of Herron Thompson Whitfield (1914 AR-living 1995 AR).
15. Mary Elizabeth Whitfield (b. AR-). She was Mrs. James William Clark, daughter of William Bradley Whitfield (1830 TN-1881 AR).
16.

....Madeline Whitfield of McAlester, Oklahoma did the research for her family tree for 30 years and formed Whitfield Family Groups. Herron Thompson Whitfield has worked on his family tree and is an authority on Whitfield families at Pineville, Arkansas. Nerva Trimble who is Mrs. Carlton Trimble of Thayer, Missouri has contributed Whitfield family groups.

Note: George Whitfield was the first Whitfield from England to the new colony of Georgia in 1738. He settled at Wilkes Territory of Georgia. A man named George Whitfield, Jr. lived in the area in 1781.

Arkansas Record. Angela Whitfield Davis, age 27, in Nov. 1995 moved from Illinois to Arkansas to Marrilton, AR. A daughter of Joyce Congenia Whitfield.

HEALY WHITFIELD was born 1813 in Georgia, the daughter of John G. Whitfield and Kizziah Whitfield. Her name is found as Haley and Mahalia.

Healy Whitfield married Coleman Porter, a native Indian, about 1831 in Tennessee. He left his wife Healy and their two sons. Healy Whitfield Porter returned to the home of her parents in Cannon County, Tennessee. Healy took back her maiden name and named the two sons Whitfield. Children:
1. Coleman Porter b. 1832 and d. 1870 in Arkansas. He was Coleman Whitfield, and raised in the home of John G. and Kizziah. He is on the census as a child of John G. Whitfield.
2. David Becton Porter born 1833 in Tennessee, and died 1895 in Oklahoma. He was David Becton Whitfield.

Healy Whitfield married Cary Jarnagin in December 1838.

Tennessee Marriage License Issued November 29, 1838

Cary Jarnagin — Marriage License
To — Issued The 29th day of November
Healy Whitfield — 1838. Saml C Garrisonett

Healy Whittield Jarnagin raised the boy David Becton Whitfield. Healy Jarnagin and Cary Jarnagin had two daughters. They had Mahalia Jarnagin and another daughter ____ Jarnagin. The family resided in Tennessee.

POLLY WHITFIELD born 1814 in Georgia, the daughter of John and Kizziah Whitfield. Polly married Eli Whitfield seventh cousin who was born July 2, 1807 TN. They were married in Cannon County, TN, and appear on 1840 census. They appear on the 1850 and 1860 census of Izard County, Arkansas. Eli Whitfield died between 1860 and 1870. Polly known as Mary Polly and Eli Whitfield had two children:
1. Willie Wiley Whitfield born 1834 and died December 31, 1862. Willie married Elizabeth Henderson.
2. Rhoda Allen Whitfield born 1835 TN and died 1868 Arkansas. Rhoda Whitfield married William Jasper Trimble. He was born 1830 and died 1863 in Arkansas.

WILLIE WILEY WHITFIELD born 1834 in Tennessee, and died December 31, 1862 in Murfreesboro, Tennessee in the Civil war. Corporal killed in Action. Infantry Company G.8 Arkansas. C.S.A. Joined September 23, 1861. Cleburne's Division Hardee's.

Willie Wiley Whitfield and Elizabeth Henderson who was born 1836, Arkansas were parents of two daughters Rhoda and Mary.
1. Rhoda Whitfield born ca. 1858 Izard County, Arkansas. She may have married Mr. Franks, son William Franks was born 1878.

Record of Marriage License

2.   Mary R. Whitfield born October 12, 1861, Izard Co., AR.,
and died February 18, 1937, Izard Co., AR. Mary Staggs is
buried at Wise's Chapel Cemetery, Izard Co., AR.   Mary was
married when she was age twenty-one to Samuel A. Staggs.   They
had children:
    1.   Daughter was Mrs. John Fountain, Pineville, AR in 1937.
    2.   Wiley Staggs, Wild Cherry, AR in 1937.
    3.   Daughter was Mrs. Henry Ball, Calico Rock, AR in 1937.
    4.   Jordon Staggs, Chase, KS in 1937.
    5.6. Two girls died in infancy.

Mary R. Whitfield Staggs departed this life February 18, 1937,
age 76 four months and six days.   She was survived by three
daughters and a son, and seventeen grandchildren, and eleven
great-grandchildren.   Mary Staggs was converted at an early age
and united with the Baptist Church and lived a Christian in
faith.   Elder D.A. Hively conducted the funeral service.

RHODA ALLEN WHITFIELD was born ca. 1835 in Tennessee, the
daughter of Eli Whitfield and Rhoda Whitfield, and she died ca.
1868 in Arkansas.   Rhoda Whitfield married William Jasper
Trimble who was born between July 16, and October 8, 1830,
Izard Co., Arkansas.   They were married when the Arkansas 1850
census was taken.   They had five children:
1. George Washington Trimble (1852-1939).   George had the
    grandson Carlton Trimble, husband of Nerva Trimble who did
    the family genealogy.
2. Ephraim Jasper Trimble 1855, living in 1860 and died before
    1870.
3. William Henry Trimble (1857-1936).
4. Bradley Trimble born ca. 1860, d. ca. 1878.   He died in a
    hunting accident.
5. Baby Girl.

JOHN G. WHITFIELD, Jr. was born 1826 in Tennessee, and died
1871 in Sylamore Township, Izard Co., Arkansas.   John was a
blacksmith.   John G. Whitfield was buried at mouth of Clear
Creek in Boone Co., Arkansas.

John G. Whitfield, Jr. married first to Marina Serina McCloud
and they had children:
1. Lucinda Whitfield b. 1855, AR
2. Jasper Marion Whitfield, b. 1858 AR Jasper married Eliza
    Fledmeak.   Jasper Whitfield was a Minister.

Marina Whitfield died and John G. Whitfield, Jr. married her
twin sister Malissia McCloud.   They had five children:
1. John Newton Whitfield b. 1859, Calico Rock, AR married
    Clara Esie Burnett.
2. Irving Whitfield b. 1861
3. William Whitfield b. 1863
4. Alice E. Whitfield b. 1865
5. George Washington Whitfield, b. 1868

Irving and William also had a name of Lorenzo and Dock.   Eliza
Whitfield died in 1868 when George the son was born.   Eliza was
buried Woodruff County, Arkansas in April.   Sixteen miles
Northeast of Augusta McGregory Graveyard.

JOHN NEWTON WHITFIELD was born 1859 in Calico Rock, Izard County, Arkansas. He had an interview and biographical sketch for Arkansas Pioneer.

Mr. John Newton Whitfield in Izard County, Arkansas. In the beginning of the war informed me one day in the Creek Nation that he underwent an experience just as the war was closing. Mr. Whitfield is a son of John N. Whitfield and Marina McCloud Whitfield. His father was a confederate soldier and served in the army east of the Mississippi River. 'I was too young,' he said to recollect anything about the Civil War except the last year of it when there were so many things that occurred that I do remember about. Some months before it's final ending while father was off in the army, my mother took us children and moved to Woodruff County where we stopped some sixteen miles northeast of Augusta. The locality where we stopped was known as Bowdens Ridge which took its name from Tom Bowen who was an early settler there.

I and my little brother Lorenzo was sick and we both lying on the bed the tools were hid in.

John N. Whitfield told the interviewer S.C. Turnbo where his parents were buried in Arkansas. The Marauders, Volume IV, Pioneer Sketches by S.C. Turnbo. Written 1900-1910, typescript. Printed as Ridge Runners, May 1975, page 40.

ALLEN WHITFIELD was born February 2, 1823 in Cannon County, Tennessee, the son of John G. Whitfield and Kizziah Rutledge Whitfield. Allen Whitfield died June 13, 1906, two miles north of Pineville, Arkansas. Allen Whitfield was buried at Trimble Campground Cemetery, Izard County, Arkansas, near Dolph, Arkansas.

Allen Whitfield with his mother and brothers came from Cannon County, Tennessee to Arkansas. They arrived first at Yellville late in the Fall of 1850. They moved on to a location two miles north of Pineville in Izard County, Arkansas. Allen Whitfield claimed a homestead there and 160 acres were approved June 16, 1856. He remained on the farm until his death in 1906.

Grandsons and great-grandsons of the Whitfield name have been on this place ever since to this date 1996, and will continue to be there. All of Allen Whitfield's family belonged to the Cumberland Presbyterian Church at the Trimble Campground at Dolph, Arkansas.

Allen Whitfield married November 13, 1856 MARGARET LANGSTON. She was born March 15, 1842 in Izard County, Arkansas. She married and was the mother of nine daughters and six sons. When laid to rest she was buried at Trimble Cemetery near Dolph, Izard County, Arkansas.

Allen Whitfield has a biographical sketch in Izard County Arkansas Historian. Volume six. Number three.

Children of Allen Whitfield (1823-1906) and Margaret Langston Whitfield (1842-1929).

Birth	Death		
1. Pernecia Whitfield (Adams)	July 1, 1858	Dec 4 1897
2. Sophronia Whitfield (Sanders)	April 8, 1860	Mar 24 1946
3. Frances Whitfield (Sanders)	Feb. 4, 1862	Jul 25 1887
4. Margaret Whitfield (Moody)	Mar. 6, 1864	Sep 14 1904
5. Mary Whitfield (Moody)	May 15, 1866	Jan 18 1951
6. Tennessee Whitfield (Ivie)	Feb. 2, 1869	Mar 17 1945
7. Porter Whitfield	Oct. 16, 1871	Apr 24 174
8. Andrew B. Whitfield*	Feb. 19, 1874	Apr 27 1923
9. Young Whitfield*	Dec. 18, 1876	Dec 21 1958
10. Martha Whitfield	May 8, 1878	Aug 8 1878
11. Julie Whitfield (Mrs. Radar)	Jun. 14, 1880	Oct 17 1898
12. Jasper Whitfield	Sep. 30, 1881	Aug 6 1955
13. Daniel Whitfield	Nov. 29, 1882	Sep 2 1883
14. Casey Whitfield	Aug. 23, 1884	Nov 15 1975
15. Alice Whitfield (Mrs. Clark)	Nov. 28, 1885	Jan 17 1965

YOUNG WHITFIELD was born December 18, 1876 the son of Allen Whitfield and Margaret Whitfield and the ninth child born. Grandson of John G. Whitfield, Sr. and Kizziah Whitfield.

Young Whitfield worked hard as a farmer all his life. He felt a calling to preach the gospel. He only had an elementary education, so when his children could help on the farm, Young Whitfield attended Mount Olive Academy. He was thirty-eight years old at the time. He became a candidate for ordination in 1915 and was ordained in 1917.

A preacher's life was not easy at that time as there was little or no pay for services, and it was necessary to work at another trade in order to support a family. Young Whitfield served as pastor in many Cumberland Presbyterian Churches throughout that area during his life time.

Young Whitfield married Mary Gabriella Herron on December 25, 1898 in Iuka, Izard County, Arkansas. Mary Gabriella was born February 14, 1884 in Norfolk, Baxter County, Arkansas. They had six children. Five boys and daughter Gracie.

1. George Herman Whitfield b. Sept. 21, 1900-d. Dec. 22, 1977
2. Gracie Alma Whitfield b. May 10, 1905-d. Sept. 23, 1912.
3. Willie Jaden Whitfield b. Mar. 13, 1908-Oct. 20, 1983.
4. Asa Dale Whitfield, boy. b. Mar. 24, 1911-
5. Herron Thompson Whitfield b. Sept. 24, 1914-Living in 1995 at Pineville, Arkansas.
6. Finis Howard Whitfield b. July 31, 1919-d. Jun. 5, 1986.

Albermarle Sound, a large water area, and line between Bertie and Chowan Counties of North Carolina. Near there were many with the name of Whitfield who moved from Virginia and after leaving the water area to North Carolina and Tennessee they moved.

A book: Old Albermarle And Its Absentee Landlords by Worth S. Ray, Published in 1947, reprint in 1976.
Whitfield appears on pages 607-614-656 to 658-682.
This book also has the families who lived near Whitfield families in Virginia.

THE WHITFIELDS
By
Herron T. Whitfield
Pineville, Ark.

REV. YOUNG WHITFIELD

The first Whitfield to settle in Izard County was Wiley Whitfield. He homesteaded land in Izard County April 24, 1820, lot No. 4. This is located at the junction of Highway 223 and the Corinth Church Road in Pineville. We do not know what, if any, connection there was between Wiley and great grandfather, John, but we believe they may have been brothers. Whitfields have lived in the Pineville area for 155 years.

My grandfather, Allen Whitfield was born in Canon County, Tennessee February 2, 1823. He was the son of John Whitfield, born in North Carolina. John married Kizzie Rutledge (sometimes spelled Kizzia) and to them were born the following children: Allen; John, Jr.; James; William; Margaret; George and Haley.

In 1850 Allen along with his brothers, James and William, and his mother, made the arduous trip overland to Arkansass, arriving at Yellville late in the Fall of 1850. John, Jr. located permanently near Yellville. Allen, James and William, along with their mother, moved to a location two miles north of Pineville.

It was at this location that Allen decided to make a permanent settlement in 1851. He claimed a homestead on what is now called the Lovelace place. The homestead of 160 acres was approved June 16, 1856. There's a small level field just before you get to the Lovelace house. This was the first field Grandfather Allen cleared. He moved there in March, cut the timber and made the rails by day, burned the brush by night and cleared three acres of land to plant corn. He also built his first cabin which was built of logs and split boards made with a froe. The boards were weighted down with logs. The only nails used were a few nails to nail the door together. He remained on the same farm until his death in 1906.

At the time of Allen Whitfields arrival at what is now Pineville, there were only five families in a radius of five miles. They were James McNeill, James A. Claiborne, Michael Henderson, Curtis Brown and William Ware. Others coming soon afterward were the Dillards, Creswells, Andersons, Matthews, Hivelys, Staggs, Guthries, Sanders, Smiths, Killians, Duckers, and many others who had much to do with the development of the community.

77

The second building Allen built was a big, double-log house with a hallway or "dog trot" as they were called. They lived in that house until, as was the custom in those days, Grandfather Whitfield gave the old homestead to the four boys in return for their taking care of him and grandmother in their old age. He divided the land south of the creek between two of the boys and the land north of the creek to the other two boys.

The Whitfield home at Pineville.

Uncle Andy wanted to move to Calico Rock and go into business so my father bought him out. Then, Uncle Jasper decided he wanted to go to school in Mountain View so he bought him out. Uncle Casey also wanted to go to school, so Father bought him out, too.

All of grandfather Allen's family joined the Cumberland Presbyterian Church at the Trimble Campground at Dolph. The congregation met at the old schoolhouse which was halfway up the hill between the present church building location and the cemetery. There was only a brush arbor at the present church site. They lived halfway between Trimble Campground and the Spring Creek Methodist Church and attended services at both churches.

One thing I admired in my grandmother and grandfather was that even though they couldn't read or write, they were very industrious. At the time grandfather went off to the Civil War, he had lots of cattle and horses. There was only one mare left when he came home from the war and she was so wild that grandmother was the only one who could catch her. But they accumulated another supply of stock and gave each girl a mare and cow when they married.

Several years after the Civil War, Allen's brother, William, moved to Jackson County and lived there until his death.

YOUNG WHITFIELD

By Herron T. Whitfield

Father worked hard as a farmer all his life but also felt a calling to preach the Gospel. He had only received an elementary education in the Pineville school and later when his children were able to help out on the farm, he attended two terms at the Mount Olive Academy. He was then 38 years old.

He became a candidate for ordination January 2, 1915 and was ordained at Pineville on January 7, 1917 by the following: Rev. J. S. Bone; Rev. R. L. Keathley; Rev. G. W. Thompson; Rev. A. M. Colson; Rev. D. R. Robertson and Rev. W. A. Rogers.

A preacher's life in the early 1900's and before was not an easy one. It was necessary to work hard at some trade, often teaching, but in father's case it was farming, in order to support a family. They had to travel long distances, often receiving no payment for their services. Payment was often made in produce such as vegetables. I remember one time he received a car load of grapes.

Churches which he served at various times were Hopewell, near Cord; Caney Springs, near Sage; Mt. Pisgah, in Fulton County; Trimble Flats, in Baxter County; Glade Community, north of Dolph; Rodney; New Hope, in Independence County; Barren Fork, now Mt. Pleasant; Strawberry; Harrison; Perogue; Pineville; Oxford; Bexar; Iuka; Spring Creek; Union; Mountain Grove, at Byron; Calico Rock; Mt. Olive and Sidney. He also held revivals as far away as Checotah, Oklahoma.

The first wedding he performed was Gulley Seay and Stella (Wayland) Seay in 1917.

I remember him telling many of his experiences, a few of which will be included here. One early incident occurred when he was serving the Hopewell Church at Cord, Arkansas, about 20 miles east of Bastesville. He went down on the train on Saturday, preached Sunday and Sunday night and came home on the train on Monday. He had a good riding horse so, some time in 1917 or 1918, he decided to ride horseback to Cord which was ordinarily a day and a half ride. But on Sunday night at the close of church services he received a telephone call that Mother was sick. He was aiming to come home right away but it being his first trip on horseback in that area, the natives advised him to stay over until Monday morning. They feared he'd get lost at night.

He took their advice and started home very early the next morning, followed the old Jacksonport Road to Sidney, stopped at Porter Bones, fed his horse, ate lunch at noon and by sundown that night he was home at the old homestead. The horse he rode that day was a wonderful saddle horse, used to being rode and gave everything he had that day. He was such a good horse that Philip Wayland offered Father a pair of good work mules in trade. At the same place he made his famous ride from, the Hopewell Church, he was later offered $260 for one of the mules.

Another of Father's experiences as a minister was in the early 1920s. He'd been over to the old Caney Springs Church east of Melbourne. It was halfway between Melbourne and just north of the Sage road. That time it was in the Spring of the year and the creeks were up. There was no bridge over Piney Creek and he drove into the Piney Creek ford and the quicksand had washed into the ford. The water came through the floorboards of the buggy. Both mules went under. One mule just had her nose sticking out. Father got out and cut the tugs. One mule broke singletree and got out. Father went up to the top of the hill which is now the Atlantic Estes place to where "Uncle" Tom Rhoades lived. "Uncle" Tom went with him to help. They took a chain and pulled the buggy out. needless to say he was late getting home that night.

Another of his early experiences was in 1923 when he bought his first Model T car. He was proud of his new car and wanted to take Mother, myself and baby brother on a trip. My brother was about 4 and I was 9. Early one Saturday morning we started out for the Hopewell Church at Cord. It rained on us all day and it took us all day long to get to the church. We stayed all night with "Uncle" Charley Pickens. Sunday morning it was still raining hard. We drove by the church - no one there - no one appeared. We drove over to "Uncle" John Pickens and spent Sunday night there. Monday morning we started back home and we never did even go into the church.

There was little in the way of monetary reward for a preacher in those early days. There were many, many long trips made when he received nothing for his services or sometimes less than a dollar. But there was plenty of good food and fellowship and the knowledge he was doing the Lord's work.

As I mentioned before, Father farmed in order to support his family. He also raised some of the very best cattle. I remember when he went to an auction at Mountain Grove, Missouri and bought some of the first Jersey cows seen in this area and he had one of the first dairies here.

Father was proud of the fact that he had been a life-long Democrat. He voted at the Pineville precinct, Union Township, for 60 years without ever missing a general election.

Young Whitfield bought out other heirs and lived on Allen Whitfield's homestead land. The wife, Mary Gabriella Herron died August 11, 1941 at Pineville, Arkansas. The husband, Young Whitfield died December 21, 1958 at Pineville, Arkansas. Both parents were buried at Pineville, Arkansas Cemetery.

Young Whitfield has a biographical sketch in Izard County Arkansas Historian. Volume Six. Number three.

ANDREW B. WHITFIELD born February 19, 1874 was the son and eighth child born of Allen Whitfield and Margaret Langston Whitfield. He was called Andy Whitfield. He married Sarah Francis Paralee Lackey on September 19, 1895. They had three daughters and four sons. Andrew B. Whitfield died April 27, 1923. Children:
1. Flora A. Whitfield (Osse) b. Oct. 1896.
2. Roe J. Whitfield, b. March 1898.
3. Porter Whitfield
4. Claudia (Clgia) Whitfield (Osse)
5. Mammie Whitfield (Punell Korff)
6. Lackey Whitfield
7. Andrew B. Whitfield, Jr.

WILLIAM BRADLEY WHITFIELD was born 1830 in Tennessee. He was born in Cannon County, the son and seventh child of John G. Whitfield and Kizziah Whitfield. He was a brother to Allen Whitfield. William B. Whitfield left Tennessee and went to Izard Co., AR with his mother Kissiah Whitfield and brothers Allen and James in 1850. 1860 census has William and wife, Elizabeth with two children, and his wife's brother and sister at Izard Co., AR.

The 1870 census of Oregon County, Missouri has William B. and wife, Elizabeth with children, and the three sons of William Jasper Trimble and wife, Rhoda Allen Whitfield Trimble.

William Jasper Trimble died during the Civil War and his wife soon after. The three Trimble boys were related to both William B. Whitfield and his wife.

The 1880 census has William Bradley Whitfield in Jackson County, Arkansas, and his wife was dead.

William Bradley Whitfield married Elizabeth Hively who was born 1831 in Arkansas. Elizabeth first married Young Henry Yeary. She was a widow when she married William Whitfield. Elizabeth was the daughter of Daniel Hively and wife, Martha Trimble Hively.

Children: Elizabeth Hively Yeary had a son born June 24, 1849 in Tennessee. Son was Young Henry Yeary, Jr. William Bradley Whitfield and Elizabeth had seven children of their union. They also raised the orphans, George Trimble who was born 1853, and Mary Trimble who was born 1858, and 3rd Trimble. William and Elizabeth had these children:
1. Alexander Whitfield, born 1859, AR.
2. Levine Whitfield married John Masengale age 23 on April 20, 1874 in Jackson Co., Arkansas. She was called Vina Whitfield Masengale. Levine was born 1862.

3. Kizzia Whitfield was born 1863 in Izard Co., Arkansas. She was called "Kisey".
4. Margaret E. Whitfield was born 1864 in Izard Co., Arkansas. She married Martin L. Woodcock.
5. Blake Sedgley Whitfield was born September 10, 1866 in Izard Co., Arkansas, Iuka township.
6. Mary Whitfield, born 1872 in Arkansas. She is named on census.
7. Frances B. Whitfield, born 1873 in Arkansas. She is on census.

There were 11 children raised in the household of Elizabeth and William Bradley Whitfield. 1 Yeary, 7 of their own, 3 Trimble boys.

William Bradley Whitfield went to Oregon County, Missouri, and the County Recorder of Deeds has these records: *W.B. Whitfield bought land from H. Stogsdill on April 21, 1870.*

W.B. Whitfield and wife sold their land to S.S. Cypret on December 29, 1874, and deed record filed April 6, 1875. 160 acres, 14th section 22nd township 3rd range. 11th section 22nd township 3rd range.

William Bradley Whitfield and family did not stay in Missouri but returned to Arkansas. They were at Couch, Missouri.

William Bradley Whitfield was born on September 10, 1830 in Tennessee and died 1881 in Arkansas.

Elizabeth Hively was born on August 12, 1831. She married Young Henry Yeary, then married William B. Whitfield. Elizabeth Hively Yeary Whitfield died 1874 in Arkansas.

MARGARET E. WHITFIELD the daughter of William B. and Elziabeth Whitfield born 1864. Margaret Whitfield married Martin Luther Woodcock 1887. They had twelve children and only four lived.
1. Laura Woodcock (Russell).
2. Mae Woodcock (Hamlet).
3. Elizabeth Woodcock (Stone)
4. Hattie Woodcock (Banwig)
Margaret E. and Martin L. Woodcock both died in 1947.

SARAH ELIZABETH HENDERSON born 1836 in Arkansas. She used her second name Elizabeth. She married Willie Wiley Whitfield (b. 1834 TN-d. 1862 TN) and had two daughters Rhoda and Mary R. William called sometimes Wiley Whitfield was the brother of Rhoda Allen who married Jasper Trimble. After his death in the Civil War she married Josiah Morgan and had son Henderson Morgan.

PETERS
One of Blake S. Whitfield's
sisters married a Peters.
From the Peters' family
Bible.

BLAKE SEDGLEY WHITFIELD born Sept. 10, 1866 in Iuka, Izard County, Arkansas was the son of William Bradley Whitfield (1830-1881) and Elizabeth Hively Whitfield (1831-1874). Blake was the grandson of John G. and Kizziah Whitfield of Cannon Co., Tennessee.

Sedgley is a surname for his middle name. Blake S. Whitfield married Calladona Ann Woodcock on July 25, 1889 in Baxter County, Arkansas. She was born January 7, 1874 in Pineville township, Izard County, Arkansas. They had twelve children. Nine boys and three girls. Blake Whitfield lived in AR and moved to OK 1902 or 1903.

1. Thomas Andrew Whitfield b. April 29, 1890 near Mt. Home, Baxter County, AR.

2. Jonathan L. Victor Whitfield b. Jan. 24, 1892 near Mt. Home, Baxter Co., AR.

3. Mary Elizabeth Whitfield b. Jan. 22, 1894 near Mt. Home, Baxter co., AR.

4. Bessie Rachael Lee Whitfield b. March 29, 1896, near Mt Home, Baxter Co., AR.

5. Leah Pearl Whitfield, girl b. Feb. 13, 1899 Weldon, Jackson County, AR.

6. Lucius Herman Whitfield b. Oct. 13, 1901 Weldon, Jackson County, AR.

7. F. or P. Drannon Whitfield b. April 21, 1904 Stroud, Lincoln County, OK.

8. Calvin Blake Whitfield b. April 20, 1907 Stroud township, Lincoln County, AR.

9. Eugene Vernon Debs Whitfield b. Dec. 21, 1909 Vera, Washington County, OK.

10. Basil Phifer Whitfield b. Jan. 25, 1912 Okemah, Okfuskee County, OK.

11. Keller Creel Whitfield b. Sept. 7, 1915 Okemah, Okfuskee County, OK. He died Aug. 24, 1932 in same county.

12. Ralph Junior Whitfield b. Oct. 21, 1917 Okemah, Okfuskee County, Oklahoma.

Whitfield males, descendants of John G. Whitfield and Kizziah Whitfield marry at Arkansas and are in-laws in these families: HENDERSON, TRIMBLE, MCCLOUD, LANGSTON, HERRON, HIVELY, WOODCOCK, RUTHERFORD, ALLEN, BURNETT, BLAND, MCKINNEY, FLEMING, LACKEY.

AMERICAN INDIANS WITH SURNAME WHITFIELD

COLEMAN PORTER-WHITFIELD

Coleman was born 1832 in Rutherford County, Tennessee. He was son of Coleman, a Native American. When he was very young Kissiah and John G. Whitfield took him into their home. He is counted as a son on the census of Cannon County, Tennessee later. Rutherford County was split to form Cannon County.

Coleman left the mother with two sons named Coleman and David; and she changed the family name to Whitfield. She later married Cary Jarnagin who is on Cannon County, Tennessee census. Coleman's brother David was buried in Choate Prairie Cemetery in Olohoma. Indian Territory was Choctaw Nation.

Coleman Porter-Whitfield married Jane Hively. They had children.
1. David Andrew Whitfield, born in Arkansas. He married and had a son. And this son had a son. Descendants were LLOYD VERNON WHITFIELD and his son Jack Whitfield, physician at Tullahoma, Tennessee in 1989.

....Submitted by Jack Whitfield of Tullahoma, Tennesee in 1989.

DAVID BECTON WHITFIELD

He was born April 15, 1833 to the Native American Coleman Porter and wife, Healy Whitfield Porter of TN. He had a brother named Coleman Porter who lived with John G. Whitfield and Kissiah Whitfield and the family.

David lived with his mother, and her husband Cary Jarnagin. In 1860 the Jarnagin family lived in Union township, Izard County, Arkansas. At age 27 David joined the Confederate Army at Pocahontas, Arkansas on September 26, 1861. David received a medical discharge from Confederate Army on December 20, 1861 at Bowling Green, Kentucky. His Army record described his physical appearance: Height 5 feet and 8 inches, complexion dark, eyes dark, hair black.

After healing in Civil War area, David enlisted in Confederate Army on July 2, 1861 in Izard County, Arkansas. He deserted July 15, 1861 at Camp Bragg, Arkansas.

David Whitfield married Mary Jane Rutherford on October 29, 1862 at Izard County, AR. Mary Jane was born May 25, 1847 in Benton County, Missouri. They lived in Missouri for four years and then moved to Arkansas and settled later in Oklahoma.

David joined the Union Army September 20, 1864. Private F Company, 46 Regiment Missouri. He was discharged March 31, 1865 at Springfield, Missouri.

David and Mary Whitfield and family were settled 1880 at Prairie Township, Boon County, Arkansas where David farmed.

North Carolina. The first major engagement of the Revolutionary War in North Carolina occurred at what became Moore's Creek Bridge, northeast of Wilmington, NC. Here a small patriot force routed several thousand Tories and spoiled the British plan to mobilize local supporters of the King.

COLEMAN PORTER WHITFIELD born 1832 in Tennessee. He was a Native American from father Coleman Porter, and English from his mother Healy Whitfield who was the daughter of John G. Whitfield, Sr. and Kizziah Whitfield, his grandparent raised him in their home. Coleman had a brother named David Becton Porter Whitfield who lived with his mother Healy Porter Jarnigan and was raised by Healy and the step-father Cary Jarnagin. Cary had two daughters. Coleman's name and his brother's were changed to Whitfield, and they lived in Cannon County, Tennessee.

Coleman Whitfield married Jane Hively who was born November 15, 1844. Coleman Whitfield died March 1870 at age 38, Izard County, Arkansas with small pox. He was buried in Old Criswell Cemetery, Pineville, Arkansas. Jane Hively Whitfield died in 1920 in Oklahoma. The parents had three children:
1. David Whitfield.
2. Jackson Whitfield.
3. Nicely Ellen Whitfield b. Aug. 27, 1864 Arkansas, and died March 20, 1945, Oklahoma

NICELY WHITFIELD married Issac Henry Williams November 16, 1882.
1. Elsie Francis Williams b. October 6, 1853 Izard Co., AR. d. September 19, 1952.
2. John Henry Williams b. Jan. 27, 1885. d. Aug. 2, 1975.
3. Tate Eyander Williams b. Dec. 6, 1886. d. Jan. 17, 1910.
4. William Monroe Williams b. Jan. 22, 1889. D. March 8, 1975.
5. Cora May Williams b. April 4, 1891. d. May 6, 1960
6. Edith Levah Williams B. Jan. 19, 1893. d. Oct. 21, 1915.
7. Addie Clercie Williams b. Nov. 5, 1894. d. Jan. 21, 1904
8. Margaret Elizabeth Whitfield b. Dec. 20, 1896. d. April 12, 1980.
9. Clara Alba Williams b. Jan. 22, 1899.
10. David Colman Williams b. Jan. 18, 1901.
11. Austin Sammy Williams b. June 25, 1902. d. March 25, 1977.
12. Lewis Vernon Williams b. June 26, 1904. d. July 8, 1948.
13. Hayes Victor Williams b. May 26, 1907. d. Dec. 21, 1941.

All the children of Isaac and Nicely Whitfield Williams children were born in Izard County, Arkansas.

Willis Whitfield b. 1761 Nash Co., NC and died Sept. 3, 1836. Willis Whitfield married Rhoda Allen b. Dec. 1, 1767, and marriage date Nov. 1, 1788. They had son Eli Whitfield, b. 1807 the tenth child, and he married Mary Polly Whitfield, daughter of John G. Whitfield and Kizziah Whitfield. We are the descendants of John G. Whitfield line and Willis *Whitfield line. Except for Eli Whitfield, we don't have other decedents of Willis and Rhoda Allen Whitfield coming to Arkansas. So many of the same unusual names appear in all families.*

John G. and Kizziah's great grandson still living on same place in Izard County, Arkansas where Allen Whitfield settled with mother Kizziah Whitfield when they came to Arkansas. He is Herron T. Whitfield of Pineville, Arkansas.

....Submitted by Nerva Trimble (Mrs. Carlton Trimble) on May 12, 1995.

Children of David Becton Porter-Whitfield (1833-1895) and Mary Jane Rutherford Whitfield (1847-1924).
1. James Wortham Whitfield b. December 19, 1863, Izard Co., AR, and died January 6, 1949, Indianola, Oklahoma.
2. Mary Ann Whitfield b. June 7, 1866 and died Sept. 6, 1867 AR.
3. Malhala Ann Whitfield b. Sept. 21, 1867 and died March 31, 1952, Oklahoma.
4. William Thomas Whitfield b. January 26, 1867 Arkansas and died October 4, 1967 Oklahoma. Life of a hundred years.
5. John Colman Whitfield b. January 26, 1867 and died April 1950 in Oklahoma. William Thomas and John C. were twins.
6. Robert Lewis Whitfield b. September 30, 1875 and died OK.
7. Nancy Lucinda Whitfield b. September 30, 1875 Arkansas and died January 5, 1957. Nancy L. and Robert L. were twins.
8. Laura Octovie Whitfield b. January 5, 1883 and died 1967 in Texas.

David Becton Whitfield served in Civil War.

The father, David Becton Whitfield received a government pension, October 30, 1890. $12.00. Thurman, Tobucksy County, Indianola, Oklahoma. Pension from the Union Army.

David Becton Whitfield died January 25, 1895, Pittsburgh County, Oklahoma. He was buried at Choate Prairie, Oklahoma Cemetery.

The mother, Mary Jane Whitfield received a widow's pension March 18, 1895. $8.00 monthly for her. $2.00 monthly for one child. Pension raised September 8, 1916 to $20.00 a month. Pension raised in 1920 to $30.00 monthly.

Mary Jane Rutherford Whitfield, John Whitfield, and George York and wife Nancy Whitfield York after the death of David Becton all went to New Mexico to homestead. They stayed six or seven years, and then all came back to the Indianola area. They were unsuccessful in getting a homestead in New Mexico. The Osborne family went with them, and on the way back they stopped in Texas.

Mary Jane Whitfield in 1900 lived on Indian Territory, Choctaw Nation Township Number 8 N R 14. She lived in the house of Arthur Osborne and Laura Osborne, her daughter.

Mary Jane Whitfield died Sept. 11, 1924, and was buried at Choate Prairie, Oklahoma Cemetery.

Seven children of the eight born to Mary Jane survived her.

Lavaca County, Texas. John Wilkins Whitfield, born March 11, 1818, Williamson County, TN, and died 1879 in Lavaca County, TX. He is buried at Halletsville Cemetery. John Wilkins Whitfield was married to first wife, Catherine Dansby in Maury County, TN, on April 13, 1839. They had two girl children. She died in TN. John W. Whitfield married second wife, Sarah B. Dibrell, daughter of General George Dibrell. Sarah was born December 11, 1827, in White County, TN. John W. Whitfield married Sarah B. Dibrell in 1853. The license issued April 27, 1853.

1900 Census Indian Territory Choctaw Nation was the place where children and grandchildren of Mary Jane Whitfield lived.

James W. Whitfield   William T. Whitfield
Lucinda   Annie A.   Birtha
James M.   Rubin L.   Mary L.
Mary E.   Robert E.J   John Whitfield
David J.

Robert Whitfield   Arthur Osborne   George York
Edna M.   Laura   Nancy L.
Rosa L.   Edmond   Virgil
    Mary Jane Whitfield

JAMES WORTHAM WHITFIELD (1863-1949)

James Wortham Whitfield was born December 19, 1863 the son of David Becton Porter Whitfield, Izard County, Arkansas. James Whitfield married first Lucia Lucinda Bland. Lucia died young at the birth of twins. They lived at Indianola, Oklahoma. Children:

1.   James Michael Whitfield (Jim) was born May 24, 1887 in Oklahoma and died January 29, 1959 Oklahoma. Buried Choate Prairie Cemetery.
2.   Mary Elizabeth ("Lizzie" Dunagan). She was born at Indianola. She was buried at Okmulgee, Oklahoma.
3.   David Jackson Whitfield born in the month of June at Indianola and died at Oklahoma City, Oklahoma.
4.   Anna Adeline ("Addie" Bynum) was born April 20, 1894 at Indianola.
5.   Ruby Lee Whitfield (Bynum) born Oct. 5, 1898 at Indianola.
6.   Robert Edward Whitfield born March 13, 1899. He was called Dick. He died November 6, 1979 at Dustin, Oklahoma and buried at Carson Cemetery.

James Wortham Whitfield second marriage was to Sally McKenny. James was called Jim Whitfield.

Whitfield daughters and granddaughters married men with surnames and their in-laws were names of Porter, Jarnagin, Franks, Stagg, Fountain, Trimble, Adams, Sanders, Moody, Ivie, Radar, Clark, Osse, Korff, Masengale, Woodcock, Williams, Dunagan, Bynum, Peters.

References:
1.   Nerva Trimble (Mrs. Carlton Trimble) of Thayer, Missouri researched and wrote the families groups for descendants of John G. Whitfield (1770-1850) and Kizziah Whitfield.
....Submitted by Nerva Trimble May 12, 1995.

2.   Madeline Whitfield of McAlester, Oklahoma researched on families of John G. Whitfield (1770-1850). She contributed the family group of John G. Whitfield, Sr., and Coleman Porter Whitfield and James Wortham Whitfield.

Austin County, Texas. Henry W. Whitfield living in 1965 in Austin County, TX, was the son of Henry W. Whitfield, the oldest son of Wilkins Whitfield and Martha Loftin Whitfield of TN. He was married to Susanna DeMoss Oliphant in Maury County, TN, on June 13, 1850. ———

SCHEDULE 1.—Free Inhabitants in *Union Township* in the County
of *Izard* State of *Arkansas* enumerated by me, on the *14th*
day of *July* 1860. *W.J. Eagle* Asst Marshal.

Post Office *Bentrick Mill* PAGE 282

ORIGINAL 1880 CENSUS OF ARKANSAS

Profession, Occupation, or Trade of
each person, male and female, over
15 years of age.

farmers

No. 7 *Blacksmith*

No. 22 *Farm Laborer*

		The name of every person whose usual place of abode on the first day of June, 1860, was in this family.	Age	White, black, or mulatto.	Value of Real Estate.	Value of Personal Estate.	Place of Birth, Naming the State, Territory, or Country.	Married within the year.	Attended School within the year.	Persons over 20 yrs of age who cannot read & write.
1	2	3	4	5	6	8	9	10			
7	517 521	Jno. G. Whitfield	36	m		100	Tennessee			1
8		Serena A.	21	f			Missouri			1
9		Lucinda	1	f			Ark.			
10		Jasper M.	1/2	m			"			
11	530 522	Alden Whitfield	34	m	7.50	800	Tenn.			1
12		Margaret	17	f			Ark.			1
13		Vernesa	2	f			Ark.			
14		Sophronia	2	f			"			
15		R.B. Whitfield	16	m			Georgia			
16	531 523	Nash Whitfield	45	m	750	300	Georgia			1
7		Elizabeth	39	f			Tennessee			1
18	522 524	Wm. B. Whitfield	26	m	1000	400	Tennessee			1
19		Elizabeth	24	f			Ark.			2
20		Henry	10	m			"			
21		Alex	1	m			"			
22		Michael Hively	20	m			"			
23		Jane	16	-			"			1
24	523 525	Eli Whitfield	35	m	130	400	Tennessee			
25		Mary A	40	f			Georgia			1
26	526	Wm. Whitfield	26	m	550	100	Tennessee			
27		Elizabeth	24	f			Arkansas			1
28		Rhoda	2	f			"			
29		Mary	6/12	f			"			
30	524 527	W.J. Trimble	29	m	750	300	Ark.			
31		Rhoda A	25	f			Tennessee			1
32		George W.	7	m			Ark.			1
33		Ephraim	4	m			"			
34		Wm. H.	2	m			"			

TRIMBLE

88

Indians lived on the land but people immigration brought the changes to the Indians. Reservations formed and the land was held in common by the tribes. Changes with new government laws and acts affected the lives of the Indians. Indian children went to strictly government schools. Children were taught the elementary subjects and agriculture and industrial work. Passing of the frontier occurred. Four states had sixty-one per cent of Indians in Oklahoma, Arizona, New Mexico, and South Dakota.

THESE BROWN PEOPLE SPREAD OVER THE LAND. EACH SMALL TRIBE WITH RELATED FAMILIES KINSHIP SPOKE A LANGUAGE DIALECT OF THEIR OWN TRIBE. THEY STAYED AS LARGE TRIBES OF PEOPLE ON THEIR HUNTING GROUNDS, THUS THE MANY DIFFERENT TRIBE NAMES FOR INDIANS.

1910 CENSUS INDIANOLA TOWNSHIP , PITTSBURG COUNTY, OKLAHOMA

NAME	AGE	MARRIED	BORN
James W. Whitfield	45	5 years	Arkansas
Sarah Mc Kenny	42	5 years	Missouri
Addie Whitfield	16		Oklahoma
David Whitfield	15		Oklahoma
Ruby Whitfield	13		Oklahoma
Edward Whitfield	11		Oklahoma
Step-children			
Iva Mc Kenny	14		
Vernie Kenny	12		
Virgil Kenny	9		
William T. Whitfield	36	12 years	Missouri
Birtha Whitfield	27	12 years	Tennessee
Mary L. Whitfield	10		Oklahoma
William T., Jr "	8		Oklahoma
Dovie M. Whitfield	6		Oklahoma
Albert E. Whitfield	4		Oklahoma
Lindsey Whitfield	10 months		
Robert Whitfield	37	12 years	
Edna Whitfield	28	12 years	
Roselee Whitfield	11		Oklahoma
James Whitfield	9		Oklahoma
Harvey Whitfield	7		Oklahoma
Cecile Whitfield	5		Oklahoma
Wallace York	41	3 years	Tennessee
Eula York	22	3 years	Alabama
Myrtle York	14		Oklahoma
Clinton York	17		Oklahoma
Alice York	8		Oklahoma
Elsie L. York	1		Oklahoma
John E. York	72	55 years	Georgia
Mandy J. York		55 years	South Carolina

ARKANSAS

Arkansas admission into the Union of the States was in 1836 when a migration of people started going to Arkansas. Earlier the country had Indians who moved into Oklahoma and westward. Beginning in the 1850's the Whitfields left Tennessee. About six male members of families started the Whitfield families there. They were early families to Izard County, AR. This county had land split off to form Stone County, Arkansas.

Whitfields were small farmers to begin with but with the large families the children helped the father who was the farmer. These farmers owned relatively small farms on which they raised diversified crops, doing much work themselves. A farmer lived on his own land which was cultivated by him and his family.

This group worked hard and fared rather well. They were on land suited to growing a variety of crops. These families and new Whitfield families stayed in Arkansas for several generations and some younger generations are there today. While some went west to Texas, they are few. *Continued page 93*

PIONEERS TO ARKANSAS

Arkansas was the twenty-fifth land territory that had admission into the Union of the United States in 1836. Indians lived there in the beginning. There was a Fort in Lafayette, Arkansas and it was taxed in 1830 and was located at Lafayette County. F.C. paid taxes in 1837. In 1836 Francis E. Whitfield lived in Lafayette County, Arkansas and paid taxes.

<u>Arkansas Censuses with Whitfield Heads of Household</u>
1840 and 1850 censuses. William Whitfield, Izard County, Arkansas. He was from Rutherford County, Tennessee and had a family. He was the brother of Benjamin Whitfield. They lived at Blue Mountain Township named Mountain View, Arkansas.
1850 Census. Benjamin Whitfield, Izard County, Arkansas.
1850 Census. E. H. Whitfield, Ouachita County, Arkansas, Camden City.
1850 Census. Eli Whitfield, Arkansas, Richwoods township. Arkansas. Eli Whitfield appears on the 1880 census with wife Mary A. who was born in Georgia.
1850 Census. George Whitfield, Lafayette County, AR, La Grange Twp.
1850 Census. James E. Whitfield, Crittenden County, AR, Jasper Twp.
1850 Census. Nancy Whitfield, Jefferson County, AR, Pine Bluff Twp.
1850 Census. William Whitfield, Pulaski County, AR, Rocky City.
1850 Census. Willie W. Whitfield, Izard County, AR, Franklin Twp.

The pioneers to Arkansas are from Tennessee, Georgia, and other states.

HERRON THOMPSON WHITFIELD born September 24, 1914, Pineville, Arkansas. Son of Young Whitfield and Mary Gabriella Herron. Herron T. Whitfield married Nellie Doris Hively December 25, 1931, Pineville, AR. Nellie Herron was born May 20, 1915, Hendrix, Bryan County, Oklahoma. Nellie Whitfield died June 2, 1993 at Calico Rock, AR. Burial at Pineville, AR. Nellie Doris was the daughter of Joseph Washington Hively and Minnie Brown. Herron and wife, Nellie Whitfield, had six children.

1. Mary Katherine Whitfield, born February 19, 1934, Dolph, AR, Mary married Thomas Junior Owens, November 17, 1950.
2. Minnie Joyce Whitfield, b. July 5, 1936, Dolph, AR. Minnie married Lawrence Victor Klein, July 24, 1959.
3. Carl Dean Whitfield, b. August 10, 1938, Dolph, AR. Carl married Joyce Ann Tackett on September 5, 1959.
4. Gladys Fern Whitfield, b. August 25, 1942, Pineville, AR. Gladys married William Earl Estes on September 14, 1962.
5. Betty Gaye Whitfield, b. November 12, 1944, Pineville, AR. Betty married Ronnie Waymon Floyd on July 13, 1963.
6. Noel Rex Whitfield, b. January 7, 1947, Pineville, AR. Noel married Carol Beth Simpson on September 4, 1965.

Herron Thompson Whitfield was living 1995 and farming. He does some carpenter work. Herron was the survivor of all the children of Young Whitfield.

Allen Whitfield (1823-1906) and Margaret Langston were his grandparents. History of the family was written for the Izard County Historian, volume six, July 1975 by Herron T. Whitfield of Pineville, Arkansas. Herron Whitfield wrote about his father and grandfather.

Grandfather Allen Whitfield was inducted into Confederate Army at Benbrooks Mills, Arkansas. He was in the Civil War from Izard County and returned home.

Great-grandfather was John G. Whitfield and the grandmother was Kizziah who was born in Georgia. Kizziah Whitfield traveled from Georgia with her family and settled at Rutherford County, Tennessee and was at Cannon County when the land boundary was set for the counties. When she was a widow in 1850, she and three sons traveled to Izard County, Arkansas. She lived with her son Allen Whitfield.

ARKANSAS RECORDS AND LETTERS

My great, great, grandfather was Mathew Whitfield. My great grandfather was William Whitfield, born in North Carolina. My grandfather was Jasper Newton in Mountain View, Arkansas. My father was John Franklin born in Bartlett, Texas.
....Submitted by James E. Whitfield of Ponca City, OK in 1990.

I had a grandmother who was Mrs. Whitfield, and the grandfather was James Henry Whitfield, born in Virginia, and migrated to Arkansas in the middle of the 1800's. James Henry Whitfield died with son Harvey, and both are buried at Adona, Arkansas. Harvey's son was Harvey Henry Whitfield, and he died about 1987.
....Submitted by Katherine McKay of Vancouver, WA in 1988.

GEORGE HERMAN WHITFIELD born September 21, 1900 at Cross Roads, AR. Son of Young Whitfield (1876-1958) and Mary G. Herron. George died December 22, 1977 at Calico Rock, Arkansas. Burial December 24, 1977 Pineville, AR. George H. Whitfield married Ada Elizabeth Richardson in June 1918. Ada was born October 26, 1899 and died July 27, 1949 in Pineville, AR. Ada's parents were James Richardson and Emma Clark.

George H. Whitfield married a second wife named Laura. George and Ada Whitfield had eight children.
1. Cecil Havron Whitfield, b. September 22, 1919 and d. December 28, 1919
2. Daisy Pauline Whitfield b. March 23, 1921, Pineville, AR. She married Narce (Bud) Majors on April 20, 1935.
3. Dessie Lorene, b. April 15, 1923, Pineville, AR. Married Harold Stroud.
4. James Roe Whitfield b. November 30, 1929, Pineville, AR. James married Gelene Thomas July 19, 1947.
5. Dale George Whitfield b. March 21, 1931 at Calico Rock, AR. Dale married Marie Stuart on September 3, 1950.
6. Twins: Billy and Bobby. Billy Leo Whitfield b. May 19, 1933 at Calico Rock, AR. Billy married Faye Jessen.
7. Bobby Cleo Whitfield b. May 19, 1933 at Calico Rock, AR. Bobby married Deloris Doty July 2, 1954.
8. Ada Mae Whitfield b. August 6, 1936 at Calico Rock, AR. Ada died November. 18, 1936.

WILLIE JADEN WHITFIELD born March 13, 1908, Cross Roads. Third son of Young Whitfield (1876-1958) and Mary G. Herron. Willie died October 20, 1983, Calico Rock, AR. Burial October 23, 1983, Pineville, AR. Willie J. Whitfield married Ruth Mae McClellan on May 23, 1930, Calico Rock, AR. Ruth Whitfield was born April 1, 1909, Iuka and died August 1, 1986, Calico Rock, AR. Burial at Pineville, AR. Ruth's parents were Willie McClellan and Cora Thrasher. They had child, Grace Naomi Whitfield, b. May 8, 1936, Pineville, AR.

ASA DALE WHITFIELD b. March 24, 1911 at Cross Roads. Son Young Whitfield (1876-1958) and Mary G. Herron. Asa Whitfield married Oris Mildred Dockins March 27, 1932, Calico Rock, AR. She was born August 28, 1911, Crossroads, AR., daughter of James (Jim) Dockins and Mary Emmaline Lovelace. Children:
1. Harold Dale Whitfield, b. May 31, 1941, Searcy, AR. Harold married Barbara Ann Penfield on May 1, 1965.
2. Paul Douglas Whitfield b. July 8, 1948, Little Rock, AR. Paul married Rebecca Wavrin on August 17, 1968.

FINIS HOWARD WHITFIELD b. July 31, 1919, the sixth child of Young Whitfield (1876-1958) and Mary G. Herron, Pineville, Arkansas. Finis died June 5, 1986, Little Rock AR. Burial at Pineville, AR. Finis H. Whitfield married June 26, 1937 to Bernice Sanders, the daughter of David M. Sanders and Malita Arnold. Bernice was born August 4, 1919, Pineville, AR. She died March 30, 1988, Little Rock, AR. Finis and Bernice Whitfield had children.

1. Jimmy Howard Whitfield b. August 29, 1938, Pineville, AR. He married Jonnie Jean Decker on May 5, 1956.
2. David Max Whitfield b. October 25, 1944, Pineville, AR. David married Judith (Judy) Leonard on May 20, 1967. Judith died August 6, 1991. David Max Whitfield married second Valerie Elaine Vaughn on June 18, 1993.
3. Charles Allen Whitfield B. August 24, 1948, Batesville. Charles married Delia Rodriguez on June 4, 1976.

1880 Arkansas Census, Boone County, Prairie Township

NAME	AGE	POSITION	BORN
Whitfield, David B.	47	Farmer	Tennessee
May Jane	33	Housekeeper	Missouri
James W.	16	Farmer	Arkansas
Mahala A.	10		Missouri
William	7	Twin	Missouri
John	7		Missouri
Robert L.	5	Twin	Arkansas
Lucinda	5		Arkansas

CARL DEAN WHITFIELD b. August 10, 1938, Dolph, AR. Carl D. Whitfield married Joyce Ann Tackett September 5, 1959, Newbern Tennessee. Joyce was born March 24, 1938, Newbern, Tennessee. Daughter of Cecil E. (Buster) Tackett and Mildred H. Flatt Tackett. They had children. 1. Scott Harris Whitfield, b. August 18, 1962, Kennett, Missouri. 2. Elizabeth Lynn Whitfield b. September 23, 1964, Kennett, Missouri.

NOEL REX WHITFIELD b. January 7, 1947, Pineville, AR. Noel married Carol Beth Simpson on September 4, 1965, Pineville, AR. Carol was born January 9, 1846, Creswell, AR., daughter of Wiley Simpson, a Preacher, and Imogene Smithson. They had children: Sarah Beth Whitfield, b. June 4, 1974, Jacksonville, AR. Nancy Diane Whitfield, b. Sept. 20, 1975, Jacksonville, AR.

GLADYS FERN WHITFIELD b. August 25, 1942, Pineville, Arkansas. Her parents were Herron Thompson Whitfield and Nelli Drosi Hively Whitfield. Gladys Fern married William Earl Estes who was born February 23, 1941., Cross Roads, AR, the son of William Earl Estes, Sr. and Ruby Atlantic Partee. They had William Eric Estes, born December 9, 1964, Calico Rock, AR. In July 1995 William and Gladys Fern reside in Wideman, AR.

Reference: Family Tree Whitfield of Herron Thompson Whitfield of Pineville, Arkansas. Contributor of the Family Tree was Gladys Fern Whitfield Ester, July 5, 1995. Ancestors were John G. and Kissiah Rutledge Whitfield.

Continued from page 90.
   There was little manufacturing in the south. The principal reason was probably the region lacked free capital. Since the money and credit of its wealthy men were tied up in land and slaves, there was little surplus available for building factories or for buying expensive machinery.

Continued page 104.

DESCENDANTS OF HERRON THOMPSON WHITFIELD (1914-living 1995) AND NELLIE DORIS HIVELY OF PINEVILLE, ARKANSAS
MARRIAGE RECORDS

Thomas Junior Owens md. Mary Katherine Whitfield Nov. 17, 1950. Children: Kenny T. Owens, Jimmy W. Owens, Larry G. Owens, Kathie A. Owens.

Kenny T. Owens md. Palma Ann Lenex June 12, 1970. Children: Gayln Denise Owens and Angela Renee Owens. Ken People md. Gayla Denise Owens b. Dec. 7, 1968.

Bradley Harold Emerson md. Angela Renee Owens June 20, 1992.

Jimmy Wayne Owens md. (1) Marilyn Kay Williams on Dec. 4, 1974 (2) Gloria Jean Grice on July 14, 1983. Jimmy W. Owens d. Oct. 5, 1983, Pineville, AR.

Larry Gene Owens md. (1) Debra Crotts (2) Barbara E. Kelton on Dec. 24, 1974 (3) Traci Lee Miller on Dec. 11, 1987.

Rickey Eugene Grigg md. Kathie A. Owens July 1, 1983.

Lawrence Victor Klein md. Minnie Joyce Whitfield July 24, 1959. Children: Brent A. Klein and Ron D. Klein.

Ron David Klein md. Rhonda Dell Nyberg Mar. 5, 1988.

Ronnie W. Floyd md. Betty Gaye Whitfield July 13, 1963.

Steven Paul Marshall md. Jill Kristine Floyd Dec. 7, 1985.

Brent A. Klein md. Amy Kay Spielvogel Aug. 24, 1990.

ARKANSAS RECORDS

Many people have contributed to making Whitfield Families Group pages in Arkansas. Occasional Family Reunions have taken place. All the Whitfield Families Group's history, genealogy, records have been sent to Vallie Jo Whitfield for the purpose of knowing Whitfields in Arkansas. The ancestor is mainly John G. Whitfield and Kizziah Whitfield descendants, but there are a few who come from other ancestors unknown. The ancestor is mainly Willis Whitfield and Rhoda Allen Whitfield of Cannon Co., TN. The ancestor is Mathew Whitfield born 1772 and died 1827 and Levina Whitfield of Rutherford Co., TN. Willis Whitfield and Matthew Whitfield from Nash Co., NC are brothers. They were the sons of Thomas Whitfield (1741 ca.-1800 ca.) and Elizabeth of Nash Co., NC, and grandsons of Thomas Whitfield (1721-81) and Mary _____ Whitfield of Edgecombe Co./Nash Co., NC. Reference to North Carolina and Tennessee chapters of this book. Lineages are twelve generations.

Great-Great-Grandparents.
John G. Whitfield (1770 NC-1850 TN) and Kizziah (Kizia) (1785 GA-1860's AR) had a son named William Bradley Whitfield, (b. 1830 Cannon Co., TN, d. 1881)

Great Grandparents.
William B. Whitfield md. Elizabeth Hively, and they had a daughter, Mary Elizabeth Whitfield, b. Sept. 21, 1872, AR.

Grandparents.
Mary Elizabeth Whitfield lived in Arkansas. She md. Victor Parrion Clark, b. Jan. 31, 1854, Brownville, Haywood Co., TN. James William Clark b. May 27, 1909 at Davenport, OK was the son or grandson of Victor Parrion Clark.

Grandparents.
James William Clark b. 1909 in Oklahoma md. Eunice Flossie Langston who was b. June 19, 1909. Jacksonville, AR. They had a daughter named Wilma Jean Clark b. Nov. 7, 1929, Stroud, OK.

Eunice Flossie Langston Clark md. first Mr. Brookes and had a daughter Lynn Allyn Brookes b. Sept. 10, 1948, Los Angeles, CA. Eunice Brookes md. second Ralph Posten, adopted child who became a Police Officer for thirty-five years in Southern California.

Lynn Allyn Brookes md. Mr. Hoomalu and had two daughters Kim Hoomalu and Michelle (Shellee) Hoomalu, ages 21 and 17 in 1995. The surname Hoomalu is Hawaiian. Lynn and husband have been practicing physical therapists at Ukiah, CA since 1987.

Daniel Hively 1800 was from York Co., PA and his wife was Martha Trimble of Izard Co., AR. They had the daughter Elizabeth Hively.

.....Submitted by Lynn Allyn Brookes Hoomalu on June 1, 1995.

OTHELLA WHITFIELD PETERS has shared the following:

Mathew Whitfield and Olive's marriage record of license was destroyed in the courthouse fire in 1889 in Arkansas County and all records lost. Mathew Whitfield's Civil War Federal records showed he joined the military on July 6, 1862 and on Sept. 11, 1863 he was shown as "deserted."

Mathew Whitfield application for a pension dated August 12, 1915 reads he was left behind at Delhi, Louisiana Hospital in August 1863. The Arkansas pension was granted for $100.00 per year.

ALBERTA WHITFIELD HANNA of Fayetteville, AR in 1982 had a great grandfather named JOHN WHITFIELD. He went to Arkansas from Scotsboro, AL after the Civil War, and he settled at Wattensaw, AR, Lonoke Co. Her grandfather was PIERCE H. WHITFIELD.

In 1996 the United States naturalized 180,000 immigrants. United States Department of Immigration.

Arkansas Record -
ODEAN C. WHITFIELD b. Aug. 9, 1925, son of Wanie R. Whitfield
(b. April 27, 1900-d.Feb. 6, 1990) and Minnie May Burroughs (b.
May 25, 1904-d. Oct. 14, 1989). He was raised in Bismarch, AR.
He was a bank teller retired Feb. 21, 1993. His home was at
Benton,AR. His brothers and sisters: 1. Clifford Whitfield b.
Nov. 17, 1921, 2. Farrell Whitfield b. Feb. 2, 1923, 3. Wilson
"Bill" Whitfield b. Jan. 5, 1928, 4. Oneeda Whitfield Beebe b.
June 9, 1924, 5. Faye Whitfield Powell b. Feb. 13, 1927, 6.
Opal Whitfield Castleberry b. June 29, 1935.

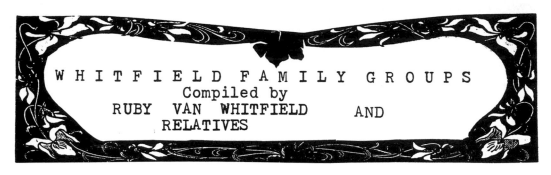

WHITFIELD FAMILY GROUPS
Compiled by
RUBY VAN WHITFIELD AND
RELATIVES

FAMILY GROUP

BENJAMIN WHITFIELD (b. 1806 Sumner Co., TN and d. 1900 Rutherford
Co., TN)
Wife: ELIZABETH HERROD (b. 1810 TN, and d. circa 1870)
Thirteen Children: six sons, six daughters, and one child named
Diuzella. Children born in Tennessee and some died in Arkansas.

FAMILY GROUP

MATTHEW WHITFIELD (b. 1772 NC and d. 1827 TN)
Wife: LEVINA ROBINSON (b. 1776 NC and d. after 1860 TN)
Five Children: three sons, two daughters.

FAMILY GROUP

MATTHEW (Nathney) WHITFIELD (b. 1834 IL, and d. in AR)
Wife: OLIVE DILLARD (b. 1838 MS and d. 1922 AR)
Eleven Children: seven girls and four sons.

FAMILY GROUP

WANIE RUBEN WHITFIELD (b. 1899)
Married 1921 MINNIE M. BURROUGHS in Arkansas. Minnie Whitfield
was born 1904.
Seven Children: three sons, four daughters.

FAMILY GROUP

CLIFFORD L. WHITFIELD (b.1921 AR)
Married 1946 to LENA E. SUGGS in Arkansas.
Children: two sons.

.....Submitted by Ruby Van Whitfield of Benton, AR in 1993.

Whitfields went from Virginia Colony to North Carolina, and many were born in North Carolina. Three moved to Rutherford Co. and Cannon Co., TN, and then they moved to Arkansas. In Arkansas Izard Co. land was split with land portions in Stone Co. and Marion Co.

MATTHEW WHITFIELD was b. 1772, and his brother WILLIS WHITFIELD was b. 1760, the sons of Thomas Whitfield (d. 1800) and Elizabeth Whitfield of Nash Co., NC. They had sisters Mary, Sarah, Chloe, Nancy. Grandsons of Thomas Whitfield (1721-1781) of Nash Co., NC, and Mary Whitfield (d. 1792). Matthew d. 1827 in Rutherford Co., TN. Willis Whitfield d. Sept. 3, 1836 in Rutherford Co., TN. Willis Whitfield md. Rhoda Allen on Nov. 1, 1788. In 1792 they moved to Sumner Co., TN from Nash Co., NC. Also living there were William Whitfield, Jesse Whitfield and John Whitfield. After a stay there they moved to Rutherford Co., TN. Willis and Rhoda had twelve children. Son Eli Whitfield went to Arkansas. Son Alfred Whitfield went to Missouri.

Willis Whitfield made a declaration, Aug. 23, 1832 that he was in Revolutionary War in Army. He was at Nash Co., NC when he was drafted under Capt. Carter and served two or more tours of duty in the Revolution as a private. He was under General Greens and was stationed near Charleston, SC. He served for seventeen months. After his death the widow Rhoda Allen Whitfield received a pension of $58.33 per annum.

"Matthew Whitfield was born 1772 in North Carolina. His wife was Levina Robinson from North Carolina. William Whitfield was my great-great-great-grandfather and he was born in Tennessee and was there in 1830."

.....Submitted by Charlotte Lawrence of Mountain View, AR in 1988. She has a genealogy and charts herein book.

Mrs. Charlotte Lawrence's chart. WILLIAM AND LEVINA AND FAMILY. Matthew Whitfield and Levina Robinson Whitfield were the parents of William Whitfield b. Nov. 28, 1800, Nash Co., NC and d. Nov. 14, 1862 in Izard Co., (later Stone Co.), AR. William was buried in Fowler Field Cemetery. Matilda was b. 1805 and d. June 20, 1879 in Izard Co., AR. Matilda was buried in Whitfield Cemetery. They had eleven children: the first seven children born in TN. The last four children born in AR. 1. Mary (Polly), 2. W. Wiley (John), 3. S. W., 4. Levina, 5. Matthew, 6. Willis M., 7. Talbert, 8. Coleman, 9. Blake, 10. Franklin, 11. Newton Jasper.

"I have obtained documents on Whitfield of Virginia. Know this. An affidavit dated Jan. 10, 1840, Cannon Co., TN. Levina Whitfield, age 67, stated that she knew Willis Whitfield, born in Nash Co., NC."

....Willie Mae Beattie of Jasper, TN made a telephone communication in 1988 to Vallie Jo Whitfield. Pleasant Hill, CA.

Ancestral Chart

Rudy Van Whitfield
father's full name

→

DAUGHTER

Meghan Elizabeth Whitfield
full name

Born July 21, 1985

Delana Gay West
mother's full maiden name

→

Clifford Lee Whitfield
paternal grandfather

Lona Evelyn Suggs
paternal grandmother

Percy Lee West
maternal grandfather

Jimmie Jo Overbey
maternal grandmother

Wane Ruben Whitfield
great-grandfather

Minnie May Burroughs
great-grandmother

John Andrew Suggs
great-grandfather

Ethel Myrtle Geneva Adkey
great-grandmother

Paris Lee West
great-grandfather

Rebecca Clementine Haney
great-grandmother

Thomas Orlando Overbey
great-grandfather

Lillie Alene Casey
great-grandmother

Finis Mathanel Whitfield
great-great-grandfather

Hattie Marie Counts
great-great-grandmother

Robert Lee Burroughs
great-great-grandfather

Carrie Talitha Whitley
great-great-grandmother

James Sam Suggs
great-great-grandfather

Martha Jane Morgan
great-great-grandmother

Eugene Albert Stout ADKO
great-great-grandfather

Mary Arkans Higgins
great-great-grandmother

Martin Van Buren West
great-great-grandfather

Martha Jane Rippetoe
great-great-grandmother

Jefferson Davis Haney
great-great-grandfather

Rememberance Ann C. Myre
great-great-grandmother

Joseph Layefette Overbey II
great-great-grandfather

Martha Ellen Cowan
great-great-grandmother

James Walter Casey
great-great-grandfather

Flora Ester Clonts

(1)

98

Ancestral Chart

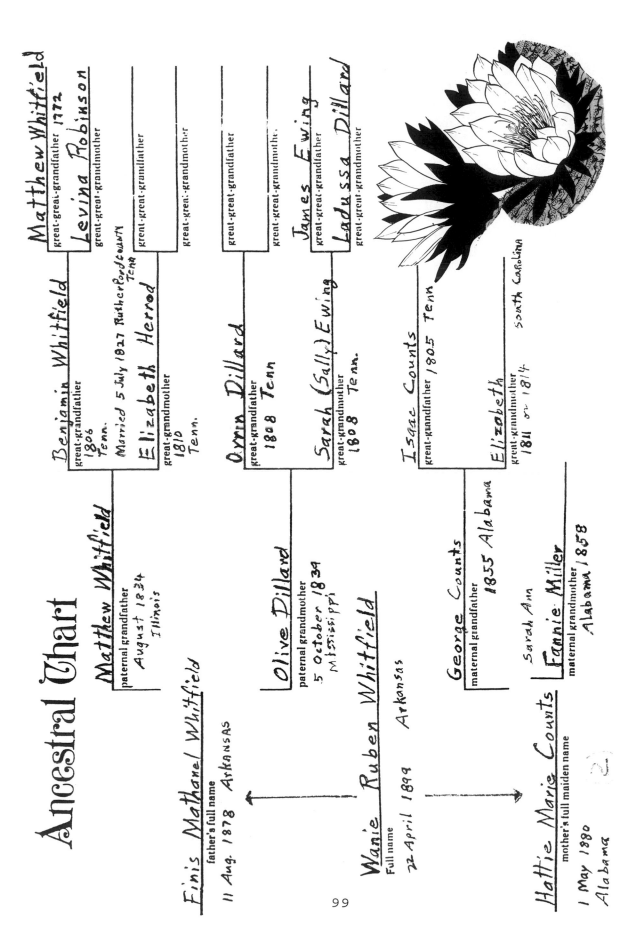

Matthew Whitfield

Benjamin Whitfield
great-grandfather
1806
Tenn.

Matthew Whitfield
great-great-grandfather 1772

Levina Robinson
great-great-grandmother

Married 5 July 1827 Rutherford County
Tenn.

Elizabeth Herrod
great-grandmother
1810
Tenn.

great-great-grandfather

great-great-grandmother

Matthew Whitfield
paternal grandfather
August 1824
Illinois

Orrin Dillard
great-grandfather
1808 Tenn

great-great-grandfather

great-great-grandmother

Olive Dillard
paternal grandmother
5 October 1839
Mississippi

Sarah (Sally) Ewing
great-grandmother
1808 Tenn.

James Ewing
great-great-grandfather

Ladussa Dillard
great-great-grandmother

Finis Mathaniel Whitfield
father's full name

11 Aug. 1878 Arkansas

Marie Ruben Whitfield
Full name

22 April 1899   Arkansas

George Counts
maternal grandfather
1855 Alabama

Isaac Counts
great-grandfather 1805 Tenn

Elizabeth
great-grandmother
1811 or 1814   South Carolina

Sarah Ann

Fannie Miller
maternal grandmother
Alabama 1858

Hattie Marie Counts
mother's full maiden name

1 May 1880
Alabama

99

MOUNTAIN VIEW, STONE COUNTY, ARKANSAS

BENJAMIN WHITFIELD was born in Sumner Co., TN, May 14, 1806, and is therefore 81 years of age. When quite young, his father moved to Rutherford Co., TN where Benjamin continued to live until he was married to his first wife, in 1827. He then removed to Shelby Co., IL, where he remained twelve years, when he returned to Rutherford Co., remaining two years, and then immigrated to Stone Co., then Izard Co., AR, where he has since continued to reside. His first wife bore him fifteen children (eight boys and seven girls). Five of his sons and one daughter are dead. The rest are scattered, some living in Arkansas, some in Texas, some in California and some in the territories.

He is a farmer by occupation and has performed hard labor all his life and can still do hard work. He owns a good farm and has a beautiful residence on it in Richwoods, a fertile mountain valley about five miles southwest of Mountain View. With the exception of slight urinary trouble he enjoys and has always enjoyed good health. He rides to town on horseback every week, descending a high and rugged mountain on the route.

In politics he has always been a Democrat, though he sometimes votes a mixed ticket, voting for the man and not the party. He is strictly a moral man, though he has never belonged to any church or made a profession of religion. He always took his dram when he felt like it, but never drank to excess. He chews tobacco and has followed the habit from early childhood. All his teeth but two or three are in a good state of preservation, and these have only begun to decay within the last five or six years. He does not know the number of his grandchildren and great-grandchildren.

Benjamin Whitfield (1806-1900) married Elizabeth Herrod on May 5, 1827 in Tennessee. They had eight boys and seven girls. Children born in Illinois and Arkansas. Their stay at Rutherford Co., TN was for three years after marriage. They moved 1828 to Shelby Co., IL and stayed to late 1840. Then they stayed two years in Tennessee. In 1842 they went to Richwoods Township, Stone Co., AR about five miles southwest of Mountain View, AR and settled there. Elizabeth Herrod Whitfield was born 1810 in Tennessee and died by 1870 in Stone Co., AR.

Benjamin Whitfield (2) married Elizabeth Birdwell on Oct. 5, 1882. She was age 50 and he was age 76.

Census has him living on Blue Mountain. He lived in Richmonds Township later, Inzard Co., AR. He is buried in Richmonds. Benjamin lived to be ninety-four years of age.

NAME Whitfield Benjamin   **NAME** Elizabeth Herrod

md #1 7-5-1827 Rutherford Co Tenn   #2 10-5-1842 Stone Co Ark

b 5-14-1806 on 94th B. Kelly   d 1900 5/14 NC

b 1810 Tenn.   d BY 1870

Father Matthew Whitfield (1772 1827 Tenn) NC
Mother Levina

#1 Elizabeth — Bridwell (Mo Zenn) (2nd John Bridwell) (Hamey)
   Other Wives 4/1830 d 5-10-1910
#2

CHILDREN	BIRTH	DIED	FIRST SPOUSE
1 Sarah Ramus	5-22-1828 T	Everts Cem. 4-28-1910	James UA Riley Rollins 2) John Harvey Gray
2 William	2-18-1831	M.V. Cem Sav'D Bernard Calif 10-30-1915	Sarah Ann Pigmire V.16-1875 M.D. 1843-1917
3 Reuben	9-9-1833	May 3-1903 Flatwoods Cem.	Mary E. Nelson
4 Mattew	Aug-10-1836	app. 86-1919 Bozeman R Co.	Olive Dillard
5 Levina "Dina"	1836	Lived in Melbourne	Hodge
6 James	1838	Williamette Mes	Elizabeth —
7 Whitmale	1840	16 Mar 1863	
8 Andrew Jackson	1841 A		
9 Diuzella	1842		
10 Elizabeth	1845		Thomas
11 Mary	1846	Lived in Texas	Richard S Decker
12 Malinda	1848		
13 Lucinda Lou	2-1849/56	Ramsey Cem 8-11-1925	Henry B. Hess

MARRIAGE LICENSE.

STATE OF ARKANSAS, }
County of Stone. } To any person authorized by law to solemnize Marriage—Greeting:

You are hereby commanded to solemnize the rite and publish the bans of matrimony between

Mr. *Benj Whitfield*, of the County of Stone and State of Arkansas

aged *76* years, and Mrs. *Elizabeth Bidwell*, of the County of Stone, and

State of Arkansas, aged *50* years, according to law. And do you officially sign and re-

turn this License to the parties herein named.

WITNESS my hand and the seal of said court, this *5* day of *October*, 188*2*

Wm H H Oyler

Clerk of the Circuit Court and Ex-Officio Clerk of the County Court.

CERTIFICATE OF MARRIAGE

STATE OF ARKANSAS, }
County of Stone. } *Arkansas*
Stone county

I, *Wade The Simpson*, do hereby certify that on the *5* day of

October A. D. 188*2*, I did, duly and according to law, as commanded in the

foregoing License, solemnize the rite and publish the bans of matrimony between the parties

named.

Benj Whitfield

Elizabeth Bridwell

Wade Th. Simpson

HUSBAND _Matthew Whitfield_

Born _____ 1772 Place _N.C._ at Nash County.

Died _____ 1827 Place _Rutherford Co., TN_

WIFE _Levina Robinson_

Born _____ 1776 near Nash Co., North Carolina

Chr. _____

Died _after_ 1860 Tennessee

SEX M F	CHILDREN List Each Child SURNAME (CAPITALIZED)	BORN YEAR	WHERE BORN COUNTY	WHERE BORN STATE OR COUNTRY	DATE OF FIRST MARRIAGE TO WHOM	
1 M	William	1800		NC	Matilda	
2 M	Benjamin	MAY 14 1806	Sumner	TN	5 May 1827 Elizabeth Herrod	
3 F	Mary		Rutherford	TN	- - - - - - - -	
4 F	(name unknown)		"	NC	- - - - - - - -	
5 M	Matthew	1814	"	TN	Fanny R. Monahan	

BENJAMIN WHITFIELD b. 1806, Rutherford Co., TN. He married ELIZABETH HERROD in Tennessee. Elizabeth b. 1810 and d. 1870, AR. They went to Arkansas 1842 and made a home there.

In 1834, they visited a Whitfield family in Illinois where a child was born. Whitfield was early neighbor in Tennessee, and not of their kinship Whitfield. Benjamin Whitfield and Elizabeth Herrod Whitfield had children.

1. William Whitfield b-1831 IL
2. Reuben Whitfield b-1833 IL
3. Matthew Whitfield b-1834 IL d. Apr. 26, 1919 AR. He married Olive Dillard.
4. Levina Whitfield b-1836 IL
5. James Whitfield b-1838 IL
6. Whitmale Whitfield b-1840 TN
7. Andrew Whitfield b-1841 TN
8. Druzilla Whitfield b-1842, AR
9. Elizabeth Whitfield b-1845 AR
10. Mary Whitfield b-1846 AR
11. Malinda Whitfield b-1848 AR
12. Lucinda Whitfield b-1850 AR

The grandfather Matthew Whitfield was born in Edgecombe Co., NC, and the land formed later as Nash Co., NC. When he went to Tennessee, he first stayed at Sumner Co., TN and located his brother Willis Whitfield and moved to Rutherford Co., TN where he died.

Refer to North Carolina chapter in this book for his ancestors at Virginia and North Carolina before he moved to Tennessee.

WHITFIELD FAMILY GROUPS
EMILY WHITFIELD
Submitted by Othello Peters of Jacksonville, AR in 1993.

FAMILY GROUP
MATHEW WHITFIELD (b. 1834 IL, d. 1919 AR). Wife: OLIVE DILLARD (b. 1838, d. 1922 AR). Eleven children: four sons and seven daughters.

FAMILY GROUP
BENJAMIN WALTER WHITFIELD (b. 1875 AR, d. 1929 AR). Wife: EMILY SHIRLEY (b. 1878, d. 1968 AR). Eleven children: seven sons and three daughters.

FAMILY GROUP
FLOYD MCKINLEY WHITFIELD (b. 1902 AR, living 1992 AR). Wife: LENA ESTELLE BROTHERS (b. 1901 AR, d. 1982 AR). One daughter.

FAMILY GROUP
EMILY OTHELLA WHITFIELD PETERS (b. 1925 AR, living 1992 AR). Husband: MURIEL HOLT PETERS (b. 1925 AR, living 1992 AR). Three children: two sons and one daughter.

A group's first search was by Dora Bell Whitfield and Thomas Hughes before 1957 by visitations to AR local cemeteries where Matthew Whitfield and Olive Dillard Whitfield and their children were buried.

One January 24, 1965 Thomas J. Hughes and daughter Pearl Hughes circulated the family births and burial places at cemetery, and places they died.

Deaths:

Olive - Hot Springs Co., AR.	Finis - Bismarck, AR.
Sarah - North Little Rock, AR.	Olive - Point Cedar, AR.
Plinia - Texarkana, TX, brd AR.	Dora Bell Whitfield Hughes -
James - Lambert, AR.	Malvern, AR.
Benjamin - Little Rock, AR.	

Continued from page 93.

Slavery had an important effect on southern society. Only one white man in five owned any slaves at all, and only one in a hundred had as many as 50 slaves. This made for a clear division of classes. It had a profound effect on Arkansas. The Negro population increased, and they needed more supervision for their labors.

The northern states were experiencing an industrial revolution and a new economy, which had several important effects. (1) Existing cities of the north grew rapidly, at power sites new cities appeared at waterfalls and rapids of the Merrimac; (2) there was a great demand for better transportation to carry food and raw materials to cities and manufactured goods to markets; (3) the cities provided new markets for farm products. In the northern states they had two new classes of people - the industrial capitalists and the industrial laborers - those who owned the factories and those who worked in them. *Continued on page 106.*

DATE 1993	SEARCH#	
ENC#		
SOURCE Whitfield Family		
Bible - held by Pearl		
Hughes, Malvern AR		

HUSBAND Matthew (Mathew) Whitfield

Born 10 August 1834 Place Illinois

Died 26 April 1919 Place Hot Spring Co. AR

HUSBAND'S FATHER Benjamin Whitfield - Tenn.

HUSBAND'S MOTHER Elizabeth Herrod - Tenn.

WIFE Olive Dillard

Born 5 Oct. 1838 Place Miss.

Chr. Place

Died 31 January 1922 Place Hot Spring Co.

Bur. Place

WIFE'S FATHER Orrin Dillard - Tenn.

WIFE'S MOTHER Sarah (Sally) Ewing - Tenn.

SEX M F	CHILDREN List Each Child (Whether Living or Dead) in Order of Birth GIVEN NAMES SURNAME (CAPITALIZED)	WHEN BORN DAY	MONTH YEAR	DATE OF FIRST MARRIAGE TO WHOM	WHEN DIED DAY	MONTH YEAR
1	Sarah Elizabeth	10	Sept. 1857			Jan. 1930
2	Mary Frances	8	Jan. 1860	Cron	14	Jan. 1927
3	Viney Adline	8	June 1863	Diffie		1866
4	Ruben Waney	8	Jan. 1865	Ava	3	July 1945
5	Plinia Ellen	21	Sept. 1867		died - 18 Oct. 1961	17 Sept 1960
6	Julie Ann	25	March 1870	Moore		1889
7	James Mathney	15	Sept. 1872		7	July 1952
8	Benjamin Walter	8	Feb. 1875			Aug. 1929
9	Finis Mathanel	11	Aug. 1878	Hattie Marie Counts		Aug. 1904
10	Olive I Deafer	10	Oct. 1880			1889
11	Dora Bell	22	Nov. 1885	Hughes	31	Oct. 1957

FAMILY GROUP

HUSBAND-Wanie Ruben Whitfield
    Born April 27, 1899
    Married January 23, 1921

Husband's Father-Finis Nathaniel Whitfield, b. August 11, 1878

Husband's Mother - Hattie Marie Counts, b. May 1, 1880

WIFE-Minnie May Burroughs
    born May 25, 1904

Wife's Father-Robert Lee Bourroughs

Wife's Mother-Carrie Talitha Whitley

CHILDREN:
1. Clifford Lee Whitfield, b. Nov. 17, 1921, md. Feb. 27, 1946
   Lena Evelyn Suggs.
2. Farrel C. Whitfield, b. Feb. 2, 1923, md. Oct. 4, 1947 Joyce
   Marie Shuffield.
3. Vivean Oneeda Whitfield, b. June 9, 1924, md. Aug. 25, 1950
   Harold Lee Beebe.
4. Clara Odean Whitfield, b. Aug. 9, 1925
5. Freeda Faye Whitfield, b. Feb. 13, 1927, md. Jan. 1, 1927
   Charles Eugene Powell
6. Odie Wilson Whitfield, b. Jan. 5, 1928, md. Mar. 16, 1947
   Dorthea Evelyn Shuffield.
7. Opal Christene Whitfield, b. June 29, 1935, md. Apr. 12,
   1952 Leo Alexander Castleberry.

Continued from page 104.
    The profits of the manufacturing and shipping of the Northeast
were great. Much of the money went back into business, but much
of it also went into the banks in the large eastern cities. Money
lent made investments all over the country. Eastern bankers lent
money to speculators in western lands, to companies that produced
what was needed for more businesses.
    Only the agriculture agrarian economy continued to exist in
the southern states. There were southern states in a
Confederation. Then four more slave holding states: Virginia,
North Carolina, Arkansas, and Tennessee joined the Confederacy.
These four slave states seceded after April 15, 1851. The states
of Alabama, Georgia, Florida, Mississippi, Louisiana, South
Carolina, and Texas were slave states, which seceded before April
14, 1851. The Civil War had many men named Whitfield who were
soldiers.   *End*

    The Flatwoods Missionary Baptist Church had minister Rubin
Whitfield (1833-1903) who donated his property March 1881 to
the people to build a church and school and a cemetary. Rubin
Whitfield gave April23, 1881, a Deed to his property located at
the Cemetery Hill in Flatwoods Community.

HUSBAND ____Clifford Lee Whitfield____
Born ___17 November 1921___ Place ___Bismarck, AR, Hot Spring Co.___
Chr. _____ Place _____
Marr. ___27 February 1946___ Place ___Hot Springs, Garland Co., AR___

HUSBAND'S   HUSBAND'S
FATHER ___Wanie Ruben Whitfield___ MOTHER ___Minnie May Burroughs___

WIFE ___Lena Evelyn Suggs_____
Born ___23 March 1925___ Place Casaia Conway Co., AR (Route 1)

WIFE'S   WIFE'S
FATHER ___John Andrew Suggs___ MOTHER ___Ethel Myrtle Geneva Adney___

CHILDREN List Each Child In Order of Birth SURNAME	WHEN BORN DAY MONTH YEAR	WHERE BORN TOWN	COUNTY	STATE OR COUNTRY	DATE OF FIRST MARRIAGE TO WHOM
Rudy Van	5 Oct. 1950	Hot Springs	Garland	AR	23 April 1976 Delana Gay West
Don Wade	27 Oct. 1953	Hot Springs	Garland	AR	17 Dec. 1971 Vickie Faye Hill

GEORGIA

Georgia Censuses

Burke County, GA, 1850 Census. In a household were George Whitfield age 20, Cathrine Whitfield age 20, Benjamin Whitfield age 22. On page 587 of Census.

Cass County, GA, 1850 Census. Frances M. Whitfield, age 25, Mary S. Whitfield age 19; William P. Whitfield, seven months. 1850 Census. Margaret Whitfield, age 67, born SC; Sterling T. Whitfield, age 20; James Whitfield, age 17.

Polk County, GA, 1870 Census. Lucy Whitfield, age 56, born SC; John Whitfield, age 17, born in GA. Sterling Whitfield, age 15.

Georgia Records

William C. Whitfield was in the Georgia Land Lottery a winner in 1833. On Oct. 21, 1837 he was in Dooly County, Ga.

Whitfield (Whitefield) family went to Georgia to live. In the family were Alexander Whitfield, Darby Whitfield, James Whitfield, Sarah Whitfield, Tucker Whitfield.

George Whitefield of Whitefield and Brown Company was a real estate company. George Whitefield was a real estate agent from 1747 to 1803 at Abbeville County, South Carolina.

Husband's Full Name-FLOYD MCKINLEY WHITFIELD
    Born-January 10, 1902, Bismark, Hot Springs, Arkansas.
    Married-July 3, 1922, Pulaski Co., Arkansas.
    Place of Residence-Pulaski Co. Arkansas.
    Occupation-Upholsterer.
    Church-Methodist

Father's name was BENJAMIN WALTER WHITFIELD.
Mother's name was EMILY SHIRLEY.

Wife's Full Maiden Name-LENA ESTELLE BROTHERS
    Born-February 16, 1901, Olmstead, Pulaski Co., Arkansas.
    Died-April 27, 1982, Little Rock, Pulaski Co., AR.
    Buried-Bethel Cemetery
    Place of Residence-Pulaski Co., Arkansas.
    Occupation-Telephone Company. Mattress Factory.
    Church-Methodist.

Father's name was RUFUS ZIM BROTHERS.
Mother's name was OTHELLA E. DANIEL.

CHILDREN:

1. Emily Othella Whitfield, born April 22, 1925, Pearcy, Hot Springs Co., Arkansas. Married May 5, 1946, Jacksonville, Pulaski Co., Arkansas to husband: Muriel Holt Peters, b. November 19, 1925, Grand Ridge, Pulaski Co., Arkansas.

2. Infant Son, b. June 26, 1932. Died June 27, 1932, buried Little Rock, Arkansas, Bethel Cemetery, Pulaski Co., Arkansas.

Othella Peters researched the Whitfield Census in 1986 and commented on the following:

"In researching census records, I found that my Great Grandfather Mathew's records alternated his birthplace between Illinois and Tennessee. Other research leads me to believe that he was born in Shelby Co., Illinois. I rented the 1840 census from Illinois. It shows a Benjamin Whitfield, age between 30-40, with wife of same age, lived in Shelby Co., Illinois. They had 6 male children between ages 10-15 to under 5 and 2 female children between ages 10-15 to under 5. That's all that census shows-no names. In 1840 there was only one Whitfield family in Izard Co. (Mountain View). His name was William, age 30-40, born in North Carolina. I have reason to believe that he was a brother of the Benjamin in the paragraph above. They lived on adjoining farms in 1850 in Izard Co.."

Chart 1. Family Group No. 4. Source : E. Othello Peters.
Family of BENJAMIN WALTER WHITFIELD AND EMILY SHIRLEY.
CHILDREN

NAME		Day Month Year—Place	
1 *Lenia*	Birth	26 Jan. 1897	Benjamin Walter Whitfield b. Feb. 8, 1875. D. Aug. 15, 1929.
	Mar		
Full Name of Spouse	death	2 Dec. 1974	
Birdie Mae Atkins	Burial	b. 7 Oct 1903	
		Buried Bethel Cemetary, Pulaski Co, AR	
		d. 26 June 1987	
2 *Carrie J.*	Birth	29 Sept. 1898	Benjamin buried Cate Cemetery, Faulkner Co., AR. He was a farmer.
	Mar		
Full Name of Spouse	Death	16 July 1963	
Lin Bishop	Burial		
		Cate Cemetery, Faulkner Co. AR	
3 *Oscar M.*	Birth	23 Mar. 1900	Benjamin's born Hot Spring Co., AR. His parents were Mathew Whitfield and Olive Dillard Whitfield.
	Mar		
Full Name of Spouse	Death		
Cecelia	Burial		
4 *Floyd McKinley*	Birth	10 Jan. 1902	
	Mar		
Full Name of Spouse	Death		
Lena Estelle Brothers	Birth	b. 16 Feb 1901	
		Pulaski Co.	
		d. 27 Apr 1982, Buried Bethel Cematary	
5 *Ellis*	Birth	30 Apr. 1904	
	Mar		
Full Name of Spouse	Death	3 May 1984	
Blanch Garvin	Burial	12 Feb. 1908	
		Buried Bethel Cemetary, Pulask. Co. AR	
		d. 22 Dec. 1982, Bethel Cemetery.	
6 *Winnie*	Birth	24 Aug. 1907	Benjamin's wife's name Emily Shirley b. June 23, 1878. D. March 7, 1968. Buried at Cate Cemetery, Faulkner Co., AR.
	Mar		
Full Name of Spouse	Death		
Otto Schmidt	Burial		
7 *Houston*	Birth	23 June 1910	
	Mar		
Full Name of Spouse	Death		
Leona	Burial		
8 *Winfred*	Birth	25 Jan. 1912	
	Mar		
9 *Earl*	Birth	4 Mar. 1914	
	Mar		
Full Name of Spouse	Death		
Edna Owens	Burial		
10 *Raymond*	Birth	25 Apr. 1916	
	Mar		
Full Name of Spouse *Lottie Mae Garvis*	Death	2 Sept. 1991	
11. RUBY	Birth	17 July 1920	

Chart 1. Family Group 8.   Source: E. Othello Peters
Husband Name - MATHEW WHITFIELD b. Aug. 10,1834, Illinois.
Died April 26,1919. Residence Blue Mountain, Izard Co.,
and Hot Springs Co., AR. Occupation Farmer. War Service
Civil War.
Father BENJAMIN WHITFIELD. Mother Elizabeth Herrod Whitfield.
Wife's Maiden Name - OLIVE DILLARD b. October 5, 1838 and
died January 31, 1922. Both Mathew and Olive are buried at
Phillippi Cemetery, Hot Springs County, Arkansas.

CHILDREN

Name		Day Month Year	Place Co. State
1 Sarah Elizabeth	Birth	10 Sept. 1857	Mtn. View, AR Stone Co. AR
Full Name of Spouse:	Mar.		
	Death	Jan. 1930	Faulkner Co. AR
Jack Crone	Burial		Buried at Cato Cemetary, A
2 Mary Francis	Birth	8 Jan. 1860	Mtn. View, AR Stone Co. AR
Full Name of Spouse:	Mar.		
	Death	14 Jan. 1927	
Henry Diffee	Burial		Buried at Bismarck Cemetary
3 Viney Adline	Birth	8 June 1863	
Full Name of Spouse:	Mar.		
	Death	1866	
	Burial		Buried at Shilo Cemetary
4 Reuben Waney	Birth	8 Jan. 1865	Clark Co. AR
Full Name of Spouse:	Mar.		
	Death	3 July 1945	Buried at Phillippi Cemetery,
Aive C. Platts b. 1		1874 d. 18 Oct, 1961	
5 Plinia Ellen	Birth	21 Sept. 1867	Clark Co. AR
Full Name of Spouse:	Mar		
	Death	19 Sept. 1960	Buried at Amity, AR
Sumory Moore	Burial		
6 Julie Ann	Birth	25 Mar. 1870	
Full Name of Spouse:	Mar.		
never married	Death	1889	Buried at Phillippi Cemetary
	Burial		
7 James Matthew (Mac)	Birth	15 Sept 1872	Clark Co. AR
Full Name of Spouse:	Mar		
	Death	7 July 1952	Buried at Phillippi Cemetery
Mary Williams	Burial		
8 Benjamin Walter	Birth	8 Feb. 1875	Hot Sprgs Co. AR
Full Name of Spouse:	Mar		
	Death	19 Aug. 1929	Buried at Cato Cemetary
Emily Shirley	Burial		
9 Fines Nathaniel	Birth	11 Aug. 1878	Hot Sprgs Co. AR
Full Name of Spouse:	Mar		
	Death	Aug. 1906	Buried at Bismarck
Hattie Counts	Burial		Hot Sprgs Co. AR
10 Olive I. Deafer	Birth	10 Oct 1880	
	Mar	1889	Buried at Phillippi Cem.
11. DORA BELL	B.	22 Nov. 1885	Buried at FOREST HILLS
Spouse-Thomas J. Hughes	D.	31 Oct. 1957	BISMARCK, AR

110

CHART I continued-WHITFIELD FAMILY GROUP NO. 8

Father-MATHEW WHITFIELD born August 10, 1834, IL * and died at Blue Mountain, Izard Co., AR on April 26, 1919. Mathew was the son of Benjamin Whitfield and Elizabeth Herrod Whitfield of Izard Co., AR.

Mother-Olive Dillard (1838-1922) had eleven children and all the children were born in Arkansas state.

Children

1. Sarah Elizabeth Whitfield b. Sept. 10, 1857, AR and d. Jan. 1930 in AR. Sarah married Jack Crone. Mountain View, AR. Stone Co.
2. Mary Francis Whitfield b. Jan. 8, 1860, Mountain View, Stone Co., AR. Mary married Henry Diffee. Mary Francis Diffee died Jan. 14, 1927.
3. Viney Adline Whitfield b. June 8, 1863 and died at age three in Stone Co., AR.
4. Reuben Waney Whitfield b. Jan. 8, 1865 at Clark Co., AR. Reuben married Ava Platts in Arkansas. Reuben Whitfield died July 3, 1945 in Arkansas. Ava Platts Whitfield was b. Jan. 1874 and d. Ava Whitfield Oct. 18, 1961 in Arkansas.
5. Plinis Ellen Whitfield b. Sept. 21, 1867 Clark Co., AR. Plinis married Gumory Moore in Arkansas. Plinis Whitfield Moore died September 19, 1960 in Arkansas.
6. Julie Ann Whitfield b. March 25, 1870, Clark Co., Arkansas. Julie Whitfield was unmarried, and she died 1889 in Arkansas.
7. James Matthew Whitfield called Mac. James was born September 15, 1872, Hot Springs Co., Arkansas. James M. Whitfield married Mary Williams. James died July 7, 1952.
8. Benjamin Walter Whitfield b. February 8, 1875, Hot Springs Co., AR. Benjamin W. Whitfield married Emily Shirley in Arkansas. Benjamin died August 19, 1929 in Arkansas.
9. Finis Nathaniel Whitfield b. August 11, 1878, Hot Springs Co., AR. Finis married Hattie Counts in Arkansas. Finis died August 1906.
10. Olive I. Deafer Whitfield b. October 10, 1880 AR, and died at age nine years in 1889 at Arkansas.
11. Dora Bell Whitfield b. November 22, 1885 in AR. Dora Whitfield married Thomas J. Hughes, Arkansas. Dora Hughes died October 31, 1957 in Arkansas.

Parents Mathew Whitfield and Olive Dillard Whitfield had six daughters and five lived to be adults. They had five sons and four lived to be adults. Sons: Reuben, James, Benjamin, Finis have Whitfield children. Kinship with Crone, Diffee, Moore, Hughe. The family of Mathew Whitfield lived in Arkansas Counties. In 1857 they lived at Mountain View, Stone Co., Arkansas. In 1865 they lived at Clark Co., Arkansas. In 1872 they lived at Hot Springs Co., Arkansas. The adult children married and lived in various counties of Arkansas.

....Submitted by Othella Peters of Harrisburg, AR in August 1987. She was E. Othella Whitfield and married Mr. Peters.

E. Othello Whitfield Peters corresponds with JOHNIE WHITFIELD, Whitfield Road, Pearch, Arkansas Zip 71964 in 1986, and defines each genealogical relationship of Othella and Johnie the following censuses.

Census

1850	Name	Age	Born
	Whitfield, Benjamin	44	Tenn.
Your Great-Grandfather			
	Elizabeth	40	"
	William	19	
	Reuben	17	
Your Grandfather	Mathew	16	
	Levina	14	
	James	12	
	Whitmale	10	
	Andrew	9	
	Druzella	8	Ark.
	Elizabeth	5	"
	Mary	4	"
	Malinda	2	"
	Luanda	6/12	"

1860	Whitfield, Mathew	26	Illinois
Your Grandfather			
	Olive (Dillard)		Ark.
	Sarah	3	"
	Mary	6/12	

On adjoining farm lives a brother:

	Whitfield, Reuben	27	Illinois
	Mary O.	25	Tenn.
	Catherine	6/12	

On nearby farm lives:

	Whitfield, Benjamin	56	Tenn.

Your Great-Grandfather

	Elizabeth		
	Andrew		
	(Several names unreadable)		
	Mary		

1870	Whitfield, Benjamin	64	Tenn.

Your Great-Grandfather

	Elizabeth		
	Mary	22	
	Lucinda	19	
	James	17	
	(James or Jane)	13	

On adjoining farm lives:

	Reuben	36	Tenn.
	Mary E.	34	
	Catherine	10	Ark.
	Reuben W.	6	"
	Julia O.	3	"

1870

Shows Mathew moved to Clark County (It later became Hot Springs County)

Whitfield	Mathew	35	Tenn.
	Olive		
	Sarah E.	12	
	Mary F.	10	Ark.(Your father. born 8 Jan. 1865
	Reuben	6	died 3 July 1945
	Ellen P.	2	buried at Philippi Cemetary)
	Julia	3/12	

1880

Whitfield	Mathew	45	Tenn. Your Grandfather
	Olive	39	Miss.
	Sarah	23	
	Reuben	15	Your Father
	Plinia	12	
	Juli	10	
	James	7	
	Benjamin	6	Ark. My Grandfather
	Nathaniel	2	

1900

Whitfield	Mathew	65	Ill. Your grandfather
	Olive	60	Tenn.
	Dora Bell	14	Ark.

Whitfield	Benjamin	25	Ark. My Grandfather
	Emily M.	22	
	Lunia E.	3	
	Carie I.	2	
	Oscar M.	2/12	

1910

Whitfield	Benjamin	35	(born 8 Feb. 1875
	Emily	31	died 19 Aug. 1929
	Lunia	15	(born 23 June 1878
	Carrie	11	died 7 Mar. 1966
	Oscar	10	Buried Cato).
	Floyd	8	
	Ellis	5	My Father
	Winnie	2	

Whitfield	Mathew	75	Born 10 Aug.1834
			died 26 Apr. 1919
	Ollie	72	Born 5 Oct. 1838
			died 31 Jan. 1922
			Buried Philippi.

Full Name-EMILY OTHELLA WHITFIELD PETERS
Born-April 22, 1925, Pearcy, Hot Springs Co., Arkansas.
    Married May 5, 1946, Jacksonville, Pulaski Co., Arkansas.
    Occupation-Accountant.
    Church-Methodist.

Father's name-Floyd McKinley Whitfield
Mother's maiden name-Lena Estelle Brothers.

Husband's Full name-MURIEL HOLT PETERS.
    Born-November 19, 1925, Gravel Ridge, Pulaski Co., Arkansas
    Occupation-Methodist Minister.
    Church-Methodist.

CHILDREN: The grandchildren related surnames are not complete or
dates. Peters and Cribbs.

NAME		Day Month Year / City / County
1 Donald Whitfield Peters / Full Name of Spouse* Wanda Kay Morgan	Birth	26 May 1950 Little Rock Pulaski Co. AR
	Mar.	Emily Francille 14 July
	Death	Rebecca Kay 18 July
	Burial	b. 21 mar 1952
2 Deborah Lynn Peters / Full Name of Spouse* Julian Dean Cribbs	Birth	17 Sept. 1952 Little Rock 7 May 1976 Monica Ellen Cribb
	Mar.	4 mar. 1972 4 Sept. 1980 naomi Ruth Cribb
	Mar. Death	CHALMERS H. DAVIS, SR. 21 mar. 1975 julian D. Crib
	Burial	b. 1 June 19 3 Jan. 1979 Jerry Kinney 1 Jan. 1980 Julian D. Cribb
3 Dale Allen Peters / Full Name of Spouse* Ann Foster Orlicek	Birth	24 nov. 1956 Little Rock Pulaski Co. AR
	Mar	11 apr. 1982
	Death	North Little Rock, AR Pulaski Co.
	Burial	b. 15 Aug. 19 Andrew Orlicek 22, 19--

In May 1992 Othella W. Peters writes the following:
"Sometime after the 1910 Census my grandfather Benjamin Whitfield
moved his family to Pulaski Co., Arkansas, where they remained
until his death. A few Whitfields are still living, my father
being the oldest at age 90."

"There are a lot of Whitfields down around Hot Springs. We had
one family reunion which I hosted here on the farm and over 80
came."

"Pulaski Co., Arkansas is very large including all of Little Rock,
Arkansas. We are in the northern section of this county."

"We had retired here on father's farm. One of our sons lives here
also. I grew up here and attended Bethel Church, which my great-
grandfather on my mother side built. We have four generations in
church each Sunday."

114

WHITFIELD FAMILY GROUP

Submitted by Charlotte Lawrence of Mountain View, Arkansas in 1989.

FAMILY GROUP

WILLIAM WHITFIELD b. November 28, 1800 in North Carolina and died November 14, 1862 in Izard Co. (later Stone Co., Arkansas). He is buried in family plot, Fowler Field. His father was Matthew Whitfield, and his mother was Levina Robinson.

Wife was Matilda _____ who was born 1805 in Tennessee. Matilda Whitfield died June 20, 1879 in Izard Co., AR. She is buried in Whitfield Cemetery. They had eleven children: nine boys and two girls.

FAMILY GROUP

WILEY W. (John) WHITFIELD was born March 17, 1823 in Tennessee. He died May 19, 1895, Mountain View, AR, Stone Co.. Buried in Whitfield Cemetery. He married Eliza Ann Felton. Eliza was born May 12, 1831 and died December 9, 1913, Mountain View, Arkansas, Stone Co.. Her father was James Felton.

Wiley William (John) Whitfield father was William Whitfield (b. 1800, d. 1862) and his mother was Matilda Whitfield.

Wiley Whitfield and Eliza Ann Whitfield had ten children: five boys and five girls. These children when adults with their families live in Arkansas and Texas.

FAMILY GROUP

RICHARD ELLIS WHITFIELD (b. July 8, 1851 and d. May 12, 1932) resident of Mountain View, Arkansas, Stone Co. He was married to Elizabeth Ann Kemp. Richard is buried in Mountain View Cemetery, and also his wife. Wife was Elizabeth Ann Kemp, (b. May 3, 1854 and d. June 16, 1934). They had eight children: Five boys and three girls. Elizabeth Whitfield father John Jacob Kemp, Sr. Her mother was Rebecca Reeves

FAMILY GROUP

Husband was CHARLES KNOX LANCASTER (b. July 27, 1894 and d. January 29, 1972), Mountain View, Arkansas, Stone Co. He was buried at Flat Wood Cemetery. Charles Lancaster married Lillie May Whitfield on June 17, 1917, Mountain View, Arkansas. His father was Green Dink Lancaster. His mother's maiden name was George Ann King.

Wife was Lillie May Whitfield (b. July 14, 1897 and d. September 19, 1987) Mountain View, Arkansas. They had three children: two boys and one girl. Group includes names of grandchildren and great-grandchildren.

Husband Name – **WILLIAM WHITFIELD**
Born Nov. 28, 1800, Nash Co., North Carolina.
Died Nov. 14, 1862, Izard County, Arkansas.
Buried in Family Plot, Fowler Field.
His father – Matthew Whitfield
His mother – Levina Robinson.

Wife's Name – **MATILDA**
Born 1895 in Tennessee.
Died June 20, 1879, Izard County, Arkansas.
Buried Whitfield Cemetery.
Compiler of Chart Feb. 20, 1989, Charlotte
Lawrence, Mountain View, Arkansas.

	Children Birth	State	When Married to	Died	Mo	Yr	Place	Co-State
1	Mary SEPT 6 1821	T.N.	Simeon Ellis Rosson SEPT 27 1839	24	6	1912	Holland	Bell Tx
2	W. Wiley MAR 17 1823	T.N.	Eliza Ann Felton	19	5	1899	Whitfield Cem.	Stone AR
3	S. W. 1825	T.N.	Nancy Pittman MAR 11 1879					
4	Levina AUG 10 1827	T.N.	Walter J. Cagle 1850	2	12	1896	Bartlett	Bell Tx
5	Matthew NOV 41 1829	T.N.	Rhoda L. Pittman					
6	Willis M. SEPT 33 1832	T.N.		7	5	1844	Fowler Field	Izard AR Stone
7	Talbert F. 1834	T.N.	Mary S.					
8	Coleman 1836	An. Co.	Emily J. Shaw					
9	Blake S. 1841	Izard An. Co.						
10	Franklin 1844	An. Co.	Martha F. Cagle FEB 3 1859					
11	Newton Jasper SEPT 10 1847	Izard An. co.	① Martha F. Cagle ② Flora J. Hinkle	DEC 31 1890	27	3	1928 Amarillo	TEXAS

Stone Co. Marriage Records Bartlett
Independence Co. Marriage Records
Izard Co. Census 1850–1860 – 1870
Stone Co. Census 1880
Book "Whitfield History and Genealogy"
Tennessee by Willie Jo Whitfield
Stone Co. Cemetery Records
Deeds for Setting William Whitfield
Estate Stone County, Clerk Office
Information from Willie Whitfield
Lancaster

All Ten
children
born in
Mtn. View
Izard Co.,
Arkansas.

HUSBAND'S NAME Whitfield, Wiley W. (John)

When Born 17 March 1823 Where TENNESSE
When Died 19 May 1895 Where Mtn. View, Ar. Stone County
Buried Where Whitfield Cem.
His Father William Whitfield His Mother's Maiden Name Matilda

WIFE'S MAIDEN NAME Eliza Ann Felton

When Born 18 May 1831 Where TN.
When Died 9 Dec. 1913 Where Mtn. View, Ar. Stone Co.
Buried — Where Whitfield Cem.
Her Father James Felton

	CHILDREN (Arrange in order of birth)	When Born Day	Month	Year	Buried Town	County	State Cou	Married to	When Married Day	Month	Year	When Died Day	Month	Year
1	James W.	17	Nov.	1849	Lawton	Comanche Co.	OK.	Ollie McMurtry	13	Aug	1874	15	Jan	1920
2	Richard Ellis	8	July	1851	Mtn. View	Stone	Ar.	Elizabeth Ann Kemp	4	Jan	1877	13	May	1932
3	Matilda Jane	25	July	1853	"	"	"	Chris C. Beckham	15	May	1873	9	June	1931
4	Jessie Thomas	20	Sept	1855	Bartlett,	Bell	Texas	Elizabeth C. Ramsey	28	Oct	1877	8	July	1945
5	Coleman	30	Sept	1857	En Angelo	Tom Green	Texas							1954
6	Jessie T.	5	Sept	1859	Mtn. View	Stone	Ar.					3	Dec.	1858
7	Julia P.	28	Feb.	1861		Stone	Texas	C. T. Beckham	3	Feb.	1886			
8	Henry Clay	1	Feb.	1864	Mtn. View	Stone	Ar.	Jennie E. Mixon	15	Dec.	1889	13	Dec	1958
9	Mary P.	25	April	1866	"	"	Ar.	Dr. Robert P. Winston	22	Apr	1888	8	Mar	1950
10	Nancy E.	6	Nov	1868	"	"	Ar.	John Lemuel Lancaster	22	Sept	1886	14	July	1949

Husband's Full Name WiLLiAm MoRRis WHiTfiELD

FAMILY GROUP

Husband's Data	Day Month Year	City, Town or Place	County or Province. etc	State or Country
Birth	29 Aug. 1893	MouNTAiN View	SToNE	ARKANSAS
Chr'nd				
Marr.	3 JAN 1917	CoLEmAN		TEXAS
Death	13 APRiL 1966			
Burial				

Places of Residence		
Occupation	Church Affiliation	Military Rec.
Other wives. if any. No. (1) (2) etc. Make separate sheet for each marr.		
His Father RuBEN WHiTfiELD	Mother's Maiden Name MARy EsTHER NELSoN	

Wife's Full Maiden Name NoRA BuRSoN

Wife's Data	Day Month Year	City, Town or Place	County or Province, etc	State or Country
Birth	4 JuLy			TEXAS

Sex	Children's Names in Full (Arrange in order of birth)	Children's Data	Day Month Year	City, Town or Place	State or Country
	1 KATy WiLLiNE	Birth	7 DEc 1917	RocKWooD	TEXAS
		Marr.	3 cHiLDREN		
	Full Name of Spouse SCoTTy FLETcHER	Death			
		Burial			
	2 LuDiA ALLiNE	Birth	MAy	MERETA	TEXAS
	Full Name of Spouse TED DuKE	4 cHiLDREN			

SIMPSON H. WINSTON , b. 1830 Tenn. and wife, Margaret V. b. 1832 Tenn. and family is on the 1860 Census of Izard County , Arkansas , Mill Creek Township. Mill Creek Post Office # 354.

On the 1870 Census they are listed in Izard County, Arkansas, Blue Mountain Township , Riggsville Post Office.

On 1880 Census they are at Stone County, Arkansas , Blue Mountain Township.

Simpson H. and Margaret V. Winston children are the following :

> Mary Virginia Winston , b. 1860 Arkansas , married W.R. Sheffield.
>
> Sallie F. Winston , b. 1862 Arkansas , married John Wesley Humphrey.
>
> Robert F. Winston , b. 1864 Arkansas , married Mary P. Whitfield
>
> Queen E. Winston , b. 1870 Arkansas married William H. Nelson.
>
> Alberta Saline Winston , b. 1870 Arkansas married James Maloy.

118

HUSBAND'S NAME __Richard Ellis Whitfield__

When Born __8 July 1851__ Where __Mtn. View Ar. Stone Co.__

When Died __12 May 1932__ Where __"__ "__ "__

When Buried ____ Where __Mtn. View Cem.__

His Father __Wyley W. Whitfield__ His Mother's Maiden Name __Eliza Felton__

WIFE'S MAIDEN NAME __Elizabeth Ann Kemp__

When Born __3 May 1854__ Where __Mtn. View Stone Co. Ar.__

When Died __16 June 1934__ Where __Mtn. View Cem.__

When Buried ____ Where __Mtn. View Cem.__

Her Father __John Jacob Kemp, Sr.__ Her Mother's Maiden Name __Rebecca Reeves__

	CHILDREN (Arrange in order of birth)	When Born Day	Month	Year	Married to	When Married Day	Month	Year	When Died Day	Month	Year	Town or Place
1	Clarence Earl	22	Dec.	1877	Belvia Long	21	Sept.	1904	6	Jan	1949	STONE CO., AK Mtn. View
2	Edgar Poe	22	July	1879	Never Married				12	Oct	1902	" AR
3	Elbert Foster (Dock)	6	Jan	1881	Julia Emma Folks	23	Nov.	1904	3	Sept	1949	" AR
4	Abbie Walker	20	Aug.	1882	W. F. (Billie) Curry	11	Oct	1904	16	Jan	1970	Newgate AR
5	Delonia Myrtle	22	July	1885	Grover C. Hawkins	20	Dec	1914	23	Jan	1959	Mtn. View AR
6	Robert Kemp	28	May	1892	Bertha Mae Rymer	14	Mar	1920	29	Oct	1966	" AR
7	John Wyley	23	June	1894	Never Married				7	Oct	1972	" AR
8	Lillie May	14	July	1897	Charles Gray Gonzales, Sr.	17	June	1917	19	Sept	1981	" AR

119

WILL OF MATHEW WHITFIELD

" In the name of God Amen - I, Mathew WHITFIELD of the County of Rutherford and State of Tennessee, being of perfect sound mind and memory - Blessed be God, do this sixth day of September in the year of our Lord, One Thousand Eight Hundred and Twenty Three make and publish this my last Will and Testament in manner following: That is first, I give and bequeath to my wife, Levina the whole of my estate both real and personal of every description for her use entirely during her natural life or widowhood and at her marriage or death then my will and pleasure is that all my personal estate be sold at public sale and my executors and the Amt. arising from said sale to be equally divided between of my children namely, Benjamin, Mary and Mathew and all my real estate or landed property at that time, I allow to my daughter Mary and lastly I do hereby appoint and ordain my wife Levina and my son William Whitfield Executors of this my last Will and Testament and I do hereby revoke all other Wills and Testaments by me made and establish this and no other to be my last will and testament."

In testimony where of I have here unto._____

Rutherford County, Tennessee, Wills, Settlements, Inventories - Vol. 7 1827 - 1830, page 294 of State of Tenessee Library analytical index and 1820 Rutherford County, Tenessee Census set my hand and Seal the day and Year first above written.

Signed and sealed in presence of
H. ROBINSON JURAT
Jane ROBINSON
Levina ROBINSON JURAT

his mark
Mathew x
WHITFIELD

Levina Robinson WHITFIELD had a bond deed to 168 acres in Rutherford County, Tenessee on 19th June 1837. Children lived in Rutherford County, Tenessee, and the descendants are there.

Benjamin WHITFIELD married Elizabeth HERROD, 5 of July 1827 in Rutherford County, Tennessee. They are listed in the 1860 Federal Census in Blue Mountain Township, Richwood Post Office, Izard County Arkansas. Benjamin and Elizabeth had 15 children.

FAMILY GROUP

This information Obtained From

Husband's Full Name RUBEN WHITFIELD

Priscilla Atkinson Crutcher
1860 Federal Census
Izard Cty
1890
1880 #150-150
1900 #57
Stone Ct. Marriage B A
Cemetery Stone Ct. Book
Whitfield History B, Valli's Ja

Husband's Data	Day Month Year	City, Town or Place	County or Province. etc.	State or Country
Birth	9 Sept 1833	Nashville		Tennessee
Death	3 May 1903	Mt. View	Stone	Arkansas
Burial		Flatwoods Church Cemetery		

Other wives, if any. No. (1) (2) etc. Make separate sheet for each marr.

His Father BENJAMIN WHITFIELD B. 1835 Tennessee Rutherford Cty Mother's Name ELIZABETH HERRON

Wife's Name MARY ESTER ELIZABETH NELSON

Wife's Data	Day Month Year	City, Town or Place	County or Province, etc	State or Country
Birth	26 Oct 1834			North Carolina
Death	10 May 1910	Mt. View	Stone	Arkansas
Burial		Angora Cemetery		

Places of Residence

Mother's Maiden Name SUSANNAH EDWARDS

Other husbands, if any No. (1) (2) etc. Make separate sheet for each marr.

Her Father MARTIN NELSON

Children's Names in Full (Arrange in order of birth)	Children's Data	Day Month Year	City, Town or Place	County or Province	State or Country
1 JAMES H.	Birth	27 Nov 1856			
	Marr.				
	Death	Before 1860			
Full Name of Spouse	Burial				
2 LAURA A.	Birth	31 May 1858			
	Marr.				
	Death	Before 1860			
Full Name of Spouse	Burial				
3 CATHERINE (KATY)	Birth	25 April 1860	Mt. View AR		
	Marr.	13 Aug 1874	Oxley		
M. MORRISON	Death	14 June 1834	Angora Cemetery Mountain View AR		
Full Name of Spouse	Burial				
4 RUBEN WILLIS	Birth	4 Aug 1864	Mountain View AR		
	Marr.	8 July 1888			
Molly Nilsen Mary	Death	1943			
Full Name of Spouse	Burial				
5 Julia O.	Birth	2 Nov. 1867	Mountain View, AR		
	Marr.				
	Death	Before 1880			
Full Name of Spouse	Burial				
6 Joseph	Birth	7 April 1870	Mountain View, AR		
	Marr.				
	Death	Before 1880			
Full Name of Spouse	Burial				
7 Benjamin	Birth	2 Sept 1871	Mountain View, AR		
	Marr.				
	Death	Before 1880			
Full Name of Spouse	Burial				
8 William M.	Birth	29 Aug 1873	Mt. View, AR		
	Marr.	3 Jan 1917			
Nora Burson	Death	13 April 1966	Coleman, Texas		
Full Name of Spouse	Burial				

Mary Esther "Elizabeth" NELSON was born 26 October 1834 in North Carolina. She died 10 May 1910 at Mountain View, Stone, Arkansas. She is buried in Angora Cemetery that is located 7 miles south of Oxley, Arkansas in Sec. 8, T. 13 N, R 13 W. She married Ruben WHITFIELD who was born 9 September 1833, Nashville, Tennessee. Ruben died 3 May 1903, at Mountain View, Stone County, Arkansas. Ruben is buried in the Flatwood Cemetery in Mountain View, Arkansas. Ruben's first marriage was to Nancy _____ who was born in 1835 in Tennessee.

From The Stone County Leader dated the 5th of August 1965 –

FLATWOODS CHURCH RAISING FUNDS FOR MONUMENT

"The Flatwoods Missionary Baptist Church is sponsoring a drive to solicit funds for a Memorial Monument for the grave of Bro. Rubin WHITFIELD who donated the property of the Church and the Cemetery.

This generous man's grave has no marker at all, and the Church would appreciate all donations.

Anyone interested may give their donation to a member of the Church."

From "The Heritage of Stone", June 1972, Volume I, Number I;

"On the second Sunday in March 1881 the Flatwoods Church voted to secure property from Ruben Whitfield for purposes of building a church and school. The property was deeded to the church on April 23, 1881 and is the property the church now owns. It is located at what is known as the grave yard hill in the community of Flatwoods".

Ruben's father was Benjamin WHITFIELD, who was **one** of five children of Mathew and Levina WHITFIELD. Mathew was born in 1772 in **Nash Co., North** Carolina, and died in 1827 in Rutherford County, Tennessee. Benjamin **had relatives.**

    A. William   WHITFIELD b. 1800 m. Matilda
        1 Mathew   WHITFIELD b. 1830   Tenn.
        2 Talbert   WHITFIELD b. 1834   Tenn.
        3 Coleman   WHITFIELD b. 1838   Ark.
        4 Blake   WHITFIELD b. 1841   Ark.
        5 Franklin WHITFIELD b. 1844   Ark.
        6 Jasper   WHITFIELD b. 1847   Ark.

    B. Benjamin WHITFIELD b. 1805 m. Elizabeth
                                        Herrod
    C. Eli   WHITFILED b. 1807 m. Mary A.
    D. Matthew   WHITFIELD b. 1814 m. Fanny P.

```
Ruben       WHITFIELD  b . 1833  m. Mary Esther
                                       NELSON
Mathew      WHITFIELD  b. 1834  m.  Olive Dillard
Levina      WHITFIELD  b. 1836
James       WHITFIELD  b. 1838  m. Elizabeth
                                       KEMP
Whitmale  WHITFIELD  b. 1840      Tenn.
```

Whitmale died 16 May 1863. Whitmale WHITFIELD, is Whitmon WHITFIELD mentioned in the first paragraph of the journal "Where I Was - What I Saw During The War",   found on Page 4 of "The Heritage of Stone", Volume 11, Number 2, of E. C. BECKHAM where he says: "I left the home of my father............... with   Felix O. PITTMAN,   James S. NELSON,   and Whitmon WHITFIELD...... WHITFIELD died in Alabama from a wound in the thigh,   which he received in the battle of Baker's Creek, Miss. on the 16th day of May 1863."

```
G. Andrew    WHITFIELD b. 1841     Tenn.
H. Druzilla  WHITFIELD b. 1842     Ark.
I. Elizabeth WHITFIELD b. 1845     Ark.
J. Mary      WHITFIELD b. 1846     Ark.
K. Malinda   WHITFIELD b. 1848     Ark.
L. Lucinda   WHITFIELD b. 1849 m. Henry B. HESS
                                     4 Apr. 1878
```

"The Whitfield History and Genealogy of Tennessee" has been published by Vallie Jo WHITFIELD, 1964. 1841 Pleasant Hill Rd. Pleasant Hill, CA 94523.

Ruben WHITFIELD is listed in the 1860 Federal Census, Blue Mountain Township, Richwoods Post office, Izard County, Arkansas. They are also found in the 1870 Federal Census Bluemountain, Riggsville Post Office, Izard County, Arkansas and the 1880 Federal Census report Blue Mountain Township, Stone County, Arkansas. In 1900 Federal Census report for Blue Mountain Township City of Mountain View, Stone County Arkansas they are still listed.

It is noted that Ruben Whitfield filed for land described as the S1/2 of SE1/2 Sec 8 & W1/2 of SW1/4 Sec 9, Twns 14 N, Range 10W, consiting of 160 acres, for $10.00 on November 20, 1871 certificate # 5093 under the Homestead Act of 1862. It is also noted that he also filed   the W1/2 se,NESE & SE NE4, Sec 5, Twns 13 Range 11, consisting of 160 acres and 46/100th on 24 May 1894. Certificate # 23568, patent # 11060, Feby 3,1898. Patent dated June 23 1898, Volume No 5, Page 472.

Information from Rutilla (ATCHISON) CRUTCHER.
             Children of Ruben and Mary Ester (NELSON)
WHITFIELD.   123

```
A. James H.        b. 27 Nov 1856
B. Laura A.        b. 21 May 1858
C. Catherine       b. 25 Apr 1860    d. 1934
                      m. John M. Morrison
D. Ruben Willis b.  4 Aug 1864    d. 1943
                      m.  Molly Miser
E, Julia O.        b.  2 Nov 1867
F. Joseph          b.  7 Apr 1870
G. Benjamin        b.  2 Sep 1871
H. William M.      b. 29 Aug 1873
```

C) Catherine WHITFIELD was born 9 June 1856 in Izard County, Arkansas and died 14 of June 1934 as found in the Stone County Cemetery Book. She married John M. MORRISON 13 August 1874 as found in the Marriage Book A of Stone County. John Morrison was born 7 April 1850 in Arkansas. He died 23 of January 1928. Both are buried in the Angora Cemetery. Catherine was married the first time to a CANADY. According to records sent to me through the family, Catherine had one girl by the name of Eliza A. Eliza married and had one son named Edgar P.

D) Ruben Willis WHITFIELD was born 4 Aug 1864 in Arkansas and died 1943. He married Molly MISER who was born 1 June 1868, in Arkansas and died 1 April 1954. This marriage is recorded in the "Stone County Marriage Record Book A", page 24, as the following: "WHITFIELD, R.W. 24 to Mollie MISER 20 July 8, 1888". On the 1880 Federal Census we find that Mollie is listed as Mary. From the letter quoted from the family member it was stated she was a sister to Tenny Miser. Mollie's Father was Samuel H. Miser, born in Tennessee and her Mother was Caroline born in Arkansas.

From the June 1972,Volume I, Number I "Heritage of Stone", it is noted that Willis WHITFIELD served as the Flatwoods Church clerk from October 1886 to October 1898. In a letter from Rutilla L. CRUTCHER, she states "Their (Rubin Willis and Molly (Mizer)) children were:

1) Esther Tennessee WHITFIELD who was born 9 May 1889,four miles east of Mountain View, Arkansas. She died in 1915.

2) Ray Stanley WHITFIELD, (His father named him after James Stanley NELSON) was born 3 June 1894, four miles east of Mountain View, Arkansas. He married Margie BROWN 27 January 1918, at Miles, Texas in the Baptist Parsonage. Margie BROWN was the daughter of James Jackson and Mollie BROWN. They had four children. They

had   seven grand- children.

   a) Willis James WHITFIELD was born
       7 Dec. 1919, Rosedale, Okla.
       He married Belva J. WIGGINS.

   b) Lawrence Alfred Whitfield was
       born 7 April 1922 Mereta,
       Texas. He married Dee Ann
       BAKER 23 June 1955.

   c) Amy Lorain WHITFIELD was born
       11 Jan 1926 at Veribest,
       Texas. She married Jack J.
       BLACKBURN 21 May 1949.

   d) Annie Lorain WHITFIELD was
       born 11 Jan 1926. She died 2
       Nov. 1926.

     3) Dwight R. WHITFIELD was born 20 Nov.
1899. He married Lucille_____ . They adopted two girls.

All of these children of Ray and Margie (BROWN) WHITFIELD
were born 4 miles east of Mountain View, Ark.

     4) Susie Hix WHITFIELD, b. 23 Oct.1906.
She was born 3 1/2 miles west of Mereta, Texas.

All of this family is found listed in the 1900 Federal
Census of Mountain View Township, City of Mountain View,
Stone County, Arkansas except Susie Hix.

     William Morris WHITFIELD was born 29 August
1873 in Mountain View, Stone, Arkansas. He died 13 April
1966. He married Nora BURSON who was born 4 July, 3 January
1917 at Coleman, Texas. They had two girls:

     1) Katy Willine WHITFIELD was born 7 Dec
1917 at Rockwood, Texas.   She died from the measles. She
married Scotty FLETCHER and they had three children.

     2) Lydia Alline WHITFIELD, born in
       May at Mereta, Texas. She
       married Ted DUKE and they had
       four children.

Excerpt of a letter from Rutilla (ATCHISON) CRUTCHER.

"Cousin Morris WHITFIELD married Nora BURSON, sister of Cora
BURSON. Mrs. Beulah JOHNS, Rosedale, Okla, Box 74, Zip
74831 is the former Beulah WHITFIELD. Her dad and Cousin
Willis were Cousins and her mother and cousin Molly were
sisters. Their name was MISER".

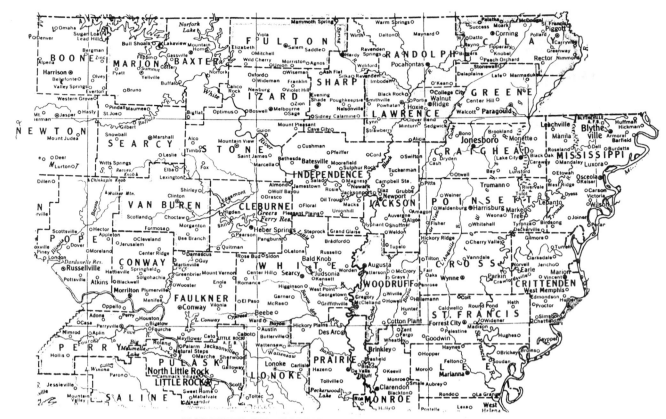

NORTHEAST COUNTIES OF ARKANSAS

Whitfield families settled at Izard, Stone Counties, and other parts of Arkansas.

BARBADOS

The Island claimed by Britain in 1625. Settlers arrived 1627 from England. Slaves were imported from Africa. British Empire abolished slavery in 1834. There were men named Whitfield who went to Barbados.

They died at Barbados, and some returned to England, and some went to Virginia, Georgia, the Carolinas, and other Colonies. There are about ten Whitfields we do glean as coming to the mainland named Whitfield. Barbados is in the West Indies.

From census of Barbados of West Indies.
1600-1700 JOHN WHITFIELD age 20, Negro.

1600-1700 SARAH WHITFIELD, Negro, christened in the St. Peter's All Saints Parish between March 25, 1678 and Sept. 29, 1679.

1600-1700 THOMAS WHITFIELD, soldier under command of Samuel Tidcom in 1679. He was buried in St. Peter's All Saints Parish, England on Sept. 29, 1670. Negro.

The economic basis of the Virginia colony was the cultivation of tobacco on large plantations, and from that single economic circumstance resulted most of the social features.

FAMILY GROUP Husband's Full Name RUBEN Willis Whitfield

This information Obtained From:	Husband's Data	Day Month Year	County or Province, etc.	State or Country
1900 CENSUS - Blue MOUNTAIN	Birth	4 Aug 1864		ARKANSAS
BETWEEN # 59 - 60	Chr'nd			
STONE CITY -	Marr.	8 July 1888	STONE county	ARKANSAS
STONE CITY MARRIAGE BOOK A	Death	1943		TEXAS

His Father RUBEN WHITFIELD — Mother's Maiden Name MARY ESTHER NELSON

Wife's Full Maiden Name Molly MISER (MARY)

Wife's Data	Day Month Year	City, Town or Place	County or Province, etc	State or Country
Birth	1 JUNE 1868			ARKANSAS
Chr'nd				
Death	1 APRIL 1954			TEXAS

Her Father SAMUEL H. MISER — Mother's Maiden Name SUSAN

Childrens Names in Full (Arrange in order of birth)		Day Month Year	City, Town or Place	County
1 ESTHER TENNESSEE	Birth	9 MAY 1889	MOUNTAIN VIEW	STONE, AR
	Marr.			
Full Name of Spouse	Death	1915		
	Burial			
2 RAY STANLEY	Birth	3 JUNE 1894	MOUNTAIN VIEW	STONE, AR
	Marr.	27 JAN 1918		
Full Name of Spouse MARGIE BROWN	Death			
	Burial			
3 DWIGHT R.	Birth	20 NOV 1899	MOUNTAIN VIEW	STONE, AR
	Marr.		ADOPTED 2 GIRLS	
Full Name of Spouse LUCILLE	Death			
	Burial			
4 SUSIE HIX	Birth	23 OCT. 1906	MERETA	TEXAS

Betty Gilbert of Tyrone, Oklahoma lives in a town with the population of 500 people in 1992. Betty researched on Martin Nelson who was born July 22, 1796 and died July 8, 1880. Nelson has descendants located at Izard Co., Arkansas. Betty has written on this family. All the people with Nelson left Hardin Co., TN in 1840's. There was sixty wagons in the train going to Arkansas.

Betty Gilbert contributed the two Whitfield family groups who resided in Texas. Ray Stanley Whitfield (b. 1894-d. 1918), and William Morris Whitfield (b. 1873-d. 1966).

Record

From the Journal of Elihu Chris Beckham in the Civil War. "I left the home of my father, Joshua M. Beckham of Izard Co. (later Stone Co., Arkansas) on October 27, 1861, in company with Felix O. Pittman, James S. Nelson and Whitmon Whitfield. We were boys together, all born in 1840."

FAMILY GROUP

Husband's Full Name RAY STANLEY WHITFIELD

Husband's Data	Day Month Year	City, Town or Place	County or Province. etc.	State or Country
Birth	3 JUNE 1894			
Chr'nd				
Marr.	1918	MILES	BAPT. —	TEXAS

His Father WilliS RUBEN WHITFIELD   Mother's Maiden Name Molly MISER

Wife's Full Maiden Name MARGIE BROWN

Wife's Data	Day Month Year	City, Town or Place	County or Province. etc	State or Country
Birth	10 July 1898			

This information From:
BiBLE RECORD oF RAY & MARGIE WHITFIELD

7 GRANDCHILDREN
Mother's Maiden Name Mollie

Her Father JAMES JACKSON BROWN   OKLAHOMA

Sex	Children's Names in Full (Arrange in order of birth)	Children's Data	Day Month Year	City, Town or Place
	1 WilliS JAMES	Birth	7 DEC. 1919	ROSEDALE
		Marr.	3 SEPT. 1949	
	Full Name of Spouse BELVA J. WiggiNS	Death		TEXAS
		Burial		
	2 LAWRENCE AlFRED	Birth	7 APRil 1922	MERETA
		Marr.	23 JUNE 1955	
	Full Name of Spouse DEE ANN BAKER	Death		TEXAS
		Burial		
	3 Amy LoRAIN	Birth	11 JAN. 1926	VERiBEST
		Marr.	21 MAY 1949	
	Full Name of Spouse JACK J. BlackBuRN	Death		TEXAS
		Burial		
	4 ANNiE LoRAIN	Birth	11 JAN 1926	VERiBECT
		Death	2 NOV. 1926	

CIVIL WAR
by Robert Whitfield (1948-1971)
Written January 30, 1960

The Civil War was created between the North and South because of slavery. The North thought all people should be free and the South thought there should be slavery. In late 1860 and 1861 the attack on Harpers Ferry lit the fuse. Then in the late middle of 1861 the outbreak came when the Confederates attacked Fort Sumter. That was the beginning of the Civil War, and it didn't end until five years later in 1865 when General Lee surrendered to General Grant at Richmond, VA. During this period of time, it was more a back and forth thing until July of 1863 when General Meade beat Lee at Gettysburg. Then the Northerners started taking over by winning the important battles. When the War was over, the South was in ruins. The free slaves didn't know what to do and the other people didn't know what to do about them. It took years afterwards to get the nation back in order.

ARKANSAS

Husband's Name-CHARLES KNOX LANCASTER
>   Born July 27, 1894 on a wagon train trip to Texas.
>   Died-January 29, 1972, Mountain View, Arkansas.
>   Buried-Flat Wood Cemetery
>   Married-June 17, 1917, Mountain View, Arkansas.
>
>   His father was GREEN DINK LANCASTER.
>   His mother was George Ann King, maiden name.

Wife's Maiden LILLIE MAY WHITFIELD
>   Born-July 14, 1897, Stone Co., Arkansas
>   Died-September 19, 1987, Mountain View, Arkansas
>   Buried-Flatwood Cemetery
>
>   Her father was RICHARD ELLIS WHITFIELD.
>   Her mother maiden name was ELIZABETH ANN KEMP.
>   They had three children: Charles, Richard, Melba.

1. Charles Knox Lancaster, b. July 3, 1918, Mountain View, AR. Charles married Jemmie Carter on Oct. 25, 1941. Charles K. Lancaster d. Feb. 12, 1972, Mountain View, AR, Stone Co.

2. Richard Dink, b. Aug. 7, 1921, Mountain View, AR. He married first wife, Jean McCurred. Divorced. No issue. He married second wife, Joann Dobbins, mother of children. Richard Dink and Joann live in Mountain View, AR in 1990.

3. Melba Louise, b. April 30, 1927, Mountain View, AR. Melba L. Lancaster married William G. Conley, and they live in Little Rock, AR in 1990.

Charlotte Katherine Lancaster married Vernon Marion Lawrence on June 9, 1962. Charlotte was b. June 7, 1944. Vernon Lawrence was b. Aug. 24, 1941, Big Flat, AR. Issue: Stephanie. Melba Susan Lancaster married Dr. William John Nixon, D.V.M. on June 2, 1969. Melba Susan Lancaster was b. March 10, 1948. Charlene Kay Lancaster was b. July 27, 1955. She married first husband Howard Younger. They had child-Heather Younger, b. Aug. 3, 1974. Charlene Lancaster-Younger married second husband Jerry Joe Stice, and they had a child, Charles Russell Stice who was b. Feb. 26, 1989.
1.   Brenda Ann Lancaster married Dwight Richardson. They had a child Elisha Marie Richardson.
2.   Paul Richard Lancaster married Judy Lewis and they had 1. David Lancaster. 2. Michelle Lancaster. 3. Bruce Allen Lancaster married first wife, Mary Jane Williams and had children: 1. Tina Lancaster. 2. Bryan Lancaster. Bruce married second wife Linda _____. Lisa Geryl Conley married William Mahlon Ogden and they had child, Andrew William Mahlon Ogden. Lisa Conley-Mahlon married second husband Jay R. Bain. Stephanie Diane Lawrence b. May 27, 1964 was daughter of Charlotte Lancaster-Lawrence. Stephanie married James A. Kirby on July 31, 1982. Divorced July 11, 1988, no issue.

CALIFORNIA

1990 Whitfield head of families living in California are five hundred and sixty people with the surname of Whitfield.

CALIFORNIA:
The National Union Catalog of Manuscript Collections. 1959-1964. Based on Reports from American Repositories of Manuscripts. Compiled by Library of Congress.

From Bancroft Library, University of California, Berkeley, Calif. "Emancipation oration by Dr. Ezra R. Johnson, and Poem by James M. Whitfield, delivered at Platt's Hall, January 1, 1867, in honor of the fourth anniversary for President Abraham Lincoln's proclamation of emancipation, 1864."

WHITFIELD LITERARY COLLECTION, compiled by Vallie Jo Fox Whitfield. Bound book-manuscript volumes. Writing of Dr. Robert Edward Whitfield (b. 1921 Tennessee-d. 1990 California), Chemist, United States Department of Agriculture, West Regional Laboratory, Albany, California.

Writings of Vallie Joe Fox Whitfield (b. 1922 Tennessee-living 1997 Contra Costa Co., California at Pleasant Hill City).

The writings of Robert Edward Whitfield (b. 1948 Mass.-d. 1971 in Ghana, Africa). Son of the above parentage. Graduate of the University of California at Davis, California, and Peace Corp teacher at Nalerigu Training College in Gambaga, Ghana (Africa-west).

HAAG AND WHITFIELD

John Christopher Haag and Rosena b. 1826 married on October 20, 1846 in Mundelsheim, Wuertemberg, Germany. In 1852 they left Kleinbottwar, Germany and went to America. They settled near Racine, Wisconsin at Theresa. John's two brothers came with them. In 1859 the Haag family moved to Jackson Co., Kansas near Holton. In 1872 they lived in Downs, Kansas in 1884. John and Rosena had eleven children. Four girls and seven boys.

A son, Frederick William Haag (Will) married Lee Jettie Whitfield November 24, 1886 at Cucamonga, California. All of their seven children were born at Cucamonga and died in California.

1.	James Edward Haag b. October 20, 1887, d. July 23, 1972. James married Mary Catherine Kennedy February 6, 1912.
2.	George Christopher Haag b. November 28, 1890, d. May 26, 1977. George married Frances Barlow Trailer February 22, 1917.
3.	Rose May Haag b. July 27, 1892, d. October 16, 1959. Rosa married Harry U. Jackson on July 12, 1920.

4.   Frank Wallace Haag b. February 15, 1894, d. October 25, 1978. He married (1) Donna Ora Maltby August 9, 1919 and (2) Zilla Mae Anderson.
5.   Carl William Haag b. February 2, 1898, d. July 21, 1982. Carl married Nevada Rebecca Anderson on August 22, 1921.
6.   Hazel Lee Haag b. December 21, 1902, d. April 21, 1991. Hazel married Walter Edward Haag on June 25, 1925. Walter b. November 8, 1894 Holton, Kansas, d. April 28, 1977, Shafter, California. They lived Rio Bravo, California. Child: Charles Robert Haag b. July 3, 1931. He married Mary Virginia Anderson August 21, 1953.
7.   Ray Theodore Haag, b. August 2, 1907, d. February 26, 1982. Ray married Elaine Gwaltney b. April 24, 1915 Berkeley, California.

Haag family lived at Cucamonga, California. In 1910 they moved to Kern Co., California. In 1927 they moved to Martinez, Contra Costa Co., California. Lee Jettie Whitfield Haag died January 30, 1942 in Martinez, California. Frederick William Haag died June 7, 1953, Rio Bravo, California, Kern Co.

_____

Reference: The Family Of Frederick William Haag by Charles Robert Haag. Pages 83. Private print January 1, 1994, Torrance, California.

Haag Family 1910. Front: Frederick, Hazel, Carl, Ray, Lee. Back: James, Rose, George, Frank.

California Topography

In the beginning there was only the California land stretching its barren slopes to the Pacific Ocean. This was about 6,000 years ago. There were no trees, only an occasional scrub. There was nothing to suggest that anything but the hardiest of sagebrush and weeds would flourish on this desolate site.

Continued on page 134.

WHITFIELD DEATHS 1905-1929 IN CALIFORNIA

REGISTER	NAME	BIRTH	DEATH IN COUNTY		Spouse Initial
8858	Mary E. Whitfield	b. Jan. 1848	Los Angeles	April 13-1922	C
4034	Mary F. Whitfield	b. Jan. 1858	Los Angeles	Dec. 16-1912	
5494	Mary F. Whitfield	b. Jan. 1851		Feb. 14-1910	
34360	Mattie Whitfield	b. Jan. 1869	Napa	July 24-1918	
42391	Nathanie C. Whitfield	b. Jan. 1866	Los Angeles	Nov. 7-1909	
38511	Phoeba B. Whitfield	b. Jan. 1885	San Joaquin	Sept. 25-1927	R
27540	Saloma Whitfield	b. Jan. 1864	Los Angeles	Aug. 27-1915	
16042	Sarah A. Whitfield	b. Jan. 1884	Los Angeles	Nov. 13-1917	W
58756	Seward Whitfield	b. Jan. 1830		Aug. 22-1925	G
54581	Sidney N. Whitfield	b. Jan. 1832	Siskiyou	July 20-1927	E
59410	Wilbert J. Whitfield	b. Jan. 1862	Los Angeles	Jan. 25-1911	
2105	Will E. Whitfield	b. Feb. 1908	Fresno	Nov. 19-1929	
23202	Willet M. Whitfield	b. Jan. 1876	Solano	Mar. 25- 1909	
7274	William Whitfield	b. Jan. 1865		Nov. 2-1906	
8212	William Whitfield	b. Jan. 1837	Madera	July 11-1915	
46057	William Whitfield	b. Feb. 1879	Orange	Feb. 22-1920	R
30209	William H. Whitfield	b. Jan. 1852	Los Angeles	May 20-1928	
21129	William W. Whitfield	b. Jan. 1884	San Bernardino	Oct. 30 -1915	
6805	Wilmot Whitfield	b. Jan. 1884	Los Angeles	Dec 25-1924	E. M.

WHITFIELD DEATHS 1905-1929 IN CALIFORNIA
California Registered Deaths by Law

REGISTER	NAME	BIRTH	DEATH IN COUNTY	DEATH	Spouse Initial
1186 A	Joseph H. Whitfield	b. Jan 1824	Placer	June 13-1913	
6266	Albert A. Whitfield	b. Jan. 1859		July 1-1922	N
15653	Barbara J. Whitield	b. Feb. 1901		June 12-1926	
2520	Benjeman Whitfield	b. Feb. 1928	Shasta	Oct. 2-1918	
61600	Charles Whitfield	b. Jan. 1842	Los Angeles	April 30- 1929	
11860	Clark Whitfield	b. Jan. 1880	Los Angeles	April 11-1929	TT
	E. B. Whitfield	b. Jan. 1858	San Bernardino	July 17-1912	
13044	Ethel Whitfield	b. Jan. 1832	Los Angeles	Feb. 1919	W. T.
20576	Eva Whitfield	b. Jan. 1872	Los Angeles	Oct. 24-1926	
61337	Francis B. Whitfield	b. Jan. 1851	Los Angeles	Oct. 10-1917	R. R.
19940	Gene I. Whitfield	b. Mar. 1913	Modera	Mar. 13-1920	
8810	George J. Whitfield	b. Jan. 1860		June 4-1922	
45667	Isaac H. Whitfield	b. Jan. 1917		Mar. 24-1922	
19219	Isaac H. Whitfield	b. Jan. 1871		Dec. 28-1927	T
20638	Isabella Whitfield	b. Jan. 1883		June 19-1911	
15105	James F. Whitfield	b. Jan. 1842		Dec. 2-1926	S
3902	John Whitfield	b. Jan. 1841		Sept. 28-1929	
17403	John B. Whitfield	b. Jan. 1878	San Bernardino	Feb. 20-1923	
23867	Joseph S. Whitfield	b. Jan. 1833	Kern	Oct. 29-1918	
8137	L. S. Whitfield	b. Jan. 1867		Dec. 24-1921	
54383	Margret Whitfield	b. Jan. 1875	Solano	Feb. 23-1910	
35355	Mary E. Whitfield	b. March 1902	Kern	June 20 - 1911	

California Topography *(continued from page 131)*

Materials resistant to weathering and erosion formed the hills and ridges. A range of mountains and hills separated some of the lower valleys. There were mountains, valleys, and a large southern desert, but on the shores of the bays and rivers were marshlands and tule weeds. As time passed, the valleys were traversed by water courses, and the banks along the streams fringed themselves with trees and shrubs. Up the slopes, in the moisture-gathering canyons, there were oaks and sycamores. California was a vast spread of land and the only people who lived there were Indians.

Water was mostly lacking in California or the upper Alta land as the Mexicans called California. It was lacking more so in the southern land. The soil was not fertile and lacking very much. It was adobe soil. It was like a soft clay decay near the surface of the ground to produce a tough soil, difficult to hoe in dry weather. This soil absorbed the small amount of rainfall that occurred and expanded in rainy season.

There was some movement in the rocks, especially during heavy rains, causing earth changes. The natural forces in the weather elements of the earth made most of the changes until people came to California and there was little force from the few human beings on the land with a low population. There was a mass of gravelly rock material containing hard boulder full of water-worn pebbles firmly cemented together with lime. This varied in the earth's elevation ranges.

Continued on page 136.

CALIFORNIA MORTALITY WHITFIELD(S) VOLUME 1904-1927
Explanation of Codes

INDEX of all deaths in California for 1905 through 1929 registered by law, arranged by surname of decedent. The Index is divided into eight volumes.

Information regarding the decedent, initials of spouse, age and place and date of death, included for identifying purposes. Units and place of death are CODED and KEYS to these CODES are on page.

The column headed "Place of Death - County" indicates the county to which the certificate is filed.

The "Stafe FILE NUMBER" is an identifying number assigned to the certificate of the office of the State registrar. In practice the number is always preceded by the last two digits of the year of date.

Original Certificates of Death are on file with the State Registrar of Vital Statistics. A copy of each certificate is on file with the County Recorder at the place of death except for those deaths which occurred in the City and County of San Francisco or the City of Los Angeles. An index entry for Whitfield surname from page 11710 and this explanation of this entry is to assist you in the use of the index.

Units of Age	*Codes*
1 - Years	*5 - Minutes*
2 - Months	*A - 100 years or over*
3 - Days	*Blank - Unknown*
4 - Hours	*Blank - Unknown*

10	Fresno Co.	36	San Bernardino Co.	70, 80, 90 For the name
15	Kern Co.	39	San Joaquin Co.	of these counties, contact
20	Madera Co.	48	S	California Deaths State
28	Napa Co.	60	Alameda Co.	File.
30	Orange Co.			

STATE OF CALIFORNIA , DEATHS , LAST NAME IS WHITFIELD

WHITFIELD — Years 1904 to 1927

Middle Initial of name

Name of Deceased — Initial of Spouse — Date Filed in California Registration Deaths State File No.

Last Name — First Name — Age Month year — Place of Death — Month Day Year

Last Name	First Name	Mid. Init.	Sp. Init.	Age	Mo/Yr	Place	Mo	Day	Yr	State File No.
WHITFELD	JOSEPH	H		124	31	6	13	13	13	19637
WHITFIELD	ALBERT	A	N	159	90	7	12	2	22	32144
WHITFIELD	BARBARA	W		201	90	6	12	26	26	30636
WHITFIELD	BENJEMIN	A		188	45	10	21	8	18	41372
WHITFIELD	CHARLES			142	70	5	30	11	11	13556
WHITFIELD	CLARA	T		180	70	5	11	29	29	25928
WHITFIELD	E	B		158	36	7	17	12	12	21415
WHITFIELD	ETHEL	JT		152	70	2	19	19	19	9734
WHITFIELD	EVA			172	70	10	24	26	26	47144
WHITFIELD	FRANCIS	SRR		251	70	10	10	17	17	33769
WHITFIELD	GENE	I		313	30	3	13	30	20	13071
WHITFIELD	GEORGE	S		160	90	6	4	22	22	28204
WHITFIELD	ISAAC	H		117	60	3	24	22	22	10523
WHITFIELD	ISAAC	HT		171	60	12	28	27	27	58521
WHITFIELD	ISABELLA	A		183	90	6	19	11	11	17439
WHITFIELD	JAMES	FS		142	90	12	2	26	26	59836
WHITFIELD	JOHN			141	90	9	28	29	29	55087
WHITFIELD	JOHN	B		178	36	2	20	23	23	8485
WHITFIELD	JOSEPH	S		133	15	10	29	18	18	34797
WHITFIELD	L	B		157	90	12	24	21	21	48927
WHITFIELD	MARGRET			175	48	2	23	10	10	5564
WHITFIELD	MARY	E		302	15	6	20	11	11	15948
WHITFIELD	MARY	EC		148	70	4	13	22	22	17285
WHITFIELD	MARY	F		158	70	12	16	12	12	35761
WHITFIELD	MARY	F		151	90	2	14	10	10	4924
WHITFIELD	MATTIE			169	28	7	24	18	18	24915
WHITFIELD	NATHANIE	C		166	70	11	7	09	09	27331
WHITFIELD	PHOEBA	B		185	39	9	15	20	20	37150
WHITFIELD	ROBERT	H		102	70	7	6	17	17	23817
WHITFIELD	ROY	R		126	80	4	25	27	27	20898
WHITFIELD	SALOMA			164	70	8	27	15	15	24764
WHITFIELD	SARAH	A	W	184	70	11	13	17	17	37646
WHITFIELD	SEWARD		G	130	80	8	22	25	25	38991
WHITFIELD	SIDNEY	N	E	152	47	7	20	27	27	38209
WHITFIELD	WILBERT	J		162	70	1	25	11	11	1289
WHITFIELD	WILL	E		208	10	11	19	29	29	56796
WHITFIELD	WILLET	M		176	48	3	25	09	09	8208
WHITFIELD	WILLIAM			165	90	11	2	06	06	26322
WHITFIELD	WILLIAM			137	20	7	11	15	15	5064
WHITFIELD	WILLIAM	R		179	30	2	22	20	20	7971
WHITFIELD	WILLIAM	H		152	70	5	20	28	28	25982
WHITFIELD	WILLIAM	W		184	36	10	30	15	15	31749
WHITFIELD	WILMOT	EM		184	70	12	25	24	24	56005

SPANISH RECORD 8153

JOSE DEL CARMEN:

EN 29 DE APRIL DE 1828, FUESTE SOLEMNUÑTI IN LA YGLESIA DE ESTALLDSO UN ESTNADENOR DIAS DE RANDO HYO___ DE AUGUSTIN DEL CARMAN NATURAL DEL NORTE AMERICA YE DE RAMONA GONZALES DE ESTA CALIFA OLQUE PURE JOSE DEL CARMAN. TUERON PADRINOS FLORENTINO ANELUSLETA YE _____ ANNA HIGUERA SU A LOS QUE INVANTE LO DUNI Y LO FISNO

FR. JOSE VIADER

TRANSLATION

ON 29 OF APRIL OF 1828, THE SON OF AUGUSTIN DEL CARMAN, NATIVE OF NORTH AMERICA AND ROMANA GONZALES OF THIS CALIFORNIA WAS BAPTIZED IN THE CHURCH (DE ESTALLSO).

JOSE DEL CARMEN

FLORENTINO ANILSISLTA AND ANNA HIGUERA WERE THE GODPARENTS.

California Topography (continued from page 134)

California, with its many hills and some mountains with slopes had a variety of scenery, and presented a charming diversity of surface. It was very different from the land soil and formations than the land of the middle United States and the eastern states. It was not that livable.

The mountain is a tower above all peaks - prominent in its complete accessibility and magnificent panoramic sweep from its top. Few men saw the tops of these mountains in the beginning of time. The coast lands were visited more often and the boats in the 1600's found the shores of California. Men came slowly to California.

The Indians survived and lived in harmony with nature for hundreds of generations, eating the many roots and seeds from the earth, the fish from the waters, and wild small animals roaming the areas.

Explorers and Expeditions

The men who ventured from their homes for search and exploring were explorers and travelers. Sir Francis Drake made expeditions with ships in 1577, 1578, 1579, and he sailed to the Bay of San Francisco.

The Spaniards of Mexico went on explorations. Padres of the Catholic Church came from Spain and started Missions for the Indians. Don Gasper de Portola became the first Mexican governor of upper California. In 1769 he came to San Francisco from Mexico. Continued on page 148.

GERTRUDES JUARES DE GUITFIL, 1876,

In the County Court of Contra Costa County State of
California
In the Matter of the Application
of
Gertrudes Juarez de Guitifield
to become a Sole Trader.
State of California
County of Contra Costa }ss.

I Gertrudes Juarez de Guitifield
do in the presence of Almighty God solemnly swear that
this application is made in good faith for the purpose
of enabling me to support myself and my said children
Marjerela Sutaro Veberoda, and Juan Jose, and not
with any view to defraud delay or hinder any creditor
to creditors of my husband: And that of the Moneys
&c to be used by me in business not more than five
hundred dollars have come either directly or indirectly
from my husband So help me god.
Subscribed and sworn to before
me this 6th day of Nov AD 1876.
L. C. Kittenmyer   Gertrudely her Juarez de Guitifield
    Clerk   mark

Judgment entered Nov 6, 1876.
                    L. C. Kittenmyer
                            Clerk

I L. C. Kittenmyer County Clerk and ex officio Clerk of
the County Court, in and for the County of Contra Costa,
State of California, hereby certify that the above and
foregoing is a full, true and correct copy of a
Judgment authorizing Gertrudes Juarez de Guitifield
to do business as a Sole trader filed in my office on
the 6th day of November 1876 and now remaining on file
therein.
Witness my hand and the Seal of said County this 6 day of Nov 1876
                    L. C. Kittenmyer
                            Clerk
Recorded at Request of J Bryant

Concord, Contra Costa County, California.

137

VIRGINIA STATE TO CALIFORNIA

AUGUSTUS WHITFIELD was a native of Virginia. He found his way to California before the land was a state of the United States. The Mexican Spanish had come with expeditions in 1776 to upper California and were mostly the people living in California when Whitfield arrived. The language spoken was Mexican Spanish. There is no alphabetical K and W in Spanish language. Vidfil is found as a spelling. Augustus Whitfield records in California are in Spanish language. Spanish archives has these records: Number 8153 Baptism of Austin De Carmel Guitfil. Number 2180 Marriage certificate of Augustin Guitfil and Ramona Gonzelas.

Whitfield changed to Guitfil has record numbers 3063 and 2180 and 8153. This number 8153 is AUGUSTIN DEL CARMEL (Whitfield) Guitfil.

Numbers 2180 and 8153 records in Spanish:
Augustin Del Carmen Vidfil, American from Virginia, married with RAMONA GONZALES, date 1825.

In 1820 Augustus Whitfield was in California and name translates to Austin Guitfil.

Number 3063 record from Helvia de Ceix Mission of Sacramento, California. Marriage in 1850, Austin del Carmel Guitfil and Ramona Gonzales. This Austin del Carmel Guitfil (Whitfield) had a son: Augustin del Carmen Guitfield married to GERTRUDES JUAREZ and they have two sons named JOSE GUITFIELD AND JUAN GUITFIELD.

Augustin Guitfil died and Gertrudes moves to Contra Costa Co. and lives on the Salvio Pacheco Rancho in Concord, CA. She spelled the name in 1876 in this record made before a County Clerk, L. C. Wittenmyer.

"I GERTRUDES JUAREZ DE GUITFIELD do in the presence of almighty God solemnly swear that this application is made in good faith for the purpose of enabling me to support myself and my said children MARGERITO SUTARO YEVERODA, JUAN AND JOSE, and not with any view to defraud, delay or hinger any creditor or creditors of my husband: And that of the moneys go to be used by me in business not more than five hundred dollars have come directly or indirectly from husband so help me God. Subscribed and sworn to before me this 6th day of November 1876, A.D.
L. C. Wittenmyer, Clerk."

GERTUREDEZ JUAREZ DE GUITIFIELD, A WIDOW. She received a license and was sole trader in Concord, California.

AUGUSTUS WHITFIELD was b. 1790. He was a native of Norfolk, VA. Came to California and married June 19, 1825.

Official Spanish record appear on following page.

En 24. de Ocubre de 1850. en la
Yglesia de esta mission; case y
veló A Agustin del Carmel
Guitfil. solters. h. l. de Agustin
Guitfil m Ramona Gondalez,
difuntos. con illa Gexterr
dis Suara. ssllena ambos recivron
hi'a lexitimd de Illa—
mul Suares of de Maria
Eximala c Ballscuna. Dog fe.

Document from Spanish Archives, University of California.
There is no letter K or W in Spanish language. Whitfield
became Guitfil.
Augustus Whitfield born 1789 or 1790 at Norfolk,
Virginia. Augustus Whitfield was baptized 1832 with the
Spanish name of Augustin del Carmen. File- Vidfil Number
1705. Augustus Whitfield with the Spanish Mexican name
married a woman of this nationality on June 19, 1825 at
the Mission Santa Clara in California to Romona Gonzales.

Augustus Whitfield born 1789 or 1790 at Norfolk, Virginia. Augustus Whitfield was baptized 1832 with the Spanish name of Agustin del Carmen. File-Vidfil Number 1705. Augustus Whitfield with the Spanish Mexican name married a woman of this nationality of June 19, 1825 at the Mission Santa Clara in California to Romona Gonzales. They had son Augustin born 1828 in Santa Clara, California. The son grew to adult and married Ana Maria Gertrudis Juares 1850. Name Guitfil in file-Number 1706. Gertrudis Juares had three children.

Miss Charmaine A. Burdell of Petaluma, California contributed the Chart, 1982. She was researcher for Los Californianos, heritage Spanish Mexican Organization in California.

Reference: 1. Archives Spanish Mexican at University of Santa Clara California. 2. Some Alta California Pioneers and Descendants by Doroth Gittinger Mutnick, Division One P-Z. Book Published 1983, Lafayette, California.

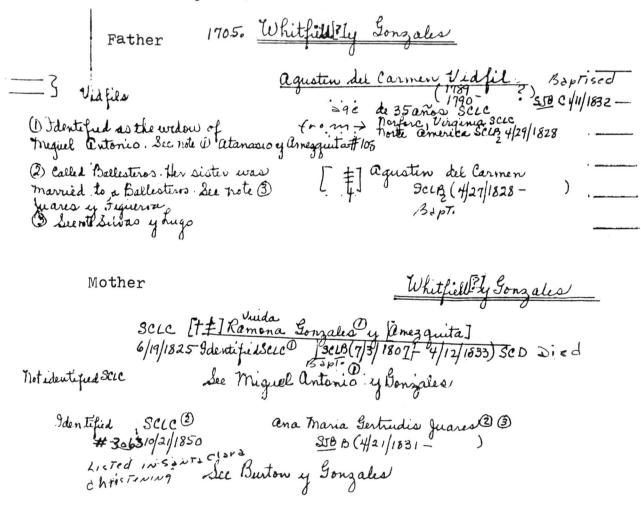

1706 Whitfield y Juarez

Father   [‡] Agustin del Carmen Guitfil [1] y Gonzales 1852 Contra
                 SCLB (4/27/1828 -   ). aged 29   Census Costa County

when his parents were married; left blank SCLB. 4/27/1828

① Spelled Vidfil SCLC 6/19/1825
② See note ② Whitfield y Gonzales ——— No children in file
③ See note Silvas y Lugo

Mother   Whitfield y Juares

Identified SCLC [‡ Ana Maria Gertrudis Juares [2] y Figueroa [3]   Census
10/21/1850]   SJB B (4/21/1831 -   )   1852
                                                    aged 20
whom | he was baptized.   1860 Contra Costa Coun
                                                    Antioch - Pacheco T-p # 1.
                                                    aged 30
                                                    called Juares with mother

Discovery of gold in 1849 brought many people to California from America and places of the English speaking world. In 1850 California became a state belonging to the United States.

1850 California Census
George Whitfield, age 30, from Australia arrived in El Dorado Co.
George Whitfield, age 26, from Virginia arrived in Sacramento Co.

1850 Census, Calavera Co., CA list three men with family.
George Whitfield, age 21, from Illinois. James S. Whitfield, age 24, from North Carolina. Martin Whitfield, age 36, from Great Britain. No women were listed on census only men in 1850.

Few Whitfields came later over the many years. Juan Guitfil, son of Augustus Whitfield, is listed on census once. Augustin Guitfield who married Gertrudis Juarez died before 1876.

William Whitfield born 1831 in Illinois and wife Sarah Prigmore who was born 1833 in Missouri came with their nine children to California in 1854, and later settled at Cucamonga, California.

141

THE FAMILY OF WILLIAM WHITFIELD
AND SARAH ANN PRIGMORE

WILLIAM WHITFIELD was born in Tennessee (so recorded in the 1880 census report), February 18, 1831. He moved with his family to Arkansas when he was ten years old and there attended school in a log school house fitted with slab benches and dirt floor. He remained in Arkansas until he was eighteen years old at which time he went to Dallas County, Texas, to farm and raise stock.

On October 28, 1852 (recorded in Volume A-B, Marriage Records, Dallas County), he married SARAH ANN PRIGMORE. She was born in Missouri, June 16, 1833, daughter of Mr. and Mrs. Joseph Prigmore. The Prigmores moved to Texas when she was a small girl and then went to California with the gold rush of 1849. They returned to Texas in 1852 satisfied that California held better prospects than Texas. Disposing of their Texas holdings, William and Sarah Whitfield, Mr. and Mrs. Prigmore and other members of the family went to California via the Utah route in 1854, travelling with ox teams. Their oldest daughter, Mary Jane, was born in a covered wagon by the Green River in Utah, July 7, 1854.

Arriving in California, the family first settled at Scott's Valley where they engaged in mining. Later they moved to Danville (Contra Costa County) where the Prigmores and Mr. Whitfield ranched and raised wheat. At that time the San Francisco Bay extended inland as far as Pacheco and wheat could be sent by boat. A walnut tree planted by Mr. Whitfield at Danville still stands.

Around 1860, they sold their holdings and returned to Texas, bought cattle and horses and began the stock business on a large scale. They had intended to bring their livestock back to California when the Civil War broke out. Mr. Whitfield enlisted in the Confederate Army and served three years, being discharged at the conclusion of the war in 1865. During his service he contracted malaria and received a bullet which he carried with him to the grave. At the end of the war, the Whitfield family had lost almost all of its possessions, Mr. Whitfield and daughter Mary were ill, and the doctor advised them to leave Texas.

In 1870 they began their second trip to California by covered wagon and their daughter Lee was born en route at Winslow, Arizona, November 2, 1870. They arrived in Cucamonga and settled on 132 acres in the foothills owned at the time of Mr. Whitfield's death by C. K. Thorpe. They raised grapes, peaches and prunes. About 1910, Mr. and Mrs. Whitfield moved to (Pico-) Rivera to be near their daughters, Mary and Sarah Pallett. Around 1914 they moved to San Bernardino to live with their daughter Lucinda Montgomery. Mr. Whitfield died of old age and dropsy October 30, 1915, and the funeral service was held in the Montgomery home. Mrs. Whitfield then lived with her youngest daughter, Belle Milner, until her death, November 13, 1917. William and Sarah Whitfield are buried in Mountain View Cemetery, San Bernardino, California.

1 MARY JANE WHITFIELD. Born July 7, 1854 on the Green River, Utah, in a
   covered wagon while the family made its first trip to California -
died December 18, 1928 and is buried in the El Monte Cemetery

Married May 24, 1876 at Rivera, California to JAMES ROBERT PALLETT - born
July 27, 1850 in Tennessee - his family moved to Rivera and the Palletts
(father and three sons) owned the largest walnut grove in the state -
died of pneumonia January 1, 1891 at his stock ranch at Rock Creek and is
buried in the El Monte Cemetery.

2 SARAH ELIZABETH WHITFIELD. Born October 22, 1856 near Danville, California - died of cancer, February 12, 1916 at Rivera and is buried in
the El Monte Cemetery

Married January 20, 1873 to WILLIAM ARMSTRONG PALLETT - born October 16,
1851 in Tennessee, son of Mr. and Mrs. George W. Pallett, and brother of
James R. Pallett (above) - family came to California in 1857 - with members of his family, went to Argentina in 1900 to found a cattle ranch (some
of his descendants still live in Argentina) - returned to Santa Ana in 1911
and died November 22, 1931 after a paralytic stroke - buried in the El Monte
Cemetery.

3 JOSEPH BENJAMIN WHITFIELD. Born September 26, 1859 - died October 31,
   1862.

4 MOHALA LUCINDA WHITFIELD. Born January 16, 1862 in Texas - died June
   12, 1932 and is buried at Mountain View Cemetery, San Bernardino

Married June 10, 1881 to MARTIN LEWIS MONTGOMERY - born April 15, 1861 -
died December 28, 1935 and is buried at Mountain View Cemetery, San Bernardino.

5 WILLIAM CROCKETT WHITFIELD. Born March 14, 1866 in Texas - died December 30, 1940 from heart trouble at his home in Esticata, Oregon and is
buried at Riverview Cemetery, Portland, Oregon

Married November 15, 1892 to ANNIE MYERS - born at Rochester Pennsylvania,
January 25, 1869 - died October 6, 1949 and is buried at Riverview Cemetery,
Portland, Oregon.

6 LEE JETTIE WHITFIELD. Born November 2, 1870 at Winslow, Arizona, in a

Sources: The obituary of William Whitfield; "History of Pomona Valley
California" with Biographical Sketches of the Leading Men and Women of the
Valley Who have been Identified with its Growth and Development from the
Early Days to the Present (published by the Historic Record Company, Los
Angeles, 1920); recollections of various descendants of William and
Sarah Whitfield.

coverea wagon, en route to California second trip -- died January 30, 1942 at Martinez, California and is buried at Union Cemetery, Bakersfield

Married November 24, 1886 to FREDERICK WILLIAM HAAG - born November 19, 1862 at Holton, Kansas - died June 7, 1953 at Bakersfield, California and is buried at Union Cemetery, Bakersfield.

7 *JAMES WHITFIELD. Born November 16, 1872 - died February 5, 1874 and is buried in the Spadra Cemetery.*

8 *HENERY ALVAN WHITFIELD. Born March 4, 1876 - died January 18, 1880 and is buried in the Spadra Cemetery.*

9 *ANNA BELLE WHITFIELD. Born January 16, 1879 - died June 22, 1968 and is buried in the Inglewood Cemetery*

Married January 17, 1900 to HARRY WAGNER MILNER - born February 19, 1876 at Springfield, Missouri - died November 21, 1957 and is buried in the Inglewood Cemetery.

Whitfield at Contra Costa County, California, 1974

Joe Whitfield married to Lillian Whitfield was from Amcafter, Canada. He came from Canada to California in 1944. He lived in Visalia, CA, and has a brother, Harker Whitfield. Joe Whitfield had parents who were citizens of the United States and they moved to Canada.

Joe and Lillian Whitfield had five children. 1. Murray Whitfield. 2. Kenneth Whitfield. 3. Arthur W. Whitfield and in 1974 he lived in Toronto, Canada. 4. Constance Lillian Whitfield lived in Halifax, Canada, in 1974. 5. Allen Whitfield. Arthur and his sister, Constance, moved to Canada the same year.

Joe Whitfield died in 1949 in California. Lillian Whitfield lived on C Street in Antioch, CA. Her sons Murray, Kenneth and Allen lived in California.

David Whitfield was born in California, age 29 in 1978. He resided for two years in Pleasant Hill, CA. He was single and worked as a paper hanger. His mother, Lila Matthew Whitfield, came to CA and lived in Stockton in 1978.

Lloyd Whitfield was born 1905 and died 1981 at Modesto, CA, while on a travel trip. Lloyd lived in Palm Springs, CA.

H. Leland Whitfield, III, served in the military service during World War II. Afterward for a short time he lived in Pleasant Hill, CA, in 1981. He was married. Obtained a real estate license, worked for a time, and then moved to a southeast state.

William Whitfield had a son Lube Whitfield, and a son, Benjamin Whitfield at Santa Monica, CA, where they lived. Family connected with South Carolina and Georgia in counties Putnam and Greene.

144

BIOGRAPHY-VALLIE JO FOX WHITFIELD

Vallie Jo Fox was b. Mar. 8, 1922 at Nashville, Davidson Co., TN. Daughter of Joseph Edward Fox (b. Dec. 1, 1880-d. July 25, 1942). Birth and passing at Nashville, TN and Valley Schiefer Fox (b. Mar. 13, 1892 Newport, KY-d. Mar. 6, 1968, Washington, D.C.). Residents of Nashville, Davidson Co., TN.

Granddaughter of Joseph George Fox (b. Apr. 2, 1832 Baden, Germany-d. June 29, 1888 Nashville, TN.) and Elizabeth Heiner (b. Dec. 15, 1840 ca Madison, IN-d. Jan. 7, 1919, Nashville, TN). Joseph G. Fox entry to NY Oct. 28, 1852, destination Madison, IN where he resided, and moved to Franklin, Simpson Co., KY in 1869, and moved to Nashville, TN in 1883.

Great granddaughter of John Heiner (b. 1811, Soniorse, Germany-d. Nov. 4, 1864, Madison, IN), and Elizabeth Outh Heiner (b. 1817 Prussia, Germany-d. July 4, 1901, age 84, Madison, IN). Heiner was shorten to Hiner. Md. was Apr. 4, 1837 Ohio Co., VA. Outh came in 1820 to US. Heiner came in mid-1830's to US. Fraternal lineage.

Granddaughter of Joseph Schiefer II (b. 1841 in Vienna, Austria-d. May 4, 1904 in Newport, Campbell Co., KY). Entry 1852 with parents to US of America. Grandmother, Elizabeth Wilkins (b. Oct. 19, 1863, Berlin, Germany-d. Dec. 28, 1925 Newport, KY). Entry 1877 to US as a girl with an aunt, and the destination was Ohio. Joseph and Elizabeth md. July 10, 1884.

Great granddaughter of Joseph Schiefer I (b. 1808 in Hungary-d. 1876, Newport, KY, Campbell Co.). Schiefer family entry 1852 to US, destination KY. Wife, Mary _____ (b. 1821 in Bohemia of Czechosolvakia-d. Oct. 1884 in Newport, KY). Joseph and Mary md. 1838 in Austria. Maternal lineage.

Vallie Jo Fox, fourth generation on American land, US, and from Heiner, and from Schiefer. The third generation from Joseph George Fox. Origin is Germany mostly.

Vallie Jo Fox received primary and high school education in parochial schools in Nashville, TN graduated 1939. She received college and univ. education from: Ward-Belmont Coll, Nashville, TN, 1940-1941, Univ. of TN, Knoxville, TN, 1941-1943, Rutgers Univ., New Brunswick, NJ, 1949-1951, DVC, Pleasant Hill, CA 1959-1963. Graduate 1963. She received business training from Anthony Bus. School, Walnut Creek, CA, 1968 & 1974.

Vallie Jo Fox md. Robert Edward Whitfield on Mar. 26, 1943, Nashville, TN. Robert E. Whitfield was the son of James Dee Whitfield (b. Feb. 10, 1877 TN-d. Sept. 14, 1954 in Waverly, TN) and Mary Hester McKeel (b. Mar. 10, 1878 TN-d. May 10, 1924 TN). Robert Whitfield called Bob was b. Aug. 11, 1921 in Waverly, TN, there was his home. The union brought two boys and two girls. Christa Marie, b. Dec. 30, 1945 Berkeley, CA. Robert Edward, Jr. b. Nov. 21, 1948 Boston, MA-d. Oct. 14, 1971 in Ghana, Africa. James David, b. Feb. 21, 1953 CA.

Joanne Vallie, b. March 14, 1955 California.
Vallie Jo Whitfield Work Experience:
1943-1945.   Chemical Laboratory Technician, Shell Development
Co., California.
1946-1948.   Harvard University Co-op Program. House and Child
Care, Chestnut Hill, and Cambridge, Massachusetts.
1952-1964.   Operated Whitfield Farm, Pleasant Hill, California
of Contra Costa Co.
1968-1984.   Real Estate Agent. Realty companies, Pleasant Hill
and Walnut Creek, California.   Licensed Broker of California.
Retired in 1984.
1960-1964 and 1976-1996 and to present date. Whitfield Books
Firm, Pleasant Hill, California.   Publisher and Writer.

Vallie Jo Whitfield worked numerous programs and projects in
community service. 1975-1996 historian and archivist with local
Historical Society, Pleasant Hill, California.

Robert Edward Whitfield died July 10, 1990 at Walnut Creek,
California.   He was Dr. Whitfield, Chemist, United States
Department of Agriculture, Albany, California.

Whitfield genealogy has been published. Whitfield's families have
been in this country from 1700 ca. to present. Virginia to
Tennessee, and this generation of Whitfields reach into others
United States.

ROBERT EDWARD WHITFIELD

Robert was born November 21, 1948 , the son
of Robert Edward Whitfield and Vallie Jo Whitfi eld.
He was born at Boston, Massachusetts of Suffolk Co.
Robert was called Bob, Jr. He resided in Pleasant
Hill, California of Contra Costa County. He attended
the Pleasant Hill Schools . Graduated from the Pleasant Hill High School in June 1966, Anthony School
of Real Estate 1968 , attended Diablo Valley College,
and graduated June 17, 1970 from the University of
California (Davis). He enrolled in the Peace Corps
of the United States Department of State , March 1970
July 1, 1970 left for Ghana in West Africa. Bob Whitfield, Jr was serving at Nalerigu Training College as
a teacher in Gambaga , Ghana . He was in the northern part of Ghana in West Africa. On October 10 ,
1971, Sunday afternoon , he was killed as a result of
sky lightning and electricity. He died October 14,
1971 at Accra, Ghana . He returned by airplane and
had interment at Pleasant Hill, California. Unmarried.

CALIFORNIA

<u>LAKE TAHOE</u>, CA, Soda Springs and Truckee Telephone Directory
1968 List

Whitfield, C.W., Aspen Drive   Whitfield, Samuel J., Capistrano Ave.
Whitfield, Chloe, Steelhead Ave.   Whitfield, W.B. Salmon Ave.

Jack Whitfield resident 1992 of Citrus Heights, CA. His grandfather Whitfield came from England around 1800 and lived at Bedford, PA. He came to the United States with two brothers. Parents are Charles Whitfield and Mary Whitfield.

Residents Living in California
Roy R. Whitfield, Solano Way, Concord, CA, in 1967.
George O. Whitfield, Magnolia Street, Martinez, CA, in 1967.
Wade Whitfield, Sutter County, CA, in 1975. Works in Agriculture.

<u>CONTRA COSTA COUNTY</u>, CA, Telephone Directory
1975 List

Whitfield, David W., Walnut Creek   Whitfield, Roy, Martinez
Whitfield, Gary R., Antioch   Whitfield, Roy R., Martinez
Whitfield, George A., Martinez   Whitfield, R. W., Martinez
Whitfield, Lillian, Mrs., Antioch   Whitfield, S.L., Concord
Whitfield, M.H. (B), Walnut Creek   Whitfield, Steve, Brentwood
Whitfield, Robert, Pleasant Hill

<u>CONTRACTORS LICENSED</u> in the State of California in the year 1972.

Whitfield, G.A., J Street, Eureka, CA
Whitfield, Kenneth, Mill Valley, CA
Whitfield, Lowell Aytes Brent, Kern Tulare, CA
Whitfield, Murray, Bakersfield, CA

<u>REAL ESTATE</u> licenses in the State of California in the year 1972.
A few named Whitfield.
Whitfield, Robert E., 1841 Pleasant Hill Rd., Pleasant Hill, CA.
Whitfield, Vallie J., 1841 Pleasant Hill Rd., Pleasant Hill, CA.
  Zip Code 94523.
Whitfield, Robert Edward (Bob Whitfield, Jr.), Pleasant Hill Road, CA, 1970.

Truman Whitfield, Laurel St., Eureka, CA. Residend 1968 in Eureka, CA, the manager for Whitfield's Boarding Home for the Aged.

Joy Klein of Martinez, CA, 1992. Her grandmother's maiden name was Geneva Whitfield. Geneva's brothers are Jay Whitfield of Vallejo, CA; Cecil Whitfield of Anaheim, CA; and sister Clarabelle at Oklahoma.

Robert Edward Whitfield and Vallie Jo Whitfield, born 1922, living 1995, came to California April 1, 1943, and stayed until June 1945; and came to reside at Pleasant Hill, CA, January 1952 and lived there until their deaths. Robert Whitfield died July 10, 1990. Children James David Whitfield and Joanne Whitfield reside in Pleasant Hill, CA, and making it their home. Christa Whitfield Bundy Buckingham resides in Walnut Creek, California.

147

Explorers and Expeditions Continued from page 136.

Don Pedro Fages came on an expedition in 1772 to the San Francisco area from the south land. The most determined man with the encouragement of the Padre was Juan Bautista De Anza who made two trips to northern California from the Presidio of Tubac in Arizona. The first time he traveled with twenty soldiers, Father Garces, and an Indian named Sebastian Terabal. The second time Juan De Anza came with the intention of selecting two mission sites and a presidio site.

Juan Bautista De Anza Expedition

The De Anza expedition consisted of the first men and women and children colonizers to settle in Upper California. In 1775 thirty Spanish-Mexican families signed up for the expedition. De Anza selected ten veteran Mexican soldiers to guard the expedition. On the 4th day of October, there were 177 people recruited from the Arizona Valley and sent to the Presidio Tubac in Arizona, where De Anza lived.

On October 23, 1775, De Anza left Tubac, Sonora in Arizona with a count of 240 persons. One hundred and fifty-five were women and children. Thirty of them had 118 children. Of 78 children on one list, 44 were under 10 years of age. On a roll call of the 240 persons who left Tubac, Monday, October 23, 1775, there was De Anza, four church fathers, two veteran guards and escorts, 10 soldiers, 28 wives, children, settlers, widows, brothers were 165. Muleteers 15, Vaqueros 3, who were servants of De Anza, Indians 5, Vidal, commissary officer. A total of 240 souls were about the first colonists to California.

People of the expedition divided into three groups: First group of people were 12 soldiers and their families led by Father Pedro Font. The second group had 12 soldiers and their families and led by Sergeant Juan Pablo Grijalva. The third group consisted of Lt. Don Joseph Joachin Moraga, 12 soldiers, and their families. These three groups traveled a very long way on horse and by foot for almost six months. They toured Arizona, Mexico, and southern California moving north until they reached the San Francisco area bay valleys in April 1776.

After reaching Monterey once, they returned to Monterey arriving on April 8. On April 14, 1776, the first settlers gathered in the plaza at Monterey and bade a fond and tearful farewell to their Commander De Anza. He had earlier explored around San Francisco Fort and Mission and it was evident that the Spanish-Mexicans found a home there. On June 17, 1776, followed the third group Don Moraga and on Sunday, June 27th, they reached the site of Mission Dolores, and settled there in San Francisco.

Never in American history had so many women and children been first colonists like this. This was an extraordinary feat of crossing 3,000 miles of California deserts with a large contingent of men, women, children, and animals on a traveling route which reached the site of the first settlement of Spaniards. The Catholic Church men did the colonization with Missions including Indians but it was the immigrant Spanish-Mexicans that filled the first colonies of people in California.

End Expeditions.

ENGLAND TO UNITED STATES

Henry Whitfield of Staffordshire, England had a son named Arthur Harvey Whitfield. The son married Marguerite Gueliesse in 1902 and then entered the Port of NY in 1908. They settled Pittsburg, PA on Turtle Creek. They had children. 1. Roy R., b. 1914 and d. Mar. 8, 1974 in Contra Costa Co., CA. Roy R. married (1) to Mary, and they had the son Roy Williams b. 1945. He married (2) Provide Kyte-Dimmick about 1961. They had children. 2. Harry Whitfield who lives in PA. 3. Margaret who married Robert Burnett and 1974 lived at Richmond, CA. 4. George who in 1974 lived in Martinez, CA.

Roy R. Whitfield came to California in 1955 to work for Shell Development Co. at Pittsburg, CA. In 1962 to 1972 he was a teacher and technician of Electronics at Diablo Valley College at Pleasant Hill, CA. Family resided at Martinez, CA.

ROBERT EDWARD WHITFIELD was b. Aug. 11, 1921, Waverly, Humphreys Co., TN, and d. July 10, 1990, Walnut Creek, Contra Costa Co., CA. Robert was the son of James Dee Whitfield (1877-1954) and Mary Hester McKeel Whitfield (1878-1924). He was the grandson of Thomas Jefferson Whitfield (1845-1908) of Hickman and Humphreys and Benton Counties, and (Martha) Mattie Jane Nicks Whitfield (1855-1930). Robert was descend of Thomas Whitfield (1735-1794) of Sussex Co., VA, and Winifer Whitfield (1740 ca-July 9, 1838). Winifer and her children with families moved 1808 to Williamson Co., TN. She lived with her son Wilkins Whitfield (1770-1851) in Franklin, Williamson Co., TN. Wilkins had the son Thomas Jefferson Whitfield (1810 VA-1873 TN) who had Thomas born 1845.

Robert Whitfield graduated from Central High School in May 1939 at Waverly, TN and was Valedictorian of his class. In 1943 he graduated from the University of TN at Knoxville, TN. Robert and Vallie Jo Fox were married on Mar. 26, 1943 in Nashville, TN. They arrived on Apr. 1, 1943, Berkeley, CA. In June 1952 they came to settle at Pleasant Hill, CA.

RON WHITFIELD-Marine World Trainer

Ron Whitfield is a trainer and performer. Ron gives shows at Marine World Africa USA's Jungle Theater in Vallejo, Solano Co., CA, 1990's.

Ron Whitfield has made a career of training animals. His lions and tigers are on 170 acres in Rio Vista, CA.

Ron Whitfield plays with cubs Bengali and Kzar.

149

PLEASANT HILL— The twang of Tennessee still drips from her lips. But it never got in the way of her telling the story of California and of becoming one of the foremost historians of Contra Costa County.

Vallie Jo Whitfield hordes old historical books and newspaper clippings, checks land deeds dating back to the 1800s and even studies notes from city council meetings.

She visits libraries more often than most women go to supermarkets. She probes county records, observes old maps, and peruses wills written 200 years ago.

VALLIE JO WHITFIELD

AUTHOR

She accumulates bits and pieces, throwing away nothing, storing and stacking like an antique dealer.

"Research is the name of the game," says Whitfield, whose latest book, "History of Pleasant Hill, California," records the birth and growth and characters of the area as perhaps no other person has ever done.

It all has to do with her passion for the past.

Pleasant Hill became a city in 1961, "but people have been living here since 1834," she says while relaxing in her rambling, 67-year-old farm house where she raised four children, fed dozens of chickens and grew thousands of almonds and walnuts.

Historical facts fill her home and head.

"Only a few houses and nine families popped up here in the late 1800s. But Pleasant Hill grew to 330 people in 1910," she quickly points out.

"I settled here in 1951 with my husband, a research chemist. The population was 4,000. Now we have more houses than that — 6,000 at last count — and 27,000 people. And we've got the space to grow."

But California growth isn't what triggered a historical book about Pleasant Hill from a woman who had spent half of her life in Tennessee.

"There was a need for it," says the graying grandmother. "Books had already been written about other Contra Costa cities — Martinez, Walnut Creek, Alamo, Crockett, El Cerrito, Richmond, Clayton, and Concord.

"But I found nothing about Pleasant Hill. So I wrote a 323-page history, published it myself and even delivered the books to Safeway in Pleasant Hill, where they're now on sale."

Whitfield, a workaholic with a quick smile, has written history books about the South and also published them herself.

"I am not a great writer," she admits. "I put together a compilation of facts. I deal in statistics."

She sells most of her work to university libraries throughout the country.

"My income is meager," she notes. "I break even. But I'm not doing it for any monetary gain. I'm reporting the history of an area. It's vital that people can read about what went on before them and know it is accurate and authentic."

Whitfield remembers former Gov. Jerry Brown saying, "We must preserve our California

Reference. "Historian Is Living Out Her Passion For The Past". Article by Ed Levitt. The Tribune newspaper, Oakland, California, September 23, 1983.

BOOK TITLES

Whitfield History And Genealogy of Tennessee

Virginia History And Whitfield Biographies

150

history. Each county has to be responsible for its own historical resources."

Pleasant Hill formed a historical society nine years ago. Whitfield helped to organize it, recruited some of its 95 members and now reigns as vice president.

She has gone on to become an active member of just about every historical society in California, touring the state five times a year, sitting in on meetings, exchanging ideas, gathering her "bits and pieces of information."

Her father, she says, was a railroad man. "I learned at an early age to go and see where those trains went."

She received an Award of Merit last year from the Conference of California Historical Societies; was selected to appear in the 1968 edition of Who's Who of American Women and has been quoted in some 27 history books.

Vallie Jo Whitfield is a celebrity in her own right. But most people don't know her, even in Pleasant Hill where the street that leads to her house is named Whitfield Road.

She smiles when explaining the bulk of her mail. It's mainly letters from librarians wanting to know, "Who is Vallie Joe Whitfield?"

But she doesn't mind.

"My mission is to get as many people interested in history and preserving our landmarks," she says.

"But it takes time, diplomacy, patience and understanding."

She thinks it is important for history students "to get out of the university, extend themselves into the community and, through an organization, help preserve historical resources."

The first thing you should know is your heritage, she says.

But, she acknowledges, some people give her a bad time. They tell her, "History is the past. I'm interested in the future."

Vallie Jo Whitfield tries to explain the significance of learning history — a subject that has dominated her life and created a career for her while she raised a family.

To get an idea of where you're going, she maintains, "you must have some knowledge of how it all started.

"The present is linked so tightly to the past."

Vallie Jo Whitfield can show you a million "bits and pieces" to prove it.

1850 census George Whitfield lived in Sacramento County, California.
1850 census George Whitfield lived in El Dorado County, California.

In a Cemetery in Mojave Desert five miles north of Daggett near old mining town of Calico is a wooden slab with Minnie B. Whitfield , born 1881, died 1885.

Whitfield living at San Diego 1964.

Barbara J. Whitfield
Barney   Whitfield
David Whitfield
Mrs. Ella B. Whitfield
Ellsworth   Whitfield
Fred A. Whitfield
Joseph Whitfield

Noble J. Whitfield and Velma purchased property at Contra Costa Co., Calif. in 1946.

Whitfield residents in 1959 at Oakland, California. Telephone Directory

---

Whitfield A R 544-34th . . . . .OLympc 5-7286
Whitfield Ben 914Linden . . . . .TEmplbr 6-2682
Whitfield Bennie 9640MaddxDr . . . .NEptn 8-2750
Whitfield Betty 5858Marshl . . . . . . .OLympc 3-8041
Whitfield Claud W r 4039 Lyon Av. . .KE llog 2-1068
Whitfield Estella 6906Morkn . . . . .LOckhvn 9-7309
Whitfield Eura Lee 2457E22d . . . . . .KElog 3-4820
Whitfield Francis J
500TheAlameda(B) . . . . .LAnscpe 6-8442
Whitfield Inez Mrs 5619Edgrly . . . . .KElog 4-3305
Whitfield Isabell 873-27th . . . . .GLncrt 2-0760
Whitfield Jack 832-16th . . . . .TEmplbr 2-5336
Whitfield Jack R Mrs 1338-93dAv. .LOckhvn 2-2725
Whitfield John D 627-62d . . . . .OLympc 5-2504
Whitfield Lillian 311B MoslyAv(A) . .LAkehrst 3-5190
Whitfield Lula 717Frankln . . . . . . .TEmplbr 6-0754
Whitfield Robt 3699DlMnteWy(SL) . . . .ELgn 1-1072
Whitfield Susie 3124Grove . . . . . . .OLympc 2-2014

Whitfield residents in 1956 at San Francisco California. Telephone Directory

---

Whitfield Albert J Dr ofc 450 Sutr .DO uglas 2-8214
Whitfield Albert J Dr r 2280 Pac Av . WE st 1-4702
Whitfield Emma 1676Grove . . . . .JOrdn 7-7642
Whitfield Enterprises
200 OnondagaAv. JUnipr 6-4101
Whitfield Geo Tiny's Bty Salon
1101GenevaAv. JUnipr 6-3700
Whitfield Gertrude 1431 Steinr . . . .Fllmor 6-0636
Whitfield Henrietta r 1618 Polk. . .PR ospct 5-0890
Whitfield Lawrence K Rev
455UrbanoDr. DElaware 4-0843
Whitfield Melva 1714Geary . . . . .WEst 1-8437
Whitfield Peter R Sr 419ThorntnAv. . .MIssn 7-9119
Whitfield Philip J 2936 Scott. . . . . . .WAlnt 1-8511
Whitfield Preston M 51TulareBrisbne. JUnipr 4-6066
Whitfield Wm 565Chenery . . . . .JUnipr 7-5024

Douglas Whitfield, b. 1951, died July 8, 1979. Son of George A. Whitfield at Martinez, California

151

1990 Whitfield head of families in   COLORADO
state of Colorado were eighty-six
people. 1880 cenuses Charles Whitfield lived in Gunnison Co.,
and 1880 Phyllis Whitfield lived in Arapahoe County, CO.

CONNECTICUT

WHYTFELD AND WHITFIELD

Grandfather, Robert WHYTFELD , died 1597 at Worth in Sussex County,
England with Will proved February 16 - 1597.

He had son Thomas Whytfeld (Whitfield), Esquire , a lawyer of the Courts
of Westminster , who resided at Mortlake, formerly called East Sheen, on
the south side of the Thames, in the County of Surrey , near London in the
country of England. His wife was Mildred Manning Whitfield.

He had a son named Henry Whitfield , born 1597 at Mortlake.
He attended Corpus Christi College , Oxford, England. He was a conformist,
a Puritan. He became a minister of religion. Then he was a congregationalist.

Henry Whitfield married Dorothy Sheaffe , daughter of Dr. Edmund Sheaffe
of Cranbrooke, County of Kent , England. They lived at Ockley, England.
There this baptismal records of nine children in the Register at Ockley,
Surrey of England.

In 1639 his family and friends emigrated to New England of the
colony in America. The ship vessel sailed from London 1639 with thirty-
seven farmers from Kent and Surrey, England. They settled at Guilford,
Connecticut.

Henry Whitfield in Connecticut was a Pastor to the Church of Christ
at Guilford in New England. A member of the Puritan Missionary Society.
He lived there from 1639 until 1650 when he returned to England.

The wife , Dorothy Sheaffe Whitfield remained in Connecticut until as
late as 1659. The sons Nathaniel Whitfield and John Whitfield remained
a year or two years after the father left for England, and then went to
England to live and died there.   Rev. Henry Whitfield died at Winchester
in 1657 in England.

Henry Whitfield and Dorothy Sheaffe Whitfield and children:
1. Dorothy Whitfield , baptized March 25 - 1619. She married Thomas
    Jordan . Dorothy Whitfield Jordan   went back to England in 1651.
2. Sarah Whitfield, baptized November 1 - 1620 . She married Rev.
    John Higginson in 1641 , and died in 1675. His first wife **was**
    (Sarah Whitfield Higginson).   He came to Salem, Massachusetts ,
    and ordained minister , August 1660 , and died December 9 - 1708.
    They had children.
3. Abigail Whitfield , baptized September 1 - 1622. She married in October
1648 at Guilford , the Rev. James Fitch . (Abigail Whitfield Fitch)
152

They had children born from 1649 to 1658.

Rev. James Fitch married second wife, Priscilla Mason, October 2, 1664.

4. <u>Thomas Whitfield</u>, baptized December 28, 1624, probably died young.

5. <u>John Whitfield</u>, baptized February 11, 1626. He came to Guilford, Connecticut but returned to England and died there.

6. <u>Nathaniel Whitfield</u>, baptized June 28, 1629. He came to Guilford, Connecticut but returned to England and died about 1655.

7. <u>Mary Whitfield</u>, baptized March 4, 1631.

8. <u>Henry Whitfield</u>, baptized March 9, 1632. He died at Ockley, Surrey Co., England, February 28, 1634.

9. <u>Rebecca Whitfield</u>, baptized December 22, 1635.

The sons of Henry Whitfield (b. 1597-d. 1657) did not leave descendants in New England, many lines may be traced through his daughters.

WHITFIELD Coat-of-Arms

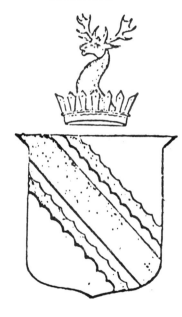

Thomas Whitfield of Mortlake, Surrey, England, was a lawyer. In 1606 the Herald's College confirmed his arms, with six quarterings, and filed his pedigree. Thomas married Mildred, daughter of Henry and Caterina Manning, January 10, 1584, at St. Magnus Church, London.

Henry was born in 1597 at Mortlake, England, the same year his grandfather died. In 1618 he married Dorothy Sheaffe, and from 1619 through 1635 we find the baptismal records of their nine children in the register at Ockley, Surrey.

Savage's *Genealogical Dictionary of the First Settlers of New England* (1862) states:

"The common account of him is that he was son of a lawyer, born about 1597, settled as minister at Ockham about 20 miles from London, in Co. Surry, but others say Ockley or Okely . . . He had property enough and disregarding the fulminating of Bishop Laud for not reading the royal proclamation for sports on Sunday, resigned his place without dispute after serving at the altar nearly 20 years in his native land."

The Rev. Henry Whitfield was one

of a company of 25 men, mostly from counties Kent, Surrey, and Sussex, in England, who came to New England in July 1639. While on shipboard, a Covenant was signed by the following: Robert Kitchell, John Bishop, Francis Bushnell, William Chittenden, William Leete, Thomas Joanes, John Jurdon, William Stone, John Hoadly, John Stone, William Plane, Richard Gutridge, John Hughes, William Dudley, John Parmelin, John Mephan, Henry Whitfield, Thomas Norton, Alexander Cruttenden, Francis Chatfield, William Halle, Thomas Naish, Henry KingsNorth, Henry Dowde, and Thomas Cooke.

The Whitfields remained in Guilford, Conn., about 12 years before they returned to England in 1650.

"Late in the autumn of 1650, he returned home, published in the two following years relations of the spread of the gospel among our aborigines, and died in the city of Winchester," Savage says.

Rev. Henry Whitfield was survived by his widow.

Rev. Henry and Dorothy (Shaeffe) Whitfield had issue:

1. Dorothy, baptized March 25, 1619. She married Thomas, son of James Jordan, an original settler of Guilford. Savage tells us:

"Thomas Jordan in Guilford in 1650, came from some part of Kent, England; went home in 1651, and was of distinction there. A daughter married Andrew Leete."

2. Sarah, baptized November 1, 1620. She married Rev. John Higginson of Guilford, as his first wife, in 1641. She died in 1675.

John Higginson was born August 6, 1616, at Claybrook Co. Leicester. He served as Chaplain, 1637, at Saybrook, but in 1641 went to Guilford as assistant to the Rev. Henry Whitfield, his future father-in-law.

John Higginson intended to go to England, but he came in 1659 to Salem. There he was prevailed on to

Arms: Argent a plain bend cotisca engrailed sable.

Crest: Out of a pallisado crown argent a stag's head or.

The above description of the Whitfield Armorial Bearing is ascribed to the Rev. Henry of Mortlake, Surrey, England and of Guilford, Conn., 1639. It is found in the *Register of the Order of Americans of Armorial Ancestry (1965)*, and is #241 in the "Roll of Arms" published by the New England Historical Genealogical Society.

remain and was ordained August, 1660. He "died among the most honored of our clergy December 9, 1708."

John and Sarah (Whitfield) Higginson had the following children: John; Nathaniel, born October 11, 1652; Thomas; Francis, baptized June 9, 1660, who went to England to study and died at London of smallpox in 1684; Henry, born December 22, 1661, died at Barbados of smallpox; Sarah, who married Richard Wharton in 1672; and Ann, who married William Dolliver of Gloucester, October 4, 1682.

3. Abigail, baptized September 1, 1622. She married in October 1648 at "The Old Stone House," Guilford, Conn., the Rev. James Fitch, son of Thomas and Anne (Reve) Fitch. Abigail died September 9, 1659 at Saybrook, Conn.

James Fitche was born December 24, 1622 at Bocking, Co. Essex, England. He died November 18, 1702 at Lebanon, Conn. He came to New England at the age of 16 in 1638, and was admitted to the ministry at Saybrook in 1646. In 1660 he removed to Norwich, Conn., with a large portion of his Saybrook congregation, and became one of the original proprietors.

He gave up his office in the ministry in 1696 and removed to Lebanon where the Indians had given him five square miles of land. Also, he was willed 5,000 acres of land in Windham, Conn., by Joshua Uncas, an Indian chief.

Rev. James Fitch served as Chaplain of the Connecticut forces in King Philip's War under Major Robert Treat in 1675 and under Major John Talcott in 1676. Rev. James Fitch also served as missionary to the Mohegan Indians and preached to them in their own language. He married second, Priscilla Mason October 2, 1664.

James and Abigail (Whitfield) Fitch had issue: James, born 1649, married first Elizabeth Mason, and secondly Alice (Bradford) Adams; Abigail, born 1650, married Capt. John Mason, Jr.; Elizabeth, born 1652, married Rev. Edward Taylor, and died in 1689; Hannah, born 1653, married Thomas Meeks/Mix; Samuel, born 1655, married Mary Anne Brewster; and Dorothy, born 1658, married Nathaniel Bissell.

4. Thomas, baptized December 28, 1624, probably died young.

5. John, baptized February 11, 1626. He came to Guilford, but returned to England with his parents.

6. Nathaniel, baptized June 28, 1629. He came to Guilford and returned to England shortly after his parents. He probably died about 1655.

7. Mary, baptized March 4, 1631.

8. Henry, baptized March 9, 1632. He died at Ockley, Surrey, England February 28, 1634.

9. Rebecca, baptized December 22, 1635.

Although the sons of Henry Whitfield apparently did not leave descendants in New England, many lines may be traced through his daughters.

Coat-of-Arms

Translated into non-Heraldic terms: A silver (argent) shield charged with a plain black (sable) band drawn diagonally from the dexter (right) chief to the sinister (left) base, between two black bendlets (cotised) edged with semi-circular incisions close together.

We describe a shield as if standing behind it. Therefore the right side of the shield is to the left of the viewer, and the left side is to the right of the viewer.

Crest: Out of a silver (argent) pallisado crown, a gold (or) stag's head.

The mantling would be black lined with silver.

References.

1. A History Of The Plantation Of Menunkatuck And Of The Town Of Guilford, Connecticut by Bernard Christian Steiner. Private published 1897.
2. "At The Sign Of The Crest" by Hazel Kraft Eiler. Article Feb. 1968. HOBBIES Magazine.
3. " Wadsworth Or The Charter Oak " by W.H. Gocher Private published 1904 , Hartford , Connecticut.
4. Henry Whitfield House. Booklet published 1970. Museum.

1850 census Robert M. Whitfield , New Haven County, CT.

the Henry Whitfield house

Photograph 1842

The exterior of the house is stone brought by Indians on hand barrows from Griswold's Rocks. The house consists of two floor stories and an attic. The walls are three feet thick. The walls of the front and back end at the floor of the attic.

The angle of the roof is 60 degrees and designed to handle snow and rain run off, and weight on the roof. At the end of two sections of the structure are chimney. The interior walls appear to be touching the chimneys. There are two closets which project beyond the lower part of the building.

There are histories written on the people who lived in the stone house and the church activities. These people sailed for forty-nine days after leaving London, England in May 1639. In September 1639 the people founded Guilford after landing at New Haven and the Connecticut Colony.

Samuel Disborow, a Lawyer, born in Cambridgeshire in 1619. Henry Whitfield, a Minister of Ockley and his family. William Leete, a London Lawyer, and thirty-seven sturdy farmers from Kent and Surrey. They had families.

In 1639, Whitfield and friends built the stone house for his family and as a fortification for the protection of the inhabitants against the Indians.

Samuel Disborrow was the first person appointed Magistrate in Guilford. Disborrow and Whitfield family members later return to England and died there.

When it was built the house served many purposes. It was the home of Reverend Whitfield and his family. It was church, meeting house, and fort to the families that came with Reverend Whitfield and founded Guilford. To travelers between the existing settlements of Saybrook and New Haven, it was shelter halfway between those two towns. Today as a state museum, the Henry Whitfield House is regarded as the oldest known stone house in New England.

During the reign of Charles I, in the early seventeenth century, the Church of England began its persecution of dissidents within the church. Separatists and Puritans alike were censured and some had to flee England. Reverend Henry Whitfield was not among the dissidents at first. His nature was conciliatory, humane, and forgiving. So he conformed to his faith during most of his term as vicar at Ockley. But as the church grew more rigid, more papist, his sympathies shifted to those who longed for reform and eventually he himself was called before the High Commission Court and censured.

Emigration to the New World

In 1638, Henry Whitfield resigned his position as head of the Ockley church. He gathered around him twenty-five families of young people (he himself was forty-six at that time) and made plans to emigrate. Most of the Puritan men he attracted were farmers of Surrey and Kent; a few came from the north of England.

Rev. John Davenport, a friend of Whitfield's, had emigrated and founded the New Haven Colony. Whitfield's college friend George Fenwick—now Colonel Fenwick—had helped found the Saybrook colony in 1635. It was natural then that Henry Whitfield should aim for the shores of what is now Connecticut.

During the rough long voyage across the Atlantic, Whitfield drew up an agreement which he required all the heads of the families accompanying him to sign. It has come down to us as the Guilford Covenant:

Robert Kitchel	John Stone	Francis Chatfield
John Bishop	William Plane	William Halle
Francis Bushnell	Richard Guttridge	Thomas Naish
William Chittenden	John Housegoe	Henry Kingnoth
William Leete	William Dudley	Henry Doude
Thomas Jones	John Permely	Thomas Cooke
John Jordan	John Mepham	Henry Whitfield
William Stone	Thomas Norton	
John Hoadley	Abraham Cruttenden	

Whitfield and his group of English farmers landed at Quinnipiac or New Haven where they were welcomed by Davenport and the settlers there. After some consultation with Davenport and Col. Fenwick (who had accompanied Whitfield from England where he had been on a visit) it was agreed that Whitfield would found a settlement about halfway between the two existing ones. Either by sea or land, Whitfield's group reached the site of what is now Guilford and in September of 1639 purchased land

"Articles of agreement, made and agreed upon the 29th of Septemb. 1639, between Henry Whitfield, Robert Kitchel, William Chittenden, William Leete, John Bishop and John Caffinge, English planters of Menunchetuck, and the Sachem Squaw of Menunchetuck, together with the Indians, inhabitants of Menunchetuck, as followeth:

First. That the Sachem Squaw is the sole possessor and inheritor of all the lands lying between Kuttawoo (East River) and Oiockcommock (Stony Creek) river.

Secondly. That the sayed Sachem Squaw (with the consent of the Indians there inhabiting, who are all, together with herself, to remove from thence), doth sell unto the forsayed English planters, all the lands within the forsayed limits of Kuttawoo and Oiockcommock river.

Thirdly. That the sayed Sachem Squaw, having received 12 coates, 12 fathom of Wompom, 12 glasses, 12 payer of shooes, 12 Hatchetts, 12 paire of stockings, 12 hooes, 4 kettles, 12 knives, 12 hatts, 12 porringers, 12 spoons and 2 English coates, professeth herselfe to bee fully payed and satisfied. In witness whereof the forsayed parties have sett their hands.

Squaw	Sachem	Hry Whitfield
her	marke	in the name of ye rest.

In presence whereof
John Higgenson
Robert Newman

Whitfield and his group of English farmers landed at Quinnipiac or New Haven where they were welcomed by Davenport and the settlers there. After some consultation with Davenport and Col. Fenwick (who had accompanied Whitfield from England where he had been on a visit) it was agreed that Whitfield would found a settlement about halfway between the two existing ones. Either by sea or land, Whitfield's group reached the site of what is now Guilford and in September of 1639 purchased land from the Menuncatuck Indians (see above). With them, too, came the "little red cattle" given them by Lady Fenwick of Saybrook, said to be some of the first cattle brought to this country.

Thus stone was used from a ledge about a quarter of a mile east of the house site, and tradition has it that the Indians helped the settlers transport it on hand-barrows. The necessary mortar was made of yellow clay and crushed oyster shells. With plenty of stone at hand, the walls were made two feet thick; joists and rafters were hand-hewn oaken timbers; the inside partitions were formed by wide planks of pine or whitewood joined with feathered edges.

In this house they worked, ate and slept; on Saturday they cleared the Great Hall for Sunday services, for no one might labor on the Sabbath.

Dame Dorothy had to reconcile herself to the fact that her home was first of all the church, second the meeting hall, third a hostel for wayfarers, and lastly her home. Everyone worked early and late to wrest a living from the New England soil, sea, and forest.

**A STATE HISTORICAL MUSEUM
GUILFORD, CONNECTICUT**

Reverend Whitfield in the decade after the founding of Guilford, was its first citizen. It was his duty to compose and deliver two long sermons and sometimes even more each week. He was in demand, then as now, for baptisms, marriages, and funerals; he helped to settle neighborhood disputes in a growing community, attended house and barn raisings, and supervised town affairs in general.

After ten or eleven years in such service, Mr. Whitfield made known his desire to return to England. He started in 1650, leaving his wife and some of his children behind. It is not certain why he left the colony never to return. Perhaps the strain of life here had been too much for him. Or it may be that with the changed political and religious conditions in England he felt the call to return home. In any event, after a roundabout journey by way of Boston he reached England about the time Cromwell was made Lord Protector and the Puritans were secure in power. Henry Whitfield remained in England and died there in 1657. He was buried on September 17th in Winchester Cathedral.

Dorothy Whitfield continued to live in the stone house on its commanding knoll long after her husband's departure. Why she remained here is not known. She may have preferred to because so many of her children did. Three of her daughters had married since coming to Guilford: Dorothy to Samuel Desborough, the town magistrate; Sarah to the Reverend John Higginson; Abigail to the Reverend James Fitch. Daughter Mary and sons John and Nathaniel lived with their mother in the stone house, but Mary and Nathaniel were with their father when he died, so they must have returned to England sometime prior to 1657. It is known that the youngest son, Henry, died in 1634, five years before the migration to this country; but whether the eldest son, Thomas, returned to England with his father, or did not come over here in the first place is unknown. Equally unknown is what became of the youngest of the nine children, Rebecca.

In 1659 Dorothy Whitfield returned to England and lived there until her death in 1669.

Owners to follow with the Stone House: Dorothy Sheaffe Whitfield, 1657. Robert Thompson 1659. Frances Thompson, wife of Robert, and the title of property to remain with male heirs Joseph, William, and Robert. The property was occupied by tenants during the absentee landlords. In 1772, the property was sold to Wyllys Eliot of Guilford. On Nov. 6, 1772 Wyllys sold the property to Joseph Pynchon and he became the first owner to actually live in the house after the Whitfields.

On June 27, 1776 he sold the property to Jasper Griffing who with his descendants owned the property until 1900. In 1868 there were made many repairs and changes in chimneys and fireplaces, and a new roof less steep than the old. In 1900 the State of Connecticut acquired the property. The Society of the Colonial Dames was in charge. The Stone House serves the people today.

James Fitch was b. Dec. 24, 1622 and d. at Lebanon, Nov. 18, 1702 in England. James Fitch married Abigail Whitfield. A daughter of James and Abigail was born at Saybrook, CT Dec. 17, 1652. The daughter married Thomas Bradford and they lived at Norwich, CT where Thomas died in 1708. Abigail Whitfield Fitch died Sept. 9, 1659. James Fitch married second wife Priscilla Mason on Oct. 1664.

Corporation of Yale College held Sept. 1774 preaching of George Whitfield. Church of Hartford.

DELAWARE

Whitfield there by 1940.
Occupation with Military service.
In 1990 there were eleven Whitfield heads of families living in Delaware. 1980 Donald Whitfield and Perry Whitfield lived in Dover, DE. 1980 R. Lloyd Whitfield lived in Lewes, DE.

FLORIDA

There are many families named Whitfield living in Florida in the 1980's.

FLORIDA federal censuses and Whitfields in Florida state and counties. Dates of censuses 1790 to 1850 which have Whitfield head of families.

    1830 William Whitfield, Jackson Co., FL.
    1830 William Whitfield, Jackson Co., FL.
    1840 and 1845 B. V. Whitfield, Jackson Co., FL.
    1840 R. P. Whitfield, Jackson Co., FL. 1845 census.
    1840 and 1845 S. B. Whitfield, Jackson Co., FL.
    1840 and 1845 W. A. Whitfield, Jackson Co., FL.
    1850 Benjamin M. Whitfield, Columbia Co., FL.
    1850 George Whitfield, Leon Co., FL.
    1850 John B. Whitfield, Columbia Co., FL.
    1850 Lawson Whitfield, Franklin Co., FL. 6th division.
    1850 Winny Whitfield, Jefferson Co., FL.

1885 Census - Jackson Co., FL.

Whitfield family members all born in Florida.
    Whitfield, William Male Age 26   Father
    Whitfield, Ann Female   Age 24   Mother
    Whitfield, Ela Female   Age 6
    Whitfield, Dock   Male Age 4
    Whitfield, Joe Male Age 1

Whitfields living in 1981 in Miami, FL. Each person lived in a house or apartment. Whitfield residents taken from the telephone book of Miami City.

Betty Whitfield	Harold S. Whitfield	Robert L. Whitfield
Beverly Whitfield	James W. Whitfield	Roy E. Whitfield
Clarence Whitfield	Kelvyn Whitfield, and	T. B. Whitfield
Cora Whitfield	his wife Gitta	Tom Whitfield
David Whitfield	Kenneth L. Whitfield	Tony Whitfield
Doris Whitfield	Lizzie Whitfield	V. L. Whitfield
Duke Whitfield	M. F. Whitfield	Vassena Whitfield
Earl E. Whitfield	Nancy Whitfield	Winnie Whitfield
Eugene Whitfield	P. T. Whitfield	

Telephone books do not indicate race. For white names in list a review can be made of the Directories that list only white race with surname for the purpose of genealogy and other studies.

Susie C. Cameron born Nov. 29, 1842 married Bryan C. Whitfield of Florida. She was daughter of William F. Cameron, Governor of Virginia 1882. They had children: 1. Evelyn Cameron Whitfield. 2. Lou Egerton Whitfield.

Fifth Generation   FLORIDA

CLINTON WHITFIELD
(Francis, William, William, William)

Clinton Whitfield was born Nov. 23, 1845. He died July 2, 1917, in Zephyrhills, Fla. He married Oct. 12, 1865, in Jefferson, Ala., Maggie Magdalene Bryan. They lived in Florida and he was buried in Adamsville, Fla.

Children:

1. Loulie Whitfield; b. March 2, 1868; m. W. T. Chapman, of Tampa, Fla.
2. Edwin Whitfield; d. in infancy.
3. Willie (dau.) Whitfield; m. J. F. Stebbins.

Fourth Generation   Sumpterville, Florida

FRANCIS EDWIN WHITFIELD
(William, William, William)

Francis Edwin Whitfield (April 28, 1813-1887 or '89) was born in North Carolina and died in Sumpterville, Fla. He was buried in Adamsville, Fla. He married (1) on Aug. 6, 1832, Margaret Ann Fort (1818-1835); (2) in Petersburg, Va., Dec. 22, 1836, Demetria Meredith Jones (1822-1860), (3) on May 16, 1867, Lucy Harrison Gay (b. Nov. 17, 1845). His first wife was the daughter of Harriet Wilson and Lewis B. Fort.

Children:

1. Francis Eugene Whitfield.
2. Edwin Whitfield; b. Sept. 6, 1841, d. Jan. 8, 1869; m. May 28, 1867, Frances Gertrude Caldwell. One daughter dying in childhood.
3. Florence Whitfield; b. Feb. 21, 1848, d. June 20, 1857.
4. Clinton Whitfield.
5. Frank Raynor Whitfield; m. Carrie Clay.
6. Lillie May Whitfield.
7. Francis Edwin Whitfield; b. 1868, d. young.
8. William Carey Whitfield; b. 1870, d. 1905; m. Nov. 2, 1898, Mary Morton Herring (1879-1902).
9. Lucy Harrison Whitfield.
10. Elizabeth Harrison Whitfield; b. Aug. 17, 1880.

First six children born of the second marriage.

Fifth Generation Dunedin, Fl and Leon   County, Florida

RICHARD BASS WHITFIELD
(George, Bryan, William, William)

Richard Bass Whitfield (July 31, 1846-1881), married Katy Palmer, of Monticello, Fla. He was a lawyer.   She lived, 1927, at Dunedin, Fla.

Children:

1. Richard Bass Whitfield.
2. Julia Whitfield.

JOHN NASH WHITFIELD (James,
Richard, James, Bryan, William, William)

John Nash Whitfield was born Sept. 25, 1897, in Tallahassee, Fla. June 9, 1920, he married Nan Ward in Plant City, Fla. Res., 1947, Jacksonville, Fla.

Children:

1. John Nash Whitfield; b. June 2, 1924, Jacksonville, Fla.[20] He attended the University of The South, at Sewanee, Tenn., and was graduated in 1944. Student in Virginia Theological Seminary, Alexandria, Va. 1944-46. Employed, 1947, in the Library of Congress, Washington, D. C. Episcopalian.

Fifth   Generation   Leon   County,   Florida

RICHARD ALLEN WHITFIELD
(James, Bryan, William, William)

Richard Allen Whitfield (1832, Wayne Co., N. C.-Nov. 28, 1906, Tallahassee, Fla.) married (1) Mary Whitfield Croom (2) July 2, 1872, Ella Talbot (d. 1873) ; (3) Sept. 14, 1875, Anna Maria Talbot, of Baltimore, Md. The last died in 1904. At the time of the first marriage Richard Allen Whitfield was living in Wayne County, but he moved to Tallahassee, Fla., in 1863. He was a student in the University of North Carolina, 1849-52, and in the Confederate Army he was a member of Scott's Battalion, 5th Florida Cavalry. 1897 found him county judge of Leon County, Fla.

Children:
1. Richard Allen Whitfield; b. 1859; Ala., d. 1885.
2. James Bryan Whitfield.
3. Hardy Croom Whitfield; b. 1862 in Fla.; d. 1914.
4. Allen Wooten Whitfield; b. 1863 in Fla.; d. 1904.
5. Bryan Croom Whitfield.
6. George Talbot Whitfield; b. July 29, 1873; m. Ruby Wilson Trammell. Living (1929) in Talahassee, Fla. Four children.
7. Mary Talbot Whitfield; b. Sept. 23, 1876; unmd. Living (1929) in Tallahassee, Fla.
8. Louis Talbot Whitfield.

Sixth   Generation   Leon County, Florida
and Tallahassee, Fla.

JAMES BRYAN WHITFIELD
(Richard, James, Bryan, William, William)

James Bryan Whitfield was born Nov. 8, 1860, in Wayne Co., N. C. He married (1) Nov. 25, 1896, Leila R. Nash and (2) June 12, 1901, Margaret H. Randolph . Leila R. Nash was the daughter of John W. and Emma T. Nash, of Tallahassee, Fla. She died Oct. 4, 1897.

James Bryan Whitfield was reared on a farm in Leon Co., Fla. After graduation in law at the University of Virginia in 1886, he began practice in his home county. Two years later he was elected county judge in the same county. In 1889 he resigned to accept the clerkship of the state Supreme Court. This was surrendered for the appointment as state treasurer in 1897, and this in turn in 1903 for the position of attorney general of the state. For a few months in 1904 he was a justice of the Florida Supreme Court and then he became chief justice. This position he continued to hold for almost forty years. He then resigned. In 1947 he was living in Tallahassee, Fla. and maintaining an active interest in Florida history.

James Bryan Whitfield died Aug. 20, 1948, in Tallahassee, Fla.

Children:

1. John Nash Whitfield.
2. Mary Croom Whitfield; b. April 30, 1902.
3. James Bryan Whitfield; b. May 20, 1904.
4. Julia Croom Whitfield.
5. Margaret R. Whitfield; b. Nov. 30, 1907, d. May 20, 1908.
6. Randolph Whitfield.

Sixth Generation   Tallahassee, Florida

BRYAN CROOM WHITFIELD
(Richard, James, Bryan, William, William)
Bryan Croom Whitfield married Feb. 12, 1897, Susie Egerton. Cameron, daughter of William Ewan Evelyn Egerton and Louisa ____. William E. E. Egerton was governor of Virginia from 1882 to 1886. Bryan Croom Whitfield was living in 1930 in Tallahassee, FL.

1.   Evelyn Whitfield
2.   Lou Egerton Whitfield

Florida Censuses. 1830 William Whitfield ,1840 B.V. Whitfield, R. P. Whitfield, S. B. Whitfield, William A. Whitfield all lived in Jackson Co., FL. 1840 Willis Whitfield in Shelby Co., FL. Benjamin Whitfield and George Whitfield in 1850 lived in Columbia Co., FL. 1850 George Whitfield in Leon Co., FL. 1850 Lawson Whitfield in Franklin Co., FL. 1850 Winny Whitfield in Jefferson Co., FL.

Whitfield families from North Carolina and Georgia moved to the State of Florida.

REFERENCES: Whitfield, Bryan, Smith And Related Families, Book I, by Emma Morehead Whitfield.
Whitfield   Florida
    Francis E., p. 95. Clinton, p. 138, 139. George, p. 147. George, p. 147. Richard B., p. 147, 148. Richard Allen, p. 148. James B., p. 210, 211. Bryan Croom, p. 211. John , p. 257

GEORGE WHITFIELD (Bryan, William, William)

George Whitfield was born June 6, 1804, and died in Tallahassee, Florida, on June 16, 1880. He is buried there. He married January 8, 1824, Louisa Ann Blackledge (b. Feb. 1, 1807). The wedding was in the home of her father, William Blackledge. His first wife dying in Athens, Ga., Feb. 5, 1846, George Whitfield married Mary Ann Brown, of New Bern. His third wife was Mrs. Lucy Winifred (Whitfield) Higgs

General George Whitfield was a member of the state legislature of North Carolina and of the militia. In 1845 he moved to Florida and entered the legislature there. The Census of 1850 shows him a resident of Leon County. A tablet was recently placed in the new chapel at Sewanee in his memory.

Children: 1. ——— Whitfield; d. in infancy.
2. Alice Wharton Whitfield.
3. William Whitfield; d. young.
4. George Whitfield.
5. Bryan Whitfield; b. Aug. 1, 1833, in N. C., d. Aug. 23, 1861 or '62. He was a lieutenant in the C. S. A. and came to his death in service, perhaps wounded in the Battle of Seven Pines near Richmond. If wounded in this battle the year would have been 1862. He married Mrs. Paralee Blavins Cook, of Selma, Ala.
6. Louisa Blackledge Whitfield.
7. Winifred Bryan Whitfield; d. in infancy.
8. William Whitfield; b. in July 4, 1842, killed in the Battle of Seven Pines, May 31, 1862.
9. Elizabeth Ryder Whitfield; b. 1844, d. 1845.
10. Richard Bass Whitfield.

FLORIDA MARRIAGES

1. Nathalie Ashe Whitfield b. Nov. 27, 1859. She married Nov. 5, 1889 Col. Norman Griffin Winn. He was born Sept. 14, 1858.

2. Alice Wharton Whitfield b. Oct. 2, 1827. She married in Tallahassee, FL. to Wade Keyes.

3. Julia Croom Whitfield was b. July 11, 1905 in Tallahassee, FL. She married Clarence Neely in Panama City.

4. Louisa Blackledge Whitfield was b. Feb. 1, 1835 in NC. With her parents she went to Leon Co., FL. She married Nov. 26, 1861 in Tallahassee, FL., to Judge William Edwin Danelly (1830-1884) and moved to Texas.

America Discovered

The decision to finance a voyage to America was made by Spain monarchs King Ferdinand and Queen Isabella. Christopher Columbus led the expedition. Three small ships sailed across the ocean: Pinta, Nina, Santa Maria. On Oct. 12, 1492 Columbus discovered land at Bahama Island (San Salvador).

Three more voyages were made in 1493, 1498, 1502. The lands found were south of Florida and in and near the Caribbean Sea. Later Spain claimed Florida. In 1705 America settlers went to Florida and revolted against Spanish rule. In 1819 Spain sold and a treaty ceded Florida to the United States.

164

GEORGIA

There were Whitfields at Georgia in the 1700's but only a few. There were many Whitfields in Georgia state from 1806 to 1850 and thereafter. They came from North Carolina, Alabama, Mississippi, and a few from South Carolina. There has not been a Whitfield compilation of all Whitfield heads of families and with the family in Georgia. There have been completed lineages but it is difficult to locate the ancestor outside of Georgia.

All four above states mentioned have to be searched to find the ancestor. Whitfield men left Virginia and went to North Carolina, and many who left North Carolina went west into Tennessee, and southwest to Alabama and into Mississippi, and then the people go east to Alabama or to Georgia for some who settle there.

Family groups and records in this book will help with some of the west to east movement.

State of Georgia-Minutes of the Executive Council, Wednesday, Dec. 2, 1778. "Resolved James Whitfield be appointed Secretary of State until the next general election of officers in the room of James Maxwee, esquire who hath resigned."

Whitefield/Whitfield references from Will book and page with name and county and a date.

WHITEFIELD, George	1770	Colonial	Will A	363
George	1813	Chatham	Will E	241
James	1793	Chatham	Will A	101
James	1796	Chatham	Will A	223
WHITFIELD, Benjamin	1832	Putnam	Will B	124
Elizabeth	1798	Chatham	Will A	310
John	1833	Chatham	Will G	192
Lewis	1859	Burke	Will A	142
Martha	1796	Chatham	Will A	254
Reuben	1856(d)	Pulaski	Will B	12
William S.	1848	Pulaski	Will A	218

Ted O. Brooke compiled Georgia Wills from 1733-1860.

In Georgia, Mary Hillyer was born 1839 and died 1921. Mary married George Whitfield and he died 1908.

Thomas Brannon Whitfield was a military man who lived in the Pacific Island on Guam many years, and in 1986 Whitfield was living in Florida. This ancestral family of his was the one that Whitfield Co., Georgia got its name.

....Submitted by Mrs. Cuykendall who was a Whitfield who knew the history of how this Georgia Co. was named, 1989.

Georgia. Jake Cook, PO Box 652, Statham, GA 30666 has a paper titled Civil War Service of Frank Burton and Uriah Burton and Bryant W. Whitfield. Franklin U. Burton served under the command of Robert E. Lee and was in all of the major battles fought in Virginia, Maryland, and Pennsylvania. Uriah Burton and his uncle Bryant W. Whitfield were members of two Companies of the 32nd Georgia Regiment. Uriah Burton, Bryant W. Whitfield and John Wesley Bell were all at the surrender at Greensboro on April 26, 1865, of the Civil War. They returned to Burke Co., GA. Bryant W. Whitfield died in 1893. John Wesley Bell died February 1, 1894. Uriah Burton died August 4, 1911.

South Carolina and Georgia. Robert D. Burton on Waldo Road in Gainesville, FL, zip 36901, has a Descendary Chart from Whitfield through Daniels and others to Burton families. He also has computer listed information on these surnames. Burton has gathered much information to support his records. Burton has submitted information on Whitfield and Burton from May to July 20, 1997, and has contributed Whitfields of South Carolina and Georgia. He has additional papers that have been found on Whitfield.

Georgia Record. Michael E. Whitfield living 1995 and with General Joseph E. Johnston, Camp 671, Sons of Confederate Veterans, Rocky Face, Georgia.

GEORGIA STATE CENSUS. WHITFIELD RESIDENTS IN COUNTIES:
1850 Antinelda Whitfield-Pulaski Co., GA
1850 Benjamin Whitfield-Morgan Co., GA.
1850 Bryant Whitfield-Harris Co., GA.
1840 Benjamin Whitfield-Cobb Co., GA.
1840 Berry Whitfield-Habersham Co., GA.
1840 Bray Whitfield-Habersham Co., GA. Cashs District
1840 Bryant Whitfield-Harris Co., GA.
1840 D. H. Whitfield-Cobbs Co., GA.
1840 E. S. Whitfield-Laurens Co., GA.
1840 G. W. Whitfield-Cobbs Co., GA., 85 1st District
1840 Hyrusbury Whitfield-Franklin Co., GA. 284 District
1840 Ivy E. Whitfield-Clarke Co., GA.
1840 Jacob Whitfield-Cherokee Co., GA.
1840 James E. Whitfield-Thomas Co., GA.
1840 J. H. Whitfield, Thomas Co., GA., Grooversville District
1840 John S. Whitfield-Loundes Co., GA.
1840 Joseph Whitfield-Camden Co., GA., St. Marys town
1840 Mathew Whitfield-Jasper Co., GA.
1840 Miles Whitfield-Emanuel Co., GA.
1840 Robert Whitfield-Washington Co., GA.
1840 Robert Whitfield-Walton Co., GA., Broken Arrow District
1840 Robert whitfield-Washington Co., GA, 92nd District
1840 Simpson Whitfield-Savannah Co., GA.
1840 Thomas Whitfield-Newton Co., GA.
1840 W.S. Whitfield-Pulaski Co., GA.
1840 William Whitfield-Habersham Co., GA., Cashs District

GEORGIA CENSUSES
WHITFIELD HEADS OF FAMILIES

1806 John Whitfield-Franklin Co., GA.
1820 and 1824 Alexander-Clarke Co., GA., Athens
1820 and 1824 Andrew-Chatham Co., GA., Savannah
1820 and 1824 Benjamin Whitfield-Putnam Co., GA.
1820 and 1824 Bryan Whitfield-Burke Co., GA.
1820 and 1824 Darky Whitfield-Jackson Co., GA.
1820 George Whitfield-Richmond Co., GA.
1824 Horatio Whitfield-Putnam Co., GA.

1820 and 1824 James Whitfield-Putnam Co., GA.
1820 and 1824 James Whitfield-Jefferson Co., GA.
1820 and 1824 Jemima Whitfield-Washington Co., GA.
1826 (Tax List) John Whitfield-Chatham Co., GA.
1820 and 1824 John S. Whitfield-Bryan Co., GA.
1820, 1824, 1830, 1840 Lewis Whitfield-Burke Co., GA.
1820, 1824, 1840 Robert Whitfield-Washington co., GA
1820, 1824, 1830 Ruben Whitfield-Washington Co., GA
1824 Tucker Whitfield-Jackson Co., GA., 3rd ward
1820 William Whitfield-Putnam Co., GA.
1820 and 1824 William Whitfield-Putnam Co., GA.
1824, 1830 William Whitfield-Putnam Co., GA.
1820 William Whitfield-Washington Co., GA.
1830 and 1840 Bryant Whitfield-Washington Co., GA.
1830 and 1840 Bryant Whitfield-Troup Co., GA.
1830 Bryant Whitfield-Burke Co., GA.
1830 and 1840 Elisha Whitfield-Habersham Co., GA.
1830 and 1840 George Whitfield-Columbus Co., GA.
1830 George Whitfield-Houston Co., GA.
1830 Horatio Whitfield-Troup Co., GA.
1830 James Whitfield-Jackson Co., GA.
1830 John Whitfield-Lowndes Co., GA.
1830 Martha Whitfield-Clarke Co., GA.
1830 and 1840 Mathew Whitfield-Jasper Co., GA.
1830 Myles Whitfield-Washington Co., GA.
1830 Robert Whitfield-Clarke Co., GA.
1830 Sampson Whitfield-Chesham Co., GA.
1830 Samuel Whitfield-Laurens Co., GA.
1830 Silvia Whitfield-Chesham Co., GA.
1830 Thomas Whitfield-Clarke Co., GA.
1830 William Whitfield-Burke Co., GA.
1830, 1840 William H. Whitfield-Dooley Co., GA. 10th District
1830 William T. Whitfield-DeKalb Co., GA.

Georgia. Betty Bailey, wife of James W. Bailey of Waynesboro, GA, age 65 in 1997, is interested in Bailey. She had information on Burton and Whitfield and Whitefield having read the papers on Reverend George Whitefield, the evangelist. She reported that no white people named Whitfield lived in Burke Co., GA, in 1997 but there were a number of African-Americans with Whitfield surname living in Burke Co.,GA. Betty Bailey said, "Lewis Whitfield, Jr., is buried in Louisville, in Jefferson County, GA, which is adjacent land to Burke Co., GA."

WHITFIELD
FAMILY GROUPS

GROUP ONE : Robert Whitfield born ca. 1770 in North Carolina, and died ca. 1854 , Washington County, Georgia.

GROUP TWO : Ruben Henry Whitfield born October 20, 1849, Dooley County, Georgia , and died December 7, 1935 Panama City, Bay County, Florida.

GROUP THREE : J.H. Whitfield born October 31, 1849, Thomas County, Georgia.

GROUP FOUR : Matthew Whitfield , Hancock County, Georgia.

GROUP FIVE : Henry H. Whitfield born April 11, 1826, and died January 28, 1886.

Robert Whitfield married Edith Jones Whitfield, and the marriage bond was dated 1792 Pitt County, North Carolina. Robert does not appear on 1800 census Pitt County, N.C. Robert and Edith Whitfield moved to Washington County, GA. by 1802.

ROBERT WHITFIELD

Robert was from Bertie County, North Carolina. He went to Washington County, Georgia about 1790.

Will dated Jun.15,1853 in Washington County, Georgia. Mentions in Will - Wife Rebecca; Son Miles Whitfield; Daughters - Cherry Whitfield, wife of John W. Pate; Almiler Whitfield, wife of John D. Paradise; Jemima Whitfield wife of Owen H. Fort; Granddaughter, Julia Ann Sheppard, wife of Zachariah Sheppard. Executors: Son Miles Whitfield, Reuben Whitfield, and Elbert D. Taylor. Witnesses: Elizabeth Norris, Arthur P. Fort, Thomas Norris, and Jemima J. Whitfield.

Robert Whitfield - May 25, 1863 - Division of estate between two heirs: Ellen Whitfield, wife of Patrick Whitfield heir of Cherry Pate, deceased and the heirs of Patrick J. Pate son of said Cherry Pate, deceased, to wit: Elizabeth R. Pate, James R. Pate, and Cherry J. Pate whose interest in said distribution was represented by W.G. Bryan guardian of said minor children.

```
Robert Whitfield------ Married to    1st
b. ca 1770 in N.C.                   2nd Rebecca _____
d. ca 1854 in Wash.Co.,Ga               b. ca 1805 in Ga.
```

Known Children

1. Miles Whitfield---Ma.   --To: Sarah _____
   b. ca 1791 in N.C.   b. ca 1802 in Georgia
   d.

   1. Cherry Whitfield-Ma.2-15-1849-To: Thomas T. Page
      b. Aug.4,1830   b. Jan.6,1828
      d. Jun.15,1872   d. Nov.11,1910

      1. Robert Washington Page-----To: Minnie Lee Meeks
         b. May 26,1865   b. Jan.6,1870
         d. Aug.7, 1950   d. Nov.17,1916

   2. Robert Whitfield--Ma.7-29-1849---To: Janet Townsen
      b. ca 1826   b. ca 1830
      d.

      1. Miles Whitfield-Ma.   ---To: Emma Meeks
         b. ca 1864   b. Mar.13,1869
         d.   d. Mar.26, 1907

   Note: The above Minnie Lee & Emma Meeks were sisters.
         They married 1st cousins Robert Washington Page &
         Miles Whitfield.

2. Cherry Whitfield---Ma.   To: John W. Pate

   1. Ellen Pate------Ma.   To: Patrick Whitfield
   2. Patrick R. Pate-Ma.   To:
      1.Elizabeth R.Pate, 2.James R.Pate, 3.Cherry J. Pate.

3. Almiler Whitfield-Ma.   --To: John D. Paradise

4. Jemima Whitfield--Ma.   --To: Owen H. Fort

5. (?) Bryan Whitfield-Ma.   --To: Martha _____
   b. ca 1790 in N.C.   b. ca 1794 in Ga.

6. Reuben Whitfield---Ma.   --To; Rhoda _____
   b. ca 1789 in N.C.   b. ca 1798 in N.C.

   Note: Not sure whether Bryan & Reuben are sons of Robert
         Whitfield. Reuben was executor of Robert's will
         along with his son Miles. Bryan lived near Robert
         and the other Whitfields in Washington County, Ga.
         and his age fits to be a son.

WHITFIELD

William Jackson (Boss) Page said that he remembered well that his grandmother's (Mrs.Thomas T. Cherry Whitfield Page) parents were Miles and Sarah Whitfield. Thomas T. was living with Boss's daddy when he died in 1910. Boss was 20 years old at that time. Miles Whitfield was born in North Carolina.

Robert Whitfield was a very close friend and neighbor of Soloman Page,Sr. in Washington County, Georgia. Soloman was born in Bertie County, N.C. and was the son of Thomas Page,Sr who made Will in 1786 in Bertie Co., N.C.. Soloman's wife, Mary Horton Page, in applying for a Rev. War Pension in 1852 obtained this statement form Robert Whitfield. He stated he was personally acquainted with Mary Horton Page and had known her since 1790 and knew her husband Soloman Page first about 1775 in Bertie Co.,N.C. where they were neighbors. He further stated that Soloman entered the Rev. War service in Bertie Co, N.C. in the Continental Line 3 to 4 years before the end of the War. Robert Whitfield moved from N.C. to Ga. circa 1790 and Page did also. Page died in Washington Co.,Ga. in Dec. 1823. He and Mary Horton were married in Washington County, Ga. in 1790.

1790 Ga. Census burned.   1810 Census Georgia burned

1820 Washington Co., Ga. Census.
```
WHITFIELD, Robert    45+
     "    , [wife]    45+
     "    , [son] 16-26
     "    , [dau's] 16-26 [2]
WHITFIELD, Bryan  26-45--Ma.1-17-1816-To:Patsy Wells in
     "    , [wife]  16-26              Jefferson Co.,Ga
     "    , [son] under 10 [1]
     "    , [dau's]  "   "   [2]
WHITFIELD, Reuben  16-26
     "    , [wife]  16-26
          , [son]    under 10
WHITFIELD, J       45+
     "    , [wife] 26-45
     "    , [dau]  10-16
WHITFIELD, Wm.     26-45
     "    , [wife] 26-45
     "    , [son's] 10-16 [2]
     "    ,   "     under 10 [3]
     "    , [dau]  10-16
     "    , [dau's] under 10 [3]
```

Marriages - Jefferson County, Georgia.
Bryant Whitfield married Patsy Wells - Jan.17,1816
James E. Whitfield "   Sarah Blackman -4-16-1815
Marriages - Emanuel County, Georgia
Aden Powell   married Ann Whitfield - 2-19-1839
Thomas T. Page   "   Charity(Cherry) Whitfield-2-15-1849
Samuel Whitfield   "   Sarah Anders - 6-29-1848
Robert Whitfield   "   Janet Townsen - 7-29-1849

```
         1830 Washington Co., Ga. Census
         WHITFIELD, Robert  50-60
              "   , [female] 15-20
              "   , [males] 5-10 [2]

         1830 Washington County census - Cont.
         WHITFIELD, Bryant  30-40
              "        (Wife)  30-40
              "    , [son]   15-20
              "    ,   "      5-10
              "    ,   "    under 5
              "    , [dau's] 10-15 [2]
              "    , [dau]   5-10
              "    , [dau's] under 5 [2]
         WHITFIELD, Reuben  40-50
              "    , [wife]  30-40
              "    , [son]   15-20
              "    ,   "      5-10
              "    , [son's] under 10 [2]
              "    , [dau]   5-10
         WHITFIELD, Myles  20-30
              "    , [wife] 20-30
              "    , [son's] under 5 [2]  (Robert + ?)
              "    , [dau]     "    " [1]  (Cherry)

         1840 Emanuel Co., Ga. Census
         WHITFIELD, Miles  30-40
              "    , [wife] 20-30
              "    , [son's] 5-10 [3]
              "    , [son] under 5 [1]
              "    , [dau]    "    " [1]

         1840 Washington Co., Ga. Census
         WHITFIELD, R        50-60
              "    , [2nd wife?] 40-50
              "    , [son] 20-30
              "    ,   "    15-20
              "    ,   "    10-15
              "    ,   "     5-10
              "    ,   " under 5
              "    , [dau]  "   "
              "    ,   "    15-20
         WHITFIELD, Robert  70-80
              "    , [wife?] 40-50
              "    , [son]  30-40
              "    ,   "    20-30
              "    ,   "    15-20
         WHITFIELD, Bryant  50-60
              "    , [wife?] 40-50
              "    , [son]  20-30
              "    ,   "    15-20
              "    ,   "     5-10
              "    , [dau]  15-20
              "    ,   "    10-15
              "    ,   "     5-10
                             171
```

1850 Emanuel Co., Ga. Census

WHITFIELD, Miles   59 M [N.C.]
     "   , Sarah   48 F [Ga.]
     "   , Mountrivil 13 M [Ga.]
     "   , Pricilla   9 F [Ga.]

1850 Washington Co., Georgia Census
627 (Shellman?) Whitfield 33 M Ga.
     Julian   "   33 F "
     Martha Ann   "   6 F "
----
628 Bryan   "   60 m N.C.
     Martha   "   56 F Ga.
     Everitt   "   25 m "
     Martha   "   21 F "
     Morning   "   19 F "
     Bryan   "   15 M "
----
641 Charlie P.N.   "   23 m Ga.
     Adeline   "   23 F "
     Ruben H.   "   1 M "
----
661 Ruben   "   61 M N.C.
     Rhoda   "   52 M N.C.
     Emily   "   17 F Ga.
     Pinkney   "   14 M "
     Josephine   "   11 F "
----
775 N. B.   "   30 M "
     Martha   "   28 F S.C.
     Armanda   "   1 F Ga.
     Wm. A.   "   27 M " Bro.
----
79 Robert   "   80 M N.C.
     Rebecca   "   45 F Ga.
     Sarah   Rogers   22 F "
     G. A.   Runhart   22 m " Boatmaker
     L. H.   Jordan   26 M France -Tailor

1860 Emanuel Co., Ga. Census
WHITFIELD, G.M.T.   31 M Ga.
     "   , Annie   35 F Ga.
     "   , Minee   6 F Ga.
     "   , Egustus   5 M Ga.
     "   , Silas   3 M Ga.
     "   , Annie E 7/12 F "

1880 Census Johnson County, Georgia

```
Whitfield, R.            54 M Ga. (Bro. to Cherry)
     "   , Jane          50 F "  (Townsen married 7-29-1849)
     "   , Nancy         19 F "  Dau.
     "   , Miles         16 M "  Son-married Emma Meeks sis to
     "   , Eli           20 M "  Son          Minnie Meeks
     "   , Nancy          2 F "  Gr.Dau.
---------------------------------------
     "   , E.            24 m Ga.
     "   , Jane          24 F "
     "   , Appley         2 F "
---------------------------------------
     "   , Samuel A.     35 M Ga.
     "   , Sarah A.      38 F "
     "   , William S.E.  13 m Ga.
     "   , Frederick      8 M "
     "   , Elizabeth S.   4 F "
     "   , Delpha         1 F "
     "   , Samuel        79 M (Father)
```

1880 Census Emanuel County, Georgia

```
Whitfield, Geo.M.T.     50 m Ga.
     "   , Ann           56 F "
     "   , Rastus        23 m '
     "   , Sylus         22 m '
     "   , Anna          20 F "
     "   , Jefferson     18 m "
     "   , Elette        13 F "
     "   , Allen         11 m "
 Boyd,    Allen          70 M (Uncle)
```

1900 Census Montgomery County, Ga.

```
Whitfield, Miles        35 Ga. Jul.1864 (ma.12 yrs)
     "   , Emma          29 "   Mar.1871 (Ch-5,4 alive)
     "   , Mountavilia 10 "         1889 Son
     "   , Walace         9 "         1891  "
     "   , Brant D.       3 "         1896  "
     "   , Rudysill       1 "         1899  "
```

1830 Census , Habersham County, G .
Elisha Whitfield head of family and household
two boys under five years of age
two boys - 10 - 15   Wife , 40-50 age range
1 boy - 15-20   1 female , 15-20
Elisha was age 40-50   2 females , 20-30

GEORGIA CENSUSES

The first three censuses of the State of Georgia were taken
in 1790 , 1800, 1810 and were destroyed by fire in the attack
on Washington by the British during the War of 1812.

1820 , 1830 , 1840 censuses of Georgia have been published
and are on microfilm reels.

173

DEVELOPMENT OF GEORGIA COUNTIES

The largest state with more counties - 159 - than
any other state East of the Mississippi River. List shows
any name change of some counties and names of certain counties that have been merged into other counties.

COUNTY	COUNTY SEAT	INITIAL	DATE FORMED
Baldwin	Milledgeville		May 11, 1803
Burke	Waynesboro	BKE	Feb. 5, 1777
Chatham	Savannah	CHT	Feb. 13, 1854
Clarke	Athens	CLK	Feb. 16, 1854
Cobb	Marietta		Dec. 3, 1832
Columbia	Appling	COL	Dec. 10, 1790
De Kalb	Decatur	DEK	Dec. 9, 1822
Dooly	Vienna	DOO	May 15, 1821
Emanuel	Swainsboro		Dec. 10, 1812
Franklin	Carnesville	FRK	Feb. 25, 1784
Greene	Greensboro		Feb. 3, 1786
Habersham	Clarkesville	HAB	Dec. 15, 1818
Houston	Perry	HST	May 15, 1821
Jasper	Monticello	JSP	Dec. 10, 1807
Jefferson	Louisville	JEF	Feb. 20, 1796
Lowndes	Valdosta	LWN	Dec. 23, 1825
Madison	Danielsville	MAD	Dec. 14, 1827
Morgan	Madison		Dec. 10, 1807
Putnam	Eatonton	PUT	Dec. 10, 1807
Troud	La Grange		June 9, 1825
Washington	Sandersville	WSH	Feb. 25, 1784
Whitfield	Dalton		Dec. 30, 1851
Wilkes	Washington	WIL	Feb. 5, 1777
Laurens		LWN	
Troup		TRP	

* Abbreviation of counties on Microfilm Reels and page numbers
for county.

1830 CENSUS GEORGIA. LIST WHITFIELDS.
Microfilm Reel page numbers.

WHITFIELD

WHITFIELD, Alexander	Clk	294
____, Benjamin	Put	190
____, Bryant	Bke	139
____, Bryant	Trp	50
____, Bryant	Wsh	252
____, Elisha	Hab	14
____, George	Col	334
____, George B.	Hst	279
____, Horatio S.	Trp	44
____, James	Jsp	370
____, James E.	Jef	412
____, John S.	Lwn	82
____, Lewis Sr.	Bke	139
____, Lewis	Bke	139

WHITFIELD

____, Martha	Clk	310
____, Mathew	Jsp	384
____, Myles	Wsh	252
____, Reuben	Wsh	244
____, Robert	Clk	311
____, Robert	Wsh	248
____, Thomas	Clk	310
____, Sampson	Cht	268
____, Samuel	Lau	9
____, Silvia	Cht	241
____, William	Bke	139
____, William	Put	190
____, William H.	Doo	89
____, William T.	DeK	40

GEORGE
WHITEFIELD
(1714-1770)

175

GEORGE WHITEFIELD (1714-1770) BIOGRAPHY

Evangelist. Born Gloucester, England Dec. 28, 1714. Son of Thomas and Elizabeth (Edward) Whitefield. Graduated from Oxford Univ. 1736 in England. A M honorary, College of New Jersey at Princeton 1754. George md. Mrs. Elizabeth (Burnell) James Nov. 14, 1741, one child James. She was a widow.

Ordained deacon Anglican Church 1736, priest 1739, preached extensively in England before 1737. He drew great crowds of people. He came to Savannah, GA 1737, preached in Savannah and area; returned to England to raise funds for orphanage in Georgia 1738; found most English churches were closed to him due to opposition, and he preached in the open air.

He returned to America 1739, and became interant preacher from GA to Massachusetts. When he was refused a pulpit in PA, Benjamin Franklin led group to build non-denominational church for him.

Whitefield received 500 acres from Georgia colony to build Bethesda Orphanage, supported by colonial funds. George Whitefield preached all along New England coast 1740-41 and produced a "Great Awakening" in Christianity. He engaged in bitter controversy with John Wesley over Calvinistic principles in England 1741-44. He preached with great success in New England 1744-48. He became domestic chaplain to Countess of Huntingdon, England 1748.

George Whitfield made four more visits to America 1751-52 and 1763-64 and 1769-70. His American trips resulted in numerous conversions to Calvinism and weakening of established church in the South.

Reverend George Whitefield became leader of the Calvinistics Methodists. Whitefield held evangelistic tours in Great Britain and in the America colonies. His last sermon was delivered at Exeter, Massachusetts on Sept. 29, 1770. Whitefield died on Sept. 30, 1770 at Newburyport, Massachusetts where he is buried. He had no children named Whitefield or Whitfield on his own.

Benjamin Whitfield in Putnam Co., GA Will Book A, 1823-1856.
William S. Whitfield in Pulaski Co., GA Wills 1816-1850.
Asa Bradley names dau Martha Whitfield, 1847, Franklin Co, GA.
Thomas Monford has in Will 1821-1823, son-in-law, Samuel Whitfield and dau., Elizabeth Whitfield, Laurens Co., GA.

MARRIAGE BOOK

Putnam Co., GA, Book A 1806-1816. Benjamin Whitfield and Matilda Smith. William B. Traylor and Molsey Whitfield in Book A.
Jackson Co., GA, Book 1806-1860. Marriage of James McClure and Nancy Whitfield.
Laurens Co., GA. Marriages. William Whitfield and Elizabeth Wallace Sept. 17, 1817. Samuel Whitfield and Margaret Outlaw Oct. 13, 1825 md. `
Wills and Marriages were submitted by Mrs. J. D. Goforth of Wichita Falls, TX in May 1977.

Source: Biographical Souvenirs of the States of Georgia and Florida.   Pages 839 and 840, 844.   F. A. Battey and Company, Chicago, IL 1887.

J. H. WHITFIELD, b. Oct. 31, 1849, Thomas Co., GA.

Mr. Whitfield's father and grandfather were both natives of Jefferson Co., GA (planters all their lives). His mother was Miss Virginia Spangler.

J. H. Whitfield was the eldest in a family of ten children, the
   others being:
      T. L. Whitfield
      W. L. Whitfield
      Sarah R. Whitfield, wife of W. S. Bullock
      Fannie E. Whitfield, wife of John Z. Fitzgerald
      E. M. Whitfield
      Julia R. Whitfield, wife of Davis Bullock
      C. S. Whitfield
      Georgia R. Whitfield, wife of J. H. Anderson

In 1879, J. H. Whitfield began railroading, followed this through Georgia to Ocala, FL.

March 1874, married Miss Jennie Deckle, daughter of John W. Deckle, a successful planter of Thomas Co., GA.

J. H. Whitfield belongs to Marion Lodge No. 19, F & A M; Ocala Chapter Royal Arch Masons, No. 13; Harmony Lodge, No. 24, IOOF, and Marion Lodge No. 3378, Knights of Honor.

MATTHEW WHITFIELD of Hancock Co., GA b. Sept. 13, 1789-d. March 23, 1867. He married three wives. Parents of: WILLIAM H. WHITFIELD, married Maria C. Breedlove of Jasper County. Children of William Hurt Whitfield.

1.   Clifton Whitfield
2.   JOHN B. WHITFIELD
3.   Hon. BOLLING WHITFIELD, b. Oct. 21, 1850, Milledgeville, GA
     married 1874, Georgia H. Brown, daughter of Hon. George A.
     Brown of Americus, GA.   She d. Sept. 1885.   Issue: 1-
     Lillian; 2-Essie; 3-Eugene; 4-Lavergne
4.   ROBERT WHITFIELD, b. Oct. 1, 1852, Milledgeville, GA married
     Mary Euphemia Harris, daughter of Judge Charles J. Harris of
     Macon, GA.

Georgia Record.   Benjamin Whitfield b. 1752-d. 1832.   He married (1) Sarah Bryan and (2) Ann Staten.

Georgia Record.   James M. Whitfield born 1824-d. 1874. James married Julia A. _____ born 1823. Georgia Record. They had son Andrew J. Whitfield born 1846.

Georgia Record.   Uriah Burton (1844-1911) married Isabelle S. Devant (1840-1909).

Source: Georgia DAR Historical Collections. Vol. 4
Bible owned by Mrs. Cobb White, Hawkinsville, GA:

MARRIAGES:
James S. Daniels, b. 7-30-1798, d. 1867
   m. 11-10-1842, Elizabeth Wilcox, b. 11-18-1826, d. 1-1810 dau.
   of John Wilcox & Polly Lea,
HENRY H. WHITFIELD, son of George B. & Sarah
   b. 4-11-1826, d. 1-28-1886
   m(1) Elizabeth J. Pipkin, 8-4-1852, who was b. 2-13-1836, d. 5-
   30-1856
   m(2) 1-19-1859, Mary W. Daniels, dau. of James S. & Elizabeth
   b. 1-28-1845, d. 12-10-1907

DEWITT CLINTON WHITFIELD, son of Henry H. & Mary
   b. 5-24-1874, d. 6-13-1915
   m. 8-8-1895, Eva Leila Allen
Howell Cobb White, son of George H. & Emma
   m. 10-9-1895, LETITIA WHITFIELD, b. 7-16-1871
JOHN JAMES WHITFIELD, son of H. H. & Mary, b. 9-29-1865
   m. 8-10-1898, Estella Baynard Willingham, dau. of Thomas H.
John Philetus Doster, son of Andrew J. Doster & Carrie Mims
   m. 11-23-1898, MARY LEE WHITFIELD, b. 8-30-1878, d. 12-10-1907
HENRY H. WHITFIELD, JR., b. 3-15-1881
   m. Bertie Louise Manne, dau. of Henry L. & Mollie

BIRTHS:
AUGUSTUS BRYANT WHITFIELD, b. 9-2-1876, son of Henry H. & Mary
NELIA BELL WHITFIELD, b. 3-18-1883, dau. of Henry H. & Mary
GEORGE WILLIAM, b. 10-17-1854, son of Henry H. & Mary
SARAH ELIZABETH WHITFIELD, b. 12-25-1863, dau. of Henry H. & Mary
JOSEPHINE REBECCA WHITFIELD, b. 11-24-1867, dau. of Henry H. &
Mary
CHARLES HENRY WHITFIELD, b. 7-20-1869, son of Henry H. & Mary

DEATHS:
CHARLES HENRY WHITFIELD, d. 6-14-1870
NELIA BELL WHITFIELD, d. 8-20-1882
SARAH ELIZABETH WHITFIELD, d. 11-8-1890
AUGUSTUS B. WHITFIELD, d. 9-30-1900

End of Genealogy.

Record from Hawkinsville, GA: Henry H. Whitfield, son of George
B. and Sarah Whitfield was b. Apr. 11, 1826 and d. Jan. 28, 1886.
He married first wife, Elizabeth J. Pipkin, Aug. 4, 1852, and she
was b. Feb. 13, 1836; d. May 30, 1856.

The child, George William Whitfield, b. Oct. 17, 1854. Henry H.
Whitfield md. second wife, Mary W. Daniels on Jan. 19, 1859. She
was the dau. of James S. and Elizabeth Daniels. Mary W. Daniels
Whitfield was b. Jan. 28, 1845, and d. Dec 10, 1907, GA. The
children (1) Dewitt Clinton Whitfield, b. May 24, 1874, d. June
13, 1915. He married Aug. 8, 1895 Eva Leila Allen.(2) John James
Whitfield (3) Augustus Bryant Whitfield (4) Nelia Bell Whitfield.

GEORGIA RECORDS AND LETTERS

GEORGE B. WHITFIELD is between the ages of 30/40 on the 1830 census of Houston Co., GA with a female age 10/15.

Susanna Shurley Whitfield was born about 1815 in Georgia. Volume I, Virginia Colonial Abstracts lists a number of children born to Richard, John, Thomas and Daniel, and Martha Shurley.
....Submitted by Phyllis Farris of Plain Dealing, LA in August 1992.

RAY WHITFIELD, son of Elisha and Zilpha, grandson of William, great-grandson of Thomas (1721-1781) on Habersham Co., GA censuses.
1840 Census. Ray Whitfield, Malissa, spelled "Melifair."
1850 Census with two sons, four daughters.
1860 Census. Ray, age 49. "Matifac," age 48. Father-farming with four sons, 24-3 and four daughters, 20-6.
Malissa for Melissa and various spellings.

"The Whitfield I am looking for is James E. Whitfield, born Feb. 27, 1790, parents and birth place unknown. He married Sarah M. Blackmon, April 16, 1815 in Jefferson Co., GA. He died Apr. 11, 1858 in Thomas Co., GA."
Submitted July 27, 1987, M. A. Clemens of Brandon FL.

Ray Whitfield born NC moved to GA and has a family born in Georgia. Family was at Habersham Co., GA in 1850 and 1860 but family members at Tennessee, Arkansas, and other places after 1870.

Ancestor of Donnie (Eades) Pickard living in 1993 in Kokomo, IN.

Submitted the family tree typed on computer and numbered family Group Record 238, Jan. 1993.

WHITFIELD FAMILY TREE

Ray Whitfield b. 1813 ca., North Carolina. Ray died between 1860 and 1870. GA or TN. (Number 1488). Ray married Malissa _____ born 1812, NC. Ray and Malissa Whitfield had children:
1. Girl Whitfield born 1835, Georgia
2. Berry Whitfield born 1836, Georgia
3. Calvin J. Whitfield born 1838, Georgia
4. Mary (Polly) A. Whitfield born 1840, Georgia
5. T. Whitfield born 1843, Georgia
6. Hannah Joseph Whitfield born March 15, 1846, Habersham County, GA: Hannah Whitfield m. Mr. _____ Dunn. Hannah Whitfield Dunn d. Oct. 10, 1918, Clark Co., AR, and buried at Rose Hill Cemetery.
7. Julia Whitfield born 1848, GA
8. William W. Whitfield b. Feb. 26, 1851, GA. He md. Missouri Frances Lockard on Nov. 24, 1869 in Monroe Co., TN. William W. Whitfield died Mar. 2, 1904 in Van Buren Co., AR and was buried in Foster Cemetery in Van Buren Co. William W. Whitfield and

Missouri F. Lockard had a son named Joseph W. Whitfield and he died at age twenty-nine, and buried in Brown Springs, AR. Joseph's wife was Dora Mary Burk, and their son was Truman Arthur Whitfield, Sr. His wife was Sarah Derenda Byrd. Truman was born in Scotland, AR in 1904. Truman had son, Harlen Dewayne Whitfield b. May 4, 1935. In 1994 Harlen resided in Cyril, OK.

9.   Marion Francis Whitfield b. 1853, GA. Marion Whitfield married Sarah Jane Cate on Dec. 12, 1878 in McMinn Co., TN. Marion had another marriage.

10.   Harriet C. Whitfield b. Jan. 11, 1854, GA. Harriet married Joseph Minyard on Dec. 17, 1873 in Monroe, TN. Harriet Whitfield Minyard d. Sept. 6, 1933 in Clark Co., AR; and buried at Jones Cemetery of Clark Co., AR.

11.   Tina Whitfield was b. 1860 in TN.

12.   Malissa Whitfield was b. 1862 in TN.

13.   Jane Whitfield was b. 1868 in TN.

The children of Ray Whitfield and Malissa were born in Habersham Co. GA.

This Whitfield lineage is the father's side for ancetral line of Whitfield, and of the family tree of Donnie Pickard of Kokomo, IN who submitted two lines of the family on Jan. 20, 1993. On his mother's side the family surname is Grady. Donnie is from ancestor William Whitfield who married Elizabeth Whitfield. John Grady married their daughter Mary Whitfield in 1733 at Windsor, Bertie Co., NC. John Grady was b. 1710 in Chowan Co., NC and John d. Mar. 12, 1787 in Albertson, Duplin Co., NC. John Grady's parents were William Grady and Anne Barfield. The wife, Mary Whitfield was b. 1715 and d. Dec. 20, 1781 in Albertson, Duplin Co., NC.

John and Mary Grady of NC had 11 children (five boys and six girls). Grady family is published in the book JOHN GRADY OF DUPLIN COUNTY, NORTH CAROLINA.

Reuben Whitfield d. 1856 at Pulaski, GA. Will Book 12.
Charles Henry Whitfield died June 14, 1870, Dooley Co., GA.

Charles P. N. Whitfield born in Washington Co., GA. Charles married Mary Adeline Hicks, and served in the Civil War and was killed in 1861 or 1862. A son, Reuben Henry Whitfield was born in Dooley Co., GA. Descendant is Gene T. Bell of Orlando, FL. Napoleon Whitfield of Georgia married in 1847 to Martha Hicks.

Georgia record: Bryant Whitfield, soldier, of Bryant's District and Nancy Whitfield, William's widow, of Roe's District drew in the 1832 Land Lottery.

Georgia Record. William Whitfield (1800-1830) m. Nancy Fryer (1800-1832). Children: 1. Benjamin Elbert Hill b. 1828 was m. to Rhoda Hill b. 1832. They had four sons and five daughters. A son was George M. T. Whitfield (1820-1900) who was married twice. (1) wife had no children. (2) wife had four sons and three daughters. The son and grandchildren of Lewis Whitfield, Sr. (1756-d. 1832). Burke Co., GA.

180

WHITFIELD - BURKE COUNTY, GEORGIA

Lewis Whitfield, Sr. was born 1750's in North Carolina, the son of Luke Whitfield and wife. He lived and died 1832 in Burke Co., Ga. Lewis Whitfield, Sr. married and had children: (1) 1. Bryant Whitfield b. 1780-d. 1830 GA. 2. Girl b. 1791-d. 1828. She married Elisha Coleman (b. 1789-d. 1860). 3. Lewis Whitfield, Jr. b. 1800 GA-d. 1859 Burke Co., GA.

Lewis Whitfield, Sr. first land grant was in 1786 Georgia. On the 1798 tax list Lewis owned 565 acres. (2). Lewis is on the 1820, 1830 censuses of Burke Co., GA.

Lewis Whitfield, Jr. was born 1800 GA-d. 1859. He lived and died in Burke Co., GA. Lewis was married to Jane _____ born 1798-d. 1860 GA. (3) children. (4) 1. James M. Whitfield b. 1824-d. 1874. James married Julia A. _____ b. 1823. Their son was Andrew J. Whitfield b. 1846. James is buried at Old Church between Waynesboro and Alexander, GA. 2. Mary Whitfield b. 1825-d. 1846 GA. Mary married Dexter Burton b. 1810-d. 1848. They had five children. 3. Bryant Whitfield b. 1836-1874. Bryant's wife was Helen Nancy Whitfield b. 1838-d. 1889. Unmarried.

Lewis Whitfield, Jr. wrote his Will and signed it on July 26, 1856. The Will was probated in 1859 (5). Franklin, Zechariah, Uriah, Mary Mozelle, Ella Fair. Lewis's Will included the names of his five Burton grandchildren.

Lewis Whitfield is on the 1850 Census, Burke Co., GA. (6)

From Georgia State Lewis Whitfield, Jr. received land grants 115 acres in 1845 and 283 acres in 1850. (7)

Reference:
1. Descendancy Chart of Robert Burton of Gainesville, FL, May 7, 1997. Submitted by Jake Cook of Statham, GA on May 17, 1997.
2. Burke Co., GA, 63rd District, Deed Books Surveyor General Office, State Archives, Atlanta, Georgia: Book KKK 1786, p. 431. (200 acres). Book SSS 1789, p. 198. (76 acres). Book YYYY 1796 p. 130 (125 acres). Book K 1815 p. 259 (34 acres).
3. Maiden name of Jane, wife of Lewis Whitfield, Jr. has not been proven. The name is Jane Whitefield, or Jane Darley, or another name.
4. Ibid. Same as number 1. Reference.
5. Burke Co., GA. Will Book A, pages 142-3.
6. 1850 Census Burke Co., GA. Lewis Whitfield, Jr. has varied spellings for first names. Louis is Lewis. Briant is Bryant. Elatara Burton is Ella Fair Burton.
7. Burke Co., GA Deed Books, State Archives. Book V-5 1845 p. 408. Book X-5 1850, p. 177.

Georgia Record. Bryant W. Whitfield (1836-1893) married (1) Helen born 1830 and (2) Rebecca Bonnell born 1831. Helen Whitfield had daughter Florida Whitfield born 1858. Rebecca Whitfield had sons Samson Whitfield born 1861 and Thomas Whitfield born 1866.

BIRTHS OF ALABAMA AND GEORGIA

Births in the Family Groups prepared by Gene T. Bell of Orlando, FL.

1-Charles P. N. WHITFIELD b. [1823]
  Mary Adeline HICKS b. [1827]
2-Ruben Henry WHITFIELD b. Oct. 20, 1849 Dooley Co., GA
  Catherine Bethney FAULK b. Mar. 18, 1844 Coosa Co., AL
3-Amelia Alice WHITFIELD b. Dec. 3, 1869, GA
  John HUDSON b. [1869]
3-Charles Ransom WHITFIELD b. Dec. 11, 1871, Ga
  Emma WILLIAMS b. 1871
3-Laurinda WHITFIELD b. Mar. 21, 1874, GA
  John B. NORWOOD b. June 19, 1878 Goodman, Cofee Co., AL
4-Anna Lee NORWOOD b. July 11, 1900 Dundee, Geneva, AL
4-Lucinda NORWOOD b. Aug. 4, 1903 Geneva Co., AL
  Loyce Zack BELL b. May 6, 1898 Geneva Co., AL
  Dewey Commodore NORWOOD b. Nov. 27, 1908 Bascoma Jackson, FL
  John Marion WHITFIELD b. Mar. 14, 1876, GA
  Maggie E. WARD b. [1876]
  George Ann WHITFIELD b. Nov. 21, 1878, GA
  Reneger KEMBRO b. [1878]
3-Martha Jane WHITFIELD b. Oct. 18, 1881 Skipperville, Dale, AL
  William HARDY b. [1881]
3-Mary Adeline WHITFIELD b. July 18, 1885 Skipperville, Dale, AL
  John Henry KEMBRO b. [1885]
3-Susan Agusta WHITFIELD b. July 18, 1889 Dundee, Geneva, AL
  Bertha MITCHELL b. [1849]

RECORD

James E. Whitfield b. Feb. 27, 1790, and d. Apr. 11, 1858 in Thomas Co., GA. James E. Whitfield m. Sarah M. Blackmond Apr. 16, 1815 in Jefferson Co., GA.
.....Submitted by M. A. Clemens in July 1987, Brandon, FL.

2600 Revolutionary Soldiers drew in Georgia Lottery.
Lewis Whitfield of Burke Co., GA received a land grant.
Lewis Whitfield in 1827 drew Lee Co., GA and granted land in Aug. 1830.

Georgia Record. George M. T. Whitfield (1829-1900). George married (1) Catharine ? Born 1830 and (2) Ann ? (1824-1890). Children: 1. Mina Whitfield, b. 1854; 2. Erastus Whitfield (1855-1896); 3. Silas Whitfield (1857-1920), Silas married Elmina B. ____ (1872-1948); 4. Annie E. Whitfield, born 1860; 5. Jefferson D. Whitfield (1861-1864); 6. Ann Elette Whitfield born 1866; and 7. William A. Whitfield (1868-1941). William married Elmina B. ____ (1872-1948) and Linnie ____ born 1837.

Pedigree Chart

Mark (X) boxes when ordinances are completed.

C = Children's ordinances completed (Mark [X]
    this box when all ordinances are completed
    for all children of this couple.)

F = Family group record (Mark [X] this box
    when this person appears on a
    family group record as a parent.)

B = Baptized
E = Endowed
S = Sealed to spouse
P = Sealed to parents

8 Zacharia BELL
(Father of #4) B E S P F C
Born/Chr 24 Dec. 1843
Place Geneva Co., Al
Married 29 Sept. 1867
Place
Died 27 Jan. 1924
Place Geneva Co., Al

9 Rodha Emaline DAVIS
(Mother of #4) B E S P F C
Born/Chr 18 Mch 1844
Place Geneva Co., Al
Died 18 Jan 1926
Place Geneva Co., Al

4 John D. Bell
(Father of #2) B E S P F C
Born/Chr 13 Sept. 1868
Place Geneva Co., Al
Married 24 Jan. 1889
Place
Died 30 Mch 1961
Place Geneva Co., Al

2 Loyce Zack BELL
(Father of #1) B E S P F C
Born/Chr 6 May 1898
Place Geneva Co., Al
Married 3 Dec 1921
Place Sanford, Seminole, Fl
Died 8 July 1967
Place Cross City, Dixie. Fl

Vivian M
PURSLEY
(Spouse of #1)

5 Carrie TATE
(Mother of #2) B E S P F C
Born/Chr 31 Aug 1868
Place Barber Co., Al
Died 18 Mch 1941
Place Fadette, Geneva, Al

10 James F. TATE
(Father of #5) B E S P F C
Born/Chr
Place
Married 12 April 1857
Place
Died
Place

11 Sarah Jane HALL

1 Gene Tunney BELL
B E S P F C
Born/Chr 26 Jul 1927
Place Orlando, Orange, Fl
Married 9 Jan 1950
Place Orlando, Orange, Fl

6 John B. NORWOOD
(Father of #3) B E S P F C
Born/Chr 19 Jun 1878
Place Goodman, Coffee, Al
Married 17 Aug 1899
Place Geneva Co., Al
Died 20 July 1952
Place Orlando, Orange, Fl

12 Daniel R. NORWOOD
(Father of #6) B E S P F C
Born/Chr
Place Coffee Co, Al
Married
Place
Died
Place

13 Elizabeth (LIZA) HURT
(Mother of #6) B E S P F C
Born/Chr
Place
Died
Place

3 Lucinda NORWOOD
(Mother of #1) B E S P F C
Born/Chr 4 Aug 1903
Place Geneva Co., Al
Died 14 Apr 1964
Place Slocomb, Geneva, Al

7 Laurinda WHITFIELD *
(Mother of #3) B E S P F C
Born/Chr 21 Mch 1874
Place   GA
Died 8 Mch 1942
Place Geneva Co., Al

14 Ruben Henry WHITFIELD
(Father of #7) B E S P F C
Born/Chr 20 Oct 1849
Place Dooley Co., Al
Married 8 Jan 1869
Place
Died 7 Dec 1935
Place Panama City, Bay, Fl

15 Catharine FAULK
(Mother of #7) B E S P F C
Born/Chr 18 Mch 1844
Place Coosa Co., Al
Died 2 Aug 1910
Place Geneva Co., Al

Person Submitting Pedigree Chart
Name
GENE T. BELL

193

CHRONOLOGY

JOHN WILKINS WHITFIELD

Resident: Tennessee, Missouri, Kansas, Texas.   Tennessee

1818 — Born on March 11, 1818. Son of Wilkins Whitfield and Polly Mary Whitfield of Franklin, Tennessee of Williamson County.

1824-1835 — John was educated on the plantation of his parents and at the local school of Franklin.

1836 — John moved to Centerville of Hickman County, TN. He joined the Hickory Guard Militia on Natchez Road.

1836 — John was a clerk in Robert Charter Mercantile Store. He also assisted with planting on the Charter farm.

1839 — John Whitfield married Catharine Dansby on April 13th. She died in 1846 at Centerville, TN. Issue, one daughter.

Texas

1846 — John was Captain of Hickory Guards which became Company A, First Tennessee Regiment. Volunteer Foot Soldiers of the Mexican War.

John's militia company reached New Orleans on June 15th. Company was in Texas June 20th to July 20th. Soldiers with dysentery disease and company discharge on July 23rd.

Mexico — October and November 1846 Whitfield was at Camp Allen in Mexico. 1847 he was with his Company.

1848 — On July 24th John Whitfield was mustered out of service in the Mexican War.

Tennessee

1848 — First Hickman County Court case, John is a juror. He was juror in three other law cases.

1849 — John Whitfield was in the 28th General Assembly of the State of Tennessee and was in the Tennessee Senate. He was a congressman from 1849 to 1852.

1851 — He was appointed major general of the Third Division of the State Militia.

1852 — He had duties as master and clerk of the Hickman County Chancery Court.

1853 — John W. Whitfield married Sarah B. Dibrell on May 28th, Nashville, TN. Sarah was born December 11, 1827, and she died April 26, 1918 in Texas.

Missouri
1853   John moved from Tennessee to Independence, Missouri, to be Agent to Pottawatomies Indians.

Kansas
1854   John crossed to Kansas in the spring. On December 5th John Wilkins Whitfield was declared by the Governor to be duly elected Delegate to the 33rd Congress, the House of Representatives of the United States.

1855   John Whitfield lived at Leavenworth, Kansas. He was an Agent from 1855 to 1856 to Arkansas Indians and in charge of Upper Agency.

            Political philosophies made public with residents of Kansas territory. They were pro-slavery party , free state party, John Brown and Sons, Law and Order Society.

1856   John Whitfield served as Democrat from December 20th, 1854, to August 1, 1856. He was elected to the 34th Congress of the United States from Kansas. In the spring, he became General of Amry Troops in Kansas. He had a duty to protect the treaties the United States had with the Indians and land holdings. Needless conflict of Kansas kept him in the army camp most of the time.

1857   Kansas is with statehood. John Whitfield in the 34th Congress of the United States served until March 3, 1857. John Whitfield was given the duty to register land grants at the office in Doniphan, KS. He served from 1857 to 1861 as Registrar.

1859   Sarah B. Dibrell Whitfield and her son, Anthony Whitfield arrived in Lavaca County, Texas. Her husband had received land grant in Texas for service in the Mexican war. At Kansas John Whitfield hears the speech of a visiting President Abraham Lincoln.

1861   John began his military career in the Confederate Army. Kansas under Wyandotte Constitution is admitted into the Union as the 34th State of the United States.

            John was in the Creek Indian battle on north side of Arkansas. In December 1861 Trans-Mississippi armies of the west of the Confederacy had sixteen regiments. John had enlisted a Company near Petersburg.

Texas
1862   The 27th Texas Cavalry of the Confederate Army became known as Whitfield's Legion. It mounted in the fall of 1862 and dismounted and was sent to reinforce an Army at Corinth, Mississippi. John promoted to Major rank while with the fourth battalion.

KENTUCKY RECORDS

Descendants of William Whitfield (born 1688 England-died NC) and Elizabeth Goodman.

JOSEPH WHITFIELD. Descend of William, William, William. He was born in North Carolina. Joseph married Mary Grady, May 2, 1790. He went to Christian County, KY. Joseph Whitfield died 1835. Children:

1. Joseph Whitfield
2. William Whitfield
3. Bryan Whitfield
4. Henry Whitfield
5. Rachel Whitfield
6. John Whitfield
7. Timothy Whitfield
8. Elizabeth Whitfield
9. Hester Whitfield
10. Sarah Whitfield
11. Charity Whitfield and she married ____ Loftin.

BRYAN WATKINS WHITFIELD. Descend of Bryan, Bryan, Nathan, Bryan, William, William. Bryan Watkins Whitfield was born Oct. 16, 1902, in Franklin County, AL. He married Sept. 10, 1924, in Harlan, KY, to Florence Clay Carter. Bryan was living 1948 in Brookside, Harlan County, KY. He was with Harlan Collieries Company. Children: 1. Bryan Watkins Whitfield born July 7, 1925; 2. Amme Keayes Whitfield born Jan. 9, 1928; and 3. John Carter Whitfield born May 17, 1930.

"Mary Whitfield of Duplin County, NC, md. Buckner Killebrew. In 1796 they moved to Christian County, KY. They had lived in Edgecombe County, NC, before moving to Kentucky. Killebrew families have many descendants in Kentucky and other places."

"Mary Whitifled and Buckner Killebrew had children. A son was Whitfield Killebrew. His daughter was Martha Pleasant Radford, and she had a son named William Whitfield Radford. His sister, Georgia Ann Radford, was mother to my great-grandfather William Whitfield Link."

....Submitted by Kathy Colson of Franklin, Simpson, County, KY, on November 5, 1991.

It was Christian Territory land in 1776. From this territory were formed two counties - Christian County, Kentucky, and Montgomery County, Tennessee. Both counties are on borders of the two states.

B.W. WHITFIELD, Jr. of Brookside, Harlan County, KY, has been a person with others that have produced works on a pedigree of the Whitfield lineage in England that links a man named William Whitfield born 1688 in England and sailed his own ship to the colony North Carolina about 1710 and made his home in America. In 1976 B.W. Whitfield, Jr. was living in Kentucky. B.W. is Bryan Watkins Whitfield.

Herman Whitfield, Nancy J. Whitfield, Pattie Whitfield, William Whitfield, Sr., William Whitfield, Jr. are listed in the Kentucky Genealogical Index, Volume One. Issues of Magazines compilation by Glenda K. Trapp and Michael L. Cook of the Company publications.

1846 - 1847 MEDICAL STUDENTS

MEDICAL INSTITUE , LOUISVILLE, KENTUCKY

Names.	Residence.	Preceptors.
Peyton, Craven	Tennessee,	Frayser & Shanks.
Phillips, T. A.	Mississippi,	J. W. Phillips, M. D.
Phipps, H.	Kentucky,	S. O. Peyton, M. D.
Pickens, A. G.	Alabama,	Newman & Robinson
Pilant, E. T.	Tennessee,	G. Drauban, M. D.
Poor, R. A.	Kentucky,	W. K. Bowling, M. D.
Porter, W. S.	Tennessee,	
Postlethwaite, Wm.	Kentucky.	F. Johnston, M. D.
Poynor, A. B.	Tennessee,	D. B. Cliffe, M. D.
Priest, Wm.	Missouri,	D. H. Davis, M. D.
Proctor, W. G.	Kentucky,	Prof. Gross.
Pugh, D. M.	Mississippi,	Pugh & Ewing.
Pyles, Madison	Kentucky,	Talbot & Wakefield.
Ramsay, M. C.	Indiana,	J. H. D. Rogers, M. D.
Randolph, Peter	Tennessee,	G. Thompson, M. D.
Ransom. M.	Tennessee,	S. B. Robinson, M. D.
Reber, Wm.	Mississippi,	S. C. Farrar, M. D.
Rees, W. T.	Kentucky,	F. Rees, M. D.
Reynolds, R. E.	Alabama,	J. E. Lewis, M. D.
Rice, H. H.	Kentucky,	F. A. Rice, M. D.
Richardson, T. G.	Kentucky,	Prof. Gross.
Richards, W. L.	Kentucky,	J. R. Buck, M. D.
Riffe, John M.	Kentucky,	Dr. W. Ray.
Rives, L.	Ohio,	L. C. Rives, M. D.
Roberts, S. P.	Mississippi,	J. L. M'Cool, M. D.
Robinson, G., M. D.	Kentucky.	
Rockett, J. B.	Mississippi,	Dr. T. T. Armstrong.
Rogers, W. E.	Tennessee,	Dr. E. Haywood.
Rowlett, Augustus	Mississippi	B. B. Buchanan, M. D.
Royster, C. G.	Tennessee.	Bayless, Buck, &
Russell, W. S.	New York.	Colescott.
Sanders, H. J.	Louisiana,	J. R. Buck, M. D.
Scruggs, J. H.	Mississippi,	Scruggs & Hodges.
Scruggs, R. L.	Tennessee.	Frayser & Shanks.
Sebastian, J. P.	Tennessee,	Dr. S. B. Moore.
Selman, Thomas	Mississippi,	Practitioner.
Sevier, B. B.	Alabama,	Dr. S. Sevier.
Shackleford, Edmund	Kentucky,	Hardin & White.
Sharman, E. L.	Mississippi,	E. W. Jones, M. D.
Shapard, J. C.	Tennessee,	J. Fitzpatrick, M. D.
Sinex, W. G.	Indiana,	H. M. Darling, M. D.
Sisson, Nelson B.	Ohio,	Morgan & Town.
Sinck, W. H.	Kentucky,	J. H. Johnson, M. D.
Smith, J. H.	Alabama,	D. Keller, M. D.
Smith, B. M. E.	Tennessee,	Dr. A. Hunn.
Smith, A. E. L.	Indiana,	J. Sloan, M. D.
Smith, W. E.	Mississippi,	Smith & Wendel.
Snelson, J. B.	Missouri,	Practitioner.
Spitler, A.	Virginia,	Pinnel & Bland.
Stage, W. B.	Pennsylvania,	L. Kinsloe, M. D.
St. Clair, A. S.	Kentucky,	Prof. Cobb.
Steele, J. Rowan	Kentucky,	Talbot & Wakefield.
Steele, R. W.	Kentucky	Dr. T. H. Gaines.
Steger, F. E. H.	Alabama,	Newman & Robinson.
Stephens, B. L.	Kentucky,	Nuckols & Knight.
Storts, Hervey	Kentucky,	
Stringfellow, William,	Alabama,	Practitioner.
Stroud, T. B.	Tennessee,	L. N. M. Cooke, M. D.
Sugg, E. C., M. D.	Indiana.	
Sullivan, O. B.	Alabama,	P. Houston, M. D.
Sullivan, H. N.	Tennessee,	Dr. J. S. M'Lean.
Summers, A. E.	Virginia,	S. Patrick, M. D.
Sumner, G. B.	Tennessee,	T. R. Jennings, M. D.
Taliaferro, G.	Tennessee,	Dr. E. Haywood.
Taylor, J. G.	Kentucky,	J. D. Winston, M. D.
Thomas, M. L.	Indiana,	J. H. D. Rogers, M. D.
Thomas, N. C.	Kentucky,	J. M. Flint, M. D.
Thomas, J. B.	Kentucky,	W. Thomas, M. D.
Thomas, A. E.	Mississippi,	G. Banks, M. D.
Thompson, Dickson	Texas,	J. Wilder, M. D.
Torrey, J. L.	Mississippi.	Practitioner.
Trimble, J. A., M. D.	Alabama,	
Tucker, J. S.	Tennessee,	J. T. Richardson, M. D.
Turner, J. S.	Kentucky,	J. M. Harris, M. D.
Wall, J. T.	Kentucky,	A. Addams, M. D.
Walling, G. H.	Kentucky,	Talbot & Wakefield.
Ward, T. W.	Mississippi.	J. K. Ward, M. D.
Ward, R. G.	Kentucky,	J. J. Taylor, M. D.
Ware, Richard	Kentucky,	H. Hopson, M. D.
Warfield, T. N.	Kentucky,	Bayless, Buck, & Colescott.
Washington, W. B	Tennessee,	A. B. Washington, M. D.
Wasson, L. M.	Tennessee,	B. W. Avent, M. D.
Wendel, B. F.	Kentucky,	Prof. Yandell.
Westbrook, R. A.	Tennessee.	
Westbrook, E. E.	Tennessee,	J. H. B. Westbrook, M. D.
Whitfield, J. M.	Tennessee,	McPhail & Cliffe.
Wilkins, M. M.	Mississippi.	
Willingham, R. S.	Alabama,	F. J. C. Heizen, M. D.
Wilson, W. H.	Tennessee,	J. H. Charlton, M. D.
Winsor, W. T.	Missouri,	W. P. Boulware, M. D.
Withers, J. V.	Kentucky,	Dr. J. Lloyd.
Wood, R. L.	Missouri,	Wm. B. Wood, M. D.
Woods, P. C., M. D.	Mississippi.	
Woods, D. H.	Tennessee,	W. P. Goodwin, M. D.
Wright, John	Tennessee,	J. M. Head, M. D.
Yandell, D. W.	Kentucky,	Prof. Yandell.
Young, A. G.	Tennessee,	J. Y. Young, M. D.
Zimmerman, R. P.	Missouri,	
Zimmerman, Philip	Alabama.	C. C. Billingslea, M. D.

TOTAL—Kentucky 98; Tennessee 91; Mississippi 54; Alabama 35; Missouri 19; Indiana 16; Virginia 8; Ohio 4; Arkansas 4; Georgia 4; Louisiana 3; Iowa 3; Texas 2; Pennsylvania 1; Prussia 1; Illinois 1; Connecticut 1.—345.

J. COBB, M. D., *Dean, &c.*

Reference Periodical.
Ninth Annual Catalogue Of The Medical Institute Of Louisville. Session 1845-1846, And Circular For The Ensuring Session 1846-1847. Published by Prentice And Weissingee, Louisville, Kentucky, 1846.

PEDIGREE CHART

NAME

VIRGINIA WHITEFIELD JOHNSON

STREET ADDRESS OF P.O.

(NORTH MERIDIAN)

CITY, STATE, ZIP CODE

MERIDIAN IDAHO 83642

1 (W)HITFIELD BRYAN

BORN ABOUT 1804
WHERE DUPLINCO, N.C.
WHEN MARRIED
DIED 6 DEC. 1863
WHERE

NAME OF HUSBAND OR WIFE

GRADY SERENA

2 WHITFIELD JOSEPH

BORN ABOUT 1770
WHERE DUPLINCO N.C.
WHEN MARRIED 1 MAY 1790
DIED 17 APRIL 1853
WHERE

3 GRADY MARY

BORN ABOUT 1772
WHERE DUPLINCO N.C.
DIED

4 WHITFIELD WILLIAM JR.

BORN 1 JUNE 1743
WHERE ROCKFORD, N.C.
WHEN MARRIED 1763
DIED MARCH 1817
WHERE

5 WILLIAMS HESTER

BORN ABOUT 1735
WHERE ROCKFORD, N.C.
DIED
WHERE

6

BORN
WHERE
WHEN MARRIED
DIED
WHERE

7.

BORN
WHERE
DIED
WHERE

8 WHITFIELD WILLIAM

BORN 20 MAY 1715
WHERE VIRGINIA OR N.C.
WHEN MARRIED 6 NOV. 1741
DIED 31 MARCH 1795

214

PEDIGREE CHART

8 WHITFIELD JOHNNY JAYBO
BORN / DEC. 1860
WHERE NORTONVILLE, HOPKINS, KY.
MARRIED 6 JAN. 1884
DIED 6 DEC. 1950
WHERE

9 DILLINGHAM ELIZABETH JANE
BORN 22 DEC., 1862
WHERE
DIED / JAN. 1929
WHERE

WHITFIELD LEWIS B. CONTINUED ON CHART.
17 JAN. 1818 BORN
DIED 14 JAN. 1884
OUTLAW CHARITY
BORN MAY, 1813 CONTINUED ON CHART.
DIED 10 APRIL, 1871

4 WHITFIELD HANNABLE JE
BORN 3 OCT. 1902
WHERE NORTONVILLE HOPKINS, KY.
WHEN MARRIED 17 SEPT, 1920
DIED 23 JULY 1979
WHERE HOPKINSVILLE, CHRISTIAN, KY

5 RAY, CARRIE MAE
BORN .19 JUNE 1903
WHERE PRINCETON CALDWELL KY.
DIED
WHERE

2 WHITFIELD WILL ROGERS
BORN 20 JUNE 1929
WHERE MANNINGTON, CHRISTIAN,
WHEN MARRIED 30 AUGUST 1948 (div)
DIED 25 MAY 1971
WHERE HOPKINSVILLE, CHRISTIAN,

1 WHITFIELD VIRGINIA RAY
BORN 4 JUNE 1949
WHERE HOPKINSVILLE, CHRISTIAN, KY.
WHEN MARRIED 23 OCTOBER, 1973
WHERE
JOHNSON DAVID CHRISTOPHER

3 HACKNEY MARGARET MURRELL
BORN 21 SEPT. 1930
WHERE HOPKINSVILLE CHRISTIAN, KY.
DIED
WHERE

KENTUCKY
Family Group Submitted In 1982 By

VIRGINIA JOHNSON
NAME
N. MERIDIAN
STREET ADDRESS OR P.O.
MERIDIAN IDAHO 83642
CITY, STATE, ZIP CODE

215

WHITFIELD LIVING RESIDENTS IN 1980 AT LOUISVILLE, KENTUCKY.
Inclusive of white race and black race.

Name, Street Address   Telephone Number, Post Office Zip

Whitfield Bob Jr 4505 Estate Dr ———————— 363-2252   —40216
Whitfield C L 403 Marshall Wk ———————— 361-0741
Whitfield Clara 2719 Howard ———————— 776-2061   ———— 40211
Whitfield David W 502 Running Creek Pl ——— 245-0173 —40243
Whitfield Debra 3810 Young Av ———————— 774-1594   —40211
Whitfield E E 3502 Capri Dr ———————— 451-2354
Whitfield Edgar H 308 Freeman Av ———————— 366-1247
Whitfield Emmitt 421 S 28th ———————— 774-5458
Whitfield F S 705 Denmark ———————— 366-6541
Whitfield Freda 4119 Hillview Av ———————— 449-1459   ———— 40216
Whitfield G A 1032 E Kentucky ———————— 634-0972   — 40204
Whitfield Hattie 431 S 32nd ———————— 776-8003
Whitfield Jacquelyn 10612 Hume Ct ———————— 933-0773 ———— 40272
Whitfield James 5808 Montfort Ln ———————— 241-7247
Whitfield Jerry H 4021 Druid Hills Rd ——— 896-0275   — 40207
Whitfield John 3606 Garind Av ———————— 778-7886
Whitfield Josie 3374 Young Av ———————— 778-6303   — 40211
                                                       40211

Whitfield Latonya 1816 Wenatchee Pl ———— 776-6449
Whitfield Leslie 1805 Cypress ———————— 772-9751
Whitfield Lucile 630 S 41st ———————— 774-8856   — 4050
Whitfield Maggie J 101 S Longworth Av ——— 778-3960   —— 40212
Whitfield Marcia 343 Glendora Av ———————— 776-0900   — 40212
Whitfield Nellie Armstrong Mrs
   924 Cecil Av ———————— 778-1583   40211
Whitfield R A 1120 Viewcrest Dr ———————— 366-0738
Whitfield Robert 4137 Larkwood Av ———————— 772-7914
Whitfield Robert A 953 Whetstone Way ——— 245-7562   — 40223
Whitfield Robert B 2011 Foxhrst Dr ———————— 447-1627 —— 40216
Whitfield Robert L 4126 Larkwood Av ——— 774-8116   — 40212
Whitfield Sammie L
   4122 Muhammad Ali Blvd ———————— 772-9722   — 40215
Whitfield Sharon F 3611 Georgetown Pl ——— 368-7501
Whitfield W E 3929 Staebir Av ———————— 895-2704   — 40207

"Mary Whitfield of Duplin County, North Carolina, married Buckner Killebrew. In 1796 they moved to Christian County, Kentucky. Mary had a son named Whitfield Killebrew, and his daughter Martha Pleasant Radford had a son named William Whitfield Radford. William's sister, Georgia Ann, was mother to my great-grandfather William Whitfield Link."

....Submitted by Kay Carlson of Franklin, KY, in November 1991.

In the old Kentucky entries and deeds there were two Military Warrants. Edward Whitfield, 100 acres. Warrant Number 3024 to a three-year soldier in Virginia line April 27, 1784.

Haynes Whitfield, 100 acres. Warrant Number 1954 to a three-year soldier in Virginia navy, November 22, 1783.

Neither Edward Whitfield nor Haynes Whitfield moved on the land granted to them. Edward Whitfield died in the Revolutionary War. Haynes Whitfield continued to serve in the navy and must have died a young man.

Herman Whitfield, Nancy J. Whitfield, Pattie Whitfield, William Whitfield, Sr., William Whitfield, Jr. are listed in the Kentucky Genealogical Index, Volume One. Issues of Magazines compilation by Glenda K., Trapp and Michael L. Cook of the Company publications.

_____

California Record.
Martinez, Concord, Danville, Pleasant Hill, Walnut Creek are towns of Contra Costa County, California in 1990. Whitfield residents living in these towns in the County were Bob and Genie Whitfield, David Whitfield, James David Whitfield, Gary C. Whitfield, I. Whitfield, Joe and Kay Whitfield, College Professor, N. H. Whitfield, an African American, R. Whitfield, Robert and Vallie Jo Whitfield, Roy R. Whitfield, Roy W. Whitfield.

KENTUCKY

ANCIENT BURIED CITY near Wickliffe Prehistoric artifacts, mounds and museum.

BARDSTOWN My Old Kentucky Home, plantation manor immortalized in song by Stephen Foster. Daily, 60c. Nearby is Wickland, home of three Kentucky governors.

CUMBERLAND GAP Historic gateway through Cumberland Mountains. Toll road up spectacular Pinnacle Mountain.

FORT KNOX Training center for armored forces. U.S. Gold Depository houses the world's greatest fortune. Patton Museum, memorabilia from World War II.

FRANKFORT State Capitol building and near-by Old State Capitol open weekdays. Daniel Boone's grave is in Frankfort's cemetery. Jefferson-designed Liberty Hall and gardens open.

HARRODSBURG Reproduction of historic Fort Harrod in Pioneer Memorial Park. Mansion Museum, log cabin in which Lincoln's parents were married are other park features.

JEFFERSON DAVIS MONUMENT Site of birthplace of President of Confederacy marked by 351-foot obelisk. Elevator to top.

KENTUCKY LAKE Vast, man-made lake a resort center. All water sports and other facilities in the area and at two state parks on the lake, Kentucky Dam Village and Kentucky Lake.

LEXINGTON Heart of the Blue Grass Region, breeding ground of thoroughbred horses. To the west is the Keeneland Race Course. Many horse farms welcome visitors. Ashland, home of Henry Clay.

LINCOLN NATIONAL HISTORICAL PARK Traditional Lincoln birthplace cabin is preserved in marble and granite memorial.

LOUISVILLE World-famous Churchill Downs is scene of Kentucky Derby in May. Several distilleries open to visitors. Zachary Taylor shrine, J. B. Speed Art Museum also in Louisville.

MAMMOTH CAVE NAT. PARK Enormous limestone caverns, underground river and lake, odd formations.

STATE KENTUCKY MAP 1970

LOUISIANA

The first Whitfields living in Louisiana begin in 1840 that a record is available on censuses.
1840, 1850   Benjamin Whitfield, Caddo Parish, Louisiana
1850   W.A. Whitfield, Orleans Parish, Louisiana
1850   William Whitfield, Oreleans Parish, Louisiana

In the 1830's Whitfields begin to arrive at Louisiana. William Whitfield, III born 1743 NC and died 1817 NC. He had the son William Alexander born 1817, a posthumous child. William Alexander grew up and married Dec. 1, 1841, Charity Helen Jones. William A. moved to Mississippi, and he died 1904 in Rayner, Louisiana. William A. Whitfield was age 87 when he died.

William A. Whitfield had a son Blanchard Kearney Whitfield born 1856 in Shelly, Mississippi, and he lived to be age 92 and more. William A. Whitfield died at Lafayette, Louisiana. He had a daughter Rosabelle F. Whitfield born 1908, and she was living in 1993 in Lafayette, Louisiana. Rosabelle Whitfield tells her own family history. She never married.

Isabella Carolina Whitfield was born in Arkansas, the daughter of George W. Whitfield and Mary Johnson Whitfield. Isabella married Joseph H. Stephens. They had the child George Whitfield Stephens of Natchitoches, Louisiana.

Joseph Henry Stephens was born 1847, Louisiana and lived in Louisiana. Joseph and Isabella married May 7, 1871. Joseph was born about 15 miles southeast of the city of Natchitoches, LA. In 1847 his birth was at the place Provencal, LA. The father of Joseph Henry Stephens was Joseph G. Stephens, a native of Darlington District, South Carolina, who was born August 22, 1818, and died 1876 in Harrison County, TX. His wife was Mary Vascocu who was a native of Red River Parish, LA. She was born 1823 and died 1878 in Texas. They had 11 Stephens children.

Records
Francis Eugene Whitfield was born June 22, 1839, in Bosier Parish, LA. December 29, 1863, he married Bessie Winifred Whitfield.

Mary Catherine Whitfield married W.H. Jack of Louisiana. Their child was George Whitfield Jack.

George Washington Whitfield born 1815, married Mary Johnston (or Johnson) of Cumberland County, NC. He moved to Holly Springs, Mississippi, and finally settled in Louisiana near Natchitoches. They had 12 children. They had the daughters Mary and Isabella who married men at Louisiana.

DESCENDANT OF WILLIAM WHITFIELD AND ELIZABETH GOODMAN WHITFIELD

William Alexander Whitfield was born May 20, 1817 after his father's death in Wayne County, NC. He married Dec. 1, 1841, in Wake County, NC, Charity Helen Jones. They had eight children. Their fourth child was Blanchard Kearney Whitfield, and he was born Sept. 6, 1856, at Shelly, Mississippi. On March 1, 1886, he bought a rice plantation near Rayne, LA.

On Jan. 12, 1898, Blanchard Whitfield married Yvonne Mouton who was born July 1, 1880. In February 1913 he moved his family to Lafayette, Louisiana. They had ten children. Rosabelle Frances Whitfield was born June 26, 1908, and was the sixth child. She never married.

ROSABELLE F. WHITFIELD has written to Vallie Jo Whitfield in 1992 and 1993. From Lafayette, Louisiana, on November 29, 1991, she sent this letter and the original letter is here.

I do appreciate very much your work in making the Whitfield books available.
I am a daughter of Blanchard Kearny Whitfield and Marie Yvonne Whitfield. My grandfather, William Whitfield was the 29th child of his father, and was born after his father's death. My grandmother was Hellen Charity Jones Whitfield.

Yours Truly,
Rosabelle F. Whitfield

Miss Rosabelle F. Whitfield
Lafayette LA 70503

California Record
Of five persons who came to Pleasant Hill, CA, to meet author Vallie Jo Whitfield, the most interesting was a man who lived in England and was new in the United States. He was Whitefield. He told the story of Whitefield in England and about cemeteries there. He said, some of the cemeteries have graveyard tombstones with both Whitfield and Whitefield in the same burial plot. For some times the name has been used in a family with both spellings. This was a Whitefield he spoke about. He made the visit in 1978.

November 29, 1991. "I am a daughter of Blanchard Kearny Whitfield and Marie Yvonne Whitfield. My grandfather, William Whitfield, was the 29th child of his father and was born after his father's death. My grandmother was Hellen Charity Jones Whitfield."

March 7, 1992. "I am a granddaughter of William Alexander and his wife, Hellen Jones, both born in North Carolina but traveled through Tennessee, Mississippi, and settled on the top rim of Bay of St. Louis, on the gulf."
...Submitted by Rosabelle Whitfield, Lafayette, LA, in letters.

William Alexander Whitfield left North Carolina about 1845. He moved to Hancock County, Mississippi, after this he established himself on head of the Bay of St. Louis, Mississippi. He called the place Shelly and lived there until 1891 when he went to Mexico, and then to Rayner, Louisiana. It was his son, Blanchard Whitfield, who moved to Lafayette, Louisiana.

Louisiana Purchase

On April 30, 1803, James Monroe and Robert R. Livingston representing the United States signed the treaty with the French government whereby the United States bought all of Louisiana for $15,000,000 minus $3,750, paid claims to U.S. cities for claims against the French government. It was a very large purchase of land from New Orleans on the south to north border of Canada and to land of the northwest and central areas of the west.

This land purchase assured the outlet through the Mississippi River to the west. It lessened the eastern states' control of the government. Following the War of 1812, the western movement took place. In 1800 the population of the west was less than 400,000, and it increased to 2,000,000. Rich soil found in the southwest produced cotton crops. In 20 years seven new lands became states of the Union.

Whitfield families migration to western, southern lands began in the 1830's and increased in the 1850's.
_____
Reference: The Development of America by Fremont P. Wirth, p. 233.

Bob Whitfield lived in 1980 on Fisher Rd., Denham Springs, LA.

WHITFIELD RESIDENTS IN 1981 AT NEW ORLEANS, LA. Addresses:

Whitfield Arthur D 1917 Laura Chalmette
Whitfield Benjamin 2044 Law —
Whitfield Corra A 5941 Tchoupitoulas -
Whitfield E J 3614 Drbgny Met ——
Whitfield Elward 3924 Delhi Metairie -
Whitfield Eugene 2815 Danneel ——
Whitfield Evelyn H 3230 Ursulines Av -
Whitfield Freda 915 Franklin Av ——
Whitfield George B 1637 Felicity ——
Whitfield George W
3605 Ole Miss Dr Kenner ——

Whitfield Gracie J 4727 Sierra Madre Dr
Whitfield Gwen 2912 Harvard Metairie —
Whitfield Herbert J 407 Bath Av Metairie
Whitfield Joan Mrs 3434 Republic ——
Whitfield John Ray
1102 N Arnoult Rd Metairie——
Whitfield Joseph A 4727 Sierra Madre Dr
Whitfield L 2409 Fenelon Chalmette
Whitfield M J 1905 S Carrollton Av ——
Whitfield Malcolm J 1619 Independence
Whitfield Mark 306 N Starrett Rd Metairie

Whitfield Martin 1232 St Mary
Whitfield Mary 405 N Turnbull Dr Metairie
Whitfield Mc Morris 3434 Republic —
Whitfield Mike 2212 34th Kenner ——
Whitfield Newton R Jr
W 1301 Center Arabi——
Whitfield P C 3425 Edenborn Av Metairie
Whitfield R Smith Clbrn Towers ——
Whitfield Rebecca Mrs 1824 Amelia —
Whitfield Richard J
1612 Severn Av Metrie
Whitfield Ricky 4831 Yale Metairie——
Whitfield Rita 2104 N Arnoult Rd Metairie
Whitfield Rose Mrs 1224 Eighth ——
Whitfield Vernon
2410 Tournefort Chalmte ——
Whitfield William J
8420 Prince Dr Chalmte ——

Inclusive of white race and black race.

220

KATHLEEN LYNCH ROLLEIGH WHITFIELD

Kathleen was born Kathleen Rolleigh on February 10, 1921, at Monroe, Louisina. Her parents had a 100-acre farm.

Kathleen married Joe Mangham Whitfield on February 5, 1943, Camp Carrabelle, FL. They had three sons and three daughters. The children grew up in Virginia and the family lived at Falls Church, Virginia. The family has lived at other locations when the military service was a long stay at a base of the father.

Kathleen was a school teacher in Virginia.

A daughter, Anne Whitfield, attended Northeast Louisiana University at Monroe, LA. Anne was born June 1947 ad died July 1970 at San Antonio.

JOE MANGHAM WHITFIELD

Joe M. Whitfield was born 1917 in Monroe, Louisiana. Son of Davis Andrew Whitfield who was born October 27, 1890, in Suffolk, Virginia, and died April 15,1957, at Vicksburg, Mississippi. Davis A. Whitfield left Suffolk of Nansemond County, VA, in 1913 when he had a state project to teach the natives of Louisiana how to grow peanuts. The Whitfield family made their home in Monroe, LA. The ancestors lived at Virginia.

Joe M. Whitfield's career was in the Army Air Corps and he had a military career. In 1945 he returned from Europe. He was head of the Oakland Army Recruiting Office in California. The Whitfield family lived in 1945 at San Leandro, California. In 1946 the family lived in Park Merced, California.

Joe Whitfield grew up on a cotton plantation in Louisiana of 1,000 acrew where his father was manager in the Mississippi Delta. Joe had brothers but no sisters.

In the Army Joe Whitfield was an Air Corps Colonel. He led the B-26 planes over Normandy on D-Day in World War II. He retired after 30 years of Air Force service and had the home place at Falls Church, Virginia. After retirement he was with American Gas Association.

Joe and Kathleen were on diplomatic tours in Rome, Italy 1952-1955 and Bonn, Germany 1965-1967.

Family Whitfield History

Jim Dillard Whitfield married Ruth Ferguson. Jim was related to Joe Whitfield. Joe Whitfield's great-grandfather had a grandson and the child's mother was Lucy Saunders.

Joe M. Whitfield's great-uncle Davis Andrew Whitfield was an attorney at age 26 in Franklin, Southampton County, VA, he died around 1892. He had been eleted to the State Legislature.

221

Cordy Clifton Whitfield
GREAT GRANDFATHER
BORN   2/4/1817
WHERE   Southampton Co, VA
MD.   3/31/1851, Southampton
         Co, VA
DIED   11/11/1888
WHERE   Southampton Co., VA
BURIED   Whitfield Homestead,
         Newsoms, VA

Lucy J. Saunders
GREAT GRANDMOTHER
BORN   1825
WHERE   VA
DIED   8/11/1895
WHERE   Suffolk, VA
BURIED   Whitfield Homestead,
         Newsoms, VA

Seth Benton
GREAT GRANDFATHER
BORN
WHERE   Gates Co., NC (?)
MD.
DIED
WHERE
BURIED

Martha Benton
GREAT GRANDMOTHER
BORN
WHERE   NC (?)
MD.
DIED
WHERE
BURIED

Thomas Japeth Whitfield
YOUR FATHER'S FATHER
BORN   1/1/1852
WHERE   Southampton Co, VA
MD.   12/6/1887, NC
DIED   3/26/1930
WHERE   Suffolk, VA
BURIED   Cedar Hill Cemetery,
         Suffolk, VA

Annie A. Benton
YOUR FATHER'S MOTHER
BORN   9/6/1865
WHERE   Gates Co., NC
DIED   12/10/1915
WHERE   Suffolk, VA
BURIED   Cedar Hill Cemetery,
         Suffolk, VA

Joe Mangham Whitfield
YOUR NAME
BORN   7/3/1917
WHERE   Monroe, LA
MD.   2/5/1943
         Camp Cannabelle, FL

Davis Andrew Whitfield
YOUR FATHER
BORN   10/27/1890
WHERE   Suffolk, VA
MD.   4/29/1914, LA
DIED   4/15/1957
WHERE   Vicksburg, MS
BURIED   Delhi, LA, City Cemetery

Pedigree Chart

222

SOURCES

Southampton Co. Courthouse Records

Tombstones - LA and VA

Carter Ref. - D.A.R. #601672 - Kathleen

Whitfield Pratt - 1975

Annie Estella Mangham
YOUR MOTHER
BORN   1/22/1892
WHERE   Monroe, LA
DIED   2/6/1945
WHERE   Vicksburg, MS
BURIED Old City Cemetery,
        Monroe, LA, Mangham Plot

Kathleen R. Whitfield (1993)
Falls Church, VA 22042

Kathleen Lynch Rolleigh
YOUR SPOUSE
BORN   2/10/1921
WHERE   Monroe, LA

Judge Joe Bertrand Mangham
YOUR MOTHER'S FATHER
BORN   11/11/1870
WHERE   Monroe, LA
MD.   2/15/1891, LA
DIED   3/16/1926
WHERE   Monroe, LA
BURIED Old City Cemetery,
        Monroe, LA

Annie Carter
YOUR MOTHER'S MOTHER
BORN   ca 1873
WHERE   Bastrop, LA
DIED   1/27/1930
WHERE   Monroe, LA
BURIED Old City Cemetery
        Monroe, LA

T. S. Mangham
GREAT GRANDFATHER
BORN   5/8/1826
WHERE
MD.
DIED   11/18/1901
WHERE   Monroe, LA
BURIED Old City Cemetery,
        Monroe, LA

Theresa Mangham
GREAT GRANDMOTHER
BORN   6/16/1836
WHERE
DIED   3/22/1901
WHERE   Monroe, LA

Enoch Preston Carter
GREAT GRANDFATHER
BORN   9/14/1845
WHERE   Alabama
MD.   2/14/1872
DIED   5/2/1920
WHERE   Guyman, OK   LA

Frances Eliz. Watson
GREAT GRANDMOTHER
BORN   ca 1854
WHERE   Alabama (?)
DIED   ca 1876
WHERE   Bastrop, LA
BURIED Carter Cemetery,
        Bastrop, LA

MAINE

Elvira Hutchinson was born July 14, 1820, at Wilton, Maine.
Elvira married May 8, 1838, to George Whitfield, the son of
George and Lydia Whitfield. They left Maine and made a home at
Francestown, New Hampshire. Yeoman. They had seven children:
1. George Edward Whitfield, b. June 1, 1840
2. Alvirah Mariah Whitfield, b. June 18, 1842
3. Emer Francis Whitfield, b. Aug. 17, 1845.
4. James Harrison Whitfield, b. Oct. 15, 1848
5. Almira Augusta Whitfield, b. April 22,1851
6. William Wilson Whitfield,b. October 24, 1853
7. Charles Warren Whitfield, b. at Lowell, May 12, 1856

George Whitfield was born in Dunstable, resided in Hollis, and
moved to Wilton, Maine, and then to Francestown in 1825. He
married Lydia Tanger on November 27, 1801.

_____

Reference: Essex Institute Historical Collections. Vol. X,
Part II. Salem, Mass. Press, 1869....Elvira Whitfield found in
the genealogy of The Hutchinson Family.

1820 Census George Whitfield lived at Oxford County, Maine.

MARYLAND

THEODORE MARSHALL WHITFIELD
(James, Theodore, Benjamin, William, William, William)
He was born in Richmond, Virginia, May 24, 1905. Attended the
University of Richmond and John Hopkins University (Ph.D.).
Author of "Slavery Agitation in Virginia," 1829-32. 1930
appointed Professor of History and head of the Department of
Western Maryland College, Wesminster, MD. September 2, 1931,
Theodore M. Whitfield married Elizabeth Denny Dixon in Rocky
Mount, VA. Children:
1. Mary Emma Whitfield, b. Nov. 18, 1933, Richmond, VA.
2. Margaret Denny Whitfield, b. Nov. 18, 1933, Richmond, VA
3. Theodore Marshall Whitfield, b. Sept. 4, 1938, Richmond, VA.
4. John Dixon Whitfield, b. June 15, 1941, Richmond, VA.
 Professor Theodore Whitfield died March 21, 1991, Maryland.

Abraham Whitfield was Archbishop of Catholic Churches in 1830
at Baltimore County, MD.

James Whitfield was born Nov. 3, 1770, in Liverpool, England.
He came to the United States. James Whitfield was ordained a
priest of the Roman Catholic Church in 1809. The clergyman,
James Whitfield died October 19, 1834, at Baltimore, MD.

Roby L. Whitfield, Librarian, lived 1967 in Hyattsville, MD.

WHITFIELD RESIDENTS IN 1981 AT BALTIMORE, MARYLAND

Whitfield A 11692 S Laurel Dr Laurel
Whitfield Adell S Mrs 2036 Kennedy Av
Whitfield Albert 1710 Ashburton St
Whitfield Alease 2668 Oswego Av
Whitfield B A 4219 Buffalo Rd
  New Windsor · · · · · · · Sykesville Tel No
Whitfield Bobby 1671 Freedomway North
Whitfield Carrie Mrs 202 N Fremont Av
Whitfield Chas E 4008 N Rogrs Av
Whitfield Charles K Lt Col Ret USMC
  648 Santa Maria Ln
  Davdsnvle · · · Bowie Glenn Dale Tel No
Whitfield Charles K Lt Col Ret USMC
  648 Santa Maria Ln Davidsonville
Whitfield Charles L ofc 721 W Redwood St
Whitfield Delmar G 805 Lannerton Rd Essex
Whitfield Delmar R 1730 Middlboro Rd
Whitfield Edward 1228 St Paul St

Whitfield Engineering Inc High Tor Hill
  Columbia · · · · · · · Ellicott City Tel No
Whitfield Ernest 260 Robert St
Whitfield Eunice 4976 Edgemere Av
Whitfield Georgianna E Mrs
  524 Normandy Av
Whitfield Geraldine Mrs 1606 N Warwick Av
Whitfield Hattie 3300 W Mulberry St
Whitfield Hubert A S Sgt
  8017 Leslie Rd Ft Meade
Whitfield James C 1200 N Curley St
Whitfield Jas T 445 Kent Av
Whitfield John D
  New Windsor · · · · · · Sykesville Tel No
Whitfield Johnney 2918 Ellicott Drwy
Whitfield Jos 2620 W Franklin
Whitfield Mae A 567 Laurens St
Whitfield Margina C 6006 Amberwood Rd

Whitfield Marlene 2918 Ellicott Drway
Whitfield Morris D
  638 Hallmark Dr Glen Burnie
Whitfield Patrick H Col 6067 Granite Knoll
  Columbia · · · · · · · · · · Laurel Tel No
Whitfield R 2400 Cub Hill Rd Parkville
Whitfield Richard A 1530 Burnwood Rd
Whitfield S Edgewood
Whitfield S 2303 Pentland Dr
Whitfield Theodore M
  237 Uniontown Rd Westminster
Whitfield Theodore R 1806 N Regester St
Whitfield William E 4805 Wrenwood Av
Whitfield Wm H 1619 N Port
Whitfield Willie C 9409 Mellonbrook Rd
  Columbia · · · · · · · · · · Laurel Tel No
Whitfill Cypert O 45 E Gordon St Bel Air
  48 E Gordon St Bel Air

The first Maryland-established settlement was at St. Mary's in 1634. George Calvert (Lord Baltimore) was a founder. The purpose of the founders was to find a feudal state and a haven for Roman Catholics but after 1688 the colony became more Protestant.

A hundred years later Maryland in 1788 was an admitted state in the Union of States. In 1960 the state had an estimated population of 3,100,689. The area in square miles was 10,577.

MASSACHUSETTS

The Pilgrims called Separatists arrived 1620 on the coast of Massachusetts and started a colony. Pilgrims were interested in freedom of religion and opportunity of self-government. The colony was promoted by Virginia Land Company, the King gave a Charter by 1629 and Cambridge Agreement. There were stockholders and twelve men controlled government locally. By 1640 no less than 16,000 people came to New England which later formed a New England Confederation with four towns. There the struggle between British Governors and Colonists began. 1773-1774 fighting and Revolutionary War.

FAMILY GROUP

Abby Maria Delano married in Fairhaven, Massachusetts, on Feb. 9, 1875, Marcellius Post Whitfield, b. April 23, 1849, at Savage District IV. Issue:
1. William Henry Whitfield, b. Sept. 19, 1875.
2. Marcellius Post Whitfield, Jr., b. Nov. 27, 1877.
3. Edgar Jenney Whitfield, b. Jan. 23, 1880.
4. Thomas Woodbridge Whitfield, b. Feb. 14, 1882.
5. Joseph Omey Whitfield, b. Sept. 16, 1883.

Whitfield In Publications:
1. New England History.
2. New England Genealogies.
3. New England Registers.
4. Genealogy Dictionary of New England 1860-1862 by J. Savage.
5. Pioneers of Massachusetts by C.H. Pope. Pub. 1900.
6. Dorchester Antiquities and History.
7. Essex Institute History Collection 1869-1870.

Major JAMES FITCH, eldest child of Rev. James Fitch and ABIGAIL WHITFIELD FITCH was born August 2, 1649, colony at Connecticut. When he was an adult, James Fitch became the owner of a vast amount of land, which he accumulated by legislative grants, by purchase from other grantees and through his intimate connection with the Indians.

In 1684 he received a large tract of land, extending from the Quinebang River north of Brooklyn, Connecticut, westwart 45 miles, and northward to beyond the northern boundary of Massachusetts. James Fitch died in Canterbury, Connecticut, November 10, 1727, at age 80.

Abigail Whitfield was one of the daughters of Rev. Henry Whitfield who settled at Guilford, CT. Henry, wife, and sons returned to England but Abigail died in the colony.

References: "Our New England Ancestors and Their Descendant, 1620-1900." Compiled by Henry Whittemore. And in book "Virginia History and Whitfield Biographies," compiled by Vallie Jo Whitfield.

Federal Census of Massachusetts
Spellings on state census of Parnalm and Parnell for first name 1800, 1810, 1820 years.

1800 PARNEL WHITFIELD, Bristol County, Massachusetts, New Bedofrd.

Ralph Root, age 50, sold land estated upon his daughter Sarah Root by Edward Whitfield. She was wife of James Balson. Deed confirmed by Boston Massachusetts General Court, February 28, 1649. This colonial America record found in book, "The Pioneers of Massachusetts" by Charles H. Pope.

MARRIAGES
Abigail Whitfield and John Fitch married October 10, 1648, Saybrook, Connecticut.

Irene L. Whitfield married Isiah J. Watts in Boston, Massachusetts, July 23, 1836.

Miss Whitfield married Mr. Collins, both of the Boston Theatre, in Boston, Massachusetts, January 25, 1794.

Lydia Whitfield married Smith Adams, III, both of Newton, Massachusetts, in Watertown, April 12, 1834.

Francis James Whitfield, an educator, born in Springfield, Massachusetts md. Cecylia Stanislawo Rudzka, March 22, 1916.

Religion played an important part in the settling of Massachusetts. The Puritans' political party asked for and received a charter from the king which was granted in 1629. During 1630 17 vessels came to America, carrying about 2,000 people to Massachusetts Bay and Boston Town was settled. In ten years 16,000 more people came.

MICHIGAN

The 26th state to join the Union on January 26, 1837, was Michigan with a land area of 57,980 square miles. In an acre there are 6,272,640 square miles. It is the number of square feet in an acre (43,560) times the number of square inches in a square foot (144).

New settlers and community and the development of roads did much to development of the state of Michigan. It had interest in the commercial and industrialization using the water ways and transportation.

C E N S U S E S

1840	Whitfield, Charles	St. Clair County, MI
1840	Whitfield, Daniel	St. Joseph County, MI
1840	Whitfield, F.	Oakland County, MI
1840	Whitfield, James	Oakland County, MI
1840	Whitfield, T.	Oakland County, MI
1840	Whitfield, W.	Oakland County, MI
1850	Whitfield, Ansella	Branch County, MI
1850	Whitfield, Daniel	Oakland County, MI
1850	Whitfield, Daniel	St. Joseph County, MI
1850	Whitfield, Fredrick J.	Ionia County, MI
1850	Whitfield, George F.	Ionia County, MI
1850	Whitfield, James	Oakland County, MI
1850	Whitfield, Mary	Berrien County, MI
1850	Whitfield, Walter	Oakland County, MI
1850	Whitfield, William	Oakland County, MI

R E C O R D S

The Pontiac Commercial on February 19, 1925, lists in print Edward Harris Whitfield, son of Thomas W. Whitfield of Waterford, MI.

Ann Marie Whitfield, born in Kalamazoo, MI, August 27, 1948. George B. Whitfield, III, born in Kalamazoo, MI, on July 28, 1959. These names in the Frisbee-Frisbie-Frizy Family Genealogy by Olin E. Frisbee. Book published 1964.

Stuart E. Whitfield was a businessman in Pontiac, MI, in 1966.

WHITFIELD—

Whitfield Anthony 5017EOuterDr	8V3-5559
Whitfield Archie 13209Lauder	838-0413
Whitfield Artha 3640Canton	925-3674
Whitfield Auto Service 6050 14th	898-6910
Whitfield Barney 18314Winthrop	838-6066
Whitfield Ben 9380Elsa	924-0189
Whitfield Ben Jr 614Chrysler	393-9404
Whitfield Bernard 9360Niver AlPrk	383-4703
Whitfield Bernard 35Trowbridge	867-8729
Whitfield Beverly 11634Robson	835-5842

Whitfield Brenda 14007Terry	493-4889
Whitfield Charles 20501Monica	341-1484
Whitfield Chemical Company Inc	
9108Freeland	838-7770
Whitfield Clinton 1201 Selden	831-2286
Whitfield Coy C 8868Wyoming	934-2957
Whitfield D S 26072Lila DeaHts	562-8387
Whitfield David Jr 19450CranbrookDr	862-7151
Whitfield David J 898Edison	868-5910
Whitfield Esther L 3626Frederick	571-1071
Whitfield Eugene 9241 SchaeferHwy	934-0784
Whitfield Forrestina 1440WBethune	872-6426
Whitfield G 7503Wetherby	834-6741

Whitfield Geneva 39Kenilworth	871-5967
Whitfield George 14007Terry	273-1263
Whitfield George Jr 2660Glendale	867-1059
Whitfield George D	
22341Madison Dea	565-5250
Whitfield George R 4140Dickerson	823-2094
Whitfield Hazel 13209Lauder	838-0413
Whitfield Henry 3017Hogarth	898-4039
Whitfield James 15729Marlowe	273-2723
Whitfield James 9008Rutland	273-0325
Whitfield James Jr 2977 Seyburn	571-9215

Louisa Belcher Clarke was born in Kendall, IL. Her first husband, Andrew Smith Church, was born in New York City. Her second husband was Thomas Whitfield, born in Ireland. Thomas Whitfield graduated at the Chicago College of Pharmacy, and was a member of the firm of Thomas Whitfield and Company, maufacturing and dispensing drugs. He was a son of Thomas and Susanna (Brown) Whitfield. His father was a farmer of Ireland. Thomas Whitfield resided in Chicago, IL, before 1897.

Reference: The Pickering Genealogy: Being an account of the first three generations of the Pickering family of Salem, Massachusetts and the descendants of John and Sarah Burrill Pickering of the third generation. By Harrison Ellery and Charles Pickering Bowditch. Vol. III. Pages 773-1284. Private print, 1897.

T.N. U.C. of M.C. Index 1959-1962 - List of Whitfield names.
T.N. U.C. of M.C. Index 1963-1964 - List of Whitfield names.
The National Union Catalog of Manuscript Collections 1959-1961. Based on Reports from American Repositories of Manuscripts, and Compiled by the Library of Congress. J.W. Edwards, Publisher of Volume, Ann Arbor, Michigan.

WESTERN ROADS

The national government in 1811 began the construction of a road to the West from Cumberland, MD, and by 1817 it was completed to Wheeling, VA. It was known as the Cumberland Road or National Road. Political disagreement interfered. The extension of the road and its western terminus at Vandalia, IL, was not reached until 1852.

The eastern portion of the road was 80 feet wide, with a 30 foot strip in the center, constructed of crushed rocks covered with gravel, while the western part was not so highly improved. This road was the most important route to the West during the period of westward migration, and it was used by a constant stream of people and animals in travel. Immigrants were on foot or on horseback, stage coaches, and Conestoga wagons.

In the West the Michigan Road from St. Joseph, Michigan, to Madison, Indiana, on the Ohio River was important. Lansing town became the capital of the state. In 1930 the population of Michigan was 4,842,325.

RESIDENTS IN 1981 AT DETROIT, MICHIGAN
Inclusive of white & black races/1981 addresses & telephone numbers

Whitfield James E 2908Hager	331-6045
Whitfield James W 2703Hogarth	894-2386
Whitfield Joan 578EFerry	875-8582
Whitfield Katie 9202Demar	883-1335
Whitfield Kevin 19952Keating	892-4552
Whitfield L 3550Cass	832-2771
Whitfield L 2908Hager	822-3157
Whitfield Lawrence 9361Fox APt	383-7189
Whitfield Leathea Y 1560Longfellow	867-0071
Whitfield Leon 999Navahoe	822-9150
Whitfield Lesley 13994Archdale	273-1319
Whitfield Linda 5001Daisy	361-0222
Whitfield Lindsey 13155Greenlawn	935-3127
Whitfield Louis 2908Hager	331-6045
Whitfield Lula 8032ECanfield	571-2591
Whitfield Lyndia B 12826Caldwell	891-5790

Whitfield Margaret 7610EHildale	368-6746
Whitfield Marie A 11634Robson	835-8542
Whitfield Morris 6403 30th	361-4706
Whitfield Ocie 578EFerry	875-8582
Whitfield Ocie F 1420Gynn	868-7857
Whitfield Oneita 18948Winthrop	493-3977
Whitfield Pearl 1004EPhiladelphia	872-3248
Whitfield Pearl E 622EPhiladelphia	875-5670
Whitfield Ralph E insman	
4201ToledoCornerOfScotten&Toledo	554-2840
Res 8319Pierson	584-5144
WHITFIELD RAY FORD INC	
10725 STelegraph Tlr	**291-0300**
Whitfield Robert 7503Wetherby	834-5147
Whitfield Rosa Lee 1619Atkinson	875-2389
Whitfield Ruth 4669Alter	885-2924
Whitfield Susie 3216Waverly	868-1897
Whitfield Sylvia 20501Monica	945-9814

Whitfield T 2752WBoston	868-2236
Whitfield Tecumseh 9645 Shoemaker	923-7308
Whitfield Thelma R 12772Corbin	928-1874
Whitfield Tommy 8976May	922-0406
Whitfield Velvia 9960 Sorrento	834-1975
Whitfield Venonia 4815Roosevelt	898-9502
Whitfield Veronica 3345Richton	865-7126
Whitfield Virginia 12634Terry	838-8029
Whitfield Wanda G 20554Plainview	538-4153
Whitfield William 5214NCampbell	895-2584
Whitfield William 14464 3rd HiPrt	869-8009
Whitfield William III 13951Terry	273-7154
Whitfield William D 22Carlton Dea	271-8667
Whitfield William O 18948Winthrop	273-1044
Whitfield William R 1422Morrell	842-7022
Whitfield Willie B 3949Coplin	822-0310
Whitfield Willis 3521JohnCLodgeExpwy	832-1307

ISAIAH J. WHITFIELD (1835-1865)

I. J. WHITFIELD *M. D.*, for the past 10 years practicing physician at Grand Rapids, is a native of Hamilton, Canada, and was born Feb. 23, 1835; he is a son of Frederick J. and Susanna (Churchill) Whitfield, the former born in England and the latter in Nova Scotia. Frederick J. Whitfield was a minister of the " Christian Church " and came to Vergennes tp., this county, in 1847, bringing his wife and family of six sons; here he remained some six months, when the family moved to the town of Keene, Ionia county, where he bought a farm which, with the assistance of his sons, he cleared. A daughter was born to them in Kent county, and the seventh son was born in Ionia county.

From 1847 until 1862 he was widely known throughout Ionia county and the northeastern part of Kent; he is still well remembered by the residents of these localities as a preacher of rare native eloquence. As a Bible scholar he was seldom surpassed. His faith in the Christian religion was unbounded, and the business of his life was to preach the gospel pure and simple, without money and without price. He was called by those who had listened to his eloquent preaching one of Nature's greatest orators, who at will, through the magnetic influence of his voice, moved whole audiences to tears. While still in harness, and discharging his ministerial duties in Canada, he was taken sick and died, Oct. 22, 1865 His wife had preceded him some three years, departing this life in Ionia county, in July, 1862.

The subject of this sketch passed his minority on his father's farm, in the meantime receiving such advantages for an education as were afforded by the district schools. At the age of 21 he made an extended tour of the Western country as far as the Rocky Mountains. On his return to Michigan in 1860 he was married in Ionia county, to Miss Kate Knapp. Soon afterward he moved to Fremont Co., Iowa, where he began reading medicine in the office of R. R. Hawley, M. D.

In July, 1861, he enlisted in Company A, 4th Iowa Vol. Inf., to serve in the Union army during the war of the Rebellion, and in consequence was obliged to leave his wife and a babe three months old among comparative strangers. This was a great trial, but his duty to his country beckoned him on, and when next he met the loved ones the babe was a prattling child of nearly three years, and lisping the name "Papa." Soon after his enlistment, the regiment was ordered to Missouri, and was in camp at Rolla until February, 1862, when they took part under Gen. Curtiss in driving the rebel army under Gen. Price out of Springfield, Mo., and beyond " Cross Hollows," Arkansas. Soon afterward occurred the battle of " Pea Ridge," at which memorable battle the Doctor participated; his comrades on either side were shot down, although he escaped without injury. During this engagement he was continually in the fight, and discharged many rounds of ammunition at the enemy, estimated to be in weight three pounds of lead. Half of his company was killed or wounded. After this battle he received the appointment of Orderly Sergeant of his company, and on the arrival of the regiment at Helena, Ark., at the solicitation of the surgeon, he was appointed "Hospital Steward," discharging the duties of that office for two years and a half. This position kept him always at the front and in constant service. The Doctor was with his regiment in 35 different engagements, beginning at Sugar Creek, Mo., and ending at Bentonville, N. C., covering a period of four years and one month. Among the most notable in which he participated was that of Chickasaw Bayou, near Vicksburg; Arkansas Post, where 7,000 rebels were taken prisoners; the Vicksburg campaign until its surrender; battle of Lookout Mountain. The first night after this battle commenced, there was but one other surgeon besides the Doctor to attend to the wounded, who comprised men from 16 different regiments.

In 1864, he, with his entire regiment, re-enlisted as veterans, and after a short visit home on furlough he again entered active service, participating in the Atlanta campaign, and was with Gen. Sherman's army in its famous "march to the sea." On the arrival of the regiment at Savannah, Ga., the Doctor received his commission as Assistant Surgeon, but had discharged the duties of that office for the two preceding years. From Savannah the regiment marched to Beanfort and Columbia, S. C., and thence to Bentonville, N. C., where it took part in the last battle of the war. The regiment paraded in the grand review of the Union army held in Washington in 1865; was then ordered to Louisville, Ky., and two months afterward to Davenport, Iowa, where it was mustered out of the service Aug. 24, 1865.

The war having ended, he returned to his family at Lowell, Mich. It may be mentioned that five brothers of Dr. W. served as soldiers in the Union army, two being severely wounded in the seven days' fight before Richmond; subsequently one, Thos. N., died at Annapolis, Maryland, while still in the service. During the whole period of the Doctor's service he lost but three days' time from sickness, and it was computed that his regiment during service traveled 8,000 miles.

On his return home he resumed the study of his chosen profession, and in the winter of 1865–'6 he attended a course of medical lectures at Ann Arbor. In the spring of 1866 he moved to Big Rapids, and engaged in the practice of his profession. In 1869 he attended lectures at the Homeopathic Medical College at Cleveland, O., where he graduated in the spring of 1870, and in November, 1871, he located permanently at Grand Rapids, where he has built up a fine practice and has won an enviable reputation as a thorough, competent, and successful physician. The doctor is distinctly a homeopathist, liberal in his views, and tolerant of other schools. He is a member of the Grand Rapids and Kent county Homeopathic Medical Societies, and of the American Institute of Homeopathy, one of the oldest medical societies in existence in this country.

Dr. Whitfield has four children living, three daughters and one son. He has three brothers that are physicians, one living in Grand Rapids, Mich.; the second in Dakota, and the third in New York.

A good portrait of Dr. I. J. Whitfield.

FAMILY GROUP - Sixth Generation

Susannah Churchill born Dec. 23, 1811, was the sixth generation of the Churchill families. Susannah Churchill married Frederick John Whitfield on Dec. 24, 1828, in Wakefield, New Brunswick of Canada.

Frederick John Whitfield was born May 9, 1800, in Woolwich, England, and died in Paris, C.W., Oct. 21, 1865. Frederick John and Susannah moved from New Brunswick to Ontario, Canada, in 1831. They lived in various towns of Canada, as the births of the children show.

1. Mariah Whitfield, b. Wakefield, New Brunswick of Canada, March 19, 1830-d. in Upper Canada, Oct. 13, 1831.
2. Dr. George Frederick Whitfield, b. in Hamilton, CW, Nov. 30, 1832. He married Phebe Brant. Dr. Whitfield was a prominent physician in Grand Rapids, Michigan.
3. John Isaiah Whitfield, b. in Selfleet, CW, Feb. 23, 1835. He married Kate Knapp of Ionia County, Michigan, in 1860. John Isaiah Whitfield was a minister and then a physician. The biography of his has name Isaiah John Whitfield in the Churchill genealogy.
4. Charles Watts Whitfield, b. in Selfleet, CW, April 17, 1837. He married first, Orphia White, and married second Phebe Fletcher.
5. Thomas Nice Whitfield, b. in Burford, CW, Oct. 29, 1839, and died in Baltimore, Maryland, Dec. 6, 1863, in Marine Hospital.
6. Nathaniel Churchill Whitfield, b. In Norwich, CW, May 7, 1843. He married first Julia Wood, and married second Amelia M. Atkins.
7. Henry Allen Whitfield, b. in Burford, CW, May 14, 1845. He married Minnie Wead.
8. Rebecca Carr Whitfield, b. Burford, CW, July 23, 1847. She married Orrin T. Fuller.
9. James Carr Whitfield, b. In Burford, CW, June 11, 1849, and died June 25, 1849. Infant.
10. Zenas Elliot Bliss Whitfield, b. July 1, 1854.

Locations England, Canada, Michigan. CW for County Wentworth, Canada.

_____

Reference: The Churchill Family of America. Volume One. Compilers Gardner Asaph Churchill and Nathaniel Wiley Churchill. Editor and associate compiler: Rev. George M. Bodge. Privately published by the family of Gardner A. Churchill.

Censuses.

MINNESOTA

Faribault County, MN
  1870 Whitfield, Catherine
  1870 Whitfield, Minnieh
  1870 Whitfield, William F.

Hennepin County, MN
  1870 Whitfield, Sarah
Hillsborough County, MN
  1850 Whitfield, Daniel

MISSISSIPPI

There were many named Whitfield who helped to develop the state of Mississippi. The first Whitfield arrived 1821, and there afterwards many followed in search of productive land for growing crops, trees, and cotton.

There was a westward movement of people for homestead lands. Rivers and the stream were there. The weather was of mild temperature.

Mississippi histories record many of these developments and give names of the people. This chapter will announce those that were part of the early history.

Columbus, MS, is where the national first Memorial Day was observed. Natches, MS was founded by the French in 1716.

John W. Whitfield, son of Benjamin Whitfield (1806-1862) and Nancy Whitfield of Tashmingo, MS served in the Civil War. John served in Company A, 2nd Mississippi Infantry, CSA. Benjamin F. Whitfield served in Company E, 17 Mississippi, CSA.

Allein Whitfield (Mrs. Martin Van Buren Miller) was b. May 26, 1880 at Gainesville, TX. Allein md. Feb. 22, 1917 Martin Miller who was b. July 22, 1886. They were residents of Meridan, MS. She wrote her heritage lineage: James Henry, James H., James, Benjamin, Luke, Luke, William (1688-1770). She filed an application 1950 with a National Society and merged two men named Luke Whitfield. She contributed these dates: Rachel Powell Whitfield was b. 1722 at NC and d. 1782 NC. Luke Whitfield d. Dec. 2, 1796. Allein Miller was the ninth generation in America.

God created all things. The earth was made for people, and the sun and moon were made to give them light. Rivers and seas were formed to provide food and to float their ships, rainbows gave them promise of fair weather, winds blew for or against their enterprisess, stars and planets circled in their orbit, to preserve inviolate a system of which they were the center.

Away in the state of Florida there were air space men called astronauts who on July 20, 1969 left the earth in a space vehicle propelled and landed on the moon for the first time.

On July 4, 1997 a mechancial vehicle called a Rover machine landed on the planet Mars without men. It was electronically and scientifically programmed on Earth by men and women of NASA called the Mars Pathfinder Team.

Immigration

Greatest number of immigrants to pass through Ellis Island in New York between 1892 and 1924 was Italy with 2.5 million. Austria-Hungary 2.2 million. Russia 1.9 million and Germany 63,000.

In 1996 there were over 9,852 Whitfield households in the United States. This figure may include white and black people for the computer program project counting included telephone directories and kinds of resource not with W and B for identifying race. Estimating two parents and three children for a household for a arithmetic average will result with 49,265 people. How many white and black people are unknown. Only Census count for all land areas could determine this. However it is reasonable to say 38,800 more white people with natives and new born and new immigrants with Whitfield in 1996. This figure could be added to the earlier count on colonists and early states and gives an uncertain figure of 64,800 Whitfield caucasians. The reason for the division of races is for genealogical history for "roots" and descendancy of blood related persons.

DESCENDANTS OF WILLIAM WHITFIELD AND ELIZABETH GOODMAN WHITFIELD

WILLIAM WHITFIELD born 1688 in England. He came in his prosperous ship to the Virginia colony, and went to North Carolina. William married Elizabeth Goodman in 1713 at a land portion called Gates Co., NC. They settled 1722 in Bertie Co., NC. They had ten children: four boys named William, Matthew, Luke, Constantine. Six daughters were named Mary, Patience, Margaret, Elizabeth, Sarah, Charity. These children were born between 1715 and 1746.

Later moving again to join their son William Whitfield in Rockford, Lenoir Co., NC when old of age, was killed by Indians in 1770. Elizabeth survived and died a few years later.

Descendants were over 1,000 persons by 1930. These people had notes prepared by many people and mainly by Bryan Whitfield, Theodore Whitfield, Emma Morehead Whitfield and Theodore Marshall Whitfield.

Glean those family Whitfield descendants who lived at Mississippi.

References:
1. Colonial Records of North Carolina. Executive Council 1734-1766.
2. North Carolina High Court Minutes 1724-1730. Colonial Records.
3. Manuscript. Life of William Whitfield 1688-1770 by Vallie Jo Whitfield, July 15, 1997. Five pages.

South Carolina Record. George Whitefield was an appraiser of estate of Higgason Barksdale, Jr., 96th District, SC, August 4, 1784.

WILLIAM WILTSHIRE WHITFIELD
(William, Needham, William, William)

William Wiltshire Whitfield was born Feb. 13, 1823, in North Carolina. He married March 3, 1847, Mary Elizabeth Whitfield. After her death he married Nov. 24, 1865, Sarah Elizabeth Phillips, daughter of Edward and Betsey Phillips, of Vaiden, Miss. William Wiltshire Whitfield apparently moved to Mississippi, for the census returns for Lowndes County, Miss., for 1860 show his property as real estate worth $55,000 and slaves, chattels, etc., worth $50,000.

Children:

1. Nathan William Whitfield.
2. William Wiltshire Whitfield; b. Jan. 19, 1851; m. April 10, 1872, Sarah Antoinette Smith. No issue. He was ordained in the Baptist ministry and served successively churches at Mt. Zion, Pleasant Hill, New Salem, Crawford, Kosciusko, McCool, and Carrollton, Miss., between 1892 and 1908.
3. Jessie Bryan Whitfield; b. 1852, d. 1859, Demopolis, Ala.
4. Turner Watkins Whitfield; b. 1857, in Miss.
Second marriage
5. Lucy Whitfield; m. Beverly Matthews. Res., 1929, Columbus. Miss. (38)

We view thirty-eight early residents of Mississippi and find that the Whitfield men went to Mississippi for more productive land. The Santa Fe Trail westward was being developed. Transportation by boat from the North Carolina shore to the southern shore of Mississippi could be managed for travel.

A few of the Whitfield men had left North Carolina and gone early to Alabama. Each new land that became a new state of the United States government provided an opportunity and homestead land, and so men moved westward.

Benjamin Whitfield (b. 1800-d. 1872) left North Carolina and moved to Clarke Co., AL, and married his cousin Lucy Eliza Hatch Aug. 21, 1821. In 1824 Benjamin and his family settled at Hinds Co., and he settled in the district later to be called Society Ridge.

Hatch Whitfield married Hephzibab Whitfield who was born 1792 and her father was Needham Whitfield (b. 1758-d. 1812). In 1835 Hatch Whitfield left North Carolina and settled near Aberdeen, Monroe Co., MS. After the death of his wife he moved back to North Carolina.

In or about 1845 William Alexander Whitfield came to Hancock Co., MS., to purchase a plantation, but for a few years he managed the Bay Place owned by Benjamin Whitfield. After this he established himself nearby on the head of the Bay Saint Louis, MS. and called the place Shelly. His first child Rosabelle Whitfield was born 1842, and died 1850 at Shelly. This family gives information on the ancestors and families.

Fifth Generation. Clinton, MS. ADONIRAM J. WHITFIELD d. in 1929. He md. Catharine McDonald. Children. 1. Katharine md. Eric David Bowie 2. Martha md. Wilbur H. Marshall. 3. Joseph Benjamin Whitfield md. Lillian Collins. (2)

Fifth Generation. Jackson, MS. ALBERT HALL WHITFIELD (Oct. 12, 1849-Nov. 12, 1918) Md. Isadore Buffaloe Dec. 13, 1876. Children.

1. Lawrence Whitfield.
2. Marina Robbins Whitfield; m. Chalmers Alexander.
3. Garland Quinche Whitfield.
4. Kate Coffman Whitfield; m. John Crumpton Hardy.
5. Albert Hall Whitfield.
6. Edith Bessie Whitfield.
7. Robert Joseph Whitfield. (3)

Albert was professor of law at Univ. of MS. He was appointed Judge of Supreme Court 1894 and served to 1912 at Jackson, MS. He was a professor of law in Millsaps College.

Fifth Generation. Shelly, MS. ALSTON JONES WHITFIELD b. Mar. 11, 1860 at Shelly, MS. He md. (1) Emma Jones and (2) Ann E. Rickey. Children.

1. Elliott Temple Whitfield.
Second marriage
2. Arthur Vohilion Whitfield.
3. Alston Rickey Whitfield; living (1929) at Mexico. (4)

Fourth Generation. NC, AL, Hinds Co., MS. BENJAMIN WHITFIELD b. Jan. 13, 1800 in Wayne Co., NC and d. June 13, 1872 Hinds Co., MS. First located in Clarke Co., AL. Md. his cousin, Lucy Eliza Hatch Aug. 21, 1821. In 1824 he with family settled at Society Ridge, MS. He had 20,000 acres and owned 140 Negroes. He manage property and aided education. Benjamin was trustee to Mississippi College and a trustee of Central Female Institute at Clinton. He d. June 13, 1872. Children. (5)

1. Benjamin Hatch Whitfield; b. 1822, in Ala.; d. 1841
2. William A. Whitfield; b. 1824, in Ala.; d. 1828.
3. Sally Ann Eliza Whitfield.
4. Edmond Whitfield; b. 1827, d. 1828.
5. Narcissa Whitfield; b. 1828, d. 1829.
6. George Whitfield.
7. Lewis Augustus Whitfield; b. 1832, d. 1833.
8. Theodore Whitfield.
9. Flora Amelia Whitfield; b. 1827, d. 1852.
10. Judson Whitfield; b. 1838, d. 1843.
11. Ella Eugenia Whitfield; b. 1840, d. 1852.
12. Benjamin Hatch Whitfield.

Fifth Generation. Hinds Co. BENJAMIN HATCH WHITFIELD b. Nov. 23, 1848. He md. in 1873 Mattie Hamilton (1852-1902). He served in Confederate Army. In 1867 he graduated from Tulane University LA. He attended Columbia of Mines, 1871, New York, NY. Dr. Benjamin Whitfield was a learned man in botany, natural science, geology and chemistry. His work was of short terms. Benjamin d. Oct. 12, 1887 at Jackson, MS. Children
1. Laura Elizabeth Whitfield.
2. Adoniram Judson Whitfield.
3. Sally Ann Whitfield. (6)

Sixth Generation. Pocahontas, MS. BENJAMIN FRANKLIN WHITFIELD b. Mar. 10, 1874 Hinds Co., MS. He md. Nov. 25, 1908 Eva McCleland. He was a graduate A. B. of Mississippi College Clinton, MS. He was a farmer and d. after 1930. Children (7)

1. Benjamin Hatch Whitfield; b. Mar. 11, 1910.
2. Rhoda Whitfield; b. Oct. 20, 1911.
3. Thomas McCleland Whitfield; b. Feb. 8, 1913.

Fifth Generation. Holmes Co., MS. CATHERINE ELIZABETH WHITFIELD (b. Apr. 15, 1812-d. 1845) She was b. in Montgomery Co., TN. She md. Aug. 12, 1830 John Farrar Williams (b. Dec. 2, 1802-d. 1872 at Marshall, TX). Catherine was the wife (2) and John F. Williams md. three more times. They had one daughter. Catherine Eliza Williams. (8)

Fourth Generation. Monroe Co., MS. EDMUND WHITFIELD b. Dec. 9, 1793 Wayne Co., NC. He d. Sept. 13, 1867. He md. (1) Susan Matilda Croom Mar. 8, 1816. (2) He md. Penelope Clinton Holmes Jan. 23, 1821. (9)

Children of Edmund Whitfield. 1. Susans Croom Whitfield d. infant. Second marriage. 2. Needham Hatch Whitfield b. June 6, 1822, NC. Md. Jan. 2, 1849 Ann Nicholas Hill (1829-1867). Needham was a physician. He moved to Monroe Co., MS. 3. Owen Holmes Whitfield b. Feb. 29, 1824 in Wayne Co., NC. He d. Feb. 14, 1884. Lived in Monroe Co., MS. 4. Edmund Richard Whitfield b. May 20, 1827 Wayne Co., NC and d. May 5, 1829. He was buried in Sampson Co., NC. 5. Hardy Holmes Whitfield b. Jan. 17, 1830 and d. Oct. 22, 1838. 6. James Alexander Whitfield b. Apr. 23, 1833 Wayne Co., NC and d. July 22, 1835. Buried near Clinton, Sampson Co., NC. 7. Mary Ann Holmes Whitfield. (9)

Fifth Generation. Corinth, MS. FRANCIS EUGENE WHITFIELD b. June 22, 1839 in Bosier Parish, LA. He md. Bessie Winifred Whitfield. He attended the Univ. of VA and the law school of Cumberland Univ., Lebanon, TN. He served in the Confederate Army and was Colonel of the Ninth MS Regiment. At Shiloh, MS. and Resaca, GA., he was wounded and captured but not before he was promoted to brigadier-general. He escaped from the prison in Alton, IL. Then he made his home in Corinth and was a farmer. He became a counsel for the business companies. One child: Edwin Nott Whitfield b. Nov. 1, 1864 in Corinth, MS. He md. Lucile Nelson Dec. 2, 1891. She was b. Apr. 1, 1870 in NY. and was living 1929 in Pasadena, CA. No issue. (10)

Seventh Generation. Jackson, MS. GARLAND QUINCHE WHITFIELD b. Sep. 18, 1880. He md. Apr. 27, 1921, Betty Henry of Jackson, MS. He went to Univ. of Chicago and received a degree in 1902, and L.L.B. at the Univ. of MS. He was a lawyer residing 1933 in Jackson, MS. Child 1. Elizabeth Henry Whitfield b. Jan. 15, 1922. (11)

Fifth Generation. Hinds Co., MS GEORGE WHITFIELD (Sep. 6, 1830-Mar. 15, 1923) was b. in Hinds Co., MS. He md. (1) Amelia Hatch Mar. 7, 1867, and (2) Mildred Foster Apr. 25, 1898. He entered Columbian (later George Washington Univ.) and graduated 1851. In 1856 he went to Newton Theological Seminary in MA. He was a pastor in 1858-59. He became a farm manager. 12 years he was secretary of Ministerial Education in the Baptist Church and was a trustee of MS College.

1. Daisy Whitfield; d. in infancy.   (12)
2. Paul Whitfield; b. 1870, d. 1930.
3. Jesse Whitfield; b. 1872, d. 1922;
    m. Sarah Ellen Robertson.
4. Benjamin Franklin Whitfield.
5. Grace Whitfield; b. 1875; m. in 1911 A. A. Duncan.
6. Theodore Whitfield.
7. Frank Hatch Whitfield; b. 1882, d. 1882.

Fifth Generation. GA. and MS. GEORGE WHITFIELD b. 1827 in GA. He md. (1) Victoria O. Meins and (2) Mary Hilliard, of GA. In 1850 he was a merchant in Lowndes Co., MS. (13) Children. 1. James Whitfield b. 1850 ca. 2. Isham H. Whitfield b. 1854, Columbus, MS. He md. Lacy Witherspoon.

Sixth Generation. Clinton, MS. GEORGE HILLMAN WHITFIELD b. June 22, 1873 in Clinton, MS. When an adult he moved to Richmond, VA. In 1948 he was at Washington, D.C. He was an engineer and graduated from Cornell Univ. He md. Laura Merryman Crane on Oct. 26, 1904 in Baltimore, MD. Father of two daughters named Clare and Anne. (14)

Sixth Generation. Rankin Co., MS. JAMES HERVEY WHITFIELD (July 23, 1834-Sep. 30, 1912) was b. at Pine Level, Johnston Co., NC., Dec. 10, 1856 he md. in TN. Sarah Jane Bourne (Dec. 10, 1838-June 18, 1916). He attended the Univ. of NC finishing in 1855. The family settled on a farm at Brandon, MS. Children: 1. Kate Whitfield 2. Eugene W. Whitfield 3. Estelle Elizabeth Whitfield (15)

Fifth Generation. Lowndes Co., MS. HENRY BUCHANON WHITFIELD b. Apr. 19, 1835 in GA., and d. Sep. 30, 1883. He md. (1) May 5, 1858, Laura Young

of Columbus, MS. Laura (1839-1877) and (2) in 1879 Mrs. Mary Montgomery. Henry attended the Univ. of MS and received A. B. and A. M. degrees in 1854 and Cumberland Univ., TN. in 1857, L. L. B. In 1860 he was living in Lowndes Co., MS. He served in the Civil War. In 1871 he was mayor of Columbus, MS., from 1872-75 he was district attorney for the 7th Judicial District of the Northern District of MS. Later he moved to Waldron, AR. Children: (16)
1. Sally Martin Whitfield b. 1859. She md. Claude H. Ayres. 2. Elizabeth Whitfield, unmd. 3. James Whitfield. He md. Ms. Ledbetter at Crawford, MS. and lived in TX.

Seventh Generation. Rankin Co., MS. HENRY LEWIS WHITFIELD b. June 20, 1868, in Rankin Co., MS. He md. Aug. 25, 1897, Mary Sampson White (b. Sep. 1, 1877). Henry received an A. B. of MS College, 1895. He studied law in the Univ. of MS. In 1898 he became state Superintendent of Education. He left this office and became president of MS College for Women, 1924-27. Henry L. Whitfield became the Governor of MS. In the midst of his term Gov. Whitfield died Mar. 16, 1927. Children. (17)

1. Robert Allen Whitfield; b. 1899.
2. Knox White Whitfield; b. 1901.
3. Henry Lewis Whitfield; b. 1909, d. 1916.
4. William White Whitfield; b. 1913.

Henry L. married Mary Dampeer White, dau. of a physician. He was 1896 a teacher at Steen's School, Florence, MS. Wife was petite, attractive, and a homemaker. Henry Jr. died with Polio. Robert and William were living in 1974 in Columbia, MS.

Reference Book.
CATCH THE VISION The Life Of Henry L. Whitfield Of Mississippi by Bill R. Baker, Published 1974.

Fourth Generation. Lowndes Co., MS. JAMES WHITFIELD was b. Dec. 15, 1791 at Elbert, GA., and d. June 25, 1875 in MS. James md. Caroline Dyer of Jasper Co., GA. James moved to MS, and at an election in 1845 James Whitfield was elected Speaker of the House. In Jan. 1852, Senator James Whitfield was elected President of the MS Senate. The family lived at Columbus, MS. James Whitfield became the Governor of the state of MS. He was a banker by occupation. Children. (18)

1. George Whitfield.
2. Julia Randolph Whitfield.
3. Luke James Whitfield.
4. Henry Buchanon Whitfield.
5. Anthony Dyer Whitfield; b. 1843. Miss. : m. Mary Baskerville, No issue.

Fourth Generation. Columbus, MS. LUKE JAMES WHITFIELD was b. Sep. 7, 1833. He md. Eleanora Harris in Apr. 1856. Luke was a student in the University of MS in 1852. He served in the Confederate Army. Children. (20)
1. Julia Whitfield. 2. Betty Whitfield, unmd., living in 1929.

Fourth Generation. Hinds Co., MS JOHN OLIVER WHITFIELD b. 1809. He md. Mary H. Boone (b. July 8, 1818). About 1835 or 1836 John moved to Hinds Co., MS. Before his death at Huntsville he had lived at Hempstead and on the Brazor River, both in TX. His wife d. while he was living on the Brazos River. Children. (19)

1. Sarah ("Sallie") Bryan Whitfield; b. ca. 1837, d. in Brazil; m. Joseph White. Two children returned to Whitney, Texas.
2. Narcissa ("Sis") Whitfield; b. ca. 1839, d. 1877; m. ——— Boyd. They had one daughter.
3. Mary Whitfield; b. ca. 1841, m. ——— Harris. Four children.
4. John Whitfield; b. ca. 1843.
5. Harriet A. Whitfield.
6. Robert Whitfield; b. 1847, d. 1887 unmarried.
7. Juliet ("Julia") Whitfield; b. ca. 1849; m. Richard Payne with whom she lived in Mexico, Texas.

Reference. Whitfield Bryan Smith, And Related Families. Compiled by Emma Morehead Whitfield. Pub. 1949.

Fourth Generation. Columbus and West Point, MS. Moved to Atlanta, GA. NATHAN WILMER WHITFIELD b. Feb. 22, 1886, at Columbus, MS. Nathan md. Winifred Alice White of Surrey, England on Feb. 18, 1918. He lived in West Point, MS but in 1936 was living in Atlanta, GA. Child. (21)

1. Nathalie Winifred Whitfield.

Fourth Generation. Monroe Co., MS. NEEDHAM WHITFIELD was June 21, 1789 in NC. He md. Mrs. Alice (James) Hall, b. about 1795, and may have d. before 1860. In 1850 the family was living in Aberdeen, Monroe Co., MS. (22)

1. Lucy Amelia Whitfield; b. Jan. 14, 1821; m. Benjamin Lemuel Hatch lived in Aberdeen.
2. Mary Catherine Whitfield.
3. Robert Donnell Whitfield.
4. Samuel Whitfield; b. 1829; m. Margie Brandon.
5. Needham James Whitfield.

Fifth Generation. Shelley and Handsboro, MS and NC OVERTUS MONTAGUE WHITFIELD b. Jan. 1, 1865, at Shelly, his father's homestead at Bay St. Louis, MS. He md. Henrietta Airey on Apr. 10, 1888 in Handsboro, MS. Overtus Whitfield spent his last years in Asheville, NC where he d. Jan. 6, 1940. Children. (23)

1. William Airey Whitfield; b. Jan. 31, 1889; m. Clifford Mock, of Ga., Jan. 8. 1916. No issue.
2. Henry Montague Whitfield.
3. Joseph Blanchard Whitfield.
4. Virginia Whitfield; m. June 23, 1938, Byron Fred Braidwood, No issue.
5. Helen Whitfield.

Sixth Generation. Meridian and Newton, MS. RICHARD HENRY WHITFIELD b. Sep. 8, 1830-d. Sep. 30, 1901. He md. Jan. 17, 1856, Emily McInnis (Jan. 20, 1837-Sep. 8, 1912) of AL. His father d. and he went to live with Nathan Bryan Whitfield. He attended and graduated from Univ. of NC. He was in AL but left for Philadelphia to study medicine. After the war he moved to Meridian, MS, and there he combined the practice of medicine with the business of druggist. During the Civil War he had been a surgeon in the Confederate Army. For a while he lived at Newton, MS. (24)

1. Robert McInnis Whitfield; b. Oct. 17, 1856, d. Nov. 8, 1884; m. Dec. 7, 1882, Ella Maria Hulburt (b. August 7, 1861).
2. John William Whitfield; b. Feb. 15, 1858, d. Oct. 12, 1863.
3. Richard Henry Whitfield; b. April 14, 1864; d. Sept. 28, 1867.
4. Annie Kate Whitfield.
5. Edith Alice Whitfield; b. July 14, 1871, d. Jan. 8, 1889.
6. Sarah Hughes Whitfield; b. Sept. 18, 1876 (or Sept. 19, 1875); m. August 10, 1898. Watson Edwin Jones (b. 1869). She had two daughters.

Seventh Generation. Florence and Jackson, MS. RICHARD NOBLE WHITFIELD b. Feb. 1, 1879. He md. Annie Belle South on June 14, 1908. Richard Whitfield attended Millsaps College in Jackson, MS, and the Medical School of the Univ. of Nashville, TN and obtained the degree in 1905. From 1910-1919 he was employed by the State Board of Health of MS. On Jan. 1, 1924 he became Director of the Bureau of Vital Statics for his state. In 1948 he was residing in Florence and Jackson , MS. Children.

1. John South Whitfield; b. March 30, 1909.
2. Richard Noble Whitfield.
3. Henry Massey Whitfield.
4. Fitzhugh Ails Whitfield; b. Sept. 22, 1915.
5. Sarah Katherine Whitfield; b. 1918, d. 1922.
6. Edmond Whitfield; b. May 14, 1921.
7. Emily Whitfield; b. March 4, 1924.
8. George Allan Whitfield; b. 1925, d. 1925.
9. Carolyne Whitfield; b. May 22, 1929. (25)
10. Mary Anne Whitfield.
11. Amelia Whitfield.

Sixth Generation. Okolona, MS. ROBERT DONNELL WHITFIELD He md. Irene Bradford. He may have been a doctor. Lived in Okolona. Child. 1. Bryan Whitfield. (26)

Seventh Generation. Smith and Chickasaw Counties, MS. ROBERT FITZHUGH WHITFIELD b. Feb. 13, 1866 in Smith Co., MS. He md. Sallie Atkinson of Chickasaw Co., MS, June 16, 1886. Sallie was b. Jan. 5, 1874. She had four children. (27)

Mississippi in 1960 had an estimated population of 2,178,141. Area in square miles was 47,170. The state had five member Representatives in Congress. Soil of grounds was very good for agriculture. There were cotton plantations covering the fertile rich bottom lands. Peanuts grew well.

1. Robert Demar Whitfield; b. April 18, 1897.
2. Mary Loraine Whitfield; b. Aug. 26, 1902.
3. Edna Earle Whitfield; b. May 13, 1906; m.— Alexander. Res., 1939, Grenada, Miss.
4. John Lewis Whitfield; b. May 15, 1910.

Fifth Generation. Hinds Co., MS.

THEODORE WHITFIELD AND ANNIE ELIZA MOREHEAD WHITFIELD. Theodore was b. in Hinds Co., Jan. 31, 1834 and d. May 28, 1894 in Richmond, VA. He attended the Univ. of NC and graduated 1854. He returned to MS. Then he entered the Newton Theological Institution, Newton Center, MA and completed the work in 1858, and sought a Pastorate.

Whitfield md. Annie Morehead on Nov. 11, 1859. After a year he moved to Aberdeen, MS. In 1864 he moved to Goldsboro, NC. He soon returned to MS to Jackson.

From 1869 to 1872 he was at First Baptist Church in Meridian, MS. In 1873 for one year he had the superintendency of the State Institution for the Blind at Jackson, MS. In 1874 Theodore returned to the ministry in Charlotte, NC. In 1878, Wake Forest College, NC conferred upon him the degree of Doctor of Divinity. In succeeding years Dr. Whitfield was occupying the pastorates near Spartanburg, SC, Goldsboro and New Bern in NC, and Richmond, VA.

Annie Morehead Whitfield was b. Feb. 1, 1836 and d. Nov. 12, 1914. Children: (28) 1. James Morehead Whitfield. 2. Lizze May Whitfield, d. infancy. 3. George Hilman Whitfield. 4. Emma Morehead Whitfield.

Sixth Generation. Hinds Co., MS. THEODORE WHITFIELD b. Nov. 23, 1877 near Jackson, MS. He md. Rebecca Taylor Hendry (b. Aug. 17 1881) in Louisville, KY

on Aug. 20, 1902. Theodore Whitfield received the A.B. degree from MS College, Clinton, MS, and Ph.D. degree at the Southern Baptist Seminary, Louisville, KY. He served the following pastorates: Norfolk, NB, Jackson, Hayti, Flat River and Poplar Bluff, MO; McComb and Gulfport, MS. He retired in 1846 and lived in Pocahontas, MS in 1948. Children.

1. George   ndry Whitfield.
2. Benjamin Whitfield; b. Nov. 26, 1904, d. Nov. 25, 1907.
3. Paul Mercer Whitfield; b. Jan. 8, 1908.
4. Grace Virginia Whitfield; b. Aug. 19, 1909.

Fourth Generation. Lowndes Co., MS. WILLIAM WHITFIELD (1783 or '87'-d. June 20, 1864). William md. Ann Turner in Nov. 1812.

1. Mary Whitfield; b. 1814, d. 1832, N C.
2. Lucy Ann Whitfield; b. 1817 ca., d. Aug. 11, 1887 in Miss where she was living with her brother William.
3. Needham Hatch Whitfield; b. 1820, d. 1825.
4. William Wiltshire Whitfield.
5. Jesse Leonidas Whitfield; b. 1826, d. 1849, or '50.
6. John Alexander Whitfield; b. June 20, 1829.

Fourth Generation. Hancock Co., MS. WILLIAM ALEXANDER WHITFIELD William, a posthumous child, was b. at Vilanow, Wayne Co., NC on May 20, 1817. His father had d. in 1817. After a short period in the US navy, William md. Dec. 1, 1841, at Pomona in Wake Co., NC. Charity Helen Jones, second daughter of Seth Jones of the same place.

About 1845 William A. Whitfield came to Hancock Co., MS. to purchase a plantation, but for a few years he managed the Bay Place owned by Benjamin Whitfield. After this he established himself nearby on the head of the Bay of St. Louis, MS and called his place Shelly. He lived there until 1891 and moved to Mexico for better weather. From there he moved to Rayner, LA, where he d. in 1904. He lived to be age 87. His wife, Charity Helen Jones Whitfield d. in 1877. Children.

1. Rosabelle Whitfield; b. 1842, d. 1850 at Shelly.
2. Irene Whitfield.
3. Iolause St. Louis Whitfield; b. 1852 at Shelly.
4. Blanchard Kearney Whitfield.
5. Alston Jones Whitfield.
6. Vohilion Carolinus Whitfield.
7. Overtus Montague Whitfield.
8. Vertalee Whitfield; b. Aug. 10, 1867. at Shelly; m Turner Baites, of Maxie, Miss.

The descent of Charity H. Jones follows: Sally Borthers md E. Kearney; Mary Hinton md. Solomon Alston; Sarah Hinton md. B. Blanchard; Eliz. Willis md. Evan Jones. Sally Alston md. Seth Jones, and Charity Helen Jones was b. of this union. (31)

Sixth Generation. AL and MS. ROBERT ALLEN WHITFIELD b. Jan. 11, 1839 in Gainesville, AL. He attended school at Harrisburg, PA; the Univ. of NC 1856-57; and the Univ. of VA. He md. Mary Ann Fitzhugh on July 3, 1860. She was from Rankin Co., MS. They settled near Brandon, MS. Robert A. Whitfield was a Minister. In 1862 Robert enlisted in the Confederate State Army. He served at hospitals at Oxford, Newton and Jackson, MS. until the close of the Civil War. Robert taught school for twenty-three years, fifteen years at Fannin, MS. Robert and Mary Ann had nine children. After her death Robert md. (2) Martha (Mattie) H.(Bishop) Williams Mar. 20, 1890, of Westville, MS. Martha (b. Oct. 27, 1840-Oct. 28, 1908) was the widow of Jeff Williams of Simpson Co.,MS.

Six of the children grew up and settled at Rocky Mount, NC and living in 1918 there.

(32)

Eighth Generation. WILLIAM WHITFIELD b. 1913 is called WILL WHITE WHITFIELD. He married Mabel Ewing and they had dau. Mary Clare Whitfield. She md., div., no issue. In 1995 she was with school district in administration. Will was in the military service. He later was a salesman, and then worked for a television station. He was the son of Governor Henry L. Whitfield. Will was age 83 in 1995 and living in Columbus, MS, on Southdown Pkwy. He is interested in Whitfield's history.

1. George Fitzhugh Whitfield; b. May 1, 1861, d. Nov. 2, 1862.
2. Frances Batte Whitfield.
3. Robert Fitzhugh Whitfield.
4. Henry Lewis Whitfield.
5. Hunter Whitfield; b. Feb. 20, 1871, d. Sept. 30, 1872.
6. James William Whitfield; b. March 21, 1874, d. July 1, 1884.
7. Drew Fitzhugh Whitfield.
8. Richard Noble Whitfield.
9. Charles Marion Whitfield; b. Oct. 8, 1883; m. Alice Deterly, sister of Jessie Deterly. They lived in Jackson, Miss. No issue.

(32)

Sixth Generation. Oxford, MS ANDREW LUCAS WHITFIELD (b. Jan. 12, 1866-June 3, 1936). He md. Helen Brank Davidson (b. 1870) in Oxford, MS. Andrew Whitfield devoted most of his life in education and the ministry in the Presbyterian Church. He served as president of a Presbyterian Academy at Columbia, KY; President of Reynolds College, Albany, TX; and professor of English in Arkansas College, Batesville, AR. Several pastorates had his time and energy. He retired from the ministry in 1932. He died in Doniphan, MO. Children. (33)

1. Margaret B. Whitfield.
2. Edwin C. Whitfield.
3. Florence Lucas Whitfield; b. Dec. 12, 1903; m. Ralph Barton, of Beaumont, Texas.
4. Anna Ruth Whitfield.

This list of thirty-three persons who were descendants of William Whitfield (b. 1688, Lancaster, England, and d. 1770 in NC) and his wife Elizabeth Goodman Whitfield were residents of the state of MS.

The fourth generation had land opened in the West and they begin settling in MS in the 1820's. Several births made fifth generation in the 1830's in MS. Several of these men came before the Civil War to MS. Many men of this lineage were in farming, ministry, and education. Some practiced law in the state.

Children born in the state of MS in early days were over one hundred new members with the surname Whitfield.

240

Continued from page 189.

CIVIL WAR SERVICE OF JOHN WESLEY BELL 1846-1896

Lived in 63rd District of Burke County near Alexander. Son of Simeon and Elizabeth Herrington Bell, he married Ella Fair Burton Bell (1844-1937) Nov. 15, 1866 in Burke County, GA, by Rev. Thomas B. Lanier. He died in 1894 as a result of a reaction to an insect bite and was buried at Habersham Methodist Church.

In 1927, she made an application for a widow's pension which was turned down. An affidavit made June 23, 1927, by E.N. Skinner of Burke County who was a confederate veteran states that he knew Bell before the war, and that Bell was in the war but not in his same company. He said that Bell was in the artillery, and that for two weeks in 1863 John Wesley Bell and his company were stationed at Cedar Creek near Jacksonville, FL, at which time deponent's company was at the same place and "deponent had several meals of parched corn with the said John Wesley Bell." John Lewis was captain of Bell's company, and Sam Robinson and H.D. Sapp were in the same company. Sapp was dead, and his wife was receiving his pension. July 19, 1927 the Commissioner of Pensions in Atlanta rejected the application and stated that Skinner knew nothing about Bell's service or discharge. (Roll GCP-40)

A muster roll for the Alexander Grays for Sept. 13, 1861 shows John W. Bell, Edward N. Skinner, and H.D. Sapp. Sapp enlisted in the Chatham Artillery in December 1861 and served with that unit until its surrender. He was in Guerand's Battery from June, 1862 until April, 1865. Skinner enlisted in Company C, 5th Georgia Cavalry near Savannah in June 1862.

Records show that Bell enlisted in the Chatham Artillery Nov. 20, 1863 in Guerand's Battery, and that John Lewis was his captain. All available roll records show him present through November and December, 1864. (Roll GCP-42). Additional records show that he served as a bugler, and was promoted to Corporal Jan. 7, 1864, but was demoted on July 5, 1864 (the same day he received six months back pay).

RECORDS OF GUERAND'S BATTERY: At White Bluff 12-31-63 (also 4-30-64). At Oatland Island (near Savannah and Ft. Jackson) May and June 64. At Combahee Ferry, SC Nov.-Dec. 64. On 2-8-64 was ordered to Lake City, FL. Went to Oulstee, and was engaged in action at Ocean Pond 2-20-64. Marched to Camp Milton, where they stayed until March 8. Ordered to front for picket duty with cavalry brigade until April 18. Took part in skirmish at Cedar Creek April 2. On 4-18-64 was ordered to march to Charleston via Callahan (FL), Trader's Hill (now Waycross), and Savannah. "Marched 96 miles to railroad in 4 ½ days in excellent order. Reached Savannah on 26th and ordered to its present camp. Clothing, shoes worn. Health good." (Microcopy No. 266, Roll No. 105)

CIVIL WAR MISSISSIPPI

Chalmer's Brigade. In the first actions of the Battle of Shiloh, Major Francis Eugene Whitfield lead the skirmish line under Colonel William A. Rankin.

Colonel William T. Shaw commanding 14th Iowa surrendered his regiment to Major Francis E. Whitfield. On the morning 7th, 1862 they were heavily attacked and compelled to retire after their ammunition was exhausted. Major Francis Eugene Whitfield was severely wounded.

Francis E. Whitfield joined the Confederate forces and was in time colonel of the Ninth Mississippi Regiment. In another battle at Resaca, GA he was wounded again. Then he was captured but not before he was promoted to brigadier-general for gallantry. He escaped from the prison in Alton, IL.

After the war F. E. Whitfield wrote up his experiences and published the story in the "Booneville Leader" of Corinth, MS where he lived. On Mar. 18, 1885 Francis died on a vacation in Florida. Francis Whitfield was born June 22, 1839, in Bossier Parish, Lousiana Dec. 29, 1863. He married Bessie Winifred Whitfield and they had one child, Edwin Nott Whitfield who was born Nov. 1, 1864 Corinth, MS. On Dec. 2, 1891 Edwin married Lucile Nelson of New York. Edwin was a lawyer in New York. He died in 1929. His widow, Lucile Whitfield, was living in 1929 in Pasadena, CA. No children.

Julia Whitfield, daughter of Governor Whitfield married Isham Harrison who was killed in the Civil War. He was with the Confederacy in Alabama when he died.

John Wilkins Whitfield was born 1818 Williamson Co., TN and died 1879 Lavaca Co., TN. John W. Whitfield was the Confederate General First Texas Legion, and was in battle at Iuka Mississippi on Sept. 19, 1862. General John Whitfield was at Thompson's Station in Mar. 5, 1863.

MISSISSIPPI RECORDS

Mary Ann Whitfield was born Dec. 14, 1836 in Wayne Co., NC. She moved to Aberdeen, MS with her parents. Mary Ann Whitfield on Feb. 12, 1856 married William Hardy Holmes.

Laura Eloise Pickett was born June 21, 1851 in Columbus, MS. Laura Pickett married Nathan William Whitfield on June 23, 1869. Nathan was born Nov. 23, 1848 or 1849 in Alabama.

Whitfield living residents in 1980 at Mississippi.
Brad R. Whitfield, Gulford, MS. Care Whitfield, Lyman, MS. Robert Whitfield, Gulport, MS. Whitfield Timber Company, Standard, MS.

DESCENDANTS OF SEABORN WHITFIELD 1805-1881

1870 United State Census, Hancock County, Mississippi

John E. Whitfield, age 40, born GA
Sarah Whitfield, age 35, born AL
Angeline, age 8, born MS.
John E. (Van) Whitfield married Sarah McCarty.

Cemetery Record

Frances A. Whitfield md. Jordan Smith. They are buried in Corinth, MS in Turtleskin Cemetery. This cemetery is located between Bay St. Louis and Picayune, MS. She may be Frances Angeline Whitfield.

....Submitted by Gene T. Bell of Orlando, FL in Oct. 1994. Research by Mrs. John H. Howard, Sr. of Picayune, MS included several pages.

Whitfield Story by Vallie Jo Whitfield

In 1983 Jesse B. Whitfield wrote to Whitfield Books, a book publishing office of writer-publisher, Vallie Jo Whitfield. Jesse Whitfield purchased a book titled Whitfield History And Genealogy of Tennessee. On Apr. 9, 1983 Vallie Jo wrote to Jesse Whitfield asking about his family. He said they came from Georgia, and his brother knew a little about family, but we have forgotten most of the old things.

On May 7, 1990, Claude Whitfield living at a rural post office box, Picayune, MS writes to Vallie Jo Whitfield and sent five pages of copied typing papers. The information announces there has been a FAMILY REUNION at Picayune, MS in 1989 and a reunion in 1990. The 1990 reunion was held at the Walkiah Bluff Park, northwest of Picayune, MS, and it was held on Apr. 14, 1990. There was an application for family information and family history, a lengthy biographical sketch on Claude Whitfield, age 83, a large list of names who were descendants of Seabron Britt Whitfield, Sr. who died 1881, and a letter saying we missed you at Reunion, and 200 persons attended and 1990 Election Results:
President-Daryl Whitfield   Secty. Asst.-Mrs. Ron Whitfield
Vice Pres.-Mrs. Perry Whitfield Reunion Recorder-Edgar Whitfield
Secty.-Mrs. Patricia Whitfield Finance Ofcr Mrs. Toby Whitfield
Trustee for the Family History Book-Claude Whitfield and Mrs. Hilda Hoffmann.

This letter asked for cooperation for family history for "The Book"-Yes, they wanted a Family History. Mrs. Rosemary Lovell was announced as genealogist, and she was Director of Heritage Family Research Center, at her home, an application for pre-order of a planned future book, enclose check for $20.00. Claude Whitfield did write in ink pen a half page saying what he believed was the location of his ancestors, and they would like to begin with Georgia where a person named Seaborn Britt was born.

243

He wrote Seabron Britt Whitfield d. 1881. He married (1) Nancy Byrd (b. 1815-d. 1860). He md. (2) Rebecca Johnson, b. 1844 and d. 1881. They had five children: 1. John Francis Whitfield. 2. Frances. Whitfield 3. William Whitfield. 4. Arthur Whitfield.

Claude Whitfield sent announcement on the Whitfield Reunion at Picayune, MS, and the Whitfield Families, Mitchell, Stockstill and other families on a listing chart. He also sent the following biography.

BIOGRAPHY OF CLAUDE WHITFIELD

Claude Whitfield was b. Apr. 8, 1907 four miles east of Picayune in Hancock Co., MS. The area became Pearl River Co. in 1908. He went to Salem High School. In 1932 he joined the Marines and served at Haiti and his troop left 1933. In 1942 Claude was drafted into the Army in World War II. He served in the Army military for twenty-four years. Then he did nine years with Civil Service.

In 1942 Claude Whitfield md. Oneita ____ of the same community. They had two sons. In 1990 they had two grandchildren and two sons. They made a home at Hobolochitta Creek in Pearl River Co., MS.

Claude Whitfield wrote a letter in 1993. He wrote that his brother Jesse B. Whitfield of Woodbury, TN had died.

A search began by several persons in the regional area. There were eighteen Whitfield families and other descendants in 1993, and they were interested in a family genealogy. Studies of states censuses took place, and research. Rosemary Lovell remained as Director of Research.

Seaborn Whitfield had three wives and twelve children. 1. Nancy Byrd Whitfield. 2. Minnie ____ Whitfield. 3. Rebecca Johnson

Mar, 24, 1995 a letter was sent to Vallie Jo Whitfield and it disclosed the following:
"William Matthew Whitfield b. 1761 and d. 1845. He had a passport record Aug. 20, 1801. A permit from North Carolina to Wayne Co., GA and thru Florida to Hancock Co., MS."

244

GA.　　　FLA.　　　MISS.

PEOPLE AT THE 1990 WHITFIELD REUNION AT PICAYUNE, MISSISSIPPI WERE GIVEN THIS CHART. IT WAS THE BEGINING OF WORK FOR FAMILY TREES.

SEABORN WHITFIELD SR. 1881

1805　BYRD 1860

1815 NANCY

JOHN F. 1840-1928

MARY ANN 1844-1921 THORNTON BROWN

LOUISA 1849-1940 MILAM A. MITCHELL

S.M.JOE 1852-1898 HESTER STOCKSTILL

ARTHUR　POLLY

GREEN

MAGNOLIA

JOHN　IDANIC　PEARL

SEBRON C.

GEORGE　RAYMON

NANCY

ELSIE　W.R.BILL　MIRANDA 1849

F. DALTON

NANCY　JOHN B.

JOHN P.

SALLY　MITCHELL MITCHELL

CATHETICA

1844 REBECCA JOHNSON 1881

FRANCES 1864-1938 EVERETTE

SARAH 1866-1949 ISAAC GRAVES

JANE 1865-1932 JEFFERSON PENTON

S.B.JR. 1873-1943 FRIESON

EMMA 1875-193: ALBERT CASANOVA

ANDREW　SARAH　PHILLIP I.CLARENCE　DALLAS　SHAPAH

FELTON

VAN A.　LOUISA　VIRGII　LEOLLA　EDITH　SEAB

MEADE

ULMAN　MINNIE　POLLY　OLIE　ETHEL　MARY

E VAN

VINIA　MELTON　LIZZIE　RANDOLPH　S.E.3rd　ILA MAE

TADD D.

CHECKER H. HERNY　HARRY　HUGO　WILLIE R. ALBERT L.

RANSON

IRENE　HARVE　EARL　ARGO　YIONNE

ARTHUR

BEN　BYRD　EDDIE　MARTHY

LUTHE

WILL　FREDDIE　LOU

CORA

NANCY　FRANK　BOYD

BARNEY

ANDY　BUFORD　LUTHER

IRENE

JOHN　LOUIS

245

DESCENDANTS OF SEABORN WHITFIELD AND MINNIE WHITFIELD

There was something about Shelly Place near the Bay of St. Louis, MS for there were other Whitfields who were residents at Shelly of Hancock Co., MS. Blanchard Whitfield lived there and later moved to Louisiana. Irene Whitfield was b. Feb. 1, 1850 as a native. George Whitfield who was b. 1827 at Georgia lived there in 1850. Robert Allen Whitfield who was b. Jan. 11, 1839 at Gainesville, AL lived there at Shelly area. Theodore Whitfield had a stay at Shelly. Theodore was b. Jan. 31, 1834 at Hinds Co., MS and d. at Richmond, VA May 28, 1894.

While these were descendants of William Whitfield and Elizabeth Goodman Whitfield who married 1713 in Gates Co., NC., there are others with surname of Whitfield who are not of this lineage. Such are the following names:

John Francis Whitfield family had a reunion on July 4, 1925 with descendants and 112 persons posed for the family picture. The Times-Picayune newspaper, New Orleans, LA, printed the following information:

JOHN FRANCIS WHITFIELD was born Sept. 27, 1840. He was the son of SEABORN WHITFIELD and his wife NANCY BYRD. John moved from Florida to Mississippi and settled near Picayune. He married (1) Harriet Elizabeth McCarthy and (2) Josephine Smith.

1850 Florida Census

Seaborn B. Whitfield, age 45 b. GA   child, age 4, b. FL
Wife (Minnie), age 30, b. GA   Miranda, age 2, b. FL
John Francis (Bull), age 9, b. FL

MARRIAGE RECORDS

John Francis Whitfield (b. 1840-d. 1928) md. Harriet Elizabeth McCarthy Feb. 20, 1861. Note: Book A, page 241 and
John Francis Whitfield (b. 1840 FL-d. 1928 MS) md. Josephine Smith Feb. 27, 1875. Note: Book BB, page 273, By J. P. Davis, JF, MS.

CHILDREN of John Francis Whitfield and Wives and Marriage Records of children.
Francis Dalton Whitfield, b. Oct. 3, 1866. Francis md. Susan Viola Stockstill, Apr. 11, 1889.
Sebron C. Whitfield md. Caroline Smith, Apr. 8, 1885.
Magnolia Whitfield md. Jack C. Craft Oct. 17, 1888. Note: Book C, page 296. L. Thigpen JF. MS.
Rachel Cathelica Whitfield md Hozie (Hosea) Flemming Sept. 24, 1888, MS.
John P. Whitfield md. Sarah Burge Dec. 12, 1892.
Mead Whitfield md. Emily Lott, Sept. 7, 1892.
Felton Whitfield (?) md. Ida Leona Harris Aug. 13, 1896.

....Submitted by Mrs. John H. Howard, Sr., of Picayune, MS in 1990s. Received 1994 from Gene T. Bell of Florida and papers from Latter Day Saints Library.

Mitchell Family Group

MARINDA Whitfield, b. 1848 md. Jan. 11, 1865. Lic. Registration Hancock Co., MS. Marinda md. John Berry Mitchell, b. July 26, 1846 and d. Mar. 24, 1918. He was son of John Berry Mitchell and Lavina West Mitchell. Issue: Nancy, Sarah, William, Andrew, Harvee, Milton, Bryd, Henry, Minnie, Louisa.

1880 United States Census, HANCOCK COUNTY, MISSISSIPPI
Post Office, Gainesville, MS.

William Aultman Whitfield, age 50, b. FL
Willfreds A. Whitfield, age 45, b. MS
S. M. Joseph Whitfield, age 28, b. MS
and grandchildren
Mary Whitfield, age 8, b. MS.
Pearl Whitfield, age 6, b. MS.
William A., age 3, b. MS.

Marriage Record

William Aultman Whitfield, b. 1830 at Florida md. Willfreds Adeline Mitchell (Aunt Sally in family) was daughter of John M. and Lavina West Mitchell. This son is buried as Joseph Whitfield, Cedar Grove Cemetery in Mississippi.
Note: Initial before name or all first names of children the same means that is child (or in this case grandchild) of fraternal father. Initial are frequently seen in old country of Europe and early records in America colonial of father's name or initial only. *S. M. for Seaborn Merritt.

S. M. Joseph Whitfield md. Hester Lavina Stockstill Oct. 4, 1870. By Reverend A M. Slaydon. Registration, Hancock Co., MS, Book BB, page 13. S. M. Joseph was age 18 when he md. for 1880 Census list his age as 28. Hester Stockstill was the daughter of John William Stockstill and Amanda Mitchell Stockstill. Issue: Mary Bond (Polly), b. circa 1872, and d. 1969. Pearl, b. circa 1874. William A., b. circa 1877.

MARY BOND (Polly) WHITFIELD, daughter of S. M. Joseph Whitfield and Hester L. Stockstill Whitfield md. Pedro David Whitney, May 18, 1892. By A. M. Slaydon, MG. Book G, page 156, Hancock Co., MS.

Pedro D. Whitney was the son of Oliver and Malinda Marsen. Oliver Whitney was resident of Kasegan, Maine. Marsen family was from Virginia. Issue: Children of WHITNEY FAMILY GROUP. Audry md. O. E. Hart and living in 1970, Ethel Vivian, Jack, Henry Crask, Angie Pearl, Pedro Corburn, Mildred Inez.

South Carolina. Vicki Ward is a descendant of Peter Madison Whitfield (1830-1907) of Anderson County, SC. A kinship ancestral is Lewis Whitfield, b. Sept. 14, 1801-d. Nov. 29, 1858, SC. The same family group at Anderson Co., SC. Linda lived in Flora Lone, FL, in 1995 and moved to Pomona Park, FL.

Whitfield Books office at Pleasant Hill, CA has this list of Mississippi people that have made inquiry on Whitfield and book publications, and the year they made the inquires.
1974. Mrs. Louise Moseley Heaton of Clarksdate, MS.
1977. Mrs. Gloyd Smith of Iuka, MS.
1980. Mrs. Jimmy Whitfield (Brenda) of Iuka, MS
1983. Maury Whitfield of Corinth, MS.
1990. Claude Whitfield of Picayune, MS.
1991. Alice Jean Dortch of Vicksburg, MS.
1991. Davis A. Whitfield of Greenville, MS.
1991. Rosemary Lovell of Picayune, MS

Brenda Whitfield, Mrs. Jimmy Whitfield of Iuka, MS searched for lineage of Joel Whitfield and submitted the following information in June 1990.

Joel Whitfield, b. circa 1750 NC had wife Lydia Crisp, the daughter of William Crisp whose second wife was Frances _____, and he md. her about 1775.

Benjamin Whitfield and Joel Whitfield are listed on 1850 Tishomingo Co., MS. Census. A county which borders on Alabama and Tennessee line. Joel Whitfield came by way of Tennessee to Mississippi.

Joel Whitfield b. circa 1804 or 1805 NC. Wife Darcus.

For the ancestry of Jimmy Whitfield, her husband, there is proof of the following: Marriages-WILLIAM SMITH WHITFIELD, b. 1822. Wife-Martha Langkford.
George Washington Whitfield. Wife-Mollie Browning.
Walter Smith Whitfield. Wife-Georgia Seago.
Noel Dosey Whitfield. Wife-Euna Mae Price.
Jimmy Don Whitfield. Wife-Brenda Phifer.

People studying ancestry of Seaborn Whitfield have a name of William Eugene Whitfield (1722-1793) and wife Genevieve Bryan that could be related to Seaborn Whitfield but the relationship has not been proven with a document. Study has been done on Hancock Co., MS, FL and GA. Connections have been done on Hancock Co., MS. Further study to be on GA and FL.

There are many William Whitfields in early NC, and many to have family trees made for them. Refer to the chapter on NC and view the early territorial lands in counties of NC. In these counties are found early Whitfield settlers not in any print except for the NC Censuses.

South Carolina Record. In 1663 King Charles II of England gave the large territory of the Carolinas to eight courtiers. In 1670 the first settlement was named Charles Town on the Ashley River, and ten years later the people had moved to the peninsula between Cooper and Ashley Rivers, and this land became city of Charleston, SC. A vital and important seaport for Carolina and Georgia.

WILLIAM W. (Dick) WHITFIELD b. Mar. 21, 1850 and d. Feb. 4, 1941 at Upshur, TX. His wife was Julie A. White, b. Feb. 15, 1851 in AL and d. Mar. 4, 1928 in Upshur, TX. They had eight children:
1. William Martin Whitfield, b. May 29, 1875 Tishomingo Co., MS, and d. Sep. 13, 1946 in Upshur, TX.
2. John Luther Whitfield, b. Mar. 28, 1877 Tishomingo, MS. and d. Apr. 23, 1945 in Upshur, TX.
3. Albert Lee Whitfield, b. Jan. 1883 in TX.
4. Marion Whitfield, b. Mar. 1884 in TX.
5. Louisa Whitfield, b. 1840 Tishomingo Co., MS. She md. Gaspar V. Grimes who was b. in Alcorn Co., MS. They had six children.
6. James Thomas (Jim) Whitfield, b. Mar. 5, 1847, and d. Dec. 3, 1935. Burial in Burnsville, Tishomingo Co., MS.
7. William W. (Dick) Whitfield
8. Mary Darcus (Molly) Whitfield, b. Jan. 14, 1853 Tishomingo Co., MS, and d. Oct. 5, 1937, Alcorn Co., MS.

....Submitted Genealogy on Descendants of Joel Whitfield I and Lydia Crisp Whitfield of North Carolina. Compiled by Carolyn Loden of Olive Branch, MS, May 1, 1995. Genealogy includes residents of Edgecombe Co., NC and Pitt Co., NC, and Haywood Co., TN, and Tishomingo Co., MS.

HENRY LEWIS WHITFIELD was b. on June 20, 1868 in Rankin Co., MS. Henry attended Mississippi College in 1895. He md. Mary White on Aug. 25, 1897. They had children: Robert Allen Whitfield, b. in 1899, Henry Lewis Whitfield b. in 1909 and d. in 1916. Knox White Whitfield was b. in 1901 and d. in 1964. Will White Whitfield was b. on Sep. 9, 1913 and raised in Missisippi. He md. Mabel Ewing on May 20, 1944. Will Whitfield was living in Columbus, MS in 1993.

Henry Lewis Whitfield (b. 1868-d. 1927) studied law and became the State Superintendent of Education in 1898 for Mississippi and served until 1907. Then he became president of what is now Mississippi University, serving from 1907 until 1920. He was Governor of Mississippi from 1924 until his death in office on May 18, 1927. Henry L. Whitfield was an educator and a prominent one in that state. He has a published biographical book CATCH THE VISION. The Life of Henry L. Whitfield of Mississippi by Bill R. Baker. University Press of Mississippi, Jackson, MS. Published 1974.

South Carolina Record. South Carolina was an original colonial colony. It was the eighth colony to join the union of states. Area square miles 30,989. Population in 1930 was 1,738,765. Capital at Columbia, SC.

Heads of Families

1850   James M. Whitfield, Tishomingo Co., MS. Southern Division.
1850   Needham Whitfield, Monroe Co., MS. Western Division.
1850   Needham Whitfield, Monroe Co., MS. Western Division.
1850   Robert D. Whitfield, Monroe Co., MS. Western Division.
1850   William Whitfield, Marshall Co., MS. Northern Division
1850   William Whitfield, Jefferson Co., MS. East 9th Twp.
1850   William A. Whitfield, Harrison Co., MS.
1850   William H. Whitfield, Monroe Co., MS.
1850   William Whitfield, Lowndes Co., MS.

These names taken from Federal Censuses 1840 and 1850 and from Mississippi Tax lists in 1841 and 1845 years. It appears a person may be counted more than once on a record, it is a father and son of the same name.

Immigrants to Mississippi state with surname of Whitfield are on the 1840 Censuses and the location of the county. In 1850 the same persons are on 1840 and 1850. The sons and descendants are on the 1850 censuses and the new immigrants to the state.

Study of Vallie Jo Whitfield shows the following:
*   Tishomingo Co., MS. borders Tennessee and Alabama states and in northeast division of state MS.
    1840 Benjamin Whitfield and 1840 Joel Whitfield.
    1850 Benjamin Whitfield and 1850. James M. Whitfield. Joel Whitfield.

*   Hinds Co., MS. near Louisiana in southwest division of state.
    1840   Benjamin Whitfield and 1840 John O. Whitfield
    1850   Benjamin Whitfield.

*   Holmes Co,. MS. Located in middle of MS. State
    1840   Duncan B. Whitfield and 1840 William Whitfield.

*   Desoto Co,. MS. Southern Division of state.
    1850 Johnathan Whitfield.

*   Jefferson Co,. MS. Border of Louisiana State. Western Division near South portion.

*   Hancock Co., MS. Southern division of state.
    1850   B. Whitfield.

SOUTH CAROLINA

In the book, South Carolina Provincial Troops, by Alexander Salley, is a footnote, Number Four, which reads, "The British officer at Fort Charlotte, a nephew of George Whitefield." The book was published in 1977.

The provincial militia troops existed before the revolutionary measures were taken. George Washington was with his army in service and moving his troops.

MISSISSIPPI COUNTIES WITH SURNAME OF WHITFIELD ON THE UNITED STATES FEDERAL CENSUS 1840 and 1850

HEADS OF WHITFIELD FAMILIES

Year
1840, 1841, 1845 Benjamin Whitfield, Tishomingo Co., MS
1845, 1841, 1840 Benjamin Whitfield, Hinds Co., MS.
1840, 1841, 1845 Boar Whitfield, Lowndes Co., MS.
1840 Duncan B. Whitfield, Holmes Co., MS.
1840, 1841, 1845 Edmond Whitfield, Monroe Co., MS.
1845 Edmond H. Whitfield, Marshall Co., MS.
1840, 1841 Edmond H. Whitfield, Marshall Co., MS.
1840 George Whitfield, Marshall Co., MS.
       1841 and 1845 living in Southern Division.
1840, 1845 Hatch Whitfield, Monroe Co., MS.
       (This name appears five times on list).
1840, 1841, 1850 Joel Whitfield, Tishomingo Co., MS.
       (This name appears five times on list.)
1840 John O. Whitfield, Hinds. Co., MS.
       1841, 1845 (This name appears five times on list).
1840, 1841, 1845 Mills Whitfield, Warren Co., MS.
1840, 1845 Needham Whitfield, Monroe Co., MS.
1840, 1841, 1845 William Whitfield, Holmes Co., MS.
       (This name appears four times on list.)
1840, 1841, 1845 William Whitfield, Lowndes Co., MS.
       (This name appears four times on list.)

1850 John Whitfield, Lowndes Co., MS. District 3.

1850 Johnathan Whitfield, Desoto Co., MS. Southern Division.
     (This name appears again on list)

1850 M. W. Whitfield, Warren Co., MS , Vicksburg.

1850 Benjamin Whitfield, Tishomingo Co., MS. 4th District
     Northern Division

1850 Benjamin Whitfield, Hinds Co., MS. Jackson.

1850 Cebern B. Whitfield, Hancock Co., MS. Hobolockitto Dist.

1850 Edmund Whitfield, Monroe Co., MS. Western Division.

1850 George Whitfield, Lowndes Co., MS. Columbus City first
     Ward.

1850 Hatch Whitfield, Monroe Co., MS. Western Division.

1850 James Whitfield, Lowndes Co., MS. Columbus City 3rd
     Ward.

South Carolina Record.

Thomas Whitfield. See Thomas Whitefield. Whitfield lived at
Georgetown County, SC.

*   <u>Harrison Co., MS.</u> Southern division of state Mississippi. 1850 William A. Whitfield

*   <u>Lowndes Co. MS</u>. Middle northeast division of state, and borders on Alabama state.
1840   Boar Whitfield and 1840 William Whitfield.
1850   John Whitfield.   1850 George Whitfield.   1850 James Whitfield.   1850 William Whitfield.

*   <u>Marshall Co., MS.</u> North division of state MS and borders on Tennessee.
1840   Edmond H. Whitfield.   1840 George Whitfield.   1850   William Whitfield.

*   <u>Monroe Co., MS.</u> Northeast division of MS state and borders on Alabama
1840 Edmond Whitfield.   1850 Hatch Whitfield.   1850 Needham Whitfield.   1850   Edmund Whitfield.   1850 Needham Whitfield (varied spellings)   1850 Robert D. Whitfield.   1850 William H. Whitfield.

*********Ten counties of Mississippi had Whitfield heads of families on the 1840 and 1850 federal censuses.

MARRIAGES .

SUSAN M. WHITFIELD was b. 1820 in Wayne Co., NC. She md. (1) D. Wiley Howe and (2) Bryan Watkins (1818-1848). In 1850 Susan was living in Monroe Co., MS. Child: 1. William Whitfield Watkins. Susan Whitfield was of the fifth generation of her lineage.

LILLIE MAY WHITFIELD (b. Oct. 27, 1857-d. Sep. 20, 1892) West Point, MS. She md. William Peyton Owen (Sep. 19,1855-June 27, 1907), son of Judge B. F. Owen, of West Point, MS. They had five children and two children lived to become adults. Demetria Whitfield Owen b. Feb. 18, 1886. She md. James Leonidas Jones, of Logtown, MS. She was living 1927 in Groveland, FL. She had a sister Dona Scott Owen. Susan Whitfield Owen was of the fifth generation of her lineage.

FRANCES (Fannie) Batte Whitfield b. Feb. 27, 1864,in Rankin Co., MS. She md. Charles S. Massey on Feb. 14, 1884. He was of Pickens, Madison Co., MS. She was seventh generation of lineage. Four children of the marriage.

IRENE WHITFIELD b. Feb. 1, 1850, at Shelly, MS., and d. Oct. 13, 1875. She md. Oct. 1, 1866, Dr. Christopher Columbus Post. They had two children.

There were many other daughters with surname of Whitfield born in Mississippi and married there with families.

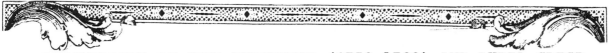

DESCENDANTS OF JOEL WHITFIELD (1750-1783) AND LYDIA CRISP

Whitfield family history of two hundred and forty-five years on a computer program. A family tree stretching from North Carolina across the lands of Tennessee and Mississippi. Many people at Tishomingo Co., MS. and others of the area in that vicinity have been makers in contributing to the design. These people came together in Whitfield Family Reunion at Mississippi.

It began when a child named Carolyn listened to her grandmother's stories of the family and then proceeded to learn more about the people that grandmother spoke about. Carolyn grew into woman and had her own family. She learned keyboard typing of the computer machine, and put the program design to written form as a genealogy. She began with grandmother's family and then moved back in time listing the family members, giving each a number, and collected family groups. She researched and found the ancestor that began all of this Joel Whitfield. He was the first and only person in Colonial American colonies to be named Joel. His son, Benjamin Whitfield, and wives have children that are branches on the Whitfield family tree.

Carolyn Loden of Olive Branch, MS. submitted the computer form of the family tree, May 1995.

Technology of 1995 with computer programs yields computerized genealogy in a simple and specific format. The program used by Carolyn Loden is printed accordingly using numericals of the program to identify people in the particular computer system with data storage.

AMANDA LOU WHITFIELD

My earliest memories of my grandmother are of her sitting in a straight back cane bottomed chair and reading her bible by the light of a kerosene lamp. She was a wonderful woman. She did not preach. She just lived what she believed. She had black hair she usually wore on top of her head in a bun. I loved to watch her at night when she took it down and combed it. She was one of the cleanest people I ever knew. I know I washed my hands until they were raw before meals. And speaking of food she made the best fried pies and canned vegetable soup in the history of the world.

She never talked bad about anyone that I can remember, and I know that she told me at least one thousand times when I was working my family tree "Child, I wish you hadn't found that out". And in almost every case it was not anything bad at all. She and my grandfather were very happily married. I never heard them raise their voices in anger, and they spoiled me and my brother and first cousin Billie Jane Bingham.

I miss my grandmother very much. My only daughter is named for her, Amanda Carol Loden Hill.

253

FAMILY GROUP RECORD-1

Husband-Charles Michael (Mike) Loden-4
    Born June 4, 1940, Winborn, Benton Co., MS.
    Died Sept. 30, 1989, Memphis, Shelby Co., TN. Buried Oct.
    2, 1989, New Albany, Union, MS, Wilkins Cemetery. Charles
    M. Loden md. Carolyn Sue Barnett May 10, 1965 (div.), Twin
    Bridges, Tipton, TN.

    Father-Oliver Lawrence Loden-2027
    Mother-Georgia Helen Lee Booker-2028

Wife-Carolyn Sue Barnett-1.
    Born Jan. 12, 1943, Booneville, Prentiss Co., MS.
    Other marriage of Carolyn S. Barnett to Charles Raleigh
    Heflin-3379. June 1, 1958-divorce.

    Her Father-William Clayton Barnett-5.
    Her Mother-E Marie Bingham -6.

Children:
1. Amanda Carol Loden-2. B. Mar. 12, 1963, Memphis Shelby
    Co., TN. Md. Richard Lee (Dick) Hill-67.
2. Michael Shawn Loden-3. B. Feb. 18, 1966, Knoxville, Knox
    Co., TN.

FAMILY GROUP RECORD-2

Husband-William Clayton Barnett-5.
    Born June 19, 1920, Iuka, Tishomingo Co., MS.
    William C. Barnett md. May 8, 1940 (divorce), Iuka,
    Tishomingo Co., MS.

    Father-James Malcolm Barnett-38.
    Mother-Mary Ethel Underwood-39.

Wife-E Marie Bingham-6.
    Born Mar. 21, 1922, Burnsville, MS.
    Her Father-William Marion Bingham, Jr.-8

Children:
1. Carolyn Sue Barnett-1. B. Jan. 12, 1943, Booneville,
Prentiss, MS. Carolyn Sue Barnett md. May 10, 1965 (div.)
Charles Michael (Mike) Loden-4. Marriage took place at Twin
Bridges, Tipton, TN. Carolyn Barnett Loden md. Charles
Raleigh Heflin-3379 (div.).

2. Gary Michael Barnett-7. B. Sep. 30, 1950, Memphis, Shelby
Co., TN. Gary M. Barnett md. Vick Marie Langston-68. They
were md. at Memphis, TN.

Joel Whitfield married Darcus, maiden name and place unknown. I have always felt she was a Smith because they named their only son William Smith, but of course that is only conjecture. Joel first settled in Haywood Co., TN. On Jan. 28, 1837 Joel Whitfield bought 400 acres from Samuel Woods Surveyor's District 10 range 4 section 11. But for some reason Joel decided to move on because on Oct. 17, 1837 he was buying land in Tishomingo Co., MS. In 1840 he and Benjamin Whitfield both bought land in Tishomingo Co.

Tishomingo Co. was formed from the Chickasaw session in 1836. So our Joel and Benjamin were truly some of the first settlers.

Joel was not as affluent as his brother. I have always assumed he was somewhat of a gambler. At one time we see him taken to court by Banks Ledbetter, his niece's father-in-law, to collect on a gambling debt. In 1850 their only son was married, and they were alone. They signed a power of attorney to brother Benjamin and left.

Family tradition always said he went to Arkansas and was robbed of his gold. Which just may be true because I finally did find him in Sevier Co., AR with his wife Darcus Whitfield on the 1860 census. Why he left Mississippi and his only child has always been a mystery to me. But after much thought I remembered the gold rush started in 1849, so I guess Joel was looking for gold.

In 1870 he, or his wife, was not on the census. I lost them at this point. But William Smith Whitfield did go to visit them at least once. Rethel Whitfield, daughter of George W. Whitfield, remembers her father and her uncle, John Whitfield, talking about the time their daddy went to Texas to visit his parents. His daughter Mary Darcus Whitfield was born while he was gone and was a big baby about a year old. When he came back, he said his mother begged and begged him not to leave. Sevier Co., AR is on the Texas border.

Tishomingo Co., MS is the county at the northeast corner of the state and borders on Tennessee and Alabama.

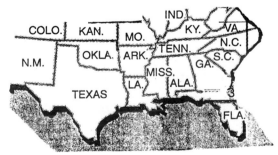

Joel moved across Mississippi and Arkansas to reach Sevier Co., AR. Joel Whitfield died and buried at Sevier Co., AR after 1860 and before 1870.

May 1, 1995   By Carolyn Loden

Husband-William Marion Bingham, Jr.-8.
        Born June 1, 1880, Burnsville, Tishomingo, MS.
        Died March 18, 1966, Burnsville, MS. Buried at Burnsville
        Cemetery.

        William M. Bingham md. Amanda Lou Whitfield Dec. 24, 1907
        at Burnsville, MS.

        Father-William Marion Bingham-7.
        Mother-Sarah Elizabeth Johnson-18.

Wife-Amanda Lou Whitfield,
        Born Feb. 4, 1888, Burnsville, MS.
        Died June 13, 1976, Burnsville, MS, and buried at
        Burnsville Cemetery.

        Father-James Thomas (Jim) Whitfield-31.
        Mother-America Elizabeth (Meck) Woodley-32.

Children: All born at Burnsville, Tishomingo Co., MS.

1.   Edna Opal Bingham-10. B. Jan. 31, 1917. D. Oct. 6, 1918.
     Tishomingo Co., MS.
2.   Troy Whitner Bingham-11. B. Aug. 27, 1919, Burnsville, MS.
     Troy Bingham md. Dec. 21, 1940 Orene Milisaps-13.
3.   E. Marie Bingham-6. B. Mar. 21, 1922, Burnsville, MS. E.
     Marie Whitfield md. May 8, 1940 William Clayton Barnett-5.
     Marriage at Iuka, MS.
4.   Wilton Leroy Bingham-12. B. Sep. 7, 1928. D. May 15,
     1989, Burnsville, MS. Buried at Burnsville, MS. Buried
     Rowland Mills, MS. Wilton Leroy Bingham md. June 5, 1963
     Launa Ross-16. They were md. at Belton, Bell Co., TX.

ANCESTOR

The name Whitfield is of English origin. Whitfields emigrated
from that European country. Joel Whitfield's birthplace is
unknown. Joel Whitfield and wife Lydia Crisp lived at Pitt Co.,
NC. Lydia Crisp Whitfield birth place was at Martin Co., NC.

Joel Whitfield may have been a native but his parentage is
unknown. The emigrant ship records for passengers to North
Carolina colony has not been seen by researchers.

The root of the family tree involves ancestor. Joel Whitfield
(b. 1750-d. 1783) is the ancestor known for this family tree and
family groups.

Husband-Gasper W. Grimes-311. Born Dec. 1840 TN. He was
buried in Alcorn Co., MS, Old Danville Cemetery.

     Father-Henry Young Grimes-4284
     Mother-Elizabeth Fuson-4285

Wife-Louisa Whitfield-155, Born Nov. 1840, Tishomingo Co., MS.

     Father-William Smith Whitfield-153
     Mother-Martha Ann Marilda Lankford-154

Children:
1. Martha E. Grimes-312. Born Oct. 1874, MS.
2. James Gaspar (Jim) Grimes-313. Born June 1869, MS.
    James Grimes md. Rebecka Ray-5285
3. Mary Lou Grimes-5247. Born May 1877, MS.
4. Thomas J. Grimes-314. Born June 187_, MS.
5. Henry Luther Grimes-316. Born Dec. 1880, MS.
6. Lizzie A. (Lou) Grimes-315. Born June 1884, MS.

Husband-William W. (Dick) Whitfield-156.
    Born Mar. 21, 1850 Tishomingo Co., MS.
    Died Feb. 4, 1941, Upshur Co., TX. Buried Upshur Co.,
TX, Morris Cemetery.

    Father-William Smith Whitfield-153.
    Mother-Martha Ann Marilda Lankford-154.

Wife-Julie A. White-317.
    Born Feb. 15, 1851, AL.
    Died Mar. 4, 1928, Upshur, TX. Buried Upshur, TX, Morris
Cemetery.

Children:
1. William Martin Whitfield-318. Born May 29, 1875,
    Tishomingo, MS. Died Sep. 13, 1946, TX. Buried Upshur,
    TX, Morris Cemetery.
2. John Luther Whitfield-319. Born Mar. 28, 1877, Upshur,
    TX. Buried Upshur, TX, Morris Cemetery, for he died Apr.
    23, 1945.
3. Albert Lee Whitfield-320. Born Jan. 1883, TX
4. Marion Whitfield-321. Born Mar., 1884, TX.
5. James E. Whitfield-322. Born May 1888, TX.
6. Frederick (Fred) Whitfield-323. Born Feb. 1890, TX

Husband-Joel Whitfield-160. Year of Birth 1804.
Wife-Darcus-161.

Child-WILLIAM SMITH WHITFIELD.
    William S. Whitfield was b. Dec. 27, 1822 in NC. When he
was about 14 his father headed west. Can you imagine what an
adventure that would be for a boy that age? The rivers that had
to be crossed, the storms, and wild animals. And this was just
at the time the Indians were still here but were being pushed
westward. It must have been a great adventure even with women
living in wagons on the trail. I know it must have been hard to
get settled.
    On Jan. 11, 1838 at the age of 15 years and 15 days, he sold
a pair of black and white oxen, marked with a bix on the right
ear and a crop and a split on the left. They had to be sold
because he owed his uncle Benjamin Whitfield $55.93. Boys were
men at an early age during those times.
    William Smith Whitfield was a farmer and a gunsmith, he was
also a sharp shooter, and he made a lot of his living going to
turkey shoots, etc., and taking home the prize.
    When William was age 21, he married Martha Lankford. She
was a midwife and delivered all the neighborhood babies. She was
a hard person to live with it is said, she ran him off, and the
children had to sneak off to go to see their father. Martha was
busy helping with childbirths in other houses.
    William S. Whitfield was said to be a good and kind man.
William Smith and his first cousin, William who was Benjamin's
son, were close friends. To tell them apart he ended up with the
nickname Monkey Bill, and his cousin was Hacker Bill.
    William Smith served his country in the Civil War between
the North and South. He was in Morelands Alabama Cavalry. His
widow applied for his pension in 1900.
    William Whitfield died at the home of William Williams in
1871 and is buried in the woods in the Whitfield Cemetery near
the old home place now known as the Crain place. It is said the
reason for his death was an accidental gunshoot wound in the leg
that he later died from. He and his son and most of the
Whitfield men were great fox hunters.

Husband-Joel Whitfield
    Born 1804, Pitt Co., NC and died after 1860 in Sevier Co.,
    AR. Joel Whitfield-160. Father-Benjamin Whitfield Sr.-162.
    Mother-Susanna Wilkinson-163.
Wife-Darcus-161. Child-William Smith Whitfield-153.
    Born Dec. 27, 1822, NC and died Feb. 18, 1871, Tishomingo
    Co., MS, and buried at Whitfield Cemetery. He was md. Nov.
    23, 1843 to Martha Ann Marilda Lankford-154.

Husband-William Smith Whitfield-153. Born Dec. 27, 1822, North Carolina. Died Feb. 18, 1871, Tishomingo Co., MS. Buried Tishomingo Co., MS. William Smith Whitfield md Nov. 23, 1843 to Martha Ann Marilda Lankford.
Father-Joel Whitfield-160.
Mother-Darcus-161

Wife-Martha A. M. Lankford-154,
Born Nov. 9, 1823, and died Apr. 16, 1913, Tishomingo Co., MS, and buried at Old Lebanon Cemetery.
Her father was John Lankford-3085. Her mother may have been _____ Luster ?-3086.

William Smith Whitfield and Martha Lankford Whitfield had six children:
1. Louisa Whitfield, b. 1840, MS.
2. James Thomas (Jim) Whitfield, b. 1847-d.1935.
3. William Whitfield, b. 1850-d. 1941, MS.
4. Mary Darcus Whitfield, b. 1853-d. 1937.
5. John H. Whitfield, b. 1855-d. 1948 MS.
6. George Washington Whitfield, b. 1857-d. 1935, MS.

FAMILY GROUP RECORD-8

Husband-James Thomas (Jim) Whitfield-31. Born Mar. 5, 1847, Burnsville, Tishomingo Co., MS. Died Dec. 3, 1935, Burnsville, MS.
Father-William Smith Whitfield-153.
Mother-Martha Ann Marilda Lankford-154.
Wife-America Elizabeth (Meck) Woodley-32. Born Dec. 14, 1849 MS-GA. Died July 7, 1925, Burnsville, Tishomingo Co., MS., and buried Woodley Cemetery.
Father-David D. Woodley-539.
Mother-Narcissa Dean-540.

Children: Six boys and three girls. Township-Burnsville, MS. All children born in Tishomingo Co., MS.
1. Anna Belle Whitfield-33. B. Sep. 26, 1875
2. Martha Ella Whitfield-34. B. May 26, 1878. D. Nov. 21, 1957, Burnsville, MS. Buried Rowland Mills Cemetery. Martha Whitfield md. Bert U. Watkins-178 on the day of Feb. 24, 1901.

South Carolina Provincial Troop Soldier.

Lewis Whitfield served in the militia and was at the fall of Charles Town. Yearbook 1897.

Lewis Whitefield, son of Luke Whitfield and Chloe Whitfield of Georgetown County, SC. He was born about 1756 in Carolina's and died 1832 in Burke County, GA.

3. William Whitner (Will) Whitfield-35. B. May 29, 1880. D. June 25, 1964, Tishomingo Co., MS, New Lebanon Cem. William Whitfield md. Ora Alice Jourdan-186, and on the day Oct. 1, 1909.

4. Arthur David Whitfield-36. B. Feb. 2, 1882. D. Sep. 26, 1976, Tishomingo Co., MS, Buried Belmont Cemetery.

5. George Washington Whitfield-37. B. Mar. 16, 1883. D. Mar. 6, 1968, Burnsville, MS. Buried Rowland, MS. George W. Whitfield md. in 1911 to Cora Dee Peterson-208.

6. James Franklin Whitfield-150. B. Mar. 4, 1886, Glen, MS. D. Mar. 21, 1966, Winona, MS. James F. Whitfield md. on July 28, 1907 to Myrtle Alice Bingham-26 in Mississippi.

7. Amanda Lou Whitfield-9. B. Feb. 4, 1888. D. June 13, 1976. Born and died at Burnsville, MS. Amanda L. Whitfield md. on Dec. 24, 1907 to William Marion Bingham, Jr-8.

8. Samuel Benning Whitfield-151. B. Aug. 31, 1891. D. Dec. 1, 1970, MS. Samuel B. Whitfield md. on Mar. 19, 1922 to Effie McCoy-258.

9. Code Dean Whitfield-152. B. July 22, 1897, Tishomingo, MS. D. Nov. 13, 1968, Grenada, MS. Buried in Carroll Co., MS, Mt. Pisgah Cemetery. Code D. Whitfield md. on Aug. 17, 1919 Tishomingo, MS. Code D. Whitfield md. again on May 10, 1925 to Vera Woods-265.

CENSUS 1840 of Tishomingo County, Mississippi
Benjamin Whitfield

2 males-5-10	3 females-0-5
1 male-30-40	1 female-10-15
	1 female-20-30

CENSUS 1850 of Tishomingo County, Mississippi
Benjamin Whitfield, age 44, male, Farmer, Property value $1,000, b. NC. Nancy Whitfield-wife, age 40, female, b. NC.

Husband-William C. L. Burcham-324. Born July 11, 1860, MS. Died
Nov. 16, 1938, Burnsville, Tishomingo, MS.
        Father-Levi H, Burcham, Jr.-520.
        Mother-Elizabeth Hays-538.

Wife-Mary Darcus (Molly) Whitfield-157. Born Jan. 14, 1853,
Tishomingo Co., MS. Died Oct. 5, 1937, Corinth, Alcorn Co., MS
        Father-William Smith Whitfield-153
        Mother-Martha Ann Marilda Lankford-154

Children:
1. Arthur P. Burcham-326. Born March 2, 1882, MS. D. in
    Tishomingo Co., MS, and buried in Little Flock Cem. Arthur
    was md. to Mary Rebecca (Pent) Bingham-22
2. William Kirby (Kirb) Burcham-325. Born May 3, 1892, Durant,
    Bryan Co., OK. Died Dec. 4, 1986, Atmore, AL. Buried at
    Burnsville, Tishomingo Co., MS, Rowland Mills Cemetery.
    William was md. to Minnie Belle Ross-328.
3. Benjamin F. Burcham-327. Born 1887. Died 1918, Tishomingo,
    Co., MS., Little Flock Cemetery buried. Benjamin md. Sue
    Thomas-497

Husband-John H. (Tink) Whitfield-158. Born Sep. 23, 1855,
Tishomingo Co., MS. Died FeBorn 12, 1948, Burnsville,
Tishomingo Co., MS, and buried at Rowland Mills Cemetery.
        Father-William Smith Whitfield-153.
        Mother-Martha Ann Marilda Lankford-154.

Wife-Mary Jane (Molly) Carter-335.

Children:
1. Evie E. Whitfield-336. Born Sep. 8, 1882, TN. Died May
    12, 1907, Henning, TN. Buried Henning, TN, Poplar Grove
    Cemetery. Evie Whitfield md. Jack Raines-376
2. Claude Whitfield-337. Born Mar. 8, 1895, TN. Died Nov.
    5, 1911, Henning, TN. Buried Henning, TN., Bethlehem
    Cemetery.
3. Carrie Roberta Whitfield-338. Born Aug. 23, 1887, TN.
    Died Sep. 8, 1908, Henning, TN. Buried Henning, TN.
    Poplar Grove Cemetery.
4. William Carl Whitfield-339. Born Nov. 20, 1890, TN. Died
    Nov. 13, 1936, Tishomingo Co., MS. Buried Cookvile, TN,
    Dyer-Billingsly Cemetery. William Whitfield md. Arpha C.
    Dyer-377.

South Carolina Provincial Troop Soldier.

Thomas Jordan Whitefield served 12 months as a sergeant and
four months as a forage-master in the cavalry under Colonel
Daniel Horry. N 425.

Continued Family Group Record-101

5. Willis Lane Whitfield-340. Born July 27, 1893, TN. Died after 1974. Willis Lane Whitfield md. Ada Pittman-378. William or Ada Pittman Whitfield had other marriages.
6. Walter Bowman Whitfield-341. Born July 27, 1893, TN.
7. Baby Whitfield-342. Born and died one month later. Infant child buried Henning, TN, Cemetery.

JAMES THOMAS WHITFIELD
1847-1935

Computer program for over three thousand names. A single lineage collected over periods of time and put into the data program system gives varied numbers when withdrawn from storage discs. Numbers stay with the name. Carolyn Loden of Olive Branch, MS submitted May 1, 1995 the following computer chart.

Husband-Benjamin Whitfield, Jr., born July 18, 1806 NC. Died Mar 30, 1862, Tishorningo Co., MS.
      Father-Benjamin Whitfield, Sr.
      Mother-Susanna Wilkinson

Md. Jan. 5, 1826, Edgecombe Co., NC.
Wife-Nancy Council, born Nov. 10, 1811, NC and died Jan. 1, 1901, Tishomingo Co., MS. Buried at Holder Cemetery

Eleven children: Five boys and six girls.
1.   William C. Whitfield Born June 21, 1831 NC and died May 11, 1903, MS. Buried Little Flock Cemetery. William C. Whitfield md. Nov. 10, 1853 to Elizabeth J. Welch. Elizabeth was born Feb. 17, 1838 in TN. She d. on May 11 or 16 day and 1897 or 1917. Buried in Little Flock Cemetery.

2.   Josiah Whitfield, born ca. 1834, in NC. Josiah Whitfield md. Feb. 24, 1859 to Sarah E. Robinson.

3.   Mary Whitfield, born ca. 1836, NC.

4.   Eliza Whitfield, born ca. 1838. Eliza md. John Morris. Wayne Co., TN. burial place of one of them. Eliza md. Oct. 27, 1853 to James H. Ledbetter. James died before 1860 and buried in MS.

5.   Narcissa Whitfield, born Jan. 18, 1840 in TN, and died May 21, 1881, Prentiss Co., MS. Narcissa Whitfield md. Dec. 13, 1866 to Wiley Baxter Pollard. Wiley was Born July 18, 1845, AL and he died Sept. 22, 1922, MS, buried at Mt. Pleasant Cemetery.

6.   John W. Whitfield, born Feb. 11, 1843, MS. and died May 19, 1923, MS. Buried Little Flock Cemetery. John W. Whitfield md. Emily Pratt Oct. 3, 1867. Emily was born Dec. 2, 1841 and died Oct. 26, 1923. John W. Whitfield served in Company A, 2nd Mississippi Infantry, CSA. Civil War.

7.   Benjamin Whitfield, born ca. 1844, MS. Benjamin F. Whitfield was young when he served in Company E 17th Mississippi CSA. Civil War. Benjamin md. June 27, 1867 to Rachel Swimm.

8.   Susan Whitfield born ca 1846, MS.

WHITEFIELD - SOUTH CAROLINA ROSTER ARMY OFFICERS 1777

Benjamin Whitefield. See Benjamin Whitfield (1752 NC-1836 GA).

Joshua Whitefield. He served in the second Regiment during 1777. S.C.H. & G., XVI 31.

9. Nancy Whitfield born ca. 1848, MS.

10. Joel Whitfield born ca. 1851, MS.   Joel md. Mary J. Shill.

11. Amanda Whitfield born ca. 1853, MS.   She md. Charles L. Morris. Died in Wayne Co., TN.

_____
References:
    Alcorn Co., Mississippi Marriages
    Cemeteries of Tishomingo Co., MS.
    Cemeteries of Prentiss Co., MS.
    History Of Old Tishomingo Co. MS
    1845, 1850, 1860 Censuses Tishomingo Co., MS.
    North Carolina Marriage Bonds on Microfide Centioplex
    Library.

....Submitted by Lucille Hastings Thompson of Wynne, AR, May 1995.

FAMILY GROUP-45

Husband-Benjamin Whitfield SR-162.   Born circa 1780 in Pitt Co., NC and died 1840, Pitt Co., NC.
    Father-Joel Whitfield SR-166
    Mother- Lydia Crisp-167.   Parents MRIN-46

Benjamin Whitfield had three marriages. Refer to North Carolina for the other marriages.

Wife-Susanna Wilkinson-163.   She was born in 1787. NC or VA. Susanna Whitfield died in Pitt Co., NC.
    Father-Joshua Wilkinson-176
    Mother-Sarah Knight-177

Children:
1. Albena Whitfield-165. Born in 1803, NC. Died after 1846 in TN. Albena md. William Nelson-373. On Nov. 24, 1822 they were wed in Edgecombe Co., NC. She had another marriage to Obediah Carson and had six children.   MRIN 109

2. Joel Whitfield-160. Born 1804 in Pitt Co., NC. He died after 1860 and before 1869, Sevier Co., AR. Joel Whitfield md. Darcus ____ 1825.   MRIN-44

3. Benjamin Whitfield, Jr.-164. Born July 18, 1806, NC. Died Mar. 30, 1862, Burnsville, Tishomingo Co., MS. Buried in Tishomingo Co., MS, Holder Cemetery.   MRIN-453

South Carolina Provincial Troop Soldier.

Thomas Whitefield served 25 days in the militia under General Marion during 1782. A.A. 8446; Q615.

Husband-Joel Whitfield SR-166.   Year of Birth - 1750
Wife-Lydia Crisp-167.   Year of Birth - 1755

Husband-JOEL WHITFIELD
     Joel Whitfield md. Lydia Crisp of Martin Co., NC about 1775.
     After their marriage he bought 200 acres of land in Pitt
     Co., NC, in the northern part of Bethel. This land is still
     in the hands of Whitfields today.

Wife-LYDIA CRISP

Child-Benjamin Whitfield SR-162

Benjamin Whitfield, Sr. md. about 1802. His wife evidently did
not live long; her last child was born in 1806. In 1817 he
remarried to Clara Council Cherry, a widow. I have not been able
to prove any children of this marriage. Clary, as she was
called, also only lived a few years after her marriage, for on
June 8, 1825 Benjamin Whitfield md. again to Temperance Manning.
At this time he would be in his fifties of age, and Temperance
is a young woman. To this union three more children are born.
The children of his first marriage are grown. The daughter
Albena Whitfield is married and settled.

I think Benjamin Whitfield, Sr., more or less, paid the older
children their inheritance because of his new young family. This
is when he gave them land. Joel headed west. First he was in
Haywood Co., TN in 1830. On Feb. 28, 1837 a deed was recorded
for the purchase of 400 acres of land, purchased from Samuel
Woods, 10th Surveyor's District, range 4, section 11. Benjamin
soon joined him.

FAMILY GROUP RECORD-46
May 1, 1995   Page 1 of 2
Husband-Joel Whitfield, born ca. 1750, NC and died ca. 1783 in
Pitt Co., NC.

Wife-Lydia Crisp, born ca. 1755, North California at Martin Co.
and died as Lydia Crisp Whitfield Baden in Edgecombe Co., NC.
Father-William Mansel Crisp-168, Martin Co., NC.
Mother-Frances Crisp.

Child-Benjamin Whitfield SR-162 born 1780 ca, born in Pitt Co.,
NC, and died 1840 in Pitt Co., NC.
His spouse-Susanna Wilkinson-163.
Benjamin had three marriages.

Note - Land early is Edgecombe territory and land splits made
Pitt Co. Whitfield is on the same land site.

Wife		Husband
Nancy Council	Name	Benjamin Whitfield Jr.
NC 11-10-1811	Born	7-18-1806 North Carolina
	Married	1-5-1826 Edgecombe Co. N.C.
Tishomingo Co. Miss. 1-1-1901	Died	3-30-1862 Tishomingo Co. Miss.
Holder Cemetery	Burial	Holder Cemetery, Tish. Co, Ms.
	Father	Benjamin Whitfield
Date married & spouse	Mother	Susanna Wilkinson Born 16 Oct. 1787

#	S	Children in order of birth	Born Day Month Year	Where born	Died Day Month Year	Where died
1	m	William C. Whitfield	6-21-1831	NC	5-11-1903	Little Flock
11-10-1853		Elizabeth J. Welch	2-17-1838	Tenn.	5-11-19170 / 5-16-1897	Little Flok
2	m	Josiah Whitfield	ca. 1834	NC		
2-24-1859		Sarah E. Robinson				
3	F	Mary Whitfield	ca. 1836	N.C.		
4	F	Eliza Whitfield	ca. 1838			WAYNE CO. TN
10-27-1853		James H. Ledbetter			bef 1860	MS
5	F	Narcissa Whitfield	1-18-1840	Tenn	5-21-1881	PRENTISS CO.
12-13-1866		Wiley Baxter Pollard	7-18-1845	AL	9-22-1922	MT. PLEASANT
6	m	John W. Whitfield	2-11-1843	Miss.	5-19-1923	LITTLEFLOCK CEM.
10-3-1867		Emily Pratt	12-2-1841		10-26-1923	
7	m	Benjamin F. Whitfield	ca. 1844	Miss.		
6-27-1867		Rachel Swimm				
8	F	Susan Whitfield	ca. 1846	Miss		
9	F	Nancy Whitfield	ca. 1848	Miss		
10	m	Joel Whitfield	ca. 1851	Miss		
11-5-1869		Mary J. Shill				
11	F	Amanda Whitfield	ca. 1853	Miss.		

FAMILY GROUP RECORD

Sources : 1. Lucille Hastings Thompson. 2. Alcorn Co., Miss.
Marriages. 3. Cemeteries of Tishomingo, MS. 4. Cemeteries
of Prentiss County. 5. History Of Old Tishomingo County.
6. Censuses 1845 - 1850 - 1860 Tishomingo Co., MS. 7. North
Carolina Marriage. 8. Bonds. Microfilm, Centiplex Library.

DESCENDANTS OF BENJAMIN WHITFIELD (1806-1862)
AND NANCY COUNCIL

Benjamin was born son of Benjamin Whitfield (1780-1840) and Susanna Wilkinson Whitfield.

Ruby Whitfield, wife of Lanier A. Whitfield, and mother of Jerry Whitfield, age 42 (1995) of Gatesville, NC had these families as descends of Benjamin Whitfield, Jr, Mar. 1995.

John Wesley Whitfield md. Emily Pollard, and family lived in Tishomingo Co., MS. Son follows.

Joseph Lou Allen Whitfield md. Minnie G. Ross, and family has lived in Corinth and Burnsville, and in 1995 lives in Iuka, MS. Son follows.

Artis Odell Whitfield md. Sarah Elizabeth Gable, had only one son who moved to Arizona in 1942. Both parents are buried in Rest Haven Cemetery in Glendale, Arizona near Phoenix.

Lanier Artis Whitfield md. Ruby Arien Beights, born 1927. They had the son, Jerry Whitfield. The father, Lanier was born 1925.

Mississippi Records

Elizabeth Whitfield, sister of Honorable James Whitfield of Columbus, MS, Governor of Mississippi, was md. to John Goode Oct. 8, 1801. John Goode d. Aug. 28, 1846. Elizabeth Goode d. June 17, 1847, aged 66 years, 3 months and 11 days. ....Submitted by Kathleen Rich of Tallahassee, FL on July 27, 1968. The information came from the Goode family Bible. The family came from Virginia to Georgia and settled at Upson Co., GA.

Henry L. Whitfield (1868-1927) was Governor of Mississippi.

Governor of Mississippi, James Whitfield (b. 1791-d.1847).

CENSUS 1860 of Tishomingo Co., MS.

Benjamin Whitfield, age 55, male, Farming, 3,000-4,000, b. NC.
Nancy Whitfield, wife, age 50, female, b. NC.
Children all b. in Mississippi.
Narcissa Whitfield, age 20, female, b. 1840
John Whitfield, age 18, male
Benjamin F. Whitfield, age 16, male.
Susan Whitfield, age 15, female
Nancy Whitfield, age 13, female
Joel Whitfield, age 9, male, b. 1851
Amanda Whitfield, age 7, female, b. 1853
Elizabeth Whitfield Ledbetter, age 22, female
Grandaughter, Mam Ledbetter, age 5, female, b. MS.
Grandson, James P. Ledbetter, age 3, male, b. MS.

Certificate No. 8847

The United States of America

To all to whom these Presents shall come, Greeting:

WHEREAS *Joel Whitfield of Ittawamba County Miss* ha.. deposited in
the GENERAL LAND OFFICE of the United States, a Certificate of the REGISTER OF THE LAND OFFICE
at *Pontotoc* In several treaties with the Chicasaw Indians dated Oct. 20, 1832 and May 24, 1824 , whereby it appears that full payment has been made by the said
Joel Whitfield , according to the provisions of the Act of Congress of the
24th of April, 1820, entitled "An Act making further provision for the sale of the Public Lands," for *the*
South East Quarter of Section 4 in Township 4 of
Range 7 East in District of Lands subject to sale at
Pontotoc Miss. Containing 159 7/100 acres

according to the official survey plat of the said Lands, returned to the General Land Office by the SURVEYOR
GENERAL, which said tract has been purchased by the said *Joel Whitfield*

NOW KNOW YE, That the UNITED STATES OF AMERICA, in consideration of the Premises, and in
conformity with the several acts of Congress, in such case made and provided, HAVE GIVEN AND GRANTED,
and by these presents DO GIVE AND GRANT, unto the said *Joel Whitfield*
and to *his* heirs, the said tract above described; TO HAVE AND TO HOLD the same, together with all
the rights, privileges, immunities, and appurtenances of whatsoever nature, thereunto belonging, unto the said
Joel Whitfield and to *his* heirs and assigns forever.

IN TESTIMONY WHEREOF, I *Martin Van Buren* , PRESIDENT OF
THE UNITED STATES OF AMERICA, have caused letters to be made PATENT, and the SEAL, of the
GENERAL LAND OFFICE to be hereunto affixed.

Given under my hand, at the CITY OF WASHINGTON, the *6* day of *October* ,
in the Year of Our Lord One Thousand Eight Hundred and *Forty* , and of the IN-
DEPENDENCE OF THE UNITED STATES the *65th* .

BY THE PRESIDENT *Martin Van Buren*
By M. Van Buren Jr Secy

Joseph S. Wilson
acting Recorder of the General Land Office.

(Seal)

Filed for Record Dec. 29th 1917
Record in Land Patent Record
P.14. Page 16, Dec. 21 1917.

Recorded, Vol. *P/4* , Page *16*

E. A. Payne, Clerk. By I. I. Stormont D.C.

268

```
      P E D I G R E E              8 Joel WHITFIELD-160----------------:   16 Benjamin WHITFIELD SR-162
                                   ¦ B:        1804                       : B: Abt     1775
          C H A R T                ¦ P: Prob,EC,North Carolina            ¦ D: Aft     1840
4 William Smith WHITFIELD-153-------¦ M:       --44                       17 Susanna WILKINSON-163-
¦ B: 27 Dec 22                     ¦ P:                                      B: 16 Nov 1787
¦ P: ..North Carolina              ¦ D:                                      D: 1 Aug 1818
¦ M: 23 Nov 1843   --43            ¦ P: Pro,Sevier Co,Ark
¦ P: .Tishomingo Co,Ms                                                       32 Joel WHITFIELD
¦ D: 18 Feb 1871                   9 Darcus-161                             ---!
¦ P: .Tishomingo Co,Ms             ¦ B:                                      33 Lydia CRISP-167-
¦                                  ¦ P:
2 James Thomas [Jim] WHITFIELD-31---- P:                                     34 Joshua WILKINSON
¦ B: 5 Mar 1847                    ¦ D:                                      ---!
¦ P: Burnsville,Tishomingo Co,Ms   ¦ P:                                      35 Sarah KNIGHT-17?
¦ M:     --8                                                                 44 John Burton ENLOW-928
¦ P:                               10 John LANKFORD-3085                     ---!
¦ D: 3 Dec 1935                    ¦ B:                                      45 Margaret Ann HILL-929
¦ P: Burnsville,Tishomingo Co,Ms   ¦ P: ,,Georgia                            46 Thomas Franklin DENTON-922-
¦                                  ¦ M:     --1080                          ---!
5 Martha Ann Marilda LANKFORD-154---¦ P:                                     47 Mary Ethelinda ELLIS-923
¦ B: 9 Nov 1823                    ¦ D:                                      50 UNKOWN TAYLOR-1399
¦ P: ,,GA/S/C/S/C                  ¦ P:                                      ----!
¦ D: 16 Apr 1913                                                             51 Jerutia-1398
¦ P: .Tishomingo Co,Ms             11 UNKOWN LUSTER ?-3086                   54 John WILSON-3087----
¦                                  ¦ B:                                      ---!
¦                                  ¦ P: ,,Georgia                            55 Sarah UNKOWN-3088---
¦                                  ¦ D:
1 Amanda Lou WHITFIELD-9---------- ¦ P:                                      56 Joel WHITFIELD-160--
¦ B: 4 Feb 1888                                                             ---!
¦ P: Burnsville,Tishomingo,Ms                                                57 Darcus-161----------
¦ M: 24 Dec 1907   --3
¦ P: Burnsville,Tishomingo,Ms                                                58 John LANKFORD-3085--
¦ D: 13 Jun 1976                                                            ---!
¦ P: Burnsville,Tishomingo,Ms      12 John WOODLEY-551                       59 UNKOWN LUSTER ?-3086-
¦William Marion Jr BINGHAM-8----    ¦ B:       1790/1800
¦ Spouse                            ¦ P:                                      60 John WOODLEY-551-----
¦                                  ¦ M:     --189                           ---!
¦  6 David D WOODLEY-539------------¦ P:                                      61 Mary Jane [Polly] FARRIS-5
¦  ¦ B: 28 Jul 1823                ¦ D: Abt    1835
¦  ¦ P: ,,Ala                       ¦ P:                                      62 Griffith DEAN-547--
¦  ¦ M:    --186                                                            ---!
¦  ¦ P:                             13 Mary Jane [Polly] FARRIS-552          63 Annice BISHOP-548--
¦  ¦ D: 5 Feb 1896                 ¦ B:       1805
¦  ¦ P: .Tishomingo Co,Ms          ¦ P: ,,Ala/Tn
¦  ¦                               ¦ D:
3 America Elizabeth [Meck] WOODLEY-32- P: .Tishomingo Co,Ms
   ¦ B: 14 Dec 1849
   ¦ P: ,,Ms-Ga-S/C
   ¦ D: 7 Jul 1925                        Part One                           Part Three
   ¦ P: Burnsville,TC,Mississippi
```

269

PEDIGREE CHART

```
                                                                28 Samuel DEAN-549-----
                                                                !  B:       1751
                                14 Griffith DEAN-547----------------!  D: 22 May 1826
                                !   B:       1794
                                !   P: ,AD,South Carolina
                                !   M: Abt    1818   --187        29 Gwendolyn JANES-550--
                                !   P:                               B:       1754
   !                            !   D: 22 Dec 1858                   D: Aft 22 May 1826
 7 Narcissa DEAN-540-----------!   P: ,Tishomingo Co,Ms            30
   B:  4 Oct 1825              !
   P: ,,South Carolina         !
   D: 31 Jan 1908              !
   P: ,Tishomingo Co,Ms        15 Annice BISHOP-548
                                  B:
```

```
                                                                16 Luther Alfred BARNETT-50--
                                                                !  B:    Jun 1828
                                 8 William H [Billy] BARNETT-44------!  D: Aft    1910
                                 !   B:       1867
                                 !   P: ,Tishomingo Co,Ms
                                 !   M: 29 Dec 1887   --10        17 Martha Elvira REID-51------
                                 !   P: ,Tishomingo Co,Ms            B:    Nov 1828
 4 James Malcolm BARNETT-38----------!   D: Abt    1905             D: Bef    1910
   ! B: 14 Jun 1897             !   P: ,Tishomingo Co,Ms
   ! P: ,Tishomingo Co,Ms       !                                18 John A MARONEY-110---------
   ! M: 25 Dec 1918   --9       !                                !  B:       1848
   ! P: ,Tishomingo Co,Mississippi  9 L Cordelia [Cordie] MARONEY-45----!  D:
   ! D: 18 Jun 1960             !   B:    Feb 1873
   ! P: Iuka,Tishomingo Co,Ms   !   P: ,,Ms                      19 Susan Jane HARRIS-111------
 2 William Clayton BARNETT-5----------   D: Abt    1933             B:    Dec 1844
   !    B: 19 Jun 1920              P: ,Tishomingo Co,Ms          D: Aft    1900
   !    P: Iuka,Tishomingo,Ms
   !    M:  8 May 1940(div)  --2                              20 Martin Van Buren UNDERWOOD-926
   !    P: Iuka,Tishomingo,Ms                                    !  B:  5 Sep 1835
   !    D:                        10 Samuel Huskey UNDERWOOD-58--------!  D: 19 Jan 1927
   !    P:                        !   B: 24 Sep 1869
   !                              !   P: ,Bradley Co,Tn-Tn-Ga     21 Sarah C INGRAM-927
   !                              !   M: 26 Jan 1889   --12          B:  1 Apr 1841
   5 Mary Ethel UNDERWOOD-39-----------!   P: ,Tishomingo Co,Mississippi  D:  6 Apr 1888
     B: 16 Jul 1902               !   D: 24 Aug 1924             22 Richard Fairlander ENLOW-696
     P: ,Tishomingo Co,Ms-Tn-Ms   !   P: Dennis,Tishomingo Co,Ms
     D: 12 Feb 1992               !                                !  B:  4 Mar 1845
     P:                          11 Etha Ann ENLOW-59----------------!  D: 22 Sep 1927
                                    B: 19 Jul 1872
                                    P: ,,Ala/Tn/Ala              23 Margaret Jane Amanda DENTON-921
                                    D:    Mar 1940                  B:  6 Sep 1848
                                    P: ,Tishomingo Co,Ms           D: 17 Aug 1924
```

Part Two

270

2

```
1 Carolyn Sue BARNETT-1----------------
    B: 12 Jan 1943
    P: Booneville,Prentiss,Ms
    M: 10 May 1965(div)    --1
    P: Twin Bridges,Tipton,Tn                         24 Hugh M BIGHAM-553
    D:                                                   B: Abt   1800
    P:                            12 William Marion BINGHAM-17---------! D: Abt   1887
   Charles Michael [Mike] LODEN-4-   B:  7 Dec 1836
    Spouse                           P: ,,Ms                           25 Rebecca TAYLOR-554
                                     M: Abt   1877   --6                  B: Abt   1812
       6 William Marion Jr BINGHAM-8-------! P:                           D: Abt   1884
         B:  1 Jun 1880            D:  5 Jan 1915
         P: Burnsville,Tishomingo,Ms  P: Burnsville,Tishomingo Co,Ms 26 John JOHNSON-3108
         M: 24 Dec 1907    --3                                           B:
         P: Burnsville,Tishomingo,Ms 13 Sarah Elizabeth JOHNSON-18--------! D:
         D: 18 Mar 1966               B: 23 Aug 1855
         P: Burnsville,Tishomingo,Ms  P: ,,Tn-Ms\Nc\Tn                 27 Mary N WILSON-1835
                                      D:  2 Oct 1920                      B: 10 Jan 1826
    3 E Marie BINGHAM-6--------------------  P: Burnsville,Tishomingo Co,Ms  D: 13 Apr 1907
       B: 21 Mar 1922
       P: Burnsville,Tishomingo,Ms                      28 William Smith WHITFIELD-153
       D:                                                  B: 27 Dec 1822
       P:                           14 James Thomas [Jim] WHITFIELD-31---! D: 18 Feb 1871
                                      B:  5 Mar 1847. 29 Martha Ann Marilda LANKFORD-154
                                      P: Burnsville,Tishomingo Co,Ms.
                                      M:     --8                          B:  9 Nov 1823
       7 Amanda Lou WHITFIELD-9-----------! P:                            D: 16 Apr 1913
         B:  4 Feb 1888            D:  3 Dec 1935
         P: Burnsville,Tishomingo,Ms  P: Burnsville,Tishomingo Co,Ms 30 David D WOODLEY-539
         D: 13 Jun 1976                                                  B: 28 Jul 1823
         P: Burnsville,Tishomingo,Ms 15 America Elizabeth M WOODLEY-32----! D:  5 Feb 1896
                                      B: 14 Dec 1849
                                      P: ,,Ms-Ga-S/C                  31 Narcissa DEAN-540
                                      D:  7 Jul 1925                      B:  4 Oct 1825
                                      P: Burnsville,TC,Mississippi       D: 31 Jan 1908
```

Part Three

Refer to Part Three on Part One

Whitfield Family Reunion 1989

MISSISSIPPI

One hundred, ten people came to the Whitfield Family Reunion which was held at the Carroll County Community House in Carrollton, MS, on June 11, 1989.

Many Whitfield families were represented; however, William Whitfield and Martha Langford Whitfield's descendants made up the majority of the group. Approximately ninety family members represented William and Martha's son, James Thomas "Jim" Whitfield, born March 5, 1847, and married America Elizabeth Woodley, (daughter of David Woodley and Narcissus Dean Woodley). Jim died in 1935 and was buried in Tishomingo County, MS.

Scott Caulder of Grenada was recognized for having been named 1989 Mr. Grenada High School, a handsome, campus cutie, homecoming escort, Exchange Club Student of the Month, class favorite, and several other honors.

Billy Whitfield of Holcomb won Grenada High School's Most Outstanding Student in Drafting.

Ken Robinson of Guntown was also recognized for receiving Mississippi's Most Outstanding Farm Award.

Achievements and accomplishments of other family members were reported.

Silent meditation was held for Wilton Bingham, a favorite fun-loving cousin, who died at Burnsville, MS recently.

Fun, food, and fellowship were enjoyed by all participants. It was decided to have the reunion in Carrollton again next year.

Descendants of James Thomas "Jim" and America Woodley Whitfield were represented by families of their children Code, James Franklin, George, Will and Lou.

Representing Code Dean Whitfield, Sr.; Mr. and Mrs Talmadge Whitfield of Iuka; Mr. and Mrs. C.D. Whitfield, Jr. of Carrollton; Mr. and Mrs. Paul Whitfield of Hernando; Mr. and Mrs. Jack Hemphill and Mr. and Mrs. John Caulder & Scott of Grenada; Mr. and Mrs. Charles A. Whitfield, Charlie & Billy of Holcomb;Mr. W.C. "Bud" Whitfield and Mrs. Patsy Earnest of Greenwood; Mr. and Mrs. Mike Chamness & Beth of Delta State University; Mr. and Mrs. Terry Whitfield & Code of Greenwood; Mr. and Mrs. Rob Edwards of Grenada and Mr. and Mrs. Bill Ivy of Clarksdale.

Representing James Franklin Whitfield: Mr. and Mrs. Audry Whitfield of Winona; Mr. and Mrs. Bill Heath of Pearl; Mr. and Mrs. Mark Heath & Emily of Florence; Cindy Bumgardner of Pearl; Mr. and Mrs. Frank Vaughn, Jr., Frank III, Cole, & Ryan Mrs. Margarita Vaughn of Winona; Kathy Gehrett, Kari, & Ricki III of Southaven; Tammy Vaughn & Mickey of Winona; Mr. and Mrs. Jeff James, Jeff, Jr. and Johua of Winona and Susan Welch of West.

Mr. and Mrs. Donald Whitfield, Susan & Patty of Guntown; Mr. and Mrs. Michael Snider, Jon Michael, & Lynsey of Columbus; Mr. and Mrs. Gerald Whitfield, Joey, Michael, and Felicia of Saltillo; Mrs. Ollene Guthrie of Glen; Kerry, Josie, Randy, & David Trim, Sarah Jane Wildman of Corinth.

Representing Will Whitfield: Mr. and Mrs. Grady Whitfield of New Albany, Indiana; Mr. and Mrs. Melton Whitfield of Iuka.

Representing Lou Whitfield Bingham: Mr. Troy Bingham of Blue Springs; Mrs. Billie Bingham Robinson & Ken of Guntown; Mrs. Marie Bingham Barnett of Memphis, TN; Mrs. Carol Loden & Shawn of Memphis, TN; Mrs. Wilton Bingham of Burnsville; Amanda and Rick Hill of Memphis, TN; and Mr. Mike Barnett of Bartlett, TN.

Descendants of Mackey D. Whitfield: Oscar Whitfield, Mary Darkas Whitfield Burcham, and Eliza Whitfield Ledbetter were also present.

Representing Mackey D. Whitfield: Dr. and Mrs. B.A. Sims & Don of Greenwood Mrs. Bula Hatcher Watkins of Burnsville.

Representing Oscar Whitfield: Mr. Terry Whitfield of Corinth and Mr. Morris Whitfield also of Corinth.

Representing Mary Darkas Whitfield Burcham: Mr. and Mrs. Leroy Burcham of Meridian.

MISSOURI

CENSUS

1840 Whitfield, Edom A.   Macon County, Missouri
1840 Whitfield, William A.   Allegancy County, Missouri
1850 Whitfield, George W.   Pettis County, Missouri

WHITFIELD, AN INDIAN AGENT

John Wilkins Whitfield was b. March 11, 1818, in Franklin, Williamson Co, TN. John was the son of Wilkins Whitfield (b. ca. 1781 Sussex Co, VA, & d. 1841 Franklin, TN) and Polly Mary Whitfield.

In 1853 John W. Whitfield moved from Hickman County, TN to Independence, Missouri, to serve as an Indian Agent to the Pottawatomies Indians at Westport and Jackson, MS.

1853.

John W. Whitfield was the agent of the Pottawatomies this year. The agency was evidently maintained at Westport, Mo., though the report gives no location. It says: "The agency is located so far from the nation that it is impossible for the agent to prevent many disturbances that he might do if his location was near to them."

The Prairie band is spoken of in the report as the "Council Bluffs band." Of this band Whitfield said:

"The Pottawatomies, principally the Council Bluffs band, while out on their summer hunt came in contact with the mountain Indians, and after a hard-fought battle, lasting more than half a day, succeeded in putting them to flight, leaving some twenty or thirty of their dead on the battle field. At least the Pottawatomies brought in about that number of scalps, over which they have been dancing for the last month. I learn from various sources that the mountain Indians came down expressly for the purpose of having a fight with the frontier Indians. They first came in contact with the Pawnees, and but for the timely aid of the Pottawatomies (who happened to be but a few miles off) would have killed the last one, as they had them surrounded and had killed some ten or fifteen before the Pottawatomies reached the scene of action. All parties give the Pottawatomies great credit for their gallant conduct on that occasion. They lost in killed and wounded some four or five. From the best information I can get, the frontier Indians are not to blame, as they were fighting in self-defense. We anticipate a renewal of hostilities next summer if they should meet on the plains."

Speaking of the Baptist Manual Labor School, the report says that it encountered many difficulties and was not in a prosperous condition for some time. The Rev. "David" Lykins was in charge of it when the report was written.

The report of J. D. Duerinck, superintendent of the Catholic Manual Labor School, shows prejudice against the Prairie band. The children of this band attended the Baptist school, which was not kindly taken by the superintendent of St. Marys. He said: "The Prairie Indians of the Pottawatomie tribe, an infidel sect of medicine men, are as yet but little civilized, and are in every respect far behind their Catholic brethren." This good brother was something of a politician, understanding the value of flattery, saying in his report to Whitfield: "The Pottawatomies at large are wonderfully taken up with you."

1854.

The Pottawatomie agency was wholly neglected this year, so far as reports show—or rather there are no reports, except that from the St. Marys school. It was said to be in fine condition and to be doing excellent work.

Whitfield had been sent as a special agent far out upon the plains to settle difficulties among the plains tribes. He made two reports, both dated Westport, Mo., one September 27 and the other October 2.

"I am officially advised that on the arrival of agent Whitfield at Fort Atkinson, on the Arkansas river, with the annuity goods for the Comanches, Kiowas and Apaches, in July last, he found that they had all gone on a war party against the tribes of the north, confident from their numbers, estimated at 1,500, to gain an easy victory over any tribes they should encounter. In the vicinity of Smoky Hill they came up with a party of Sacs and Foxes and a few Pottawatomies, the whole not exceeding 200 in number. The Comanches believing (to use the words of one of their chiefs) that they could eat up so small a force in a few minutes, made a general charge. The Sacs allowed them to approach until within a hundred yards, when they opened upon them a well-directed fire from their rifles, which, being unexpected, appalled and for the moment checked their assailants. Three times these charges were repeated, and each time with a like fatal result. The Comanches at length retired, crestfallen and dispirited, having twenty-six killed and over one hundred wounded. On their return to Fort Atkinson their appearance and deportment were quite changed; they seemed humble and dejected, and quietly and submissively received their annuities and retired. The loss of the Sacs and Foxes is reported to be very inconsiderable."

Whitfield's report makes no mention of the Pottawatomies. But the following may prove of interest:

"The Indians were encamped on Pawnee fork, at the crossing of the Santa Fe road, where they were collected in larger numbers than have ever been known to assemble on the Arkansas river before. Old traders estimate the number at twelve to fifteen hundred lodges, and the horses and mules at from forty to fifty thousand head. The entire Kiowa and Prairie Comanches were there; several hundred of Texas or Woods Comanches had come over; the Prairie Apaches, one band of Arapahoes, and two bands of Cheyennes, and the Osages, composed the grand council. They had met for the purpose of forming their war party, in order, as they in their strong language said, to 'wipe out' all frontier Indians they could find on the plains. Two days previous to my arrival they broke up camp and started north. As soon as I heard that they were gone I sent two runners to try and bring them back. They, however, declined coming, and sent word that they would soon return, as it would take but a short time to clear the plains of all frontier Indians. They were doomed to be disappointed, as other great nations in their own imagination have been. At some place near Kansas river they met about one hundred Sac and Fox Indians, and the fight commenced, and, from their account, lasted about three hours, when to their great surprise the combined forces were compelled to retreat, leaving their dead on the field, which Indians never do unless badly whipped. They report their loss at about sixteen killed and one hundred wounded. From the best information I can get, the Sacs and Foxes were as much surprised at the result as the others, for there is no doubt but that they would have run too if they could have seen a hole to get out at. They had taken shelter in a ravine, and were for a long time surrounded. The Prairie Indians were armed with the bow and arrow, while the others had fine rifles. One is a formidable weapon in close quarters, but worthless at more than about fifty yards. The rifle told almost every shot, either on rider or horse. It is easily accounted for why one hundred whipped fifteen hundred. The former had a weapon to fight with; the latter had none at the distance they were fighting. I learn that the Sacs and Foxes lost six killed, but they were killed with the rifle.

1855

George W. Clarke was the agent for the Pottawatomies in 1855. The Kansas Indians had been taken out of the agency; that is, they had been given an agent of their own. The agent's report is an arraignment of the Prairie band. Judged by the Indian policy of the government, the report is a good one. It is a plea for the allotment system. This system has always failed to benefit the Indian. He invariably loses his land to the white man by ownership in severalty.

The custom has been to divest the Indian of his land in the interest of the white settler.

"A portion of these people have for a long time had intercourse with the whites, and in a measure adopted the civilized mode of life, and they manifest a desire for the improvement of themselves and their people.

"The 'Prairie band' adheres to the hunter life, nearly all of whom despise the arts and principles of civilization, who regard it as disgraceful for men to work, and they spare no language in denouncing those of the tribe who cultivate the soil or follow the peaceful arts. This band arrogantly claims ownership of all the land and declares that the other bands have no rights here, nor to the annuities, they being *permitted* to participate in them only on the *courtesy* of their condescending brothers.

The land of Missouri held native Indian people for a long time before the white settlers came. These Missouri Indian tribes were Pottawatomies, Pawnees, Comanches, Kiowas, Apaches, Sacs, Foxes, Arapahoes, Cheyennes, and Osages.

Reference: The Kansas Historical Quarterly, Vol. II, Number One. Published Feb. 1933, Kansas Magazine.

TENNESSEE AND MISSOURI FAMILIES

Generation One. Thomas Whitfield born 1735 and died 1794 in Sussex County, Virginia.

Generation Two. Wilkins Whitfield born 1781 and died 1841 in Franklin, Tennessee. He moved to Tennessee in 1808 from Sussex County, Virginia.

Generation Three. Thomas Jefferson Whitfield born 1810 TN and died, 1873, TN.

Generation Four. Thomas Jefferson Whitfield born 1845 TN and died 1908 TN.

Generation Five. Jefferson Lafayette Whitfield born 1867 TN and died 1937 Steele, MO. He married first wife in TN who died young; they had no children. Jefferson Whitfield married second wife Lou Ellen Matlock. Lou Ellen Whitfield had 17 children born to her and Jefferson Whitfield. She had four sets of twins. She had 13 pregnancies. Three sets of twins died young and two children died young. Jefferson Lafayette Whitfield and Lou Ellen Whitfield raised nine children to adulthood.

JEFFERSON LAFAYETTE WHITFIELD 1/28/1867 - 6/2/1937

He was born in Benton County, TN, on the Tennessee River at Pavatt's landing five miles away at Eagle Creek where he resided until he moved to Steele, MO, in 1916.

He married Lou Ellen Matlock on 10/14/1888 at Benton County, TN. Lafayette was a merchant and farmer. They came to Missouri with three covered wagons and three cows tied to them. They moved to Nute Maxwell's place in 1917 which they rented to farm.

They planted sunflower for the seeds. Aunt Veatrice and Olie beat the seeds out with sticks. Neely and Ollie drove the team and pulled up the flowers. Grandpa was a hard worker. He was sick with arthritis. They moved to a farm near Steele, MO, which they bought. They built a home and settled there. The children were married by now. They visited regularly for he was bed confined. He died in 1937. Grandma died one year later.

They are buried at Mount Zion Cemetery. The 61 Highway runs by the cemetery. There are several of the children, grandchildren, and daughters-in-law buried there, also.

To this marriage were born 17 children; four sets of twins. Eight children died young and are buried at Pavett's Cemetery at Benton County, TN.

There are only two children left of this original family, Veatrice Thornton and Ollie May. But there are a lot of grandchildren and relatives scattered everywhere.

DESCENDANTS OF JEFFERSON LAFAYETTE WHITFIELD (1867 TN - 1937 MO) and LOU ELLEN MATLOCK

Virginia Rose Whitfield Quinn compiled the Whitfield Family Tree. Aunt Veatrice gave me some information and David and Montana Whitfield gave the other.
Courthouse record, Steele, MO. Land Survey and description of property of Jefferson Lafayette Whitfield and Lou Ellen (Matlock) Whitfield.
> Pemisent County, Missouri. Survey Number 115.
> Section 20, Township 17, County Road
> Range 12 East. 46.7 acres.
> NY 2 of the Swy 4. West of County drainage ditch.
"December 3, 1936, property owned by Lou Ellen Whitfield. She willed to Jennie L. Whitfield Ward and children the land. The highway took a large part of the land dividing it. The son, Claude Ward, and wife, Sara Ward, took small acres for themselves. There is no house on the land site in 1994 for the house was torn down."
....Submitted by Virginia Rose Whitfield Quinn (Mrs. Noel Quinn) on February 8, 1994.

"My name is Virginia Rose Whitfield, the daughter of N.H. Whitfield and Era Warren Whitfield. There were five small children born to them, and I am one of them. My mother's name was never mentioned. My step-mother was Earlene Owens Bostic. She married him after mother died."
....Submitted by Virginia Rose Whitfield Quinn of Cruthersville, MO, on August 21, 1990.

Jefferson L. and Lou Ellen Whitfield Family. 1925 Steele, Missouri. Front Row–Clara, Clarence, Jennie Lou, Ellen, Lawrence, Lillie, Veatrice, Jefferson L., Lou Ellen , Annie, Neeley, Howard, Era, Ila Mae. Center Row– Arie, James, Herschel, Carlie, Harlie, Irene, Bell, Dowthitt, David, Thomas, Christeen, Wilson, John Dye, Back Row– Thomas C., Jefferson L., Ollie Mason, Mary Quay, Mary Bell.

WHITFIELD AND KINSHIPS

Whitfield children and **PICTURE**
In-laws .

FRONT ROW (left to right) Married surnames

1. Clara Ellen
2. Clarence
3. Jennie Louellen (daughter)
4. Lawrence
5. Lillie
6. Veatrice (daughter)
7. J. L. Whitfield (grandfather)
8. Lou Ellen Whitfield (grandmother)
9. Annie Wilkins (daughter)
10. Neely Howard (son)
11. Howard
12. Era   Warren
13. Ila Mae

MIDDLE ROW (left to right)

14. Arie   Baker
15. James
16. Hershel
17. Carlie Letton (son)
18. Harlie
19. Irene
20. Bell   Hatley
21. Douthitt
22. David
23. Tom Wesley (son)
24. Christine   Yates
25. Wilson Durwood
26. Olie May (daughter)
27. John Dye

BACK ROW (left to right)

28. Thomas C.
29. J. L.
30. Ollie Mason (son)
31. Mary Quay   Warren
32. May Bell

The book Eagle Creek Heritage Notes. The Saga of Ten Pioneer Families, compiled by F.B. Cain. Published in the 1990's. Private print. F.B. Cain is a resident of Holladay, TN

The book has family trees and lineages of these families of the Eagle Creek off of the Tennessee River in Benton County, TN: FRY, HENRY, HUBBS, MALIN, McDANIEL, MATLOCK, MERRICK, SANDERS, WHITE.

This book has a complete lineage of Thomas Jefferson Whitfield (1845-1908). Thomas was a native of Hickman County, TN. Later in marriage he was found in Humphreys County, TN, and in 1908 in property ownership in Benton County, TN

FAMILY BIBLE RECORD

Father: J.L. Whitfield   Mother: Lou Ellen Matlock
        Jefferson Lafayette Whitfield

Married Sunday, October 14, 1888, at 10:00 a.m.
Benton County, TN, by H.A. Green, J.P.
Witnesses: W.L. Phillips & Dock Allison

Children

1. T. W. Whitfield (Tom Wesley) 08/02/1889 - 1942 (1st son)
2. C. C. Whitfield (Cleather Cummins) born 09/30/1891 (son)
3. H. W. Whitfield (Hermon Wesley) born 02/17/1894 (son)
4. C. L. Whitfield (Carlie Letton) born 09/06/1895 (son)
5. W. B. Whitfield (William Brient) born 05/26/1897 (twin
6. J. B. Whitfield (Jennie Brient) born 05/26/1897 (twin
7. L. A. Whitfield (Lela Ann) born 06/07/1898 (daughter)
8. B. M. Whitfield (Bula May) born 12/17/1899 (twin - daughter)
9. B. L. Whitfield (Birdie L.) born 12/18/1899 (twin - daughter)
10. J. L. E. Whitfield (J. Lou Ella) born 01/20/1901 (daughter)
11. N. H. Whitfield (Neely Howard) 11/03/1902 - 10/18/1978 (son)
12. O. M. Whitfield (Ollie Mason) born 02/11/1904 (twin - son)
13. O. M. Whitfield (Olie May) 02/11/1904 - 11/02/1982 (twin - dau)
14. V. A. Whitfield (Veatrice A.) born 02/06/1906 (daughter)
15. Golden Whitfield born 09/11/1908 (twin - daughter)
16. Jewel Whitfield born 09/11/1908 (twin - daughter)
17. A. W. Whitfield (Annie W.) born 09/01/1910 (daughter)

Baptized

Carlie Whitfield   age 19 was baptized 8/6/1915

Jennie Whitfield   age 13 was baptized 8/15/1914

Veatrice Whitfield age 14 was baptized 9/19/1920

Olie May Whitfield age 16 was baptized 9/19/1920

Annie W. Whitfield was baptized 10/3/1923

General Thomas Jefferson Whitfield

Thomas Jefferson Whitfield (1810-1873) served as Colonel of the militia of Davidson County, TN, in the Civil War, and was later named Brigadier. He appeared in Hickman County Court minutes of Tennessee several times. Thomas did not live in Benton County. He was wounded and taken prisoner in the Civil War, and was being prepared for burial one time when it was realized that he was still alive. He was nursed back to health and was later engaged in other battles during the war. He appears as General Jeff Whitfield in some of the Tennessee books.

Thomas J. Whitfield had three sons, John (Jack), George Monroe, and Thomas Jefferson, Jr. who were in the Confederate Army. It was the son, Thomas, Jr., who later moved to Eagle Creek off the Tennessee River and bought the property in 1908.

FAMILY GROUPS

1. **Thomas Jefferson Whitfield** (1810-1873) married (1) Eliza Nolen and they had two children. He then married Sarah Dillahunty (1817-1885) and they had seven children.

A. Henry W. Whitfield
   born 1830
B. Martha Eliza Whitfield
   born 1832
C. Silas Dillahunty Whitfield
   born 1836
D. John W. Whitfield

E. George Monroe Whitfield
F. Thomas Jefferson Whitfield, Jr. born 1845
G. Sarah Virginia Whitfield born 1849
H. Mary Delilah Whitfield
I. Josephine Whitfield

A. HENRY W. WHITFIELD born July 1830 was a son and he married Nancy Porch of Humphry's Co., TN. Children:

1. Mary Ann Whitfield
2. John D. Whitfield
3. Nancy Whitfield

B. MARTHA ELIZER WHITFIELD born Nov. 1832. She married J.D. Murray.

C. SILAS DILLAHUNTY was born May 1836. He married Eliza Richardson (1848-1917). Children:

1. Jefferson M. Whitfield
2. James H. Whitfield
3. Robert Whitfield
4. William Whitfield
5. Kit ? Whitfield

1. Jefferson M. Whitfield was born Jan. 1, 1866, and died in 1905. He married Annie Porch. She was Oct. 27, 1868, and died in 1960. They lived in Holladay, TN, for a time and operated a hotel.

a. Gus Whitfield 1892-1972.

    b.   Foster Whitfield
    c.   Leonard (Lynn) Whitfield 1899-1958
    d.   Mary Whitfield

    2. James H. Whitfield born in 1868, died in 1933. James
married Delia Gibson who was born in 1877.

    3.   Robert E. Whitfield married N.E. Woods on 5/3/1894.
    4.   William Whitfield
    5.   Kit ? G. Whitfield married Eura Briggance on 5/17/1915.

    D.   JOHN W. WHITFIELD

    E.   GEORGE MONROE WHITFIELD

    F.   THOMAS JEFFERSON WHITFIELD, JR. was born Feb. 25, 1845, and
died in 1908.   Thomas married (1) Martha Lillie America
Cunningham, and (2) Mattie (Martha) Jane Nicks who was born Sept.
28, 1845 and died in 1930.   The burial was in Pavatt Cemetery.
Mattie died on April 16th.   Four children were born to first wife:
    1. Sally Whitfield, b. Nov. 28, 1868. Md. Lee Franscisso.
    2. Lillie May (Lizzie) Whitfield born Aug. 13, 1871.
    3. Mary Whitfield
Mother's maiden name is found as Cunningham and
Cunmingham.   Six children were born to the second wife called
Mattie.   Martha Cunningham was born 1847 and died March 1,
1874, in Benton County, TN.
    4. Jefferson Lafayette Whitfield born Jan. 28, 1867, and
    died June 2, 1937. He was born in Tennessee and died in
    Missouri.
The following were children of Mattie Nicks and Thomas
Jefferson Whitfield, Jr.:
    5.   James Dee Whitfield born Feb. 10, 1877, and died 1954
    in Humphreys County, TN.
    6.   John Regan Whitfield, Oct. 18, 1880.
    7.   Thomas Cleveland Whitfield born Nov. 8, 1884.
    8.   Henry Edward Whitfield born May 1, 1888, in Benton
    County, TN.
    9.   Delie Ann Whitfield born Dec. 2, 1891, in Decatur
    County, TN.
    10. Clara May Whitfield born June 10, 1894, in Decatur
    County, TN.   She never married.

    1.   Sally Whitfield married Lee Franscisso on Jan. 17,
    1897.
    2.   Lillie Whitfield married Martin Phillips n Dec. 19,
    1888.   They lived on Lower Eagle Creek where they farmed
    for a living.   Children: (1) Henry Cletus Phillips. He
    married Mary Henry, daughter of Enoch and Eliza White
    Henry.   They had four children:
    a.   Ralph Phillips died 1956
    b.   Edith Phillips never married.

c. Boyd Phillips md. Lois Bell, daughter of John Bell.
d. Henry Phillips married Topps Hicks, and they had
son Dennis Phillips.
There were a total of 11 children. Seven boys and three
girls residing in Humphreys and Benton Counties, TN. They
were children of Lillie Whitfield and M. Phillips. (2) Thomas
(3) Clarence; (4) Dennis; (5) Melvin; (6) Marshal; (7) Billie;
(8) Stella; (9) Ora; (10) Mary Ellen; and (11) infant died.
All the children were born in Humphreys County, TN.

4. Jefferson Lafayette Whitfield married the daughter of
Wesley and Elizabeth Flowers Matlock named Lou Ellen.
Jefferson operated a general merchandise store on Eagle Creek
for several years. He then went to farming the river bottom
land near the mouth of Eagle Creek. They lived in Happy
Hollow. In September 1916 the river flooded and raised all
the crops in the river bottom. Jefferson loaded the family up
and set out for Missouri. He found land to rent near Steele,
MO. This family raised their children there to adulthood.
Jefferson died June 2, 1937, and Lou Ellen died Sept. 2, 1938.

Following are records on the adults. Their generation.
G6 a.
Thomas Wesley Whitfield born 8/2/1889 married Liza Bell Hatley
on 12/1/1907. She was born 7/1887 on Eagle Creek, TN. She is
the daughter of James R. and Eliza Harris Hatley. They were
married on 12/1/1907. Children are:

1) Gladys Irene Whitfield born 8/24/1908, married William
G7 Leslie Hatley on 8/6/1937. Children are:
   a) William Leslie Hatley, Jr. born 11/13/1938, married
June Schmitt on 4/13/1959. Children are:
      (1) Sally Ann Hatley born 11/13/1959
      (2) Pamela Louise Hatley born 6/6/1961
   b) Gladys Naomi Hatley born 12/27/1939, married Michael
McCormack II on 12/5/1958. Children are:
      (1) George Michael McCormack III born 12/9/1959
      (2) Naomi Lynn McCormack born 2/7/1962
   c) Ketha Lynne Hatley born 11/1/1941
   d) Thomas Whitfield Hatley born 12/21/1943

2) Thomas C. Whitfield, a Church of Christ minister, lives in
G7 Nashville, TN. Children are:
   a) Thomas Clark Whitfield
   b) Jefferson David Whitfield

3) Naomi Christine Whitfield married Emmett Yates.
   a) Jerry Yates
   b) Judy Yates

4) James Lafayette Whitfield born 1912 married Estell
G7 Hamilton on 1/25/1934, lives in Hayti, MO. Children are:
   a) Sandra Lynn Whitfield b. 2/22/1936, md. Jimmy Jones.

b) James Wesley Whitfield married Brenda.　Children G8.
　　　　(1)　Terry Lynn Whitfield
　　　　(2)　Tracy Whitfield
　　　　(3)　Kimberly Whitfield
　　　c)　Janie Sue Whitfield
　　　d)　Dwane Whitfield

G7
　　5)　David Samuel Whitfield born 1920 married Montana Crawford
in 8/1941, and they live in Steele, MO.　Children are:
　　a)　David Kay Whitfield born 11/29/1943, married James Carey
on 6/6/1961. G8
　　b)　Roy Lee

G7
　　6)　Wilson Durwood Whitfield born 10/24/1923, married Betty
Ruth Fromes on 8/7/1943.　They live in Steele, MO.　Children
are:
　　a)　Gary Whitfield born 10/18/1944　G8
　　b)　Gwen Whitfield

G7
　　7)　Douthitt Glendall Whitfield born 1/19/1928, married Laura
Moare in 1947.　They live in Camden, TN.　Children are:
　　a)　Douglas Whitfield　　G8
　　b)　Charles Whitfield
　　c)　Mark Whitfield
　　d)　Lou Whitfield
　　e)　Ann Whitfield

G6
b.　Cleather Cummins Whitfield born 9/30/1891, married Mary Crabb
on 10/13/1909.　Children are:　G7
　　1.　Edna Whitfield
　　2.　Ruby Whitfield
　　3.　Herman Whitfield
　　4.　Dalton Whitfield
　　5.　Reva Whitfield
　　6.　Louise Whitfield married a Ladd and lives in St. Louis, MO.

G6
c.　Hermon Wesley Whitfield born 2/17/1894, died 1899 Pavatt
Cemetery.
d.　Carlie Letton Whitfield born 9/6/1895, died 1925, married Arie
Baker on 8/13/1916.　Children are:
　　1.　Nathan B. Whitfield
　　2.　Hershel James Whitfield.　Child.
　　a)　Patsie Cachron Whitfield
　　3.　Carlie Lincoln Whitfield
　　4.　James Harold Whitfield.　Children are:
　　a)　Linda Whitfield
　　b)　JoAnn Whitfield
　　c)　Jill Whitfield
　　d)　Cindy Whitfield

G6
e.　William Brient Whitfield born 5/26/1897, died 7/10/1897 Pavatt
Cemetery
G6
f.　Jennie Brient Whitfield b. 5/26/1897, d. 7/10/1897 Pavatt
Cemetery.

G6
g. <u>Lela Ann Whitfield</u> born 6/7/1898, died 7/3/1898 Pavatt Cemetery

G6
h. <u>Bula May Whitfield</u> born 12/17/1899, died 2/24/1900 Pavatt Cemetery

G6
i. <u>Birdie L. Whitfield</u> born 12/18/1899, died 6/14/1900 Pavatt Cemetery

G6
j. <u>Jennie Lou Ella Whitfield</u> born 1/20/1901, died 7/13/1986. Married Clarence Ward. Children are:
   1) Lillie Lockwood Ward   4) Elizabeth Ward   G7
   2) Lawrence Ward   5) Claude Ward
   3) Clara Ellen Ward   6) Sallie Ward

G6
k. <u>Neely Howard Whitfield</u> born 11/3/1902 in Tennessee and died 10/18/1978. Married Era Vernon or Lavern Warren on 7/3/1920. Children are:
1) <u>Howard Layette Whitfield</u> born 10/13/1921, died 4/11/1945. Married Lula May Mathenia. Children are: G8
  a) Howard Layette Whitfield, Jr. born 10/30/1942, married Barbara Sue Jacob (first wife) on 3/30/1964. Children are:
      (1) Debbie Whitfield born 11/8/1967.
      (2) Laura Whitfield born 12/22/1968, married Len Herr.
  - Married Sara Ann Kemp (second wife) on 10/27/1985. Children are:
      (3) Aaron Wesley born 3/4/1986.
  b) James Rufas Whitfield born 9/23/1944, married Betty Wilson. Children are: G8
      (1) Beth Whitfield
        i) James Kevin born 1/11/1989.
      (2) Rebecca Ann Whitfield born 10/20/1967.

G7
2) <u>Ila Mae Whitfield</u> born 8/14/1924. She married Ken Beuchel Tschannen on 2/11/1950. He was born on 1/29/24. Ila Mae was an RN at Baptist Memorial Hospital in Memphis, TN, from 1943-1946. Ken was a purchasing agent until he retired on 2/1/1989. Children are: G8
a) Kenneth Beuchel Tschannen, Jr. born 11/20/1951, married Sandra Ruth Baird on 8/7/1976. She was born on 10/5/1954.
b) Pamela Ella Tschannen born on 1/26/1956.
c) Cameron Reinhold Tschannen born 12/14/1956, married Debra Mae Anderson on 8/3/1979. She was born on 6/2/1957. Children are:
      (1) Nadine Mae Tschannen born 8/26/1980.
      (2) Cameron Reinhold Tschannen, Jr. born 2/21/1984.
      (3) Nicole Elisha Tschannen born 7/11/1986.

G7
3) <u>Austin Pay Whitfield</u> born 3/6/1928, married Louise. Children are: G8
a) Howard Whitfield

b) Sheila Whitfield, she has children
- Austin Pay Whitfield remarried a woman named Dorothy.

G7
4) <u>Virginia Rose Whitfield</u> born 2/1/1930, married Noel Quinn on 6/27/1948. Children are: G8
a) Noel Quinn, Jr. born 1/18/1953, married Sheila Huffine on 12/22/1976. Children are:
    (1) Heather Noel Quinn born 10/3/1978.
    (2) Elizabeth Rose Quinn born 2/11/1981.

G7
5) <u>Veatrice Whitfield</u> born 7/28/1931, married Timothy Vickers. Children are: G8
a) Sarah Claudia Vickers born 11/25/1951, married Tommy Wayne Hogen. Children are:
    (1) Jeanette Ann Hogen born 9/17/1976.
    (2) Elizabeth (Beth) Dawn born 1/19/1981.
b) Thericia Ann Vickers born 7/19/1953, married Vincent Holmes. Children are:
    (1) Jefferie Allen Holmes
    (2) William Timothy Holmes
- Neely Howard Whitfield's wife, Era Vernan or Lavern, died in Memphis Hospital in 1933. He remarried Lerlene Owens Bostic on 10/14/1934. She had two children from a previous marriage. Their children are:
6) <u>Patricia Ann Whitfield</u> born 6/22/1936, married William Ray
G7 Turner on 5/15/1955. They were divorced on 3/1/1959. Children are: G8
a) William Glen Turner born 8/11/1957, married Becky Futrell on 5/15/1982. Children are:
    (1) Allen Whitfield Turner born 7/9/1985.
    (2) Brooke Elizabeth Turner born 12/18/1987.
- Patricia Ann married Dorce W. Pirtle on 12/18/1959. Children (twins) are:
b) Harold Don Pirtle born 9/19/1960, married Delana Ann Watson on 5/30/1984. Children are:
    (1) Christopher Don Pirtle born 7/27/1988.
    (2) Whitney Ann Pirtle born 2/2/1991.
c) Darryl Jon Pirtle born 9/19/1960, married Michalino Holcomb on 7/29/1987.
d) David Neal Pirtle born 7/6/1963, married Donna Marie Wright on 6/23/1984. Children are:
    (1) Nathan Andrew Pirtle born 2/9/1988.
    (2) Michael Neal Pirtle born 4/7/1990.

G7
7) <u>Ronnie Glen Whitfield</u> born 2/19/1939, married Barbara Ann Holloway in 1960. Children are: G8
a) Cynthia Gale Whitfield born 3/1961, married Roger Rowe on 8/11/1990.
b) Michael Whitfield born 1/13/1964.
- Ronnie Glen Whitfield married a second time. Her name was Stephanie. Children are:
c) Lindsey Whitfield born 2/3/1939.

G7
8) <u>Carolyn Jo Whitfield</u> born 5/27/1940.

Children are:
(1) Mark Thornton, children are:
  i) Latishia Thornton
(2) Wesley Paul Thornton, children are:
  i) Paige Thornton

o) <u>Golden Whitfield</u> born 9/11/1908, died 10/7/1098 Pavatt Cemetery.

p) <u>Jewel Whitfield</u> born 9/11/1908, died 10/7/1908 Pavatt Cemetery.

q) <u>Annie Wilkins Whitfield</u> born 9/1/1910, md. Tommy Henley. Children are:
  a) Margaret Henley married Paul Weeks.
  b) James Henley married Barbara.
  c) Minnie Bell Henley married Bill Chalk.
  d) Emma Lou Henley married Jack Kirk.

Left to Right
Brothers and Sisters
Olie May, Ollie Mason,
 and Veatrice   1980

Left to Right. Brothers &
Sisters. Arthur, Louis, Fadie
May, Oliver   1995

Jefferson L. & Lou Ellen Whitfield
1925

FAMILY GROUPS

Children of Jefferson Lafayette Whitfield (1867-1937)   G7

<u>Olie May Whitfield Dye</u> - Twin of Ollie Mason Whitfield. Olie May was born 2/11/1904. She married John Dye and had two boys: 1) Wilson Dye and 2) George Dye. The family resided in Benton Harbor, Michigan. John Dye died in 1969. Olie Dye died 8/27/1994, buried at Mt. Zion, MO.

<u>Ollie Mason Whitfield</u> was born a son on 2/11/1904. He was a twin to olie May. He retired from farming and moved to Hayti, Missouri, with his third wife, Irene Umphrey. Ollie Whitfield died 11/2/1982 in Hayti, mO. Irene Whitfield died 5/21/1987. She was born 3/3/1917. They were buried at Mt. Zion Cemetery in Steele, Missouri.

G8

<u>Arthur Junior Whitfield</u> was born 12/25/1927 in Steele, Missouri, to Ollie Mason Whitfield and Mary Quay Warren. She died when son was very young.

Arthur Whitfield married Nora Lee ____ in 1950 in St. Joseph, MI. They had three daughters.   G9

  1. Brenda Kay Whitfield b. 4/7/1951
  2. Deborah Quay Whitfield b. 6/24/1952
  3. Pamela Lee Whitfield b. 10/27/1953.

The father, Arthur Whitfield, and Nora Lee divorced in 1963.

Arthur Whitfield married second Judith Ann Mooney who was b. 6/29/1939, in Chicago, IL. They married 7/8/1967 in St. Joseph, Michigan. Judith had a daughter from a previous marriage. Arthur then adopted her. She was Cinthia Sue Whitfield born 8/6/1962. Arthur and Judith Whitfield had one daughter by birth: Sharon Ann Whitfield born 3/19/1969.

Sharon Ann Whitfield married Peter Slittar. Divorce one year later. In April 1995, Sharon was age 26, and working for Asphalt Seal Coating Company in Scottsville, Michigan.

Arthur Whitfield and Judith Mooney ____ Whitfield lived in Coloma, Michigan, until they died. Arthur Whitfield died 9/1/1984. Judith Whitfield died 8/18/1986.

Arthur Whitfield worked at Modern Plastics, Inc. for 35 years, until he died. He was an avid fisherman and liked gardening. Arthur Whitfield had three daughters and one step-daughter.

Judith Mooney was age 28 the first time she married. Judith md. 2nd husband Reno Rigozzi, and they had one child, who is half-sister to Sharon Whitfield. Judith married 3rd husband, Arthur Whitfield. Judith Whitfield had three daughters. Sharon Whitfield was age 17 when her monther died. All children of Arthur and Judith b. in MO. Grandfather was Ollie Mason Whitfield who raised children: 1. Arthur Whitfield, 2. Jefferson Whitfield, 3. Lou.

DAUGHTERS AND GRANDCHILDREN OF ARTHUR WHITFIELD (1927-1984)

- Brenda Kay Whitfield Ames had children: 1. Elliot Ames, 2. William Ames, 3. Arthur Ames.   G10
- Deborah Quay Whitfield ____ Sanders had one child: Caroline Suesane Wednt.
- Pamela Lee Whitfield Duncan had children: 1. Kerry Duncan, 2. Tonya Duncan, 3. Derek Duncan.
- Cinthia Sue Whitfield (adopted child with Whitfield name) married ____ Thomas and had children: 1. Heather Sueanne Thomas.

2. Kristopher Duane Thomas, 3. Holly Marie Thomas.
Brother of Arthur Whitfield.
Benny Mason Whitfield born 7/28/1944. His mother was Attic Paye born 5/12/1907 and died 10/19/1950.

Benny W. Whitfield and wife, Barbara had two boys: 1. Steven Ray Whitfield born 6/16/1965, 2. Gregory Lynn Whitfield born 5/28/1970. Parents Benny and Barbara divorced in early 1980's.

Benny Mason Whitfield married second Etta Faye Summerford. Etta died in 1993. No child. Benny W. Whitfield lives in Coloma, MI, and works for Modern Plastics, Inc. in Benton Harbor, MI. Son of Ollie Mason Whitfield (1904-1982).
Oliver May Whitfield (Pete) was born 8/6/1933 in Caruthersville, MO to Ollie and Attic Paye Whitfield.

Oliver May Whitfield married Robbie Jean Sherrillon 7/15/1955 in Michigan, City, IN. They had six children all born and grew up in Michigan City.

1. Gary Lynn Whitfield	4. Timothy Wayne Whitfield
b. 5/15/1957	b. 5/6/1964
2. Jimmy Ray Whitfield	5. Jeffery Dale Whitfield
b. 11/2/1959	b. 2/15/1966
3. Neil Allan Whitfield	6. Marianne Whitfield
b. 3/24/1963	b. 3/25/1971

The father worked for Joy Manufacturing Company and retired 1995.
....Submitted by Sharon Whitfield of Scottsville, MI on 9/6/1995, the descendants of Ollie Mason Whitfield and family of Olie May Whitfield Dye.

Reference:
1. Whitfield Family Bible, Home of David Whitfield, Steele, MO.
2. Williamson County Historical Journal, #17, Anniversary 10th Edition, 1966-1976. Article by Mrs. Eilene Plummer.
3. Whitfield History and Genealogy of Tennessee by V.J. Whitfield. Second edition published 1979.

DEATHS

Pavatt Cemetery along the Tennessee River, Benton County, TN had burial of first wife of Jefferson Whitfield before 1888. There are 8 children of Lou Ellen Whitfield in Pavatt Cemetery, including two sets of twins.

William Brient Whitfield died at age 2 months, 7/10/1897.
Jennie Brient Whitfield died at age 2 months, 7/10/1897.
Lela Ann Whitfield died at one month, 7/31/1898.
Hermon Wesley Whitfield died at age 5 in 1899.
Bula May Whitfield died at one year 2/24/1900.
Birdie Whitfield died at 6 months 6/14/1900.
Golden Whitfield died 9/11/1908.
Jewel Whitfield died 10/7/1908.

Deaths in Missouri and Tennessee
Naomi Christine Whitfield Yates died in 1995.
Olie May Whitfield Dye died 8/27/1994 and buried at Mt. Zion.

Genealogy lineage of Jefferson Lafayette Whitfield (1867-1937) continued on page 551 in Appendix.

CEMETERY AT STEELE, MISSOURI.

Gladys Irene Whitfield Hatley died Aug. 27, 1990. Her father,
  Thomas Wesley Whitfield died 18, 1942.
Jefferson Lafayette Whitfield (1867-1937) lived fourty-nine
  years in Tennessee and twenty-two years in Missouri. He and
    his wife both died at age 70. They were parents of nine
girls and eight boys. Sons who lived to be adults were Thomas
Wesley, Cleather, Carlie, Ollie, and Neely. All children of
Jefferson and Lou Ellen had died by 1995.
CEMETERY AT MEMPHIS, TENNESSEE.

Veatrice Whitfield Thorton died Oct. 28,1992. Her sister,
  Annie Whitfield Henley is buried at Memphis. Veatrice
  and Annie lived in Memphis, Tennessee.
  XXXXXXXXXXXXXXXXXXXXXXXXXXXXXXXXXXXXXXXXXXXXXXXXXXX

M O N T A N A

A state in the northwest of the United States.
There is no record of Whitfield family there before 1850.

XXXXXXXXXXXXXXXXXXXXXXXXXXXXXXXXXXXXXXXXXXXXXXXXXXXXXXX

N E B R A S K A

A state in the west and northern part of the United States.
There is no record of Whitfield family there before 1850.

XXXXXXXXXXXXXXXXXXXXXXXXXXXXXXXXXXXXXXXXXXXXXXXXXXXXXXX

N E V A D A

C E N S U S E S

1870	Whitfield	, C. H.	Elko County, Nevada
1875	Whitfield	,C. H.	Elko County, Nevada
1880	Whitfield	, Isabella,	Storey County, Nevada
1882	Whitfield	, Isabelle,	Storey County, Nevada
1880	Whitfield	, James A.	Storey County, Nevada
1882	Whitfield	, James A.	Storey County, Nevada
1880	Whitfield	, Robert A.	Storey County, Nevada
1882	Whitfield	, Robert A.	Storey County, Mevada

XXXXXXXXXXXXXXXXXXXXXXXXXXXXXXXXXXXXXXXXXXXXXXXXXXXXXXX

NEW HAMPSHIRE

1820	Whitfield, Joseph	Rockingham County, New Hampshire
1837	Whitfield, Nathaniel	Hillsboro County, New Hampshire
1840	Whitfield, Nathaniel	Hillsboro County, New Hampshire
1850	Whitfield, George	Hillsboro County, New Hampshire
1850	Whitfield, George, Jr	Hillsboro County, New Hampshire
1850	Whitfield, James	Hillsboro County, New Hampshire
1850	Whitfield, Nathaniel	Hillsboro County, New Hampshire

NEW JERSEY

CENSUSES

1830	Whitfield, Daniel	Essex County, New Jersey
1830	Whitfield, George	Essex County, New Jersey
1830	Whitfield, William, Jr.	Essex County, New Jersey
1830	Whitfield, William L.	Essex County, New Jersey
1840	Whitfield, George	Essex County, New Jersey
1840	Whitfield, J.R.	Essex County, New Jersey
1840	Whitfield, John	Essex County, New Jersey
1840	Whitfield, John	Essex County, New Jersey
1840	Whitfield, William	Essex County, New Jersey
1840	Whitfield, William, Jr.	Essex County, New Jersey
1850	Whitfield, Allis	Somerset County, New Jersey
1850	Whitfield, Anna	Camden County, New Jersey
1850	Whitfield, Betsey	Atlantic County, New Jersey
1850	Whitfield, Daniel	Monmouth County, New Jersey
1850	Whitfield, David	Monmouth County, New Jersey
1850	Whitfield, Edward	Monmouth County, New Jersey
1850	Whitfield, Emeline	Monmouth County, New Jersey
1850	Whitfield, Francis A.	Essex County, New Jersey
1850	Whitfield, George	Essex County, New Jersey
1850	Whitfield, George	Essex County, New Jersey
1850	Whitfield, John	Essex County, New Jersey
1850	Whitfield, John	Essex County, New Jersey
1850	Whitfield, John A.	Atlantic County, New Jersey
1850	Whitfield, John R.	Essex County, New Jersey
1850	Whitfield, Joseph L.	Essex County, New Jersey
1850	Whitfield, Robert	Monmouth County, New Jersey
1850	Whitfield, William M.	Essex County, New Jersey
1850	Whitfield, William L.	Essex County, New Jersey
1850	Whitfield, William S.	Essex County, New Jersey
1850	Whitfield, William, Sen.	Essex County, New Jersey
1850	Whitfield, William, Jun.	Essex County, New Jersey

Bryan Whitfield married Ellen White in 1865. Richard Allen
Whitfield was a son and he had son John who married Frances.
John H. Whitfield had daughter Mary Ellen Whitfield who md.
Ernest Bailey of Sacramento, Calif. Wife, Mary Bailey was a
librarian in the California State Library in 1971.

NEW MEXICO

Native Indian tribes inhabited the land later called New Mexico. This land was north of the country of Mexico and a part of the Texas state south side. Navajo Indian Reservation was later made at San Juan County, NM. Western lands were slow in becoming a state of the United States. New Mexico borders on the east by Texas, and borders on the west by Arizona, and on the north by Colorado.

There was no person named Whitfield in the open land before it became a state. Whitfields came late to New Mexico, and they seem to find the state after World War II.

WILLIE J. WHITFIELD lived in Albuquerque, NM. He was born about 1919 in Eola, TX, the son of Ray Stanley Whitfield of Mereta, TX.

Whitfield was a 1937 graduate of Eola High School and an alumnus of Hardin-Simmons University. He was supervisor of the planetary quarantine system support division at Sandia Laboratories, Albuquerque, NM. He was employed by the firm in 1954.

In 1961 he received the Holley Medal, one of the nation's top engineering awards, for his invention of the laminar air flow clean room.

The medal was bestowed by the American Society of Mechanical Engineers. A certificate award cited Whitfield "for the unique concept in the laminar flow clean room principle to eliminate air borne contamination in closed space; application of the new concept created new industry; and permitted advances in electronics and microbiological control. The laminar flow system with filters in structures is a means of producing ultra clean environments for business operations."

293

1810	Whitfield, Joseph	
1810, 1820	Whitfield, Thomas	
1820, 1830, 1840	Whitfield, George	
1830, 1840	Whitfield, George B.	
1830, 1840	Whitfield, George	
1830, 1840	Whitfield, George	
1830, 1840, 1850	Whitfield, Joseph	
1830	Whitfield, William	
1840	Whitfield, Abigail	
1840	Whitfield, Samuel	
1850	Whitfield, Andrew	
1850	Whitfield, Ashbury	
1850	Whitfield, James	
1850	Whitfield, John	

* CENSUSES *

Albany County, NY
1840   Whitfield, Edward

Columbia County, NY
1850   Whitfield, Thomas

Erie County, NY
1840   Whitfield, J.H.
1850   Whitfield, George S.

Dutchess County, New York
1810   Whitfield, James

Courtland County, NY
1810   Whitfield, John

Ontario County, NY
1830   Whitfield, Edward
1850   Whitfield, Edward

Cayuga County, NY
1830, 1840, 1850
              Whitfield, George
1850   Whitfield, George
1850   Whitfield, William

Herkimer County, NY
1850   Whitfield, Alfred
1850   Whitfield, Walter

Kings County, NY
1850   Whitfield, James

Jefferson County, NY
1850   Whitfield, Margaret

Lewis County, NY
1850   Whitfield, William

There were approximately twenty-eight Whitfield heads of families in counties of New York state 1810 to 1860.

There were four widow females heads of families on censuses.

In New York City, NY, there were twelve of these men in the City. One widow on census.

Many immigrants were from Ireland in New York City.

Descendent of Edward Doty, an emigrant on the Mayflower, 1620. Ida Albertine Doty, Dau. of Abner Elverton Doty and Caroline Hooker Harrington, born Ilion, NY, on Nov. 16, 1847. Ida married James Alfred Whitfield on Dec. 8, 1864. He was born at New Hartford, Oneida Co., NY, on Jan. 3, 1840, the son of Alfred Whitfield and Sarah Kirkham. They lived in Ilion.

Children born in Ilion, NY:
1. Inez Harrington Whitfield, b. May 2, 1867. She graduated with the class of 1889, Smith College, Northampton, Mass. Inez was a teacher in partnership with Caroline E. Bliss in 1897. Miss Bliss had a widely known girls school in New York City.

2. Erie Winfred Whitfield, b. July 13, 1873. She graduated from Cornell University, 1895.

Monroe County, NY
1850 Whitfield, Phebe

Niagra County, NY
1840, 1850 Whitfield, John
1840, 1850 Whitfield, William
1850 Whitfield, Jane
1850 Whitfield, Sarah A.

Onedia County, NY
1830 Whitfield, William
1850 Whitfield, George

Rensselaer County, NY
1850 Whitfield, George
1850 Whitfield, Hamilton W.
1850 Whitfield, Simon

St. Lawrence County, NY
1840 Whitfield, John
1840, 1850 Whitfield, William

Suffolk County, NY
1850 Whitfield, Holloway

Warren County, NY
1830, 1840, 1850
    Whitfield, John
1850 Whitfield, Sarah

Wayne County, NY
1840 Whitfield, Edward

Many of these families stay in New York state and some have Whitfield generations in New York state.

There continues to be immigrants with surname Whitfield coming from England over many years.

Telephone directories give information in cities of New York state as to Whitfield families. Inclusive of white and black people with telephone directories.

WHITFIELD RESIDENTS IN 1961 AT MANHATTAN, NY
Telephone numbers reveal the districts in Manhattan

WHITFIELD

Whitfield A	3657Bway	AU 6-8849
Whitfield Addie	245LenoxAv	MO 6-7540
Whitfield Alletha Mrs	310W142	AUdbn 3-0550
Whitfield Alvenia	17W129	SA 2-5354
Whitfield Anne J Mrs	157-10RivDrW	WA 8-0199
Whitfield Arthur	64W84	TR 3-2375
Whitfield Augusta	536W158	SW 5-8052
Whitfield Charlotte Mrs	2465 7Av	AUdbn 1-6858
Whitfield Frank A	222EdgcmbAv	AU 1-1314
Whitfield Harriet Mrs	26ConvntAv	MO 6-3678
Whitfield Hattie M Mrs	39W128	ENright 9-8748
Whitfield Helen	927MadAv	RH 4-5831
Whitfield Henry A	35W110	LE 4-4981
Whitfield Herman	620LenoxAv	AU 1-7352
Whitfield Hugh Jr	789WstEndAv	AC 2-6336
Whitfield Hugh Studio drama	359W38	LO 5-9255
Whitfield Jas J	430E57	TE 2-9392
Whitfield John	230E102	LE 4-2909
Whitfield John Jr	306W135	AD 4-5184
Whitfield John E	12BeekmnPl	PL 8-0691
Whitfield John K	306W135	AD 4-5184
Whitfield Johnnie M	2040 7Av	MO 6-6815
Whitfield Juanita Mrs	75W118	SA 2-0937
Whitfield L Mrs	464W152	WAdswth 6-7913
Whitfield L L	525W150	TO 2-3158

WHITFIELD

Whitfield Louis C	52StNchlasPl	AU 6-3122
Whitfield Louis C phtogphr	132Nasau	CO 7-1504
Whitfield Louise Mrs	128W137	TO 2-1870
Whitfield M J	466W151	AU 6-3824
Whitfield Mae Carrie	15W139	FO 8-1140
Whitfield Margaret Mrs	424StNichAv	WA 6-2438
Whitfield Mildred	620LenoxAv	AU 1-7352
Whitfield Mortimer	188E101	TR 6-7332
Whitfield Myrtle Mrs	41W112	AT 9-4004
Whitfield Omega	545EdgcmbAv	WAdswth 8-7367
Whitfield Oscar N	2181MadAv	AUdbn 1-2908
Whitfield Oscar N	2200MadAv	AD 4-1996
Whitfield Patricia	109E73	UN 1-0457
Whitfield Paydon W	117W141	ADrndak 4-2646
Whitfield Robt W Jr lwyr	1ChseManhPlz	HA 2-2660
Res	375RivDr	MO 3-2817
Whitfield Sally Mrs	555W151	AUdbn 6-9546
Whitfield Silas A	54Cathrn	WO 2-1309
Whitfield Stanley MD	133E58	HA 1-3588
	421W113	UN 5-3000
Whitfield Thos	478CntrlPkW	UN 6-1978
Whitfield Walter E	315W113	MOnumnt 2-0026
Whitfield Wm D	72HmltnTer	AUdbn 3-7628
Whitfield Willie	445E120	HA 7-3674

Archbishop of Catholic Church: James Whitfield was at Crosby Hall in England on September 10, 1816. On November 5, 1817, Rev. James Whitfield arrived In New York from England.

"My father's mother was a Whitfield. Whitfields in Ilion and Mohawk area of New York all originated from England."

....Submitted by Marcia winters Peebles of Carthage, NY, in December 1990.

295

Powerful and interesting is the story of iron made into steel and the development of steel mills and changes with new technologies.

LOUISE WHITFIELD CARNEGIE and ANDREW CARNEGIE

Louise was born March 7, 1857, New York, NY, the daughter of John and Fannie M. Davis Whitfield. Louise attended Miss Haines School, 1864-76, New York University, 1921, Doctor of Law Degree (LLD). She was a quiet, serious, sensitive woman. Andrew liked talking to her. They were married April 22, 1887. They had one daughter Margaret (Mrs. Roswell Miller).

Louise Carnegie received many awards certificates in her lifetime. Carnegie family lived in New York and at Skibo Castle in Dornoch, Scotland, on 40,000 acres.

Louise Carnegie died June 24, 1946, and was buried in Sleepy Hollow Cemetery, N. Tarnytown, NY. She appears in Who Was Who In America. Volume Two, 1943-1950.

Andrew Carnegie was born 1835 to parents Will and Margaret Carnegie and had one brother Thomas. When age 12 Andrew came with the family to Pittsburgh, PA. There was an industrial revolution in the United States in 1847. 190,000 people left Scotland.

When young Andrew was a telegraphic messenger. He learned about railroads. Andrew saw the conversion of iron into steel. In 1865 he moved to New York. He handled finances in steel mills and he bought steel mills. Carnegie dominated plants with laborers and steel production for railroads. Carnegie became one of the richest men in America. In 1889 he became a benefactor of libraries and pension plans for teachers. He was an industrialist. Andrew died in 1919.

EDWIN WHITEFIELD, artist, born 1816 England. He came to the United States about 1840 and painted scenes of Hudson Valley Esstates, 1841-42. He worked in New York City and illustrated American wildflowers in publications. In 1845 a series of the views he painted was published with the title North American Scenery, 1847.

Edwin Whitefield made several trips to Minnesota to promote his real estate interests, 1856-59. There he painted several water color landscapes which were placed with the Minnesota Historical Society. Edwin Whitefield lived in Boston and Reading, Massachusetts during the 1880's. The Homes of Our Forefathers was published and showed early New England houses, eight volumes. Whitefield died 1892.

RECORD

GEORGE WHITFIELD had a grandson named Samuel Whitfield, and a grandson named George Whitfield, age 19, on the 1870 census of Darrytown, NY. George Whitfield may have had a daughter named Nellie Whitfield of Flushing, NY.

....Submitted by Jay Nelson of La Cres, CA, near Glendale, CA, on 8/2/1994.

Lester Mason Whitfield ,Jr. shares this information:
"My family tree goes back to Jackson,Mississippi where my
great-great-great-great-grandfather MASON WHITFIELD, an author and college dean, had to the best of my knowledge eight
children: Beatrice, May Lou, Julia, Ida, Lester I , Mimmie,
Mable and his wife's name was Matirda Whitfield."

Lester Mason Whitfield, Jr. was born July 2,1933 and was
raised in New York. He worked as a car inspector for the New
York City authority. He was born as the fourth generation
with the name in lineage. In 1933 he was retired and lived
at Henderson, Nevada. He married and had three children. His
parents were Lester Mason Whitfield, Sr. and Adeline Louise
Howe.

NEW YORK MARRIAGE BONDS

1761 , Jan. 10 . Elizabeth Whitfield , widow , and Richard
Robinson -   Richard Robinson , John Osborn .

1768, May 11. John Whitfield of New York City, Mariner ,and
Catherine Burger of New York City, Spinster - Jacob
Shafer , Abraham Swart .

1775, Nov. 3 . Catharine Whitfield and Thomas Ogilvie.

1765 , Sept. 12 . Elizabeth Whitfield and Giles Cooper.

1768 , May 11 . John Whitfield and Catherine Burger.

1764 , March 29 . Thomas Whitefield and Hannah George.

FANNY MINER DAVIS   was married in New York City, to
John William Whitfield, son of George B. and Elizabeth Augusta
(Stevens) Whitfield, of New York City, who was born in New York
City, July 20, 1832, and died in New York, April 25, 1878. Their
children were:

   i. Louise, b. in New York City, Mar. 7, 1857.
  ii. George B., b. in New York City, Apr. 4, 1859, d. in New York,
        Sept. 19, 1861.
 iii. Estelle, b. in New York City, Sept. 17, 1862.
  iv. Henry Davis, b. in New York City, Oct. 7, 1874.
   v. Mary Elizabeth, b. in New York City, Jan. 22, 1877, d. June

An account of the descendants of
John Davis, a native of England,
who died in East Hampton, Long
Island, New York ,in 1705.
Reference. <u>History Of The Davis Family</u>
by Albert H. Davis. Published 1888
New York ,N.Y.

There is a Whitfield buried in the cemetary yard of United States
President James Monroe. Eastern state of United States.
There is a Whitfield burial in California and the information from
a certificate. This date is 1880. John Monroe was a first cousin of President James Monroe.

HUSBAND'S NAME _John Monroe_

When Born _____ Where ____ _N.Y._

Cal. N.Y. 7th Sept 1851-1803

When Married _6 Aug 1846_ Where _446 Albany St, N.Y._

WIFE'S MAIDEN NAME

Esther Josephine Whitfield

When Born _____ Where ____ _N.Y._

When Died _25 Jan 1880_

Where _College ca._

Where _burial cemetery Vallejo, ca_
Dept Solano Co. School

Other Husb. (if any)
Number (1) (2) etc. _Geo. W. Simonton_

John Monroe
(Husband's Full Name)

Esther Josephine Whitfield
(Wife's Maiden Name)

This information obtained from

Max Cutter - cemetery
the whole lists from
J grand daughter Esther
Max cut for
Esther Josephine Whitfield
& John Monroe
our children Monroe Scott
Geo Perry Monroe & Scrap

Date _13 Sept 1953_
Compiler _Mrs Ruthland Dellinis_
Address _1325 Kheadage Place_
City _Denver Place_ State _Co. 95404_

		State or Country	WHEN DIED*			Married
			Day	Month	Year	
F 1	Geo Perry Monroe	2 Aug 1850 N.Y.			1933	To Theckless Murray Scott 1869
					Date	Date 13 Nov 1873
F 2	Hattie Clida (Clida) Monroe	2 Nov 1855 conn	22 Jan 1880			To Lewis Benjamin Clark

298

From:
    "The New York Times Obituaries Index," 1858-1968, page 1093,
New York, New York.

DEATH RECORDS

    Whitfield, James B. 1948, Ag 21, 15:4.
    Whitfield, Arthur 1947 F 5, 23:1
    Whitfield, B.W., Sr. 1949, Ja 6, 23:1
    Whitfield, Frederick E. B. 1940, O 16, 23;5
    Whitfield, Harold B. 1965, S 8, 47:4
    Whitfield, Henry D. 1949, F 14, 19:3
    Whitfield, Howard 1938, S 22, 23:3
    Whitfield, Inez 1951, Je 28, 25:2
    Whitfield, J. Randolph 1939, My 11, 25:5
    Whitfield, Jacob H. 1944, 14, 23:5
    Whitfield, James A. (Bill Lewis) 1961, Ap 2, 76:1
    Whitfield, James P. 1950 Jl 28, 7;1; 1953, Jl 18, 14-8
    Whitfield, Owen H. 1965, My 6, 88:4.
    Whitfield, Robert 1951 Mr 15, 29:5
    Whitfield, Susan B. 1946, O 20, 60:4.
    Whitfield, William L. 1955, Ag 13, 13:7.
    Whitfield, William Mrs. 1956 D 15, 25:1.

MARRIAGE RECORDS

From Book: "The Whitney Family of Connecticut," by S. Whitney,
Phoenix, Private Print, 1878, New York.

#3011. Moses Osborn Curtis, b. at New York City, 23 Nov. 1801; a
dealer in boats and shoes; married in 7/1824, REBECCA WHITFIELD.
WHITFIELD, born in 10/1806, dau. of Thomas Whitfield and ____
(Godfrey) Whitfield. They settled in New York, where he died on
Hudson Street, in 4/1850, without children.

Rebecca Whitfield died at Fort Lee, NJ, 11/5/1873, aged 67 years.
They were buried in the family vault in St. Mark's Churchyard, NY.

Ella Miranda Howard, born at Pierrepont, NY, 11/15/1851; married
to Herbert Wood, a farmer, son of James and Charlotte Griffin
Wood, of Potsdam, NY, where he was born on 7/29/1850. Married by
the Rev. WILLIAM WHITFIELD. Free Baptist, 11/15/1870.

#2712. Miranda Lydia Brooks married Charles Chamberlain at Madrid,
NY, 12/4/1846, by Rev. William Whitfield. Free Baptist.

Robert Parr Whitfield, b. May 27, 1828, New Hartford, NY, and died
April 6, 1910, in NY. Son of English parents. He married 1848
Mary Henry. Robert was a Paleontologist. He was an illustrator,
lecturer, curator, and assistant to state geologist at Albany, NY,
in science of paleontology and geology.

New England. As early as 1623 a settlement was made in New
Hampshire. The region which now comprises Maine, New Hampshire
and Vermont was granted by the Council for New England to Sir
Ferdinando Gorges and Captain John Mason and their associates.
In 1629 Mason and Gorges divided their territory. Some of the
early settlements were unsuccessful but in time people of
Massachusetts moved in these regions.

NORTH CAROLINA

Indian tribes inhabited the land of a place for a long time near the Atlantic Ocean. Later the place was called Carolina.

The Spaniards left Europe and went on a sailing expedition in 1492 that took them to America. Englishmen began this route with expeditions in the century of 1500. Spanish sailors first discovered the short of Florida. English sailors discovered the Barbados island of America in the century of 1600. In 1608 they landed on the coast of Virginia.

Virginia land companies were formed in England. Charters were issued from the English authority for the purpose of colonization in America. March 12, 1617, the exploration of Virginia began.

Charters to the Lord Proprietors of Carolina began 1663 and others in 1665. Constitutions for Carolina began July 1669, and five written versions followed until 1698. Charters and Constitutions were the two groups of documents. First, Charters by English sovereigns authorizing colonization area of North Carolina. Second, group of documents comprised the constitutions issued by the Lord Proprietors of Carolina.

In an explorers' expedition they visited Roanoke Island between Pamlico and Albermarle Sounds. Then the English authority issued land patents beginning in 1700. These land patents went to Englishmen of distinction and financial capabilities. Often the men were noblemen. In 1706 the land patents were issued to individuals who could carry out the plans of the British sovereigns in their authorities.

At Carolina a few men and ships were involved with the first efforts of colonization of the land. For government of England the Council was formed and General Assembly was designed as precincts. Vestry parishes became a place where men could gather and make public records of their activities. Land could be bought for a price and certain conditions were to be met by a landowner. 1706 is a date for land acquisitions and homesteading.

Immigrants came to Carolina and many people of the coastal area of Virginia found young families moving into Carolina. The land was identified as North Carolina and South Carolina and both ocean shores were accessible to a seaport.

First record in North Carolina is one of William Whitfield and land transaction group. Several named William Whitfield made the first farms in North Carolina beginning in public record 1710. Large acres were given to patent land holders up to 600 acres. Earl of Granville received a very large tract of territory land with Indians. When land was ready, it was opened to the people for settlement and purchase.

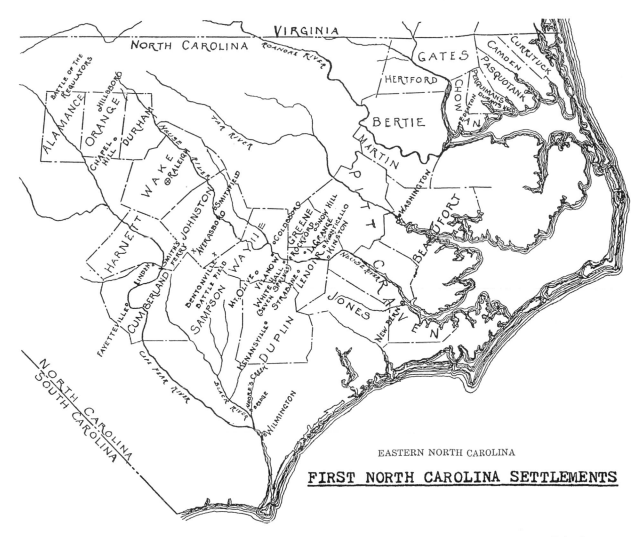

EASTERN NORTH CAROLINA

FIRST NORTH CAROLINA SETTLEMENTS

In the colonization of the North Carolina Colony, Englishmen were given land grants of large acres. These first owners sold land to people who were residents of the area and to immigrant people. Surveyors found boundaries for acre parcels and these survey descriptions were written into deeds which were legal papers filed with authority of parishes.

Maps have the owners names to parcels. This map shows the first development land areas which later were defined as counties of the precincts.

Granville District of North Carolina, 1748-1763, included these land areas:

Anson, Beaufort, Bertie, Bladen, Bute, Chowan, Cumberland, Currituck, Dobbs, Edgecombe, Granville

EARLY SETTLERS

1715 Granville District. William Whitfield, J. Davison, Thomas Cope, on 10/20/1715 were witnesses to two land deeds concerning 91) Thomas Dyall, wife Mary Dyall, Henry King, Leonard Langstone of 100 acres...Also witnesses to letter addressed to attorney.

301

Richard Moore of Nansemond Co., VA, concerning the above owners
and representatives on 220 acres. (2)

1721 - Chowan Precinct
John Beverley, planter, and wife Margaret Beverley sold 325 acres
more or less to William Whitfield on 10/14/1721. Registered in
Chowan Precinct Jan. 18, 1721. (3)

1757 - Edgecombe County
Warrants dated October 1752 and later 10/21/1762 to survey lands
of Thomas Whitfield (1721-1781) in a county land survey of 600
acres by Colonel John Haywood. (4)

1750 - New Bern, North Carolina
Matthew Elvy was a Justice of Peace. Land grant of detained
Number 403 Petition for Warrant for New Hanover. Matthew
Whitfield and other men of the area New Bern were at the Council
Chamber to prove their ownership and rights which was granted
videlicet...so what they were interested in when warrant petitions
were made to Council.... Warrants did allow under the law the
right of surveyors to do surveying of property lines, and it was
the right of authority to do the surveys on people's land.

Northampton County, North Carolina
William Whitfield lived at Northampton County, NC, before 1776.
William Whitfield sold the land to John Lawrence before 1796.
When John Lawrence wrote his will January 1796, he mentioned the
land purchase from William Whitfield and gave his land to his son
David Lawrence, 100 pounds current money of Virginia. Will
probated at Court, December 1796. (7)

1723 - Bertie County, North Carolina
William Whitfield (1688 England-died NC) and wife, Elizabeth
Whitfield, settled in Bertie County to live in 1723. (8)

1775 - Dobbs County, North Carolina
William Whitfield (1715-1795), husband of Rachel Bryan, held a
meeting with the Council of Safety of North Carolina at his house.
May 3, 1779, William Whitfield was elected to the Council of
State. Local area councils with precinct met at Kinston, Halifax,
and New Bern. (9)

▬▬ ▬▬ ▬▬ ▬▬ ▬▬ ▬▬ ▬▬ ▬▬ ▬▬ ▬▬

Records are important, both the public government source,
published public source, and the private source. Each reader
and researcher has to make the conclusion on the materials.

▬▬ ▬▬ ▬▬ ▬▬ ▬▬ ▬▬ ▬▬ ▬▬ ▬▬

Reference:
1. North Carolina, Granville District. Deed Book Number 768, page
191.
2. Ibid. Deed Book Number 769, p. 191.
3. Ibid. Deed Book Number 596, p. 200. Chowan Precinct.
4. The Granville District of North Carolina 1748-1763 by Margaret
Hoffman. Abstracts of Land Office Records, Vol. Four.
5. Pitt County, North Carolina, Deed Book 18, p. 371.
6. Johnston County, North Carolina, Deed Book 20, p. 270.
7. Northampton County, North Carolina 1759-1808, by Margaret M.
Hoffman. Abstracts of Wills.
8. Whitfield, Bryan, Smith and Related Families by Emma Morehead
Whitfield, p. 53.
9. Ibid. p. 57.

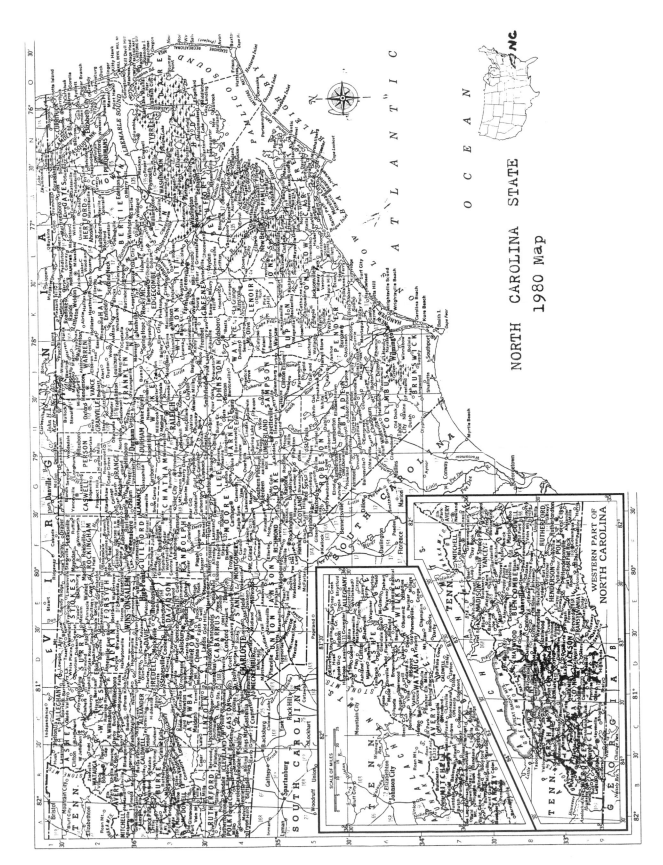

NORTH CAROLINA STATE
1980 Map

WESTERN PART OF
NORTH CAROLINA

Counties with Whitfield on Censuses before 1850.

COUNTY MAP FOR THE STATE OF NORTH CAROLINA

Alamance Co.
Anson Co.

Beaufort Co.
Bertie Co.

Craven Co.
Caswell Co.
Chowan Co.

Dobb Co.
Duplin Co.

Edgecombe Co.

Franklin Co.

Granville Co.

Halifax Co.
Hertford Co.

Lenoir Co.

Montgomery Co.
Martin Co.

Nash Co.
New Hanover Co.
Northampton Co.

Onslow Co.
Orange Co.

Person Co.
Pitt Co.

Sampson Co.
Stokes Co.
Surry Co.

Tyrrell Co.

Wake Co.
Wayne Co.

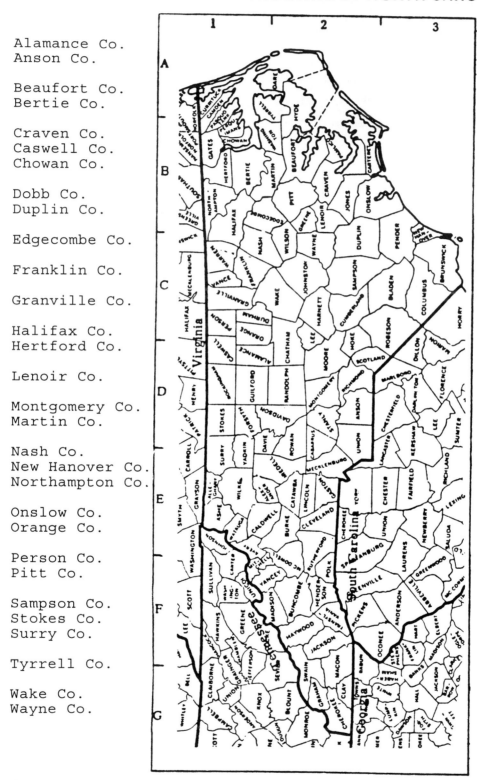

ELIZABETH CITY COUNTY, VIRGINIA

To know the first development of the Englishmen from England at Virginia in 1608 and later, a person must go back to the beginning of the country inhabited by the Indians. These records and the history are from England. The shippers with boat records are from England. These ship records list the immigrants to America.

Blanche Adams Chapman compiled the Wills and Administration of Elizabeth City County, Virginia, 1688-1800. Study and research have been done in these records. Thus there is documentation to produce factually historical information on Thomas Whitfield who died in Elizabeth City Co., VA, and left a will dated 1694. He could have been a native or an immigrant. His father could have been named Thomas Whitfield. However, since most of the early immigrants 1600's shippers records show several John Whitfields who were immigrants, his father could have been named John.

Thomas Whitfield lived on Elizabeth City land along the Atlantic Ocean and off the shore of VA with the James River to the west of the land. Thomas Whitfield married about 1681 to Ann Forgeson, daughter of Daniel and Katherine Forgeson. They had four children: John, Thomas, Mary, and Elizabeth. Thomas Whitfield died 1694 and his wife, Ann Whitfield, made his estate public in her administration of the state on 9/16/1695.

Thomas Whitfield in his 30 or 40 years of life left wife Ann Whitfield one-half of his land from George Bells and the other one-half to his oldest son. In the will he writes, "Son John Whitfield of 16 years of age is to receive his inheritance of land."

Whitfield's will was written 7/26/1694 and recorded 11/26/1694. Witnesses to the will were Thomas Tyler, Peter Manson, and Thomas Poole. The estate appraisers were Thomas House, John Bushell, Thomas Bailey, and Christopher Copeland, 11/18/1695. (1)

At Elizabeth City, VA, the names and neighbors associated with this Whitfield family were Avera, Bailey, Bells, Bushell, Copeland, Dunn, Forgeson, House, Manson, Needham, Poole, Robinson, Tyler, Williams, and others.

FORGESON - WHITFIELD

The father of Ann Whitfield left a will.
FORGESON, DANIEL-Leg. eldest daughter Ann Whitfield, land adjoining John Forgeson and Shadrack Williams. Executors: wife Katherine and son John Forgeson. Died July 28, 1697. Will recorded 10/7/1697. Witnesses, Thomas Bayly, Christopher Copeland, Mary Robinson, Mary Copeland. Probation granted John Forgeson, his son, 9/20/1697. (2) (Record is Bayly and also Bailey in another record.)

Katherine Forgeson became a widow three years after her daughter Ann Forgeson Whitfield was widowed. Katherine would have been age range 55 to 65 and also her husband of same age or few years older.

Reference:
1. Wills and Administrations of Elizabeth City County, Virginia 1688-1800 by Blanche Adams Chapman. Pages 156, 194, 224, 381, 382.
2. Ibid. Pages 217 and 272.

Ann Forgeson Whitfield, daughter of Daniel Forgeson, deceased, petitioned court for mother, Katherine Forgeson, to deliver to Ann Whitfield all goods and cattle given to her by father before decease.

Moses David was a brother-in-law of Ann Whitfield. Moses Davis sold 50 acres granted from father-in-law Daniel Forgeson 1696. His wife was deceased. Moses was of age for some time. Moses and Ann exchanged some land. (3)

DESCENDANTS OF THOMAS WHITFIELD (1660 ca-1694) and ANN FORGESON AND THE FAMILIES' HISTORY

Whitfield-Avery-Averitt-Averra-Copeland-Poole Virginia

In 1641 Henry Poole was Sheriff of Elizabeth City County. Henry Poole was the second husband of Jane Whitfield, wife of John Whitfield, Jr. and mother of Thomas Whitfield. Henry Poole was a member of the House of Burgesses 1647-1648. Henry Poole was County Clerk of Elizabeth City County, VA, in 1648-1679. (4)

In December 1695 Jane Averitt, grandmother of John Whitfield, son of Thomas Whitfield, appointed his guardian.

When an adult, Henry went to Court asking for legacy from father 11/11/1695. Henry Avery, 21 years of age, asked his mother Jane Avery, "Why did father Henry Avery (deceased) leave me in mother's custody?" Witnesses were Thomas Poole and others.

Thomas Poole, 4/26/1704, with 474 acres escheat land, late in possession of Jane Poole. Jane Averra (varied spellings) Whitfield Poole was his mother, deceased. (5)

Christopher Copeland had the eldest daughter Ann Poole. Copeland had another daughter who was Hursley Averett.

January 12, 1710-1711. Court recording March 21, 1715. Witnesses: William Dunn, Moses Davis. (6) Ann Copeland Poole was the wife of William Poole.

WHITFIELD

Ann Forgeson Whitfield's son, John Whitfield, was a farmer at Elizabeth City County, VA. He was living with his mother until of legal age to possess his land. The family stayed together. Ann and her son Thomas Whitfield, Jr. worked the land with the help of men who also did farming there. Ann was a widow for three years and a stepfather joined the family named William Dunn.

John Whitfield was not yet of age sixteen when his father died. Assuming John was age 12, his birth was in 1682. Thomas was younger than John, and his birth would have been about 1680. Mary was younger than Thomas. Elizabeth was likely the youngest child of Ann Whitfield. All children of Ann were born in Elizabeth City County, VA.

Thomas Whitfield born 1680 circa lived in Elizabeth City, Virginia. Thomas was an adult by 1701. Thomas Whitfield II married and had a son named Thomas Whitfield born in 1721 in Virginia. Thomas was married and settled for several years by 1721. There are no records there on Thomas, Jr.

WHITFIELD - DUNN FAMILY
Elizabeth City County, Virginia

It appears that Ann Forgeson was a young woman of 18 years when she married Thomas Whitfield. Their first child John may have been born about 1682. John Whitfield lived all his life at Elizabeth City County, VA.

Ann Forgeson birth was about 1664 at Virginia or her parents could have been immigrants to Virginia. Ann Forgeson married first Thomas Whitfield and she married second William Dunn at Elizabeth City County, VA. Ann Whitfield was a widow in 1694 with four children.

Ann Whitfield was a widow of at least three years. She owned land inherited from her father, Daniel Forgeson, and she owned land inherited from her husband Thomas Whitfield. Ann Whitfield married William Dunn between 1694 and 1704 at Elizabeth City County, VA.

William Dunn had 100 acres. His relative, likely a brother, Henry Dunn had 50 acres at Elizabeth City County, VA. William was a farmer. William and Ann had a family. Children were those of Thomas Whitfield and William Dunn.

1. John Whitfield
2. Thomas Whitfield
3. Mary Whitfield
4. Elizabeth Whitfield
5. William Dunn
6. Ann Dunn
7. Catron Dunn
8. Mary Dunn
9. Elizabeth Dunn

The mother of Ann Dunn died 1713 or 1714 and left a will. Abstract of the will: "Forgison, Katherine, Leg. - granddaughter Elizabeth Dunn when she is age 17; daughter Ann the wife of William Dunn. Executor, son-in-law, William Dunn. Witnesses: Thomas Needham and Charles Avera." Court has the date of the will probate January 24, 1713-1714. (7)

William Dunn died in 1724 or 1725. William left a will. Abstract of the will: Dunn, William. Leg.-Son William; daughter Elizabeth, daughter Catron, daughter Mary; to my wife. Executor, daughter Elizabeth Dunn. Overseers, Henry Dunn and Thomas Wilson. D. March 9, 1724/25. R. January 18, 1726. Witnesses: Coules Avera, Edward Williams.

Estate appraised by Edward Lattimer, James Naylor and Charles Jenings. January 28, 1726. (8)

Double dating used at Court. "Before the Gregorian Calendar was adopted by England in 1752, the legal and ecclesiastical year began on 25 March, thus resulting in two recorded dates, thus: 15 March 1698/99. When so given by the Clerk, this double-dating has been retained."

Katherine Forgison spelling of her name is different from her husband's spelling on his will. For the husband Forgeson is written by Vallie Jo Whitfield. Varied spellings exist for the surname. Furgason family at Elizabeth City County, Va. Furgason in Isle of Wight County, VA. Ferguson in Southampton County, VA. Dates 1690 to 1750. Forgeson is also found in record.

Elizabeth City on the coastline, Jamestown up the James River and Suffolk, the earliest 1600's land settlements had filled up with the natives and immigrants. Then the Englishmen and natives pushed into land on the eastern shore of America, and the Indians moved to the West. Nansemond County and the Isle of Wight County of Virginia had new inhabitants, the white and black people.

Copeland, Whitfield and a new generation of people settled at these two places of Virginia. There are 21 men names Thomas Whitfield at the Isle of Wight County, VA. It seems likely that Thomas Whitfield, son of Ann Whitfield, may have moved to the Isle of Wight County with neighbors and descendants of the people of Elizabeth City County.

There were three names Thomas Whitfield at Nansemond County, VA. Upper Suffolk Parish has a few records.

DUNN

Thirty years later Catron Dunn was living at Elizabeth City County, VA. Catron Dunn and her cousin Thomas Whitfield, born 1721, are the third generation. Catron's half brother, John Whitfield b. 1682 ca. died 1727. John died intestate and his estate was appraised June 21, 1727.

Catron Dunn was witness to Middleton Poole's will along with witness Thomas Poole. Middleton Poole died July 16, 1740. Middleton was the son of Thomas Poole who willed Middleton the tract of land given by "my mother, Jane Avera to her son John Poole." Varied spelling of Jane Averra and Jane Avera. Thomas Poole had daughters: Jane, Ann, Mary. Thomas Poole will is January 27, 1725-1762. Witness was John Whitfield (9).

References:
3. (a) Elizabeth City County, Virginia. Deeds, Wills, Court Orders, Etceteras, 1634, 1659, 1688-1701. Compiled by Rosemary Carley Neal. Published 1986.
   (b) Neal mentioned Moses Davis nine times in the compilation of Elizabeth City, VA records. Blanche Chapman mentioned Moses Davis three times in her compilation of Elizabeth City County, VA.
4. Wills and Administrations of Elizabeth City County, Virginia 1688-1800 by Blanche Adams Chapman. Pages 151, 155, 156.
5. Elizabeth City County, Virginia, Deed Book Nine, pages 141, 160.
6. (a) Wills and Administration of Elizabeth City County, Virginia 1688-1800 by Blanche Adams Chapman, page 25.
   (b) Kathleen Lynch Rolleigh Whitfield of Falls Church, VA, studied and researched the Elizabeth City County, VA, records in 1995 year and contributed the information and records on Poole, Averitt, Averra, Whitfield, Dunn.
7. Wills and Administrations of Elizabeth City County, Virginia Book 1715-1721. Page 16.
8. Wills and Administration of Elizabeth City County, Virginia Book 1704-1730. Pages 58, 91.

LIFE OF THOMAS WHITFIELD (1721-1781)
and MARY WHITFIELD (1725-1792)

Thomas Whitfield was born 1721 in Virginia. He was the son of Thomas Whitfield, and grandson of Thomas Whitfield and Ann Forgeson Whitfield of Elizabeth City County, Virginia.

Thomas Whitfield III married Mary in 1740 in Virginia. Thomas was age 19 and Mary was age 15. Thomas and Mary had four of the children born in Virginia. In 1749 they left Virginia and moved to Edgecombe County, NC. They had 130 acres there.

Thomas Whitfield and family settled at the Junction of Peach Tree Creek and Pig Basket Creek. Thomas was a farmer. He raised lambs and sold their wool and meat. He had cows and animals on the farm. He planted crops. One large crop was apples. Thomas Whitfield made the living by selling lamb products and by buying and selling real estate land.

In Edgecombe County, NC, they lived from 1749 to 1777. Edgecombe was split into Nash County and Pitt County in 1777 and then they lived in Nash County, NC, until their deaths. Their children lived in Nash County, NC.

In 1756 on June 20 Thomas Whitfield bought some property. He kept it one year and sold the land of 51 acres, June 30, 1760. The state of North Carolina opened land areas and Thomas Whitfield acquired 490 acres at the junction where he lived.

On October 5, 1765, Mary Thomas Horn and her husband sold a tract of land to Thomas Whitfield, Sr. This was the land that Earl of Granville had granted to her father, Joseph Thomas, on October 31, 1753.

In 1762 Thomas Whitfield was in court and acknowledged he had 490 acres purchased for $400 for tract of land in Halifax District, NC, and agreed to pay the heirs of Thomas Vaughan's heirs.

Thomas Whitfield bought 1,501 acres of land in North Carolina near where he lived and disposed of the land to his sons and grantees. In his late 50 years of age, he had 230 acres he retained as his farm.

Mary Whitfield, wife of Thomas, gave birth to children from 1741 to 1769 and had 13 children (nine sons and four daughters). The acquisition of land by the sons who had to be age 21 to own and have rights to land of their own tells who were the older sons.

Hardy and Ezaral were the younger sons. Mary was living with one of the sons when she died in 1792. (Ezaral pronounced Israel).

The Revolutionary War in 1776 had Thomas Whitfield, Sr. a patriot and creditor of supplies in the Revolution. The Revolutionary Supplies Commissioner was Josiah Crump, an in-law to Whitfield.

Thomas Whitfield died at his home in Nash County, NC, in 1781. He left a will.

The following records are those of Thomas Whitfield of official sources of the counties and court and of his children (10).

of God Amen. Revoking all other wills and testaments I do own and acknowledge this to be may last will and testament. In witness whereof I have signed and set my hand and seal this 6th day of July 1781.

Thomas Whitfield signed his will.

Court 1781. Sealed published declared by the above named Thomas Whitfield as his last will and testament in presence of us.
Jacob Dickinson. Willis Whitfield. Chloe Whitfield.
January Court 1781. Attest. William Hallels, Clerk. (14)

CRUMP AND WHITFIELD

During the American Revolutionary War Thomas Whitfield was a creditor of supplies. He had forage for the Continental cause. This was food of any kind for horses and cattle. Josias Crump of the Army office had Whitfield's account. (15)

The creditors of supplies had a staff officer and commissioner of specific supplies for the Northampton County, NC, in the Revolutionary War, and his name was Josias Crump. He was born June 24, 1734, in St. Peter's Parish, New Kent, VA.

Josias Crump married Mary ____ in 1760, and they had five children:
1. Richard Crump b. 1762. He married Julia Sykes.
2. Sarah Crump b. 1764. She married ____ Whitehead.
3. Penelope Crump b. 1765. She married William Edmunds.
4. Martha Crump b. 1768. She married Dave Mason.
5. Charles Crump b. 1770. He married Mary Cook. (16)

The mother, Mary Crump, was born about 1738 and died after 1812. Josiah Crump died in December 1812. The Crump family lived in Northampton County, NC.

When Crump was officer and commissioner in the 1776 war, he kept financial accounts of the creditors and wrote a brief description of the creditors. In an account record he wrote the information on Thomas Whitfield (b. 1721) who lived in Nash County, NC. He wrote the birth dates of Thomas and Mary and their marriage date 1740. He wrote that Thomas Whitfield was an in-law.

A study was made. Vallie Jo Whitfield applied to the National Society of the Daughters of the American Revolution, Washington, DC, for information.

_____

References:
9. Wills and Administration of Elizabeth City County, Virginia. Book 1740, Page 70.
10. Edgecombe County, NC, Deed Book 1750-1789.
(a) Nash County, NC, Deed Book 1777-1794. (b) Edgecombe County, NC, Court 1773 Legal Paper. Thomas Whitfield, Jr. versus Thomas Whitfield, Sr. Quiet Title and Mortgage. November 11, 1773, Court. (c) Will 1781 Court, Nash County, NC. Recording of Will of Thomas Whitfield (1721-1781).
11. (a) Edgecombe County, NC, Deed Book 1753-1777. (b) Nash County, NC, Deed Book 1777-1794.
12. (a) Edgecombe County, NC, Deed Book 1753-1777. (b) Nash County, NC, Deed Book. (c) Halifax County, NC, Deed Book 1762.

The staff member of N.S.D.A.R. replied with this information: "Our records on Thomas Whitfield, 1721-1781, do not show the maiden name of his wife. All seven members that have joined on this man descend through his son William. Alice Timberlake, number 110519, was one of these. She was also credited with ancestors William Whitfield, Josias Crump and Joshua Jones."

The study revealed both Thomas Whitfield and Josias Crump were born in Virginia. Crump was born 13 years after Thomas Whitfield. The relationship as in-law could not be determined as to the relations and who the persons were. The maiden name of the wife, Mary Whitfield, was not found and information on the father of Thomas Whitfield was not revealed.

MARY WHITFIELD was Mrs. Thomas Whitfield.

She was born 1725. In 1740 she married Thomas Whitfield in Virginia, and they lived there until 1749. They moved to Edgecombe County, VA, and stayed on the same land all their lives.

Mary was the mother to nine sons and four daughters. She was a widow in 1781. She had rights to the property as a spouse. Mary Whitfield died in 1792 in Nash County, NC. She wrote a will leaving the remaining property to her son Elisha Whitfield. She gave a cow and calf and personal property to Sookey Whitfield.

_____

References:
13. (a) Three Deeds. Edgecombe County, NC, Deed Book 1753-1777. Nash County, NC, Deed Book. Halifax County, NC, Deed Book 1762. (b) Joseph W. Watson, Abstracts Deeds. Book 1967. (c) Research Paper of M.A. Clemons of Brandon, FL, 1992.
14. Will of Thomas Whitfield, 1781. North Carolina Colonial Records, Edgecombe County.
15. Revolutionary Army Accounts North Carolina, 1776. Accounts of the Comptroller's Office, War and Revolution.
16. National Society of the Daughters of the American Revolution. Number 418903. Jane Hall Harmond Cromwell (1981) and her lineage with Crump, Edmunds, Sykes, Hall lists these documents and sources: (a) Will of Josias Crump, Northampton County, NC, (b) Kinfolks. Vol. 2, p. 1205. A Genealogical and Biographical Record by William Curry Harllee. (c) Colonial records of North Carolina, Vol. XV, p. 450. Vol. XIX, pp. 222-223. (d) D.A.R. Lineage Book, Vol. 126, p. 294.

Note. The sketches in the genealogy of Thomas Whitfield (died 1694) and Ann Forgeson Whitfield and descendants were taken from these sources: Censuses. Deeds. Wills. Colonial Records. Elizabeth City County, Virginia, Edgecombe and Nash Counties of North Carolina. The Wills of Nash County, North Carolina. Abstracts. Volume One 1777-1848. Abstracted by Dr. Stephen E. Bradley, Jr.

There is not space for a complete genealogy in this book. The purpose for this brief and profiles is to determine the number of generations of descendants.

Generation One - Father Lineage
_____ Whitfield born in 1600s.

Generation Two - Mother Lineage   (9)
Daniel Forgeson was born in 1600s, and died July 28, 1697, at
Elizabeth City County, Virginia.   Daniel Forgeson married
Katherine ____ who was born 1642 circa, and died 1713 or 1714 at
Elizabeth City, Virginia. They had children. 1. John Forgeson.
2. Ann Forgeson who was born about 1664, and died after 1725.
3. ____ Forgeson. She was Mrs. Moses Davis, and died before 1696.
The Forgesons lived at Elizabeth City County, Virginia.

Generation Two   **(Whitfield/Forgeson)**
Thomas Whitfield born in 1600s and died July 26, 1694, at
Elizabeth City County, Virginia. Thomas married Ann Forgeson, and
they had the son Thomas Whifield.

Generation Three   **(Thomas)**
Thomas Whitfield had the son Thomas Whitfield born 1721 in
Virginia.

Generation Four   **(Thomas, Thomas)**
Thomas Whitfield born 1721 and died 1781 in Nash County, North
Carolina. Thomas married Mary in Virginia, and they had thirteen
children. They had the son Thomas Whitfield born 1741 in Virginia
who died 1799 in Nash County, North Carolina.

Generation Five   **(Thomas, Thomas, Thomas)**
Thomas Whitfield (1741-1799) married Elizabeth Young in North
Carolina. They had four daughters and two sons named Mathew and
Willis. The father Thomas (1721-1781) passed a grant of land to
Thomas, Jr. on October, 1765.
The son Willis Whitfield served in the Revolutionary War and later
moved to Tennessee. The son Mathew Whitfield remained in North
Carolina until after 1800 and the death of his parents, and then
he moved to Rutherford County, Tennessee, and joined his brother
Willis Whitfield there.
In 1773 father and son are in court about the land transaction.
Thomas Whitfield, Jr. versus Thomas Whitfield, Sr. On November
11, 1773, at court claims he had paid for the property on south
side of Pig Basket Creek, and there was three appurtenances that
were his; he opposed the selling and delivery sale being presented
by his father, and he sought discharge of all manner of
encumbrances with release of mortgage judgment and any troubles.
On the same day, Thomas Whitfield, Sr. did bind and oblige
himself, and advised the land be clear from claims of any person,
and that a sale take place. In witness, he set his hand and seal
at court on the day of Nov. 11, 1773.

Signature of
Thomas Whitfield, 1773

Land is returned
to the father.

THOMAS WHITFIELD, SENR. of Edgecombe Co. to THOMAS WHITFIELD, JUNR. of same, Nov. 11, 1773, for 10 pds. Proc. money a tract of 130 acres on the south bank of Pig Basket Creek just above Worbanton's house. This land was part of a Granville grant to Joseph Thomas by deed bearing date Oct. 31, 1753 and was bequeathed by said Thomas to his daughter, Mary Horn, and William Horn, who sold the said tract to said Thomas Whitfield, Senr. by deed bearing date Oct. 5, 1765. Wit: Benjamin Whitfield, Solomon Whitfield.

Generation Five   **(Thomas, Thomas, Thomas)**

Reuben Whitfield was born in Virginia and died 1816 in North Carolina. Reuben was the head of a family with three sons and three daughters on the 1810 census of North Carolina. Whitfield's wife died before 1816. Children. 1. Miles Whitfield; 2. Ivey Whitfield; 3. Reuben Whitfield; 4. Sarah Bryant Whitfield; 5. Chloe Whitfield. She married ____ Stokes; 6. Nancy Whitfield. She married ____ Massinghill.
Reuben Whitfield witnessed a deed in 1761.

Solomon Whitfield was born in decade of 1740 in Virginia and died 1807 in North Carolina. Solomon's wife was Ann Whitfield. The family lived on Pig Basket Creek, Edgecomb Co., NC, and later Nash County, North Carolina. Solomon was in several colonial records as a witness. Solomon Whitfield served in the new army shortly after the Revolutionary War was over. Solomon and Ann had children.

Generation Six.

1. Jacob Whitfield born in the 1790s and died 1825. Jacob and his wife had three sons and one daughter; 2. Mary Whitfield was unmarried. She owned sixty acres. Mary wrote her will April 26, 1843, and her will was probated in court of February 1844. Mary left her acres to her sister Charity Whitfield. Witnesses to her will were John Ricks, Mourning (x) Strickland; 3. Nancy Whitfield was unmarried in 1825; 4. Charity Whitfield was unmarried in 1825; 5. Winney Whitfield married. She was Mrs. Nolleboy; 6. Isaac Whitfield died January 6, 1796; 7. Sarah Whitfield dated her will December 16, 1835. Will was at court in August 1836; 8. Milly Whitfield married ____ Melton. They had the child Temperance Melton.

Solomon Whitfield obtained land from his father in 1767.

Generation Five   **(Thomas, Thomas, Thomas)**

John Whitfield was born in Virginia or North Carolina. In 1779 on October 17 John Whitfield was witness to a legal paper. Edgecombe County land was split when the county boundaries were made. His father's house was now in Nash County, NC.

March 22, 1781. Matthew Carter of Johnston County, NC, was a grantor of land to John Whitfield, 380 acres, Tar River adjoining Micajah Thomas. On May 7, 1784, John Whitfield sold the 380 acres to Thomas Grover.

June 17, 1785. John Whitfield was a witness to a legal paper. In 1784 John was a witness to a will. On the 1790 census North Carolina John Whitfield was head of a family at Nash County. John and his wife had eight children.

Generation Six
1., 2., 3.   Male children over age 16.
4., 5., 6.   Male children under age 10.
7., 8., 9.   Female children
There was a female servant in the house.
In Nash County, North Carolina, was a witness to a legal paper in 1794. This is the last date he is found in Nash County for John Whitfield left the county.
On the 1800 census North Carolina there was John Whitfield at Granville County, NC, and a John Whitfield at Lenoir County, NC. John was at Granville Co., NC, in 1810, 1820, 1830.

Generation Five   (Thomas, Thomas, Thomas)
William Whitfield was born in North Carolina and died 1826 at Nash County, NC. October 25, 1782, he received a land grant from Governor Alex Martin for 300 acres on Sappony Creek. William Whitfield was on the 1790 census. William married about 1780. Wife's name may have been Elizabeth. She was two to five years older than William. The wife of William died between 1821 and 1825.
January 2, 1797, William Whitfield sold the 300 acres near Sappony Creek.
Censuses 1800, 1810, 1820 has the family of William Whitfield, the son of Thomas Whitfield (1721-1781) and Mary Whitfield.

Generation Six
William and wife had children.   2. Elisha Whitfield
1. William Whitfield, Jr.   3., 4., 5. Daughters
Nash County, North Carolina, gives the following on censuses and shows age ranges of the children and parents. William Whitfield head of family. 1800 census.
  1. Male 10/16   1 16/26 1 45+
  2. Females 16/26 1 26/45 1 45+

The sons are not at home on the 1810 census for they have their own homes and land. Another woman is in the home named Charity Ray. She was a housekeeper and servant.
William Whitfield and family. 1810 census.
  1 male 45+   1 female 16/26 2 45+
William Whitfield and family. 1820 census Nash Co., NC.
  1 male 45+   1 female 10/16 2 45+
William Whitfield purchased land in Nash County, NC. William gave some of this land in 1813 to son Elisha Whitfield.

William Whitfield left a will and wrote naming Charity Ray as heir of the remaindering estate of his. "In gratitude for good conduct, industry, council and services for forty years." William Whitfield wrote his will May 12, 1826. Will was probated in court August, 1826.

Generation Five (Thomas, Thomas, Thomas)

Benjamin Whitfield was born in Edgecombe County, NC. He was a farmer. Benjamin married three times. The first marriage was of a short time. Benjamin Whitfield is on several documents as a witness in the community. His maturity is early and indicates his birth to be in the decade of the 1750s.

The children of Benjamin are of the Whitfield sixth generation. Benjamin Whitfield's second wife was Elizabeth. They had daughters: 1. Elizabeth Whitfield; 2. Drewsey Whitfield married ____ Bunn.

Benjamin's third wife was Delilah Griffin. She was the daughter of Archibald Griffin, the Sheriff of Nash County, NC. Benjamin and Delilah had children.
1. Hardy Griffin Whitfield. Hardy left Nash County March 24, 1825, alone and died 1830.
2. Guilford Griffin Whitfield lived at Nash County, NC. He married and appears on the census.
3. Archibald Griffin Whitfield was named after his grandfather.
4. Benjamin Griffin Whitfield
5. John Thomas Griffin Whitfield.
6. Willie Griffin Whitfield.
7. Priscilla Whitfield. She married Philander Tisdale.
Benjamin Whitfield and his family lived on land on the east side of Lasiter's Branch. That land was purchased from David Strickland. Benjamin bought lands from five men named William Williams, Thomas Hart, Thomas Wilhite, Thomas Hunter. Benjamin Whitfield had six and more slaves on his land.

Benjamin wrote his will October 17 and died 1807 in Nash County, NC. The executors of his will were Nathan Gilbert, John Atkinson (Taylor), and wife Delilah Whitfield. The witnesses to Benjamin's will were James Williams, Drew Hunter, Joseph Strickland.

Delilah Whitfield had duties beyond that of a farm wife. She bought land from John Ricks and Mildred Springer of New Bern district. She had 150 acres from Hardy Whitfield.(18) Mrs. Whitfield passed her land from Mildred Springer to her father Archibald Griffin and gave a grant of 150 acres.

Generation Seven

These were the grandchildren named Martha Matilda Whitfield and Harriet Jane Whitfield who married William M. Forkner on March 19, 1850.

Delilah Whitfield died in 1818 between April and October at Nash County, NC.

Generation Five (Thomas, Thomas, Thomas)

Elisha Whitfield was born in Edgecombe Co., NC. His mother, Mary, left him her property in Nash Co.,NC, in 1792. Elisha married. He may have had a son names Elisha. Elisha lived at Southampton, Virginia, near the Great Swamp and was on the tax list in 1787. He had one horse and three cattle. Elisha's brother, Reuben Whitfield, Sr., had sons Miles and Ivey Whitfield who lived in Virginia. John Whitfield was also with them.

Who were the wife and children of Elisha Whitfield?
Uncle Elisha Whitfield had men of Generation Six with him. Elisha Sr. witnessed the will codicil of Benjamin Whitfield in 1785, and he lived next door to Benjamin in Southampton, Virginia.

321

CUMBERLAND COUNTY

William W. Whitfield = Ann Turner 10 Nov. 1812. Bryan Whitfield was Bondsman.

DUPLIN COUNTY

Henry Whitfield + Mary Ann Sutton 6 Nov. 1865. Herri Whitfield was Bondsman.

Joseph Whitfield = Mary Grady 1 May 1790. William Grady was Bondsman.

Charity Whitfield = Joshua Loftin 29 March 1832

Elizabeth Whitfield = Lewis Outlaw 19 April 1812.

Elizabeth Whitfield = Henry Grady 5 July 1830

Hester Whitfield = Alexander Grady 14 Jan. 1828

Lewis Whitfield = Sarah Bennett 18 Nov. 1854

Rachel Whitfield = James Outlaw, Jr. 29 March 1835

Sarah Whitfield = John G. Arnett 3 May 1852

Sidy Whitfield = Frederick Outlaw 24 Dec. 1836

William Whitfield = Lucy J. Williams 1 Jan. 1856

William Whitfield = Ataline (K) Eahly 10 Jan. 1856

William Min Whitfield = Mary Beck 28 Sept. 1785. Bryan Whitefield was Bondsman.

EDGECOMBE COUNTY

Albena Whitfield = William Nelson 24 Nov. 1822

Benjamin Whitfield = Temperance Manning 8 June 1825

EDGECOMBE COUNTY

Benjamin Whitfield, Jr. = Nancy Council 5 Jan. 1826. Joel Whitfield was 2nd Bondsman.

John Godwin Whitfield = Hyman Johnson 24 Dec. 1866. Married 25 Dec. 1866. Colored and Colored*.

Hasty Whitfield = Hyman Johnson 24 Dec. 1866. Married 25 Dec. 1866. Colored and Colored*.

George W. Whitfield = Mary L. Wimberly 13 Dec. 1849

Lethea Whitfield = Jerry Bunn 12 May 1868. Colored and Colored*.

Penny Whitfield = John Butler 4 Dec. 1866. Married 25 Dec 1866. Colored and Colored*.

FRANKLIN COUNTY

Franklin Whitfield = T.F. Faircloth 21 Aug. 1849

James E. Whitfield = Hexy H. Winston 12 June 1844. John H. Whitfield was first Bondsman.

John H. Whitfield = Eleanor Margaret Williams 7 Oct. 1845

GATES COUNTY

Robert Whitfield = Edith Jones 30 Sept. 1791. Robert of Pitt County

GUILFORD COUNTY

Lemuel Whitfield = Lelia Apple 13 Sept. 1867

Theope Whitfield = Annia E. Morehead 10 Oct 1859. Married 11 Oct. 1859

Minerum Whitfield = Harman Ogburn 1 Dec. 1866. Colored and Colored*.

HALIFAX COUNTY

Amarillus Whitfield = Willie Jones 3 April 1833

* Colored is African American.

NORTH CAROLINA MARRIAGE BONDS 1741 - 1868

HALIFAX COUNTY

Eugenia Addielad = Thomas Frances Anderson 8 Dec. 1865

Mary Whitfield = James H. Powers 18 March 1848

Mary Fannie Whitfield = C.H. Riddick 25 June 1866. Married 26 June 1866 by John G. Whitfield.

Nannie Whitfield = Allen Grist 17 Nov. 1865. Married 22 Dec. 1865 by John G. Whitfield.

Tabitha Whitfield = Joe Henry Whitaker 20 Sept. 1866. Colored and Colored* married 22 Sept. 1866

Travis Whitfield = Elizh Stephenson 29 Nov. 1831.

JOHNSTON COUNTY

George W. Whitefield = Catharine Hart 4 Feb. 1828

Lewis Whitfield = Patsey Bryan 9 Nov. 1816

Theophilus Whitfield = Bettie Brown 18 April 1866

Sir William Whitfield = Betsy Wimberly 27 Dec. 1808

LENOIR COUNTY

Nancy Whitfield = John Davis, Jr. 23 Oct. 1834

NASH COUNTY

Annis Whitfield = Jesse Bird 3 Feb. 1832

Eliza Whitfield = Joseph Hays 3 Dec. 1822

Elizabeth A. Whitfield = David W. Williams 21 June 1847

Harriet J. Whitfield = William W. Forkner 19 March 1850

NASH COUNTY

Isaac Whitfield = Nancy Whitehead 22 Feb. 1862

Isabella Whitfield = Gideon Coggin 22 Oct. 1856.

John Whitfield = Eveline Vick 4 Nov. 1858

John R. Whitfield = Sarah Whitley 10 Nov. 1859

John W. Whitfield = Mary Ann Taylor 17 Oct. 1854

Martha Whitfield = John Walker 7 July 1838

Martha Ann Whitfield = Willie P. Stallings 24 Dec. 1840

Martha Ann = Lafayett Williams 27 Dec. 1841

Mary W. Whitfield = William G. Murray 12 Feb. 1861.

O.H.P. Whitfield = Aribella Williams 23 Dec. 1845

Penelope Whitfield = Joel Price 31 May 1834. A. Whitfield Bondsman.

Robert C. Whitfield = Sally Ann Whitfield 22 Jan 1856

Sally Ann Whitfield = John G. Coggin 11 Feb. 1857

Willey Whitfield = James Baines 22 Nov. 1826

Willis Whitfield = Winney R. Morgan 12 Oct. 1864

NEW HANOVER COUNTY

James W. Whitfield = Virginia C. Thally. Married 7 Oct. 1851.

William J. Whitfield = Margaret N. Henry 28 Jan. 1853. Married 15 Feb. 1853.

* Colored is African American.

WHITFIELD FAMILIES, MARTIN COUNTY, NORTH CAROLINA

5. Susan Adlaide Whitfield b. June 23, 1871-d. June 13, 1960. She married Markus L. Bunting.
6. John Thomas Whitfield b. Jan. 26, 1873-d. Sept. 17, 1926. John married first Tamer ____ and had three children: 1. William Whitfield; 2. Cary Whitfield; 3. Tamer Whitfield. John married second Eva Hux and they had children: 1. Charles Whitfield; 2. Ruby Whitfield; 3. Arnold Whitfield. John Thomas Whitfield (1873-1926) had six children.
7. Martha Ida Whitfield married William Dennis Powell (1874-1928). They had three Powell children.
8. Joseph Henry Whitfield b. May 23, 1879-d. May 14, 1938. Joseph married Caddie Bell Powell (1877-1937). They had children:

   1. Joseph Henry Whitfield, Jr.
   2. Pauline Whitfield
   3. Mildred Whitfield
   4. Eleanor Whitfield
   5. Anna Belle Whitfield
   6. Blanche Whitfield
   7. Norfleet Whitfield

The father, Joseph J.R. Whitfield (1835-1914), when age 29, enlisted in Confederate Army for service during Civil War on Sept. 26, 1862, in Beaufort County, North Carolina.

Contributing persons to the Whitfield family groups were Joyce Whitfield Smith Boykin for Willis Whitfield and descendants. Virginia Whitfield for Joseph Benjamin Whitfield and Nancy (Betty) Briley Whitfield. Jewel Bunting Roberson for Joseph J.R. Whitfield and Mary C. (Polly) Leggett Whitfield.

Others who are associated with the Whitfield families groups are blood kinship, in-law kinship, and they have the surname of Whitfield and other surnames.

Addie	Elizabeth	Jessie Overton	Robert Asbury
Albena	Elsie Fleming	Joseph	Robert Latham
Angie	Emma Augusta	Mary Caney	Ruby
Arnold	Eugene	Mary Lane	Stacey
Carla	Fannie James	Mary Lou B.	Starkey
Carroll	Faye Newman	Mary Sue	Stella Roebuck
Charles	George	Matilda	Velma Britton
Charlotte	Harriet	Myrtie Lee	Wendy A.
Christy	Hattie E.R.	Nancy Council	William Anthony
David	Henry Leo	Nancy Briley	Willie
Dianne	Janet J.	Nicey	
Ella Pitt	Janet Leslie	Pauline	
Ella (Deedie)	Jennifer Lynn	Pearl Edmonds	

Reference
Editorial Tribute to the members and families of the Martin County Historical Society. Williamston, North Carolina. They published 1980 the large book with the Heritage of Martin County, North Carolina.

Reference. Martin County Heritage, Shelby Jean Nelson Hughes, Editor. Martin County, North Carolina.

North Carolina. Edith Whitfield born March 7, 1717, NC, and died Sept. 3, 1785. She married Samuel Smith about 1745.

DESCENDANTS OF JOEL WHITFIELD (1750 ca.-1783 ca.) AND LYDIA CRISP

PITT COUNTY, NORTH CAROLINA

WHITFIELD AND CRISP

Joel Whitfield was born 1750. His parentage is unknown. He lived at Pitt county, North Carolina. Joel Whitfield was a "chain bearer" on a surveyor team which processed land.

Joel Whitfield married Lydia Crisp in 1775. Lydia was the daughter of William Mansel Crisp and his second wife Frances. William Crisp had 18 children by his two wives.

William Mansel Crisp lived on land he bought in 1735 near Conetoe Creek which was land in Martin County, North Carolina, until 1792, when a small corner of Martin County was changed to Edgecombe County. Crisp family is on the same land, but the area has name changes after land processing and boundaries are changed and survey work is done over the years.

William Crisp made a will in 1783, which was recorded in Martin County at Williamston. The will names his daughter Lida (Lydia) Whitfield who inherited an interest in some slaves from her father. (1)

When Joel Whitfield married Lydia Crisp, he purchased land of a 300-acre tract at Pitt County, North Carolina and settled down. Bethel township was on three different tracts, and the original land grants were made from 1750 to 1775. Bethel was once the site of a small Indian village. Later the first tract was Andrews land of 400 acres about 1760. Joel Whitfield purchased the 300-acre tract on the north side of later Railroad Street and then east of the Andrews land. This land was later owned by Lanier Ward. The third tract was 200 acres granted to James Cattenhead. (2)

Joel Whitfield and Lydia Whitfield had a son named Benjamin Whitfield born about 1780 in Pitt County, North Carolina. The county records of Joel and Lydia are of Edgecombe County, North Carolina. Joel Whitfield died about 1783.

Lydia Crisp Whitfield married again to Thomas Bade. (3) Lydia and Thomas Baden raised the child Benjamin Whitfield. Lydia had a brother named Samuel Crisp who bought out the heirs of William and Frances Crisp. Samuel lived on Conetoe Creek, one mile north of Bethel. Samuel lived on the old home place of his father. In 1798 Lydia Baden sold the interest in her slaves to her brother Samuel Crisp. (4) On 1800 census, Lydia and Thomas had two or three children.

References
(1) Davis L. McWhorter did the research on the Crisp family. Written paper July 21, 1961. McWhorter was a resident of Bethel, North Carolina, and a descendant of Samuel Crisp. McWhorter cites for references: Deed Book C, page 34, Pitt County, NC; and Deed Book 8, page 909, Edgecombe County, NC.
(2) Copeland, Elizabeth, Chronicles of Pitt County, North Carolina, 1982. The Pitt County Historical Society, Greenville, North Carolina.

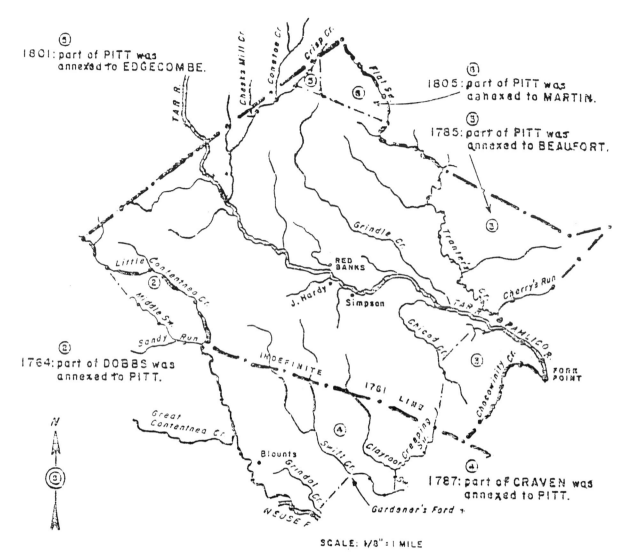

1801: part of PITT was annexed to EDGECOMBE.

1805: part of PITT was annexed to MARTIN.

1785: part of PITT was annexed to BEAUFORT.

1764: part of DOBBS was annexed to PITT.

1787: part of CRAVEN was annexed to PITT.

SCALE: 1/8" = 1 MILE

PITT COUNTY, N.C. "St. Michael's Parish"

PITT COUNTY was formed from BEAUFORT to become effective January 1, 1761

1764: part of DOBBS COUNTY was annexed to PITT ②

1784: line between PITT, EDGECOMBE and Martin established.

1785: part of PITT COUNTY was annexed to BEAUFORT ③

1787: part of CRAVEN COUNTY was annexed to PITT ④

1801: part of PITT COUNTY was annexed to EDGECOMBE ⑤

1805: part of PITT COUNTY was annexed to MARTIN ⑥

1894: dividing lines between PITT and Martin and between PITT and EDGECOMBE run.

1895: dividing line between PITT and Greene authorized to be run

PITT COUNTY FORMATION CHART:
  BATH 1696 → PAMPTECOUGH 1705 → BEAUFORT 1712 → PITT 1761

Legend: 1761 boundary lines ⚫━⚫━ ; other boundary lines ·—·—·—
  River ══════ Stream ──────

348

RECORDS OF PITT COUNTY, NORTH CAROLINA

ALEXANDER WHITFIELD

Alexander is listed on the 1790 census of Pitt Co., NC. Family-one male over 16, one male under 16, two females. He is not listed for the 1800 census. In 1790 he was in age range of 35.

Alexander Whitfield is listed in deeds both as owner and witness to deeds of others.

Jan. 30, 1790. Witnesses of deeds: Levi Nobles and Alexander Whitfield.
July 1, 1789. Alexander and Elizabeth Nelson.
May 10, 1792. Alexander Eley Whitfield to Ezekiel Parimore 100 acres. Samuel Knight was former owner of the land. Knight is the family that had a daughter who married Joshua Wilkinson and they had a daughter named Susanna Wilkinson Whitfield.

Alexander is found in records with varied spellings of name - Alex, Elleck, Alec.

March 28, 1797. Alexander Whitfield passed land to William McGowns, 100 acres. Adjoining Martin Nelson, William Edwards. Witness: Gideon Maye and John Maye.

Alexander Whitfield moved south. Alexander Whitfield appears in 1820 Georgia census in Clarke County, a family of four boys and two girls, and the parents' age range is 45 plus.

WILLIAM WHITFIELD

1790 Census, Pitt Co., NC, has listed William Whitfield and his family of three males under age 16, two males over 16, and five females, and one slave. William Whitfield had a farm. He may have had brother or relatives at Pitt Co., NC. William Whitfield was tailor who had a son named William Whitfield, Jr. He may have had son Robert Whitfield who had younger brothers Reuben, Bryan, Ivey. The wife of William Whitfield, Sr., was Jemima Whitfield. Alexander Whitfield also may have belonged to this family. These men are living and trading with the same families. Land deeds have some descriptions of adjoining land owners. This is the source used for this information and the censuses.

────
....Researcher: M.A. Clemens of Brandon, FL, 1993, received July 8, 1995.

ROBERT WHITFIELD

1800 Census of Pitt Co., NC, lists Robert Whitfield. Two males under 10 years, one male 16 to 26, one male 26 to 45, one female under 10 years, one female 16 to 26, one female 26 to 45. Family has five children.

Deed records of Robert Whitfield of Pitt Co., NC.
Feb. 16, 1802. Robert Whitfield to Robert Weatherington 355 acres. Witness: William Broome.

Sept. 30, 1801. Robert Whitfield gave a deed to Paul Herrington for 10 acres of land. It being part of a patent granted to William Whitfield, dated Sept. 30, 1801.

North Carolina

1 7 9 0   Census

Whitfield, Alexander, 148.
Whitfield, Benj., 72.
Whitfield, Benjn, 72.
Whitfield, Bryan, 137.
Whitfield, Constance, 132.
Whitfield, James, 137.
Whitfield, John, 67.
Whitfield, John, 72.
Whitfield, John, 89.
Whitfield, John, 137.
Whitfield, Joseph, 190.
Whitfield, Lewis, 151.
Whitfield, Luke, 137.
Whitfield, Matt^r, 72.
Whitfield, Nancy, 72.
Whitfield, Needham, 149.
Whitfield, Ruben, 72.
Whitfield, Sol^o, 72.
Whitfield, Thomas, 72.
Whitfield, William, 53.
Whitfield, William, 61.
Whitfield, William, 67.
Whitfield, W^m, 72.
Whitfield, William, 147.
Whitfield, William, 184.
Whitfield, William, Jr, 149.
Whitfield, William, Sr, 149.
Whitfield, Willis, 72.

North Carolina government Honorable Council meeting was held at Kingston on July 3, 1779. Among the five council members were William Whitfield, commissary to the State Regiment.
(1)

The Safety Committee of Pitt County, NC had forty-four members . Thomas Whitfield was a member of the committee. They supported the Continental provincial Congress at the Martin-borough meeting on August 23, 1775. (2)

In 1780 there were raised volunteers men and a draft of men for an expedition in Martin County, NC. Twenty-one men were drafted and among the men were William Whitfield and Willis Whitfield. (3)

CLARY COUNCIL SMITH CHERRY WHITFIELD

Clary married four times. At age 20 she married John Smith because that was only Smith on census in three counties at the time. She had children John Smith and Darcas Smith. She married (2) Solomon Cherry and had four children. She married (3) his twin brother Samuel Cherry and had one child a son. She married (4) Benjamin Whitfield. Darcas married Joel Whitfield the son of Benjamin Whitfield at Pitt Co., NC.

1800 CENSUS NORTH CAROLINA

WHITFELD, WILLIAM SEN.	NASH CO.	NC 128
WHITFIELD, BRYAN	LENOIR CO	NC 26
WHITFIELD, BRYAN, JUNIOR	LENOIR CO	NC 26
WHITFIELD, C. WILLIAM	HALIFAX CO.	NC 354
WHITFIELD, ELIZABETH	NASH CO.	NC 128
WHITFIELD, GEORGE	PERSON CO.	NC 215
WHITFIELD, JKES	ORANGE CO.	NC 607
WHITFIELD, JOHN	LENOIR CO	NC 35
WHITFIELD, JOHN	GRANVILLE CO.	NC 537
WHITFIELD, JOHN	ANSON CO.	NC 233
WHITFIELD, JOSEPH	DUPLIN CO.	NC 426
WHITFIELD, LEWIS	LENOIR CO	NC 26
WHITFIELD, LEWIS	WAYNE CO.	NC 871
WHITFIELD, MATTHEW	NASH CO.	NC 128
WHITFIELD, NEEDHAM	WAYNE CO.	NC 873
WHITFIELD, RACHEL	CRAVEN CO.	NC 251
WHITFIELD, WILLIAM	WAYNE CO.	NC 858
WHITFIELD, WILLIAM JUN.	NASH CO.	NC 128
WHITFIELD, WILLIAM	STOKES CO.	NC 591

References.
1. The State Records of North Carolina by Walter Clark. Vol. XIV 1779-1780. Pages 317-318.
2. The Colonial Records of North Carolina by William L. Saunders. Vol. X 1775-1776. P. 221.
3. The State Records of North Carolina by Walter Clark. Vol. XIV 1779-1780. Letter of Kenneth Mc Kenzie to North Carolina Governor Abner Nash, June 14, 1780.

North Carolina
1 8 1 0 Census

```
WHITFIELD, ABRAHAM          NASH 080 NO TWP L
WHITFIELD, ANN              NASH 078 NO TWP L
WHITFIELD, BENJAMIN         EDGE 052 NO TWP.
WHITFIELD, BRYAN JR.        LENO 317 NO TWP L
WHITFIELD, BRYAN JR.        LENO 312 NO TWP L
WHITFIELD, CONS.            LENO 323 NO TWP L
WHITFIELD, DELIAH           NASH 079 NO TWP L
WHITFIELD, GEORGE           PERS 146 NO TWP L
WHITFIELD, HARDY            NASH 077 NO TWP L
WHITFIELD, JACOB            NASH 078 NO TWP L
WHITFIELD, JOHN             LENO 318 NO TWP L
WHITFIELD, JOHN             GRAN 123 NO TWP L
WHITFIELD, JOHN             PERS 145 NO TWP L
WHITFIELD, JOHN             HALI 123 NO TWP L
WHITFIELD, JOSEPH           DUPL 015 NO TWP L
WHITFIELD, LEWIS            LENO 316 NO TWP L
WHITFIELD, M.               BEAU 047 BERTIE
WHITFIELD, NEEDHAM          WAYN 235 NO TWP L
WHITFIELD, RHUEBIN          NASH 080 NO TWP L
WHITFIELD, RUBIN            HERT 212 NO TWP L
WHITFIELD, W.               ORAN 154 NO TWP L
WHITFIELD, WILEY            NASH 077 NO TWP L
WHITFIELD, WILLIAM          ORAN 125 NO TWP L
WHITFIELD, WILLIAM          WAYN 235 NO TWP L
WHITFIELD, WILLIAM          CASW 512 NO TWP L
WHITFIELD, WILLIAM          HALI 123 NO TWP L
WHITFIELD, WILLIAM SEN.     NASH 084 NO TWP L
```

North Carolina

1 8 3 0 Census

WHITFEY, WYATT	NASH	173	DISTRICT
WHITFIELD, ABRAM	NASH	179	DISTRICT
WHITFIELD, ALLEN	WAYN	513	A. WHITF
WHITFIELD, ANN	NASH	166	NASHVILL
WHITFIELD, ARCHIBALD	NASH	171	DISTRICT
WHITFIELD, ARNOLD	MART	411	WILLIAMS
WHITFIELD, BENJAMIN	NASH	190	DISTRICT
WHITFIELD, BENJAMIN	EDGE	305	DISTRICT
WHITFIELD, BENJAMIN	PITT	C85	TISONS D
WHITFIELD, BRYAN	MART	398	NO TWP L
WHITFIELD, EDMUND	WAYN	513	A. WHITF
WHITFIELD, EDMUND H.	WAYN	513	A. WHITF
WHITFIELD, ELIZABETH	PERS	010	NO TWP L
WHITFIELD, EMANUEL	BEAU	C03	WASHINGV
WHITFIELD, GEORGE	LENO	302	NO TWP L
WHITFIELD, HATCH	WAYN	525	CAPT. RE
WHITFIELD, HAYWOOD	LENO	283	NO TWP L
WHITFIELD, ISAAC	NASH	172	DISTRICT
WHITFIELD, JAMES	WAYN	508	JAS. WHI
WHITFIELD, JAMES	MART	413	WILLIAMS
WHITFIELD, JAMES	PERS	009	NO TWP L
WHITFIELD, JAMES	CASW	274	NO TWP L
WHITFIELD, JERMIMAH	LENO	283	NO TWP L
WHITFIELD, JOHN	CRAN	114	NO TWP L
WHITFIELD, JOHN C.	GRAN	057	NO TWP L
WHITFIELD, JOSEPH	DUPL	148	NO TWP L
WHITFIELD, JOSEPH	DUPL	148	NO TWP L
WHITFIELD, LEMUEL H.	WAYN	518	CAPT. HA
WHITFIELD, LEWIS	NEW	151	NO TWP L
WHITFIELD, LEWIS	LENO	298	NO TWP L
WHITFIELD, MARTHA	MART	398	NO TWP L
WHITFIELD, MARY	MART	407	NO TWP L
WHITFIELD, MILLEY	PITT	085	TISONS D
WHITFIELD, NATHAN B.	LENO	302	NO TWP L
WHITFIELD, NEDHAM	LENO	279	NO TWP L
WHITFIELD, PENOLEPY	NASH	174	DISTRICT
WHITFIELD, PRECILLA	NASH	173	DISTRICT
WHITFIELD, RICHARD M.	PERS	019	NO TWP L
WHITFIELD, SARAH	NASH	174	DISTRICT
WHITFIELD, WILLIAM	WAKE	438	ST. MAPI
WHITFIELD, WILLIAM	PERS	033	NO TWP L
WHITFIELD, WILLIAM	GRAN	053	NO TWP L
WHITFIELD, CONSTANTINE	LENO	283	NO TWP L

1840 Census

North Carolina

Whitfield

```
WHITEFIELD, ABRAM          NASH 052 NO  TWP  L
WHITEFIELD, ISAAC          NASH 065 NO  TWP  L
WHITEFIELD, JAMES          CASW 126 NO  TWP  L
WHITEFFIELD, PENELOPE      NASH 073 NO  TWP  L
WHITFIELD, ALLEN           WAYN 232 INDIAN  S
WHITFIELD, ARCHIBALD       NASH 052 NO  TWP  L
WHITFIELD, ARNOLE*         MART 369 5TH DIST
WHITFIELD, BENJAMIN*       PITT 395 NO  TWP  L
WHITFIELD, BRYANT          MART 375 8TH DIST
WHITFIELD, CONSTANTINE     LENO 002 KINSTON
WHITFIELD, E.              BEAU 267 WASHINGT
WHITFIELD, EADY            NASH 065 NO  TWP  L
WHITFIELD, ELISHA          BEAU 298 GOOSE CR
WHITFIELD, ELIZABETH       PERS 281 NO  TWP  L
WHITFIELD, GEORGE          PERS 281 NO  TWP  L
WHITFIELD, GEORGE          LENO 205 KINSTON
WHITFIELD, GEORGE W.       LENO 014 KINSTON
WHITFIELD, GUILFORD G.     NASH 050 NO  TWP  L
WHITFIELD, HENRY           DUPL 172 NO  TWP  L
WHITFIELD, JAMES           MART 369 6TH DIST
WHITFIELD, JAMES B.        LENO 027 KINSTON
WHITFIELD, JAMES JR.*      PERS 291 NO  TWP  L
WHITFIELD, JAMES SR.*      PERS 281 NO  TWP  L
WHITFIELD, JOHN            PERS 280 NO  TWP  L
WHITFIELD, JOHN            NASH 052 NO  TWP  L
WHITFIELD, JOHN W.         GRAN 105 NO  TWP  L
WHITFIELD, JOSEPH          DUPL 174 NO  TWP  L
WHITFIELD, LEWIS           LENO 012 KINSTON
WHITFIELD, LEWIS           CASW 130 NO  TWP  L
WHITFIELD, LEWIS           CASW 130 NO  TWP  L
WHITFIELD, LEWIS L.        LENO 027 KINSTON
WHITFIELD, MARY            NASH 073 NO  TWP  L
WHITFIELD, MARY            MART 371 6TH DIST
WHITFIELD, NANCY A.        NASH 073 NO  TWP  L
WHITFIELD, SAMUEL H.       WAYN 200 NEWHOPE
WHITFIELD, SUSY*           PERS 280 NO  TWP  L
WHITFIELD, TABITHA         NORT 089 NO  TWP  L
WHITFIELD, THEOPHILUS      NEW  035 UPPER BL
WHITFIELD, THOMAS          PERS 282 NO  TWP  L
WHITFIELD, WILLIAM         PERS 282 NO  TWP  L
WHITFIELD, WILLIAM         GRAN 105 NO  TWP  L
WHITFIELD, WILLIAM         HALI 019 NO  TWP  L
WHITFIELD, WILLIAM         WAYN 231 INDIAN  S
WHITFIELD, WILLIAM H.      LENO 023 KINSTON
WHITFIELD, WILLIS          NASH 051 NO  TWP  L
```

1850 Census

North Carolina

Whitfield

```
WHITFIELD, LEWIS              PERS  422  NO TWP L
WHITFIELD, A. H.              CUMB  015  FAYETTEV
WHITFIELD, ARCHIBALD          NASH  318  NO TWP L
WHITFIELD, ARNOLD             MART  400  NO TWP L
WHITFIELD, B.                 CRAV  275  NEW BERN
WHITFIELD, BENJAMIN           NEW   367  NO TWP L
WHITFIELD, BRYANT             MART  426  NO TWP L
WHITFIELD, CHARITY            NASH  320  NO TWP L
WHITFIELD, CONSTANTINE        LENO  169  NO TWP L
WHITFIELD, EDWIN              PERS  420  NO TWP L
WHITFIELD, ELIZABETH          PERS  422  NO TWP L
WHITFIELD, ELIZABETH          PERS  418  NO TWP L
WHITFIELD, FRANKLIN           NASH  318  NO TWP L
WHITFIELD, GEOGANIA           WAKE  267  RALEIGH
WHITFIELD, GEORG B.           LENO  166  NO TWP L
WHITFIELD, GEORGE             PERS  430  NO TWP L
WHITFIELD, GUILFORD G.        NASH  312  NO TWP L
WHITFIELD, HAZARD             ALAM  001  SOUTH DI
WHITFIELD, HENRY H.           LENO  169  NO TWP L
WHITFIELD, HICKSY             FRAN  345  TIMBERLA
WHITFIELD, JAMES              HALI  035  NO TWP L
WHITFIELD, JAMES              PERS  418  NO TWP L
WHITFIELD, JAMES              PERS  422  NO TWP L
WHITFIELD, JEFFERSON          CASW  221  YANCEYVI
WHITFIELD, JHN B.             WAYN  236  NEUSE NO
WHITFIELD, JOHN               PERS  462  NO TWP L
WHITFIELD, JOHN               NASH  318  NO TWP L
WHITFIELD, JOHN W.            GRAN  129  BEAVER D
WHITFIELD, LOUIZA             WAKE  288  RALEIGH
WHITFIELD, MARS.              NASH  263  NO TWP L
WHITFIELD, MARTHA E.          MART  400  NO TWP L
WHITFIELD, MARY               BEAU  345  WASHINGT
WHITFIELD, MARY J.            WAYN  246  NEUSE NO
WHITFIELD, NANCY              SAMP  417  NORTHERN
WHITFIELD, NANCY A.           NASH  318  NO TWP L
WHITFIELD, NATHAN B.          LENO  165  NO TWP L
WHITFIELD, NEEDHAM            WAYN  244  NEUSE NO
WHITFIELD, OLIVER P.          NASH  312  NO TWP L
WHITFIELD, PENELOPE           NASH  318  NO TWP L
WHITFIELD, PRISCILLA          NASH  318  NO TWP L
WHITFIELD, RACHEL J.          SAMP  375  NORTHERN
WHITFIELD, RICHARD            ORAN  279  FIRST DI
WHITFIELD, RICHARD M.         PERS  428  NO TWP L
WHITFIELD, SALLY F.           LENO  165  NO TWP L
WHITFIELD, SUSAN              DUPL  008  NORTH DI
WHITFIELD, SUSAN              CRAV  284  NEW BERN
WHITFIELD, TABITHA            NORT  029  JACKSON
WHITFIELD, TEMP               HALI  034  NO TWP L
WHITFIELD, TEMPERANCE         PITT  075  ANDREWS
WHITFIELD, TEMPY              HALI  036  NO TWP L
WHITFIELD, THEOPHILUS         NEW   373  NO TWP L
WHITFIELD, THOMAS             PERS  418  NO TWP L
WHITFIELD, W. J.              NEW   871  NO TWP L
WHITFIELD, WILLIAM            HALI  034  NO TWP L
WHITFIELD, WILLIAM            PERS  418  NO TWP L
WHITFIELD, WILLIAM            WAYN  244  NEUSE NO
WHITFIELD, WILLIAM H.         LENO  168  NO TWP L
WHITFIELD, WILLIAM H.         LENO  185  KINSTON
WHITFIELD, WILLIS             NASH  263  NO TWP L
WHITFILD, RICEY               NASH  310  NO TWP L
```

WHITEFIELD 1860 CENSUS NORTH CAROLINA

WHITEFIELD,	CAROLINE A	PERSON CO.	NC 925	BUSHY FORK P.O.
WHITEFIELD,	CHARITY	RICHMOND CO.	NC 754	WOLF PITT DIST.
WHITEFIELD,	EDWIN	PERSON CO.	NC 906	BUSHY FORK P.O.
WHITEFIELD,	ELIZABETH	PERSON CO.	NC 902	BUSHY FORK P.O.
WHITEFIELD,	ELIZABETH	PERSON CC.	NC 908	BUSHY FORK P.O.
WHITEFIELD,	FRANCES	PERSON CO.	NC 925	BUSHY FORK P.O.
WHITEFIELD,	GEORGE	PERSON CO.	NC 898	HURDLY MILLS P.O.
WHITEFIELD,	GEORGE W.	EDGECOMB CO	NC 559	TARBORO
WHITEFIELD,	JAMES	PERSON CO.	NC 907	BUSHY FORK P.O.
WHITEFIELD,	JESSE J.	WAYNE CO.	NC 919	INDIAN SPRINGS DIST.
WHITEFIELD,	JOHN	PERSON CO.	NC 926	BUSHY FORK P.O.
WHITEFIELD,	LEWIS	PERSON CO.	NC 934	MOUNT TERZAH P.O.
WHITEFIELD,	MARY J.	WAYNE CO.	NC 925	INDIAN SPRINGS DIST.
WHITEFIELD,	NANCY S.	SAMPSON CO.	NC 986	PINEY GROVE DIST
WHITEFIELD,	RICHARD M.	PERSON CO.	NC 885	BUSHY FORK P.O.
WHITEFIELD,	THOMAS	PERSON CO.	NC 907	BUSHY FORK P.O.
WHITEFIELD,	THOMAS L.	PERSON CO.	NC 908	BUSHY FORK P.O.

WHITFIELD 1860 CENSUS NORTH CAROLINA

WHITFIELD,	A. H.	CUMBERLAND CO.	NC 518	FAYETTEVILLE P.O.
WHITFIELD,	A. J.	BLADEN CO.	NC 165	FRENCHES CREEK P.O.
WHITFIELD,	ALLEN A	WAYNE CO.	NC 924	INDIAN SPRINGS DIST.
WHITFIELD,	ANNA	NASH CO.	NC 517	SULLIVANTS DIST
WHITFIELD,	BETTIE W.	HALIFAX CO.	NC 819	ENFIELD P.O.
WHITFIELD,	BRYANT	MARTIN CO.	NC 886	HAMLETON
WHITFIELD,	CONSTANTINE	LENOIR CO.	NC 045	STRABANE
WHITFIELD,	DANIEL	GRANVILLE CO.	NC 401	BROOKVILLE
WHITFIELD,	ELI	EDGECOMB CO.	NC 492	TARBORO P.O.
WHITFIELD,	ELIZA	BEAUFORT CO.	NC 808	GOOSE CREEK
WHITFIELD,	ELIZABETH	NASH CO.	NC 608	COLLINS DIST
WHITFIELD,	EVELINE	CRAVEN CO.	NC 080	NEW BERN 1ST WARD
WHITFIELD,	FRANCES	CASWELL CO.	NC 764	LEASBURG P.O.
WHITFIELD,	FRANCIS J.	FRANKLIN CO.	NC 874	FRANKLINTON
WHITFIELD,	FRANKLIN	WAYNE CO.	NC 943	INDIAN SPRINGS DIST.
WHITFIELD,	G. W.	BLADEN CO.	NC 159	FRENCHES CREEK CHURCH
WHITFIELD,	GARY	NASH CO.	NC 610	COLLINS DIST
WHITFIELD,	GEORGE	FORSYTH CO.	NC 603	OLD TOWN
WHITFIELD,	GEORGE	FORSYTH CO.	NC 638	SALEM
WHITFIELD,	GEORGE F.	LENOIR CO.	NC 082	MOSELY HALL
WHITFIELD,	HANNA	WAYNE CO.	NC 905	GOLDSBORO TOWN
WHITFIELD,	HAYWOOD	DUPLIN CO.	NC 357	MOUNT OLIVE P.O.
WHITFIELD,	HENRY G.	NASH CO.	NC 620	COLLINS DIST
WHITFIELD,	ISAAC	NASH CO.	NC 517	SULLIVANTS DIST
WHITFIELD,	J.	CASWELL CO.	NC 760	LEASBURG P.O.
WHITFIELD,	J.	SAMPSON CO.	NC 992	PINEY GROVE DIST
WHITFIELD,	J. E.	WAYNE CO.	NC 942	INDIAN SPRINGS DIST.
WHITFIELD,	J. R.	MARTIN CO.	NC 850	WILLIAMSTON
WHITFIELD,	J. T.	SURRY CO.	NC 583	MOUNT AIRY
WHITFIELD,	J. W.	WARREN CO.	NC 481	WARRENTON P.O.
WHITFIELD,	JAMES	NEW HANOVER CO	NC 700	WILMINGTON
WHITFIELD,	JOEL	NASH CO.	NC 501	SULLIVANTS DIST
WHITFIELD,	JOHN	DUPLIN CO.	NC 347	MOUNT OLIVE P.O.
WHITFIELD,	JOHN	DUPLIN CO.	NC 359	MOUNT OLIVE P.O.
WHITFIELD,	JOHN	NASH CO.	NC 654	DORTCHS DIST
WHITFIELD,	JOHN	GRANVILLE CO.	NC 409	WILTON
WHITFIELD,	JOHN	HALIFAX CO.	NC 818	ENFIELD P.O.
WHITFIELD,	JOHN W	GRANVILLE CO.	NC 423	WILTON
WHITFIELD,	JOSEPH	GRANVILLE CO.	NC 410	WILTON
WHITFIELD,	K. B.	MARTIN CO.	NC 850	WILLIAMSTON
WHITFIELD,	LEWIS	DUPLIN CO.	NC 333	MOUNT OLIVE P.O.
WHITFIELD,	LEWIS	WAYNE CO.	NC 885	NEWHOPE DIST.
WHITFIELD,	LOUISA	DUPLIN CO.	NC 335	MOUNT OLIVE P.O.
WHITFIELD,	M. A.	PITT CO.	NC 030	BETHEL P.O.
WHITFIELD,	MARGETT	MARTIN CO.	NC 850	WILLIAMSTON
WHITFIELD,	MATCH	WAYNE CO.	NC 920	INDIAN SPRINGS DIST.
WHITFIELD,	MOSES	HERTFORD CO.	NC 094	MURFREESBORO P.O.
WHITFIELD,	N. B.	DUPLIN CO.	NC 359	MOUNT OLIVE P.O.
WHITFIELD,	N. G.	GRANVILLE CO.	NC 423	WILTON
WHITFIELD,	NANCY	CRAVEN CO.	NC 127	NEW BERN 5TH W.
WHITFIELD,	NATHAN	LENOIR CO.	NC 048	STRABANE
WHITFIELD,	NEEDHAM	WAYNE CO.	NC 930	INDIAN SPRINGS DIST.
WHITFIELD,	NICHODEMUS	FORSYTH CO.	NC 690	SALEM
WHITFIELD,	NICKOLAS	HERTFORD CO.	NC 046	MURFREESBORO P.O.
WHITFIELD,	OLIVE	WAYNE CO.	NC 929	INDIAN SPRINGS DIST.
WHITFIELD,	PENELOPE	DUPLIN CO.	NC 357	MOUNT OLIVE P.O.
WHITFIELD,	PHERABE	NASH CO.	NC 517	SULLIVANTS DIST
WHITFIELD,	RACHEL	SAMPSON CO.	NC 986	PINEY GROVE DIST
WHITFIELD,	RICHARD A.	WAYNE CO.	NC1031	BUCK SWAMP DIST.
WHITFIELD,	ROBERT C.	NASH CO.	NC 654	DORTCHS DIST
WHITFIELD,	ROSE A.	CRAVEN CO.	NC 136	NEW BERN 6TH W.
WHITFIELD,	S. E.	LENOIR CO.	NC 043	STRABANE
WHITFIELD,	SARAH	HERTFORD CO.	NC 066	MURFREESBORO P.O.
WHITFIELD,	SARAH	MARTIN CO.	NC 847	WILLIAMSTON
WHITFIELD,	SUSAN	CARTERET CO.	NC 587	BEAUFORT
WHITFIELD,	SUSAN	CRAVEN CO.	NC 138	NEW BERN 6TH W.
WHITFIELD,	TEMPERANCE	PITT CO.	NC 030	BETHEL P.O.
WHITFIELD,	THEODORE	BLADEN CO.	NC 164	FRENCHES CREEK P.O.
WHITFIELD,	THOMAS	DUPLIN CO.	NC 317	MOUNT OLIVE P.O.
WHITFIELD,	W. G.*	MARTIN CO.	NC 844	WILLIAMSTON
WHITFIELD,	W. J.	BLADEN CO.	NC 164	FRENCHES CREEK P.O.
WHITFIELD,	W. T.	HALIFAX CO.	NC 745	ENFIELD P.O.

1860 CENSUS NORTH CAROLINA

WHITFIELD, WILLIAM	MARTIN CO.	NC 865	HAMLETON	
WHITFIELD, WILLIAM A.	FORSYTH CO.	NC 604	OLD TOWN	
WHITFIELD, WILLIAM B.	WAYNE CO.	NC 926	INDIAN SPRINGS	
WHITFIELD, WILLIAM H.	LENOIR CO.	NC 018	KINSTON	
WHITFIELD, WILLIAM H.	LENOIR CO.	NC 084	MOSELY HALL	
WHITFIELD, WILLIAM T.	CHATHAM CO.	NC 001	GROVE P.O.	

1870 CENSUS NORTH CAROLINA
B- black   W-white

NAME	AGE	SEX	C	S	Place County		Page
WHITFIELD, A	44	M	W	NC	GREENVILLE TWP	PITT	157
WHITFIELD, A	35	M	B	NC	LIBERTY TWP	NASH	17
WHITFIELD, A J	35	M	W	NC	FRENCHES CRK TWP	BLADEN	429
WHITFIELD, A W	35	M	W	NC	TRENT TWP	LENOIR	134
WHITFIELD, Abbie	25	F	B	NC	ALBERTSON'S TWP	DUPLIN	366
WHITFIELD, Abrum	65	M	B	NC	KINSTON TWP	LENOIR	24
WHITFIELD, Aggie	25	F	B	VA	TRINITY TWP	RANDOLPH	487
WHITFIELD, Alex	21	M	W	NC	BROGDEN TWP	WAYNE	24
WHITFIELD, Allen	43	M	W	NC	CLINTON TWP	SAMPSON	175
WHITFIELD, Amons	60	M	B	NC	HARNETT TWP	NEW HANOVER	250
WHITFIELD, Ann	64	F	W	NC	MAGNOLIA TWP	DUPLIN	485
WHITFIELD, Anna	21	F	B	NC	WILMINGTON	NEW HANOVER	427
WHITFIELD, Anna	22	F	W	NC	HALLS TWP	SAMPSON	228
WHITFIELD, Anthony	51	M	B	NC	POLLOKSVILLE TWP	JONES	567
WHITFIELD, B H	45	M	W	NC	WOLFSCRAPE TWP	DUPLIN	563
WHITFIELD, B T	27	M	W	NC	GOLDSBORO	WAYNE	95
WHITFIELD, Batlemore	56	M	B	NC	3-WD NEW BERNE	CRAVEN	378
WHITFIELD, Benj	50	M	B	NC	NEW HOPE TWP	WAYNE	189
WHITFIELD, Benj	24	M	B	NC	MOSELY HALL TWP	LENOIR	111
WHITFIELD, Berry	38	M	B	NC	UPPER FISHING CR	EDGECOMBE	267
WHITFIELD, Bret	51	M	W	NC	MOSELY HALL TWP	LENOIR	110
WHITFIELD, Bryan	19	M	B	NC	TRENT TWP	LENOIR	128
WHITFIELD, Bryant	35	M	W	NC	GOLDSBORO TWP	WAYNE	80
WHITFIELD, Burton	34	M	B	NC	MIDDLETON TWP	NASH	52
WHITFIELD, Celia A	3	F	B	NC	6-WD NEW BERNE	CRAVEN	419
WHITFIELD, Charles	31	M	M	NC	6-WD NEW BERNE	CRAVEN	416
WHITFIELD, Charles	53	M	B	NC	CROSS CRK TWP	CUMBERLAND	207
WHITFIELD, Charles	41	M	W	NC	HAMILTON TWP	MARTIN	476
WHITFIELD, Chora	13	F	W	NC	FREEMAN'S TWP	FRANKLIN	549
WHITFIELD, Clabon	60	M	B	NC	KINSTON TWP	LENOIR	47
WHITFIELD, Clarrie	13	F	B	NC	GOLDSBORO TWP	WAYNE	86
WHITFIELD, Cobie	58	M	M	NC	TRENT TWP	LENOIR	130
WHITFIELD, Cyrus	28	M	B	NC	KINSTON TWP	LENOIR	30
WHITFIELD, D	40	M	B	NC	KINSTON TWP	LENOIR	24
WHITFIELD, D	40	M	B	NC	NORTH WEST TWP	BRUNSWICK	30
WHITFIELD, D C	13	M	B	NC	WINTON TWP	HERTFORD	427
WHITFIELD, Diana	23	F	B	NC	TARBORO TWP	EDGECOMBE	216
WHITFIELD, Dick	21	M	M	NC	SWIFT CRK	EDGECOMBE	180
WHITFIELD, Dixon*	69	M	B	NC	HOOKERTON TWP	GREENE	428
WHITFIELD, Dorcas	70	F	B	NC	CEDER CRK TWP	CUMBERLAND	34
WHITFIELD, Edwd	24	M	B	NC	KINSTON TWP	LENOIR	32
WHITFIELD, Edy	80	F	B	NC	KINSTON TWP	LENOIR	47
WHITFIELD, Eldrige	21	M	B	NC	SMITHFIELD TWP	JOHNSTON	513
WHITFIELD, Elias	17	M	B	NC	GOLDSBORO TWP	WAYNE	73
WHITFIELD, Elijah	39	M	W	NC	LIBERTY TWP	NASH	30
WHITFIELD, Elijah	18	M	W	NC	PAMPLICO TWP	BEAUFORT	73
WHITFIELD, Eliza	56	F	W	NC	LIBERTY TWP	NASH	14
WHITFIELD, Eliza	77	F	W	NC	WASHINGTON TWP	NASH	136
WHITFIELD, Ellen	19	F	B	NC	WILMINGTON	NEW HANOVER	365
WHITFIELD, Elvina	55	F	B	NC	LEUSBURG TWP	CASWELL	352
WHITFIELD, Emanuel	27	M	B	NC	PAMPLICO TWP	BEAUFORT	69
WHITFIELD, Faiford+	9	M	W	NC	BOON HILL TWP	JOHNSTON	347
WHITFIELD, Famos	27	M	B	NC	INDIAN SPRINGS T	WAYNE	143
WHITFIELD, Frank	18	M	W	NC	BETHANIA TWP	FORSYTH	318
WHITFIELD, General	19	M	B	NC	LOWER FISHING CR	EDGECOMBE	68
WHITFIELD, Geoge+	47	M	W	NC	LEWISVILLE TWP	FORSYTH	367
WHITFIELD, George	50	M	B	NC	NEW BERNE P O	CRAVEN	343
WHITFIELD, George	28	M	B	NC	HAMILTON TWP	MARTIN	502
WHITFIELD, George C	44	M	M	NC	6-WD NEW BERNE	CRAVEN	419
WHITFIELD, Hannah	18	F	B	NC	WILMINGTON	NEW HANOVER	373
WHITFIELD, Harkless	41	M	B	NC	SELMA TWP	JOHNSTON	479
WHITFIELD, Harriet	12	F	B	NC	NEW BERNE P O	CRAVEN	335
WHITFIELD, Harrison	44	M	B	NC	ROCKY MT TWP	EDGECOMBE	122
WHITFIELD, Henreta	17	F	B	NC	CLINTON TWP	SAMPSON	208
WHITFIELD, Henrietta	20	F	B	NC	CLINTON TWP	SAMPSON	183
WHITFIELD, Henry	13	M	B	NC	WILMINGTON	NEW HANOVER	344
WHITFIELD, Henry	50	M	B	NC	INDIAN SPRINGS T	WAYNE	154
WHITFIELD, Henry	50	M	B	NC	MOSELY HALL TWP	LENOIR	92
WHITFIELD, Henry L	7	M	B	NC	6-WD NEW BERNE	CRAVEN	420
WHITFIELD, Herring	65	M	W	NC	WOLFSCRAPE TWP	DUPLIN	563
WHITFIELD, Hiram	80	M	B	NC	CARVER CRK TWP	CUMBERLAND	223
WHITFIELD, Isaac	56	M	W	NC	SPRINGFIELD TWP	NASH	72
WHITFIELD, Isaac	39	M	B	NC	MIDDLETON TWP	NASH	53
WHITFIELD, J T	41	M	W	NC	WOLFSCRAPE TWP	DUPLIN	559
WHITFIELD, Jack	47	M	B	NC	LEUSBURG TWP	CASWELL	359
WHITFIELD, Jackson	40	M	B	NC	UPPER FISHING CR	EDGECOMBE	268
WHITFIELD, Jacob	37	M	B	NC	WOODVILLE TWP	BERTIE	331

1870 Census North Carolina

NAME	Age	S	C	S	Place	County	Page
WHITFIELD, James	72	M	B	NC	5-WD NEW BERNE	CRAVEN	393
WHITFIELD, James N	48	M	W	NC	LUMBERTON	ROBESON	102
WHITFIELD, Jane	34	F	B	NC	5-WD NEW BERNE	CRAVEN	387
WHITFIELD, Jane	39	F	M	NC	RICHLAND TWP	BEAUFORT	100
WHITFIELD, Jaret	48	M	B	NC	SMITHFIELD TWP	JOHNSTON	510
WHITFIELD, Jas	12	M	B	NC	GOLDSBORO TWP	WAYNE	87
WHITFIELD, Jessey	12	M	B	NC	TRENT TWP	LENOIR	130
WHITFIELD, Jetta	37	F	B	NC	WILSON	WILSON	611
WHITFIELD, Joel H	37	M	W	NC	SPRINGFIELD TWP	NASH	82
WHITFIELD, John	25	M	B	NC	UPPER FISHING CR	EDGECOMBE	267
WHITFIELD, John	39	M	B	NC	5-WD NEW BERNE	CRAVEN	397
WHITFIELD, John	28	M	B	NC	SWIFT CRK	EDGECOMBE	176
WHITFIELD, John	30	M	B	NC	BELVOIR TWP	PITT	2
WHITFIELD, John	60	M	B	NC	SELMA TWP	JOHNSTON	479
WHITFIELD, John	52	M	W	NC	FRANKLINTON TWP	FRANKLIN	525
WHITFIELD, John	62	M	W	NC	OLIVE HILL TWP	PERSON	642
WHITFIELD, John	61	M	W	NC	LIBERTY TWP	NASH	13
WHITFIELD, John A	21	M	W	NC	DURHAM TWP	ORANGE	209
WHITFIELD, John E	46	M	W	NC	WILMINGTON	NEW HANOVER	458
WHITFIELD, John G	54	M	W	VA	DALMATIA TWP	HALIFAX	385
WHITFIELD, John W	37	M	W	NC	WOLFSCRAPE TWP	DUPLIN	562
WHITFIELD, John W	36	M	W	NC	LIBERTY TWP	NASH	13
WHITFIELD, Joseph	12	M	B	NC	SAULSTON TWP	WAYNE	236
WHITFIELD, Joseph	46	M	B	NC	KINSTON TWP	LENOIR	45
WHITFIELD, Joseph P	34	M	W	NC	WOLFSCRAPE TWP	DUPLIN	560
WHITFIELD, Joshua	23	M	B	NC	7-WD NEW BERNE	CRAVEN	429
WHITFIELD, Kedar	30	F	B	NC	GOLDSBORO	WAYNE	98
WHITFIELD, Kedar	35	M	B	NC	BROGDEN TWP	WAYNE	27
WHITFIELD, L D H	27	M	W	NC	ALBERTSON'S TWP	DUPLIN	365
WHITFIELD, L H	31	M	W	NC	ALBERTSON'S TWP	DUPLIN	365
WHITFIELD, Lee	22	M	B	NC	GILMER TWP	GUILFORD	92
WHITFIELD, Len	28	M	B	NC	JEFFERSON TWP	GUILFORD	178
WHITFIELD, Lewis	61	M	W	NC	ROXBORO TWP	PERSON	650
WHITFIELD, Lewis	18	M	B	NC	BEAVER CRK	JONES	552
WHITFIELD, Lewis	46	M	W	NC	NEW HOPE TWP	WAYNE	195
WHITFIELD, Lewis	27	M	B	NC	KINSTON TWP	LENOIR	26
WHITFIELD, Louis	19	M	B	NC	5-WD NEW BERNE	CRAVEN	402
WHITFIELD, Manjer	28	M	B	NC	WILMINGTON	NEW HANOVER	480
WHITFIELD, Margaret	76	F	W	NC	BRASSFIELDS TWP	GRANVILLE	112
WHITFIELD, Maria	25	F	B	NC	RALEIGH TWP	WAKE	260
WHITFIELD, Mariah	40	F	B	NC	KINSTON TWP	LENOIR	31
WHITFIELD, Martha	19	F	B	NC	PIKEVILLE TWP	WAYNE	219
WHITFIELD, Mary	30	F	W	NC	GLISSON'S TWP	DUPLIN	410
WHITFIELD, Mary	30	F	W	NC	MOSELY HALL TWP	LENOIR	93
WHITFIELD, Mary	30	F	B	NC	KINSTON	LENOIR	68
WHITFIELD, Mary J	30	F	W	NC	INDIAN SPRINGS T	WAYNE	153
WHITFIELD, Mary Z	70	F	W	NC	NEW HOPE TWP	WAYNE	195
WHITFIELD, Miley	55	F	B	NC	SMITHFIELD TWP	JOHNSTON	511
WHITFIELD, Miley	50	M	B	NC	GOLDSBORO	WAYNE	104
WHITFIELD, Moses	16	M	B	NC	WINTON TWP	HERTFORD	425
WHITFIELD, Moses	103	M	B	NC	KINSTON TWP	LENOIR	47
WHITFIELD, N A	34	M	W	NC	TRENT TWP	LENOIR	133
WHITFIELD, N G	50	M	W	NC	BRASSFIELDS TWP	GRANVILLE	116
WHITFIELD, N J	43	M	W	NC	FRENCHES CRK TWP	BLADEN	440
WHITFIELD, Nancy	58	F	B	NC	LOWER CONTOE TWP	EDGECOMBE	48
WHITFIELD, Nickles	42	M	W	NC	MIDDLEFORK TWP	FORSYTH	376
WHITFIELD, Nicy	19	F	W	NC	BROGDEN TWP	WAYNE	13
WHITFIELD, P L	42	M	W	NC	LIBERTY TWP	NASH	18
WHITFIELD, Pauline	13	F	B	NC	ELIZABETH CITY T	PASQUOTANK	352
WHITFIELD, Penelope	23	F	W	NC	1-WD NEW BERNE	CRAVEN	361
WHITFIELD, Peter	25	M	B	NC	MOREHEAD TWP	GUILFORD	236
WHITFIELD, Peter	20	M	B	NC	MOREHEAD TWP	GUILFORD	229
WHITFIELD, Peter	54	M	B	NC	FAISON'S TWP	DUPLIN	386
WHITFIELD, Pompy	50	M	B	NC	MOSELY HALL TWP	LENOIR	103
WHITFIELD, Prince	60	M	B	NC	MOSELY HALL TWP	LENOIR	87
WHITFIELD, R	22	M	B	NC	MOSELY HALL TWP	LENOIR	84
WHITFIELD, Rachael	39	F	W	NC	CROSS CRK TWP	CUMBERLAND	38
WHITFIELD, Rachel	22	F	B	NC	GOLDSBORO TWP	WAYNE	86
WHITFIELD, Rebecca	70	F	B	NC	GOLDSBORO TWP	WAYNE	87
WHITFIELD, Rhoda	31	F	B	NC	3-WD NEW BERNE	CRAVEN	378
WHITFIELD, Richard	31	M	B	NC	KINSTON	LENOIR	69
WHITFIELD, Richd	38	M	W	NC	LIBERTY TWP	NASH	17
WHITFIELD, Richd	40	M	B	NC	BROGDEN TWP	WAYNE	27
WHITFIELD, Rick	10	M	B	NC	HAMILTON TWP	MARTIN	481
WHITFIELD, Robt	38	M	W	NC	LIBERTY TWP	NASH	17
WHITFIELD, Rubin	30	M	B	NC	NEW HOPE TWP	WAYNE	184
WHITFIELD, Sallie	40	F	B	NC	INDIAN SPRINGS T	WAYNE	152
WHITFIELD, Sally	27	F	B	NC	CONTENTNEA NECK	LENOIR	10
WHITFIELD, Saml	23	M	W	NC	LIBERTY TWP	NASH	25
WHITFIELD, Samuel	72	M	W	NC	GOLDSBORO TWP	WAYNE	66
WHITFIELD, Sarah	40	F	B	NC	2-WD NEW BERNE	CRAVEN	366
WHITFIELD, Sarah	60	F	B	NC	BRASSFIELDS TWP	GRANVILLE	114
WHITFIELD, Sarah C	38	F	W	NC	WOLFSCRAPE TWP	DUPLIN	552
WHITFIELD, Shepard	40	M	B	NC	NEW HOPE TWP	WAYNE	185
WHITFIELD, Solomon	46	M	B	NC	DALMATIA TWP	HALIFAX	385
WHITFIELD, Susan	39	F	B	NC	6-WD NEW BERNE	CRAVEN	418
WHITFIELD, Susan C	70	F	W	NC	FAISON'S TWP	DUPLIN	381
WHITFIELD, Theoplius	40	M	B	NC	SMITHFIELD TWP	JOHNSTON	507

1870 Census North Carolina

Name	Age	S	C	S	Place	County	Page
WHITFIELD, Thomas	66	M	M	LA	CROSS CRK TWP	CUMBERLAND	198
WHITFIELD, Thomas	51	M	W	NC	RAPIDES TWP	HALIFAX	554
WHITFIELD, Thomas	20	M	B	NC	PANTEGO TWP	BEAUFORT	85
WHITFIELD, Thos Jr	23	M	M	NC	CROSS CRK TWP	CUMBERLAND	43
WHITFIELD, Tina	45	F	B	NC	WILMINGTON	NEW HANOVER	344
WHITFIELD, Tom	28	M	B	VA	SALISBURY TWP	ROWAN	568
WHITFIELD, Trim	10	M	B	NC	BRASSFIELDS TWP	GRANVILLE	118
WHITFIELD, Turner	50	M	B	NC	MIDDLETON TWP	NASH	64
WHITFIELD, Valentine	50	M	B	NC	CYPRESS CRK TWP	JONES	558
WHITFIELD, Virgil	40	M	B	NC	NEW BERNE P O	CRAVEN	350
WHITFIELD, W	17	M	M	NC	HARRELLSVILLE TW	HERTFORD	344
WHITFIELD, W B	42	M	W	NC	INDIAN SPRINGS T	WAYNE	153
WHITFIELD, W G*	39	M	W	NC	HAMILTON TWP	MARTIN	502
WHITFIELD, W H	19	M	W	NC	KINSTON TWP	LENOIR	46
WHITFIELD, Walter	27	M	B	NC	OCCONEECHE TWP	NORTHAMPTON	594
WHITFIELD, Washington	37	M	B	NC	UPPER FISHING CR	EDGECOMBE	269
WHITFIELD, Westley	40	M	B	NC	SMITHFIELD TWP	JOHNSTON	513
WHITFIELD, William	18	M	B	NC	LOWER FISHING CR	EDGECOMBE	68
WHITFIELD, William	22	M	B	NC	OCCONEECHE TWP	NORTHAMPTON	597
WHITFIELD, William	25	M	B	NC	FAISON'S TWP	DUPLIN	394
WHITFIELD, William	45	M	W	NC	HAMILTON TWP	MARTIN	486
WHITFIELD, Willis	62	M	W	NC	SPRINGFIELD TWP	NASH	72
WHITFIELD, Wily	47	M	B	NC	TRENT TWP	LENOIR	134
WHITFIELD, Winifred	40	F	W	NC	ALBERTSON'S TWP	DUPLIN	366
WHITFIELD (Farm Laborer)	35	M	R	NC	PAMPLICO TWP	BEAUFORT	67

COUNTY NAMES NORTH CAROLINA WILLS

Caswell - James Whitfield 1859. Sarah F. Whitfield 1865.

Craven - Constantine Whitfield 1798.

Duplin - Charlotte Whitfield 1880. John Whitfield 1825.
John T. Whitfield 1876. Joseph Whitfield 1852. Joseph
Whitfield 1835. Sally Whitfield 1837.

Edgecombe - Mary L. Whitfield 1879.

Forsyth - Sarah Whitfield 1899.

Granville - John Whitfield 1833.

Halifax - John G. Whitfield 1879.
William Whitfield 1806.

Hertford - Tabithy Whitfield 1867.

Lenoir - Bettie G. Whitfield 1896.
Demaris Whitfield 1879.
Lewis Whitfield 1848.

Martin - Arnold Whitfield.
Kenneth B. Whitfield 1864.

New Hanover - William Whitfield 1776.

Orange - Sallie J. Whitfield 1898.

Person - Edwin Whitfield 1885. Lewis Whitfield 1884. Martha
Whitfield 1885.

Tyrell - William Whitfield 1761.

Union - W. L. Whitfield 1897.

Wayne - Allen Whitfield 1845. John B. Whitfield 1835. Mary
Whitfield 1871. Needham Whitfield 1812. William
Whitfield 1795. William Whitfield 1817.

Nash County

WHITFIELD: Benjamin 1808.
Charity 1854. Delilah 1818.
Henry E. 1886. Isaac 1796.
Mary 1792. Mary 1844.
Penelope 1816. Reuben 1816.
Sarah 1836. Solomon 1808.
Thomas 1781. Thomas 1800.
William 1826.

Reference. (1) (2) North Carolina Wills A Testor Index
1665-1900 by Thornton W. Mitchell.

National Society of the Daughters of the American Revolution,
D.A.R. Patriot Index, published 1966. List of Soldiers in the
Revolutionary War.

RECORDS

My 3g/f was William WHITFIELD KING. He was the son of Charles KING, b 20 Dec 1753 Sampson Co., NC, d 23 Sept 1824 Madison Co, AL, and Penelope WHITFIELD, b ca 1746 in Clinton, NC, d 1841 in Madison Co., AL.

She was the daughter of   Luke WHITFIELD, b 19 Feb 1719 Chowan Co., NC, d *SEPT.* 1767 m on 12 Jan 1740. PeeDee River, St David's Parish, SC, d ca 1782 *to 1839.*

Luke WHITFIELD was the son of William WHITFIELD b ca 1688 in Lancashire, England; d Rockford, Lenoir Co., NC, killed by Indians, m on 13 Mar 1713 Elizabeth GOODMAN, b Gates (Chowan) Co., NC, also killed by Indians Rockford, NC.

We know nothing about Susanna Shurley WHITFIELD, other than she was born ca 1815 and married Job W. SMITH, b 1810 in NC, according to "family tradition". There is nothing to prove this in our possession.

Submitted by Phyllis Strayhan Farris of Plan Dealing, Louisiana on July 21, 1992.

Alstons and Allstons Have Whitfield Descendants
Marriage Records

Helen Jones married William A. Whitfield, 1740 year.
Margaret Williams married _____ Whitfield, 1740 year. They had these children:
  1. Mary Whitfield
  2. Joseph John Whitfield
  3. Nereston G. Whitfield

Margaret Williams was the daughter of Major, Joseph John Williams and Martha James Alston.

Reference: The Alstons And Allstons Of North and South Carolina By Joseph A. Groves, M.D., Selma, Alabama. Published Atlanta, Georgia, 1901. Pages 283, 464, 465.

Marriage Records

Martha Whitfield (widow) married Isaac Glesson on June 1762, Tyrell County, North Carolina.

William Whitfield married Rachel Bryan on Nov. 6, 1741, Bertie County, North Carolina.

....William Montgomery clemens, Editor of Genealogy Magazine, published in New York

National Society Of The Daughters Of The American Revolution, D. A. R. Patriot index, published 1966. List of Revolution Soldiers in the Revolutionary War.

North Carolina. Elizabeth Whitfield of North Carolina married Lt. John Beck and Colonel John Smith.

North Carolina Record. Catharine Whitfield was wife of George W. Whitfield of Johnston County, NC, Feb. 1, 1832.

1840 CENSUS FOR UNITED STATES

State: _Virginia_ County: _Isle of Wight_

Page 14

Head of Family	Free White Males						Free White Females					
	Under 5	5-10	10-15	15-20	20-30	30-40	Under 5	5-10	10-15	15-20	20-30	30-40
John G. Whitfield Church Minister					1		1				1	

John Godwin Whitfield was born 1810 and died 1879 North Carolina. In 1840 the Household had a female slave named Godwin.
..... Submitted by Jack Strickland of Universal City, Texas.

NORTH CAROLINA

1860 Census , Halifax County, North Carolina

NAME	AGE		Birthplace	
John G. Whitfield	49	Male	VA	
Martha C. Whitfield	35	Female ...	N.C	
Anna H. Whitfield	21	Female ...	VA	**Property Value**
Mary F. Whitfield	19	Female ...	VA	
Eveline W. Whitfield	13	Female ...	VA	$250,000-
Roberta Whitfield	11	Female ...	VA	$180,000
Bettie W. Whitfield	10	Female ...	VA	
Sarah Whitfield	3	Female ...	N C	
Samuel G. Whitfield	1	Male ...	N C	

1870 Census, Halifax County , North Carolina

NAME	AGE		Birthplace	Property Value
John G. Whitfield	54	Preacher	...VA	$13,000-
Martha C. "	46	Female	...N C	$ 300
Roberta "	21	Female	...VA	
Bettie W. "	20	Female	...VA	
Sarah C. "	13	Female	... N C	
Samuel G. "	11	Male	... N C	

.... Submitted by Kathleen Whitfield (Mrs. Joe M. Whitfield) of Falls Church, Virginia in 1993. Assisted with federal Census search by Jack Strickland of Universal City, Texas.

TERRITORY LANDS FORMING COUNTIES IN NORTH CAROLINA

Edgecombe County formed 1741 from Bertie County... Granville County formed 1746 from Edgecombe County... Halifax County formed 1758 from Edgecombe County ... Hertford County formed 1759 from Chowan, Bertie and Northampton Counties ... Lenoir County formed 1791 from Dobbs County ... Martin County formed 1774 from Halifax and Tyrrell Counties... Nash County formed 1777 from Edgecombe County ... New Hanover County formed 1729 from Craven County... Person County formed 1792 from Caswell County... Wayne County formed 1779 from Dobbs County.

Years.	Nash County, North Carolina Censuses	Pages.	
1800	William Whitfield, Sr.	N C 128	
1800	Elizabeth Whitfield	N C 128	Nash Co.
1800	Matthew Whitfield	N C 128	with no
1800	William Whitfield, Jr.	N C 128	townships.
1810	Abraham Whitfield	080	
1810	Ann Whitfield	078	
1810	Delilah Whitfield	079	
1810	Hardy Whitfield	077	
1810	Jacob Whitfield	078	
1810	Rueben Whitfield	080	
1810	Wiley Whitfield	077	
1810	William Whitfield, Sr.	084	
1830	Abram Whitfield	179	
1830	Ann Whitfield	166	Nashville
1830	Archibald Whitfield	171	
1830	Benjamin Whitfield	190	In 1830
1830	Isaac Whitfield	172	Nash was
1830	Penelope Whitfield	174	the District
1830	Percilla Whitfield	173	with 2,7.
1830	Sarah Whitfield	174	

Censuses North Carolina

1880 Census. Whitfield cannot be found.
1900 Census. Halifax County, North Carolina
Samuel G. Whitfield age 41 Male Born NC.
Roberta Whitfield age 51 Female Born VA.
Bettie Whitfield age 50 Female Born VA.

ROSTER OF SOLDIERS FROM NORTH CAROLINA
IN THE AMERICAN REVOLUTION

National Society of Daughters of the American Revolution published the list in 1932. Land Grants, 1778.

William Whitfield to Heir of Jesse Whitfield 640 acres.
Jesse Whitfield, Land Do.
Willis Whitfield. Soldier Number 90934. Private in Raiford's Company, his date of enlistment and commission 1782, period of service 18 months.

These men William Whitfield, Jesse Whitfield, Willis Whitfield from North Carolina went to Sumner County, Tennessee, in search of their lands in Tennessee.

Nash County, North Carolina Censuses with Whitfield
Heads of Families. Censuses.

1782	Benjamin
1782	Hardy
1782	Israel
1782	John
1782	Mary
1782	Reuben
1782	Thomas

1790	Benjamin
1790	Matthew
1790	Nancy
1790	Thomas
1790	William

1840	E.S.	
1840	Mary	
1840	Nancy A.	1850
1840	Willis	1850

1850	Franklin
1850	Guilford G.
1850	John
1850	Oliver
1850	Penelope
1850	Priscilla
1850	Ricey

1830 Census of Edgecombe County, North Carolina

Benjamin   Whitfield, Jr.

1 male -20-30 age range
1 female -0-5
1 female - 15-20

Son of Benjamin Whitfield,Sr.
(1780-1840)

1840 Census Pitt Co., N C

Benjamin   Whitfield , Jr.

1 male -5-10
2 females - 10-15
1 male -50-60

1850 Census , New Hanover County, North Carolina
Benjamin Whitfield Male , age 23 .

WHITFIELD HEADS OF FAMILIES ON NORTH CAROLINA CENSUSES.
There were more Whitfield families not found by census takers.

1790 Census had   twenty-eight (28) Whitfield Families.
1800 Census had   Nineteen (19) Whitfield Families.
1810 Census had   twenty- seven (27 Whitfield Families.
1820 Census had   Whitfield Families.
1830 Census had   forty-three (43) Whitfield Families.
1840 Census had   forty-five (45) Whitfield Families.
1850 Census had   sixty (60) Whitfield Families.
1860 Census had   (78)   Whitfield Families.
1870 Census had   one hundred and ninety (190) Whitfield
    Families.   1860 had (17) Whitefield Families.

1980 Census conducted Whitfield project for a computer
    Company had seven hundred and nineteen (719) Whitfield
    Heads Of Families living in North Carolina state.

North Carolina. Dobbs County, NC, was formed from Johnston
County in 1758. In 1791 it was divided to make Lenoir County
and Glasgow, the latter becoming eight years later Greene
County. From Wheeler, II, p. 223.

WILLS OF NASH COUNTY, NORTH CAROLINA . Bradley's Abstracts.

SOLOMON WHITFIELD   8 Dec 1807   Nov Ct 1808
Wife ANN WHITFIELD - lend to her my house & 20 acres(excepting where my son JACOB occupies), etc.
Son JACOB WHITFIELD - all my lands & possessions, etc. Daughter SARAH WHITFIELD - $1. Daughter
MARY WHITFIELD - bed & furniture, the chairs I bought from J. MELTON, etc. Daughter NANCY
WHITFIELD - bed & furniture, etc. Daughter CHARITY WHITFIELD - bed & furniture, table I bought
from J. MELTON, etc. Daughter WINNEY NOLLEBOY - $1. Residue of estate to go to my 3 daughters
MARY, NANCY, & CHARITY WHITFIELD.
Ex.   son JACOB WHITFIELD, friend JOHN VICK
Wit.   SAML. WESTRAY, WM. SHORT

THOMAS WHITFIELD   6 Jul 1781   Jan Ct 1781
"tho weak in Body"
1 silver dollar each to: Son THOMAS, son REUBEN, son SOLOMAN, son JOHN, son WILLIAM, son
BENJAMIN, son ELISH. Son EZARAL - 115 acres on north side of Peachtree Creek joining Pigbasket
Creek, RICHARD THOMAS; etc. Son HARDY - 115 acres, etc. 1 silver dollar each to: Daughter MARY,
daughter SARAH, daughter MILDRED. Daughter ELISABETH - bed & furniture. Wife MARY - bed &
furniture, etc. Residue of estate to my 2 sons EZARAL & HARDY.
Ex.   son SOLOMAN WHITFIELD, HARDY WHITFIELD
Wit.   JACOB DICKINSON, WILLIS(x)WHITFIELD, CHLOE(x)WHITFIELD

THOMAS WHITFIELD   21 May 1798   Nov Ct 1800
Wife ELIZABETH WHITFIELD - lend to her the land where I now live; then to be sold & money to go to
my 2 sons WILLIS & MATTHEW WHITFIELD; other items lent to wife. Negro man Jack to be sold &
money used to pay my debts. Daughter MARY WILLIS - $1. 3 daughters SARAH BRYANT, CHLOE
STOKES, NANCY MASSINGILL - other property lent to my wife.
Ex.   wife, friend SAM WESTRAY
Wit.   MARY VICK, SOPHIA VICK

WILLIAM(x)WHITFIELD SR.   12 May 1826   Aug Ct 1826
"am Sick and Weak in Body"
Son WILLIAM WHITFIELD - horse. Granddaughter WILLEY WHITFIELD - cow & calf, etc. Son ELISHA
WHITFIELD - bed & furniture called CHARITY RAY's bed, after sd CHARITY's death. Friend CHARITY
RAY - remainder of estate for her maintenance "in gratitude for good Conduct her Industery and Coanesull
and Services Rendered to me for the space of 40 years."
Ex.   son WILLIAM WHITFIELD JR.
Wit.   ABSALOM B. BAINS, JAMES B.(x)BAINS

WILLIAM(x)WHITFIELD JR.   27 Apr 1826   May Ct 1828
"am sick and weak in Body"
Wife EDY W. WHITFIELD - 200 acres, livestock, etc. 3 sons - 348 acres which is my Simmons tract.
Wit.   WILLIAM JOHNSTON, ANDREW(x)JOHNSTON

JOSIAH(x)WHITLEY   12 Mar 1831   May Ct 1831
Son WILLIE WHITLEY - negro man Skipper. Daughter MOURNING BATCHELOR - a note against JOEL
WHITLEY; woman Rose. Son SION WHITLEY - my land. Daughter MOURNING BATCHELOR, son
SION WHITLEY - woman Dinah. Out of remainder of estate, MOURNING BATCHELOR to have $50 &
remainder to son WILLIE WHITLEY, JOEL WHITLEY, MOURNING BATCHELOR, SION W.
WHITLEY.
Ex.   TIMOTHY TERRELL

366

BENJAMIN WHITFIELD   17 Oct 1807   Feb Ct 1808
Wife DELILAH WHITFIELD - lend to where I live with land on east side of Lasiter's Branch; also land that was purchased from DAVID STRICKLAND; also negro man Ben Thorn, woman Moll, woman Rhoda, boy Davy, girl Chany, girl Charlotte; etc. After her death, all to be sold & proceeds to go to my 5 sons: JOHN, GUILFORD, ARCHIBALD, BENJAMIN, JOHN THOMAS GRIFFIN WHITFIELD, all children of my present wife DELILAH. Daughter ELIZABETH WHITFIELD(child of my 2d wife ELIZABETH) - $100. Son-in-law PHILANDER TISDAL - land I purchased from WILLIAM WILLIAMS that I have not already deeded to him. Daughter DREWSEY BUNN - land I purchased from THOS. HART & THOS. WILHITE that I have not already deeded away. 4 sons WILLIE, GUILFORD, ARCHIBALD, BENJAMIN GRIFFIN WHITFIELD - residue(excepting the land I bought from THOS HUNTER); WILLIE & GUILFORD GRIFFIN WHITFIELD each to each a horse. Son JOHN THOS. GRIFFIN WHITFIELD - land I lent to his mohter, after her death. Granddaughter MARTHA MATILDA WHITFIELD - land I bought from THOMAS HUNTER.
Ex.   friends NATHAN GILBERT, JOHN ATKINSON(Taylor), wife
Wit.   JAS. WILLIAMS, DREW HUNTER, JOSEPH STRICKLAND

DELILAH(x)WHITFIELD   26 Mar 1818   Nov Ct 1818
"sick of body"
My land on east side of Lassiter's Branch to be sold & the money to pay my debts. 5 shillings each to: Daughter PRISSCILLA TISDALE, HARDY G. WHITFIELD, DRUSILLA DORTCH, WILLIE G. WHITFIELD, GUILFORD G. WHITFIELD. My 3 sons ARCHIBALD G., BENJAMIN G., & JOHN T. G. WHITFIELD - the land I purchased from JOHN RICKS & the balance of my estate.
Ex.   HARDY G. WHITFIELD
Wit.   BATSON SMITH, ASA(x)SNEED

ISAAC WHITFIELD   6 Jan 1796   (no probate date)
Wife EASTER WHITFIELD - bed & furniture, painted chest. Father SOLOMON WHITFIELD - remainder of my estate.
Ex.   SOLOMON WHITFIELD
Wit.   JOHN HAYS, HENRY D. BUNN, DREW HUNTER

MARY(x)WHITFIELD   19 Feb 1792   (no probate date)
SOOKEY WHITFIELD LONG - cow & calf, etc. Son ELISHA WHITFIELD - remainder of my estate.
Ex.   ARCHD. GRIFFIN
Wit.   LUCY(x)GRIFFIN, SOOKEY(x)WHITFIELD

MARY(x)WHITFIELD   26 Apr 1843   May Ct 1844
"old infirm and weak in Boddy"
Sister CHARITY WHITFIELD - my title to 60 acres where I live; also 1/2 of negro man Abram; etc.
Wit.   JOHN RICKS, MOURNING(x)STRICKLAND

REUBEN(x)WHITFIELD   5 Feb 1816   Feb Ct 1816
"sick and weak of Body"
Daughter MOURNING WHELES - black mare. Daughters CATHARINE WHITLEY & MOURNING WHELES - remainder of estate.
Ex.   friend RICHARD HOLLAND
Wit.   ISAAC SESSUMS

SARAH(x)WHITFIELD   16 Dec 1835   Aug Ct 1836
"old and Infirm and Very low in health"
Niece TEMPERANCE MELTON - bed & furniture, painted chest, etc. My 2 sisters MARY & CHARITY WHITFIELD - balance of my property.

ANCESTORS OF JOSEPH WHITFIELD (D. 1835) AND MARY GRADY OF NORTH CAROLINA

WI   WILLIAM WHITFIELD born in Lancaster, England. He is on a British passenger ship record. Not long after arrival in the new world, 1713, he married Elizabeth Goodman, and settled in Bertie Co., NC, where they were living in 1723. Moving again to join their son William at Lenoir County, NC, they were killed by Indians.

WII   William Whitfield II was born May 20, 1715, and died March 31, 1795. They had nine children and the son named William Whitfield.

WIII   WILLIAM WHITFIELD was born June 1, 1743, and with his parents he moved across the Neuse River to White Hall, in Seven Springs, NC. He married four wives and had a large number of children (29). William had the son named Joseph Whitfield.

WIV   JOSEPH WHITFIELD married May 2, 1790, Mary Grady. The parents had 11 children. Joseph died in 1835 NC. His Will gives the names of his children. There were six sons and five daughters. Daughters married: Elizabeth Outlaw, Hester was Mrs. Henry Grady, Charity Loftin.

Reference: Book - Whitfield, Bryan, Smith and Related Families, compiled by Emma Morehead Whitfield.

WHITFIELD
Nancy Council
Nancy Ann Elizabeth Briley
Nicey
Pauline
Pearl Edmonds
Robert Asbury
Robert Latham
Ruby
Stacey
Starkey

WHITFIELD
Stella Roebuck
Velma Marie Britton
Wendy A.
William Anthony
Willie

Martin County, NC

People named Whitfield associated there 1870 to 1970.

Samuel Canady, grantor to Stephen Stephens, grantee, Jan. 14, 1757, five pounds of Virginia money. One hundred ten (110) acres more or less on the south side of Sappona Swamp, joining the Great Branch and Spring bottom. Witnesses: Thomas Whitfield and Richard Thomas. Registered deed Edgecombe Co, NC, May court 1757, Montford County Court, NC.

Catharine Whitfield was wife of George W. Whitfield of Johnston County, North Carolina, Feb. 1, 1832. Deed Book 20, p. 270.

Joseph Booth married Nancy K. Whitfield 1814, Granville, North Carolina.

Jennie Crisp born Macon County, North Carolina, in 1881, and near the Georgia boundary line. Jennie was the mother of Ruth Wigfield Phillip of Montana state.

DESCENDANTS OF WILLIAM WHITFIELD (1688-1770) AND ELIZABETH GOODMAN WHITFIELD OF NORTH CAROLINA.

Whitfield—One branch of the Whitfield family came originally from Lancaster, England. This record begins with the first Whitfield who came to North Carolina. William Whitfield came from England in the early part of the Eighteenth century and settled in Nancemond county, Virginia. He married Elizabeth Goodman, of Gates county, North Carolina, in 1713. (Gates county was a part of Chowan until 1779.) After his marriage William Whitfield settled in Bertie county, North Carolina, but eventually moved to Rockford, Lenoir county, North Carolina. He had a family of four sons and six daughters, viz: William, Matthew, Luke, Constantine, Mary, Margaret, Sarah, Patience, Elizabeth and Charity.

The second William Whitfield (son of William and Elizabeth Goodman Whitfield) was born May 20, 1715, and died March 31, 1795. He married Nov. 6, 1741, Rachel Bryan, daughter of Needham Bryan, and his first wife, Ann Rombeau Rachel (Bryan) Whitfield was born June 10, 1723; died November, 1780.

The children of William Whitfield II and Rachel Bryan were William Whitfield, born June 1, 1743, died March, 1817; Elizabeth Whitfield born March 16, 1746; Sarah Whitfield, born April 16, 1749, died Jan. 22 1780; Charity Whitfield, born April 6, 1756; died Aug. 21, 1818; Needham Whitfield, born Feb. 20, 1758, died April 6, 1812; Bryan Whitfield, born Feb. 9, 1754; Rachel Whitfield, born Sept. 16, 1760; Mary Whitfield, born May 18, 1763; Lewis Whitfield, born 1766.

William Whitfield III, son of William and Rachel Bryan Whitfield, married three times. His first wife was Lucy Hatch; his second wife was Betsy Hatch, sister of his first wife; his third wife was Sally Watkins, daughter of Levi Watkins and Edith Hilliard, of Duplin county, North Carolina.

William and Needham Whitfield were both in the Battle of Moore's Creek Bridge. Needham Whitfield was clerk to Col. Caswell, who commanded the whigs, and William served as a private in the Light Horse. William and Needham Whitfield both served in Col. John Miller's company of North Carolina troops during the Revolution.

An extensive account of this North Carolina family may be found,

(1)

William and Needham Whitfield and their brother-in-law, Joseph Green entered 2,500 acres of land in what is now Rhea County in 1786. This land lay on the north bank of the Tennessee River at the mouth of Muddy Creek. The land was surveyed in September 1786 by Thomas King, deputy surveyor under Stockley Donelson, and Alexander E. Outlaw served as chain bearer.

Needham Whitfield died in 1812 and the following year William and Edmund Whitfield as executors, brought suit to recover the above land which had been settled on by people holding their deed under an over-lapping grant. It was stated in the testimony that John A. Smith, Joseph Williams, David Beck, Allen Murphree, George Walker, Jeremiah Jones, Seymour Kitchen,

Alexander Watson and Mrs. Carter were living in 1813,within the bounds of the 2,400 acre survey.

Alexander E. Outlaw, a prominent citizen of Jefferson Co. was summoned as a witness in the case ,and gave his testimony in the Rhea County Court on June 14, 1813. (2)

References.
(1) <u>North Carolina Historical And Genealogical Register.</u>
(2) Leaves From The Family Tree. Answer section ,number nine, page 368. Magazine.

Genealogy Clearing House in Oakland, California , sent the query of that office. Note the reference from Virkus and Notable publications.

Virkus 6 - 160 ; Notable 2-51 . Mrs. Garner Shannon.

Issue:

William (1) Whitfield

B.   1688
B.   1690 (Virkus 6-517)

D.   ca 1770
Where?
Parents:
  q.v.
Matthew Whitfield

William (2) Whitfield   q.v.
  B. 29 May 1715 Bertie Co., N. C.
  D.   1795
  Md.   1741
    Rachel Bryan
    1723-1780
  of Bertie Co., N. C.
  of Rockford, Lenoir Co., N.C.
          (Virkus 6-517)

Patience (2) Whitfield
  B.
  D.
  Md.
      Edward Outlaw III   q.v.
      D. 1759
(Mrs. Garner Shannon records)

Elizabeth Goodman
  of Gates Co., N. C.

  B.   ca 1697

  D.   1773
  Where?

From England in his own ship, "The Providence" in early part of the 18th Century, & settled at Nansemond, Va., finally in Lenoir Co., N. C.

Lewis Outlaw b. Feb.9,1788 and died July 19,1859. Lewis Outlaw married Elizabeth Whitfield b. Dec.2,1795 and died August 1876. Their son was William Henry Outlaw b. Jan. 24,1834 Duplin Co. North Carolina, and died Oct. 24, 1883 , Hopkins County, KY. William Henry Outlaw married Susan Isabel Oates b. Sept. 25, 1843 and died July 31, 1885. Birth and death in Hopkins Co., KY. .... Submitted by Zora A. Outlaw Evans of La Marque, Texas.

Zora Anne Outlaw was born Dec. 24, 1926 , Ralls Crosby Co.,TX. Zora Outlaw married Oct. 21, 1949, Orange Co., Texas.

Zora Outlaw Evans has worked on several families and applied to charts with Outlaw and Graddy records.

William Whitfield (b. 1688, d. 1770)
married 1713
Elizabeth Goodman (b. 1697, d. 1773)
|
Constantine Whitfield (b. March 6, 1728, d. April 1, 1798)
married November 30, 1756
Barbara Williams (b. March 24, 1736, d. April 3, 1796)
|
John Whitfield (b. March 28, 1765, d. February 28, 1815)
married February 19, 1786
Jemima Haywood (b. June 21, 1766, d. February 26, 1837)
|
Constantine Whitfield (b. October 1, 1788, d. February 17, 1867)
married Abt 1810
Elizabeth Jones (b. December 13, 1792, d. Abt 1865)
|
Augustus Washington Whitfield (b. May 15, 1833, d. January 12, 1905)
married November 25, 1869
Delila Ann Jones (b. April 1, 1846, d. October 29, 1892)
|
DeLeon Augustus Whitfield (b. October 27, 1870, d. January 9, 1944)
married January 14, 1897
Addie Campbell Davis (b. February 11, 1873, d. September 1, 1933)
|
Ralph Alonza Whitfield (b. June 4, 1908, d. December 12, 1974)
married December 23, 1936
Alice Harper (b. March 7, 1913)
|
James Augustus Whitfield (b. December 21, 1937)
married May 18, 1958
Allie Rouse Shepherd (b. March 25, 1941)
|
James Andrews Whitfield (b. July 16, 1959)
married November 26, 1983
Monique Renee' Crevier (b. October 2, 1959)

---

(1) I have found the graves of John Whitfield, his wife Jemima Haywood, and two of their sons. Each are clearly labelled with marble slabs and are located in a small plot near Strabane, Lenoir County, NC.

(2) Alice Harper Whitfield, my grandmother, is living near Strabane, Lenoir County, NC.

James Andrews Whitfield, July 6, 1995

WILL AND TESTAMENT OF JOSEPH WHITFIELD
Duplin County, North Carolina

APRIL 1835

In the name of God Amen--

I Joseph Whitfield being weak in body but of sound disposing mind and memory do make ordain constitute and publish this my last will and testament in manner and form following

Knowing that it is appointed for all men to die first I commit my body to the (illegible) my soul to god that gave it

Item first my wish and desire is that my just debts be paid out of my estate

Item 2nd My wish and desire is that further that my beloved wife Mary Whitfield have April, Allen, Curtis, Hannah, Primer and Bias to her during her natural life. The balance and remainder of my perishable property I give unto wife Mary Whitfield Also my land lying on the South side of Mill pond I give to my wife Mary during her life and after the death of my wife my wish and desire is that my land that is before named and the negroes that is named above and all the perishable estate if any be sold at six months credit by my executors which I shall hereafter name and that my son Joseph Whitfield have one hundred dollars of the money arising from the sale of the before named land and negroes as before named, that balance of the money be equally divided into eleven shares, that my son William Whitfield have one share that my daughter Elizabeth Outlaw have one share, that

my son Bryan Whitfield have one share that my son Joseph Whitfield have one share that my son Henry Whitfield have one share that my daughter Hester Grady have one share that my daughter Sally Whitfield have one share that my daughter Charity Loftin have one share that my daughter Rachel Whitfield have one share, that my son John Whitfield's children have one share and my son Timothy Whitfield's children have one share lastly I nominate and appoint my son William Whitfield and my friends Daniel Jones and Giles T. Loftin Executors to this my last will and Testament etc.

In witness whereof the said Joseph Whitfield have published and declared this to be his last will and testament- February 11th day 1835

Jos Whitfield

Signed sealed and delivered in presence of

James (Illegible)

(Illegible) Outlaw

State of North Carolina, Duplin County

Court of Pleas and Quarter Sessions

April term 1835

the (illegible), the Last will and Testament of Joseph Whitfield is brought into court and offered for probate and is proved in due form of Laws by the oath of James Sullivan.

North Carolina Department of Archives and History in Raleigh.

Outlaw Whitfield. Grady. Ivey. Barfield. Goodman.

LEWIS OUTLAW b. Feb. 1788, Duplin Co., NC-d. July 19, 1859, Hopkins Co., KY. Lewis Outlaw married Elizabeth Whitfield b. Dec. 1795, NC-d. Aug. 1876, Hopkins Co., KY.

Lewis was the son of JAMES OUTLAW b. 1744-d. Apr 22, 1826, b. and d. in Duplin Co., NC. The mother was Patience Whitfield b. Bertie Co., NC. James Outlaw's wife.

Lewis Outlaw was the son of Elizabeth Grady Whitfield b. Feb.9,1750-d. Sept. 3, 1830. She was b. and d. at Duplin Co., NC. The father of Elizabeth was John Grady (Graddy) b. 1703, Bertie Co., NC. d. March 12, 1787, Duplin Co., NC.

MARY WHITFIELD b. ca. 1718-d. Dec. 1791 was the mother of Elizabeth Grady Whitfield. Mary Whitfield was the daughter of William Whitfield, b. 1688 in England-d. ca. 1770 North Carolina, and she was the daughter of Elizabeth Goodman Whitfield b. ca. 1697-d. ca. 1770 North Carolina. Elizabeth was the daughter of Henry Goodman b. ca. 1662 probably in Europe. The Goodman parents came to Virginia and moved to the watery slough land south which became North Carolina. Henry Goodman died circa 1745.

EDWARD OUTLAW III b. ca. 1712-14-d. 1759, Duplin Co., NC. Edward Outlaw married 1736 or 1737. Edward was the son of Edward Outlaw II b. ca. 1685, Norfolk Co., Virginia-d. by the date of Feb. 5, 1739, Bertie Co., NC. Edward Outlaw II married Anne Ivey b. circa 1688 or 1689, Norfolk Co., VA. Anne Outlaw died in North Carolina. Anne's parents were George Ivey and Hannah Sibsey who married about 1666 or 1667. The dates indicate they were probably immigrants to Virginia. George and Hannah died in Virginia.

WILLIAM GRADDY who died 1790 was married to Andrea (Ann) Barfield whose parents were Richard Barfield and Mary Evans Barfield.

GEORGE IVEY b. ca. 1640-1645 and d.in 1670's or 1680's at Norfolk Co., VA. His wife Hannah Sibsey Ivey b. ca. 1652-d. 1691.

EDWARD OUTLAW I was born about 1652 probably in Europe. Edward was married about 1684 to Elizabeth Davenall. Edward died circa Dec. 1719. Elizabeth died 1727 at Norfolk Co., VA.

Submitted by Zora A. Evans of La Marque, Texas in 1992.

Whitfield. Outlaw. Williams. Graddy. Bryan.

ELIZABETH WHITFIELD OUTLAW was born Dec. 2, 1795 in NC. Elizabeth Whitfield married Lewis Outlaw April 21, 1812 in Duplin Co., NC. Elizabeth died August 1876 in Hopkins Co., Kentucky. Elizabeth Whitfield was the daughter of JOSEPH WHITFIELD who was born circa 1763 in NC and died April 17, 1835 in Duplin Co., NC.

California Record.
In 1980 sixty-one Whitfield Families had a telephone in the house at Los Angeles, California. This includes white and black people in telephone directory.

HESTER WILLIAMS WHITFIELD married William Whitfield III (1743-1817) and became the mother of Joseph Whitfield (1763-1835 NC). Hester Williams Whitfield died about 1774, Wayne Co., North Carolina.

HESTER WILLIAMS who married Whitfield was born Sept. 19, 1747, Sampson Co., NC. Hester's father was JOSEPH WILLIAMS b. ca 1720-22, Bertie Co., NC and died after 1780, Duplin Co., NC. Joseph Williams was married Aug. 8, 1746 to MARY HICKS who was born about 1725 Brunswick Co., Virginia. The father of Joseph Williams was THEOPHILUS WILLIAMS who was b. about 1695 and died by 1760-1770. Theophilos married Christian.

Mary Hicks Williams' father was DANIEL HICKS who died circa 1735, Brunswick Co, Virginia. Daniel's wife and Mary's mother may have been Edith Fonville.

LINEAGE GRADDY

The wife of Joseph Whitfield (1763-1835 NC) and mother of his daughter Elizabeth Whitfield was MARY GRADY (GRADDY). Mary's father was WILLIAM GRADDY b. ca. 1735, Bertie Co., NC and d. after July 4, 1803, Duplin Co., NC. Mary's mother may have been Elizabeth Kornegay (?).

William Graddy's father was JOHN GRADDY b. ca. 1710-d. March 12, 1787, Duplin Co., NC. John Graddy married before 1733 to Mary Whitfield, the daughter of William Whitfield (1688-1770) and Elizabeth Goodman Whitfield.

John Graddy's father was WILLIAM GRADDY who died ca.1790. John Graddy's mother was ANDREA (ANN) BARFIELD.

LINEAGE WHITFIELD

William Whitfield (1688-1770) and Elizabeth Goodman b. ca. 1695-d. ca 1773 NC had the son WILLIAM WHITFIELD II b. May 20, 1715 NC-d. March 31, 1795, Wayne Co., NC. William II married RACHEL BRYAN Nov. 6, 1741, NC. Rachel's parents were Needham Bryan b. Feb. 23, 1690-d. 1767 Bertie Co., NC. NEEDHAM BRYAN married ANNIE ROMBEAU Nov. 11, 1711. Annie Bryan d. Jan. 16, 1730.

William Whitfield (1688-1770 NC) has a daughter who married John Graddy and they had a son William Graddy who was father of Mary Grady (Graddy) who married a fourth generation man named Joseph Whitfield (1763-1835 NC) and they had the daughter Elizabeth Whitfield (1795 NC-d. 1876, Hopkins Co., KY.) ....Genealogy Chart submitted by Zora A. Evans of La Marque, Texas in 1992.

The descendants and generations are known of William Whitfield (1688 England-1770 North Carolina) and Elizabeth Goodman Whitfield. They had ten children. Their son William Whitfield II and Rachel had eight children. They had the son William Whitfield III who married four wives and had twenty-nine children with births and nineteen of the children became adults with marriages and families.

Thirty-seven with name of Whitfield begin early 1713-1728 in North Carolina. All of the descendants and generations are published in the book Whitfield Bryan Smith And Related Families. Compiled by Emma Morehead Whitfield. Edited by Theodore Marshall Whitfield.

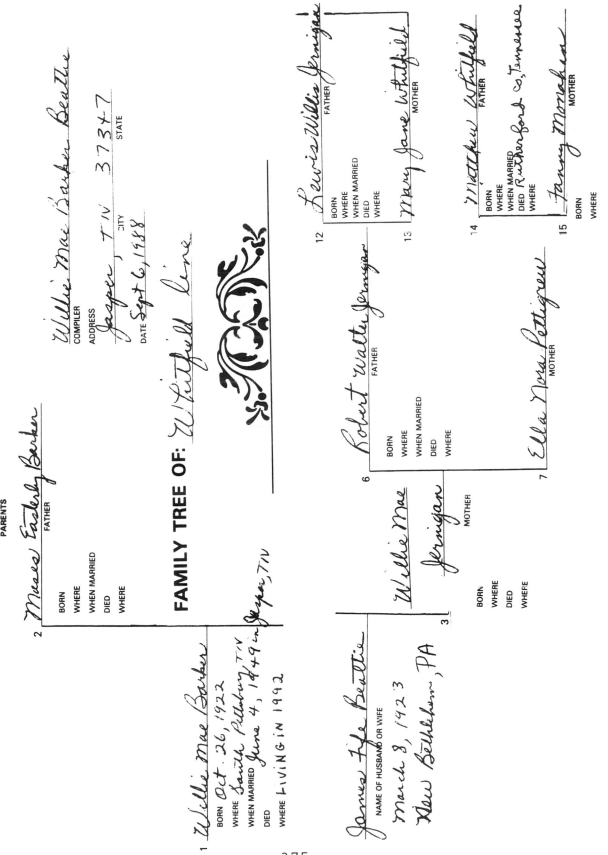

FAMILY TREE OF: W. Whitfield Beattie

PARENTS

2 Moses Easterly Barber
FATHER

BORN
WHERE
WHEN MARRIED
DIED
WHERE

1 Willie Mae Barber

BORN Oct. 26, 1922
WHERE South Pittsburg, TN
WHEN MARRIED June 4, 1949 in Jasper, TN
DIED
WHERE LIVING IN 1992

James Kyle Beattie
NAME OF HUSBAND OR WIFE
March 8, 1923
New Bethlehem, PA

3 Willie Mae
Jernigan
MOTHER

BORN
WHERE
DIED
WHERE

Willie Mae Barber Beattie
COMPILER

ADDRESS
Jasper, TN 37347
CITY   STATE
DATE Sept 6, 1988

6 Robert Walter Jernigan
FATHER

BORN
WHERE
WHEN MARRIED
DIED
WHERE

7 Ella Nora Pettigrew
MOTHER

BORN
WHERE
DIED
WHERE

12 Lewis Willie Jernigan
FATHER

BORN
WHERE
WHEN MARRIED
DIED
WHERE

13 Mary Jane Whitfield
MOTHER

14 Matthew Whitfield
FATHER

BORN
WHERE
WHEN MARRIED
DIED Rutherford Co, Tennessee
WHERE

15 Fanny Monahan
MOTHER

BORN
WHERE

375

FAMILY TREE OF: WHITFIELD LINE

Willie Mae Barker Beattie
COMPILER

His will is in Will Book 1
Nash Co., NC 1778-1868
Page 229

Same book p. 194

PARENTS

2 Mathew Whitfield
FATHER
BORN about 1792
WHERE VA or NC
WHEN MARRIED
DIED 1827
WHERE Rutherford Co., TN

GRANDPARENTS

4 Thomas Whitfield
FATHER
BORN
WHERE
WHEN MARRIED
DIED may 21, 1798
WHERE Nash Co. NC.

5 Elizabeth
MOTHER

GREAT GRANDPARENTS

8 Thomas Whitfield
FATHER
BORN
WHERE
WHEN MARRIED
DIED July 6, 1781
WHERE Nash Co. NC.

9 Mary
MOTHER

1 Matthew Whitfield
BORN about 1814
WHERE TN
WHEN MARRIED July 30, 1834 Rutherford Co., TN
DIED Eli Whitfield was witness,
WHERE Eli who his first cousin
son of Willie Whitfield

Fanny R. Monahan
NAME OF HUSBAND OR WIFE

3 Lavina Roberson
MOTHER
BORN 1773
WHERE NC
DIED
WHERE Cannon Co., TN

Willie Barker Beattie
submitted the Chart
in 1988.

Willie Beattie did research on
Whitfields in North Carolina and
Tennessee records. She found the
records of Thomas Whitfield of
Nash County, North Carolina and
records of Thomas Whitfield b.
1721 native of Virginia and d.
Nash County, NC.

This connected with records on
Whitfields of Rutherford County,
Tennessee.

Then this connected with descendants in Inzard-Stone Counties in Arkansas.
Lineage 1746 to 1992. Nansemond Co., VA to Nash Co., NC
to Tennessee and Arkansas.

376

WHITFIELD,

Bryan: b 2-19-1754 d 6-23-1817 m (1)Nancy Bryan (2)Winifred
    Bryan Capt NC
Constantine: b 3-6-1728 d *p*. 10-28-1797 m Barbara Williams Sgt
    CS NC
John: b 1743 d 1-2-1832 m Milly Grimsley Sol NC
Joseph: b 1722 d *c*. 1790-1800 m Parnel Jenne Pvt MA
Luke: b 2-9-1746 d 12-2-1796 m Rachel Powell Capt SC
Matthew: b *c*. 1717 d *p*. 1785 m — Warren PS SC
Needham: b 2-20-1758 d 4-6-1812 m (1)Lucy Hatch (2)Betsey
    Hatch (3)Sallie Watkins (4)Mrs Penelope Burk PS NC
Thomas: b 1721 d 1781 m Mary — PS NC
Wm., Sr.: b 5-20-1715 d 3-31-1795 m Rachel Bryan PS NC
Wm., Jr.: b 6-1-1743 d 3- -1817 m (1)Hester Williams (2)Sallie
    (Oliver) Hurst (3)Hepsiba Hatch (4)Sarah Hatch Cmsry NC
Wm.: b 1759 d 1806 m Elizabeth — Sol NC
Wm.: b 1- -1751 d 1833 m Mary Towler Pvt VA ★

Whitfield in The Revolutionary War Period

Name	Vol.	Page	Folio	Book of Reference.
WHITFIELD—				*Revolutionary Army Accts.*
———	4	66	2	,, ,, ,,
Ben	7	65	3	,, ,, ,,
Bryan	7	28	3	,, ,, ,,
Bryan	7	39	2	,, ,, ,,
Bryan	7	45	2	,, ,, ,,
Bryan	9	10	1	,, ,, ,,
C	6	94	2	,, ,, ,,
C	8	17	2	,, ,, ,,
Const.	7	55	1	,, ,, ,,
Hartwell	7	63	3	,, ,, ,,
Israel	1	77	2	,, ,, ,,
J	6	94	4	,, ,, ,,
Jacob	7	64	1	,, ,, ,,
James	7	64	1	,, ,, ,,
James	9	122	3	,, ,, ,,
Jesse	3	46	2	,, ,, ,,
John	9	10	4	,, ,, ,,
John	9	113	1	,, ,, ,,
John	11	49	2	,, ,, ,,
N.	9	74	2	,, ,, ,,
Needham	1	21	2	,, ,, ,,
Needham	9	69	3	,, ,, ,,
Needham	9	77	4	,, ,, ,,
Reuben	9	100	3	,, ,, ,,
W.	11	66	4	,, ,, ,,
W.	11	69	1	,, ,, ,,
William	1	33	2	,, ,, ,,
William	4	88	1	,, ,, ,,
William	4	101	1	,, ,, ,,
William	5	14	4	,, ,, ,,
William	5	15	1	,, ,, ,,
William	5	50	1	,, ,, ,,

William	7	53	3	"	"	"
William	8	63	1	"	"	"
William	8	63	2	"	"	"
William	8	64	2	"	"	"
William	8	64	3	"	"	"
William	8	65	4	"	"	"
William	8	78	1	"	"	"
William	8	89	2	"	"	"
William	10	2	2	"	"	"
William	10	9	3	"	"	"
William	11	4	3	"	"	"
William	11	4	4	"	"	"
William	11	5	3	"	"	"
William	11	6	4	"	"	"
William	11	10	4	"	"	"
William	11	18	1	"	"	"
William	11	83	3	"	"	"
William	11	84	1	"	"	"
William, Jr.	5	14	4	"	"	"
Will B.	7	68	3	"	"	"
Willis	6	30	1	"	"	"
William	EG	4	....	"	"	"
William	EG	17	....	"	"	"
William	EG	56	....	"	"	"
William, Jr.	EG	6	....	"	"	"
Jesse	28	107	....	*Book of Settlements*		
Wilson	28	106	....	"	"	"
Benjamin	K	100	....	*Accts. of Comptroller's Off.*		
Copeland	K	220	....	"	"	"
Needham	K	61	....	"	"	"
Constantine	B	219	....	"	"	"
Needham	B	227	....	"	"	"
William	B	16	....	"	"	"
		24	....	"	"	"
		41	....	"	"	"
		78	....	"	"	"
		243	....	"	"	"
William, Jr.	B	16	....	"	"	"
Wm., Capt.	B	19	....	"	"	"
Bryan	D	179	....	"	"	"
Capt.	1-6	4	....	*Public Accounts*		
William	B	243	....	*Comptroller's Off.-Kinston*		
William, Jr.	B	16	....	"	"	"
William, Capt.	B	19	....	"	"	"

Catherine E. Whitfield was the daughter of Bryan Whitfield born in North Carolina. She moved to Montgomery, Tennessee in 1793. She had grandparents of several generations with the name William Whitfield. Catherine's father Bryan Whitfield died in 1817.

"My great-grandfather, Charlton Hines Williams, was the son of Catherine E. Whitfield, wife of John T. Williams and the daughter of Bryan and Catherine Bailey Whitfield. I recently came in possession of the records of the Bryan Whitfield and Lewis Whitfield families which my great-grandfather had written and given to a member of our family 1913."
.... Submitted by Mrs. David Walshak of Gonzales, Texas on Jan. 16, 1975.

_____

Penelope Mann, daughter of Thomas Mann and his wife Elizabeth (Denton?) was born about 1752. She married John Nicholson of Nash County, N.C., son of Lemuel Nicholson, in Nov. 1770. John Nicholson (d.1799) served as a lieutenant and then as a captain in the Revolutionary War (Loosing, vol. II, p. 638). On Jan. 3, 1787, he was appointed Lt. Col. in the Edgecombe County Militia (Turner. History of Edgecombe County, p. 90).

Children:
I.   Letitia Nicholson m. Samuel Crowell.
     Children:
     1. Samuel Crowell.
     2. Asbury Crowell.
     3. Peggy Crowell m.   Wooten.
     4. Letitia Crowell m. Dr. Alexander Jelks.
II. Matilda Nicholson.
III. Timothy Mann Nicholson (d.1808) m.   Exum.
     Child:
     1. Sally Nicholson, under 21 at father's death.
IV. Penelope Nicholson m Hardy Whitfield. She died 1861.
     Children:
     1. Matilda Whitfield m.   Joyner.
     2. Eliza N. Whitfield.
     3. Mary Philips Whitfield.
V.   Mary Nicholson m. Dr. Robert Jelks (see later no. 7)
VI. Pherby Nicholson m.   Shelton.
     Child:
     1. Calvin Shelton.
VII. Elizabeth Nicholson.
VIII. Ann Nicholson.

Hardy G. Whitfield and Penelope Whitfield.

Southside Virginia Families. by John B. Boddie. Vol.2, Print 1966.

_____

November 9, 1814, Pitt County, North Carolina Constantine Whitfield and Charles Jinkins. Half tract of land, $ 1,000. Witnesses: Robert Dupree and William Adam. Constantine b. Oct.1,1788-d.Feb.17,1867 was the son of John Whitfield, and grandson of Constantine Whitfield who was born 1728 in Bertie Co.,N C and died Craven Co.NC April 1, 1798. He was married to Elizabeth Jones of Kinston, Lenoir Co., N C.

_____

EARL GRANVILLE grant to John Greenleese of Edgecombe Co., N C, June 1, 1762, a tract of 696 acres bounded by the lands of Thomas Barnes, Bunn, Edward Moore, Jacob Flowers, Rodger Allen, and John Barnes. Witness: W. Churton J. Montfort.

RICHARD ALLEN WHITFIELD , a son of Bryan Whitfield married Ellen White in 1865 . Richard was the father of John Whitfield. John was married to Frances Whitfield.
... Submitted by Frances Whitfield of High Bridge , New Jersey in August 1971. Letter was post marked Washington, N J.

JEAN WHITFIELD married John Lett November 24 , 1779, Brunswick County, Virginia.

PATTY WHITEFIELD married James Isham Lett who was born in 1747. James I. Lett was in the American Revolutionary War. He died November 20 , 1828 in Guilford , North Carolina... On the Atlas map the town is spelled Guilford, N C.
.... Submitted by Tom Lett of Girardeau, Missouri on Dec.1, 1991.

" I am another descendant of William Whitfield III through the twenty-nineth child named William Alexander who is my great-grandfather."
Submitted by Gilbert Bolles Whitfield of Tennessee Ridge, Tennessee on Oct. 13, 1989.

Constantine Whitfield born March 5, 1728 and died Oct. 28, 1797. Sgt. CS North Carolina . He married Barbara Williams.

1870 Census, Springfield township, Nash County, North Carolina. Joel H. Whitfield, age 37.

1870 Census, Pitts County, North Carolina. John Whitfield.

1810 Census, Halifax County, North Carolina. John Whitfield.

1800 Census, Halifax County, North Carolina. C. William Whitfield.

MR. JOHN STEVENS WHITFIELD

Mr. John Stevens Whitfield, age 68, of 201 West Hall Street in Wallace, died Friday night, Nov. 8, in New Hanover Regional Medical Center in Wilmington after a brief illness.

He is survived by his wife, Mrs. Carolyn Worthington Whitfield; one daughter, Mrs. Alfred (Jeri Lynn) Bridgers of Riegelwood; one son, Sgt. Thomas William Whitfield of the U.S. Army in Germany and four grandchildren.

A native of Duplin County, Mr. Whitfield was the son of the late James Vivian and Sallie Vick Stevens Whitfield. He was a veteran of World War II having served in the U.S. Army. He was a graduate of Wake Forest University and held a Juris Doctorate Degree from Valparaiso University and for the past several years had taught at Cape Fear Community College in Wilmington.

John was President of the Society Of The Whitfields 1989 and 1990. John S. died November 8, 1991.

Reuben Whitfield of Edgecombe Co., NC, sold personal property to Mathias Manning, Jr., Oct. 17, 1774, for 60 pounds. Process money a list of livestock with their marks described household and kitchen furniture, and one set of blacksmith tools. Witness: Arthur (X) Oneall and Juda (X) Hollon. Deed Box 2, p. 191. Edgecombe Co., NC.

Mrs. Mary W. Padgett wrote to author on August 16, 1988, from Rocky Mount, North Carolina. She descended from father's people who settled in White Hall, North Carolina, now called Seven Springs.

DAVID WILSON WHITFIELD, age 28, around 1990 sent a second crest on Whitfield. David lived at Mt. Olive, North Carolina. He was a graduate of Mt. Olive College. He is a descendant of William Bryan Whitfield. Mt. Olive is a small town near Goldsboro, NC.

Carleton N. Hughs of Houston, Texas, wrote to tell his wife was of Whitfield lineage of North Carolina. Luke Whitfield served in South Carolina Militia in Revolution. Luke born 1748 and died 1832. Benjamin Whitfield moved to Georgia.
....Submitted letter October 24, 1979.

PHILIP WHITFIELD was born 1818 in Nash County, North Carolina. "His father was supposed to have been WYATT WHITFIELD." Wyatt moved to Alabama and living there in 1838, and he was in Texas in 1847. Philip Whitfield was the great-grandfather of Mary E. Hopkins who was living in 1966 in Texas."
....Submitted by Mary E. Hopkins (Mrs. James G. Hopkins) of Garwood, Texas, who resided here in June 2, 1966.

ANN WHITFIELD appears in a deed, Person County, North Carolina.

MARTIN W. CLAYTON, born October 1808 and died December 10, 1882, at Roxboro of Person County, North Carolina. Martin had married Nancy Hudgins who was born 20 / 11 day / 1813 and died 1/8/1898 at Roxboro, Person County, North Carolina. Martin and Nancy had ten children. The seventh child was Lucy Ann Clayton, born 1845, who married George Whitfield.
....Letter sent by Mrs. E.J. Andersen of Humboldt, Iowa, on March 29, 1967, to V.J. Whitfield.

"JOhN WHITFIELD born 1743 and died 1832. John Whitfield and his wife Mildred Grimsley of Granville County, North Carolina, were my great-great-grandparents through their daughter Nancy Whitfield who married Joseph Booth (e). John had a will and it is on a micro-film record in Raleigh, North Carolina."
....Submitted by Alice H. Short (Mrs. J.Q. Short) of Gonzales, Texas, on November 3, 1971.

Craven Precinct existed in North Carolina. Craven County came after county boundaries were set on map. In 1700's there were Prince Frederick Parish and St. Stephen Parish and Price George's Parish. Most of the Craven land was annexed to Pitt County, North Carolina, in 1787. That was the upper northern part. Dobbs County annexed the lower part of Craven County. The name Dobbs was later abolished for a new county name.

NORTH CAROLINA RECORDS AND LETTERS

"I have a great-great-great-great-aunt, Lydia Crisp, who married a Whitfield. I found her name in my great-great-great-great-grandfather's will of 1789 - William Mansel Crisp of Martin County, North Carolina. My crisp ancestors went to Tennessee, then returned to western North Carolina."

"The Crisps and Whitfields came from Groton, Connecticut, area. My Lydia Crisp Whitfield's second husband was a Mr. Baden. Lydia's sisters married into these families: Wilkinson, Ross, Edmondson, Prescott, Little, Gibbs, Whitley, and Bullock."
"William Mansel Crisp was married twice and had 18 children."
....Submitted by Ruth Phillip of Missoula, Montana, on March 31, 1971 (Mrs. M.F. Phillip).

"I am a granddaughter of WILLIAM A. WHITFIELD and Charity Jones who are on the marriage records of North Carolina. They left North Carolina and resided at Bay St. Louis, Mississippi, for years and where Charity Jones Whitfield died. William A. Whitfield died in Mexico years later and is buried in Monterrey, Mexico."
....Submitted by Rosabelle F. Whitfield of Lafayette, Louisiana, on July 16, 1990.

"My father was THOMAS ALLEN WHITFIELD, Jr., who married Virginia Pope of Halifax County, North Carolina....I know another descendant of Whitfield, Mrs. Martha Holloman, who manages the Halifax County Library, Granville Street, Halifax, North Carolina, in 1988."
....Submitted by Mrs. Mary W. Padgett of Rocky Mountain, NC, on September 7, 1988.

"I am a grandson of WILLIAM HAYWOOD WHITFIELD who was born in North Carolina in 1852 and moved with his family that same year to Dime Box, Burleson County, Texas. I recently visited the Grainswood mansion at Demopolis, Alabama. B.W. Whitfield of Brookside, Kentucky, whom I Wrote to suggested that I contact you about Whitfield Books. Signed, Herschel Whitfield."
....Submitted by Herschel Whitfield of San Angelo, Texas, on October 24, 1990.

"I found your name Vallie Jo Whitfield and address in the family registry card file at the Georgia State Archives. I have traced my Whitfield line back to Robert and Edith (Jones) Whitfield who were on the Pitt County, North Carolina, census in 1800. Their marriage bond is dated 1791. They had moved to Washington County, Georgia, by 1802. They were married September 30, 1791."
....Submitted by Mrs. Lynda Jernigan of Snellville, Georgia, on March 9, 1989.

Society of Whitfields is a non-profit organization founded in 1961 in North Carolina by J. Vivian Whitfield. The Society has an annual Whitfield reunion held in Seven Springs, NC. This meeting is held during the weekend of the Columbus Day holiday in October of each year and meets at the Spring Creek School, three miles west of Seven Springs, NC, at the intersection of North Carolina Highway 111 and the old Mount Olive Seven Spring Road. Three hundred members pay membership fee annually of $10.

The Society was formed as a tribute to William Whitfield II (b. 1715, NC-d. 1795, NC) and his wife (1) Rachel Bryan to whom he married November 6, 1741, at Snowfield, NC. In 1745 they moved to White Hall later Seven Springs, Wayne County, NC, and lived there.

North Carolina. Several early Whitfield families settled in Wayne County, NC. The first settlements of white people were in 1738 and slowly progressed until 1750. In 1989 about 6,000 people lived in the County.

Wayne, Wayne County, NC, is 36 miles long and 28 miles wide. The land is level. Neuse River runs there. The County land is a watered area and there are three bridges across Little River.

ALDINE H. WHITFIELD, born between Mt. Olive and Seven Springs in North Carolina. He at age 66 in March, 1981. He married Eunice Waller, and they had four sons and one daughter.
1. Ril Whitfield. Worked for Construction Company.
2. Doyle Whitfield. Teacher and coach, Southern Wayne High School.
3. Aldine Whitfield, II. Tobacco Auctioneer.
4. Olivia Whitfield. Librarian at the High School in Wilmington, NC.
5. Roy Whitfield. Teacher and coach, Spring Creek Junior High School near Seven Springs, NC.

Number One

WHITFIELD, N. Papers 1874-1905. Sixty-five items. In North Carolina State Department of Archives of History Collections. Resident of Lenoir County, North Carolina. Correspondence, Memorandum book (1881-1904), Reports, Resolutions, Certificates, Newspapers, Printed matter and other papers dealing with the Grange and Farmer's Alliance movement in North Carolina, particularly on a local or county level.

WHITFIELD, N. (B). Papers 1874-1905. Patrons of Husbandry, Farmers State Alliance of North Carolina, Knights of Honor of the Supreme, Grand and Subordinate Lodges, Civil Subdivision of County, State or territory of the Southern Cotton Association, Correspondents include Alexander Q. Halladay, first President of North Carolina College of Agriculture, and Mechanic Arts, and U.S. Senator Zebulon Vance of North Carolina....Gift of Mrs. Nattie Lou Whitfield, 1955.

And Number Two

WHITFIELD FAMILY. Papers 1803-1918. One hundred fifty-eight items. In University of North Carolina Library, Southern Historical Collection (1257).
Correspondence, Deeds, Accounts, Estate papers, students notebooks of four generations of the Whitfield and Wooten families in Wayne and Lenoir Counties, North Carolina. Includes letters from branches of the family in Alabama, Mississippi, and Florida. Names represented include Nathan Bryan Whitfield (1835-1914), his wife, Elizabeth Green (Cobb) Whitfield, his parents Sarah Elizabeth (Wooten) and James Bryan Whitfield (1809-1841). Unpublished description in the library. Gift of Junie and Hattie Whitfield, 1947.

1830 Census Martin County, North Carolina
  Obedish Carson. One male age range 15 to 20 (born 1810-1825).
  Albena, wife. One female 20 to 30. She was born in Pitt Co.
  Jane Carson. One female under 5 (born 1829 or 1830).

North Carolina Marriage Records

1762 to 1800 — County

WHITFIELD, ANN	=	SMETHWICK, LANIER	MD	30 APR 1800	BERTIE	NC
WHITFIELD, BARBARA	=	TOOLEY, WILLIAM	MD	29 APR 1789	CRAVEN	NC
WHITFIELD, BENJAMIN	=	AVIS, ELIZABETH	MD	13 FEB 1777	BERTIE	NC
WHITFIELD, FEREBE	=	PERSELL, JAS.	MD	20 AUG 1793	CRAVEN	NC
WHITFIELD, JAMES	=	MINSHEW, SUSANNAH	MD	02 DEC 1798	PERSON	NC
WHITFIELD, JAMES	=	BRYAN, RACHEL	MD	17 NOV 1795	CRAVEN	NC
WHITFIELD, JOSEPH	=	GRADDY, MARY	MD	01 MAY 1790	DUPLIN	NC
WHITFIELD, LUKE	=	SLADE, SALLY	MD	04 NOV 1796	CRAVEN	NC
WHITFIELD, LUKE	=	FONVEILLE, TERESIA	MD	20 JAN 1789	CRAVEN	NC
WHITFIELD, MARTHA	=	GLESSON, ISAAC	MD	03 JUN 1762	TYRRELL	NC
WHITFIELD, MARTHA P.	=	MILBURN, HENRY C.	MD	26 JUL 1796	BERTIE	NC
WHITFIELD, MARY	=	HESTER, JOHN	MD	29 DEC 1796	GRANVILLE	NC
WHITFIELD, MILLY	=	ALLISON, JAMES	MD	06 SEP 1800	GRANVILLE	NC
WHITFIELD, POLLEY	=	RIMMER, JOHN	MD	21 JUN 1800	ORANGE	NC
WHITFIELD, ROBERT	=	JONES, EDITH	MD	30 SEP 1791	GATES	NC
WHITFIELD, WILLIAM M.	=	BAKER, MARY	MD	28 SEP 1785	DUPLIN	NC

NORTH CAROLINA

T.N. Union Catalog for Manuscript Collections. 1963-1964
    Published by the Library of Congress.
Whitfield, Elizabeth Green (Cobb),64-668. In University of North
    Carolina Library (158 items).
Whitfield, F.E., 64-1112. In University of North Carolina Library.
    He is of Corinth, Mississippi, and an Inventor of making
    Yarn.
    The following in the University of North Carolina:
Whitfield, James Bryan, 1809-1841--64-668.
Whitfield, Nathan Bryan, 1835-1914--64-668.
Whitfield, Robert P., 64-100. Correspondence, University of
    Chicago, IL.
Whitfield, Sarah Elizabeth (Wooten), 64-668.
Whitfield Family, 64-668.
Genealogy, 64-1188 of Joseph Buckner Killebrew - 1831-1906.

Exum Philip Whitfield, born in 1818 in Nash County, North
Carolina. His father was supposed to have been Wyatt Whitfield.
He was born in Alabama in 1838, and he was in Texas in 1847.

Ann Whitfield, Reg. of Deeds, Person County, Roxboro, North
Carolina.

Martin W. Clayton, born 10/1808, d. 12/10/1882 Roxboro of Person
County, North Carolina. He married Nancy Hudgins, b. 20/11/1813,
d. 1/8/1898 Roxboro, Person County, North Carolina. They had ten
children, and one child (7th) Lucy Ann Clayton, b. 1845 married
George Whitfield.

Addresses and tele-
phone numbers.

Inclusive of White
and black race.

Whitfield Carr B 1118 Easton-----274-5190
Whitfield Christine Miss
                308 B Cumberland St-275-8969
Whitfield Dale R 5307 Gulda Dr---292-8169
Whitfield E W 412 Crestland Av--272-2989
Whitfield Edward 709 Park Av----274-5697
Whitfield Fred W Hickory Tree Ln--697-8006
Whitfield Horace Church Ext------288-3120
Whitfield Howard G 4027 Hewitt--299-0241
Whitfield J A 1905 Trogdon St----292-6932
Whitfield J F 3 Yester Oaks Cir---288-7648
Whitfield Jeri L atty
                101 W Friendly Av-378-1450
Whitfield Julia D
                829 W Bessemer Av-274-3553
Whitfield Margaret D
                1501 Marion St-272-5216
Whitfield Margaret J
                305 Melbourne Rd-373-8241
Whitfield N 209 Woodlwn--------273-5939
Whitfield S 1124 Westridge Rd-299-4198
Whitfield T P Mrs
                207 E Bessmr Av--274-1746
Whitfield Toussaint P 1112 Logan--275-2851
Whitfield Viola 115 N Luther St---274-0793
Whitfield Walter L
                2440H S Holden Rd-292-3166

Inclusive of white
and black race.

Whitfield A 4619PerthCt ------------568-6088
Whitfield Eddie R 340BradfordDr -------399-6441
Whitfield Grace ofc 5415SouthBlvd------523-1220
Whitfield Henry D 100MatadorLn ------527-2850
Whitfield James E 415NMyersSt -------333-5207
Whitfield L Gale 2636WeddingtonAv ---333-1063
Whitfield Larry A 517RoyalCt ---------372-5624
Whitfield Lee S 3607ColonyRd -------364-3817
Whitfield Owen H CPA
    6525MorrisonBlvd ----------------366-9672
    Res 2523RedFoxTrail ------------366-6103
Whitfield Owen H Jr 524HawthorneLn ---376-6181
Whitfield P W 1624EastwayDr --------536-7816
Whitfield Paul L PA atty 1500E4thSt----372-8322
    Res 6028BentwayDr -------------542-3184
Whitfield R L 1154WendoverRd --------364-5885
Whitfield Sam 2441SedleyRd ----------364-0958
Whitfield Sam 5415SouthBlvd --------523-1220
Whitfield Wilhelmina 1009W6th ------

Addresses and tele-
phone numbers.

Inclusive of white
and black race.

All names have post
office zip 27530.

WHITFIELD

Whitfield Al 608 Gloucester----------------734-8038
Whitfield Albert Central Hts--------------778-1237
Whitfield Anna 506 Hinson----------------735-2672
Whitfield Annie 508 Hinson St-----------736-0512
Whitfield Annie Frances 617 Sherrard Ct-----734-5868
Whitfield Arnie Rt 5--------------------734-2060
Whitfield Arthur 800 S Slocumb----------734-3058
Whitfield B R Jr 1209 S Andrews Av---------735-2493
Whitfield Barbara Jean 717 Bryant St--------736-7156
Whitfield Bettie Mrs Rt 4----------------734-7969
Whitfield Billy 121 Seymour Johnson Homes--734-2052
Whitfield Carla 1505 Green Acre Ct--------736-7830
Whitfield Charley Sr 411 Hollowell Av-------735-2776
Whitfield Clara Hillcrest Trailer Pk--------736-4049
Whitfield Claude L PE 600 Oak Forest Rd-----778-4374
Whitfield D J 205 Alpha Ct---------------735-7028
Whitfield Davis 1926 Carolina Cir----------734-9485
Whitfield Denise 121 Seymour Johnson Homes-734-2052
Whitfield Ed Russell Rt 1----------------735-9697
Whitfield Effie B Mrs 1905-B E Maple------735-1567
Whitfield Elizabeth 411 S Herman---------735-8574
Whitfield Ella 338 Alabama Av-----------734-7617
Whitfield Elveta Mrs 903 E Pine----------734-0703
Whitfield Enterprises Equipment Yard contr
                203 Robin Lake Rd-735-8952
Whitfield Evelyn 900 National Dr---------778-1656
Whitfield Faye W 116 Erick Dr-----------731-2714
Whitfield G T Rev 513 Gulley------------735-1103
Whitfield Geo 614 S Herman-------------735-1592
Whitfield Henry 704 Isler St-------------734-0336
Whitfield Jas 506 Hinson----------------735-2672
Whitfield Jas Mt Olive Hwy-------------734-7702
Whitfield Janice A Rt 8-----------------734-4504
Whitfield Johnnie Mt Olive Hwy----------734-7702
Whitfield Johnny 619 Isler St------------735-7424
Whitfield K C 108 N Slocumb St----------736-2139
Whitfield Kathryn H Rt 2----------------736-2985
Whitfield Kyle 116 Erick Dr-------------731-2714
Whitfield Leon 411 S Herman-----------735-8574
Whitfield Mary 1904 A E Edgerton---------735-3627
Whitfield Mary 411 Hollowell Av----------735-2776
Whitfield Mary Jane 506 Rollingwood Dr----735-7741
Whitfield Mattie 704 Isler St------------734-0336
Whitfield Morris Rt 1------------------734-3140
Whitfield Nancy 619 Isler St------------735-7424
Whitfield Narcissus 915-A Carvr Dr--------735-3004
Whitfield Paul Mt Olive Hwy-------------734-4756
Whitfield Pearlie Mae 717 Bryant St-------736-7156
Whitfield Rex S 203 Robin Lake Dr--------736-1033
Whitfield Robt 409 S Herman------------735-1332
Whitfield Ronald Rt 3------------------736-4599
Whitfield Ruby Rt 1-------------------734-3140
Whitfield S 412 E Beech St-------------735-8152
Whitfield Shirley Rt 5-----------------734-2060
Whitfield Teresa Rt 3-----------------658-3879
Whitfield Ural L 1908 Elton Dr----------735-1349
Whitfield Victor 307 Hollowell St--------735-6743

PITT COUNTY, NORTH CAROLINA, AND GEORGIA

ALEXANDER WHITFIELD b. 1770 is on the 1790 census of Pitt Co., NC, with one male over 16 years of age, one male under 16, and two females.

Alexander Whitfield and family moved to Georgia before 1820. There is a 1810 Tax List - Jefferson County, GA, Cobb District. Alexander Whitfield and family are on the 1820 census of Georgia. He is age range 50 to 60 years. One female age range 40 to 50. One female 10 to 25.

A family Bible record has children:

1. James E. Whitfield
   b. 2/27/1790
2. Thomas Whitfield
   b. ca. 1805
3. Robert Whitfield
   b. ca. 1808
4. Ivey E. Whitfield
   b. ca. 1810

Letter E. is for Eley.

WILLIAM WHITFIELD is on 1775 census of Pitt Co., NC. He was born about 1750. On census he was with one male over 16. One male under 16. One female over 16. Two females under 16.

Wife had the name of Jemima Whitfield. In 1796 William Whitfield was a tailor. 1797 was the last date of his in Pitt County, NC.

William Whitfield, Jr. b. ca. 1760. In 1786 William Whitfield, Jr., had a land grant. In 1787 William was a school teacher. In 1801 William was a farmer.

The two named William Whitfield, father and son, moved to Washington County, Georgia.

On the Washington County, GA, census of 1820 Jemima Whitfield was the widow of William Whitfield, Sr. On the 1820 same census her son, William Whitfield was living in Washington County, GA.

ROBERT WHITFIELD was on the 1800 census of Pitt County, NC. He was of age range 26 to 45 years. His wife was of the same age range. They had two males under 10. One male 16 to 26 age range. One female under 10. One female 16 to 26 age range.

Robert Whitfield sold ten acres to Paul Herrington. Witness was William Brsome. Land description conveys it being a part of a land patent granted to William Whitfield to have and to hold, and transfer of land to Robert Whitfield.

On the 1820 census of Washington Co., NC, Robert Whitfield appeared on the census. Reuben Whitfield was in the same county. Bryan Whitfield was in Burke County, GA.

North Carolina Record. William (Whitfield) Whitefield of Goochland County, Virginia, had a descendant named Albert Pinckey Whitefield born Dec. 12, 1848, in Caswell County, NC, and he died Sept. 24, 1914.

386

RECORDS
PITT COUNTY, NORTH CAROLINA

Joel Whitfield (1750-1783) and Lydia had the son Benjamin Whitfield born ca. 1780 who died 1840. Benjamin Whitfield married (1) Susanna Wilinson born October 16, 1787. She died when a young woman. Benjamin married (2) Clary Cherry, the widow of Samuel Cherry. Benjamin Whitfield married (3) Temperance Manning. She lived twenty-six years after his death and had her children living near her. Elizabeth Whitfield married and with one child was a widow. She married (2) J.O. Nelson. The younger daughter, Artemisia Whitfield was unmarried. The son, Jesse Thomas Whitfield, was born 1829 and died October 25, 1857. Jesse married in 1853.

Patience (Mary Ann) House born 1836; later married Matthews Manning. Patience had a sister named Adaline House who was born 1840, and she later married Wallace Edmondson.

Marriages

George Ben Whitfield born February 4, 1855, and died October 9, 1909. George married July 30, 1945. Georgianna Whitehurst born July 27, 1884, and died April 7, 1966.

Grantors and Grantees

Joel Whitfield bought 200 acres in Bethel from John Brown July 3, 1779...Benjamin Whitfield sold 200 acres to Charlie Whitehurst December 19, 1807....Benjamin Whitfield bought 215 acres from Thomas Ross February 12, 1825....Benjamin Whitfield, Jr., and his brother Joel Whitfield sold 215 acres to Silas Wilkinson on April 3, 1828.

Variances in the use of birth, death, or dates on this family can be found. Refer to the information in the Mississippi section of book for names that are the same family.
....Information submitted by Louise Whitfield Trytko of Merritt Island, Florida, on March 28, 1996.

The children of Benjamin Whitfield moved to Tennessee; Joel, Benjamin, Jr., and Albena. Joel and brother Benjamin, Jr., moved to Mississippi. Albena was a widow and married (2) Obediah Carson in 1829. She was widow of William Nelson whom she married in 1822. No issue. Albena and Obediah Carson made a home in Haywood County, Tennessee. They died there. Refer to the Tennessee chapter herein book for the censuses and names of the Carson children.

Albena Whitfield nelson Carson was born in Pitt County, NC. There she lived with William Nelson. When she married Obediah Carson, they made their home in Martin County and ten years later were in Haywood County, Tennessee.

Albena Carson was older than Obediah.

North Carolina Record. Onslow County, NC. Will of Thomas Johnston Aug. 31, 1751, Court April 1752. Wife Ann. Sons: Thomas, Benjamin, John. Daughters: Sarah Powell and Ann Whitfield. Granddaughters: Mary, Ann, and Priscilla Keel. Ann was wife of Luke Whitfield on Onslow County, NC.

Pitt County was formed from Beaufort as early as 1760, and named in compliment to William Pitt, Earl of Chatham, who was a distinguished and devoted friend to America in the English Parliament.

In the beginning this small parcel of land annexed land from Edgecombe and Martin, Beaufort and Craven on the south. It was in 1787 that the northern part of Craven County, North Carolina, was annexed to Pitt County. The Craven land grant was a long north to south strip of narrow land.

Craven County, NC, Marriage Bonds have the following: Luke Whitfield and Teresia in 1789. Then Luke Whitfield and Sally. John Whitfield and Mary in 1827. William Whitfield and Lana in 1845. There were two colored people with bond in 1865.

Some of the early land grant areas and first county formations are extinct and do not appear on later maps.

Forty Years of Searches and Speculating on the Parentage of William Whitfield

The beginning of Whitfield in England has been the work of C.V. Whitfield of Middlesex, England. Mr. Whitfield was, in 1931, the head of the Senior Northumberland Line in England.

The beginning story has David I, King of Scotland, married first wife Maud (also Matilda). She was heiress of the Earl Waltheof, Sr., Earl of Northumberland, England. David and Maud's son married Countess Ada. It was the Countess Ada who gave her chaplain, Robert Whitfield, the land of "Witefield," the western part of Northumberland, some 12,157 acres. The years were 1124-1153.

Another early branch existed of Whitfield and descended from the holders of the living of the church at Whitfield. The difficulty is the greater by reason of the presence of two branches of the family living in the presence one of the other.

The district of the king has its Court, 1279. There are the Whitfield records with varied spellings of old Anglo Saxon language. The Great Charter of Inspectimus granted by Edward I, 1280 circa to the Prior and Convent of Hexham mentions a Whitfield and his holdings.

In an Inspectimus of Charter is a granting of lands at Alston (Cumberland) to the Prior and Convent of Hexham there are found the signature of Roberto persona de Whitefield, and Johanne de Whitefield. One hundred fifty years later the name Whitefield is found. There were very few using the name Whitefield. The Manors of Whitfields existed and a Manor of Whitefield.

Charts compiled by Ralph C.V. Whitfield, Esquire, of Red Car, York, and Middlesex, England, show a repetition of the names of William, Matthew, and Thomas. C.V. Whitfield of England could not find any connection of the immigrants to America as being of the Senior Line.

To further the story in the year 1600 there were three branches: the senior branch remained at Whitfield. The second branch settled in Durham, and the third at Wadhurst, County Sussex. Whatever family branch or lines there were, many named Whitfield in southern part of England.

Society of the Genealogists has four Whitfield lineages of about 150 pages per families line on Whitfield houses of influence in England.

In southern England at Bristol seaport, the Whitfield emigrants in 1600s depart for the America colonies. They came from many shires of England. There have been work and studies by a few persons to find a link to establish the relationship between ancestral lines in America and England but the efforts lack success.

Emma Morehead Whitfield (1874 NC-1932 VA) gathered materials on Whitfield from many people for 12 years, 1920 to 1932. In this material were sources on England on early Whitfield and descendants. She compiled this material and her nephew, Theodore Marshall Whitfield, continued the work. He edited the manuscript, carried on correspondences, and published the book Whitfield, Bryan, Smith, and Related Families in 1949.

Theodore Whitfield had a preference for their progenitor of William Whitfield to be Matthew Whitfield of England. Theodore (1905 VA - 1991 MD) and wife Elizabeth Denny Dixon Whitfield resided at Westminster, Maryland.

Bryan W. Whitfield, Jr., of Brookside, Harlan County, Kentucky, produced an artistic chart with pedigree of the Senior Line of England and added Matthew Whitfield and William Whitfield of North Carolina. The Chart on Whitfield is of size 81 inches wide and 29 inches in height. It is an impressive pedigree in the enlargement size. It is a private chart. Date of January 17, 1955.

In 1963 Vallie Jo Fox Whitfield researched at the Tennessee State Library and Archives in Nashville, Davidson County, Tennessee. The Librarian presented a Library vertical file with the following information: "William Whitfield, Sr., was born in England 1688; died 1770. He came from England in his own ship, The Providence, in early part of the 18th century and settled at Nansemonie, Virginia. Later in Lenoir County, NC, he was married to Elizabeth Goodman (1697-1773) of Gates County, North Carolina, in 1713." She published this record of the book Whitfield History and Genealogy of Tennessee in 1964, first edition.

In 1975 on October 6, B.W. Whitfield, Jr., does another chart with Sr. Thomas Smith, first Governor of East India Company. A John Smith married a Elizabeth Whitfield and the connecting marriages are on the chart. This chart includes William Whitfield married 1713 to Elizabeth Goodman. The chart includes surnames Bryan and Whitfield and others. This chart includes Sir Thomas Whitfield 15th generation from Robert the Chaplain (1154). This chart was published in a booklet on the Gaineswood Mansion of Demopolis, Alabama.

Retracing on researched work there was reviewed 11 men named Matthew Whitfield of England. There was reviewed 13 men named Matthew Whitfield in the English colonies. The search narrowed to four men. However, the fact existed that identification of an immigrant on a ship record, land records, court records, and other records examined could not be determined if records were of one man and were the same. Thus people and editors made a final determination on William Whitfield who married Elizabeth Goodman.

Continued on Page 391

LAND PROPERTIES

JOSEPH WHITFIELD, Pitt County, NC. Pitt County was formed in 1760. In 1762 JOSEPH WHITFIELD was listed as a tax payer.

B-85. Nov. 24, 1761. WALTER BRYANT to JESSE JOLLY 210 acres; f30. Witness Joseph Whitfield.

B-303. Nov. 4, 1762. JOSEPH WHITFIELD to JOHN BARNHILL in 1761, 150 acres; f35. Adjoining ROBERT KNOX, former owner was JESSE JOLLY.

B-349. EARL GRANVILLE to JOSEPH WHITFIELD (BEAL) 100 acres, 10 shillings.

C-294. Feb. 15, 1765. ARTHUR OLDS (on SW) to JOSEPH WHITFIELD 100 acres. Former owner WALTER BRYANT, PATENT 1759.

E-250. Oct. 1772. JOSEPH WHITFIELD to JESSE JOLLY, 35 acres, f7. Former owner, ARTHUR OLDS, witness EDMUN ANDREWS.

JESSE JOLLY bought land from both JOEL WHITFIELD and JOSEPH WHITFIELD. Who could have been relatives. Like a father and son.

South Carolina early marriages 1700's were compiled at Charles Town, SC, by a militia man named Colonel Issac Hayne who kept records of the marriages.

Jerry Whitfield lived 1995 in Anderson City, Anderson County, South Carolina. Jerry had ancestor Peatr Mathon Whitfield born April 10, 1838, who died October 7, 1915. Jerry Whitfield collected on surname Whitfield of South Carolina.

National Society Daughters of the American Revolution has forty-eight applications in reference to Luke Whitfield born February 9, 1719, and died December 2, 1796. Letter to Vallie Jo Whitfield from D.A.R. Registrar General's Office, Washington, DC, on August 22, 1997.

Vallie Jo Whitfield concluded this is a range of age inclusive of two men named Luke Whitfield who were father and son. Luke, Sr., father, died Sept. 1767. Luke Whitfield, son, born about 1746 NC and died 1796 in SC. Perhaps the research done so far has not been extensive enough in getting documents on the two men. Extensive lacking in thoroughly factual records. D.A.R. published Luke Whitfield married Rachael Powell in 1740. This cannot be verified by colonial records.

This information was printed: "William Whitfield (1688-1770) came in his own ship The Providence." He was from Lancaster, England. Hobbies Magazine had print with the same information in February, 1968.

Frederick Adams Virkus was an editor. The abridged edition Compendium of American Genealogy. A genealogical encyclopedia of the United States. Edited by Frederick A. Virkus under direction of Albert Nelson Marquis. Volumes 4-7. Baltimore, Maryland, Genealogical Publishing Company, 1968.

Wills of Nash County, North Carolina, 1778-1868
Abstracts of Will Book One, by Ruth Smith Williams and Margarette Glenn Griffin. Published by Joseph W. Watson.

> WHITFIELD, PENELOPE
> P. 576. Oct. 20, 1858 - Nov. Ct. 1861. Mother:
> PENELOPE NICHOLSON. Daus: 1. MARY J. WHITFIELD,
> 2. MATILDA JOYNER, 3. ELIZA WHITFIELD. Gr. dau: MARTHA
> FRANCES JOYNER. Ex: REDMUN BUNN. Wit: JAMES F. ODUM,
> ELIAS BUN. Codicil, April 5, 1859, wit. by: JAMES F. ODUM,
> EDWIN EDWARDS.

> WHITFIELD, SARAH
> P. 413. Dec. 16, 1835 - Aug. Ct. 1836. Sis:
> MARY WHITFIELD, CHARITY WHITFIELD. Niece: TEMPERANCE
> MELTON. Ex: JOHN RICKS. Wit: RICHARD RICKS, DREWSEY DORTCH.

JOHN M. WINSTEAD came from Northumberland Co., Virginia, in 1799 to Williamson County, TN. John was a Colonel in the military service. John, wife, and three girls and nine boys moved in a log cabin for their first house. In 1858 they had a mansion built and moved into the house.

WELDON JASPER WHITFIELD was born February 10, 1862, and his wife, Elizabeth Mitchell Whitfield was born September 16, 1863. They had the son ROBERT ASBURN WHITFIELD who was born January 12, 1866. Robert married Jessie Overton who was born October 26, 1901, and their home place was Roxboro, NC. They had sons named James Thomas Whitfield and Hugh Thomas Whitfield.

James Thomas Whitfield married Evelyn Gooch. Hugh T. Whitfield was born March 29, 1968, and was raised in Butner, NC. In 1994, Hugh Whitfield resided in Linwood, NC.

WENDE GAIL WHITFIELD was born July 10, 1967, and raised in Spring Hope, NC. She was a registered nurse in 1994. Wende's parents are CARL EDWARD WHITFIELD, Jr., and Myrtle Ruth Harris Whitfield. Carl Edward Whitfield, Sr., was the son of James Haywood Whitfield and Nettie Briley Whitfield. James H. Whitfield was the son of Robert Lue Whitfield and Annie Whitfield.

NORTH DAKOTA

Indian country. No Whitfield there. In 1980 one Whitfield family lived in North Dakota.

North Dakota admission to the States was November 2, 1880. The land was admitted as a new state of North Dakota in 1889. Area was a part of northwest territory. 70,837 area square miles. Population in 1930 was 680,845. Bismark is the Capital.

In 1804 an expedition of thirty-five men spent the winter in North Dakota.

OHIO

The Whitfields' migration to Ohio is different from the flow of people moving in the southeast of the United States. Some of these Whitfield people are going west from northeastern states. Some of the people are immigrants to seaport of New York, Pennsylvania, and other northeastern seaports. Some are descendants of the northeastern settlers of New York, Pennsylvania and other states.

There is not found Whitfield crossing the Ohio River to go north from Kentucky. State census have birthplaces of the individuals listed on censuses, and this is a good source for finding the birthplace of a person. The number of Whitfields is small compared to the settlers in the southern colonial states.

James Whitfield is the first name found on 1820 census, and he and the family lived in Montgomery County, Ohio. James Whitfield's children would be on later Ohio censuses. James Whitfield I had a son named James Whitfield on the 1830 census in the same county.

In 1830 Sharper Whitfield and family lived in Lexington township in Stark County, Ohio. In 1830 Widow Whitfield lived in Columbiana County, Ohio. The state census will tell if this is a male name or a widow of a husband who has died. The state census has age of female and male. The 1850 census list for the first time the names of each family member. The census of 1790 lists only male names and those with families. The census of 1800, 1810, 1820, 1830, 1840 years list the male or widow who is head of the family. Census gives a count of males and females in the household by age ranges. Counting of people in each dwelling takes place. A record is made of the population in a district in a county of each state.

In 1840 in Ohio state lived Sharack Whitfield in Barlow township in Washington County, Ohio. In 1840 in Ohio Sharper Whitfield or his son of the same name was living in Laney township, Logan County, Ohio.

In 1850 the descendants of the first settlers named Whitfield and new immigrants to the state appear on the census of Ohio. The family groups are on Ohio 1850 censuses. The heads of families are the following Whitfields in Ohio for 1850:

Sampson Whitfield lived in Erie County, OH.
Eliza Whitfield lived in Summit County, OH, Talmadge Twp.
Elizabeth Whitfield lived in Knox County, OH, Danville Twp.
Ellen Whitfield lived in Lake County, OH, Painesville Twp.
Essex Whitfield lied in Clermont County, OH, Ohio Twp.
Fanny Whitfield lived in Logan County, OH, Monroe Twp.
John Whitfield lived in Lucas County, OH.
Joseph Whitfield lived in Lorain County, OH.
Leonard Whitfield lived in Logan County, OH.
Shadrack Whitfield lived in Washington County, OH.

North Carolina. Thomas Whitefield was witness to Will of Edward Litchfield on Sept. 12, 1768, Sept. 1769. Wife, Mary. Sons: Abraham, Jacob. My six children. Will book, Currituck County, NC.

1850 Ohio Census.
    Thomas Whitfield, Hamilton County, OH.
    W. Whitfield lived in Seneca County, OH.
    W. L. Whitfield lived in Preble County, OH.

LETTERS AND NOTES

"I am searching for any descendants of Wilson L. Whitfield who was born 1822 in Ohio. He married Jane Kuhn in Preble County, OH, on November 6, 1842. In 1850 they had the following children living in their home:

    1. Emily Whitfield age 7 born in Ohio.
    2. Julia A. Whitfield age 5 born in Ohio.
    3. Sarah E. Whitfield age 2 born in Ohio
    4. Candies Kuhn Whitfield age 12 born in Ohio.

Wilson Whitfield's occupation was listed as wagon maker. They lived in Eaton, Ohio.

Wilson, along with Jane's brother, John Wilson Kuhn, was the administrator of Jane's father's estate. Her father, Christian Kuhn, died in Preble County, Ohio in 1851. In July of 1852 Wilson and Jane receipted for her share of her father's estate.

Jane Kuhn Whitfield was a sister to my great-great-grandfather, J. Wilson Kuhn, who died in Preble County, Ohio, in 1854.

I have an ancestor chart for my grandfather, John Franklin Kuhn, Jr." Signed - Jo Ann Johnson.
....Submitted by D. Jo Ann Johnson of Loretto, Michigan, on February 22, 1990.

OKLAHOMA

The state of Oklahoma was Indian country for a very long time. Land at Oklahoma was set aside as an Indian Reservation. David Becton Porter-Whitfield made his residence there. Later his brother, Coleman Porter-Whitfield, made his residence there. Both men died there and had family members living there. These brothers were grandsons of John George Whitfield and Kizziah Rutledge Whitfield of Cannon Col, Tennessee.

A descendant named Madeline Whitfield made her home in McAlester, OK, and was living there in 1989. Madeline for a long time searched for her family tree and did a lineage with blood kinships.

James E. Whitfield lived in Ponca City, OK, in 1990. He kindly submitted his family groups on August 15, 1990. He was descendant of Matthew Whitfield and Levina Whitfield of Nash Co., NC.

The following ancestral family groups were done by him. His groups show a family member in Missouri, Massachusetts, Kansas, Arkansas. James E. Whitfield wrote my "great-great-grandfather was Matthew Whitfield. My great-grandfather was William Whitfield born in North Carolina. Grandfather was Jasper Newton in Mountain View, Arkansas. His father was John Franklin born in Bartlett, Texas."

OKLAHOMA FAMILY GROUP

JOHN FRANKLIN WHITFIELD born February 19, 1893, at Bartlett, Bell County, TX, the son of Jasper Newton Whitfield and Flora Jane Hinkle. John Franklin Whitfield married Mary Catherine Callahan on July 20, 1920, Hominy town, Osage County, OK. Mary Callahan was born October 7, 1902, at Pawhuska, Osage County, OK, the daughter of William Callahan and Minnie Bridges. John died May 18, 1966. John F. and Mary Whitfield had six children and four were born in Oklahoma and two in Arkansas.

1. John Franklin Whitfield, Jr., b. Dec. 24, 1921, at Hominy, Osage Co., OK. John married Ruth Talley and they had children Sarah Whitfield and Eliz Whitfield.
2. William Andrew Whitfield b. Nov. 6, 1923, at Hominy, Osage Co., OK. William married Angela Forte on March 29, 1954, Maryland, in the state of Massachusetts. They had children William John Whitfield and Gary Mark Whitfield.
3. Eula June Whitfield b. June 13, 1925, at Hominy, Osage Co., OK. She married Bonner B. Cantley on April 25, 1948, at Fairfax, Osage Co., OK. They had children.
4. James Eugene Whitfield b. Feb. 13, 1932, at Pleasant Grove, Stone County, Arkansas. James E. Whitfield married Lois Nell Sober on Dec. 31, 1959, Ponca City, Kay County, OK. They had children.
5. Mary Elizabeth Whitfield born Oct. 12, 1934, at Pleasant Grove, Stone County, Arkansas. Mary Elizabeth Whitfield married Leonard Buchanan and John Ray Moore. Mr. and Mrs. Moore were divorced.
6. Henry Coleman Whitfield b. May 5, 1939, at Fairfax, Osage Co., OK. Henry C. Whitfield married Susie Northsteen, Dec. 5, 1964, at Glouchester, Virginia. They had children: Kevin Whitfield and Jason Whitfield.

....Submitted and prepared by James E. Whitfield, Ponca, Oklahoma, Kay County. Date August 15, 1990. All Oklahoma family groups.

WHITFIELD FAMILY GROUP

JOHN FRANKLIN WHITFIELD, Jr., was born Dec. 24, 1921, at Hominy, Osage County, OK. John F. Whitfield married Ruth Janet Talley on June 10, 1951, at Molina, Missouri. John F. Whitfield's occupation was Tax Income Preparer. He was a member of the Baptist Church.

Ruth Janet Talley's father is Jennings B. Talley. Ruth Talley Whitfield is a nurse. She is a member of the Baptist Church. They have one child named Sarah Elizabeth Whitfield.

WHITFIELD FAMILY GROUP

WILLIAM ANDREW WHITFIELD b. Nov. 6, 1923, at Hominy, Osage Co., OK. He was the son of John Franklin Whitfield and Mary Catherine Callahan Whitfield. William Andrew Whitfield married Angela Forte on March 29, 1954, at Maryland, Massachusetts.

North Carolina. Marriage Bond of John Whitfield and Mary Slade dated Sept. 28, 1827, Craven County, NC.

Angela Forte was born Oct. 20, 1921, at Newton, Massachusetts. Her father was Nicholas Atonellis and her mother was Conceho Chmpmb. William and Angela Whitfield had children:

1. William John Whitfield b. June 23, 1955, Newton, Massachusetts. William was called Billy Whitfield. William married Linda Sartell in April, 1979.
2. Gary Mark Whitfield b. April 3, 1957, Newton, Massachusetts. He was Gary A. Whitfield and was called Christopher or James. Gary M. Whitfield married Donna Rousso in April, 1982.

OKLAHOMA WHITFIELD FAMILY GROUP

JAMES EUGENE WHITFIELD b. Feb. 13, 1932, Stone County, Arkansas. James married Lois Nell Sober. His father was John Franklin Whitfield. Her parents were Rolla Eugene Sober and Naomi Irene Ivic. Lois Whitfield was born August 23, 1937, Ponca City, Kay County, Oklahoma.

James Eugene Whitfield worked for Conoco Oil Company. James was in the Army 1952 to 1956. James had places of residences at Arkansas, California, Utah, Oklahoma, and two foreign places. These staying places were due to his occupation.

Lois Nell Whitfield lists the family residences at Oklahoma and Kansas. She had children: 1. Naomi Nell Whitfield b. Sept. 29, 1960, Ponca City, Oklahoma, Kay County. Naomi married first Jerry Warren Padgett. Naomi married second Michael Earnest Melichor. 2. William Rolla Whitfield b. March 5, 1942, Ponca City, Kay County, Oklahoma.

BONNER BEN CANTLEY was born Sept. 11, 1921, Hominy, Osage County, Oklahoma. His father was Barnard Ben Cantley and his mother was Ida Mae Wolf. Bonner Cantley's wife was Eula June Whitfield and they had three children:

1. Carol Katherine Cantley b. Aug. 1, 1950, Fairfax, Osage Co., OK. Carol married Mark Lowlin.
2. Patricia Cantley was born May 19, 1954, Fairfax, Osage Co., OK. She married Fred souther and they divorced.
3. Benny Cantley. He was born May 23, 1956, Fairfax, Osage Co., OK.

MARY ELIZABETH WHITFIELD b. Oct. 12, 1934, Pleasant Grove, Stone Co., OK. Her parents were John Franklin Whitfield and Mary Catherine Callahan. Mary Elizabeth Whitfield married first Leonard Carl Buchanan. They had three children:

1. Leonard Karl Buchanan b. Aug. 8, 1955, Tulsa, OK. He married Laurie ____ on April 3, 1979, San Diego, CA. The child was Evan.
2. Lorry Keith Buchanan b. May 1, 1958, Tulsa, OK. Lorry married Tammy Mahany on June 10, 1975, Tulsa, OK. Children were: Mitchell, Nicholas, Shannon.
3. Debbie Lizabeth Buchanan b. Dec. 10, 1959, Tulsa, OK. Debbie married James Monrue Gibson. Children were Brady and Graven.

Mary Elizabeth Whitfield Buchanan married second John Ray Moore and they had children:

1. Mary Ann Moore b. April 25, 1965, Tulsa, OK. Mary Ann married Roger Linn Rarick on Feb. 20, 1982, Paolo, KS. The children were Jacob and Jordan.
2. Diania Marie Moore b. July 3, 1968, Tulsa, OK. Diania married Michael L. Peoples on Nov. 25, 1986, Otahe, KS. Children were Sandra and Barbara.

OKLAHOMA WHITFIELD FAMILY GROUP AND VIRGINIA

HENRY COLEMAN WHITFIELD born May 5, 1939, Fairfax, Osage Co., OK. The son of John Franklin Whitfield and Mary Callahan of Oklahoma. The father John Franklin Whitfield died May 18, 1966, at Pratt, Kansas. John was buried at Fairfax, Osage County, OK.

Henry Coleman Whitfield married Dec. 5, 1964, at Gloucester, VA, to Susie Harriet Northsteen. Susie was born April 11, 1938, at Gloucester, VA. Susie's parents were Harold Herry Northsteen and Mary Helen Northsteen. Susie was a member of the Baptist Church. She was also married to Oliver ____. Henry and Susie Whitfield had children:
1. John Kevin Whitfield b. Nov. 10, 1965, Newsport News, VA.
2. Jason Todd Whitfield b. Nov. 18, 1967, Hampton, VA.

Whitfield Not In
Oregon Before 1850. # OREGON

1993 marks the sesquicentennial of the Oregon Trail. In the spring of 1843, Marcus Whitman led the "great migration" of 1,000 men, women, and children along the full route of the trail, from Independence, Missouri, to the Oregon country. Traveling for six months in wagon trains, they crossed over 2,000 miles of prairies, deserts, and mountain terrain.

The Oregon Trail was the longest of the great overland routes to the West. Its main section ran west and then northwest from Independence to Fort Kearney in Nebraska. It then resumed a westward course along the Platte and North Platte rivers to Fort Laramie in Wyoming. After cutting through the Rockies via South Pass, it turned north to Fort Hall and followed the Snake River to Fort Boise in Idaho. Finally, it moved northwest to the Columbia River. Rafts were usually used to navigate the river to the final destinations, Fort Vancouver and the Willamette Valley of Oregon.

Trappers, traders, explorers, and missionaries opened parts of the Oregon Trail in the early 19th century. In 1805, Meriwether Lewis and William Clark traveled its western sector on their way to the Pacific Ocean. The first wagons passed through South Pass in the 1830s and, in 1842, John Fremont surveyed a portion of the trail for the U.S. Army.

The 1843 migration effected a break-out of "Oregon fever." Soon the trail was crowded with wagon trains of settlers anxious to stake their claims in the rich farmland of the Willamette Valley. It was an arduous trek with many hazards. Attacks by Indians were common. There were also cholera epidemics, grass fires, storms, and floods. Fatigue and hunger were constant companions.

During the 1840s and 1850s, about 12,000 settlers traveled the Oregon trail to a new life in the Willamette Valley. They established the first provisional government in Oregon in 1843.

1845 S. J. Whitfier on Census, Clatsop County, OR.
In 1980 Ohio state had 217 Whitfield families living in state.
In 1980 Oklahoma had 122 Whitfield families living in state.
In 1980 Oregon had 29 Whitfield families living in state.
In 1980 Pennsylvania had 159 Whitfield families living in state.

PENNSYLVANIA

IMMIGRANT RECORDS

1692 Richard Whitfield. 1683 Richard Whitfield and his wife, Mary Whitfield, arrived at Philadelphia, PA, in 1683. Two women, Susanna Whitfield arrived in Philadelphia, PA, 1746. Barthia (convict) arrived, 1746.

Pennsylvania has had several immigrants in 1900s, and some of these people went west. Immigration national office has names of immigrants.

The 1790, 1800, 1810 federal census of each state has names of men who were heads of families named Whitfield. These heads of families repeat themselves every ten years on censuses. When the name does appear, it usually means the person has died or has moved to another state.

A few immigrants in 1600s and 1700s named Whitfield, but births and family groups named Whitfield are natives of the Colony of British authority in the southeast colonies and later states.

Pennsylvania has an excellent collection of early history and records at the State Library and Archives.

1810 Census Pennsylvania lists Charles Whitfield, Philadelphia County, PA, Pennsylvania Township.

1830 Census Pennsylvania, Bedford County, East Providence township lists three men:
    Elias Whitfield, age range 25
    William Whitfield
    Joseph Whitfield.
Elias Whitfield in Belfast Township.

1840 Census Pennsylvania lists these men:
    William Whitfield, East Providence township, Bedford County.
    George Whitfield, Allegheny County, PA, Birmingham Borough.
    Nicholas Whitfield, Allegheny County, PA, Birmingham Borough.

"ELIAS WHITFIELD was born 1805. He resided in East Providence township, Bedford County, PA, and married Ann Clevenger who was born 1807. Elias died in 1880. His parents may have come from New Jersey or New York. Elias was born in Pennsylvania and died in Bedford County, PA."
....Submitted by Barbara A. McLane of Fort Worth, TX, January 18, 1989.

1774 Census. Charles Whitfield. Philadelphia County, Pennsylvania and Pennsylvania township.

1840 Census. Henry Whitfield. Allegheny County, Pennsylvania, Birmingham Borough.

H. Leland Whitfield, III, a Pennsylvanian, was graduated from the United State Naval Academy where he earned a degree in Aerospace Engineering before 1977. In May 1977 he resided at Pleasant Hill, California, Contra Costa County. H. Leland Whitfield worked for Coldwell Banker Commercial Brokerage Company, Oakland, California, office and was in sales.

William Franklin Whitfield was born April 10, 1927, and raised in Pennsylvania. William F. married Sue Trammel on May 29, 1954. Sue Whitfield was born August 5, 1933. Sue was raised in Houston, Texas. William and Sue had four children.

William and Sue have done some research on the name Whitfield. They share this information. "The surname Whitfield has been traced to England and confirmed in Oxfordshire, England, in the 1400s." They search for the family of ELIAS WHITFIELD and have a gap or breach to close in their search from 1775 to the 1804 birth of Elias Whitfield. They suggest maybe in Georgia.

William F. Whitfield and Sue were residing in Houston, Texas, in 1993.

William's parents were James Henry Whitfield and Lillian Minerva Cutschall Whitfield.

EMIGRANTS FROM ENGLAND TO PENNSYLVANIA

1683	RICHARD WHITFIELD n.a. ; Philadelphia, Pennsylvania
1746	SUSANA n.a. ; Philadelphia, Pennsylvania. Irish person.
1844	JOSEPH WHITFIELD n.a. ; Philadelphia, Pennsylvania
1848	JOHN P. Y. WHITFIELD n.a. ; Philadelphia, Pennsylvania
1852	FREDRICK WHITFIELD n.a. ; Philadelphia, Pennsylvania

1746, July 30, Accounts of Servants Bound and Assigned Emigrants of England and Ireland to America, Port Philadelphia, Pennsylvania

George House, Isaac Jones and Peter Robertson, overseers of the poor of Philadelphia, Pennsylvania, bind SUSANNA WHITFIELD an apprentice to Ruth Adams of Philadelphia, Shopkeeper for eight years and 10 months from this date, to be taught to read and write and sew plain work and housewifery and when free to have two suits of apparel, one whereof to be new.

1850 Census

Abraham Whitfield, Mercer Co., PA, Coldspring Township

Abraham, Philadelphia Co., PA, Spring Garden Ward One.

Charles Whitfield, Schuylkill Co., PA, Tamaqua Borough N Ward.

In 1990 year there were 56 heads of families named Whitfield living in Massachusetts.

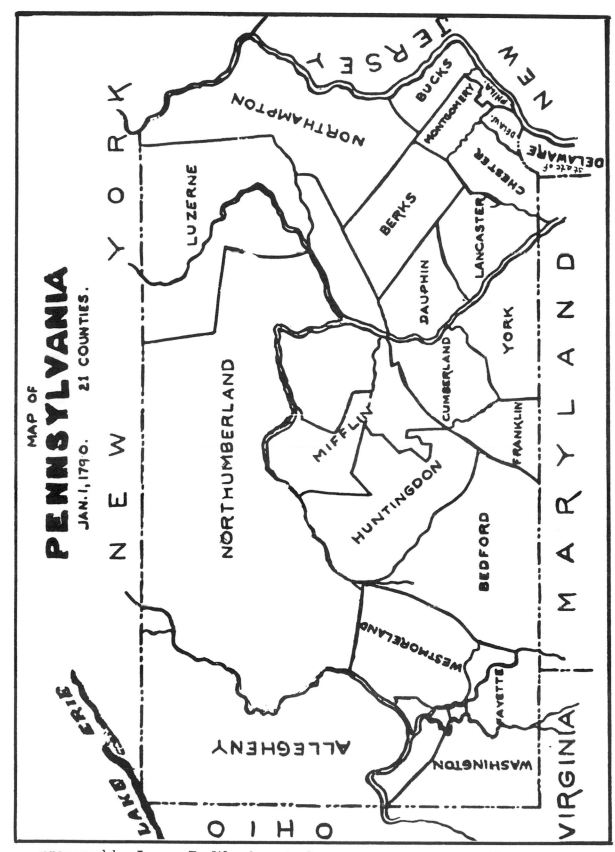

prepared by James F. Woodward, Secretary of the Land Office Bureau.

David Whitfield, Bedford Co., PA, West Providence Twp.
E. Whitfield, Philadelphia Co., PA, High Street Ward.
Elizabeth Whitfield, Allegheny Co., PA, Birmingham Borough.
George Whitfield, Washington Co., PA, Carroll Twp.
Henry Whitfield, Washington Co., PA, Carroll Twp.
Henry Whitfield, Philadelphia Co., PA, upper Delaware Ward.
S.N. Whitfield, Bedford Co., PA, East Providence Twp.
William Whitfield, Allegheny Co., PA, Skarpsburgh Borough.
William Whitfield, Bedford Co., PA, East Province.

EMIGRANTS

Whitfield came from England and Ireland and they had as a destination Pennsylvania. They came into the seaport of Philadelphia or the seaport at New York. These settlers were farmers but they had land and cultural communities different than the Whitfields at Virginia and North Carolina. There were many people that came from Germany settling in Pennsylvania. There was not, in early days, the travel very far from their community, and they did not have family ties to those named Whitfield in the southern lands.

JOHN W. WHITFIELD AND LOUISE WHITFIELD CARNEGIE

Andrew Carnegie was a man remembered for his benevolent character. Andrew Carnegie married Louise Whitfield April 22, 1887. They lived in Pittsburgh, Pennsylvania.

The biography of Louise's father was published soon after his death. JOHN W. WHITFIELD was a genial, companionable gentleman. He was an upright man who was honest and honorable. He was highly respected by those under him for he had executive ability.

When a boy, he entered business. In 1858 his merit and worth were acknowledged and rewarded, and he was admitted to the partnership, and the firm became Dowd, Baker, Whitfield and Company. In 1870 Dowd and Baker retired from active interest, remaining as specials, and the firm became Whitfield, Powers and Company.

Whitfield was a member of several mercantile boards and gave considerable attention to them. It was through the exertions of John W. Whitfield that the New York Ophthalmic Hospital achieved success.

John Whitfield was a member of Dr. Chapin's church, and he took a deep working interest in the Chapin Home. Whitfield was reserved in manner, yet gifted, in a commercial sense, friendly enough, and possessed his certain ability.

John, when only 15 years old, entered the employ of the Lyman Cooke and Company, in the notion business. The firm was located at 60 Broadway in 1848 and did a business of about $250,000 a year.

When a young man, Whitfield married and there were three children.
Louise Carnegie was a daughter.

In 1870 Whitfield and Powers were heads of the Company. In 1876
Mr. Powers died. John W. Whitfield died in 1878. The business
had new owners and executives and continued as a leading house of
business in Pennsylvania.

RHODE ISLAND

1820 Census. Samuel Whitfield, Providence County, RI.

1840 Census. Charles Whitfield, Newport County, RI, Newport Twp.

1850 Census. George Whitfield, Providence County, RI, Ward Six.

In 1980 there were ten men named Whitfield and they had families
living in Rhode Island state.

Death Records

Elizabeth Whitfield, widow of Charles Whitfield, Newport Co.,
Rhode Island, died January 16, 1796, age 70 years. Elizabeth was
the daughter of Abraham Whitfield and Elizabeth Borden.

Benjamin Whitfield, son of Charles and Elizabeth Whitfield, died
Newport Co., RI, Dec. 16, 1808, age 59 years.

Reference. Rhode Island Friends Records. Page 129.

SOUTH CAROLINA

The seaport of South Carolina opened later than the Virginia and
North Carolina seaports. There was late migration from North
Carolina into South Carolina. Once Charlestown seaport was
established, then South Carolina and Georgia 1743 had some early
colonists.

Carolinas were colonies of England and under rule of authority in
England. They were governed by precincts, councils, and trustees.
Whitfield before 1790 may appear in court minutes, tax records,
and land deeds.

WHITFIELD - CENSUS SOUTH CAROLINA

1779
George Whitfield, Ninety-six Dist.

1790
George Whitfield, Abbeville Co.
Thomas Whitfield, Georgetown Co.
Thomas Whitfield, Georgetown Co.

William Whitfield, Georgetown Co.
William Whitfield, Marion Dist.

1800
George Whitfield, Charleston Co.
Mary Whitfield, Pendleton Dist.
William Whitfield, Liberty Co.

WHITFIELD - CENSUS SOUTH CAROLINA

1809, 1810 William Whitfield, Marion District, S C.
1810 Benjamin Whitfield, Pendleton District, S C.
1810 Elijah Whitfield , Laurens District , S C.
1810, 1820 George Whitfield, Abbeville District, S.C.
1810 Lewis Whitfield , Pendleton District , S C.
1810 William Whitfield , Malboro District , S C.

1820 Benjamin Whitfield , Pendleton District, S C.
1820,1830 Benjamin Whitfield , Williamsburg County, S C.
1820 Elijah Whitfield , Lauren County, S C.
1820 George Whitfield, Abbeville County, S C.
1820 George Whitfield, Charlestown District, S.C.
1820 George Whitfield, Marlboro District, S C.
1820 Lewis Whitfield, Pendleton County, S C.
1820 Peter S. Whitfield , Williamsburg County, S C.

1830 Benjamin Whitfield , Anderson County, S C.
1830 Elijah Whitfield , Spartan burg County, S C.
1830 Joseph T. Whitfield , Anderson County, S C.
1830,1840 Lewis Whitfield , Anderson County, S C.
1830 Mary Whitfield , Laurens County, S C.
1830 Tinsly Whitfield , Anderson County, S C.

1840 James Whitfield, Chesterfield County, S C.
       St. James Goose Creek.
1840 Jeptha Whitfield , Pickens District , S.C.
1840,1850 Lewis Whitfield, Anderson District, S C.
1840 Sarah Whitfield, Greenville District, S C.
1845 Elizabeth Whitfield , Anderson County, S C.

1850 Benjamin Whitfield , Anderson County, S C.
1850 Drury Whitfield , Anderson County, S C.
1850 Helena Whitfield , Anderson County, S C.
1850 John C. Whitfield , Anderson County, S C.
1850 J.T. Whitfield , Anderson County, S C.
1850 Lewis Whitfield , Anderson County, S C.
1850 Lewis Whitfield, Jr., Anderson County, S C.
1850 Martha Whitfield , Anderson County, S C.
1850 Peter Whitfield , Anderson County, S C.
1850 Peter S. Whitfield , Anderson County, S C.
1850 Rebecca Whitfield , Anderson County, S C.
1850 Silvester Whitfield , Charlestown County, S C.
1850 William Whitfield , Anderson County, S C.

1850 Census , Anderson County, South Carolina

Lewis Whitfield, age 55, born in North Carolina
Helena Vandiver Whitfield, age 55, born in South Carolina
Rebecca Whitfield , age 28
William Whitfield, age 26   Drury Whitfield, age 11
Martha Whitfield , age 26   Peter Whitfield, age 11.
Lewis Whitfield , age 22   He died at age seventy-seven.

402

Census. District. parishes. Whitfield and Whitefield.

Name and District and Parish	Head of family & free white	Free white males under 16 yrs	Free white females & heads of family	All Free persons	Salves	Book Page
Thomas Whitfield Georgetown District Prince Fredericks		2	2			53
.... Thomas & Henry Rhodes under JOHN WATIES head 3 heads		2	6		94	53
William Whitfield Georgetown District Prince George Parish			1		4	56
William Whitfield Georgetown District Prince Frederick Parish		2	1	10	11	52
George Whitfield		3	4		24	58
Thomas Whitfield Georgetown District Prince Frederick Parish		2	2			52
Thomas Whitefield Camden District Clarendon County 2 free white males		3	3			18
Whitefield and Brown Charleston District 4 free whites & head of families St. Phillips and St. Michael's Parish						

"Head Of Families At The First Census Of
The United States Taken In The Year 1790,
South Carolina ."
  Book published by Genealogical Publishing
  Company , 1978 .

In 1980 South Carolina had 230 Whitfield families living
in the state.

There were South Carolina residents that moved to Georgia.
There were Georgia residents that moved to South Carolina,
Alabama , and Tennessee.

SOUTH CAROLINA RECORDS

Lewis Whitfield born 1790 had a descendant named JEPE who was Jeptha Whitfield. In March 1995, Bill Mitchell of Atlanta, Georgia, was searching for the family ancestors.

Mary Whitfield born SC and later married in 1778 to Buchner Killebrew who was born 1853, South Carolina.

Betsy Whitfield married Aaron Daniel of Peedee District, SC, and was living there in 1770.

NOTE: It is estimated that there are over 1.5 million last names in the United States in 1988.

The 1790 Census of South Carolina has this information...
William Whitfield, Georgetown District, SC, Prince George Parish, had four slaves and at later date had 11 slaves.

Thomas Whitefield, Georgetown District, SC, lived in Prince Fredericks Parish.

George Whitfield at one year had 24 slaves.

Thomas Whitfield was in Camden District, Clarendon County, SC.

Whitfield and Brown. Charleston District, St. Phillips and St. Michael's Parishes had three slaves.

Benjamin Whitfield born 1752 North Carolina, and his parent Luke Whitfield lived along Peedee River of South Carolina. Benjamin Whitfield left South Carolina and moved to Hancock and Putnam Counties in Georgia. Benjamin Whitfield died 1836 in Eatonton Georgia.
....Submitted by Floyd Whitfield of Charlestown, SC, in June 1993.

Floyd Whitfield in 1993 had sons named Matthew Whitfield and Benjamin Whitfield. Floyd Whitfield, Charlestown, SC, worked on the Lewis Whitfield (1791-d. after 1860) of Anderson County, SC. Floyd Whitfield submitted this information:
Benjamin Whitfield (1752-1836 GA) had the son Horatic Staten Whitfield who was born 1797 or 1800 in Troupe County, GA. He married Anne Taylor Gibson and died in 1843.

Children of Lewis Whitfield (b. 1789) and Helena Vandiver (b. 1794 SC) had children born in Pendleton District and in Anderson County of South Carolina.

Jephtha Whitfield appeared first on the 1840 census and he was age 26 in 1840. Jephtha Whitfield married Vanna Lasinana who was born 1809 in South Carolina. The first child, Adaline Whitfield, was born in 1841. The Civil War in South Carolina brought many deaths to its citizens.

South Carolina. Mary Whitfield had sons Benjamin Whitfield and Lewis Whitfield born in 1789, NC. They moved to Andersen County, SC. The husband of Mary is unknown.
....Submitted by Jerry Whitfield, Andersen, SC, June 1997.

WHITFIELD FAMILY GROUP - North Carolina and South Carolina

<u>Father - LUKE WHITFIELD</u> born Feb. 9, 1719, Chowan District, Gates County, NC. Son of William Whitfield (1688 England - 1770 NC) and Elizabeth Goodman (1695 VA - 1773 NC). Luke, Sr. died Sept. 1767 in Craven Co., SC. In 1723 he lived in Bertie County, NC, and moved to Craven Co., NC, in 1746. Left from there and moved about 1753 to Craven Co., SC. Six children born in NC, two in SC.

<u>Mother - CHLOE WARREN</u> born in 1720's in VA. Married about 1740. Birthing 1741 to 1757 Craven County, NC and SC. She died after 1768 in SC.

1. ELIZABETH born between 1741 and 1744 in NC. She married Charles Moody. Moody families long in Marion Co., SC. They died in SC. (1)
2. LUKE, Jr., born about 1746 in NC. Luke, Jr., may have married about 1773. He purchased two parcels of land with each 50 acres. The land was near Pee Dee River and his parents' plantation in SC. Luke, Jr. died December 2, 1796, in St. David Parish, SC. He was a farmer and a provincial soldier in the 1770's. (1) (3) (4) (5) (6)
3. WILLIAM born in the 1740's in NC and died after 1820 in Cheraws District, SC. He married and had a family. William lived in Cheraws District.
4. PENELOPE was born in 1750 in NC. She died at age 89 on May 18, 1839, in Madison Co., AL. She married a man of Sampson Co., NC. (1) (12)
5. TERECY (Lucretia) born 1750's in NC and lived at Pee Dee River area with parents. She married a man who lived at Sampson Co., NC. (1)
6. BENJAMIN was born in Craven Co., NC, and died 1836 at Eatonton, Putnam Co., GA. He served in the Revolutionary Army in SC in 1782. He married two times and had 13 children. Two children born in SC and eleven born in GA. (1) (8) (9)
7. LEWIS was born about 1756 in SC. He served in the Revolutionary War in SC and was at Fall of Charleston, SC, with Troop in 1777. Lewis and brother Benjamin may have gone to Georgia about 1788 together. (1) (10) (11) Lewis died 1800 in Waynesboro, Burke Co., GA.
8. MATTHEW was born in 1759 in SC. He died 1788 and lived in SC. He had work of farming. He was married.

References: (1) Will of Luke Whitfield (1719 NC-1767 SC, Craven County, SC. South Carolina Will Book 1767-71, page 141.
(2) (NSDAR) The National Society of the Daughters of the American Revolution. Anne Whitfield Dowdel. Nat'l No. 26608. Filed 1899.
(3) <u>Journal of Council of Safety, 21 Feb. 1776.</u> Colonel G.G. Powell, Regiment Eleven. St. David's Parish.
(4) <u>South Carolina Provincial Troops</u> by Alexander S. Salley, pages 5, 8, 10, 11. Luke Whitfield, Jr., at Fort Charlotte. Commander George Whitefield of Fort Charlotte.
(5) <u>Council of Safety, 21 Feb. 1774. Heitman Year Book</u> Roster of Provincial Soldier, 1893 year. Page 588.
(6) National Society Daughters of the American Revolution application in reference to Luke Whitfield born Feb. 9, 1719, Registrar General's Office. Letter Aug. 22, 1997, to Vallie Jo

Children of Benjamin Whitfield and Ann Staten Whitfield:

1. Sarah Whitfield	7. James Whitfield
2. Elizabeth Whitfield	8. Susannah Whitfield, born Nov.
3. William Whitfield	16, 1793. She married Thomas
4. Benjamin Whitfield	Keeling Smith.
5. Genjamin Whitfield	9. Molsey Whitfield
6. Matthew Whitfield	10. Horatio Staten Whitfield
	11. Bryan Whitfield

Children of Benjamin Whitfield second marriage:

12. Martha M. Whitfield, b. 1801, d. 1805.
13. Achsah Whitfield, b. 1804. She married Luke Morton and they
    lived and died in Troupe County, Georgia.
14. Matilda Whitfield.

ELIZABETH WHITFIELD, daughter of Benjamin and Ann Staten
Whitfield, was born March 6, 1781, Putnam County, Georgia.
Elizabeth Whitfield married John Goode, son of Francis Hunter and
John Goode. They were married Oct. 8, 1801. They had seven Goode
children. Elizabeth lived in Putnam County, Sparta City, and
Upson County, Georgia. Elizabeth died June 17, 1847.

JAMES WHITFIELD, son of Benjamin Whitfield, and grandson of Luke
Whitfield of South Carolina, was born Dec. 15, 1791, at Georgia
and died June 17, 1847. James Whitfield married Caroline Dyer of
Monticello, Jasper County, Georgia. James and the family moved
to Mississippi, and he became the Governor of that state. He was
a banker.

Children:

1. George Whitfield.	3. Luke James Whitfield.
2 Julia Randolph Whitfield.	4. Henry Buchanon Whitfield

5. Anthony Dyer Whitfield who was born 1843 in Mississippi.
   Anthony married Mary Baskerville. No children. She was the
   daughter of Charles Baskerville and Margaret Haynes Freear.

RECORDS

Peatr Mathon WHITFIELD, born April 10, 1838, SC, and died
October 7, 1915, SC. Certificate of Death, Registered No. 59,
SC State Registrar file only Number 22135. Place of death was
Ocone, Township Center, SC. Place of Burial was Yownville 8 C.
Burial October 8, 1915. Information from C.A. Whitfield at
Westminster.

George Whitfield lived in Abbeville County, South Carolina. He
appears in Judge of Probate Court Fragments, Minutes of the Court
of Ordinary. Book B, 1776-1783.

Residents of Columbia, South Carolina, in 1980 were E.R.
Whitfield, R.E. Whitfield, Richard A. Whitfield, Row Whitfield.

William J. Mitchell has had several people to assist on the
information of Jeptha Whitfield.

William J. Mitchell of Acworth, Georgia, has compiled the
Descendants of Lewis Whitfield of Anderson County, South Carolina,
in 1995. W.J. Mitchell submitted Whitfields of South Carolina on
August 16, 1995.

The Descendants of Lewis Whitfield
Listing 51 descendants for 4 generations.

1. **Lewis WHITFIELD**[1] was born 14 September 1789 in North Carolina. He married **Elena VANDIVER**. She was born 17 June 1794 in South Carolina.

    M   i.   Jephtha WHITFIELD, born 3 September 1814.

    F   ii.   Phoeba G. WHITFIELD, born 29 May   in Pendleton Dist. County, South Carolina. She married John HENDRIX. He was born 1817.

    F   iii. Mary Ann WHITFIELD, born 5 December 1817.

    F   iv.   Rebecca WHITFIELD, born 21 January 1820 in Pendleton Dist. County, South Carolina.

    M   v.   William WHITFIELD, born 16 August 1823 in Pendleton Dist. County, South Carolina. He married Druscilla _____. She was born about 1823.

    M   vi.   George WHITFIELD, born 29 January 1826 in Anderson County, South Carolina. He married Varsh _____. She was born about 1826.

    M   vii. Lewis WHITFIELD, Jr., born 25 May 1828 in Anderson County, South Carolina. He married Martha _____. She was born about 1828.

    M   viii. Benjamin WHITFIELD, born 15 March 1831 in Anderson County, South Carolina. He married Caroline _____. She was born about 1831.

    F   ix.   Martha WHITFIELD, born 12 November 1833 in Anderson County, South Carolina.

    M   x.   Drury WHITFIELD, born 28 June 1836 in Anderson County, South Carolina. He married Elizabeth _____. She was born about 1836.

    F   xi.   Mary B. WHITFIELD, born 28 July 183_ in Anderson County, South Carolina.
    ....Peatr appears in print and census as

    M   xii. Peter Madison WHITFIELD, born 10 April 1838 in Anderson County, South Carolina. He married Sarah Ann SULLIVAN. She was born about 1839.

2. **Jephtha WHITFIELD**[2] (1. Lewis) was born 3 September 1814 in Pendleton Dist. County, South Carolina. He married **Vanna (LASINANA)**. She was born about 1809 in South Carolina.

ISSUE:

    F   i.   Adaline WHITFIELD, born 1841 in South Carolina.
    M   ii.   George WHITFIELD, born 1843 in South Carolina.
    M   iii. John Henry WHITFIELD, born about 1847.
    F   iv.   Frances (Lasinia) WHITFIELD, born 1848 in South Carolina.
    M   v.   Andrew P. WHITFIELD, born 1850 in South Carolina.
    M   vi.   Samuel C. WHITFIELD, born 1850 in South Carolina.
    F   vii. Ada WHITFIELD, born 1853 in Pickens County, South Carolina.

According to the 1860 census, he lived in the 2nd Regiment of Pickens Dist., South Carolina. At this time he was a farmer. The value of his real estate in 1860 was $375 and his personal property was $300. Living next door in 1860 was William Whitfield (age 37) and family.

5. John Henry³ WHITFIELD (2.Jephtha², 1.Lewis¹) was born about 1847 in Pickens County, South Carolina. He married (1) **Rachel CORN** in Pickens County. She was born 27 September 1848 in Pickens County, South Carolina, the daughter of Silas Andrew CORN and Sarah (Sally) BUTTS.

ISSUE:

F i. R. E. WHITFIELD, born 1868 in Oconee County, South Carolina.

F ii. Effie Vada WHITFIELD, born 19 October 1869, died 19 February 1908.

F iii. Eugenia Jennie WHITFIELD, born 11 August 1876, died 4 March 1957.

M iv. Henry WHITFIELD. He married Lela CRAWFORD.

M v. Silas W. WHITFIELD, born 25 December 1878 in South Carolina. He married Hester "Dora" HOLLIFIELD. She was born 23 September 1875. Hester died 23 September 1973 in Greenville, South Carolina. Hester is buried in the Graceland Cemetery in Greenville Co., South Carolina.Silas died 1 April 1961 in Greenville, South Carolina, and was buried April 1961. Silas is buried in Graceland Cemetery in Greenville, South Carolina.

M vi. Hansel Kytle WHITFIELD, born in South Carolina. He married Mary Etta MIZE. Wife's mother was MARTHA ROZELLA HENDERSON and Martha's brother might be WILLIAM HENDERSON who married JENNIE WHITFIELD.

M vii. Robert WHITFIELD, born 20 September 1891, died in childhood 12 December 1894.

Rachel died 20 November 1892 in Georgia.

In 1850, she lived in the Western Dist., Pickens Dist., South Carolina. The 1860 census shows her living in the 2nd Regiment, Pickens Dist., South Carolina (P.O. -LongCreek). In 1870, we find her in Pulaski Twp., Oconee Co., S C .

John married (2) **Josie NICHOLS** about 1912. She was born 2 June 1894.

ISSUE:

F viii. Doll WHITFIELD.

M ix. Buster WHITFIELD.

F x. Eunice Evie WHITFIELD.

F xi. Jessie WHITFIELD.

F xii. Annie Mae WHITFIELD.

M xiii. Carlton WHITFIELD. Carlton was the half-sister of Jennie Whitfield.

F xiv. Lula WHITFIELD.

Josie died 19 November 1950.

Josie is buried at Antioch Baptist Church, Hartwell, Hart Co., Georgia. She was 18 years old when she married John H. Whitfield.

7. Effie Vada⁴ WHITFIELD (5.John³, 2.Jephtha², 1.Lewis¹) was born 19 October 1869 in Oconee County, South Carolina. She married **James Hampton WATKINS** 28 February 1892. He was born 12 August 1867. ISSUE:

F i. Tena Vada WATKINS, born 1 March 1902, died 7 October 1987.

James died 30 January 1939.

Effie died 19 February 1908, and was buried 1908 in Liberty Hill.

8.   **Eugenia Jennie**[4] **WHITFIELD** (5. John[3], 2. Jephtha[2], 1. Lewis[1])
     was born 11 August 1876 in Oconee County, South Carolina.
     She went by the name of Jennie. She married **William Calvin
     HENDERSON** about 1895. He was born 27 January 1871 in Blue
     Creek, White Co., GA, the son of Goolesberry B. HENDERSON and
     Mary SMITH.

ISSUE:

M   i.   John J HENDERSON, born July 1895.
F   ii.   Mattie HENDERSON, born 2 January 1897, died 20 June 1988.
M   iii. Joe Berry HENDERSON, born 21 November 1898, died 24 March 1972.
M   iv.   Bill HENDERSON, born 2 September 1906, died 20 July 1932.
M   v.   Albert William HENDERSON, born 6 June 1911, died 2 November 1970.
M   vi.   Frank HENDERSON.   F   ix.   Ida Viola HENDERSON.
F   vii. Rachel HENDERSON.   F   x.   Decie HENDERSON.
F   viii. Jessie HENDERSON.   M   xi.   Owen HENDERSON.

William died 9 September 1950 in Greenville, Greenville Co., SC,
and was buried September 1950 in Greenville, Greenville Co., SC.

William Calvin Henderson spent most of his life in Cleveland, GA,
and during that time was a farmer. During the last 15 years of
his life, he lived with his family in Greeneville, SC. He was a
member of the Chattahoochee Baptist Church in Cleveland and during
his residence there was active in all forms of church work. After
going to Greeneville he attended City View Baptist Churches as
long as his health permitted. He is buried either in Graceland
Cemetery or Beth Israel Cemetery.

Jennie died 4 March 1957 in Greenville, SC, and was buried March
1957 in Greenville, Greenville Co., SC.

She is either buried in Graceland Cemetery or Beth Israel
Cemetery.

25.   **Mary Ann**[2] **WHITFIELD** (1. Lewis[1]) was born 5 December 1817 in
      Pendleton Dist. County, SC. She married **Andrew Jackson
      GIBSON**. He was born 7 February 1817 in Pendleton Dist.
      County, SC.

ISSUE:

F   i.   Rebecca Susan GIBSON, born 1843 in Fairplay, Pickens Co., South Carolina.
           She married Wesley CAMPBELL. He was born 1843.
F   ii.   Martha Elena "Lena" GIBSON, born 10 May 1845 in Fairplay, Pickens Co.,
           South Carolina. She married Jefferson CAMPBELL. He was born 1845.

South Carolina Record. Joseph T. Whitefield. Will Book 2,
1855-1857. Page 389.

Will of Luke Whitfield, Sr. Craven County, South Carolina. Recorded
in Charleston Co.,S.C. Will Book RR 1767-1771, page 141

F iii. Mary Jane GIBSON, born 17 August 1848 in Fairplay, Pickens Co., South
Carolina. She married (1) Harrison ABLES. He was born 1848.
Mary married (2) J. S. LAWLESS. He was born 1848.

M iv. William John GIBSON, born 7 September 1850 in Fairplay, Pickens Co., South
Carolina. He married (1) Mary Handy MASON. She was born about 1850.
William married (2) Reedie CROMER.

M v. George Robert GIBSON, born 7 November 1859 in Fairplay, Pickens Co.,
South Carolina. He married Clarissa CARROLL. She was born about 1853.

vi. Anna Louiza GIBSON, born 15 October 1856.

F vii. Eliza Pickens GIBSON, born 28 August 1862 in Fairplay, Pickens Co., South
F Carolina. She married Henry Melton CAIN. He was born about 1862.

31. **Anna Louiza³ GIBSON** (25. Mary², 1. Lewis¹) was born 15 October
1856 in Pickens County, SC. She married **William Handy Pickens
CAIN**. He was born 15 October 1852 in Pickens County, SC.

M i. Samuel Aaron CAIN, born 23 August 1873.

F ii. Ada Johanna CAIN, born 29 June 1876 in Cartersville, Bartow Co., Georgia.
She married (1) Sylvester TREEST. He was born about 1876.
Ada married (2) _____ OVERSTREET. He was born about 1876.

F iii. Ida Marium CAIN, born 18 May 1879 in Cartersville, Bartow Co., Georgia.
She married Tom RENEAU. He was born about 1879.

M iv. Walter Jackson CAIN, born 28 August 1881 in Gadsen, Etowah Co., Alabama.
He married Paralee HINSLEY. She was born about 1881.

M v. Homer Stiles CAIN, born 24 October 1884 in Gadsen, Etowah Co., Alabama.
He married (1) Nanny POLLARD. She was born about 1884.
Homer married (2) Oma Jewll THORMAHLEN. She was born about 1874.
Homer married (3) Louise _____. She was born about 1884.

F vi. Mary Jane CAIN, born 29 March 1888 in Gadsen, Etowah Co., Alabama. She
married Curtis R. KAY. He was born about 1888.

M vii. Claud CAIN, born 18 August 1892 in Van Alstyne, Grayson Co., Texas.
M ʹiii. Maud CAIN, born 18 August 1892 in Van Alstyne, Grayson Co., Texas.
M ix. Earnest CAIN, born 31 May 1895 in Van Alstyne, Grayson Co., Texas.
M x. Laura Evaline CAIN, born 9 May 1896 in Van Alstyne, Grayson Co., Texas.
F She married John Ezra BLAKE. He was born about 1896.

32. **Samuel Aaron⁴ CAIN** (31. Anna³, 25. Mary², 1. Lewis¹) was born
23 August 1873 in Cartersville, Bartow Co., GA. He married
Amanda Lou Jennie MURDOCK. She was born 8 May 1878 in
Prentiss County, Mississippi.

ISSUE:

F i. Mineola CAIN, born 15 August 1897.

ii. Merel Jessie CAIN, born 19 March 1899.

M iii. Robert Altus CAIN, born 7 April 1901.

410

South Carolina Records continue on page 516 to end of Appendix.

M	iv.	Deward Deleware CAIN, born 14 August 1902.
M	v.	William Elmo "Jim" CAIN, born 7 March 1904.
	vi.	Thelbert CAIN, born 23 August 1905.
	vii.	Rowe CAIN, born 20 September 1906.
M	viii.	John Calhoun CAIN, born 10 March 1910.
M	ix.	Infant CAIN, born 20 January 1912.
M	x.	Herbert CAIN, born 4 May 1913.
M	xi.	Albert Lee CAIN, born 21 November 1914.

SOUTH DAKOTA
WHITFIELD - CENSUS SOUTH DAKOTA

1880 Amelia Whitfield, Pennington Co., SD
1880 J.S. Whitfield, Rapid Capid City, Pennington Co., SD
1880 N.C. Whitfield, Pennington Co., SD

After these Whitfields at Pennington County, South Dakota, had left or died, there have not been Whitfield residents at South Dakota before 1980. There were no Whitfields there before 1850. The area was Indian country.

TENNESSEE

In 1770 the Holston south of the Virginia fall line was free of the Cherokee Indians title by a treaty. Before the close of the Revolutionary War, October 7, 1780, 440 East Tennesseans, under Colonel John Sevier and Isaac Shelly, gave frontier fights to the English men at King's Mountain. They defeated the British people.

In 1783 James Robertson was Davidson County's first representative in North Carolina.

In 1789 the North Carolina Legislature passed the Act ceding to the United States territory embracing the present State of Tennessee. On April 2, 1790, the Territory was accepted by Act of Congress.

On June 26, 1792, Ziegler's Station in Sumner County, Tennessee, was captured and burned by the Creek Indians.

The Continental and Revolution men of North Carolina land warrants were ready and granted in 1793. Several Whitfield men with families were recipients of these Tennessee land warrants.

On January 11, 1796, at the Constitutional Convention at Knoxville, the State was named Tennessee. On June 1, 1796, the new state Tennessee was admitted into the Union.

Tennessee Record. On the 1850 census TN is Mathew Whitfield, age 38, living next door to Levina Roberson Whitfield, age 75. On Tennessee 1860 census, Levina Whitfield was age 65. She was the widow of Mathew Whitfield of Rutherford Co., TN.

Tennessee
Census Year - population - Increase over preceding Census

Census Year	population	Number	Per Cent
1790	35,691		
1800	105,602	69,911	195.9
1810	261,727	156,125	147.8
1820	422,823	161,096	61.6
1830	681,904	259,081	61.3
1840	829,210	147,306	21.6
1850	1,002,717	173,507	20.9

Since 1769 there were a few people in settlements near the eastern boundary at Tennessee. Whitfield pioneers came to Tennessee from 1787 to 1810. Many Whitfield old records and documents lay in thirty Tennessee counties in courthouses and places.

In the 1930s there was a Tennessee State Authority Work Project to do preservation work on the old records in counties. All the old county records were copied and abstracted. The typed materials were indexed by county and bound in book volumes. These indexed analytical records of the Tennessee State Library and Archives at Nashville, Tennessee, were sponsored by Mrs. John Trotwood Moore.

In November 1963 Vallie Jo Whitfield studied the indexed analytical records at the Tennessee State Library. She searched and compiled all of the Whitfield records found in sixteen counties. A book was published entitled Whitfield History and Genealogy of Tennessee by Vallie Jo Whitfield. References should be made to this book for records on Whitfield at Tennessee. Also there are many local histories written on Tennessee places and people.

Since Tennessee records have been compiled in a book, in this chapter are only the collective materials obtained since the book was written. The censuses were read on microfilm and compiled in this chapter for Tennessee. Censuses provided family groups and heads of Whitfield families.

The emigrants from North Carolina mostly filled the Tennessee state and a few emigrated from Virginia with destination Tennessee. Kin folks and neighbors came from eastern settlements to the backwoods and river basins. They came at first and found Indians and new ways and learned the seasons and the land. Nature made the state a place to do farming, and it was mostly the occupation of the first people. However in the nineteenth century many were in medicine, in ministry, allied industries, and some in the service of the government.

Many of the descendants still inhabit the Tennessee land in the region their forefathers settled in Tennessee over 195 years ago. The automobile and World Wars have caused some Tennesseans to go to the four corners of the state and to many other states for land use, work and job and opportunities.

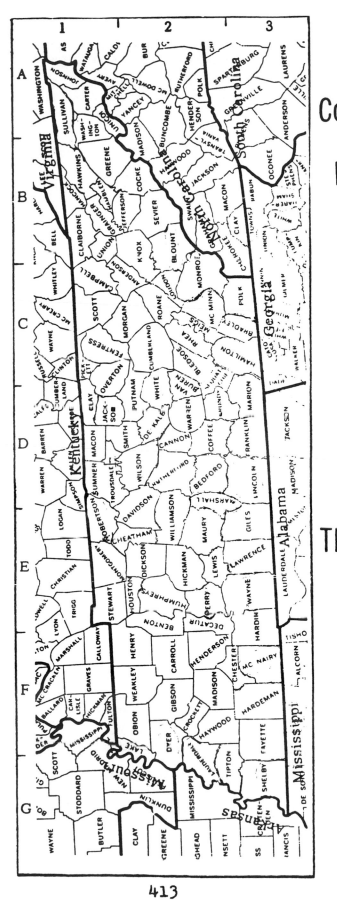

County

Map

For

The

State

Of

TENNESSEE

413

Descendants of William Whitfield and Elizabeth Goodman and William Whitfield and William Whitfield

Brothers Needham Whitfield, Bryan Whitfield and Lewis Whitfield all born in North Carolina left North Carolina for new open land 1793 in Tennessee.

LEWIS WHITFIELD

He married (1) Elizabeth Wimberly and (2) Sarah Wall, a widow.

1. Needham Whitfield; m. Sallie Bourne.
2. Lewis Whitfield; m. Ann Williams, a cousin.
3. Robert Whitfield.
4. Sarah Whitfield.
5. Elizabeth Whitfield; m. (1) Ila Metcalf,

   (2) Thomas Trigg.
   Six children by her first husband.
6. George Whitfield.
7. Joseph W. Whitfield; b. Aug. 23, 1806

   ; m. Mrs. Miriam Richardson Whitfield Fort, Second marriage.
8. Bryan Whitfield.
9. Susan Whitfield; m. Joseph Fort.
10. Catherine Whitfield

    ; m. James Buckner Osborne.
    Their children moved to Texas.

MIRIAM RICHARDSON WHITFIELD

She was born 1808 and died 1888. In 1827 she married John Diggs Fort (1804-1829). After his death she married her cousin Joseph Whitfield. Children.

1. Elizabeth (Bettie) Fort; m. Buck Williams.
2. Jack Ann Fort; b. 1829; d. 1882; m. in 1849 Joseph Marston Fort (1828-1906), s. of Josiah W. and Diana Coleman (Ligon) Fort. Joseph Fort and his wife moved to Texas not long after their marriage.
3. Joseph N. (or M.) Whitfield; b. 1833 ca., d. 1859. He was a graduate (1854) of Louisville University and of the Medical School of the University of Pennsylvania. He practiced medicine in Clarksville, Tenn.
4. Constantine Whitfield; b. 1835 ca.; m. Laura Waller, of Todd County, Kty.
5. Needham Lewis Whitfield.
6. Robert Christian Whitfield; b. 1839 ca.; killed Dec. 13, 1862, possibly in the Battle of Fredericksburg, Va. C. S. A.
7. Sarah Cornelia Whitfield.
8. Mary L. Whitfield.
9. James W. Whitfield; b. 1848 ca.; m. 1873 Margaret M. Carney.
10. Henry C. Whitfield.

SARAH WHITFIELD

She was born in Montgomery Co., TN. She married A. Dudley Bourne and gave birth to 12 children. Her child, Catherine Louise Bourne married Needham Lewis Whitfield. Another child was Charlemagne Bourne.

LAND

On 9/20/1787 Needham Whitfield and All received the land warrant and deed on the north side of Tennessee River near Green Co. In 1788 The Company and Needham Whitfield purchased several sections of land in a long flat lying between Clinch Mountain near Bull Run River.

These families left the Clinch Mountain area and went to Christian County, KY, and to Montgomery County, TN.

Jesse Whitfield went to East Tennessee in 1793.

Zelphie Whitfield at Watauga settlement in 1776 was a black person.

NEEDHAM WHITFIELD

He was born 1776 NC - died 1858 in TN. In 1798 he married Miriam Neville (1776-1852) and she gave birth to 15 children.

1. George Neville Whitfield; m. Mary Anne Killebrew. She was a descendant of Mary Whitfield and Buckner Killebrew. Possibly this Mary Ann was the same as the Mary Killebrew that married William Radford.
2. Sarah Collier Whitfield.
3. Miriam Richardson Whitfield.
4. Needham Bryan Whitfield.
   Eleven others as indicated above.

414

HERVEY WHITFIELD
(Needham, Needham, William,
William, William)

Hervey Whitfield was born July
3, 1847, in Montgomery Co.,
TN.

For many years he was editor
of the Leaf-Clarion, in
Clarksville, TN, and was in
newspaper work.

Hervey Whitfield married (1)
Oct. 20, 1875, Ella Trigg
(1852-1900) and (2) Mrs.
Jennie (Vaughan) Price.
Children.
1. Arthur G. Whitfield.
2. Roy Whitfield b. June 8,
   1878.
3. Thomas B. Whitfield b.
   Dec. 8, 1882, d. Dec. 23,
   1899.

LAND
In 1794 John Whitfield,
William Whitfield, Willis
Whitfield and the families
went to Sumner County, TN.

Thomas Whitfield, Esther
Whitfield, John Whitfield in
1794 went to Davidson Co., TN.

William Whitfield, wife Mary
Beck and family went to
Steward Co., TN, and to
Christian Co., KY

Wilkins Whitfield, Harrison
Whitfield, John Whitfield were
settled 1808 at Franklin,
Williamson Co., TN.

(William, William, William)
BRYAN WHITFIELD
Bryan was born in North
Carolina and moved to
Montgomery, TN, in 1793. He
married about 1797 (1) Anne
Neville and (2) about 1798 to
Catherine Bailey. Bryan died
in 1817. Children.
1. William Whitfield.
2. James Whitfield.
3. Mary Jane Whitfield; m. Charles
   Minor.
4. Bryan Whitfield.
5. Margaret Whitfield; m. ____
   Harrington.
6. Duncan Whitfield; m. Lettie
   Scott.

7. Catherine E. Whitfield; m. John
   F. Williams.
8. Ann Maria Whitfield.

HERBERT TERA WHITFIELD
(Needham, Joseph, Lewis,
William, William, William)
Herbert T. Whitfield was born
June 22, 1864, near
Clarksville, TN. He married
Jan. 22, 1902, Leslie Hicks
Johnson of Clarksville.
Children.
Justine Louise Whitfield; b. Dec. 7,
1902. She married Nov. 6, 1928, in
Paris, France, Bailey Wallys Diffie,
the son of William O. and Mary
(Jones) Diffie of Detroit, TX.
Dailey W. Diffie was born June 27,
1902. Res., 1930, NY.

WILLIAM WHITFIELD
(William, William, William)
William Whitfield (1764-Aug.
8, 1825) born in Wayne Co.,
NC. He married in Duplin Co.
In 1785 Mary Beck. They moved
to Christian Co., KY, and
later to Steward Co., TN,
where he died. His widow
moved to Fayette Co., IL, and
was living in Ewington,
Effingham Co., IL, in 1844.
They may have had 13 children
but only ten are known.
1. William Whitfield.
2. Needham Whitfield.
3. Joseph Whitfield.
4. Lewis Whitfield.
5. Hester Whitfield; m. Charles
   Whitfield, son of William
   Whitfield, III.
6. John Beck Whitfield.
7. Harriet Whitfield.
8. Mary Whitfield.
9. Lucy Whitfield; died unmarried
   at the home of her brother Bryan
   in Nauvoo, IL.
10. Bryan Whitfield.

LINEAGE

Robert Lee Whitfield born 1883 in Tennessee had a son. He was Hugh H. Whitfield born May 1909 in Nashville of Davidson County, Tennessee. Hugh H. Whitfield married Thelma Eunice Knight who was born January 22, 1912, Chicago, Illinois, Cook County. She died February 18, 1959, in Illinois. They had a son.

Arthur Jack Whitfield born June 8, 1934, Chicago, Illinois, Cook County. Arthur Whitfield married July 9, 1955, to Grace Valentine Falk who was born February 13, 1936, in Chicago, Illinois. They had a son.

Robert John Whitfield born February 14, 1958, in Albany, Dougherty County, Georgia. Robert J. Whitfield was married August 27, 1976, in Chicago, Illinois, to Sylvia Marie Sodders who was born Dec. 5, 1957, in Virginia. They had a child Jeremiah Christopher Whitfield born June 26, 1978, Chicago, IL. ....Submitted by Robert John Whitfield (1958-living 1992) in Chicago, Illinois.

MATTHEW WHITFIELD (1772 NC - 1827 TN)

Matthew Whitfield and Willis Whitfield were brothers born in Nash County, North Carolina. Their genealogy is of 12 generations with Whitfields of Virginia, North Carolina, Tennessee, and Arkansas.

These brothers had Tennessee land and settled at Rutherford County. Matthew Whitfield is on the 1800 census of Nash County, North Carolina. In 1806 he was in Tennessee with the family.

Matthew Whitfield was born 1772 in Nash County, NC, and he died 1827 in Rutherford County, Tennessee. Matthew Whitfield and Levina Robinson were married before 1800 in North Carolina at Nash County. Levina was born 1776 and died after 1860. Both wife and husband died in Rutherford County, TN. They had five children.

1. William Whitfield b. Nov. 28, 1800, NC, and died Nov. 14, 1862, in Izard County, Arkansas. He married Matilda _____ in Tennessee.
2. Benjamin Whitfield was born May 14, 1806, in Sumner County, TN. Benjamin Whitfield married first Elizabeth Herrod on May 5, 1827, at Rutherford County, TN. They had children. They moved to Arkansas and settled there. Benjamin married second Mrs. Elizabeth Birdwell and had no children.
3. Mary Whitfield born 1809, Rutherford County, Tennessee.
4. Girl born at Rutherford County, Tennessee.
5. Matthew Whitfield born 1814, Rutherford County, Tennessee. Matthew Whitfield married (1) Fannie R. Monahan on July 30, 1834. Matthew Whitfield married (2) Sarah _____.

....Submitted by Charlotte Katherine Lancaster Lawrence (Mrs. Vernon Lawrence) of Mountain View, Arkansas, in 1994.

Mrs. Charlotte Lawrence families groups for her lineage are the same families as that of Ruby Van Whitfield of Arkansas.

DEATH RECORDS

Matilda Whitfield d. June 20, 1870, in Arkansas. She was wife of William Whitfield (1800-1862).

Benjamin Whitfield born 1806 died May 14, 1900, at Stone County, Arkansas.

Levina Robinson Whitfield was born 1776 in North Carolina and died after 1860 in Tennessee. She was wife of Matthew Whitfield (b. 1772 NC - d. 1827 TN).

WILLIS WHITFIELD (1761-1836) and RHODA ALLEN WHITFIELD

Willis Whitfield born 1761, Nash County, NC. Willis served two or more tours in the Revolutionary War under General Greene stationed near Charleston, SC. Willis Whitfield married Rhoda Allen in 1788 in North Carolina. Rhoda was born Jan. 12, 1767, and died after 1840 at Cannon County, TN. In 1793 Willis Whitfield and family were at Sumner County, TN, with other Whitfield families, and he moved later to Rutherford County, TN, where he had land. The men named Whitfield at Sumner County were all from North Carolina.

Willis and Rhoda had 12 children who were Tennessee residents at Cannon County, Tennessee.
1. Ansil Whitfield, born Aug. 25, 1789, Nash County, NC.
2. Wright Whitfield, born March 20, 1791, Nash County, NC.
3. Christian Whitfield, born Nov. 1, 1793, Sumner County, TN.
4. Sally Whitfield, born May 5, 1795, TN.
5. Temperance Whitfield, born Feb. 26, 1797, TN.
6. Rhody Whitfield, born Dec. 27, 1798, TN.
7. Thomas Yough Whitfield, born Feb. 5, 1801, TN.
8. Arthur Allen Whitfield, born Jan. 30, 1803, TN.
9. Willis Whitfield, born Jan. 30, 1805, Rutherford Co., TN.
10. Eli Whitfield, born July 2,1807, Rutherford Co., TN.
11. Eliz. Eason Whitfield, born Feb. 26, 1810, Rutherford Co., TN.
12. Alfred Whitfield, born Jan. 19, 1812, Rutherford Co., TN.

Rutherford County land split off making Cannon County and the Willis Whitfield family and children later lived in Cannon County on the same land and home place.

Eli Whitfield, born May 2, 1807, in Tennessee, married Mary A. (Polly) Whitfield in Tennessee, and they moved to Izard County, Arkansas. Eli Whitfield died between 1860 and 1870 in Arkansas.

State of North Carolina. Willis Whitfield, wife Rhoda W 1013.

Declaration of Rhody Whitifled, January 10,1840, Cannon County, Tennessee. She was a resident of said County, age 72. She declared that she was the widow of Willis Whitfield, who was a pensioner of the United States and drew his pension in Nashville, Tennessee, for Revolutionary War service. They were married Nov. 1, 1788. Willis Whitfield died September 3, 1836. Rhody Allen Whitfield was the daughter of Arthur Allen and Elizabeth his wife, and was born Dec. 1, 1767.

THOMAS WHITFIELD AND WINIFER AND CHILDREN
All born in Virginia. Family lived 1760 to 1807
Albemarle Parish, Sussex County, Virginia

THOMAS WHITFIELD, born ca. 1735, Virginia, and died 1794 at Sussex County, Virginia. Thomas was a tobacco planter. Thomas married Winifer ____ about 1759. All children born in Albemarle Parish.

In 1808 widow Winifer and all the Whitfield families and daughters left Sussex County, Virginia, and moved to Franklin, Williamson County, Tennessee.

Thomas Whitfield (1735 ca VA-d. 1794 VA) had descendants that lived in Tennessee and Texas.

Children of Thomas and Winifer. Winifer Whitfield died 1838 in Franklin, Williamson County, Tennessee, at age 98. She lived with son Wilkins.

Children

1. MARY WHITFIELD b. Sept. 21, 1760. She married Lauren Hobbs in 1778 Sussex County, Virginia.
2. WILLIAM WHITFIELD, b. Aug. 6, 1762, VA. William married Elizabeth Tomlinson. They had four boys and four girls. William Whitfield moved to Franklin, Williamson Co., TN, with the Whitfield families, 1808.
3. ELIZABETH WHITFIELD married Benjamin Sturdivant Jan. 20, 1783, in Virginia, Sussex County. Sturdivant moved to Franklin, Williamson County, TN, with the Whitfield families, 1808.
4. FRANCIS WHITFIELD, b. Feb. 4, 1765, was called Franky. She was unmarried in 1794 when her father died. She went with the mother and brothers to Tennessee. She lived in a relative's home.
5. MARTHA PATTY WHITFIELD, b. March 16, 1767. Martha married William Hobbs in 1789, Virginia.
6. WILKINS WHITFIELD, b. 1781, VA. Wilkins married Polly Mary Sturdivant in 1801 in VA. Wilkins and the family moved to Franklin, Williamson County, Tennessee, in 1808. Wilkins died 1841 in Franklin, Tennessee.
7. BETTY WHITFIELD, b. 1774, and she was called Betsy. Benjamin Sturdivant in 1793 in Virginia married Elizabeth Betsy Whitfield.
8. NANCY WHITFIELD, b. 1774. Nancy married William Knight in 1799 in Virginia.
9. JACK WHITFIELD, b. 1780, VA. He was Jack Whitfield in his father's will and received one-third of the land. Since Jack has so few records, the name is probably Jack "John." Jack went to Franklin, Tennessee, with his brothers and mother.
10. HARRISON WHITFIELD, b. 1783, VA, d. 1864, Franklin, Tennessee. Harrison married Polly Mary Sledge in 1804 in Virginia. Harrison in 1808 to his death lived at Franklin, Williamson County, TN, and is buried there.

References
1. County records of Sussex County and census.
2. Albermarle Parish records, Sussex County, Virginia.
3. Whitfield History and Genealogy of Tennessee by Vallie Jo Whitfield, second edition published 1979.

TENNESSEE WHITFIELD BROTHERS AND CHILDREN

Sons of Thomas Whitfield, b. 1735 ca. VA-d. 1794, Sussex County, VA. Thomas married Winifer ___ before 1760 VA. Winifer b. 1740 ca.-d. 1838, Franklin, Tennessee. Winifer Whitfield and children moved from Albemarle Parish, Sussex County, Virginia, in 1808 and went to Franklin, Williamson County, Tennessee. Whitfield families made their home.

BROTHERS

WILKINS WHITFIELD b. 1781 VA-d. 1841 Franklin, TN. He md. Mary Sturdivant 1801 Virginia, Sussex Co., VA.

Children

HENRY b. 1802, VA-d. before 1850, TN. Md. with Children.

GEORGE WASHINGTON b. 1806 VA-d. 1894 Dallas Co., TX. Spouses: 1. Louisa King md. 1836 with 1 son, 2 dau. 2. Sarah Bond md. 1849 with 2 sons and 3 dau. Lived Hickman Co., TN, and Garland, Dallas Co., TX.

WILLIAM 1820 lived Hickman Co., TN, d. After 1850.

THOMAS JEFFERSON b. 1810 TN-d. 1873 TN. Married: 1. Eliza Nolan 1829 with 1 son, 1 dau. 2. Sallie Dillahunty 1835, with 4 sons, 3 dau. Lived Hickman Co., TN, and Perry Co, TN.

MARTHA ANN b. 1812 Franklin, TN, d. 1847 TN (Charter).

THEODOSIA b. 1816, TN-d. 1839 TN. No children (Clagett).

SARAH b. 1817 TN-d. TN (McPhail) (Nichols)

JOHN WILKINS b. 1818 TN-d. 1879 Halletsville, Lavoca Co., TX. Married: 1. Catharine Dansby 1839 with 1 dau. She died 1846, TN. 2. Sarah B. Dibrell 1853 TN, with 1 son, John Anthony.

JAMES MONROE b. 1819 TN-d. TX. Married with children.

VIRGINIA C., b. 1821 ca.-d. TN. No children (Cliffe).

HARRISON WHITFIELD b. 1783 VA-d. 1864 Franklin, TN. Md. Polly Mary Sledge 1804 VA, Sussex Co., VA.

Children

THOMAS b. 1827 Franklin, TN-d. July 13, 1879, TN.

REBECCA b. 1807 VA-d. TN (Allen)

JOHN b. 1815 ca. TN. Boy died young.

NANCY b. Aug. 5, 1811 TN-d. Feb. 7, 1885 TN (Winstead)

LUCY b. 1810-d. 1892 TN (Criddle).

FELIX b. 1816 TN-d. TN. Md. with children.

HARRISON b. 1825 TN-d. 1895 Dexter, TX. Md. Sophronia with children.

MARY ANNE b. 1826 TN.

WILLIAM WHITFIELD b. Aug. 6, 1762 VA-d. TN. Md. Wife died age 45 VA and had children. William went to Franklin, TN, in 1808.

JACK ("John") WHITFIELD b. 1780 VA-d. TN. He md. and had son John.

Brothers all born Albemarle Parish, Sussex County, VA. All moved 1808 to Franklin, Williamson County, TN. All died in area of Williamson Co., TN. Sons of Thomas Whitfield (1735-1794) were Wilkins, Harrison, Jack. William was raised in family, but father does not mention him as son in his will.

HARRISON WHITFIELD AND POLLY M. SLEDGE

Harrison Whitfield, born 1783, Virginia, and died 1864 in Williamson County, Tennessee. Son of Thomas and Winifer Whitfield of Sussex County, Virginia. Harrison married Polly Mary Sledge Aug. 29, 1804, in Sussex County, Virginia. Albemarle Parish. They moved with the Whitfield families of Winifer Whitfield, widow of Thomas Whitfield in 1808 to Franklin, Williamson County, Tennessee. They had five sons and five daughters. Eight of the children lived in maturity. All of the children except the first or second child were born in Williamson County, Tennessee, at Franklin. Harrison was a farmer. He had brothers Wilkins, William, and Jack for neighbors. The mother, Winifer, lived in the house of Wilkins Whitfield.

Children:

1. Thomas Whitfield b. 1827 Franklin, TN-d. July 13, 1879, Williamson County, TN.
2. Rebecca Whitfield b. 1807 ca. VA, died Tennessee. Rebecca married Lewis Allen on Oct. 11, 1823. In 1850 they had nine children. Allen children made their home in Tennessee and Texas.
3. John Whitfield born between 1810 and 1820.
4. Boy, died young.
5. Nancy Whitfield, b. Aug. 5, 1811-d. Feb. 7, 1885 in Franklin, TN. Nancy married John M. Winstead on March 8, 1827, in Williamson County, TN. They had three daughters and nine sons: Mary E., Lucy T., Ida, James M., Harrison, Walker, William, Robert O., Meredith, Thomas E., Winfield, John W. All Winstead children.
6. Lucy Whitfield, b. 1810-d. 1892. Lucy in 1832 married Smith Criddle, b. 1808-d. 1845.
7. Felix G. Whitfield, b. 1816. Felix married Minerva Williamson on June 3, 1837. In 1850 they had children: Mary E., Thomas H., Martha S., James H., Smith C., and Felix.
8. Girl, died young.
9. Harrison Whitfield, b. 1825 TN-d. 1895, Dexter, TX. Harrison married Sophronia M. Coon on March 5, 1848. They moved to Texas. They had child Agatha in 1850 in Tennessee and other children in Texas.
10. Mary Anne Whitfield, b. 1826. Mary Anne married Alonzo Avery and moved to New York.

References:
Census of Tennessee and Texas.
Whitfield History and Genealogy of Tennessee by Vallie Jo Fox Whitfield list the family and genealogy.

....Submitted by James P. Bass of McLean, Virginia. In 1989 Harrison Whitfield and Sophronia family group. In 1990 James Whitfield (b. 1851-d. 1915) family group.

In Bass family group, Sallie Whitfield married James Peter Bass, II.

WHITFIELD   CRIDDLE   SCRUGGS   JARED

Grandchild of Thomas Whitfield or great-grandchild was Lucy Whitfield who married Smith Criddle on Sept. 4, 1832. Her father was a resident of Williamson County, Tennessee. Thomas, ca. 1735-d. 1794, VA, and his family moved to Franklin, Tennessee.

First Harrison of record was Thomas' son but other Harrison Whitfields are in the family. Wilkins Whitfield did not have a son with name of Harrison for no records have been found. Harrison and Wilkins were brothers, and William and Jack (John) were the four sons of Thomas Whitfield. Censuses will provide information.

....Virginia Scruggs, a descendant, has submitted the following material. Virginia Scruggs (Mrs. B. Shaw Jared) of Hillsboro, Tennessee, provided this material in August, 1983.

"My father's Whitfield people was HARRISON WHITFIELD. His daughter LUCY WHITFIELD married SMITH CRIDDLE (b. 1808-d. 1845). Lucy Whitfield Criddle was born 1813 or 1814 and died 1892. They had child Mary Eliza Criddle (b., 1833-d. 1929) who married John Scruggs (b. 1827-d. 1911). Mary and John Scruggs had child Edward Criddler Scruggs (b. 1854-d. 1948). Edward married Mary Stuart (b. 1865-d. 1941)."

"Edward and Mary Scruggs had the child Edward Criddler Scruggs, Jr. (b. 1902-d. 1973), and he married Annie Mimms (b. 1902). They had the child Virginia Elizabeth Scruggs (b. 1937). Virginia married B. Shaw Jared, and they had the children Eliz. Shaw Jared (b. 1963) and Anne Marie Jared (b. 1960)."

Virginia Scruggs Jared has some old papers and writes what she has in these papers....

"MARY writes that in the year that LUCY WHITFIELD and SMITH CRIDDLE married (1832), Lucy's mother died leaving a six-year-old, MARY ANNE WHITFIELD. Mary Anne, the child, had some inheritance for she had money and was a slave owner at six."

"She first went to live with her brother-in-law, John M. Winstead, but this small child made to free with her toys, and in spite of a bribe of a 'pretty pony,' Mary Anne and her servant insisted on going to live with her sister Lucy and husband Smith who had just moved to Henry County, Tennessee, and had no children."

"Mary tells many delightful stories about Mary Anne who first married Ewing Criddle who was Smith Criddle's half-brother. He, too, was orphaned at 13 and came to live with Smith and Lucy. When Ewing died, Mary Anne married Alonzo Avery and went to live in New York - (Orlando)."

"Harriet Whitfield and John M. Winstead's children are listed in John M. Winstead obituary as _____ Winstead who married John M. Hart... One of John M. Winstead's sons lost a leg at Gettysburg and was treated by Dr. Dan Cliffe... Dr. D.B. Cliffe was president of Franklin Bank in 1888."

TEXAS AND TENNESSEE

Harrison Whitfield and Polly Mary had a son named Harrison Whitfield, Jr. (b. 1825 TN-d. Feb. 14, 1895 TX). Harrison and Sophronia Whitfield lived at Williamson County, TN. In 1851 the family lived in Hickman County, TN. Then they moved from Williamson County, TN, in 1870 to Lincoln County, TN. After a while they moved to Cooke County, TX. They had five children:
1. Agatha ("Aggie") Whitfield 1848.
2. James Whitfield, b. Jan. 16, 1851. He married Martha Travis.
   4. Thomas, born 1859.
3. 'N.P.' Pallie, born 1854. 5. Ada Rebel, b. 1863-d. 1883.

The children of James Whitfield (b. 1851 and d. Feb. 19, 1915) and Martha Angeline Travis (b. July 21, 1855-d. Feb. 2, 1916) were seven in numbers:
1. Medora, b. 1875-d. 1940.   5. Roger, b. 1890-d. 1953.
2. James E. Whitfield,   6. Sallie, b. 1888-d. 1966.
   b. 1877-d. 1930.   7. Harrison "Pat," b. 1896-d.
3. Thomas L., b. 1880-d.1949.   1958.
4. Leland E., b. 1885-d. 1948.

These members of James Whitfield's family are buried in the Whitfield-Deaton plot at Fairview Cemetery in Gainesville, TX, except for Roger and Harrison who are buried at Ardmore, OK.

PLEASANT HILL article from A Heritage Of Grandeur, James A. Chutchfield. Franklin, Tennessee, 1981, Cornton Association.

WILLIAMSON COUNTY, TENNESSEE

Williamson County and its county seat of Franklin were brought into being simultaneously by an act of the Tennessee Legislature on October 26, 1799, although the town of Franklin was not incorporated until 1815.

Carved from a portion of neighboring Davidson County, Williamson County was named in honor of Dr. Hugh Williamson, a Colonel and Surgeon-General of the North Carolina Militia, a member of the Continental Congress, and signer of the North Carolina Constitution.

There were no permanent settlements before 1798 due to Indian depredations. Ewin Cameron built the first house in Franklin while it was still an untouched wilderness in the fall of that year or early 1799.

Major Anthony Sharpe sold a 640-acre section of this enormous grant in this area to Abram Maury. On some 109 acres of this property, Maury laid out the town of Franklin with a square reserved for the erection of a courthouse and for public use. The site was surveyed by Henry Rutherford in 1800. The plat contained some 200 lots with most of the land on which Franklin now stands owned by Maury who rapidly sold lots to enterprising settlers.

The little town was encircled by the beautiful and historic Harpeth River.

The first few years the pioneers cut cane, felled trees, and lived off bear, deer, turkey, fish, and small game. They craved bread, but there was only a little corn from which the precious meal was made on a piece of tin punched full of holes and nailed on a board. Wild nettles substituted for turnips, and cows were cherished for their milk and butter. Hogs were difficult to pen.

After 1799 families started pouring in with every social strata represented. The greater number of them came to take up grants rewarded for Revolutionary services. Some were the younger sons of noble sires with the Cavalier blood of England fresh in their veins, forced by the rigid law of primogeniture to seek lands of their own. Many settlers were fresh from the Old Country.

McPhail-Cliffe Office

McPhail-Cliffe Office

Little of Franklin's long and eventful history has escaped this brick office building located on East Main Street. Thought to have been built as early as 1813, it was the office of at least two distinguished physicians, and it is said the first anesthetic successfully used in Middle Tennessee was administered by Dr. McPhail about 1831 when he treated a man for gunshot wounds in this building.

Born in Inverness, Scotland, in 1799, Dr. Daniel McPhail and members of his family settled in Williamson County where the name soon acquired considerable prominence. On October 11, 1831, Dr. McPhail married Sarah Whitfield. Her parents, Wilkins and Mary Sturdivant Whitfield, had emigrated to this county around 1806 from Sussex County, Virginia, where they had married in 1801. In 1846 Daniel McPhail died while serving as a surgeon in the United States Army in the Mexican War. A monument in old City Cemetery in Franklin marks his final resting place.

In 1849 Sarah Whitfield McPhail married James Nichols and moved to Hickman County where two of her sisters, Martha Ann (Mrs. Robert Charter) and Theodosia (Mrs. William G. Claggett), had previously moved. Their seven brothers were prominent residents in Williamson County for many years. The youngest sister, Virginia C. Whitfield, married Dr. McPhail's nephew, Dr. Daniel B. Cliffe, November 15, 1842.

Daniel Bonapart Cliffe (1823-1913) had come from Ohio as a boy of 13 to live with his uncle in Franklin. He began the study of medicine under Dr. McPhail's guidance and developed into one of the leading physicians in this area. Dr. Cliffe was the son of Joseph Stephen Cliffe who was born in London, England, in 1799 and Isabella McPhail Cliffe born in Scotland that same year. They were married in Wooster, Ohio, in 1822. That Joseph Stephen Cliffe died young is surmised from the fact the 1850 census lists Isabella and her second husband, R.W. Smith of Vermont, as living in Franklin in the household of her son, Dr. Cliffe, with a daughter, Julia A. Smith, who had been born in Ohio in 1828. Old City Cemetery listings record Isabella Smith's death in 1891.

At Dr. McPhail's death Dr. Cliffe had inherited a part of his uncle's estate under a partnership agreement. He lived in the house where his grandson Joe Cliffe resided in recent memory and used Dr. McPhail's office adjoining the yard to see his patients. Dr. and Mrs. Cliffe were the parents of a number of children, few of whom survived the parents.

When war broke out in 1861, Dr. Cliffe served in the Twentieth Tennessee Regiment as General Felix Zollicoffer's Brigade Surgeon.

The name of Daniel B. Cliffe has always been synonymous with the highest medical knowledge in Franklin. Skilled and kind, Dr. Cliffe was respected as a gentleman and physician by the Franklin people. The tradition of medical excellence started by him was carried on by his grandson under the same name.

Dr. Cliffe's eyesight was impaired during his stay in the Confederate army, and before his death he was blind.

Pleasant Hill

It was the Winstead homestead of generations ago when they first came here from Northumberland County, Virginia, and settled on Mill Creek between Brentwood and Nolensville in 1799. It continued their home until a majestic brick house, tree embowered and white-columned, was constructed on higher ground to the north between 1855-58.

John Matthews Winstead was born in the old log cabin to the pioneer parents on March 9, 1807. When he was twenty years old he married Nancy Whitfield (1811-1885), the daughter of Harrison Whitfield (1783-1864), and to this union were born three daughters and nine sons, five of whom were soldiers in the Confederate army.

Pleasant Hill, home of Colonel John Matthews Winstead

An old brown ledger found on a closet shelf some years ago revealed that Colonel John M. Winstead and his family moved in the brick house in the spring of 1858. It was, and is, one of the county's most beautiful and elegant ante-bellum homes with its long shady ell and stately pillars.

Colonel Winstead died in 1896 and the children moved away over the years; but the old place drew them back. They always made a quiet visit to the family cemetery near the house where parents, grandparents, other relatives, and their best loved servants rest. _____

Whitfield associated families at Williamson County, Tennessee, were the following surnames:

Elizabeth Whitfield Greene	Alexander Campbell
Theodosia Whitfield Clagett	Martha Ann Charter
Virginia C. Whitfield Cliffe	Sarah Whitfield McPhail

Cemeteries. Record of City Old Cemetery about 1810.
Rest Haven Cemetery after 1810. Williamson Co., Tennessee.
Hightower Cemetery is in Brentwood, TN, near Williamson Co., Tennessee.

Marriage Bond at Sussex County, Virginia.
23 December 1801. Wilkins Whitfield, born 1781, Albemarle Parish of Sussex County. Son of Thomas Whitfield of Sussex County, Virginia.
Wilkins Whitfield and Polly Sturdivant. Surety, Harrison Whitfield.

424

JOHN WILKINS WHITFIELD
Son of Wilkins Whitfield and P. Mary Whitfield of Franklin, Williamson Co., TN. Grandson of Thomas Whitfield (1735-1794 VA) and Winifred (1740-1838 TN). John was born 1818 in Franklin, TN.

John Whitfield settled at Centerville (Whitfield town) in Hickman County, Tennessee, in 1836. John was a planter on land from 1839 to 1845.

John married Catherine Dansby April 13, 1839. Issue, two daughters. Catherine died 1846.

In 1846 John Whitfield was Captain, Company A, First Tennessee Regiment of Mexican War.

In 1849 John Whitfield was elected to the 28th General Assembly of Tennessee, Senate. In Tennessee Congress 1849-1852.

In 1851 John Whitfield was appointed Major General, Third Division of Tennessee militia.

John Wilkins Whitfield
1818- 1879

Portrait of a Civil War Soldier"

John Wilkins Whitfield married Sarah B. Dibrell May 28, 1853, at Nashville, TN. They had a son John Anthony Whitfield (1855-1909). In 1853 John W. Whitfield and Sarah moved to Independence, MO. and John became Agent to the Pottawatomes Indians.

On December 5, 1854, John W. Whitfield was elected Delegate to the thirty-third Congress, House of Representative of the United States. John Whitfield was elected to the thirty-fourth Congress and served until March 3, 1857.

John Whitfield had duty of registering land grands in Doniphan, KS, from 1857 to 1861.

John Whitfield was in the Confederate Army and fighting in the Civil War in 1861. He was in battles at KS, TN, MS.

May 9, 1863, John Whitfield was Brigadier General of the 27th Regiment in the Army of the West. He was in the Army until 1865. John went to Texas. In 1866 settled in Lavaca County, TX, with his family and became a planter. The farm was near Hallettsville, TX. There are many accounts of John Whitfield in the state of Texas. John Whitfield was a member of the Texas State Constitutional Convention in 1866, and several trusts of the Texas people. John Whitfield died on October 27, 1879, in Lavaca County, TX, at his home.

In 1890 Sarah Dibrell Whitfield was living in Medina Co., TX. Sarah was born Dec. 11, 1827 and died April 26, 1918, in Texas.

425

DESCENDANTS OF THOMAS WHITFIELD (b. 1735-d. 1794, Sussex County, VA) **and WINIFER WHITFIELD** (b. 1740-1838 d. Tennessee). They had a son named WILKINS WHITFIELD (b. 1781 VA-d. about 1841 TN). He married 1801 Polly Mary Sturdivant. She lived and died in TN. They had a son named THOMAS JEFFERSON WHITFIELD (b. February 10, 1810, Williamson County, TN, and died January 10, 1873, Perry County, TN). He married 1835 second wife, Sallie L. Dillahunty. They had a son named THOMAS JEFFERSON WHITFIELD (b. February 25, 1845, TN, and died 1908, TN). He married (2) Mattie Jane Nicks. They had a son named Jefferson Lafayette Whitfield who had 17 children born to wife, including four sets of twins. A photograph of Jefferson Lafayette and his wife, Lou Ellen Matlock Whitfield, was taken in 1925 at Steele, Missouri.

JEFFERSON LAFAYETTE WHITFIELD (01/28/1867-06/02/1937)

He was born in Benton County, TN, on Tennessee River at Pavatt's Landing five miles away at Eagle Creek where he resided until he moved to Steele, Missouri, in 1916.

He married Lou Ellen Matlock on 10/14/1888 at Benton County, TN. Lafayette was a merchant and farmer. They came to Missouri with three covered wagons and three cows tied to them. They moved on Nute Maxwell's place in 1917 which they rented to farm.

They planted sunflower for the seeds. Aunt Veatrice and Olie beat the seeds out with sticks. Neely and Olie drove the team and pulled up the flowers. Granpaw was a hard worker, He was sick with arthritis. They moved to a farm near Steele, Missouri, which they bought. They built a home and settled there. The children were maried by now. They visited regularly for he was bed confined. He died in 1937. Grandma died one year later.

They are buried at Mount Zion Cemetery. The 61 Highway runs by the cemetery. There are several of the children, grandhcildren, and daughters-in-law buried there also.

To this marriage was born 17 chilren: four sets of twins. Eight children died young and are buried at Pavatt's Cemetery at Benton County, Tennessee.

There are only two children left of this original family, Veatrice Thornton and Olie Mae. But there are a lot of grandchildren and relatives scattered everywhere.

....Submitted by Mrs. Noel Quinn of Caruthersville, Missouri, in 1992, who is Virginia Rose Whitfield Quinn.

ANCESTRY AT WILLIAMSON COUNTY, TENNESSEE

Mrs. Annabel S. Kropff of Gilroy, California, writes in February 1992: "My grandmother, Ada Whitfield Kerr, b. 1863 in Lincoln County, Tennessee, died in 1883 when my mother was eight months old. My mother, Katie Kerr was born 1882 and lived with her grandparents until her grandfather died when Katie was age 13. She lied with her uncle Thomas Whitfield and uncle James Whitfield until she married Lemuel Sawyer, Dec. 1, 1901."

"My husband, John W. Kropff, died Dec. 3, 1987. He was almost 87 years old and was born January 5, 1901. I have a daughter, Helen Moser, who lives in Gilroy, and a son who lives in the country near Gilroy, California. The children and their families get together often, and there are forty of us, and two new great-grandchildren born this summer. I am age 81 and was born Aug. 29, 1910."

She writes to Vallie Jo Whitfield the following: "I admire your ability to get that much material put together so well, that you wrote in the book WHITFIELD HISTORY AND GENEALOGY OF TENNESSEE. We should all be grateful for the work you have done, I say, thanks for all of us." Letter is signed Annabel Sawyer Kropff.

She tells in the letter - "I have my daughter, Ruth Marie Wolf and her son, Brian Wolf, working on the genealogy. Also, a cousin Jim Bass, age 71."

James Bass submitted the following records in 1990:

DIRECTORY. WILLIAMSON COUNTY, TENNESSEE BURIAL Vol. 1, p. 355. Whitfield - Winstead Cemetery location is 16th district, Hugh Edmondson farm, Concord Road.
> Alston Cemetery. Martha A. Whitfield, born April 19,1852, and died October 8, 1855.

DIRECTORY. WILLIAMSON COUNTY, TENNESSEE BURIAL Vol. 2.
Mt. Hope Cemetery. City Cemetery - "Rush Haven"
> Whitfield marker, City Cemetery, Franklin, TN, p. 229.

Mother	Father
Sarah A. Whitfield	Smith O. Whitfield
b. 1839 d. 1919	b. July 4, 1845 d. Dec. 27, 1927

M.B. Whitfield 1886-1945. Father.

Sarah C. Whitfield married Dr. Daniel McPhail on Oct. 11, 1831. They lived in Franklin, and Dr. McPhail's office was on Main Street, Franklin, TN.

Sarah C. Whitfield McPhail has portrait in plume colored velvet. It is a family tradition that the artist was Washington Cooper.

James Bass ("Jim") and wife Bernie Bass visited Nashville, TN, in 1990. Jim Bass visited the Winstead Place in Williamson County, TN, in 1990 and found the old house, and had a good view of rolling country side.

....Annabel Kropff submitted history and pedigree chart on Feb. 18, 1992. She made her home in Gilroy, CA.

GENEALOGY
CHART
Hand written by
Annabel Kerr Sawyer Kropff
February 1992

Thomas Whitfield b 1735
Winifer b 1740
D 1838 Franklin, Tn.

1. Mary 1760
2. William 1762
3. Elizabeth 1764
4. Francis 1765
5. Martha Patty 1767
6. Wilkins 1770
7. Betty (Betsy) 1774
8. Nancy 1776
9. Harrison 1778 ⟶
10. Jack (John) 1780

Harrison Whitfield m 29 Aug 1804
b 1778 D 1864
Polly Sledge
1. Thomas
2. Rebecca
3. "
4. "
5. "
6. Harrison Whitfield 1826 ⟶
7. "
8. Nancy W. Winstead
9. "
10. "

Harrison Whitfield
b 1826 m 16 Sept 1845 D 14 Feb 1895
Sophronia M. Conn

1. Agatha (Aggie) 1848
2. James 1851 m 21 July 1455 d 2 Feb 1916
3. Mr Pallie 1854
4. Thomas 1859
5. Ada Rebel 1 Nov 1863 D 25 Jan 1883

5. Ada Whitfield b 1 Nov 1863
m. 1881
D 25 June 1883
James Kerr b. 1852
One child, Katie = Lemuel Sawyer
   b 29 Oct 1882
   M 1 Dec 1901
   D 28 Oct 1941

Children:
1. Mollie Lucille
2. Wesley Alton
3. Flora Elizabeth
4. Lilian Irene
5. Annabel
6. Ruby Faye
7. Lemuel James
8. Ida May Kathryn

5. Annabel Sawyer b 29 Aug 1918
m 14 April 1929
John W Kropff - b 5 Jan 1901
   D 3 Dec 1989
Children:
1. Roy William
2. Ruth Marie Wolf
3. Helen Ann Mozer
4. James John Kropff
5. Kathryn Pearl

Great grand + Grandchildren of Annabel & John Sawyer Kropff

1. Rex Kropff - Annancia
2. Laura Lynn = Barry Latham Poy & Linda
   A. Melinda
   B. Blake
3. Brian Wolf
4. Eric Wolf = Jo Ann
   A. Amy Marie
5. Gary Lee Wolf = Sheila
6. Mark Mozer
7. Ann Mozer
8. Carol Mozer = Ken Nelson
   A. Joseph
   B. Christopher
9. Michael Kropff = Leslie
   A. Kevin
10. Kathleen Kropff = Scott Morgan
   A. Matthew
11. Steven Kellogg
12. Scott Kellogg
13. Ryan Kellogg
14. Robert Mozer

Ruth Marie & Dave

Helen & Leo

Jim and Doris

Kathryn & Larry

Helen & Leo

Annabel Kropff, 1992

WHITFIELD AND BECK of
North Carolina, Kentucky, Tennessee, Illinois

ELIZABETH WHITFIELD (b. 1746-d. 1779) married Jonathan Taylor in 1761. Elizabeth Whitfield Taylor married second husband JOHN BECK. John served as a lieutenant in Duplin, NC. John was in the militia and died in 1790. Elizabeth and John had ten children. The ninth child was Mary Beck.

Elizabeth Whitfield Beck's daughter, Mary Beck, married WILLIAM WHITFIELD (b. 1764-d. 1825) in Duplin County, NC. They had these children: William, Needham, Joseph, Lewis, Hester, John, Harriet, May, Lucy, and Bryan.

When Mary Beck Whitfield was a widow, she went with her sons who moved to Illinois.

Stephen W. Stokes living in June 1993 in Fort Worth, TX, writes he is the great-great-great-great grandson of William Whitfield IV who lived in Tennessee.

Tennessee: William and Mary Beck Whitfield lived.
            Elizabeth Whitfield married John Perry.

Kentucky: Arthur Whitfield Hazard Perry married Sarah Jose.
            Harriet Ellen Perry married Thomas Allen Stokes.
            Cave Stokes married Minnie May Whitis.

Texas: Clint Leon Stokes married Martha Eloise Johnson.
            Stephen Wayne Stokes, born April 27, 1951.
            Unmarried.
....Submitted by Stephan Wayne Stokes of Forth Worth, TX, in June 1993.

The children of Hermon Whitfield and wife:
1. Mary Francis Whitfield (McDonald) b. July 21, 1941.
2. Glenda Fay Whitfield (Freeman) b. January 9, 1943.
3. Nancy Kay Whitfield (Johnson) b. Dec. 27, 1953.
4. Marcia Sue Whitfield (Thornberry) b. July 9, 1955.
5. Hermon Dan Whitfield b. May 6, 1961.

The father, Hermon Whitfield, was the son of Cleather Cummins Whitfield who was born Sept. 30, 1891, and died Sept. 16, 1974. His father was Jefferson Lafayette Whitfield. In 1995 Hermon Whitfield lived in Clarton, Missouri.

Jefferson L. Whitfield's store was at Bird Hill between Dry Branch and Sycamore Landing in Tennessee.

Marriage Records

Thomas Whitfield and Eliza Bell Hatley both married in Tennessee.

Cleather Cummins Whitfield married Mary Crobb in Tennessee.

Cartie Seltton Whitfield married Arie Baker in Tennessee.

Virginia Whitfield married Noel Quinn in Missouri. Noel was born in 1923. Noel Quinn had a pawn shop in Missouri at Caruthersville area. Virginia was born in 1930.

Tennessee to Illinois

1. MATTHEW WHITFIELD ("Mat") was born 1855 in Tennessee, assumed at Williamson County. His wife had the name CORA. The children were Benjamin and Lesley and others.

2. ROBERT LEE Whitfield was born 1883 Tennessee and died about 1906 in Tennessee. He was an electrician. His wife, Lervesa G. Whitfield, was born 1889 in Tennessee, and died about 1917. They had six sons:

   Ersell b. 1905   Robert b. 1912   Chester b. 1915
   Hugh H. b. 1910   Jessie b. 1913   James R. b. 1917

3. HUGH H. WHITFIELD, b. May 1909 at Nashville, TN, Davidson County. Hugh died in one of these years 1980, 1981, or 1982. Hugh Whitfield married Thelma Eunice King who was born Jan. 22, 1912. Thelma died Feb. 18, 1959, Chicago, IL. They had children.

4. ARTHUR JACK WHITFIELD was born June 8,1934, the son of Hugh and Thelma Whitfield, at Chicago, IL. Arthur Whitfield married Grace Valentine Falk on July 9, 1955. Grace was born Feb. 14, 1958, in Chicago, IL. They had the son, Robert John.

5. ROBERT JOHN WHITFIELD was born Feb. 14, 1958, at Turner Air Force Base in Albany, Dougherthy, Georgia. Robert J. Whitfield married on August 27, 1976, to Sylvia Marie Sodders. She was born Dec. 5, 1957, in VA. They were divorced in 1979.

6. Robert J. and Sylvia Whitfield had the son named Jeremiah Christopher Whitfield who was born June 26, 1978, at Chicago, IL.

....Submitted by Robert John Whitfield of Chicago, IL, in 1993.

Hester Rozelle Whitfield
Daniel (1916-1982)

Rozelle W. Daniel

WAVERLY-Services for Mrs. Rozelle Whitfield Daniel, 66, will be held at 3 p.m. Sunday at the Waverly Church of Christ. Burial will be in the Richlawn Cemetery in Waverly.

Mrs. Daniel died Friday in Benton County General Hospital after a long illness.

She was a native of Humphreys County and a daughter of the late James and Mary McKeel Whitfield. She was married to Billy R. Daniel of Waverly.

Mrs Daniel was a retired Licensed Pratical Nurse.

She was a member of the Spann Church of Christ near Waverly.

Survivers besides her husband include two brothers, James R. Whitfield, New Johnsonville and Robert E. Whitfield, Pleasant Hill. Calif.

John Whitfield, b. 1817, TN. Wife was Martha.

Nancy Ellen Whitfield, born July 25, 1855, TN. She married May 13, 1874, Dickson County, TN. Nancy died Oct. 15, 1931, Nashville, TN.
....Submitted by Robert J. Puckett of Littleton, CO, in 1992.

MARY BECK was a descendant of William Whitfield and Elizabeth Goodman of NC. Mary Beck married William Whitfield and lived in TN at Kentucky and in Steward Co., TN. William Whitfield b. 1764 Wayne Co., NC, d. Aug. 8, 1925, TN. His widow Mary Beck Whitfield moved to Fayette Co., IL, and lived in Effingham Co., IL, in 1844 and died shortly after this date.

431

William Whitfield and Sarah Ann Prigmore Whitfield were among the first to come to California named Whitfield in 1854. A travel from Tennessee to Arkansas and then to Texas and westward to California.

About 1910 William Whitfield and Sarah Whitfield moved to Pico-Rivera in California to be near their daughters, Mary Jane Whitfield Pallett and Sarah Elizabeth Whitfield Pallett. Around the time of 1914 they moved to San Bernardino to live with their daughter, Mohala Lucinda Whitfield Montgomery. William Whitfield born in 1831 in Tennessee then died October 30, 1915.

The widow Sarah Ann Prigmore Whitfield lived with her youngest daughter Belle Milner. Sarah Whitfield died November 13, 1917. William Whitfield and Sarah Whitfield are buried in Mountain View Cemetery, San Bernardino, California. (1)

These records have three with the name of Whitfield who had a stay at Arkansas and several others who moved to Texas from 1849 to 1865.

Reference: (1) "History of Pomona Valley California," pub. by Historic Record Co., Los Angeles, California, 1920.

TENNESSEE RECORDS

Enlisted Tennessee men in the War of 1812. Ancil (Ansil) Whitfield, Private in miliary service in the Cavalry. In troop of Colonel Thomas Benton and Captain McFerrin. Volunteer Infantry.

Killebrew Whitfield, Private in the Cavalry Military Service Infantry. In the troop of Colonel John Wynne and Captain Bayless Prince.

Reference: Tennesseans in the War of 1812 by Byron Sistler and Samuel Sistler.

DAVIDSON COUNTY, TENNESSEE MARRIAGES

William Whitefield of Elle Green on Nov. 6, 1847.
America Whitfield married William Gallaher on Jan. 15, 1842.
Esther T. Whitfield married John Fletcher on Nov. 5, 1799.
George Whitfield married Wareena Spence on Oct. 24, 1843.
Henry Whitfield married Martha Ann Loftin on Oct. 22, 1823.
John Whitfield married Susan Phipps on March 8, 1823.
John Whitfield married Mary G. Hutton on Sept. 1, 1835.
Mary L. Whitfield married John H. Allen on Nov. 23, 1843.
Thomas Jefferson Whitfield married Sallie L. Dillahunty on Jan. 2, 183___.
William Whitfield married Elizabeth Newson on Dec. 4, 1832.
William Whitfield married Emeline Carington on Feb. 19, 1847.

Reference: Marriages of Davidson County, Tennessee 1789-1847, Compiled by Edythe Rucker Whitley.

TENNESSEE RECORDS

Franklin Skillern a Deed of Trust to R.B. Cox, his interest in the estate of his deceased brother, Edmon G. Skillern, securing debt to Cope Whitfield. Recorded March 5, 1868.

Reference: Giles County, Tennessee Deed Book, page 435.

Trust Deed from M.B. Skillern to James A. P. Skillern to A.C. White land in 8th District bought from Hopkins bounds George Ballentine, Mrs. M. Mason, C. Whitfield, Mrs. M.B. Skillern's dowee, securing note to White. Recorded Jan. 9, 1868.

Reference: Giles County, Tennessee, Deed Book DD, page 359.

Rebecca Whitfield and Lewis C. Allen's marriage date was Oct. 11, 1823, in Williamson County, Tennessee. My great-grandparents Henry Harrison Allen and Margaret E. Warren married in 1863 in Tishomingo County, Mississippi. They were there in 1870 and in Williamson County, Tennessee, in 1880. Shortly afterward they moved to Robertson County, Texas, and both are buried there in the Owensville Cemetery. Margaret Warren came from Hardeman City, Tennessee, and the Warrens came from North Carolina.

I have started to work on Allen and Whitfield names in Virginia.
....Submitted by Estelle Corder of Dallas, Texas, on Jan. 5, 1975. Mrs. Corder researched the following records and sent them.

WILLIAMSON COUNTY, TENNESSEE MARRIAGES
Lewis C. Allen to Rebecca Whitfield, 11 Oct. 1823 by Levin Edney, M.B. Bondsman: Jeter Perkins.

On the 1850 Census Williamson County, Tennessee, Lewis C. Allen was age 49. Rebecca was age 44. Children: Seletha E. age 24, Searcy D., age 20, Felix age 18, Wilkins age 16, Harrison age 15, John W., age 13.

TISHOMINGO COUNTY, MISSISSIPPI MARRIAGES
Captain Henry H. Allen married Margaret M. Warren 24, Dec. 1863. Children: Lula Edna (Ernestine, first but Grandmother changed her name). Wilkins Cross Allen. Hortense Allen.

According to the courthouse records in Tishomingo Co., MS (now in Alcorn County), the Warren family was wealthy but lost most of their land by 1880. They also had many slaves earlier.

1880 WILLIAMSON COUNTY, TENNESSEE. Vol. 35, E.D. 242, page 10.

H.H. Allen	49 b. TN		W.C. (Son) Allen	9
M.M. Allen	35 b. TN		Hattie Allen	3
L.E. Allen	12			

Marriage Tennessee
Andrew P. Davis (1807 ca.-1881 ca) married (1) Betty Simmons and (2) Mrs. Mary (Perkins) Whitefield (b. July 4, 1812-d. Dec. 3, 1900). She was widow of Dr. Carter B. Whitefield of Jackson County, TN. Andrew P. Davis came to Jackson County, TN, in 1839 from Alabama.
....Submitted by John Paul Grady of Midland, TX, June 3, 1996.

On the 1830 census list for a neighborhood were these names for Franklin, Tennessee. Alexander Brown, John Holladay, Thomas Gillu, Joel Jones, John Evans, Henry Night, Henry Whitfield, William Evans, William Whitfield, Harrison Whitfield, Abraham Taylor, Lambert Forehand, John Forehand, Joseph Horton, Robert Hill, Alexander Porter, David Hill, Williams Byrs.

"My grandparents were all dead before I was born in 1919. My grandfather, Dr. James Whitfield, was born in Tennessee, January 16, 1851. He attended school in Murfreesboro and later Vanderbilt Medical College. My mother told me that they came to Cooke County, Texas, and settled in Dexter, Texas, near Gainesville. My brother has a large ranch next to Dexter in the Walnut Bend area. My grandfather died in Gainesville, TX, February 19, 1915, and is buried in Fairview Cemetery there."

"His father, Harrison Whitfield, was also born in Tennessee. He served as an assistant surgeon in the Confederate Infantry of Tennessee. He died in Dexter, Cooke County, in 1895 and is buried in the family lot there. Sophronia Conn (born 1826 or 1828) Whitfield died in 1894 or 1901 and is also buried there."

....Submitted by James P. Bass of McLean, VA, in March, 1989.

Paper refers to Denton, Texas, for cemetery in Gainesville, TX, and not Dexter.

JOHN ("Jack") REGAN WHITFIELD married Betty Jane Hubbbs, daughter of Elijah C. Hubbs and Arabelle McDaniel Hubbs. There children were Nancy Whitfield, Hattie Whitfield, Willie Whitfield, James Whitfield, John R. Whitfield.

....Submitted by F.B. Cain of Benton County, TN, in 1992.

Virginia Rose Whitfield Quinn of Missouri State wrote on June 11, 1992, the following: "My grandfather named LAFAYETTE WHITFIELD of Tennessee and Steel, Missouri, had a business. "I have been told he had a ferry also with his name on it. He had a store in Tennessee. He went broke and went out of business. He gave too much credit. When we were small children, we met at his home in Steel, Missouri, with our cousins. We were busy playing."

"My grandfather had coins which he made with name on them of his business. He paid labor off with them, plus money." The store was groceries and hardware.

JAMES M. WHITFIELD of Tennessee

J. M. Whitfield is listed as a student of the Medical Institute of Louisville in Kentucky in the class of 1845-1846. His residence was listed as Tennessee and his Preceptors were Doctors McPhail and Cliffe of Franklin, TN.

....Submitted from University of Louisville, Louisville, KY. Kornhauser Health Sciences Library. Secretary, Darlene Newlin, August 1978.

J. M. Whitfield attended the Medical College of Ohio for the
session 1847-1848 and was granted the Medical Doctor degree in
1848. When he registered for the course of study, he gave his
residence as Franklin, Williamson County, Tennessee.

....Submitted from University of Cincinnati Medical Center,
College of Medicine of Cincinnati, Ohio, on January 10,1979.
Marion H. Flym, Assistant to the Dean, Office of Medical
Alumnal Association.

Doctor James. M. Whitfield is shown as a physician on the 1850
Tennessee Census.

There were several men named Doctor Whitfield in early
Tennessee:
Dr. Thomas W. Whitfield married Sarah M. Berry, March 3, 1885.
     He practiced medicine West Tennessee and was from Franklin.
Dr. Harry Whitfield married Mary F. Baker.
     Issued license Feb. 26, 1856.
Dr. Henry W. Whitfield was a physician and is on 1850 Census
     of Humphreys County, Tennessee.

Dr. Dan B. Cliffe Medical Office 1850
Historic Site Landmark. Franklin, Tennessee
Photograph taken 1990

James Whitfield born Jan. 16, 1851, in Tennessee attended
schools in Murfreesboro, TN, and later Vanderbilt Medical
College. Dr. James Whitfield practiced medicine in Cooke
County, Texas.

Virginia Whitfield and Sarah Whitfield, sisters, and daughters
of Wilkins Whitfield.

Rev. John W. Whitfield, MD and DD, died 1820. He taught at
Washington College, later Washington and Lee University,
Lexington, VA.

RESIDENCES OF PARENTS THOMAS JEFFERSON WHITFIELD (b. Feb. 25, 1845 Hickman County, TN-d. July 22, 1908 Benton, TN) and MATTIE (Martha) JANE NICKS (b. Sept. 28, 1845-d. 1930) of Benton Co., TN, and JAMES DEE WHITFIELD (1877-1954) a son.

Thomas J. Whitfield moved 1886 to Rockport when James Dee Whitfield was age nine. Went to Pegram School. James Dee Whitfield was born above Bakerville, TN. On map. Thomas Jefferson Whitfield moved to Davidson Landing in about three years. From there to Vernon in Hickman County for three months and back to Davidson Landing. From there to fork of river. From these to Bakerville at Denton Bone place. From there to above Bakerville. From there to Rockport in December 1886. From there to Camden. From Canden to Pavatts in summer of July 1890. January 1891 to Parkers Landing in Decatur County, January 1895, back to Pavatts where Uncle Thomas Cleveland lives. About December 20, 1895, moved on a ferry boat up to Dixie below Cuba Landing and all in Tennessee the middle district. Married in 1899. January 1900 Thomas Jefferson Whitfield moved back to Rockport, and James Dee Whitfield moved to Rockport November 15, 1900. James Dee Whitfield moved down on Eagle Creek at Matlock place January 1902. Bought two shares of Matlocks. 1903 moved to Pavatts at Uncle Thomas Cleveland place. Thomas Jefferson Whitfield moved to Pavatts in January 1902 at the home place. Moved to Waverly Jan. 12, 1912. Moved back to Pavatt's Jan. 1, 1916, on a ferry boat leaving out at cold branch at Duck River. July 1916 moved back to Waverly to his house and lot. Bid the river goodbye. Moved to Rockdale Farm, the Whitfield-Daniel Farm at Waverly, TN, of Humphreys County 1919. Jan. 6, 1944, moved three miles from McKenzie. April 25th went to Detroit, Michigan, the only time he was outside the state of Tennessee, and it was during the World War II in 1944. August 25 came back to Henry, TN, and rented at Felts house Jan. 2, 1945. Then moved to Oakdale farm he bought at Henry, TN. He sold that farm and bought another farm at Puryear, TN, near there, and he called that farm Shadygrove. He sold that farm and retired when the sons left the farm life. Henry and Puryear town are both in Henry County, TN. He rented a house in Paris town the last year of his life. He died at the retirement rental at Brown Street in Paris, TN, and he was interned in the Tennessee Blue Creek McKeel Cemetery Sept. 19, 1954, of Humphreys County, TN.

State of Tennessee, Middle District.

....A Family Record of Vallie Jo Whitfield.

Tennessee Record. Willie Mae Barker Beattie of Jasper, TN, submitted the following lineage in 1988. Willie's father was Moses Easterly Barker and her mother was Willie Mae Jernigan and her father was Robert Walter Jernigan and his father was Lewis Willis Jernigan and his mother was Mary Jane Whitfield.

Willie Mae Jernigan's mother was Ella Nora Pettigrew whose parents were Mathew Whitfield born circa 1814 and died 1834, and her mother was Fanny Monahan. Mathew Whitfield was born 1812 or 1814 in Tennessee and died July 30, 1834, at Rutherford County, TN. He was the youngest son of Mathew Whitfield b., 1772 Nash Co., NC, and died 1827 in Rutherford Co., TN. His wife was Levina Roberson who was born 1775 in NC and died after 1860 and before 1870 in Cannon Co., TN.

436

Miss Ruth Whitfield, 1012 W. Mistletoe, San Antonio, TX, 78201, was the granddaughter of general John Wilkins Whitfield (1818-1879).

His son by his second wife, Sarah Bates Dibrell Whitfield, was John Anthony Whitfield. He married Helena Briscoe of Augusta, Arkansas. She and John met while she was visiting relatives near Hallettsville, Lavaca County. JOHN ANTHONY WHITFIELD died on April 19, 1909, at the age of fifty-four (54) years at Devine, Medina County, Texas. He was born in 1855.

John Anthony Whitfield (1855-1909) and Helena Briscoe Whitfield had four children:
1. George Dribell Whitfield lived 1965 in Devine, TX. Born 12th day, May 1887 in Tennessee.
2. Miss Sadie Whitfield lived 1965 in San Antonio, TX. Worked at bank in San Antonio.
3. Miss Ruth Whitfield lived 1965 in San Antonio, TX. Retired teacher of San Antonio.
4. Mrs. Mamie W. Moore, whose husband was a doctor and W.C. Moore who was deceased in 1965. Mrs. Mamie Moore lived in San Antonio, TX, in 1965.
These Whitfield children moved to Texas in 1859.

This report was made by granddaughter of General John W. Whitfield in a letter to Vallie Jo Whitfield on May 30, 1965.

Frances B. Starr, wife of William T. Starr, on North Lake Drive, Dallas, TX, in 1965, month of April says her great-grandfather was James Monroe Whitfield, son of Wilkins Whitfield of Williamson County, TN. James M. Whitfield was married on January 3,1845, in Maury County, TN, to Mary Dansby Oliphant, daughter of Tabitha and Samuel Oliphant. They had eight children and five of these children were born in Texas.

John Whitfield was married to Catherine Dansby in Maury County, TN, April 13, 1839, and they had two children.

George Washington Whitfield went to Texas about 1849. He has Tennessee record in 1850 there. He married Louisa King and she died 1848 and they had three children. The second wife was Sarah Hunter Bond, and there were eight children of this marriage. They are buried in Texas.

Wilkins Whitfield, oldest son, Henry Whitfield, had a son named Henry. Henry W. Whitfield was married to Susanna DeMoss Oliphant in Maury County, Tennessee, on June 13, 1850. He had a son Henry W. Whitfield who lived in Austin, Texas, in 1965.

Tennessee Record. To Reynoldsburg, TN, four miles northwest, where Dry Creek enters Tennessee River, this town was first settled from 1800 to 1805. It became the County Seat of Humphrey County, TN, in 1812, with the first court meeting at the home of Samuel Parker on Trace Creek Road. The Memphis-Nashville stage line ran through here. The County Seat moved to Waverly, TN, in 1837. From a Historical Monument in Waverly Town of Tennessee.

TENNESSEE RECORDS AND LETTERS

"Two families of mine were closely related to the Whitfields in Montgomery County, TN, and even as far back as early North Carolina, when William Whitfield married Elizabeth Goodman in Gates County, North Carolina, in 1713. Elizabeth was a sister of an ancestor of mine, MARTHA GOODMAN, wife of JOHN PIPKIN of Chowan County who left a will there in 1745."

"From that time forward, the Whitfields, the Pipkins, and sometime later the Taylors, are to be found together in the records from Lenoir Co., NC, on to the settlement and the Tennessee frontier. The name Needham Whitfield is especially intertwined with my families. With Joseph Pipkin in Lenoir County, who was the son of John and Martha Goodman Pipkin, later in Montgomery County, TN, when Needham and Bryan Whitfield were purchasers of the estate sale of Samuel Taylor in the 1820s. The wife of Samuel Taylor was a Pipkin, a great-granddaughter of John and Martha Pipkin of Chowan County; daughter of Lewis Pipkin of Smith County, TN."

"Zilpha Pipkin married Jeremiah Fly. There are instances of Whitfields and Pipkins naming one another after themselves - Needham Pipkins abounded, for instance."

"My ancestor Steward Pipkin, born 1784 in North Carolina, lived in Dickson County, TN, in 1820, Lowndes Co., MS, in 1830 and died in Yalobusha Co., MS, in the 1850s. His daughter Elizabeth married Lewis P. Taylor, who was without a doubt a son of Samuel Taylor of Montgomery Co., TN, and one of Steward's sons was named Minor, and another was named Alexander Smith Pipkin. Another of Needham Whitfield's sisters, Elizabeth, married Alexander Smith."

....Submitted by Mr. Chris Morgan of Memphis, TN, on November 3, 1971.

Zelphia Whitfield was a black woman and she died 16 June 1798 in Nashville, TN, in Davidson County.

Reference: Census of Tennessee.

Ercell Hayes Whitfield born July 23, 1907. His parents were Robert Lee Whitfield and Laversa Orace Hunter Whitfield. The family lived in Nashville, TN. Ercell H. Whitfield married Elizabeth Louise Louge, Aug. 7, 1923. They resided in Nashville, TN.

The fifth son of Nancy Whitfield Winstead was William E. Winstead (b. 1837-d. 1911). William married Ann E. Bradley (b. 1843-4.1923). They had two daughters: Maggie and Katie. Maggie Winstead married Ben D. Ewin. Katie Neil married Dr. Sam Webb White.

Williamson Co., TN. Alston Cemetery has Martha A. Whitfield b. 1852 and d. 1855.

County	Land area in Square mile	Population 1910	1900	1890
Contra Costa	714	31,674	18,046	13,515

California Thirteenth Census of United States. Taken in 1910 year.

In 1980 Ellis M. Murphy of Nashville, TN, was married and his wife's birth date was February 18, 1922. He was the son of Bessie May Whitfield, and the grandfather was Thomas Sledge Whitfield. The great-grandfather was Jacobur M. Whitfield. He was a doctor and the name was taken from his medical degree which he earned and received from Cincinnati Medial School in the year 1848. He practiced in Franklin, TN.

Thomas Sledge Whitfield once said, "Jacobur died about a year before the battle of Franklin."

There are records which show that he also had another son, Matt Whitfield, and a daughter, Lella Whitfield, according to Ellis Murphy, and he resides at Nashville, TN, and gave this information.

In 1980 Mrs. Carolyn Whitfield Pickering lived in Franklin, TN, and she is a descendant of Wilkins Whitfield.

In Williamson County, TN, at estate sales appeared Wilkins Whitfield and others. Account of sales show Wilkins Whitfield, a buyer from inventory of Samuel McCutchen, July 1816.

Wilkins Whitfield, a buyer from inventory of Thomas L. Atkins, January 1817.
Wilkins Whitfield, a buyer of inventory of Elijah Hunter, October 1817.
Wilkins Whitfield, a buyer of inventory of Thomas S. Adkins, October 1818.

Maury County, Tennesseans, who lived in Texas.

Account	Purchaser	Item	Price
James Whitfield	Bessie		
James Whitfield	Mary	1 spool thread	.05
James Whitfield	Mat		
James Whitfield	Sarah	8 # sugar	.50
James Whitfield	Stella	1 box snuff	.05
James Whitfield	Wife	5 # honey	.50
Mary Whitfield		1 yd. veiling	.20

Lewis C. Allen married Rebecca Whitfield Allen. Their births in Virginia, and they resided in Williamson County, TN, in the 1850s and 1860s. A son, Henry Harrison Allen, moved to Texas in 1881 or 1882.

Williamson County, TN, Census 1850

Lewis C. Allen	49 VA		Harrison Allen	15 TN	
Rebecca Allen	44 VA	Female	John W. Allen	13 TN	
Seleth Allen	24 TN	Female	Mary U. Allen	9 TN	Female
Searcy D. Allen	20 TN		Ewing Allen	5 TN	
Felix Allen	18 TN		Joe Allen	1 TN	
Wilkins Allen	16 TN				

TENNESSEE MARRIAGES

James Rudder Cliffe married Cornelia Stith Nichol.
Daniel Bonaparte Cliffe married Virginia Whitfield.

....Stephen G. Cliffe of Augusta, GA, in Dec. 1990, was a descendant.

DAVID LIPSCOMB COLLEGE 1976
Nashville, Tennessee

President Athens Clay Pullias conferred B.A. or B.S. degrees on 238 graduates in June and an additional 110 graduates in August, 1976, thereby adding 348 men and women to its alumni roster.

As the only other presentation at commencement, the Valedictorian's medal was presented by Dean Mack Wayne Craig to Miss Kotora in June and to Whitfield in August.

Mrs. Athens Clay Pullias presents Frances Pullias Awards, sterling silver goblets, appropriate engraved, to Jeff David Whitfield, valedictorian, and James David Haradison, salutatorian of the August graduating class. Tennessee State Senator Douglas Henry,

August commencement speaker, with Mrs. Henry and President Athens Clay Pullias are onlookers at the presentation.

Scholarship was so high in David Lipscomb College's June graduating class the two salutatorians with identical grade point averages of 3.95 were topped by the valedictorian by only two one thousandths of a point - 3.97 - all graduating summa cum laude. Mrs. Athens Clay Pullias, third from right, presents Frances Pullias Awards, highest honors conferred on Lipscomb graduates.

In August the valedictorian and salutatorian also graduated *summa cum laude* with averages of 3.94 and 3.90 each.

Mrs. Pullias presented Frances Pullias Awards, sterling silver goblets appropriately engraved, to the three top scholars of the June class and the two leaders in August. These included Jenny Kotora, English major from Washington, PA, June valedictorian; Karen Kerce Laine and David Taylor, both of Nashville, June co-salutatorians; Jeff David Whitfield, Nashville, August valedictorian; and James David Hardison, Columbia, TN, August salutatorian.

Mrs. Laine majored in home economics; Taylor in pre-medical studies; Whitfield, pre-medical studies; and Hardison, pre-dental studies.

Dr. Thomas C. Whitfield was in the Department of Education in 1965 at David Lipscomb College, Nashville, Tennessee.

MARRIAGES

Wilkins Whitfield and Mary Sturdivant had a daughter named Virginia C. Whitfield. She married Daniel Bonaparte Cliffe, Sr.
James Rudder Cliffe married Cornelia Stith Nichol.
Daniel Bonaparte Cliffe married Martha Elise Jones.
....Submitted by a descendant, Stephen G. Cliffe, of Augusta, GA, in December 1980.

John Matthews Winstead, b. 1807 and d. 1896. John md. Nancy Whitfield (b. Aug. 5, 1811, Williamson Co., TN-d. Feb. 7, 1885, Nashville, TN). Nancy was the daughter of Harrison Whitfield (b. Nov. 5, 1783, VA-d. July 21, 1864, at Nashville, TN).

TENNESSEE

Nathan James Thomas Whitfield, born 11/19/1856 and died 1/18/1939. His wife was living in 1963. The granddaughter is Milly E. Knox Hamer (Mrs. James S. Hamer), 4722 Benton Smith Road, Nashville, TN, 37215, in March 1976.
....This is some lineage from Charles Whitfield. It is some related branch line from North Carolina or Virginia.

Lombard Suburban Genealogical Society, Lombard, IL, 60148. Certified the genealogy of Vallie Jo Whitfield on "Whitfield Family Tree" and issued a Bicentennial Citizens Certificate to her daughter, Joanne Vallie Whitfield in March 1976. Thomas Whitfield b. ca. 1735-d. 1794 was the ancestor in Revolutionary Service.

Tennessee Marriage Records

Linda Gale Pendergrass, daughter of Ben Frank Pendergrass, was married to Richard Lewis Whitfield on 23 December, 1967, Chattanooga, TN. He was the son of Ralph Wilson Whitfield and Mildred Whitfield of Paris, TN.

Vivian Gale Brewer, daughter of Elmo Mitchell Brewer, married Ralph Wilson Whitfield on 11 June, 1966, Crossville, TN. Both were students of the University of Tennessee.

Janice Whitfield married Larry White of Tennessee. At Waverly, TN, the son James Ray White was born March 23, 1967. A son, John David White, was born Feb. 8, 1969, to Larry and Brenda White. Brenda Whitfield White married second husband in Tennessee.

Jack W. Whitfield and his wife, Linda Whitfield, had twin children: Melissa Ann Whitfield and Marc Wilson Whitfield on April 15, 1967, in TN. Another son, Michael Lee Whitfield, born April 15, 1968, in TN. Parents were divorced and Linda Whitfield married second time, and the three children live in Michigan.

Ralph Wilson Whitfield, graduated from Grove High School 1961 and was salutatorian of the class. He graduated from the University of Tennessee.

Richard Lewis Whitfield graduated from Grove High School and from the University of Tennessee June 10, 1969.

Rita Ann Whitfield graduated from Grove High School, Paris, TN, May 13, 1969, and she later graduated from the University of Tennessee. They are brothers and sister.

James Dee Whitfield purchased the Farm at Waverly, Humphreys Co., TN, in 1919. James Dee b. 1877-d. 1954. The Whitfield farm passed to his daughter Rozelle Whitfield Daniel and Billie Daniel her husband. Then after they died the land with house and barns were sold in 1994. The land and house of 90 acres was sold and a second parcel of land of 260 acres was sold. Whitfield Farm was 350 acres from 1919 to 1994.

JOHN WHITFIELD

Who was the man named John Whitfield who received acres of land at Coffee County, TN? This question has been asked many times and without documents to historically write an authentic biography. Was he a Revolutionary War soldier? Was he an applicant for open land in Tennessee?

LAND GRANTS, COFFEE COUNTY, TENNESSEE

John Whitfield, Numbers 42, 42, 44, 45 Grants, to John Whitfield for family, and all. Grant No. 6840, 5,000 acres, May 9, 1839, Book M, page 90.

John Whitfield, May 8, 1839. Grant Number 6847, 5,000 acres, Book M, page 89.

John Whitfield, May 9, 1839. Grant Number 6849, 5,000 acres, Book M, page 91.

John Whitfield, May 9, 1839. Grant Number 6850, 5,000 acres, Book M, page 92.

The County was named for John Coffee who was born June 2, 1772, at Prince Edward County, Virginia. Coffee moved to Davidson County, TN, in 1798. Coffee was Colonel and Brigadier-General of Tennessee Volunteers. He served in the War of 1812 and the Creek War. He was appointed surveyor of public lands in March 1817. He died July 1834 in Alabama.

The above list of land grants appears on a Tennessee State list of Land Grants. The log book was seen at the Tennessee State Library Archives at Nashville, Tennessee in 1962 by Vallie Jo Whitfield.
The Library had no information on who John Whitfield was, and their search yielded no Whitfields settling in Coffee County, Tenn. Librarian searcher said "most of the land grants were to North Carolina men for service in a war."

Land grants were usually for much less acres when a soldier was given a grant for service in war. Men could purchase land for sale. The state government announced open land for occupation.

The entry appears to be a duplication for maybe one grant of 5,000 acres. Whatever a John Whitfield had to do with this is not known.

Many of the land grants made to the western lands made by the Land Commissioner for use were not picked up or used by the grantee. This large amount of land usually required a colonization for many people with a purpose of raising revenue for the state.

444

Dear Mrs. Vallie Whitfield:

Your note of 2 May 1977 has been read with some perplexity. As Editor of the Coffee County Historical Society Quarterly, I do research almost constantly about Coffee County and its residents of past years. With no relatives who ever lived here, I can be totally objective in my searching, and I think it might safely be added that I probably do more research about the County than anyone else at this time. Your comments about "John Whitfield...the person with the land grant for most of Coffee County" are very strange, in fact. We have records of many people who held numerous grants for tracts in this County before and after its formation. No grant was allowed by state law for more than 5,000 acres, but one person could and did hold numerous grants for the maximum amount allowed. These men included John Gray and his brother Thomas Blount, Jonathan Webster, Joel Webster, Thomas Hopkins, Thomas King, Samuel B. Barrell, Joseph Anderson, Andrew Erwin, the Purdoms, the Hickersons, Waterson, and others. But I assure you no one by the name of Whitfield held any large grant.

In the first Minute Book of the County Court, 1836-1841, there is not one single reference to any Whitfield - which surely would not be the case were he ever involved in many land transactions here. In the first Tax List, taken in 1836, not long after the formation of the County, which we published in Vol. VI, in 1975, we found in Civil District 6, two men named Whitworth, not Whitfield - no one named Whitfield appeared.

If you really think that Coffee County was the site of these supposed grants, do send us what you have. Our files are indeed incomplete if your information is correct. You might transcribe the grants in question and send to us so that we can judge if they really refer to Coffee County. We should be very appreciative if you would do this.

I am sorry that we have nothing at all on Whitfields of any name in our files.

Yours truly,

Mrs. John R. Bridgewater
Manchester, TN 37355
8 May 1977

VIRGINIA LAND BOUNTIES. To stimulate enlistments and to give reward for military service, the government issued warrants for grants of land to ex-servicemen. Allotments follow:

Major-Generals received	15,000 to 17,500 acres
Brigadier-Generals received	10,000 acres and upwards
Colonel received	5,000 to 8,888 acres
Lieutenant-Colonels received	4,500 to 6,666 acres
Majors received	4,000 to 5,333 acres
Soldiers and Sailors received	200 acres
Privates received	50 acres

When any officer, soldier or sailor was killed or died in service, his heirs or legal representatives became entitled to receive the same quantity of land was would have been due the one in service had he survived.

Land grants were also issued from North Carolina. Many of the land grants did not have applications filed or did not take the land in the west and south.

TENNESSEE NEWSPAPER CLIPS

District of West Tennessee Court, November term 1804. Needham Whitfield versus John Hanks. Jn. Dickinson, clerk.

Rutherford County, TN, April Court session 1805. Land was a double tax for 1804 year. Reputed owner, Bryant Whitfield, 640 acres.

Court of Rutherford County to expose sale of land in Jefferson County on June 27, 1805. Property to satisfy double taxes, charges and cost for 1804. Samuel M. Bridge, Sheriff and Collector.

A letter about land was received in May at Nashville, TN, from Harrison Whitfield.

Bryan Whitfield, John Keathley occupied land which had public sale October 3, 1807. Clarkesville, TN, 500 acres.

William Whitfield and John Stone of Knoxville, TN, had patent of land in the counties of Jefferson and Knox, formerly Greene County, TN. (Vol. 3, No. 9, William Whitfield, April 10, 1794.) (1)

REVOLUTIONARY WARRANTS

Number 1778. Bryant Whitfield, 365 acres, May 20, 1793, as an assignee of Hugh Stephenson, private, North Carolina Continental Line, Davidson Co, TN, above Stones Lick Creek. (2)

Land Warrant. John Boyd to William Whitfield. Deed Book.

Land Transfer. John Boyd to Willis Whitfield. Deed Book.

George Whitfield Robinson born Aug. 30, 1822. He was son of Ezekiel Robinson and wife Neely. George married Aug. 3, 1848, Mary Elizabeth Mankind. Mary was born Oct. 18, 1832, in VA and died Dec. 17, 1869, at Big Spring, Rutherford Co., TN. George and Mary lived at Murfreesboro, TN. George was in the Civil War, and he died Nov. 25, 1862, at Lexington, KY. His children were William, Elizabeth, John, and Virginia.

John Murphy Butler, born 1/31/1874, married at Clarkesville, TN, on 1/14/1902, daughter of Malcolm E. Whitefield and Aurelia Leslie Garrott, and they had five children with surname of Butler.

---

(1) Genealogical Abstracts from Tennessee Newspaper 1791-1808. Compiled by Sherida K. Eddlemon. Pages 88, 102, 125, 185, 195, 264.
(2) Tennessee Genealogical Records. Records of Early Settlers from State and County Archives, compiler - Edythe R. Whitley. Book published 1980.
(3) Deed Book One, 1793-1797. (Second Book of Deeds, Court House, Gallatin, TN).

Thomas Whitfield born about 1735 and died 1794 in Sussex Co., VA. He married Winifer ____ before 1760. Winifer Whitfield was born ca. 1740-died 1838 in Franklin, Williamson County, TN. Thomas Whitfield I names three sons in his will: Wilkins, Harrison, and Jack and six daughters, 1. Mary (Hobbs); 2. Elizabeth (Sturdivant); 3. Francis Whitfield; 4. Martha Patty (Hobbs); 5. Betty (Sturdivant); and 6. Nancy (Knight). They raise a child named William Whitfield. Widow Whitfield and adult children moved 1808 to Franklin, Williamson County, TN.

Brothers

Wilkins Whitfield (b. 1781 VA-d. 1841 Franklin, TN). Wilkins married Polly Mary Sturdivant (b. ca. 1780-d. After 1850, TN). Wilkins Whitfield had the son Thomas Whitfield (b. 1810 TN-d. 1873 TN). Thomas (1810-1873) had the son Thomas Jefferson Whitfield (b. 1845 TN-d. 1908 Eagle Creek, Benton Co., TN).

Harrison Whitfield, the brother of Wilkins Whitfield (1781-1841) had the son Thomas Whitfield who became a doctor. He was brother to Nancy Whitfield Winstead (b. 1811-d. 1885) and she leaves written record her brother was a physician. Dr. Thomas Whitfield had brothers John, Felix G. (b. 1816) and Harrison Jr. (B. 1825-d. 1895 Dexter, TX).

Dr. Thomas Whitfield married and had a family. Dr. Whitfield practiced medicine in Davidson Co., TN, and moved to Henry Co., TN, and had his medical practice for 15 years there. Thomas was born 1827 at Franklin, TN, and died July 13, 1879, at Hill Side Home. He died at Williamson Co., TN.

Wilkins Cliffe Whitfield b. Jan. 29, 1916, lived at Scottsdale, AZ, in 1994. Wilkins was raised in Franklin, TN. He was employed in the US Army for 30 years. He was the son of Daniel Cliffe Whitfield b. 1872 and d. 1921 and Iola May Vaughn b. 1897-d. 1965. The parents married 1914 in Franklin, TN. Wilkins writes that Daniel C. Whitfield's father was Wilkins Whitfield, a doctor during the Civil War. He was married to Dorothy Roberta (b. Sept. 6, 1921-d. before 1994). Wilkins and Dorothy married Nov. 22, 1941, and they had four children:

1. Wilkins C. Whitfield, Jr, born 9/18/1944. He is an automotive engineer and in 1994 lived in Sacramento, CA.
2. John Cliffe Whitfield was born 7/27/1966 and died later.
3. Caroline R. Whitfield was born 1/9/1951. Caroline married Michael MacNeilly and in 1994 they resided in Capistrano Beach, CA.
4. Deborah Anne Whitfield b. 9/1/1962; is a lawyer in Mesa, AZ, in 1994.

....Submitted by Wilkins Cliffe Whitfield of Arizona in 1994.

The second person named Wilkins Whitfield at Franklin, TN, was married to Elizabeth Ridley on 9/3/1846. Wilkins Whitfield appears on the 1850 census of Williamson Co., TN.

James M. Whitfield, age 27, was a physician in 1850 at Williamson Co., TN. He was married to Rebecca and had a child named Sally M. He appears on 1850 Williamson Co, TN, Census.

References: 1. Whitfield History and Genealogy of Tennessee by Vallie Jo Whitfield. Second edition, 1979. Pages 168, 200, 206.
2. Letter to Vallie Jo Whitfield from Wilkins Cliffe dated Aug. 4, 1994.
3. The Whitfield Family, Who's Who In America. Published 1994. Family Archive Press, Phoenix, AZ.

EAGLE CREEK, BENTON COUNTY, TENNESSEE

THOMAS JEFFERSON WHITFIELD was born Feb. 25, 1845, the son of Thomas Jefferson Whitfield, Sr. (b. 1810-1873) He married (1) Martha L. Cunningham April 4, 1866. She was born 1847 and died 1874. He married (2) Mattie Jane Nicks (1845-1930) and they had nine children. Five Sons: Jefferson L., James Dee, John Regan, Thomas Cleveland, Henry Edward.

Thomas Jefferson Whitfield, Jr. lived in Hickman, Humphreys, Decatur, Benton Counties of Tennessee. He was a farmer. Thomas had grown children and some younger children who were young adults living with the parents. He first went to Decatur County and later to Benton. He moved across the Tennessee River and in 1900 to Benton County. He purchased 164 acres on the left bank of the Tennessee River at the mouth of Eagle Creek. Thomas Jefferson Whitfield died 1908. Public Pavatt Cemetery was the burial place for several of the family members.

Mattie Jane Nicks Whitfiled lived on the land and some of the children who now had families. In 1930 she died. In 1943 further fee title to land was filed. They lived on the lower reaches of Eagle Creek. Down the north side is the old Whitfield home place and cemetery. With the coming of the Tennessee Valley Authority their land was condemned. The water authorities of the Tennessee state start in 1932 looking at the river and its uses.

In 1957 on July 3 the Court case was filed. Tracts of land of Whitfields were GIR 5869 and other tract hearings at Court. The final Court case was "Whitfield of Benton County, TN, and US District Court for the Western District of Tennessee."

There were attorneys for defendants Delia Ann Whitfiled Sykes and her husband J.A. Sykes, and daughter Mattie A. Sykes. Also for Clara May Whitfield and Henry Edward Whitfield. Sykes' claim was one approved for farm and payment at court. There were defendants, Jennie Whitfield Ward, Ollie Whitfield and other defendants for land parcels.

Forty Whitfield kinships of blood lines and in-laws were listed at Court and all termed heirs of Thomas Jefferson Whitfield (1845-1908). The Court cases have 141 pages of script. Historically the Court Cases are interesting with the relationship determined of the Defendants and all. This included 34 persons both living and dead. This list of names had two Sykes, one Holliday, two Matlock, nine Phillips and 20 persons named Whitfield.

The Whitfield families were on the east side of the Tennessee River, and Thomas Jefferson Whitfield, Jr. and kinship moved to the west side of the Tennessee River. Whitfields married into some of the old pioneer families of the lower Eagle Creek. These Whitfield families have a family tree and history published in the book Eagle Creek Heritage Notes, The Saga of Ten Pioneer Families, F.B. Cain. Published about 1993. F.B. Cain with his book at Route 2 Box-1-B, Holladay, TN, 38341.

Pioneer families were Fry, Henry, Hubbs, Malin, Matlock, McDaniel, Merrick, Sanders, Thornton, and White.

TENNESSEE CENSUSES

1820 Whitfield, William, Stewart County, 109
1820 Whitfield, William, Stewart County, 109

Whitfield brothers appear on the 1830 Tennessee Census as Whitefield, also there are fathers and sons, Whitfield Place of Hickman County, Tennessee.

Whitfield, Harrison lived Williamson Co., TN, 214 No Township.
Whitfield, John lived Davidson Co., TN, 204, No Township.
Whitfield, John T. lived Whitfield of Hickman Co., TN, 042.
Whitfield, Thomas lived Whitfield of Hickman Co., TN, 042, No Twp.
Whitfield, Thomas, Jr. lived Hickman Co., TN, 265, No Twp.
Whitfield, William lived Whitfield Place of Hickman Co., TN, 051, No Twp.

1830 Tennessee Census.
Whitfield, Joel, Haywood County, TN, 441, No township. He was born in Pitt County, NC. Joel Whitfield was also on the 1840 Census. His brother, Benjamin Whitfield, joined him for a short time in Haywood County, TN. He followed his brother Joel Whitfield to Mississippi.

Joel Whitfield's sister, Albena Whitfield, married William Nelson 1822, and he died soon afterwards. Albena Nelson married (2) Obediah Carson and was living in Martin Co., NC, in 1830. The Carson family moved to Haywood County, TN, and appears on the 1840 census.

Obediah Carson, b. 1810-1815, NC, Occupation Agriculture.
Albena Carson, born 1803, NC
Jane Carson   1 female, 15 to 20, born NC
Lucy Carson   1 female, 5 to 10, born TN
Penny Carson   1 female, 5 to 10, born TN
Alfred Carson   1 male, under 5, born TN
John Carson   1 male, under 5, born TN
Nancy Carson   1 female, under 5, born TN

1850 Census Haywood County, TN, District 11, M 432-883, p. 55.October 16 Census taken. Six orphan Carson children living with Abel Thomas and Almenece Thomas in the house.
Abel Thomas, age 42, Hatter, Real estate value $500. born NC, Pitt County - Williams   John Carson, age 10
Almenece Thomas, age 41, b. NC   Penny Carson, age 8
Jane C. Moore, age 19, b. NC   Nancy Carson, age 7
Alfred Carson, age 14, b. TN
Lucy Carson, age 12, b. TN

1860 Census Tennessee. Abel Thomas had an order Martin County, NC.

Albena Whitfield Nelson Carson born 1803, NC, died after 1843 in TN. She was daughter of Benjamin Whitfield, Sr., and Susanna Wilkinson.

Robert Edward Whitfield (b. 1921 TN - d. 1990 CA) married March 26, 1943, to Vallie Jo Fox (b. 1922) at Nashville, TN. Marriage License Davidson County, TN. The marriage was performed at St. Mary Church in downtown Nashville.

449

WHITFIELD, John 38, Sarah 40, John H. 13, George B. 11,
    Wm. C. 9, Emily STINNET 9, Va.Va, Gi-1091-965
WHITFIELD, John 33, Sarah J. 21, William H. 18, James
    B. 1, NC T, B-19-265
WHITFIELD, John 32, Elizabeth 33, Mary 10, William 9,
    James 8, Martha 4, Needham 2, Elizabeth 1/12, T
    NC, Hn-102-766
WHITFIELD, John 33, Martha 32, Henry 13, John 11, Mary
    9, Eliza 9, Lucy 4, Thomas 2, T T, Wi-201-262
WHITFIELD, Joseph W. 44, Mirian R. 42, Joseph M. 17,
    Constantine 15, Needham 13, Robert C. 11, Sarah C.
    6, Mary 6, James W. 2, T T, Mt-41-499
WHITFIELD, Lewis 33, Rebecca 32, Eliza 13, James 16,
    T Ky, Hn-128-769

WHITFIELD, Lovina 74, Mary 41, NC T, Ca-299-824
WHITFIELD, Mathew 38, Angeline 15, Matilda 13, Effa 11,
    Lovina 9, Lenna 7, Mary J. 5, Martha O. A. 2, T T,
    Ca-298-824
WHITFIELD, Needham 30, E. H. 27, Henry 3, M. E. 2,
    John E. 6/12, T T, Mt-42-499
WHITFIELD, Needham 39, Agnis 32, Charity 12, Catharine
    4, Thomas 1, Ky Ky, Mt-129-510
WHITFIELD, Needham 29, Araminta 20, William 22,
    Sarah 20, Martha Ann 11/12, David GRAY 17, Eliza-
    beth ROBERTS 13, T T, Hn-9-752
WHITFIELD, R. D. 36, Susan A. 25, Arimetta 8, Eliza-
    beth 6, Adelia 4, Susan 2, T T, Mt-185-292
WHITFIELD, T. J. 40, Sarah 32, H. W. 20, Silas 14,
    John 11, George 9, Thomas 5, Sarah 1, T T, Hu-499-
    253
WHITFIELD, Thomas 49, Mary 50, Dalley 13, John 10, NC
    NC, Dk-723-101
WHITFIELD, Thos. 35, Emma 32, Martha 12, Rebecca
    WANDATE 23, Rom CANAELA 30, England.England
    Sh-462-58
WHITFIELD, Thomas Y. 49, Malinda 45, Sarah L. 25, T
    Ga, Ca-327-829
WHITFIELD, Wilkins 24, Elizabeth 22, Mary E. 3, Martha
    8/12, T T, Wi-760-586
WHITFIELD, Willis 46, Martha 15, William S. 13, Va T,
    Gi-62-624
WHITFILD, Alford 36, T. Ca-328-829

Census   1850 Year. Tennessee

LIVING IN HOUSEHOLD OF DIFFERENT SURNAME.

WHITFIELD, Alfred 20, James Carnahan, Ru-727-600
Whitfield, Benj. 23, David W. Williams, Sh-310-194
Whitfield, Christina 23, Peterson Gilley, Ru-724-600
Whitfield, Cliff A. 5'12, Tabitha Oliphant, Mu-64-315
Whitfield, Cynthia 24, Elizabeth Lee, Hn-110-766
Whitfield, David B. 14, Cary Jarnigan, Ca-259-819
Whitfield, Harrison 65, James M. Winstead, Wi-874-603
Whitfield, Henry 6, Allen Neely, Sh-809-263
Whitfield, James 33, John B. Arnold, Ca-323-828
Whitfield, James M. 30, Tabitha Oliphant, Mu-64-315
Whitfield, John W. 31, Martha Charter, Hi-541-77
Whitfield, Julia 15, David W. Williams, Sh-310-194
Whitfield, L. A. D. 17, Tabitha Oliphant, Mu-64-315
Whitfield, L. L. S. 25, William Harrelson, Mt-1364-453
Whitfield, Malvina 15, Wm. Carnahan, Ru-722-600
Whitfield, Martha 15, Roger Simpson, Gi-106-629
Whitfield, Mary 28, Joseph Carter, Ca-335-830
Whitfield, Mary D. 23, Tabitha Oliphant, Mu-64-315
Whitfield, Missouri M. T. 19, Lewis Wimberly, Hn-127-769
Whitfield, Tenada 2, Tabitha Oliphant, Mu-64-315
Whitfield, Willis 9, Roger Simpson, Gi-106-629
Whitfield, Willis 23, Wm. Carnahan, Ru-722-600

1850 Year. Tennessee. WHITEFIELD Compilation
Census

WHITEFIELD, Benjamine 25, Louisa 25, Caladona 2,
    Vasty 1, NC T, J-184-497
WHITEFIELD, Carter 46, Polly 38, Levi 21, John 19,
      Lucy 17, Josiah 12, Dicy 10, James 3, Cyntha 1,
   NC.T, J-563-551
WHITEFIELD, Henry 19, John H. Allen, D-291- Martha 43
WHITEFIELD, John 40, Emilia 30, George 12, Josiah 8,
    John 4, Elizabeth 2, NC T, J-231-503
WHITEFIELD, Josiah 36, Dicy 28, William 10, Lucy 9,
    John 6, NC T, J-182-496
WHITEFIELD, William 40, Charlotte 20, Moses 1, T T,
    D-336-581
WHITEFIELD, William 48, Sally 39, John 19, Helen 17,
    Lucetta 15, William 12, James 10, Jo siah 8,
    Tabitha 4, George 1, NC NC, J-389-527

1840 Census Tennessee had John Whitefield, John Whitefield, Josiah Whitefield, Carter B. Whitefield,
Thomas Whitefield, William Whitefield.

WHITFIELD AND CIVIL WAR

JOHN WILKINS WHITFIELD born March 11, 1818, Franklin, Williamson Co., TN. He was at Hickman Co., TN, then moved to Independence, MO, then to Kansas, and to Lavaca Co., TX in 1863. John W. Whitfield enlisted a company near Petersburg and became Captain of the 27th Texas Cavalry of the Confederate Army. He went with Army Missouri to join Ben McCulloch and commanded the force known as Whitfield's Legion. This Lavaca County, Texas Company combined with Hunt Company under E.R. Hawkins, a Company from Arkansas.

In January 1862 E.R. Hawkins returned to Texas and recruited eight other companies which were combined with the original five to form the Legion in April 1862.

The Arkansas battalion participated in the battle of Elkhorn Tavern in Arkansas. The Arkansas Company was transferred to another command, and the Legion remained at twelve companies with John W. Whitfield as Colonel, Hawkins as Lieutenant Colonel, and John H. Broochs as Major.

The Legion dismounted and joined units of Earl Van Dorn's Army to reinforce P.G.T. Beauregard at Corinth, MS. Then the Legion was mounted as the 27th Texas Cavalry Regiment. John W. Whitfield was promoted to Brigadier General, and the third, sixth, and ninth Texas Cavalry Regiments were added to his command to form a brigade. When John Whitfield retired because of ill health, L.S. Ross assumed the command on Dec. 16, 1863 and it became Ross Brigate.

John W. Whitfield had a brother, Thomas Jefferson Whitfield (1810 - 1873) who was a Brigadier General in Tennessee and in battle in Tennessee with the Legion at Nashville and in Kentucky. He was called Jeff Whitfield in the Army.

John Wilkins Whitfield had brothers in Texas. George Washington Whitfield (1806 VA - 1894 Dallas, TX) and James Monroe Whitfield (b. 1819 TN - d. in TX). John W. Whitfield had several nephews that were with him in his travels and army service.

John T. Whitfield was with his uncle and commanding officer in Whitfield's Legion at Texas. John T. was a daring Cavalry officer and promoted to Lieutenant Colonel in 1862. T.W. Whitfield was also with John Wilkins Whitfield.

Whitfield's Legion was 4th battalion in TX. By Dec. 1861 Trans-Mississippi troops were organized all over the southwest of Texas. There were 16 regiments placed - two battalions under De Bray, John W. Whitfield, and the 6th battalion formed, and the three independent companies in the field totaling 17,338 men.

The Trans-Mississippi Army of the West included Arkansas, five regiments and five battalions of 5,145 men, the Indian territory, five Regiments, two battalions, and one independent company of 5,460 men and Louisiana one regiment.

In 1865, John W. Whitfield buys a farm in Lavaca Co., TX and became a Planter. John W. Whitfield died October 27, 1879 near Hallettsville, TX.

Whitfield descendants of Thomas d. 1694, Thomas, Thomas d. 1781, Thomas d. 1799, Matthew, Benjamin, Reuben, William Morris ....Submitted by Lydia Aline Whitfield Duke of McCamey, TX, in 1998.

*Matthew Whitfield b. 1772, NC; died 1827, TN. He md. Levina Robinson, b. 1776, d. after 1860, TN. William, Benjamin, Mary, a girl, Matthew. Children (5) Mary Whitfield b. 1809, girl, b. NC.
*Matthew Whitfield b. 1814, TN Md. Fanny R. Monahan,

*William Whitfield, b. 11/28/1800, NC; d. 11/14/1862, AR. He md. Matilda Pittman, b. 1805, d. 6/20/1870. Children (11)
*Benjamin Whitfield b. 5/14/1806, TN, d. 5/14/1900, AR. He was a farmer. Stone Co., AR. Md. Elizabeth Herrod, b. 1810, d. by 1870. Children (13). Reuben was one of them. Md. Elizabeth Bridwell, b. 1831, d. 11/5/1882.
*Rueben Whitfield b. 9/9/1833, TN, d. 5/3/1903, AR. Children (8): James H., Laura A., Katherine, Benjamin, Rueben Willis, Julia, Joseph, William Morris. Md. Mary Ester Nelson, b. 11/26/1834 near Nashville, TN. D. in AR. Father: Martin Nelson, b. 7/22/1796, NC, d. 7/2/1852. Mother: Susannah Edwards, b. 7/26/1805, d. 9/4/1886 (her parents were John & Esther Edwards).
James H. Whitfield b. 11/27/1856.
Laura A. Whitfield b. 5/21/1858.
Katherine (Katy) Whitfield b. 4/25/1860.
Benjamin Whitfield b. 9/2/1862.
Rueben Willis Whitfield b. 8/4/1864, d. 4/13/1966.
Julia Whitfield b. 11/2/1867.
Joseph Whitfield b. 4/7/1870.
*William Morris Whitfield b. 8/29/1873, AR, d. 4/13/1966, Crane, TX. Md. Nora Belle Burson, Rockwood, TX, 1/3/1916. B. 7/4/1893, Coryelle Co., TX, d. 7/1/1985, San Angelo, TX.

Children (2): Katy Willene & Lydia Aline.
Nora Burson Whitfield has a BURSON LINEAGE. (1) Burson, George b. 1624, Scarborough, England. In 1684 moved to PA, d. 1715, PA. Wife - Hannah Goode. (2) Joseph b. 1689, PA. Wife - Rachel Potts. (3) Joseph b. 1730, PA, d. 1801, GA. Wife - Mary ? (4) Joseph b. 1771, SC, d. 1851. Wife - Winny. (5) Enoch b. 1796, AL, d. 1843. Wife - Mary ? (6) Jonathan b. 1838 AL, d. 1900, TX. Wife - Mary Jane Stewart. (7) William Henry (b. 1866 AL, d. 1942, TX). Wife - Sarah Jane Johnson. These were the parents of Nora Burson.
Katy Willene Whitfield b. 12/7/1917, Rockwood, TX, d. 6/8/1996, McCamey, TX.
*M. J. Scott Fletcher, 12/24/1934, San Angelo, TX. Children (3): Carol Willene, Robert William, Scott Gayle. Nine grandchildren; two great-grandchildren.
Lydia Aline Whitfield, b. 5/5/1924, Mereta, TX. Md. Teddy Francis Duke, 6/11/1941, Paint Rock, TX.
*Teddy Francis Duke, b. 3/25/1923, Paint Rock, TX, d. 1/14/1953, Llano, TX. Father: James Hill Duke, b. 5/1894, d. 4/12/1980. Mother: Tiny Clarette Nichols b. 2/12/1903, d. 2/9/1985. Children (4): Janet, Billy, Eugene, Bobby. Seven grandchildren; six great-grandchildren.

6. James William Whitfield born February 16, 1879 and died July 29, 1953 at Amarillo, TX. James married Maratha Ann Snider.
7. Child of Jasper and Flora Whitfield
John Franklin Whitfield born February 19, 1892, Barlett, TX, and died May 17, 1986, Pratt, KS. John F. Whitfield md. Mary Catherine Callahan July 20, 1920 at Mominy, OK.
James Whitfield of Oklahoma prepared the family group. Submitted by Charlotte Lawrence November 8, 1995.

Biography Of Whitfield

GEORGE WASHINGTON WHITFIELD was born Feb. 12, 1806 in Sussex Co., VA, the son of Wilkins Whitfield and Polly Mary. Parents moved to Franklin, Williamson Co., TN in 1808. George grew up at Franklin, TN. George went with his brothers to Hickman Co., TN when an adult. Centerville town of Hickman Co., TN was formed in 1823. Whitfield town was on Beaver Dam to the west of Centerville about 1830. At Council's Bend George had 600 acres.

In 1836 George W. Whitfield married Louisa King (b. 1823 - d. 1848) and they had children:
1. Daniel Whitfield
2. Virginia Whitfield who married Rev. Oliver Parker
3. Sarah Whitfield

George W. Whitfield married Sarah Bond. She was seventeen years younger than husband. On Dec. 5, 1849 they moved to Harrison Co., TX. Virginia Whitfield was born in Tennessee and Daniel Whitfield was born in TN. Another child J. Whitfield born in Texas. Whitfield family stayed four years in Harrison Co., TX, and then moved to Limestone Co., TX and stayed one year. Whitfield family moved in 1856 to Dallas Co., TX and they settled at Garland town. Children of George and Sarah Whitfield:
1. John Whitfield
2. Thomas Whitfield
3. Dundenah Whitfield
4. Belle Whitfield
5. Walter C. Whitfield
6. Davis Whitfield, daughter
George Washington Whitfield knew his ancestor to be John De Whitfield of England but left no information on his grandfather Thomas Whitfield who died 1794 at Sussex Co., VA.

George Whitfield purchased 160 acres located a mile northwest of Garland town. He increased his land to 900 acres. In 1892 he was eighty-five years of age and living at Garland, TX. George died Aug. 12, 1894 near Garland.

Reference:
1. History Of Hickman Co., TN, by W. and D. Spence.
2. Whitfield History And Genealogy Of Tennessee, by Vallie Jo Whitfield. Pages 69 Biography, 158, 159, 160, 161, 226. Second Edition. Pub. 1979.
3. Memorial And Biographical History Of Dallas Co., TX. Biography. Pages 615, 616. Book published 1892.

DWIGHT WHITFIELD

He was born four miles
east of Mountain View,
Arkansas . He lived in
San Angelo, Texas.

Dwight Whitfield, 90, of San
Angelo, died at 12:51 a.m., Feb.
13, 1990, in St. John's Hospital.

Service will be at 2 p.m. Friday
in Johnson's Funeral Home
chapel with the ' Rev. Jimmy
Rogers, pastor of Pecan Baptist
Church, the Rev. Olen Frasure
and the Rev. Derwood Rutland,
officiating. Burial will follow in
Lawnhaven Memorial Gardens.
Johnson's Funeral Home is in
charge of arrangements.

Dwight was born Nov. 20, 1899,
in Little Rock, Ark. He married
Lucille Heneritta Miller on Aug.
5, 1939, in San-Angelo. He was a
farmer and a member of Mereta
Baptist Church, where he served
as a deacon since 1943.

Mr. Whitfield is survived by his
wife, Lucille of the home; two
daughters, Mrs. Gene (Barbara)
Mowrey and Sharon Jones
Parker, both of San Angelo; one
sister, Susie Hix Whitfield of San
Angelo; three grandchildren,
Mrs. Tom (Teresa) Hamilton of
Mereta, Michael Mowrey and
Jimmy Don Jones, both of San
Angelo; two great-
grandchildren, Ann Elyce
Hamilton and Trayce Raby
Hamilton, both of Mereta; and
several nieces and nephews.

SUSIE HIX
WHITFIELD

Susie Hix Whitfield, 84,
of the Mereta community
died at 9:30
Baptist Memorials Hospital.

Graveside service will be at 2
p.m. Friday in
Mereta
Cemetery with
the Rev. O.L.
Frasure of-
ficiating.
Johnson's
Funeral Home is
handling the
arrangements.

Miss Whitfield
was born Oct. 23, 1906, in Mountain View, Ark. She was engaged
in farming, and was a member of
Mereta Baptist Church.

Survivors are several nieces
and nephews, including Sharon
Parker and Mrs. Gene (Barbara)
Mowrey, both of San Angelo, Mr.
and Mrs. Laurence Whitfield and
children, Mr. and Mrs. Willis
Whitfield and children, Mrs. Amy
Blackburn and children; great-
nieces and nephews, Mrs. Tom
(Teresa) Hamilton, Michael
Mowrey and Jimmy Don Jones;
great-great-nieces and nephews,
Anna Elyce Hamilton and Trayce
Raby Hamilton and Ashley Shy-
Ann Mowrey; and numerous
cousins.

She will always be in our hearts
and remembered by her kind-
ness, gentle nature and generous
personality. She was always
timid and quiet in a crowd, but
had a radiant smile that seemed
to calm a small child as he passed
by.

Few knew of her jolly laugh or
her reassuring hug or how she
could make a joke and cheer the
sad.

She received much joy from
watching her crops grow on the
farm near Mereta where she lived. She enjoyed quilting and loved to give her needlework to
others.

471

WHITFIELD RESIDENTS 1981 YEAR AT HOUSTON, TEXAS

Addresses and telephone numbers inclusive of white and black race. Whitfield name change to Whitfill.

WHITFIELD

WHITFIELD A L 1046 Richelieu ———— 681-9720
Anna Rae Mrs 8902 Springview ———— 462-2040
Annie Mae 3545 Dreyfus ———— 747-4307
Annie Pearl 10310 Cossey ———— 376-2809
Anthony 2820 Broadmead ———— 667-7182
Bennie L 314 Cartersville ———— 674-1720
Bertha—
　1205 O'Neil ———— 526-4117
　1205 O'Neil ———— 526-4119
Bessie 5119 Floyd ———— 862-2872
Brenda Hasting Oil Field ———— 331-8468
C W 2612 King ———— 695-6654
Carl L 10017 Hazelhurst Dr ———— 468-0413
Charles atty 2617 Richmond At Kirby ——— 222-0144
Clifton 4829 Paradis ———— 733-0523
D 12831 Crickett Hollow ———— 373-1192
D 9330 Long Point ———— 932-8911
D Kirk 7400 Stella Link ———— 661-0023
D L 8664 Wilcrest Dr ———— 495-5703
D W 4830 Southwind ———— 733-0066
David E 717 Mason ———— 351-0010
Dorothy 75 Lyerly ———— 691-3110
Doyle 12426 Palmbeach ———— 941-7845
Duane L 7930 Corporate ———— 771-4798
E C 1843 Bethlehem ———— 686-2759
E E 21622 Park Green ———— 492-2837
Earnest 11815 Murr Way ———— 734-0537
Edna 7542 Satsuma ———— 926-8940
Edward 12917 Kluge ———— 376-4535
Elnora 3612-1/2 Canfield ———— 748-0514
Frank 14422 Stuebner Airline Rd ———— 444-8255
Fred D 3818 Wayne ———— 673-3741
G M 1822 Locksford ———— 868-3167
Gary L 10903 Stroud ———— 495-4376
Gary Lee 7400 Bissonnet ———— 777-7307
Gary W 14307 Holly Park ———— 453-4853
　Children's Telephone
　14307 Holly Park ———— 453-6754
George Jr 10310 Cossey ———— 376-2809

WHITFIELD

Geo Sr 12907 Kluge ———— 376-4445
Gerald 12413 Ledger ———— 453-2867
H S 6419 Skyline ———— 783-1582
Harold 12103 Adams Run ———— 890-4132
Harold L 6327 Briar Glade ———— 495-8257
Herman 8024 Cannon ———— 734-2644
Hortense 4463 N MacGregor Way ———— 748-6081
Howard E 12631 Westella ———— 493-9078
J B MD—
　Residence 3617 Rio Vista ———— 748-4656
　Office 5445 Almeda Rd ———— 529-6101
J C Mrs 7807 Bankside ———— 771-7502
J Charles atty—
　2617 Richmond At Kirby ———— 222-0144
　Residence 5808 Charlotte ———— 668-8601
J E 3608 Creekmont ———— 682-2031
J Frank 7722 Dawn Ridge ———— 721-3258
J Frank bkkping service 3801 Kirby Dr ———— 523-1752
J H 8406 Shady Dr ———— 633-6762
J Harry 5310 Robertson ———— 695-1817
J Harry Jr 7030 Lacy Hill ———— 774-2908
J Tucker 9719 Ravensworth ———— 495-7138
J W Rev 6220 Kashmere ———— 635-1233
James 4923 Apollo ———— 681-4472
Jas 14023 Duncannon ———— 455-5142
James 11815 Murr Way ———— 738-0910
Jas B Jr 1206 Peach Spring ———— 448-9452
Jas E 16606 Castlefraser ———— 463-1326
James R 3511 Link Valley ———— 668-4575
Jim 7826 McLean ———— 734-7759
Jimmy W 8314 Oak Moss ———— 376-1625
John 12703 Island ———— 376-6824
John Eugene 2123 Kowis ———— 449-5143
John H 5407 Northridge ———— 738-0825
John K 505 Richey ———— 475-8062
Johnnie M 1530 W Donovan ———— 681-6328
Jon L 2426 Tannehill ———— 869-3933
Juanita Mrs 3617 Rio Vista ———— 748-3260
Judy 6407 Tautenhahn ———— 449-2634
K A 1422 Richmond Av

WHITFIELD
WHITFILL

WHITFILL D Leo 1530 W Donovan ———
Lena Mrs 8413 Safeguard ———
Leonard T 15734 Rolling Timbers Dr —
Leone Thelma 2303 Libbey ———
Lillie 304 E 43
Lola Lee Miss 2125 Chew
M J 8664 Wilcrest Dr ———
M S 2711 Teague
March E 5901 Selinsky
Maurice 10105 Cossey ———
Mike 970 Bunkerhill
Odis R 3705 Darden ———
Pamela A 1002 W 14
Pamela L 3445 Seabrook ———
Pete 4134 Sarong
Pete M 909 W Gardner ———
R A 10800 Fondren
Ramon 1046 Richelieu ———
Ronald 110 E Rosamond
Ronald 3106 Stratford ———
Roscoe Jr 2506 Arbor
Simon D 5003 Los Angeles —
Simon D 5003 Los Angeles —
T W 8807 Lomax ———
Tena 4516 Rawley ———
Teryl C 3617 Rio Vista
Thos 10511 Carter ———
Thomas 802 Schurmier
Tom W 1725 Lillian
Tracy 11346 Colonial Trail —
Waldo 830 Legreen
Western Jr 6319 Meredith —
Wm B 9201 Clarewood ———
Wm O 3025 Bowser Rd ———
Willie J 6869 Arto
WHITFILL B J 6161 Reims
Bill 4409 Tonawanda ———
Gerald 4205 Vista Rd ———
James R 2719 Raspberry ———
Jamie 4201 Fairmont Pkwy ———
Preston A 7331 Belle Pk ———
R K 8818 Brae Acres ———
Robt K Jr 9898 Club Creek Dr —
W A Jr 4409 Tonawanda ———

WHITFIELD RESIDENTS 1981 AUSTIN, TEXAS

WHITFIELD Beverly 1910 Santa Clara ———— 459-8410
Cecelia 5217-D Tahoe Trail ———— 892-0864
Charlotte 5401 Darlington Ln ———— 926-7822
D E 1120 E Oltorf ———— 447-7588
Debby Jan 2326 Montclaire St ———— 441-3392
Eugene D SGT 1310 Hyman Ln ———— 385-5698

WHITFIELD Flannigan 9600 Hansford ————
G W(Wheat) 2804 Cedarview ————
J 11915 Acorn Creek Tr ————
Jas Major 4705 Delores ————
James T 821 East 53 ————
K A 7113-A Dan-Jean ————
Ken 9929 Chukar Bend ————
Mark 1717 Morrow ————
Melanie 9001 Northgate ————
Pinckney N 1800 Basin Ledge ————
R L 11500 Chapel Ln ————
R W Leander ————
Ray P 4508 Knapp Hollow ————
Wheat Camp Ben McCullough ————
WHITFILL Amatene 1401 St Edwards Dr ————

WHITEFIELD Bobby D Trail Driver ———— 288-0660
K P 1000 Alta Vista ———— 444-8837

WHITEFIELD RESIDENTS 1981 DALLAS, TEXAS

WHITEFIELD Billy R 1230 La Fiesta —— 264-6894
Carey 801 James Dr ———— 235-1196
Carolyne
　1800 Josephine McKinney Tx ———— 542-6612
Fred 8620 Park Ln ———— 369-2472
G A 4151 Glenwick ———— 522-9672
Jas 1206 Horizon ———— 783-9707
　Childrens Telephone
　1206 Horizon ———— 644-5352
L K 9737 Lanshire ———— 348-9650
Lance & David 311 W Stark ———— 287-5834
P K 16000 Bent Tree Forest Cir ———— 387-4156
P K 16000 Bent Tree Forest Cir ———— 387-4156
P K 801 James Dr ———— 231-9843
R C 7714 Aurora St ———— 391-1930
Ronald R 311 W Stark ———— 287-1105
Ronnie R 1430 Deborah ———— 224-4283
W W Bill—
　1711 Whitedove ———— 337-6682
　1711 Whitedove ———— 337-8856

472

WHITFIELD LIVING RESIDENTS AT DALLAS, TEXAS IN 1981 YEAR

Addresses.   Inclusive of white race and Black race.
WHITFIELD
Whitfield, Lance and David
Whitfield, P. K., 801 James Drive
Whitfield, R. C., 7714 Aurora Street
Whitfield, Ronald R., 311 W. Stark
Whitfield, Ronnie R., 1430 Deborah Street
Whitfield, W. W. Bill, 1711 Whitedove

TEXAS

HAROLD NEAL WHITFIELD residing 1993 in Belton, TX was born February 19, 1918, son of Maude and Hubert Whitfield who lived at Eden, TX. Harold married Frances Jean Lacy who was born on December 31, 1920 and raised in Millersview, TX. Harold was a career army officer 1935 to 1968. Frances and Harold had three children: Martha, Neal, and Hubert.

Harold's parents were Hubert Leon Whitfield, Sr. who died on March 12, 1930 and Martha Maude Roberts Whitfield who died on October 24, 1978.

Harold Whitfield had a family tree. He considered that Matthew Whitfield who came from Lanchestershire, England on his ship in 1679 to the Virginia. He considered that probably his ancestor removed seven generations.

Harold and Frances Whitfield appeared in the book The Whitfield Family Who's Who In America, published 1994.

WILLIAM FRANKLIN WHITFIELD was residing 1993 in Houston, TX. William was born on April 10, 1927 and raised Altoona, PA. William married Sue Trammell who was born on August 5, 1933. Sue was raised in Houston, TX.   William and Sue had four children:
1.   Susan born 1956
2.   Bill, Jr. born 1958
3.   Celia born 1960
4.   W. Trammell born 1963

William Whitfield parents living in 1993 are James Henry Whitfield and Lillian Minerva Cutschall Whitfield.

Brothers of William are Malcolm Dean Whitfield age 65 in 1993. James Edward Whitfield deceased. Patrica Seitz Peabody, age 56 in 1993.

This family has researched on Whitfields. They compiled a list of early Whitfield immigrants to Colonial America from 1620 to 1775.   They could not identify relationship from any of the immigrants to ELIAS WHITFIELD who was born 1804.

Their brief on their research work can be seen in the book The Whitfield Family Who's Who In America.

RECORDS

William Whitfield married Elizabeth Goodman in 1713 in North Carolina. They had a son, Luke Whitfield, who married Chloe. They moved to South Carolina. They had a daughter who married. Lucretia Whitfield married Charles King of Sampson Co., NC. Steven Allen King married Sarah Ellington Dupree who was born 1811 Georgia. James Madison Solomon born circa 1822 married Tabith Elizabeth King 1846 Alabama. Lucius Samuel Lightfoort married Sarah Anna Solomon, born 1861 in Texas. John Henry Kobusch married 1908 Illinois to Alice Imalea Lightfoot who was born 1884 in Texas. John Bruce married 1931 Louisiana and married Princess H. Kobusch who was born 1909 in Texas. David Leonard Compton married 1956 at Texas to Virginia Lea Bruce who was born 1938 in Texas.
....Submitted by Ginger Compton of Webster, TX in March 1992.

Alice Hall Whitfield born Feb. 22, 1868. Alice married Levin Sledge Compton on Feb. 12, 1890. Levin was born April 30, 1858. They lived in San Angelo, TX in 1915. Alice Hall Whitfield grandfather was Bryan, Nathan, Bryan, William, William who married Elizabeth Goodman.

"My great grandfather, Exum Philip Whitfield was born 1818 in Nash Co., NC. His father was suppose to have been Wyatt Whitfield who was in Alabama in 1838 and in Texas in 1847." Submitted by Mary E. Hopkins of Garwood, TX on June 2, 1966.

JOHN ANTHONY WHITFIELD was born 1855 and died April 19, 1909 at Devine, Medina Co., TX. John married Helena Briscoe who was from Augusta, AR. They had children George D., who resided 1965 in Devine, TX. Sadie Whitfield, unmarried. Ruth Whitfield, unmarried. Mamie Whitfield who married Dr. W. C. Moore and he died before 1965. Mamie and W. C. Moore had three daughters.

John's mother, Sarah, a widow moved to Medina Co., TX and lived there until her death. In 1965 the three daughters lived together on Mistletoe Street in San Antonio, TX. Three sisters Sadie, Ruth, and Manie stayed together until they died.
....Submitted by Ruth Whitfield of San Antonio, TX on May 30, 1965.

UTAH

A few people with Normon religious intention founded Nauvoo, IL in 1836 and left there on Feb. 4, 1848 moving westward. The families settled at Salt Lake City, UT.

There were nine heads of Whitfield families living 1985 in Utah, and five of the men named Whitfield lived in Salt Lake City, UT.

VERMONT

The state of Vermont has had no residents living there named Whitfield.

Vermont admission to the states was on March 4, 1791. Area of 9,564 square miles. Population in 1930 was 359,611. Capital is Montpelier.

WHITFIELD, BURTON, AND BELL FAMILIES
63RD DISTRICT OF BURKE COUNTY, GEORGIA

Mary Whitfield (c.1825?-c.1846)was a daughter of Lewis Whitfield, Jr. (1800-1859) and Jane Whitfield. Mary married Dexter Burton (c.1810-c.1848) who is believed to have also lived in the 63rd District (1). The children of Dexter and Mary Burton were:

1. Franklin E. ("Frank") Burton was born September 28, 1840, and died in Waynesboro March 13, 1913. He married Ella I. Herrington (1850-1926) March 8, 1866. Both are buried at Magnolia Cemetery. He was a Civil War veteran serving as a private in the 3rd Georgia Regiment under Lee's command in Virginia and was one of only eleven (out of over 110) men in his company who was present at Appomattox.

2. Zechariah Burton (c.1842-November 5, 1855), a twin of Uriah.

3. Uriah Burton (c.1842-1911). He married Isabella S. Devant in 1866 and had two sons: Benjamin and Dexter ("Deck"). Uriah was known for his sense of humor and enjoyment of children. He was also a Civil War veteran serving as a private in the 32nd Georgia Regiment in coastal defenses in Georgia, Florida, and the Carolinas (the film "Glory" portrays at least two battles he was in). Benjamin has descendants presently residing in Burke Co. Through his daughter Ola Mae Burton Bailey (1900-1985) of Vidette. "Deck" lived in Augusta. He was married and had no children. Uriah and Isabella are buried in the city cemetery at Midville, GA.

4. Mary Mozelle Burton (c.1843-c.1856). (2)

5. Ella Fair (Elafair) Burton Bell (1844-December 8, 1937). In 1866 she married John Wesley Bell I (1846-February 1, 1894). He was a private in the Chatham Light Artillery of Savannah during the Civil War (the oldest active military unit in Georgia) that often fought alongside the 32nd Georgia Regiment in which Uriah Burton served. John and Elafair are buried at Habersham United Methodist Church near Perkins in Jenkins (formerly Burke) County, as are all of their children except Nannie and Emma.

The children of John Wesley and Elafair Burton Bell: 1. Nannie Bell Moore; 2. Minnie Lee Bell Jenkins (1873-1952); 3. Seaborn O. "Buster" Bell (1876-1934); 4. Emma Bell (Mrs. Kem) Johnson (buried at Garfield, GA; 5. William Thomas "Bill" Bell (1882-1952); and 6. John Wesley Bell II (1889-1954).

The 1850 Census of Burke County shows that the Burton orphans were living in the household of Lewis Whitfield, Jr. He was one of the largest landholders in the 63rd District and was "Agt. For D. Burton's children." In 1877 the three surviving orphans were deeded land that had belonged to him. (Bill Bell and John Wesley Bell II owned farms west of Alexander in the 63rd District.) (3)

The lineage and generations in this study reveal the following: G1 William Whitfield (1688 England-1770 NC). G2 Luke Whitfield (1719 NC-1767 SC). G3 Lewis Whitfield, Sr., RS (1755 or 1756) NC-c.1832 GA). G4 Lewis Whitfield, Jr. (1800 GA-1859 GA). G5 Mary Whitfield (Mrs. Dexter) Burton (c.1825?-c.1846). G6 Ella Fair Burton (Mrs. John Wesley) Bell (1844 GA-1937 GA). G7 William Thomas "Bill" Bell (1882 GA-1952 GA). G8 Ella Ruth Bell (Mrs. Harold H.) Cook (1924 GA. Living 1997, Chamblee, GA). G9 Jake Cook (1952 GA. Living 1997, Statham, GA).

_____

References:
(1)   1850 Census of Burke County, Georgia
(2)   Burke County, Georgia Deed Book B, pages 118-122.
(3)   Lewis Whitfield, Sr. and Jr. and Descendants of Burke County, Georgia. Research paper (1997) by Jake Cook of Statham, GA with the assistance of Robert Burton of Gainesville, FL, and Betty S. (Mrs. James W.) Bailey of Waynesboro, GA.

VIRGINIA

At the dawn of the seventeenth century three distinct groups of Indian tribes were on the coast. They had three different linguistic stocks which occupied the territory of Virginia. Algonquian group, Powhatan Indians, Siouan stock, Monacan and Manahoac, Iroquoian stock, Conestoga (Susquehanna) tribe.

The colonists of the London Company of England found along the rivers and coast some 200 villages. Displacement of the Indians began with the finishing of the first stockade and fort at Jamestown. Hostility between the Indians and colonists existed for many years. The Indian tribes had battles with other Indian tribes. The Indians and colonist had wars and massacres occurred.

The French and Indian War went on from 1754 to 1763. The Shenandoah Valley was the last frontier for tribes. The Cherokee Indians, as the white settlements pressed upon them in their mountain fortress, moved gradually westward.

In 1768, the Indians residing in the Virginia Colony had a small population. The Indians that remained were residing in the Colony became civilized wearing European clothes and in part did follow the customs of the planters.

England's 1682 Record of Virginia Colony Land Description

Old English script. Copy of words not readable or understood in transcribing are as found in the 1682 paper.

"To all go greetings whereas for now know you.
In the P S H Henry Company sent doputio Governor of all gentlemen
C. Grecipis unto Mr. Mathew Whitfield six hundred and fifty acres
land sie shore att the herd of his of the Southern Branch of
Elizabeth Branch of Elizabeth River in the county of lower Norfolk
in the wood called sandy harbor beginning at a gum (y isses) C
Beach growing together in a gum swamp and running east 4 by north
four hundred point again four the to beach
and gum swamp C by east two hundred and sie by point by marker had
to all holding standing in a Swamp Shore east to by north four
hundred point shore north by point woft two hundred C sie by point
to the end of the property E C R N line
the P land brought due and for the transportation of thirteen
persons unto this colony (colony) to have and to hold go to creek
hifd gr glilding the paying dues the 22 d of December 1682."

Hon. Pabre	Eliz. Pabre	Elder Atkin
Ann Hartin	Jon Foitty	Ann Smith
Robt. Cock	Ann Mattocks	John Boggus
Wm. Jolly	Robt. Jermain (Germin)	
Jo (John) Jolly	Susan Krott	

Land description of Virginia colony near Nansemond County,
Virginia to/for Mathew Whitfield who brought thirteen paying
colonists to the land of America at Virginia colony.

Words of 1682 Document Interpretation of the Paper from England

PSH Henry Company of England.
Dophin - fishery word meaning of the sea
doputio - deputy governor
gent - gentlemen
grecipis - name

C - creek
sie - site
att - at the
gum - tree

y isses - unknown. This could mean issue specific place.
point - survey point.
woft - could mean direction, to west?
P land - the company's land for the harbor needed to land a
ship.
CR - creek
hifd - for whitfield
gr - great
yeilding - granting some right or object
dowd - dues for cost of travel on ship
scrip - noun - a corruption of word script, a writing form.

MATHEW WHITFIELD received 650 acres at Sandy Harbor, a
location in the county of Norfolk on the Elizabeth river.

Location after Vestry Parish established was Nansemond Co.,
VA.

WHITFIELD COUNTY, VIRGINIA

# 1. .Abraham	Elizabeth City County , Va.	born 1708?
# 2. .Abraham....	Elizabeth City County, Va.	b. 1735 - d. 1787?
# 3... Africa	Nansemond Co., Va.....	b. 1765? living 1810.
# 4... Ann W....	Elizabeth City Co., Va...	b. 1710?
# 5. .Ann F.W. ...	Elizabeth City Co., Va..	b. 1655?
# 6. .Ann J.W....	Henrico County., Va....	b. 1795?
# 7... Atkinson....	Isle of Wight County, Va..	living 1823
# 8... Anne	Isle of Wight County, Va.	living 1765
# 90 ..Ann	Isle of Wight County, Va.	living 1745
# 91... Ann	Isle of Wight County, Va.	living 1675
# 49... Betty	Sussex County, Va.......	living 1774
# 9 ... Benjamin..	Southampton County, Va.	died 1787
# 10 ... Benjamin..	Isle of Wight County, Va.	b. 1850?
# 11. .. Benjamin..	Isle of Wight County, Va.	b. 1815?
# 12. .. Benjamin..	Isle of Wight County, Va.	b. 1730?
#13. .. Augustine..	Sussex County Virginia	living 1789
#50. .. Benjamin..	Southampton Co. , Va.	living 1809
#14. .. Catey	Isle of Wight Co., Va.	living 1780
#15. .. Charles...	James City Co., Va....	born 1780?
#16. .. Charles P.	Henrico Co., Virginia	b. 1795-living 1849
#17. .. Copeland, Sr.	Isle of Wight Co., Va.	b. 1745? - d. af.1799
#18. .. Copeland, Jr	Isle of Wight Co., Va.	b.1770? -living 1800.
#20... Copeland..	Isle of Wight Co., Va.	b. 1770?
#21. .. **Catherine Davis**	**Southampton Co., Va.**	**b.1770?** **b.1789**
#22... Edward ...	Nansemond Co., Virginia	b. 1755?-d. 1777
#23... Efrica ...	Isle of Wight Co., Va.	b. 1750?
#24... "Eine". **Ivey**	Nansemond Co., Va.....	b. 1730?
#25... Elisha	Isle of Wight County, Va.	d. 1792?
#26... Elijah.....	Southampton Co., Va.	b. 1760?
#27... Elizabeth .	Isle of Wight Co., Va.	b. 1795-d. 1817
#28. . Elizabeth	Isle of Wight Co., Va.	b. 1745?
#29. . Eliz	Northumberland Co., Va.	living 1664
#30. . Elizabeth ..	Southampton Co., Va.	living 1787
#31. . Elizabeth ..	Virginia	living 1703
#32. . Elizabeth W.	Henrico Co., Virginia ...	b. 1815 ?
#33.. Elizabeth..	Isle of Wight Co., Va..	b. 1720? -living 1758
#34.. Elizabeth ..	Elizabeth City Co., Va..	b. 1700-living 1725
#35.. Elizabeth ..	Isle of Wight Co., Va.	b. 1805?
#36.. Elizabeth ..	Isle of Wight Co., Va.	b. 1836
# 37.. Elizabeth	Isle of Wight Co., Va.	b. 1871, Nov.13
#38.. Elizabeth	Norfolk Co., Va.......	b. 1765?
#39.. Elizabeth	Elizabeth City Co., Va.	b. 1690?-d.1727
#40.. Elizabeth	Elizabeth City Co. , Va.	b. 1660. -living 1694

WHITFIELD	COUNTY, VIRGINIA	Living ? circa Birth, Death
#41. .. Elizabeth ..	Isle of Wight Co., Va.	b. 1755?
#42. .. Elizabeth ..	Sussex and TN	b. 1770? -living 1806
#43... Elizabeth..	Sussex Co., Va & TN	b. 1762? -living 1830
#44... Elizabeth..	Isle of Wight Co., Va. .	b. 1850?
#45... Lucy	Sussex Co., Virginia...	living 1789
#46... Rebecca ..	Sussex Co., Virginia....	living 1819
#47... Elizabeth ..	Virginia....	17th Century
#48... Francis ..	Sussex Co., Virginia....	living 1765
#49... Betty.....	Sussex Co., Virginia....	b. Oct 10-1774
#50... Benjamin	Southampton Co., Va. ..	living 1809
#51. .. Elizabeth	Isle of Wight Co., Va. ..	living 1745
#52... Eady H.W.	Southampton Co., Va. ..	b. 1770?
#53... Esther ...	Nansemond Co., Va. ...	b. 1750?
#54... Frances ..	Isle of Wight Co., Va ..	b. 1755?
#55... Frances..	Nansemond Co., Va. ...	b. 1820-d. 1841
#56... Fanny	Isle of Wight Co., Va...	living 1782
#57... Fanny W.K.	Isle of Wight Co., Va..	b.1778
#58... Fanny W.P.	Isle of Wight Co., Va. ,	b. 1800?
#60... George B. W	Isle of Wight Co., Va.	b. 1730?
#61. .. George	Henrico Co., Va.	b. 1845?
#62... George	Montgomery Co., Va.	living 1796
#63... George.....	Virginia	living 1792
#64... George	Norfolk Co., Virginia	b. 1765
#65... George....	Nansemond Co. Va..TN	living 1800
#66... George	Isle of Wight Co., Va.	b. 1735-living 1784
#67... George	Henrico Co., Va.	living 1849
#68... Gilbert ...	James City	living 1621
#69... Hannah	Elizabeth City	born 1737?
#70... Hardy	Virginia & NC	living 1781
#71.. Hardy	Isle of Wight Co., Va.	living 1795
#72. ...Harrison	Isle of Wight Co., Va.	b. 1750? ca-living 1781
#73. .. Harrison	Sussex Co., Va. & TN	b. 1783? -living 1850
#74... Haynes	Isle of Wight Co., Va.	b. 1748? ca
#75... Henry	Isle of Wight Co., Va.	b. 1758-d. 1823
#76... Henry E.	Isle of Wight Co., Va.	living 1835
#77... Henry	No. Carolina & TN	living 1806
#78. ... Herbert	Lancaster Co., Va. ..	living 1657
#79. .. Hester	Nansemond Co., Va.	living 1752
#80... Hester....	Isle of Wight Co., Va.	living 1750
#81. .. Hester	Isle of Wight Co., Va.	living 1798
#82... Isham	Isle of Wight Co., Va.	living 1750

#83. . Ivey	Nansemond Co., Va.	living 1784 -d. 1810 ca.
#84. . Ivy	Nansemond Co., Va.	living 1783
#125. . Jack	Sussex Co., Va. & TN . .	living 1800
#85. . Jacob	Isle of Wight Co., Va.	living 1796
#86. . James	Isle of Wight Co., Va. . . .	b. 1731
#87. . James	Isle of Wight Co., Va. . . .	living 1820
#130. . Jane Allen. . .	. Greensville Co., Va.	living 1809
#88. . Janet G. W. . .	. Phoebus, Va.	b.1862-d. af. 1920.
#123. . Jeanny	. Sussex Co., Va.	living 1755
#92. . Jemima . . .	. Isle of Wight Co., Va. . . .	living 1786
#93. . Jemima . . .	Isle of Wight Co., Va. . . .	b. 1745? ca. -d. af.1790
#94. . John	Virginia	b. 1615
#95. . John	Norfolk Co., Va.	living 1667
#96. . John	Isle of Wight Co, Va.	d. before 1672
#97. . John	Isle of Wight Co., Va. . . .	b. 1666-living 1682
#98. . John	Elizabeth City Co., Va. . .	b.1682?-living 1727
#99. . John	Elizabeth City Co&York . .	b.1680?-living 1705
#100. . John	Elizabeth city & York Co.	b. 1705
#101. . John	Nansemond Co., Va.	living 1747
#102. . John	Isle of Wight Co., Va. . . .	b. 1736
#103. . John	Va. & N	living 1760
#104. . John.	Spotsylvania Co., Va.	b. before 1738?
#105. . John.	Isle of Wight Co., Va.	b.1740 ?ca
#106. . John.	Isle of Wight Co., Va. . . .	b. before 1743?
#107. . John.	Isle of Wight Co., Va. . . .	living 1757
#108. . John	Isle of Wight Co., Va.	b. 1750? ca d. 1796
#109. . John.	Isle of Wight Co., Va.	living 1787
#110. . John W.	Isle of Wight Co., Va.	living 1782
#111. . John	Isle of Wight Co., Va.	living 1795
#112. . John	Virginia	living 1784
#113. . John	Nansemond Co., Va.	living 1763
#114. . John	Isle of Wight Co., Va&NC	. b.1800-d. 1879
#115. . John.	Greensville Co., Va.	living 1808
#116. . John.	Nansemond Co., Va.	living 1810
#117. . John	Isle of Wight Co., Va. . . .	living 1819
#118. . John P. . . .	Isle of Wight Co., Va. . . .	b. 1858
#119. . John	Sussex Co., Va & TN	b. 1770? ca-d. bef. 1820
#120. . John	Sussex Co., Va & TN	b. Va-living 1820 TN
#121. . John	Southampton Co., Va. . . .	living 1789
#122. . John F. . . .	Henrico Co., Va.	living 1849
#123. . Jeanny	Sussex Co., Va.	living 1755
#124. . Julia	Southampton Co., Va.	living 1809
#125. . Jack	Sussex Co., Va.	living 1800
#128. . Joseph	Elizabeth City Co., Va. . . .	b. 1715 ?ca.
#129. . Joshua	Isle of Wight Co., Va.	b.bef.1785-d. af. 1835

. Jean	Brunswick Co., Va.	living 1779
#130. Jane A. ...	Greensville Co., Va.	b. 1790? ca
#131.. Kernhappuch	Isle of Wight Co., Va.	living 1740
#132.. Leucretia	Isle of Wight Co., Va.	b. 1851-d. 1928
#133.. Louisa	Princess Anne Co., Va.	living 1776
#134.. Louisa	Lunenberg Co., Va.	living 1797
#135.. Lucy	Isle of Wight Co., Va.	living 1815
#136.		
#137..		
#138.. Macon	Isle of Wight Co., Va.	living 1798
#139.. Margaret A.	Isle of Wight Co., Va.	-d. 1852
#140.. Margaret W.	Virginia & Tennessee	living 1806
#141.. Margaret	Isle of Wight Co., Va.	living 1758
#142.. Martha	York Co., Va	b. 1729
#143.. Martha Patty	Sussex Co., Va.	living 1789
#144.. Martha	Southampton Co., Va	living 1784
#145.. Martha	Isle of Wight Co., Va.	living 1835
#146.. Martha	Isle of Wight Co., Va.	living 1854
#147.. Mary	Elizabeth City Co., Va.	living 1694
#148.. Mary	York Co., Virginia	b. 1705
#149.. Mary	Isle of Wight Co., Va.	living 1772
#150.. Mary	Isle of Wight Co., Va.	living 1775
#151. Mary	Isle of Wight Co., Va.	living 1781
#152.. Mary	Isle of Wight Co., Va.	living 1784
#153.. Mary	Isle of Wight Co., Va.	living 1777
#154.. Mary	Isle of Wight Co., Va.	living 1782
#155.. Mary Anne	Elizabeth City Co., Va.	living 1727
#156.. Mary Ann	Isle of Wight Co., Va.	living 1820
#157.. Mary Ann	Henrico Co., Va.	living 1843
#158.. Mary	Isle of Wight Co., Va.	living 1791
#159.. Mary	Isle of Wight Co., Va.	living 1828
#160.. Mary	Sussex Co., Va.	living 1778
#161.. Mary	Isle of Wight Co., Va.	living 1835
#162.. Mary F.	Isle of Wight Co., Va.	living 1835
#163.. Mary G.	Isle of Wight Co., Va.	living 1806
#164.. Mary H.	Isle of Wight Co., Va.	living 1830
#165.. Mary C.	Isle of Wight Co., Va.	living 1741
#166.. Mary D.	Isle of Wight Co., Va.	living 1755
#167.. Mary	Isle of Wight Co., Va.	living 1725
#168.... Mary H.	Isle of Wight Co., Va.	living 1809
#169.. Mary	Sussex Co., Va........	living 1768
#170.. Mary ...	Sussex Co., Va.	b. 1760
#171.. Mary H.	Isle of Wight Co., Va.	living 1751
#172.. Mary W. S.	Isle of Wight Co., Va.	living 1799
#173.. Mary	Sussex County , Va.	living 1765

#174..Mary	Sussex Co., Va.	living 1760
#175.. Mary	Isle of Wight,Va.	living 1791
#178.. Nancy B.	Southampton Co., Va.	living 1801
#179.. Mathias ...	Isle of Wight Co. ,Va.	b. 1735 ?
#180.. Mathew ...	Norfolk Co.,Va.	living 1664
#181..Matthew ...	Eng. West Indies. Va.	living 1679
#182..Matthew ..	Nansemond Co. &Norfolk	living 1682
#183..Matthew ..	Isle of Wight Co., Va.	living 1684
#184..Matthew ..	Nansemond Co.,Va.	living 1693
#185.. Matthew..	Nansemond Co.,Va.	living1758
#186.. Matthew ..	Isle of Wight Co., Va.	living 1706
#187.. Matthew ..	Isle of Wight Co., Va.	b. 1754
#188.. Matthew..	Nansemond Co.,Va.	living 1752
#189.. Matthew ..	Isle of Wight Co., Va.	living 1782
#190.. Mathew ..	Isle of Wight Co., Va.	living 1780
#191.. Mathew ..	Isle of Wight Co., Va.	living 1781
#192.. Mildred ..	Isle of Wight Co., Va.	living 1775
#194.. Miles	Isle of Wight Co., Va.	b. before 1740
#195.. Milley(Milla)	Isle of Wight Co., Va.	living 1765
#196..Milla(Milley)	Isle of Wight Co., Va.	living 1789
#197.. Miriam ...	Virginia	b. 1807 ?ca.
#198.. Molly	Isle of Wight Co., Va.	living 1782
#199.. Nancy	Isle of Wight Co., Va.	b. 1779 ?ca.
#200.. Nancy	Isle of Wight Co., Va.	living 1797
#201.. Narcissa	Isle of Wight Co., Va.	living 1858
#204.. Pamelia ...	Isle of Wight Co., Va.	living 1790
#206.. Peggy	Isle of Wight Co., Va.	living 1871
#208.. Peter	Southampton Co., Va.	living 1792
#209..Phebe W.	Southampton Co., Va.	living 1785
#210.. Polly D.	Isle ofWight Co., Va.	living 1797
#211.. Polly W.	Southampton Co., Va.	living 1789
#212.. Polly S.	Sussex Co., Va.	b.1780ca-d. af. 1830
#213.. Polly	Isle of Wight Co., Va.	living 1827
#214.. .Polly ...	Sussex Co., Va. & T	b. 1780? ca
#215.. Priscilla	Nansemond Co., Va.	living 1708
#216.. Priscilla	Isle of Wight Co., Va.	living 1791
#217.. Priscilla	Southampton Co., Va.	living 1798
#218... Rachelle	Isle of Wight Co., Va.	living 1799
#219... Rebecca	Isle of Wight Co., Va.	living 1849
#220... Reuben	Nansemond Co.,Va& Nash	Co.,N C. b.1745?
#221... Reuben	Nansemond Čo., Va.	b. 1767? living 1823
.. Reuben	Southampton Co., Va.	living 1785
#223... Reuben	Southampton Co., Va.	living 1801

#224..Richard	Henrico Co.,Va.	living 1849
#225..Richard	Norfolk Co.,Va.	living 1635
.. Robert	Sussex Co., Va.	living 1753
#226.. Robert	Isle of Wight Co., Va.	living 1748
#227.. Robert	Elizabeth City Co., Va.	living 1765
#228.. Robert H.	Isle of Wight Co., Va.	b. 1795- d. 1868
#229.. Ruth	Virginia	living 1635
#230.. Sally	Southampton Co., Va.	living 1781
#231. Sallie W.	Virginia	living 1800ca.
#232..Sally H.	Southampton Co., Va.	living 1782
#233..Sally W.	Sussex Co., Va.	living 1801
#234... Samuel	Isle of Wight Co., Va.	b. 1714-d.1758
#235.. Samuel	Isle of Wight Co., Va.	d. Dec. 1784
#236.. Samuel	Isle of Wight Co., Va.	b.1755?-d.1799
#237.. Samuel	Isle of Wight Co., Va.	living 1778
#238.. Samuel	Isle of Wight Co., Va.	living 1765?
#239.. Samuel	Isle of Wight Co., Va.	b. 1785-d. Feb.1842
#240.. Samuel	Isle of Wight Co., Va.	b. 1785ca. -d. 1842
#241.. Samuel	Isle of Wight Co., Va.	b. 1812- d. 1833
#242.. Samuel	Isle of Wight Co., Va.	b. 1854
#244.. Sarah	Isle of Wight Co., Va.	living 1755 ca.
#245.. Sarah	Isle of Wight Co., Va.	living 1820
#246.. Sarah	York Co., Va.	living 1729
#247.. Sarah E.	Isle of Wight Co., Va.	b. 1846
#248.. Sarah	York Co., Va.	living 1702
#249.. Seymore	Southampton Co., Va.	living 1798
#250.. Solomon	Nansemond Co., Va.	living 1747
#251.. Solomon	Nansemond Co., Va.	living 1775-d.1836.
#252.. Solomon	Nansemond Co., Va.&	living 1790
#253.. Susan	Isle of Wight Co., Va.	b.1861-d. 1863
#254..		
#256..Thomas	Elizabeth City Co., Va.	d. 1694
#257..Thomas	Elizabeth City Co., Va.	b. 1684 ?
#258.. Thomas	Nansemond Co. & N C.	b. 1721- d. 1781
#259.. Thomas	Nansemond Co., Va.	living 1775
#260.. Thomas	Isle of Wight Co., Va.	b. 1700?-d.1781
#261.. Thomas	Isle of Wight Co., Va.	living 1736-
#262.. Thomas	Isle of Wight Co., Va.	living 1751
#263.. Thomas	Nansemond Co.& N C.	living 1781
#264.. Thomas	Isle of Wight Co.,Va.	living 1797
#265.. Thomas	Sussex Co.,Va.	living 1740-d.1794

#266..Thomas ···	Nansemond Co., Va.	living 1790
#267..Thomas ···	Virginia	living 1798
#268..Thomas ···	Sussex Co., Va. ·····	living 1819
#269..Thomas ···	Henrico Co., Va. ·····	living 1894
#270...		
#271.. Wesley ···	Virginia ······	living 1798
#272..Wilkins ···	Sussex Co., Va. & T N.	b. 1783-d. af. 1840
#273..Wilkinson	Isle of Wight Co., Va.	living 1795
#274..William ···	England. Elizabeth City	living 1636
#275..William ···	Elizabeth City Co., Va	living 1675
#276..William ···	Lancaster Co., Va ····	living 1663
#277.. William ··	England. Isle of Wight co.	living 1671
#278.. William ··	Nansemond Co., Va&N. C.	living 1723
#279.. William ··	Nansemond Co., Va &N C	b. 1715 - d. 1795
#280... William..	Elizabeth City Co., Va.	living 1727
#281.. William ..	Elizabeth City Co., Va.	living 1735
#282..William ..	Isle of Wight Co., Va.	died 1750
#283..William ..	Goochland Co., Va. ····	living 1775
#284... William..	Sussex Co., Va. ······	b. Jan 16, 1757
#285..William ..	Sussex Co., Va. & T N.	b. Aug 6, 1762-
#286..William ..	Virginia ·······	1751 ?
#287.. William	Nansemond Co., Va. ···	b. 1750?-d. aft 1800
#288.. William ..	Princess Ann Co., Va. ··	living 1776
#289.. William ..	Lunenberg Co., Va. ···	living 1797
#290..		
#291., William ..	Isle of Wight Co., Va. ···	d. Jan 12, 1787
#292.. William ..	Isle of Wight Co., Va. ··	living 1815
#293.. William ..	Nansemond Co., Va & N C	b. 1759 - d. 1806
#294.. Willis ···	Norfolk Co., Va. ······	living 1790
#295.. Wilson ..	Isle of Wight Co., Va. ··	living 1782
#296..Winnifred	Southampton Co., Va. ···	living 1788
#297..Winifred	Sussex Co., Va. ······	living 1740 -1794
#298..Wrenn ···	Isle of Wight Co., Va. ··	living 1782

**Research and study of Virginia colonial records
and publications led to the book titled
Virginia History And Whitfield Biographies
by Vallie Jo Whitfield . Published 1976 .
Whitfield Books Company, Pleasant Hill, California.
Library Of Congress Number 77 - 357760.
International Standard Book Number 0-930 920 - 09-0.**

17 named WHITFIELD, Virginia 1790 Census

Whitfield, Abraham, 31, I.W.
Whitfield, Africa, 73
Whitfield, Catey, 31, I.W.
Whitfield, Copeland, 32, I.W.
Whitfield, Frances, 31, I.W.
Whitfield, Ivey, 73, Nan.
Whitfield, Ivey, 57, I.W.
Whitfield, John, 32, I.W.
Whitfield, Mary, 31, I.W.

Whitfield, Matthew, 31, I.W.
Whitfield, John Wren, 31, I.W.
Whitfield, Samuel, 32, I.W.
Whitfield, Solomon, 73, Nan.
Whitfield, Thomas, 31, I.W.
Whitfield, Thomas, 44, Nan.
Whitfield, William, 31, I.W.
Whitfield, Wilson, 31, I.W.

15 named WHITFIELD, Virginia 1810 Census

Whitfield, Benjamin, 54
Whitfield, Edward, 68
Whitfield, Hannah
Whitfield, Jane, 87
Whitfield, John, 66
Whitfield, John, 60
Whitfield, Lewis, 87

Whitfield, Milly, 53
Whitfield, Peter, 129
Whitfield, R., 66
Whitfield, Reuben, 65
Whitfield, Seymore, 54
Whitfield, Sharpee, 64
Whitfield, Viney, 56

All Southampton Co., VA

11 named WHITFIELD, Virginia 1810 Census

Whitfield, Atkinson, IW, 161
Whitfield, George, Norfolk, 134
Whitfield, John, IW, 145
Whitfield, Littleberry,
  Sussex Co, 670
Whitfield, Wilkinson, IW, 144

Whitfield, Copeland, IW, 147
Whitfield, John, IW, 145
Whitfield, John, IW, 151
Whitfield, Samuel, IW, 151
Whitfield, Sarah, York Co, 885
Whitfield, William,
  Sussex Co, 670

Elizabeth City Co.   Isle of Wight Co.   Norfolk Co.
Sussex Co.   York Co.

IW - Isle of Wight Co., VA   Rcy-Richmond, Henrico Co., VA
Ecy - Elizabeth City Co., VA   Hnco - Henrico Co., VA
Nan - Nansemond Co., VA   Eliz - Hampton Co., VA
Nrk - Norfolk Co., VA

Name on Census is a Head of A Household. 1790 to 1850 list only the male or female head of family. Wife and children are a number with an age range. White color. Black color has only the first name of the person, and under the white male or female head of the family with surname. Slaves were counted in the censuses. After the Civil War, all had same status of freedom, and W for white and B for black means American or African-American. All persons in a household or dwelling names are listed.

Virginia Record. Elisha Whitfield, Jr., of Southampton Co., VA, married Nancy Hart and they had four children.

Virginia Record. Peter Whitfield married Eady Rush. His bondsman was Josiah (F) or Herguson, the father of Harriet who married Argill Whitfield, the son of Cordy Clifton Whitfield, Southampton Co., VA.

30 named WHITFIELD, Virginia 1820 Census

WHITFIELD

Adkisson, I.W., 133
Benjamin, Sou, 129 A
* Cordall, Sou, 129 A
Elisha, Sou, 129 A
George, Nan, 81
George, Sou, 130
Henry, I.W., 119
Holland, Sou, 130
John, Sou, 129A
John, Jr., Sou, 130
John W., Sou, 130
John, Ecy, 119
Joshua, Nan, 81
* Lewis, Nfk, 138 A
Mills, I.W., 126

WHITFIELD

Milly, Sou, 129 A
Nathan, Sou, 129 A
Peter, Sou, 129 A
Reuben, Nan, 85 A
Richard, Ecy, 118
Richard, Rcy, 195
Robert, Sou, 129 A
Sampson, Sou, 130
Samuel, I.W., 108
Solomon, Nan, 76 A
Susan, Sou, 129 A
Wilkinson, I.W., 117
William, Ecy, 135 A
William, Sux, 115 A
William W., Sou, 129 A

*Cordell not Cordall or Gordy. Mills is Miles.

21 named WHITFIELD, Virginia 1830 Census

Whitfield, Atkinson, IW, 227
Whitfield, Benjamin, Sou, 246
Whitfield, Bennet K., Sou, 253
Whitfield, Edward, Nan, 228
Whitfield, Elisha, Sou, 255
Whitfield, Cordy, Sou, 248
Whitfield, Holliday, IW, 253
Whitfield, Jack, Norf, 412
whitfield, Jerry, Nan, 242
Whitfield, John, Sou, 247
Whitfield, Littleberry, Suss, 029
Whitfield, Louisa, IW, 258
Whitfield, Nathan, Sou, 250
Whitfield, Patty, Sou, 251
Whitfield, Reuben, Nan, 211
Whitfield, Richard, Rich, 405
Whitfield, Samuel, IW, 260
Whitfield, Solomon, Nan, 228
Whitfield, Thomas, Suss, 014
Whitfield, Sout, 249

18 named WHITFIELD, Virginia 1840 Census

Whitfield, Benjamin, IW, 004 No TWP
Whitfield, Benjamin, Sout 102 St Lukes
Whitfield, Bennet K., Sout 102 St Lukes
Whitfield, Cordy, Sout 102 St Lukes
Whitfield, Dorson, Sout 102 St Lukes
Whitfield, Edward, Nans 033 No TWP
Whitfield, Elisha, Sout 087 Nottoway
Whitfield, George, Sout 102 St Lukes
Whitfield, John G., IW 013 No TWP
Whitfield, King, Nans 010 No TWP
Whitfield, Lett T., Suss 254 No TWP
Whitfield, Mary, IW 014 No TWP
Whitfield, Nat, Sout 102 St Lukes
Whitifled, Nathan, Sout 102 St Lukes
Whitfield, Patience, Sout 102 St Lukes
Whitfield, Richard Henr 175 Richmond
Whitfield, Samuel, IW 015 No TWP
Whitfield, Thomas, Eliz 112 No TWP

52 named WHITFIELD
Virginia 1850 Census
Southampton County and Counties

Whitfield	, Allen	, Sout	262	St. Luke	
Whitfield	, Armin	, Sout	254	St. Luke	
Whitfield	, Ben	, Sout	329	Nottaway	
Whitfield	, Benjamin	, I W	161	Eastern	- Isle Of Wight Co.
Whitfield	, Cordy	, Sout	261	St. Luke	
Whitfield	, Crecy	, Sout	275	St. Luke	
Whitfield	, Dawson	, Sout	266	St. Luke	
Whitfield	, E .	, Dinw	411	Petersbu	- Dinwiddie Co.
Whitfield	, Edward	, Nans	209	No TWP	- Nansemond Co.
Whitfield	, Elias	, Sout	270	St. Luke	
Whitfield	, Elias	, Sout	270	St. Luke	
Whitfield	, Elizabeth	, Sout	277	St. Luke	
Whitfield	, Elizabeth	, Sout	328	Nottaway	
Whitfield	, George	, Norf	120	Norfolk	
Whitfield	, Jane	, Norf	067	Norfolk	
Whitfield	, Jesse	, I W	162	Eastern	
Whitfield	, John	, I W	163	Eastern	
Whitfield	, John G.	, P AN	207	No TWP	- Powhatan Co.
Whitfield	, Margaret	, I W	119	Smithfie	- Smithfield town.
Whitfield	, Margaret	, Norf	103	Norfolk	
Whitfield	, Maria	, I W	163	Eastern	- Eastern Shore
Whitfield	, Mariah	, Sout	252	St. Luke	
Whitfield	, Martha	, Sout	269	St. Luke	
Whitfield	, Mary	, Sout	279	St. Luke	
Whitfield	, Mary	, Sout	259	St. Luke	
Whitfield	, Mary	, Sout	246	St. Luke	
Whitfield	, Mary A.	, Sout	275	St. Luke	
Whitfield	, Milly	, Sout	262	St. Luke	
Whitfield	, Nancy	, Sout	285	Nottaway	
Whitfield	, Nat	, Sout	262	St. Luke	
Whitfield	, Nathan	, Sout	269	St. Luke	
Whitfield	, Nicholas	, Sout	280	St. Luke	
Whitfield	, Nicholas	, Sout	257	St. Luke	
Whitfield	, Norphlet	, Sout	262	St. Luke	
Whitfield	, Patience	, Sout	270	St. Luke	
Whitfield	, Patty	, Sout	269	St. Luke	
Whitfield	, Richard	, Hnco	424	Richmond town	
Whitfield	, Richard	, Ches	160	Lower DI	- Dinwiddie Co.
Whitfield	, Robert	, Nans	175	No TWP	- Township
Whitfield	, Robert H.	, I W	115	Smithfie	- Smithfield town
Whitfield	, S.	, Dinw	330	Petersbu	- Petersburgh town
Whitfield	, S.	, Dinw	330	Petersbu	
Whitfield	, Silas	, Sout	278	St. Luke	
Whitfield	,Solomon K.	, Nans	207	No TWP	
Whitfield	, Tabitha	, Sout	281	St. Luke	
Whitfield	, Tempa	, Sout	269	St. Luke	
Whitfield	, Thomas	, Norf	086	Norfolk	
Whitfield	, William	, Sout	265	St. Luke	
Whitfield	, Willis	, Sout	307	Nottaway	
Whitfield	, Winey	, Sout	250	St. Luke	
Whitfield	, Wright	, Sout	268	St. Luke	

50 named WHITFIELD, Virginia 1860 Census

Whitfield,	Allen,	Sout 170	Whitfield,	Mason,	Sout 137
Whitfield,	Benjamin,	I.W. 402	Whitfield,	Mason,	Sout 143
Whitfield,	Cordy,	Sout 175	Whitfield,	Mila A.,	Nans 571
Whitfield,	Dawson,	Sout 165	Whitfield,	Miliy	Sout 169
Whitfield,	Drucilla,	Sout 142	Whitfield,	N.,	Sout 033
Whitfield,	Edward,	Nans 586	Whitfield,	Nathan,	Sout 169
Whitfield,	Elisha,	Norfolk 112	Whitfield,	Patience,	Dinw 297
Whitfield,	Elizabeth,	Sout 090	Whitfield,	Richard,	Henr 324
Whitfield,	Emeline,	Norfolk 200	Whitfield,	Richard,	Sout 147
Whitfield,	Garrison,	Sout 143	Whitfield,	Richmond,	Nans 592
Whitfield,	H.,	Sout 134	Whitfield,	Wright,	Sout 174
Whitfield,	Henry,	Sout 066	Whitfield,	Robert,	Nans 571
Whitfield,	James,	Sout 596	Whitfield,	Robert H.,	I.W. 434
Whitfield,	James,	Dinw 222	Whitfield,	Roderick,	Dinw 241
Whitfield,	John,	Sout 175	Whitfield,	S.,	Sout 062
Whitfield,	John,	Pwhtn Co 826	Whitfield,	Samuel,	Norf 043
Whitfield,	Lazarus,	Dinw 288	Whitfield,	Sarah,	Alex 803
Whitfield,	Lucy,	Sout 162	Whitfield,	Seymour,	Dinw 297
Whitfield,	Margarett,	I.W. 403	Whitfield,	Susan,	Nans 592
Whitfield,	Martha,	Sout 147	Whitfield,	Thomas,	Alex 803
Whitfield,	Martha,	Sout 165	Whitfield,	Thomas,	Nans 600
Whitfield,	Mary,	Sout 136	Whitfield,	William,	Dinw 191
Whitfield,	Mary,	Sout 148	Whitfield,	William,	Nans 591
Whitfield,	Mary A.,	I.W. 440	Whitfield,	Winny,	Sout 250

Alex - Alexandria Co., VA   Suss - Sussex Co., VA
Rich - Richmond Co., Virginia-town

WHITFIELD FAMILY GROUP. 1860 Census of United States.
State-Virginia / County-Henrico \Town-Richmond, Ward 2, pg. 324
Census dated July 1, 1860. Dwelling 731.

Names	Age	Sex	Birthplace
Richard Whitfield	82	M	England
George Whitfield	35	M	Virginia
Elizabeth A. Jones	40	F	Virginia
Virginia A. Jones	17	F	Virginia
Ella Jones	10	F	Virginia
Richard W. Jones	20	M	Virginia

Richard Whitfield II, the father. George Whitfield, son, and widow Elizabeth Ann Whitfield Jones lived with their father. Elizabeth had three children and they lived there.

Virginia Record

George Thomas Whitfield, born 1842, son of Elisha Whitfield and Nancy Hart. On May 3, 1861, he joined the Army in the Civil War. He served in two Regiments. He was captured by the North and held a prisoner at Newport News until the end of the war. He married (1) Mary Betty Johnson on April 21, 1868. George married (2) Cora Stortz. No issue. George T. was the brother of John William Whitfield, great-grandfather of Samuel Whitfield (b. 1924 VA-d. 1994, VA). George T. joined Capt. William H. Hood's Company (Southampton Grey), Virginia Volunteers at Jerusalem (now Courtland, VA).

VIRGINIA 1870 CENSUS

WHITFIELD W - White persons and B for Black persons.

Federal Census since 1860 list both persons.
Once non-free persons took masters names when freedom from ownership old rules of laws.

1870 Census of Virginia has 42 black persons, and 20 black persons, and 3 mulatto persons.

NAME	AGE	SEX	C	B-PL	LOCALITY	COUNTY	SERIES	ROLL	PAGE
WHITFIELD, ---	8	M	B	VA	GOODSON TWP	WASHINGTON	M593	1681	79
WHITFIELD, Albert P	21	M	W	NC	DANVILLE	PITTSYLVANTA	M593	1671	424
WHITFIELD, Alfred	65	M	B	VA	NEWPORT TWP	ISLE OF WIGH	M593	1657	268
WHITFIELD, Allen	48	M	B	VA	SLEEPY HOLE TWP	NANSEMOND	M593	1664	281
WHITFIELD, Arthur*	36	M	W	VA	CHATHAM P O	PITTSYLVANIA	M593	1671	200
WHITFIELD, Benj	30	M	B	VA	NEWSOMS DEPOT TW	SOUTHAMPTON	M593	1679	272
WHITFIELD, Benj	33	M	B	VA	NEWSOMS DEPOT TW	SOUTHAMPTON	M593	1679	263
WHITFIELD, Benj	40	M	B	VA	NEWSOMS DEPOT TW	SOUTHAMPTON	M593	1679	268
WHITFIELD, Benja	60	M	W	VA	WINDSOR TWP	ISLE OF WIGH	M593	1657	302
WHITFIELD, Benjmn	24	M	B	VA	KEMPSVILLE TWP	PRINCESS ANN	M593	1673	257
WHITFIELD, Bithey	80	F	B	VA	NEWSOMS DEPOT TW	SOUTHAMPTON	M593	1679	251
WHITFIELD, Cordy	56	M	W	VA	NEWSOMS DEPOT TW	SOUTHAMPTON	M593	1679	264
WHITFIELD, Dawson	52	M	B	VA	NEWSOMS DEPOT TW	SOUTHAMPTON	M593	1679	272
WHITFIELD, Dick	60	M	B	VA	1-WD PETERSBURG	DINWIDDIE	M593	1643	198
WHITFIELD, Doctor	32	M	B	VA	TANNERS CRK TWP	NORFOLK	M593	1667	503
WHITFIELD, Edward	42	M	B	VA	SOUTHFIELD TWP	ELIZABETH CI	M593	1644	62
WHITFIELD, Elijah	60	M	B	VA	CEDAR RUN TWP	FAUQUIER	M593	1645	415
WHITFIELD, Eugenia	20	F	W	VA	WHITMELL P O	PITTSYLVANIA	M593	1671	79
WHITFIELD, Frances	33	F	W	VA	HOLY NECK TWP	NANSEMOND	M593	1664	255
WHITFIELD, Francis	25	F	B	VA	NEWSOMS DEPOT TW	SOUTHAMPTON	M593	1679	259
WHITFIELD, Garrison	30	M	B	VA	HOLY NECK TWP	NANSEMOND	M593	1664	261
WHITFIELD, Geo	30	M	B	VA	NEWSOMS DEPOT TW	SOUTHAMPTON	M593	1679	253
WHITFIELD, George T	28	M	W	VA	BERLIN & IVOR TW	SOUTHAMPTON	M593	1679	127
WHITFIELD, Georgianna	14	F	W	NJ	GUILFORD TWP	SURRY	M593	1680	139
WHITFIELD, Gilbert	24	M	B	VA	BOYKINS DEPOT TW	SOUTHAMPTON	M593	1679	162
WHITFIELD, Giles	30	M	B	VA	BOYKINS DEPOT TW	SOUTHAMPTON	M593	1679	170
WHITFIELD, Harold	30	M	M	VA	NEWSOMS DEPOT TW	SOUTHAMPTON	M593	1679	250
WHITFIELD, Henry	23	M	B	VA	TOTARO TWP	BRUNSWICK	M593	1637	109
WHITFIELD, Henry	19	M	B	VA	CEDAR RUN TWP	FAUQUIER	M593	1645	415
WHITFIELD, Jas	39	M	B	VA	1-WD PETERSBURG	DINWIDDIE	M593	1643	199
WHITFIELD, Jennie	60	F	B	VA	BOYKINS DEPOT TW	SOUTHAMPTON	M593	1679	171
WHITFIELD, Jesse	60	M	B	VA	HARDY TWP	ISLE OF WIGH	M593	1657	241
WHITFIELD, Jinnie	10	F	B	VA	TOTARO TWP	BRUNSWICK	M593	1637	172
WHITFIELD, Jno	60	M	W	VA	WINDSOR TWP	ISLE OF WIGH	M593	1657	301
WHITFIELD, Jno F	30	M	W	VA	HUGUENOT TWP	POWHATAN	M593	1672	466
WHITFIELD, John W	30	M	W	VA	BERLIN & IVOR TW	SOUTHAMPTON	M593	1679	115
WHITFIELD, Joseph	15	M	B	VA	SLEEPY HOLE TWP	NANSEMOND	M593	1664	295
WHITFIELD, Judith	17	F	B	VA	CEDAR RUN TWP	FAUQUIER	M593	1645	415
WHITFIELD, Lazarus	25	M	B	VA	6-WD PETERSBURG	DINWIDDIE	M593	1643	370
WHITFIELD, Mac	23	M	B	VA	NEWSOMS DEPOT TW	SOUTHAMPTON	M593	1679	178
WHITFIELD, Marget	50	F	W	VA	HOLY NECK TWP	NANSEMOND	M593	1664	264
WHITFIELD, Martha	60	F	M	VA	1-WD PETERSBURG	DINWIDDIE	M593	1643	212
WHITFIELD, Mary	22	F	B	VA	WARRENTON P O	FAUQUIER	M593	1645	497
WHITFIELD, Mary	49	F	W	VA	HOLY NECK TWP	NANSEMOND	M593	1664	254
WHITFIELD, Matilda	65	F	B	VA	CHUCKATUCK TWP	NANSEMOND	M593	1664	175
WHITFIELD, Milly	60	M	B	VA	NEWSOMS DEPOT TW	SOUTHAMPTON	M593	1679	253
WHITFIELD, Nat	60	M	B	VA	NEWSOMS DEPOT TW	SOUTHAMPTON	M593	1679	262
WHITFIELD, Nellie	55	F	B	VA	BLACKWATER TWP	PRINCE GEORG	M593	1673	164
WHITFIELD, Nichols	43	M	B	VA	BOYKINS DEPOT TW	SOUTHAMPTON	M593	1679	164
WHITFIELD, Patience	62	F	B	VA	6-WD PETERSBURG	DINWIDDIE	M593	1643	379
WHITFIELD, Rebecca	42	F	W	NC	NEWPORT TWP	ISLE OF WIGH	M593	1657	268
WHITFIELD, Richard	34	M	B	VA	HOLY NECK TWP	NANSEMOND	M593	1664	259
WHITFIELD, Richd	62	M	B	VA	1-WD PETERSBURG	DINWIDDIE	M593	1643	222
WHITFIELD, Richmond	34	M	W	VA	HOLY NECK TWP	NANSEMOND	M593	1664	254
WHITFIELD, Roderick	37	M	B	VA	6-WD PETERSBURG	DINWIDDIE	M593	1643	408
WHITFIELD, Sarah	21	F	W	VA	SLEEPY HOLE TWP	NANSEMOND	M593	1664	231
WHITFIELD, Sarah A	52	F	W	VA	WYTHE TWP	ELIZABETH CI	M593	1644	73
WHITFIELD, Stephen	70	M	B	VA	KEMPSVILLE TWP	PRINCESS ANN	M593	1673	257
WHITFIELD, Susan	48	F	W	VA	HOLY NECK TWP	NANSEMOND	M593	1664	244
WHITFIELD, Susan	58	F	W	VA	HOLY NECK TWP	NANSEMOND	M593	1664	254
WHITFIELD, Tho	16	M	B	VA	BOYKINS DEPOT TW	SOUTHAMPTON	M593	1679	169
WHITFIELD, Virginia	15	F	M	VA	SUFFOLK	NANSEMOND	M593	1664	307
WHITFIELD, Watson	57	M	B	VA	TOTARO TWP	BRUNSWICK	M593	1637	109
WHITFIELD, William	20	M	B	VA	JERUSALEM TWP	SOUTHAMPTON	M593	1679	248
WHITFIELD, William E	20	M	W	VA	HOLY NECK TWP	NANSEMOND	M593	1664	243
WHITFIELD, Wright	45	M	B	VA	NEWSOMS DEPOT TW	SOUTHAMPTON	M593	1679	264

RECORDS SEARCH

Isle of Wight Co., VA, Marriages, 1628-1800, Blanche Adams Chapman, 1933. 137 pages. Grooms alphabetized; Brides indexed.

Southampton Co., VA, Marriage Bonds and Ministers Returns, VA, Catherine Lindsay Knorr, 1955. 145 pages. Index to brides; Grooms alphabetized. Three grooms of the name Reuben Whitfield, Benjamin Whitfield, Davis Whitfield (Whitney).

Douglas Register, ed. W. Mac Jones, Goochland, VA., 1928. P 317: Children of Will Whitefield and Mary Towler.

Now as to the D.A.R. members.

   Kathleen Whitefield Towler, Ancestor: William Whitefield (Whitfield). This application includes the Pension record of William Whitefield and names four children - in 1829 soldier stated he reared 12 children. Na. No. 80439, Add Volume 371. Bible and other records corroborating this are in the file cases of the Library. I examined this cursorily and there are twelve pages of the Bible and other records. They are all in the name Whitefield.

   Na. No. 523756, Mrs. Imogene Whitfield Solarek, 1967. Ancestor Thomas Whitfield, Sussex Co., VA. Entire paper copied. There are many inter-lineations which cannot be read on the microfilm copy - evidently census data and so on which the DAR genealogist added as she checked the paper.

   Na. No. 568149, Juniata Montgomery Vietrie Silvey, accepted 1974
      This paper not yet microfilmed. I had one of the employees go to the basement and obtain the book it was in and examined it. All names are given as Whitefield except son of William Whitefield is shown as James Towler Whitefield (Whitfield) - and then from him down Whitefield.

The DAR Patriot Index shows only the surname Whitfield and no Whitefield at all.

William Whitfield is shown marrying Mary Towler.

William Whitfield changed his name to William Whitefield for either taxpayer's purpose or religion.

....Submitted by Mabel Van Dyke Baer of Washington, DC in March 21, 1975. She did a research at the National Daughters of American Revolution Library.

Virginia Record. Copeland Whitfield married Feb. 19, 1791, Catharine Howard, Isle of Wight County, VA.

494

RECORDS

Jean Whitfield married JOHN LETT November 24, 1779, Brunswick Co., VA. Jean was born March 10, 1753, in Virginia, the daughter of Robert Whitfield and Mary Whitfield of the Albemarle Parish of Sussex Co., VA. Also written as Whitefield.

AND

(Martha) Patty Whitfield married James Isham Lett who was born 1747. James Lett I was in the American Revolutionary War. James died in Guilford, NC, November 20, 1828. Patty Whitfield was a head of the family on the 1830 United States federal census of Southampton Co., VA.

....The two records were submitted by Tom Lett of Cape Girardeau, MO, in December 1991.

William Whitfield Alexander was born Rockbridge, VA, a son of John B. Alexander and Ann Whitfield Alexander.

....Submitted June 27, 1987, by Wesley E. Pippenger of Alexandria, VA.

Marriage Bonds and Ministers' Returns of Sussex Co., VA 1754-1810, compiled by Lindsay Knorr, 1952, are published records.

The following records are the ancestry Whitfield family relatives of Robert Edward Whitfield (b. 1921 - d. 1990), resident of Tennessee and California.

January 3, 1793. Benjamin Sturdivant and Elizabeth Whitfield, daughter of Thomas Whitfield. Married January 20 by Rev. Henry Moss. Sur. James Knight, page 70.

August 18, 1804. Harrison Whitfield and Polly Sledge, ward of Mary Sledge. Married 29 August by Rev. James Rogers. Sur. Benjamin Sturdivant, page 115.

December 23, 1801. Wilkins Whitfield and Polly Sturdivant. Sur. Harrison Whitfield, page 104.

DESCENDANTS OF BENJAMIN WHITFIELD AND WIFE

Benjamin Whitfield was born in Virginia. His father's name has not been determined because of the fragmented Virginia colony records. His ancestor came from England. Nansemond County split into two parts, the southern part became Southampton Co., VA. They moved south to North Carolina and the son was named Benjamin Whitfield.

Virginia Record. Louisa Whitfield married Samuel S. Luffingwell before 1800.

JOHN GODWIN WHITFIELD

John G. Whitfield was born 1810 in Isle of Wight Co., VA. John became a church minister and did preaching. John G. married first wife Eugenia Woodhouse who has born in Princess Anne Co., VA. John and wife had six children. They were Anna, Mary, Eugenia, Eveline, Roberta, and Betty. These children were born in Virginia.

John Whitfield left Virginia after 1850 and moved to North Carolina. John married second wife Martha Cofield. They had two children. The family appears on the 1860 census in Halifax Co., NC. The daughter Sarah Whitfield was born in Edgecombe Co., NC. The only son Samuel G. Whitfield was born in Halifax Co., NC. Samuel was not named for father Henry Whitfield but for grandfather Samuel Whitfield. The family remained in Halifax Co., NC.

When Samuel Whitfield was an adult of age forty-one he was living with his half-sisters, Roberta age fifty-one and (Bettie) who was Betty and age fifty. The three adults made their home in Halifax County.

There were many records on John all written as John G. Whitfield. John Godwin Whitfield died in 1879.

In 1992 Jack Strickland of Universal City, Texas, submitted the 1870 Census.

1870 CENSUS OF UNITED STATES					
State: No. Carolina			County: Halifax		
Date of Enumeration: 2 Sept. 1870					
Township: Dalmatia		Page: 385		Color: White Family	
Real Estate Value - 130.00		Personal property value - 300			
	Names	Age	Sex	Occupation, etc.	Birthplace
40	John G. Whitfield	49	M	Preacher	VA
	Martha C. Whitfield	46	F	(Cofield)	NC
	Roberta Whitfield	21	F		VA
	Bethie Whitfield	20	F	(Betty)	VA
	Sarah C. Whitfield	13	F		NC
	Samuel G. Whitfield	11	M		NC

(Dwelling No. — leftmost column for dwelling 40)

VIRGINIA

ALEXANDRIA (L-1). Atmosphere of bygone days is reflected in such venerable places as Gadsby's Tavern, Christ Church, Stabler-Leadbetter Apothecary Shop and the Old Presbyterian Meeting House. All open weekdays. Admissions charged. The George Washington Masonic National Memorial, open daily, overlooks the city.

APPOMATTOX COURT HOUSE NAT. HIST. MON. (K-2). Scene of Lee's surrender to Grant, April 9, 1865. McLean House where terms were drafted, has been restored. Open daily.

BLUE RIDGE PARKWAY (J-2). When completed, scenic parkway will connect Shenandoah and Great Smoky Mountains national parks.

CHARLOTTESVILLE (K-2). Seat of the University of Virginia. Monticello, Thomas Jefferson's home; Ash Lawn, James Monroe's residence, and Michie Tavern, are in the vicinity. Open daily, admissions 75-90c.

FREDERICKSBURG (L-1). Kenmore, home of Washington's sister, Betty Washington Lewis; Mary Washington House, the home of his mother, and James Monroe law office are open daily, admissions 30-60c. The National Park Service maintains four battlefields of the War Between the States in the area. Museum open 9-5. 25c.

GARDEN WEEK. Many privately owned antebellum homes opened to visitors during annual tour last week in April. Details from Garden Club of Virginia, Jefferson Hotel, Richmond, Va.

JAMESTOWN (L-2). Site of first permanent English settlement in America (1607). Old church tower, reconstructed church, graveyard, museum. Daily, 35c.

LEXINGTON (K-2). Home of Washington and Lee University. Tomb of Robert E. Lee is in the Lee Memorial Chapel; chapel open daily. Virginia Military Institute also in Lexington.

MARINERS' MUSEUM near Newport News (L-2). One of the world's largest collections of ship figureheads, models, prints, paintings and other nautical material. Daily, afternoon only on Sun.

MOUNT VERNON (L-1). Washington's beautiful estate overlooking the Potomac River provides a glimpse of the life and times of our first President. Tomb of George and Martha Washington. Open daily. 50c.

NATURAL BRIDGE (K-2) near Lexington. Massive rock arch carrying U.S. 11 has 90-foot span 315 feet above creek in gorge below. Daily, $1.20.

NATURAL TUNNEL. Near Clinchport (H-2). Railroad and creek pass through tunnel. Trail leads to entrance and 700-foot overlook. Daily $1.10.

RICHMOND (L-2). Among the points of interest are the Capitol, the White House of the Confederacy (30c), St. John's Church where Patrick Henry made his "liberty or death" speech, Edgar Allan Poe Shrine (50c) and ornate Maymont with its famous gardens.

SHENANDOAH VALLEY. Historic and scenic area in northwestern Virginia traversed by U.S. 11. Natural Chimneys (K-1), towering monoliths of weathered stone, and many limestone caverns (Crystal, Endless, Grand, Luray, Massanutten, Shenandoah, Skyline) are open to public. Most caverns open daily, admissions charged.

SKYLINE DRIVE. Spectacular scenic highway follows crest of Blue Ridge Mountains for over 100 miles in Shenandoah National Park (K-1). Beautiful views of surrounding region. Toll 25c.

STRATFORD HALL (L-1). Birthplace of Robert E. Lee. Mansion and gardens of this old Colonial plantation have been restored. Open daily, 50c.

TOBACCO. Oldest and largest market in Virginia is in Danville (K-2). Visitors welcome at sales here from mid-September into the Winter and in other Old Belt markets. Guided tours at tobacco plants in Richmond and Petersburg.

VIRGINIA BEACH (M-2). Seaside resort. Old Cape Henry lighthouse stands at site of first landing place of Jamestown colonists in 1607.

1879 Students at the
University of Virginia

Robert Whitfield. Isle of Wight Co. (Robert)VA. B L M.C., C.S. Comm. Atty. Lawyer. D. 1868. Smithfield, VA.

Eugene, 1839. Memphis, TN. Lawyer. Corinth, MS.

Henry Ethelred Whitfield. 1850 Smithfield, VA. Lawyer. Smithfield, VA.

1892 MARRIAGES

Marriage Notices in the Religious Herald with Dates of Publication. Virginia State Archives, Richmond, VA.

Whitfield, Fanny J., d. of Rev. George W. Whitfield, and George L. Wimberly, by Rev. B. Manly, Jr., Oct. 22, 1857.

WHITFIELD, Mary L., and George N. Gardner, by Rev. Jno. R. Watkins, Jan. 4, 1872.

WHITFIELD, W.C., and Minnie M., d. of George H. And M.B. Hening, by Rev. J.H. Longcrier, Nov. 24, 1898.

EARLY EMIGRANTS. Compiled by Peter Wilson Coldham.

First emigrant listed is 1607.

John Whitfield, 1635.

George Whitfield
Clovelly Road, Richmond, VA
Resident in 1966.

WASHINGTON BIRTHPLACE NAT. MON. (L-1). Memorial Mansion on the site is a reproduction of a typical Colonial home. Open daily.

WILLIAMSBURG (L-2). Colonial capital of Virginia, extensively restored. The Capitol, lavishly furnished Governor's Palace and garden, the Public Gaol and several other exhibition buildings and Craft Shops open daily. $2.50-3. "The Common Glory" pageant presented in Summer.

YORKTOWN (L-2). Lord Cornwallis surrendered here in 1781 ending the Revolutionary War. Reconstructed fortifications and Moore House (10c). Open daily.

LETTER FROM THEODORE M. WHITFIELD

Dr. Theodore M. Whitfield, Professor of History and Political Science, became professor emeritus in 1972. Professor at Western Maryland College, Westminster, MD, wrote Vallie Jo Whitfield on October 1, 1974, and gave this information. "I did very little work to gather material for the early Whitfield families. Most of it was by my Aunt Emma Morehead Whitfield or some of our ancestors. I gathered some odds and ends about the Virginia Whitfields other than those in Isle of Wight. I visited Isle of Wight both with my Aunt and since her death. More recently I have studied the Isle of Wight records on microfilm, thanks to the Mormons."

"The most interesting old documents — in duplication — to reach me have been the Tennessee records of a suit brought by Samuel Smith in Knox Co., TN. and a copy of a very dust-covered book in England" which had this record:

'May second 1679. Whitfield Mathew in the Ketch Prosperous for Virginia. David Goff Commander time out.'

"....It is difficult to believe he was an indentured servant serving time in any period close to 1679, and a man of sufficient means to pay later for the passage of 13 persons."

"Mrs. Louise Moseley Heaton of Clarksdale, Mississippi, went to the Public Records Office in London, England and finally went to the Round Room and came on the record." He further mentions in this letter that he had numerous references to General John Wilkins Whitfield. Also that State Archivist in Richmond, VA, was one of his former students, Louis H. Manarin. The letter is signed Yours Truly, Theodore M. Whitfield.

Mathew and Matthew Whitfields

Several men have looked at the list of men to early Virginia of those men named Matthew Whitfield. Several men have speculated as to the parentage of men named Matthew Whitfield who were early residents of Virginia colony. There was no person successful in establishing parentage in England.

EMMA MOREHEAD WHITFIELD was born Dec. 5, 1874, in Greensboro, NC, and died in Richmond, VA, May 6, 1932. Emma attended the Woman's College. Art early caught the attention of Emma M. Whitfield and drew her to its service. She did portraitures and teaching as her profession. However, the death of her sister-in-law changed plans for her. She turned aside to assist her brother James Whitfield to rear three sons. She was active in the Baptist Church and gave time, talents, and means for her church. She was a donor of art drawings.

Into the hands of Emma M. Whitfield came the family records and personal journals of her father and mother. With these as a start she began a search on the Whitfield family to the end of publishing a genealogy of the same. For more than a dozen years she worked in searches on Whitfields. Working unto the end until she took to bed, she glimpsed the task complete for two volumes on Whitfield and Bryan.

WHITFIELD,	CATEY	[MRS]	DAVIS, WILLIAM	MD	07 FEB 1783	ISLE OF WIGHT	VA
WHITFIELD,	COPELAND		HOWARD, CATHERINE	MD	19 FEB 1791	ISLE OF WIGHT	VA
WHITFIELD,	COPELAND JR		WILLS, PAMELIA	MD	23 JAN 1790	ISLE OF WIGHT	VA
WHITFIELD,	DAVIS		FRANCIS, POLLY	MD	25 OCT 1789	SOUTHAMPTON	VA
WHITFIELD,	ELIJAH		WHITFIELD, MARTHA	MD	25 APR 1784	SOUTHAMPTON	VA
WHITFIELD,	ELIZABETH		STURDIVANT, BENJAMIN	MD	03 JAN 1793	SUSSEX	VA
WHITFIELD,	FANNY		KING, JOHN	MD	15 JAN 1798	ISLE OF WIGHT	VA
WHITFIELD,	GEORGE		KINLEY, ELISABETH	MD	20 NOV 1789	NORFOLK	VA
WHITFIELD,	JEMIMA		DRIVER, DOLPHIN	MD	29 OCT 1786	ISLE OF WIGHT	VA
WHITFIELD,	JEMIMA		DRIVER, DOLPHIN	MD	29 OCT 1786	ISLE OF WIGHT	VA
WHITFIELD,	JOHN		WREN, POLLY	MD	15 JAN 1789	SOUTHAMPTON	VA
WHITFIELD,	MARTHA		HOBBS, WILLIAM	MD	21 DEC 1789	SUSSEX	VA
WHITFIELD,	MARTHA		WHITFIELD, ELIJAH	MD	25 APR 1784	SOUTHAMPTON	VA
WHITFIELD,	MARY		DICKINSON, JACOB	MD	03 DEC 1791	ISLE OF WIGHT	VA
WHITFIELD,	MARY		HOBBS, LABURN	MD	21 MAY 1778	SUSSEX	VA
WHITFIELD,	MILLY		BRYANT, MATTHEW	MD	13 AUG 1789	SOUTHAMPTON	VA
WHITFIELD,	NANCY		KNIGHT, WILLIAM	MD	24 DEC 1799	SUSSEX	VA
WHITFIELD,	PETER		HUSK, EADY	MD	18 FEB 1792	SOUTHAMPTON	VA
WHITFIELD,	PRISCILLA		DRIVER, JOSEPH	MD	26 JAN 1790	ISLE OF WIGHT	VA
WHITFIELD,	REUBEN		BARRETT, WINNIFRED	MD	02 AUG 1788	SOUTHAMPTON	VA
WHITFIELD,	REUBEN		WILLSON, PHEBE	MD	23 JUL 1785	SOUTHAMPTON	VA
WHITFIELD,	SALLY		REVELL, HOLLIDAY	MD	25 SEP 1781	SOUTHAMPTON	VA
WHITFIELD,	SAMUEL		NORSWORTHY, FANNY	MD	27 MAR 1783	ISLE OF WIGHT	VA
WHITFIELD,	SEYMOR		WHITEHEAD, PRISCILLA	MD	14 MAR 1798	SOUTHAMPTON	VA
WHITFIELD,	SOLOMON		HOWELL, SALLY	MD	25 JUL 1782	SOUTHAMPTON	VA
WHITFIELD,	WILLIAM		TOMLINSON, ELIZABETH	MD	19 JUL 1782	SUSSEX	VA

....Credit to Liahona Research, 1991.

RECORD

James Morehead Whitfield b. Nov. 7, 1867, Jackson, M , and died Sept. 4, 1936, Richmond, VA. James married Mary Graham Whitfield (1870-1908). They had five children. 1. Mary Whitfield b. 1894-d. 1895. 2. James M. Whitfield b. 1898. 3. Theodore Marshall Whitfield b. 1905-d. March 21, 1991. He was a Professor at Western Maryland College. 4. Philip Whitfield b. 1906. He was a lawyer. 5.William Whitfield died at infancy.

Theodore Whitfield (1834 MS-1894 VA) and Annie Eliza Morehead were the parents of James Morehead and Emma Morehead Whitfield. These families collected the Whitfield materials of family groups and many people assisted. Theodore Marshall Whitfield edited the materials and published the book in 1949."Whitfield, Bryan, Smith and Related Families." All copies of the book sold by 1964.

The Whitfield brothers who were born, lived, and died in Nansemond Co., VA had these families:

EDWARD WHITFIELD (b. 1805)	ROBERT WHITFIELD (b. 1808)	SOLOMON KING WHITFIELD (b. 1815)	
Sarah Jones, wife	Margaret, wife	Susan, wife	
Mila A.	William	Richmond	
Rebecca	John H.	Dempsey	
Robert	Elizabeth	Frances	
Sarah	Emmeline	James L.	
Virginia	Georgiana	Thomas	
Jordan	Edward	Sarah E.	William E.
	Mary	Benjamin	Martha Jane
	Margaret		

CENSUSES OF ELIZABETH COUNTY, VIRGINIA

1810 Census. JOHN WHITFIELD lived in Hampton City limits. He was age range 26-45, wife same age range, 1 boy and 1 girl under age 10. Another male age 26-45 and a female age 16 to 26 were in the house.

1810 Census. SARAH WHITFIELD age range 26 - 45. Three females ages 10-16 and one male age 10-16 range. Sarah Whitfield lived in Williamsburg, York Co., VA.

1820 Census. JOHN WHITFIELD and wife age range 45 and over. 1 male of 10-15 age range. One girl under age 10. Resided in Hampton, VA.

1820 Census. RICHARD WHITFIELD and wife were age range 26-44. 1 female age range 16-25. 1 female under age 10. 1 male under age 10. 1 Family resided in Hampton, Elizabeth City Co., VA.

1820 Census. WILLIAM WHITFIELD and wife age range 26-44. 2 females 16-25. Elizabeth City Co., VA. Not in City limits.

1840 Census. THOMAS WHITFIELD age range 20-30, and 1 female age range 15-20. 1 male slave. Resided in Elizabeth City Co., VA.

1850 and 1860 Censuses. No Whitfield or Whitefield appears on the Censuses of Elizabeth City Co., VA.

1870 Census. SARAH A. WHITFIELD, widow, age 42 with sons. Thomas Whitfield age 20, William Whitfield age 18, and Lenora Whitfield age 15. At Elizabeth City Co. in 1870, the town of Wythe, Virginia, had the post office Hampton.

ISLE OF WIGHT COUNTY, VIRGINIA RECORDS

Copeland Whitfield, Jr. And Parmelia Whitfield witnessed the will of John Jordan, February 15, 1790. (1)

Johannah Scott: Inventory and appraisal of the estate returned by Thomas Whitfield, John Gibbs, John Marony and Nicolas Miller, Sept. 17, 1756. (2)

Peter Ballard, deceased, October 13, 1718. (3)

In June 1975 Joe Whitfield and Ralph Whitfield resided in Williamsburg, VA, and were listed in the telephone book.

References:
(1) Edward Pleasant Valentine Papers, Vol. 2, p 673.
(2) E.P. Valentine Papers, Vol. 3, p 1528.
(3) E.P. Valentine Papers, Vol. 1, p 146.

....Valentine papers searched by Linwood H. Warwick of Charlotesville, VA on April 10, 1976.

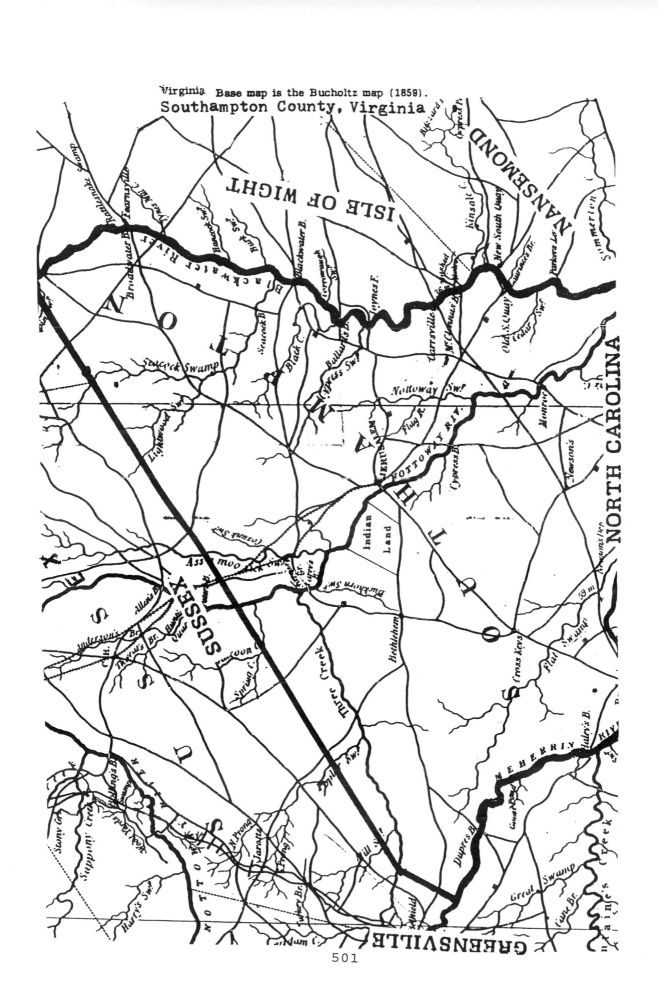

Southampton County, Virginia

Virginia Base map is the Bucholtz map (1859).

1800 WHITFIELDS IN VIRGINIA

Cordell (Cordy) Whitfield, Reuben Whitfield, Benjamin Whitfield were brothers who settled on James River in Isle of Wight Co., VA. They were Quakers with their faith, according to print in the book Makers of America by B.F. Johnson. Volume One. Published 1915 in Washington.

A descendant, Thomas Japheth Whitfield gave the oral history. Thomas has a biography in the book. He is found in the lineage of Cordell Whitfield.

THOMAS JAPHETH WHITFIELD was born January 1, 1852 in Southampton, VA, and died March 26, 1930 in Suffolk, VA. He was named by his mother Lucy Saunders Whitfield for his father. This was her first child and Cordy Clifton's fourth. When an adult Thomas J. married first wife and they later divorced. On December 6, 1887 in Gates Co., NC, Thomas Japheth Whitfield married Annie A. Benton, a native of that county. Annie was the daughter of Seth Benton and Martha Benton. They had children.

1. Davis Andrew Whitfield- He was given a business education.
2. Marjorie Whitfield- She completed Peace College, Raleigh, NC.
3. Gladys Whitfield
4. Quitsna Whitfield
5. Thomas Japheth Whitfield, Jr.
6. Otto Kermit Whitfield

Thomas Japheta Whitfield, Jr. had a son named Fred Whitfield. Fred was age 87 living in 1995 and residing in Richmond, VA. Fred Whitfield was the uncle of Joe Mangham Whitfield who was born in 1917.

Benjamin Whitfield was the oldest son of Reuben and Phebe Wilson Whitfield. Benjamin married Julia Leary and had eight children. Benjamin died between 1840 and 1850 in Virginia.

Reuben Whitfield moved from Virginia to Hertford Co., NC, and was living there in 1810.

Cordy Whitfield married first wife, Nancy Hargrove, and she died after 1844 leaving children Sarah J., William H., and Argil C. Cordy Whitfield married Lucy Jane Saunders who died in 1895. Their children were Thomas Japheth, Susannah G. Bradshaw, Martha Jane Allman, Lucy Ann, John, Cordy, Davis Andrew and his twin Alice M. Cutchin, Charles C. and infant twins who died shortly after birth. Only six of the offspring reached maturity. Four married leaving descendants named Bradshaw, Allman, Cutchin and Whitfield.

References:
1. Virginia Censuses 1820, 1830, 1840. Cordell (Cordy) Clifton Whitfield appears on the Southampton Co., VA, in St. Luke Township. Cordell was misspelled as Gordy on the 1830 census. On the 1840 census Cordy Whitfield and Benjamin Whitfield both heads of families occupied the same dwelling in 1840.
2. Letters of Kathleen Whitfield 1990-1995, Falls Church, VA.
3. Makers of America by B.F. Johnson, 1915.
4. Obituary Newspaper 1895, Suffolk Co., VA. Sketch on Lucy J. Whitfield.

RELATED WHITFIELD MARRIAGES

David Andrew Whitfield married Carre Anding Jan. 1, 1946. Elizabeth Ann Whitfield was born Dec. 19, 1946.

Davis Andrew Whitfield died at Vicksburg Hospital Apr. 15, 1957 in Vicksburg, MS. Davis Whitfield married Annie E. Mangham 1914. 2. Marjorie Whitfield m. Peym Wiesant 1915 or 1916. 3. Thomas Whitfield m. Renginar King 1915 or 1916. 4. Jacell _____ Whitfield md. Raymond Petewany. 5. Gladys Whitfield md. Jimmie Moore. 6. Kermit Whitfield md. _____ .

MARRIAGES
1. David Whitfield md. Elaine Waite, June 28, 1940.
2. Joe M. Whitfield md. Kathleen Lynch Rolleigh Feb. 5, 1943.
3. Elizabeth Whitfield md. H.P. Logan, Jan. 8, 1945.
4. Mr. _____ Whitfield md. a woman native of Scotland. He was killed in active military service in 1965.

PARENTS and CHILDREN
Marjorie Whitfield Wiesant and children. 1. Peym 2. David. 3. Thomas Japheth Whitfield III. Ann Claudia. And children: Fred, Dianne.

Raymond Petewany and Q. W. and children: 1. Peggy 2. Bill 3. Raymond 4. Nancy

FAMILY GROUP
Joe Mangham Whitfield born July 3, 1917, Monroe, LA. He married Feb. 5, 1943, Carrabelle, FL. His father was Davis Andrew Whitfield b. Oct. 27, 1890-d. 1957. His mother was Annie Mangham. Occupation of Joe M. Whitfield was Pilot in United States Air Force, Colonel. Joe md. Kathleen Lynch Rolleigh Feb. 5, 1943. Kathleen was b. Feb. 10, 1921, Monroe, LA. Her father was Louis F. Rolleigh and her mother was Kathleen Lynch. They had children: 1. Kathleen Whitfield b. Nov. 16, 1943, Monroe, LA. She md. Dr. Claude S. Pratt and divorced Oct. 10, 1975. They had child Wentyd Anne Pratt b. May 17, 1972, Monroe, LA. 2. Anne Whitfield b. June 10, 1947, San Francisco, CA and d. July 14, 1970 in San Antonio, TX. 3. Joe Mangham Whitfield, jr. b. Nov. 1, 1948, Greenville, SC. Unmarried. 4. Louis W. Whitfield b. May 3, 1950, Fairfax Co., VA at Fort Belvois. Unmarried. 5. Wesley T. Whitfield b. June 16, 1951, Fairfax Co., VA at Fort Belvois. Unmarried. 6. Susan Marian Whitfield b. Jan. 22, 1954 in Naples, Italy. Susan md. Curtis L. McCabe, May 27, 1989, at Fort Belvoir, VA. Curtis was a Major in the U.S. Army. They had the daughter Megan Kathleen McCabe b. Apr. 4, 1990, Washington D.C.

Thomas Japeth Whitfield I b. 1852-d. 1930. When age 22 Thomas md. (1) Rosa Johnson. They had daughter Laura Whitfield. They were divorced. Thomas Japeth Whitfield went on an expedition to Peru in South America and stayed eight years. Thomas returned to Virginia and md. (2) Annie Benton.

Whitfield Families of Virginia

Between 1990 and 1995 Colonel and Mrs. Joe Mangham Whitfield of Falls Church, Virginia made twenty trips to the southeastern part of the state to research their Whitfield ancestors. The results of their search are a priceless legacy to posterity.

During this period of time Kathleen Whitfield wrote many letters describing their progress to Vallie Jo Whitfield. Through the information printed here readers can learn more of Whitfield history in the "Old Dominion" and particularly Southampton County.

Joe and Kathleen Whitfield located the homestead on Virginia State Route 683 near Sunbeam, formerly Joynersville, that Reuben and Phebe Wilson Whitfield gave to third son Cordell in 1811 when he married Sally Boon. The property passed to Cordy's son Cordy Clifton Whitfield, Joe's great-grandfather, ca. 1839. The family cemetery contains seventeen known burials representing four generations. As was customary, the graves faced the East, and crepe myrtles were planted at the foot of each almost a century ago. Joe Whitfield cleared and fenced the plot and with a son's help is maintaining it.

Not far from the homestead is the 1771 Royal Grant of George III of 198 acres to Benjamin Whitfield, Sr. The plantation was extended and willed to son John in 1787. The codicil added in 1796 the day before Benjamin died was witnessed by Elisha Whitfield, Sr. who lived next door. John and Polly Wren Whitfield and later Bennett K. Whitfield were neighbors. Barnes Methodist Church is a few miles away in the old Piney Grove section, now called Sands.

The home of Cordy Clifton's daughter Sarah Saunders is off State Route 684. It was built in 1800 by Clements Rochelle, the founder of the town of Monroe (1818-1824) on the Nottoway River at Brown's Ferry which he owned. Sarah was murdered by her husband in 1858 leaving young children Mollie and James Bray who were raised by her father. The house is in excellent condition today.

The George Washington Whitfield home is on Route 682 and borders Cordy Clifton's property on Route 683. George was the son of Bennett Kilroy and Mary Anne Hargrove Whitfield. During the Civil War Mary Anne, a widow, ran the family plantation while sons George W. and William H. were in Confederate service.

In 1876 Cordy Clifton gave the old homestead to daughter Susannah Bradshaw and bought Monroe Farm at Brown's Ferry which was birthplace of General William Mahone, the Confederate hero of the Battle of the Crater at Fredericksburg. Cordy Clifton died there in 1888 leaving four plantations to his children. Wife Lucy Jane Saunders died in 1895 in Suffolk, VA where her last remaining son, Thomas Japheth, resided. Lucy outlived all but three of her eleven children.

John William and George Thomas Whitfield, sons of Elisha Jr. and Nancy Hart Whitfield, lived at Berlin. Both served in the Civil War and their father in War of 1812. John William had fifteen children and added to the house built by Elisha off Route 641. George T.'s is on Route 616 between Courtland and Berlin. Both houses are inhabited today.

The Courthouses at Courtland and Isle of Wight and the Municipal Building at Suffolk yielded wills, deeds of land transfers, marriage, birth, death and guardianship records. The Morgan Memorial Library in Suffolk and Walter Cecil Rawls Library in Courtland have extensive genealogical resources that proved helpful. Sycamore Baptist Church Cemetery near Franklin, Mt. Horeb Baptist Church Cemetery near Sunbeam and Cedar Hill Cemetery in Suffolk were all visited by Joe and Kathleen Whitfield for a few moments of reflection and silent tribute to the brave men and women who had forged a livelihood from the sandy loam soil and raised sons and daughters to carry on the Whitfield name.

The five year search was satisfying and rewarding with a wealth of material that had never been gathered before.

APPENDIX ITEM 1
WHITFIELD and WHITEFIELD of SOUTH CAROLINA 1722 to 1825

GEORGE WHITFIELD on the 1800 Census was living in Charleston County, SC. George Whitfield was also on the 1820 Census of Charleston Co., SC.

GEORGE WHITEFIELD MARRIED REBEKAH ____ 22 Jan. 1807 in SC.

GEORGE B. WHITFIELD was on the 1820 Census in Maralboro District, SC. George B. received a court judgement on Bond due and twenty-five hundred and fifty in Estate of William B. Thomas who died and lived at Maralboro County, SC...March 30, 1818 George B. qualified as Executor of the Will of Henry Hodges in Maralboro County Court....March 17, 1820 George B., James R. Ervin and Samuel Townsend entered into Bond $10,000 for Townsend to be Admn. of estate of Margaret Britton....June 21, 1823 Barak Thomas at Maralboro Court versus Gadi Crawford and George B. Whitfield, Judgement.
("South Carolina Magazine of Ancestral Research," Vol. 16, page 14) ("Maralborol County, South Carolina Minutes of the County Court 1785-1799 and Minutes of the Court of Ordinary 1791-1821" by Brent Holcomb. pages 125-126). (SC Dept. of Archives and History ARSMR 980 CAI pages 22653, 22654, 22664, 33347).

JAMES WHITEFIELD 1763 versus Alexander Mackay in Court, SC.
(SC Dept of Archives and History ARSNR980 CAI pages 22653, 22654, 22664, 33327).

JAMES WHITEFIELD in 1778 was Justice of the Peace, Charleston, SC. James witnessed marriages.

JOHN WHITFIELD 1722-1734 had a mortgage for 325 land acres on John's Island. The Island later had a Fort for soldiers.
(SC Dept. of Archives and History. ARSMR980 CAI).

JOHN WHITFIELD 1731-1734 had mortgages and releases to four parcels of land. Release for 60 acres, Charles Town Neck. In 1731-1734 lease and release of 500 land acres at Colleton County, South Carolina. Lease and release for 400 acres in Christ Church Parish. Lease and release of 526 land acres in Berkeley County, SC. John Whitfield had a total of 1,436 land acres. In addition to this John Whitfield and his copartners got a Court Judgement on about 400 acres in 1735-1736 against David Arnett on the 400 acres in Christ Church Parish. In addition, JOHN WHITFIELD had two land grants on Feb. 24, 1736 in Williamsburg Township to 700 acres and 850 acres. On April 9, 1736 John Whitfield had a land grant for 500 acres in Colleton County, SC on April 9, 1736.
(SC Dept. of Archives and History. ARSMR980 CAI page 33348).

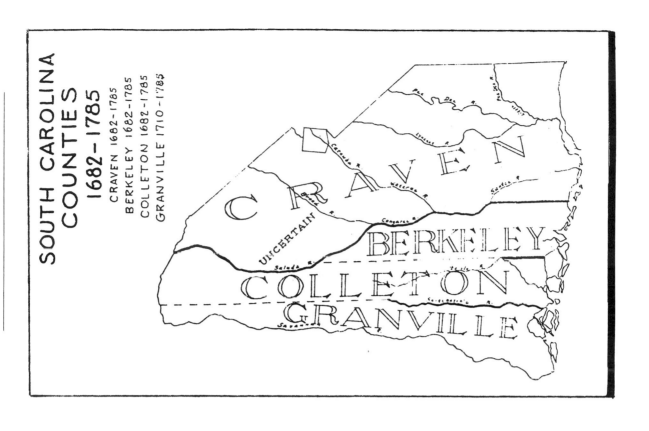

SOUTH CAROLINA COUNTIES 1682–1785

CRAVEN 1682–1785
BERKELEY 1682–1785
COLLETON 1682–1785
GRANVILLE 1710–1785

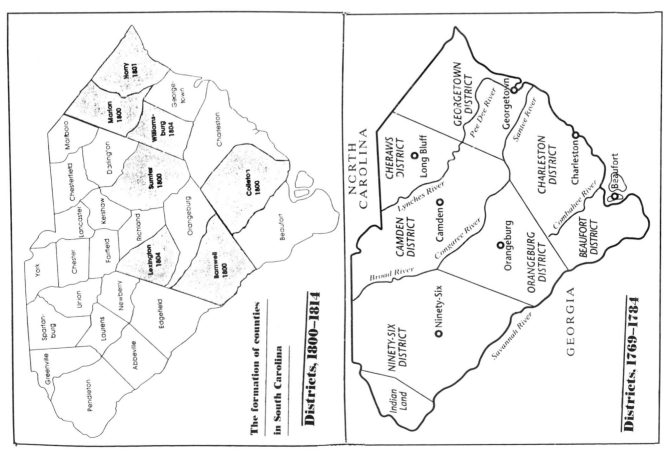

The formation of counties in South Carolina

Districts, 1800–1814

Districts, 1769–1784

APPENDIX ITEM 1
WHITFIELD and WHITEFIELD of SOUTH CAROLINA 1722 to 1825

W. WHITEFIELD (William Whitfield) was witness to marriage of Obadian Hand and Sarah Butler, widow. Jan 10, 1792, Georgetown Co., SC. Obadian Hand was a carpenter.

WILLIAM WHITFIELD 1790 Census Williamsburg Co., SC. One male under age 16, two males over age 16, and eleven slaves. ("History of Williamsburg" by William W. Boddie, p. 169).

WILLIAM WHITFIELD was the son of Luke Whitfield (1719 NC -1767 SC)and Chloe Warren Whitfield. His father in his Will referred to William as one of the younger children. William was born between 1744 to 1758 in Craven County, Carolinas. The Whitfield family moved to Craven Co., South Carolina. William Whitfield had a brother named Luke, Junior who had two plat maps and Deeds along Pee Dee River and Tobys Creek in 1773. William's property was in Cheraws District. In 1800 this land became Chesterfield Co, SC. Court record of July 1, 1803 has Mary Bass and William Whitfield with Citation of Court June 24, 1803 on the Estate and Effects of John Bass late of Tobys Creek deceased. This was Mary Bass deceased husband. On July 1, 1803 Mary Bass and William Whitfield qualified to handle the Estate and Effects.

Brothers Luke, Jr., Benjamin, and William all lived at Pee Dee River in northeast, SC. Benjamin and William supplied food, materials, animal fodder to the Public on command of General Marion in 1781, 1782, 1783 of Marion County, SC. In 1781 he gave 64 weight pork, 13 bushels of corn, 18 eight bacon, 250 bundles of fodder for animals. In 1782 he furnished a use of horse for 17 days. In 1783 he furnished the public with twelve hogs at 640 weight. William's account number 8447 was with name Whitefield.

William Whitfield, Plat for 100 acres on North East side of Pee Dee River, Cheraws District Precinct was surveyed by William Powe, January 5, 1785. William received April 29, 1785 from the State Commission of the Treasury 15:10:10. W. 616 Book O for the account.

William was married and had a family. William died before 1840. ("Marion District Minute Book of the Ordinary 1803"). ("South Carolina Magazine of Ancestral Research", Vol. 9, page 77). (SC Dept. of Archives and History. SC Plat, page 22664. ARSMR 980. CAI, pages 33328, 33329).

WILLIAM WHITFIELD was on the 1800 Census Liberty District in Georgetown County, SC. Liberty District was renamed Marion District, SC. William Whitfield was on the March 29, 1809 Marion District Tax List for 5.45.
("South Carolina Magazine of Ancestral Research", Vol. 8, p. 72).

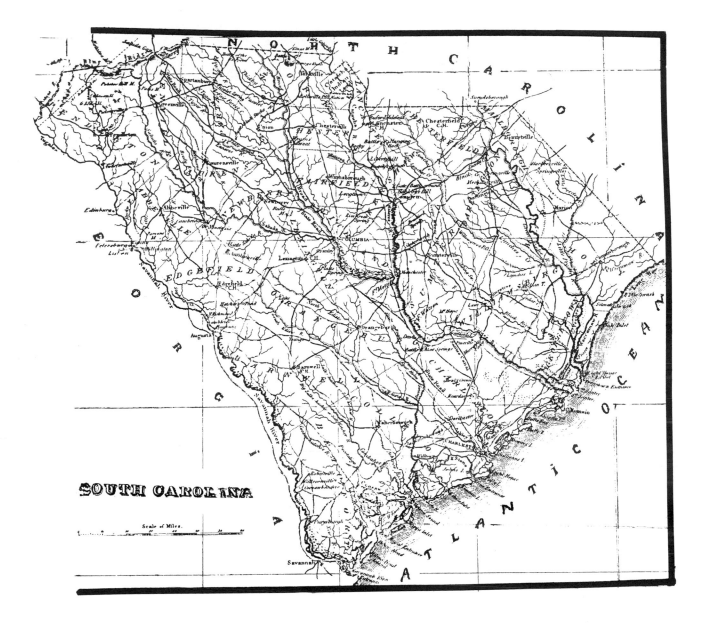

SOUTH CAROLINA

Scale of Miles.

MARION COUNTY, SOUTH CAROLINA

History of the land area of Marion County, SC, began in 1682 with Proprietor Lard Craven. Then the Angelican Church parishes formed. 1767 on Pee Dee River, All Saints Parish formed. To the north Santee River area had St. Stephens Parish. Municipal records kept at Charleston. The Northeast had Gcrogetown District, south of that area was Charleston District, and south of that area was Beaufort District. They all bordered on the Atlantic Ocean. Georgetown District changed to four new named districts in 1783. They were Liberty, Kingston, Williamsburg, Winyhan. They were Districts and Counties in 1785. These short lived named new districts were renamed Marion, 1800. Horry 1801, Williamsburg remained, and Winyhan ceased to exist and was Georgetown. Georgetwon District had Liberty District, a settlement. Liberty was renamed Marion District. Carolinas in 1682 became South Carolina and North Carolina, two colonies.

529

WHITFIELD and WHITEFIELD of SOUTH CAROLINA 1722 to 1825

WILLIAM WHITFIELD was living 1807 in Charleston, SC. William was a mariner sailor on ship <u>Heart of Oak</u> which sailed to the coast of Africa and back to Charleston County, SC. The passengers on this ship were Africans brought to America for slave work. William was unmarried and left a Will at Charleston, SC. (Will Book 1808-1818, Vol. Three, page 57, Charleston Col, SC).

WILLIAM WHITFIELD of Maralboro County, SC. William was at court meetings 1787 to 1819. He served as a Grand Juror in 1787 three times, and once in 1788. Jurors list included Aaron Daniel, Senior from Pee Dee Township, Marion Co., SC. William was a Defendant at Court six times between 1788 and 1797. William was a Plaintiff at Court in 1788, 1789, 1791.

William attended a Legislature meeting in 1797 as a person representing Pee Dee District, SC. At this meeting William Whitfield was elected the new Representative for Maralboro Co., SC. He served one term.

On April 8, 1811 Esquire appeared with his name. He was an Attorney. William had a surveyor to survey two parcels of land 140 acres and 263 acres for Plats in 1812. One parcel 441 acres for a Plat in 1813. One parcel 410 acres in 1819 for a Plat. ("Maralborol County, South Carolina Minutes of the County Court 1785-1799 and Minutes of the Court of Ordinary 1791-1821" by Brent Holcomb. Pages 8,14,35,36,38,49,52,88,103,106,108,109, 111,112,118, 120,121). (SC Dept. of Archives and History. ARSMR 980. SC Plats, p. 22665)

References in Book - MARLBORO County, South Carolina 1785-1799 and Minutes of Court of Ordinary 1791-1821 by W.W. SELLERS, Esquire. Published 1902.

1. George B. Whitefield p. 126 (2)   George B. Whitfield p. 125
2. William Whitefield 88(2), 103, 106, 108, 109, 111, 112, 118, 120, 121.
2. Mathew Whitfield pgs. 5-8, 12, 14, 17, 25, 47, 54, 57, 58, 60
3. William Whitfield pgs. 8(2), 14, 18, 32, 35, 36, 38, 49, 52 55(2), 86, 87

Williamsburg Co., SC Record. C.H. Whitfield. Private soldier in Light Dragoons Troop, Confederate Army of Colonel R.F. Graham, 1861 Pee Dee Legion, Civil War.

Williamsburg District, SC. Cicero Whitfield and Hagard Whitfield were immigrants to North Carolina and moved to South Carolina. Both worked with trees in the field for turpentine. In the 1850's they were called "Tara Heels."

Anderson Co., SC Record. Jeptha Whitfield of Pendleton District, SC, married Vanna Lasina. Theyhad children all born in South Carolina. 1. George b. 1843, 2. John Henry b. 1847, 3. Samuel C. b. 1850, 4. Frances b. 1848, 5. Ada b. 1853, 6. Adaline b. 1841.

LIFE of WILLIAM WHITFIELD (1688-1770) and
ELIZABETH GOODMAN WHITFIELD (1695-1773)

William Whitfield became friend with the Goodman family. A family that had arrived in Virginia several years before and established themselves in Virginia history. To get their own land they moved to Chowan precinct. (2) Henry Goodman had a family. Elizabeth Goodman and William Whitfield developed a relationship and they were married in 1713.

William and Elizabeth lived in the parents' home until William had worked enough in the planting of the fields to get his own right to earning pounds. Elizabeth was a young person about eight years younger than William.

Elizabeth's first child was born 20 May 1715 and was named William. (3)

The colonial government was at Nansemond, there was a Governor and Council for the area. The Court of the territory was at Norfolk, Virginia. The country England owned the colony.

The English Legislature was interested in the property of America and had agreements with Land Companies, and there was colonization. Indian Treaty had to be obtained and once this was done the boats with immigrants began arriving at Albermarle Sound lake in what was called Carolina. Once the English Legislature approved the colonization, the Land Companies were ready to do the work. It did not take long. 1696 to 1723 were the years of development. Then Chowan Precinct appears as North Carolina with its Parish and new government working.

William Whitfield first appeared in public service when he was a witness to land transactions in 1715. He was a witness to a deed on 25th October 1715. Thomas Dyall and his wife Mary were grantors to Henry King of Chowan Precinct. 100 acres. (4) There was a letter of attorney to acknowledge to Richard Moore of Nansemond County, Virginia. Deed of 220 acres. (5) On October 25, 1715 William Whitfield was witness for Thomas Dyall and Mary granting land to Leonard Langstone, 100 acres. (6) On October 25, 1715 William Whitfield was witness for Thomas Dyall land to Richard Moore. (7) William Whitfield was witness for Sarah Odam, her attorney Jacob Odam acknowledges sale to John Callings and Moses Odam on William Branch, Chowan precinct. (8) These land transactions in the form of Deeds that William Whitfield witnessed on October 25, 1715 (Chowan) were in a public meeting place for may others witnessed these deeds with Whitfield. There were attorneys present.

William Whitfield helped to cultivate the agriculture of Henry Goodman and the other swamp farms. William has enough pounds in 1721 to purchase his own land. John Beverley of Chowan Precinct, planter, and Margaret Beverley transfer land to William Whitfield, Planter on 14 October, 1721. 25+ 300 acres. (10) This land was a cultivated crop.

William and Elizabeth were married for nine years. They had a house and farm now in 1721, Chowan Precinct. Elizabeth is kept busy with children, birthing, cooking, and preserving foods. Elizabeth gave births to three children by 1721.

APPENDIX ITEM - 3

LIFE of WILLIAM WHITFIELD (1688-1770) and
ELIZABETH GOODMAN WHITFIELD (1695-1773)

The English Government built the Courthouse at Edenton which lay to the western side of Chowan Precinct. There were some disadvantages to remaining in Chowan Precinct. The swamp land was not the best land for crop cultivation, the watery sloughs and streams had to be avoided, winter freezing weather covered the ground with blankets of snow and a stranger had a hard time knowing the land and the watery areas of this country when land was covered with snow.

Precincts boundary made for all the North Carolina lands and at Bertie Precinct the landowners and freeholders were beginning to complain about the citizens having to travel to Edenton for business. (11)

In 1723 William Whitfield was in Bertie Precinct. He did not do well and did not cultivate some property that he had. He did not improve land as required by law. He did not cultivate this land. He was a poor man. In 1723 William Whitfield was one of 137 jurymen for Bertie. In 1724 William Whitfield was in a lawsuit at court in Bertie. (12)

William got himself into a legal situation. The court wanted case with Judgement of Wirt (identification). William had an attorney named Thomas Jones. William was the defendant. Following videlicet, the court people said "we command you to take body of William Whitfield, and he prayed judgement of writ and may writ abate." Order was to take body of William Whitfield of Bertie Precinct of district Albermarle, planter alias dictus, and court case was continued until March of the year. (13)

"In 1726 the Plaintiff, Francis Pugh versus Benjamin Hill and William Whitfield of Bertie Precinct in custody, and these defendants were to render sum 216 pounds to him owned." (14)

In 1727 Hill and Whitfield took hogs from a farm. Men in need with families. This was settled with defendants getting attachment on properties.

Whitfield came to know the Higher Court very well from 1724 to 1740. He left records in North Carolina and the subjects were Juror, (15), Edenton Courthouse (16), Planter (17), Security (18), Special Bail (19).

Elizabeth Goodman Whitfield born circa 1695. When a child she lived in Virginia. Her family Goodman lived in Chowan Precinct when she married William Whitfield. Elizabeth gave birth from 1715 to 1735 and had ten children. Four sons and six daughters. The sons were William Whitfield (1715-1795), Matthew Whitfield (1717-1789), Luke Whitfield, (born 1719-died 1767), Constantine Whitfield (1728-1797 or 1798), and Daughters Mary Whitfield (born after 1723-d.1791) married John Grady (1710-1787), Patience Whitfield married Edward Outlaw III (1719-d.1759), Elizabeth Whitfield (1746-1790) married (1) Jonathan Taylor and (2) John Beck (d.1790). Sarah Whitfield married Stephen Herring. Charity Whitfield married (1) Frederick O'Daniel (2) Stephen Herring. Margaret Whitfield married (1) Solomon Barfield and (2)_____ Winkfield.

LIFE of WILLIAM WHITFIELD (1688-1770) and ELIZABETH GOODMAN WHITFIELD (1695-1773)

William and Elizabeth of Bertie Precinct had many grandchildren from these children of their own. They have a published genealogy in a book titled <u>Whitfield, Bryan, Smith and Related Families</u> by Emma Morehead Whitfield, edited by Theodore Whitfield and published in 1950 by Times Incorporation of New York, N.Y.

In 1723 the North Carolina Council on April 9th day the Council at Edenton, N.C. heard the petition of William Whitfield praying the recovery of certain lands from one John Holmes being 600 acres "lying at Beverlys on Meherrine."

In 1726 William was Juror in case of Ann Speir charged with murder of Patience Speir. William Whitfield served in several court cases as a juror. Those court cases are listed in the North Carolina Higher Court from 1724-1730, Edenton, North Carolina.

In 1728 in July William was a member of the jury in the case John Lackey. In August 1732 he appointed Thomas Jones his attorney in a case against William Badham, of Edenton, Bertie precinct. February 25, 1739/40 in a list of jurymen for Bertie and Edgecombe precincts are found the name of father and son, William Whitfield. W.L. Saunders compiled ten volumes before 1900 titled <u>Colonial Records of North Carolina II.</u>

After 1740 William Whitfield was a planter. He grew hay and probably wheat and tobacco. His agriculture crops are not listed. He was not a man with cattle. The stock for a farm came later.

Little is written about William Whitfield after 1750 and his death date is not of record. It is written William and Elizabeth in old age were moving to join his son William Whitfield in Rockford, Lenoir County, North Carolina and he was killed by an Indian. His death after many years has been set as 1770. His widow in the Indian accident survived and she died circa 1773 in North Carolina.

Emma Morehead Whitfield wrote in a letter to the South Carolina Historical Society in the 1920's this sentence: "William Whitfield was the son of Matthew Whitfield (son of Baronet Thomas whitfield) knighted in 1604, came from Lancashire, England, in 1670." This was not proven by American researches. It was accepted in the 1970's that William Whitfield was born circa 1688 and came from Lancaster Shire, England, to America.

ILLINOIS RECORD. FIRST FAMILIES OF AMERICA. Edited by Frederick Adams VIRKUS. The Virkus Company of Chicago, IL. In 1930 published a total of 29,000 lineages. Indexes of a quarter of a million names of ancestors. Vols. 1, 2, 3, 4.

APPENDIX   ITEM -

LIFE of WILLIAM WHITFIELD (1688-1770) and
ELIZABETH GOODMAN WHITFIELD (1695-1773)
By Vallie Jo Fox Whitfield
Paper written July 1, 1997, Research June 1997.

REFERENCES

1.   Compendium of American Genealogy by Frederick A. Virkus
Pub. 1968. Direction of Albert N. Marquis.
2.   Virginia Colonial Records. Deeds of Virginia Colony.
Goodman records.
3.   Whitfield, Bryan, Smith and Related Families compiled by
Emma Morehead Whitfield. Edited by Theodore Marshall
Whitfield. Printed by Times Corporation, 1950. New York, N.Y.
Pages 53, 54.
4.   Chowan Precinct, North Carolina 1696-1723 by Margaret
Hofmann. Abstracts of Deeds. Printer, The Roanoke Company,
Weldon, North Carolina. Deed Books by Sections of published
book with number for each deed.
5.   Ibid. Number 770   (Names of other Witnesses are found
6.   Ibid. Number 769.   in the Abstract of Deeds, Chowan
7.   Ibid. Number 771   Precinct. Papers were signed at one
8.   Ibid. Number 1689   Branch)
9.   Colony of North Carolina 1735-1764 by Margaret Hofmann.
Volume One. Land Patents. Whitfield and others had no land
Patent.   Whitfield lands on page 294. Number 4274. Land on
page 294 of book. Number 4774, page 96. Whitfield Line. Number
6907.
10.   Chowan Precinct, North Carolina 1696-1723 by Margaret M.
Hofmann. Genealogical abstracts of Deed Books. Printer, The
Roanoke News Company, Weldon, North Carolina, Deed Book One.
Section of book F Number 1. 1719-1721 Number 596, page 200 of
book.
11.   The Colonial Records of North Carolina. Second Series.
Volume VII. Records of the Executive Council 1766-1734, edited
by Robert Cain. P. 300.
12.   North Carolina Higher Court 1724-1730. Second Series.
Editor, Robert Cain. P. 280. See Index for list of pages.
13.   Ibid. Page 292.
14.   Ibid. Discharge from Recognition, page 280.
15.   Jurors. Pages 434, 441, 501, 505, 509, 511, 515.
16.   Ibid. Courthouse petitioners, Edenton, Chowan Precinct,
North Carolina. Pages 517, 618.
17.   Ibid. Planter. Pages 292, 493.
18.   Ibid. Security. Pages 127, 153.
19.   Ibid. Special Bail. Pages 244, 246, 429, 484. Whitfield
and   Daniel for Jonathan Clift.
20.   Whitfield, Bryan, Smith, and Related Families by Emma
Morehead Whitfield. Whitfield's children. Pages 54 to 63.

Bertie Precinct, NC.
The south line connects
to Virginia border.

From: Moseley Map of North Carolina 1733

Craven County became the center of learning and began the first public school. New Bern, NC was made the capitol. New Bern was the seat of all county courts, the supreme court of Craven, Carteret, Beaufort, Johnston and Hyde counties.

The proprietors in Carolina colony had some survey work done and each knew his territory. The British Governor and citizens on his Council gave away lands. The proprietors died and the Governors had more power and work. Government formed in several areas such as courts, church parishes, Councils of the colony; and the finance tax collecting.

The governor and elected council members in Assembly met at Edenton, Bertie precinct until 1735 and then the Assembly met in New Bern in 1736 and continued until 1749. New Bern had a harbor and shipping. Goods were imported and the local people exported goods.

Royal Governor Gabriel Johnston was sworn in office 1748. The Johnson clan began with land company interest. The three Whitfield brothers, William, Matthew, Luke knew these people. Matthew Whitfield petitioned for 100 acres May 19, 1757 in Johnston County, NC. Luke Whitfield, Senior, petitioned for 100 acres on the same side of the Neuse River May 17, 1754. Luke had petitioned the Governor and Council a total of six times for free land. Luke Whitfield had petitioned in these Council Minutes in years 1743, 1744, 1746, 1751, 1752, 1754. These Whitfield usually did not receive the land they requested in petitions. They had the patents of 1746. (4) (5)

Governor Johnston received a patent notice that the crown had given to "Samuel Johnston 24th September 1741, 3,000 acres in New Hanover county in the N Branch of the N.E. Branch of Cape Fear River, joining the head of a great marsh above the Horse Bluff, a creek, a marsh Whitefield land, and a branch on a small marsh." This means there was a place called new Hanover at Cape Fear River and it is not new Hanover County of the Carolinas and state. Johnson had the Johnston County to colonize and develop.

There were many changes in those counties that was once the property of William, Lord Carven who died in 1711. Then between 1746 and 1756 there were many changes in North Carolina. New generations of people, more immigrants, more black people and those who became free black because of some kind master. The free black persons could never return to his master's property but he could adopt the master's surname. Craven County had 1,300 free black people who worked for food crops and money pounds on farms. The taxes on owners of slaves became very high. There were new buildings and warehouses, and commissions on road building.

New Bern village was on a post road which began at Suffolk, Virginia and came down by Roanoke, Pamlico River, Bath, through New Bern on to South Carolina by New River, Wilmington of New Hanover County, and Brunswick. (6) A cut off this road would lead to Georgetown, South Carolina. Peedee River runs from old Cheraw District to Georgetown near the Atlantic coast in South Carolina. A wagon train of a few people went on this road. There was a man named Luke Whitfield with his family and a few slaves and another man named Matthew Whitfield with his wife Ann Warren Whitfield and their daughter Betsy Whitfield. It was in the summer of 1753 that the wagon trains left Craven County, North Carolina and moved to Craven County, South Carolina. It was to the original land grant of William, Lord Craven they went for more land and a new home.

Matthew and Luke, two brothers and two sisters, Ann and Chloe stayed together. They lived and died on land of Craven County, South Carolina. They would be buried near their farms. Matthew left court and records. He died at Cheraws District. Some of the addresses and descriptions on properties are to the same land site. At first Matthew Whitfield settled along the Santee River and a few years later there were two townships there. On the Northeast in Craven County he settled but in 1754 he was in Court for the Property Lease payment and received a judgement and was placed on the court Roll. Matthew was to get two more property leases to properties and each time he received a court judgement being placed on Judgement Roll or Court. This was called back country where the roots grew wild and sold at a good price.

Luke Whitfield settled at Pee Dee River and not far from the Matthew's few properties he held. He did rice growing and he did fishing on the Pee Dee River. Luke had two male slaves and one female slave with increased of black children.

In 1754-1755 William Whitfield was a militia Captain of sixty-nine men. Constantine Whitfield, his brother, was a member of a Company of soldiers commanded by William Whitfield. (7) They were established at Fort Barnwell which lay in Craven County immediately north of the line separating that county from Jones and Lenoir counties, NC which had been formed from Craven County, N.C. (8)

Luke died in September 1767. The Will Luke left tells about the people on the plantation and some philosophy of Luke, the native of Carolinas. The Will was probated Oct. 21, 1767. The Inventory of Estate took place December 1767. The Estate Inventory has been published.

These families had records but the public records of Georgetown District was destroyed in 1865. These records were burned in Cheraw, South Carolina where they had been sent for safe keeping. There is about fifteen book publications that do include something on the Whitfield from this period of 1754 to 1800 in South Carolina.

REFERENCES

1. The James Sprunt Historical Publications with two histories. The Free Negro In North Carolina by R.H. Taylor and Some Colonial History of North Carolina by Francis H. Cooper. Published 1920.
2. Ibid.
3. The Colonial Records of North Carolina. Second Series Volume Eight. Records of the Executive Council 1735-1754. Edited by Robert J. Cain, page 199.

4.   Ibid. P. 403. (3) Ibid. P 181. (4) Ibid. P. 210 (5) Ibid. P.271 (6) Ibid. P. 285

5.   Colonial Records of North Carolina by William L. Saunders, Ten Volumes.

6.   A History of New Bern and Craven County by Alan D. Watson. Published 1987.

7.   The State Records of North Carolina by Walter Clark, 16 volumes.

8.   John Wheeler, Vol. II, pages 221, 223.

9.   History of Marion County, South Carolina by W.W. Sellers, published 1902.

APPENDIX   ITEM 5

SOUTH CAROLINA

WILL OF LUKE WHITFIELD, SENIOR (1719-1767)

IN THE NAME OF GOD AMEN, I Luke Whitfield, Senior, of Prince George Parish Craven County in the Province of South Carolina being Indisposed of Body but of Perfect mind but knowing that there is nothing so certain as death and nothing so uncertain as the hour thereof. Therefore, I do make and constitute this my last Will and Testament revoking, annulling and make Void all other Wills, Codicils and Gifts in case of death but will that this my Last Will and Testament may stand and in its Force and virtue.

First of all I commit my Spirit to the Hands of Almighty God hoping for a Resurrection at Last day and my Body to the Earth to be decently Interred of my Executors hereafter Named discretion nothing doubting but I shall Receive the same at the Resurrection of the great day and be again Reunited by the Almighty power of God and as for such worldly goods as it please God Almighty to endow me with, I do hereby dispose in manner and form following.

First of all I give and bequeath to my Loving Wife Chloe Whitfield the plantation I now live on and Crop on the said plantation all my Stock of Horses Cattle and Hogs, Sheep and Geese and all my Household Furniture and One Negroe Fellow Named Molbry and my debts being paid out of my Wife Chloe Whitfield's part of my Estate.

Secondly I give and bequeath to my two youngest daughters Penelepe Whitfield and Terecy Whitfield at their Marriage or when they come of age One Negroe Wench Named Vilet and one Negroe girl Named Sal they and their increase from this day to be equally divided with the two Girls Penelepe and Terecy Whitfield. Wife Chloe Whitfield having the Use of the above Named Negroe Wench Vilet her life time.

Thirdly I give and bequeath to my son Luke Whitfield, Junior. One Negroe Boy Named Daniel.

Fourthly I give and bequeath to my daughter Elizabeth Moody One Negroe Boy Named Simon.

Fifthly I give and bequeath the following Negroes One Wench Named Cate, One Girl Named Jude, One Girl Named Dol and One Girl Named Phillis, One Boy Named Tim, one Boy Named Mingo and one Boy Named Tom they and their Increase from this day to be equally divided between my Four Youngest Sons as they come of Age, William Whitfield, Matthew Whitfield, Benjamin Whitfield and Lewis Whitfield.

Sixth I leave my Negroe Fellow Sam to be Sold and the Money arising to be applied to the Use of Schooling the four above Named Boys William Whitfield, Matthew Whitfield, Benjamin Whitfield and Lewis Whitfield. I further Request of my Executors to carry or send the four above Named Boys William

Whitfield, Matthew Whitfield, Benjamin Whitfield and Lewis Whitfield into Dobbs County in North Carolina they and their portion of Negroes to William Whitfield and Constantine Whitfield to have them in their care to raise and their portion of Negroes in their case and to give each Boy his share they come age.

I further Request of my Executors to Send or Carry the above Named Negroe Fellow Sam and to put the money the said Negroe Fellow doth fetch to the use of Schooling the four above Named Boys William Whitfield, Matthew Whitfield and Lewis Whitfield and Benjamin Whitfield and to give William Whitfield and Constantine Whitfield the Liberty of selling the above Named Negroe fellow Sam.

And for the Execution of this my Last Will and Testament and every article and condition therein contain I have and do Constitute Nominate and approve my Dear and beloved Son Luke Whitfield, Junior Executor and my beloved Friend Aaron Daniel, hoping and well assured that they will in conjunction do their utmost Endeavor to have every Article and Clause therein Contained performed and fulfilled. IN WITNESS whereof I have hereunto set my hand and Seal.

Luke Whitfield, Senior (L.S.)

Signed Sealed and published the Twenty Ninth day of August Annoque domini One Thousand Seven Hundred and Sixty Seven.

Matthew Whitfield) Proved by Virtue of a Dedimus directed by
    his   ) His Excellency The R.H.L. Charles Greville
Charles X Moody) Montagu to John Abran Esq. October 21,
    mark   ) 1767 at the same time Qualified Aaron
) Daniel and Luke Whitfield Executor of the
                   said Will.

Recorded in South Carolina Will Book 1767-71. Recorded on page 141.

CICERO WHITFIELD was an immigrant to North Carolina who moved to South Carolina. Cicero was a turpentine worker among trees in 1850s living in Williamsburg County, SC.
("History of Williamsburg" South Carolina by William W. Boddie)

O.H. WHITFIELD. Private soldier in Light Dragoons Troop in Confederate Army of Colonel R.F. Graham 1861 Pee Dee Legion, Civil War. Williamsburg Co., SC.
("History of Williamsburg" by William W. Boddie, p. 358)

HAGARD WHITFIELD was an immigrant to North Carolina and moved to South Carolina. He lived in Williamsburg District, SC. Hagard was a turpentine worker. 1850s Hagard "Tara Heel."
("History of Williamsburg" by William W. Boddie, p. 328).

JEPTHA WHITFIELD of Pendleton District, SC, married Vanna Lasina. They had children all born in South Carolina. GEORGE WHITFIELD b. 1843, JOHN HENRY WHITFIELD b. 1847. SAMUEL C. WHITFIELD b. 1850. FRANCES b. 1848. ADA WHITFIELD b. 1853. ADALINE WHITFIELD b. 1841. The District became Anderson County, SC.

PHILIP WHITFIELD colored soldier between age 21 to 31, unmarried and in Confederate Army service. Philip was a resident of Williamsburg Co., SC. Philip died on June 28, 1918.
("History of Williamsburg," by William W. Boddie, p. 513)

_____
References:
1. History of Williamsburg South Carolina by William W. Boddie, published in 1923. List Whitfield residents in this county.
2. On the 1790 Census of Williamsburg, SC, are Thomas Whitfield and William Whitfield.

MARRIAGE BOOK
Putnam County, Georgia, Book A, 1806-1816. Benjamin Whitfield and Matilda Smith. William B. Traylor and Molsey Whitfield in Book A.
Jackson Co., GA, Book 1806-1860. Marriage of James McClure and Nancy Whitfield.
Laurens Co., GA, Marriages. William Whitfield and Elizabeth Wallace, Sept. 17, 1817.
Samuel Whitfield and Margaret Outlaw, October 13, 1825, married.
....Wills and Marriages were submitted by Mrs. J.D. Goforth of Wichita Falls, TX, in May 1977.

1992 and 1994 California state was in deep recession, about 200,000 to 300,000 people were leaving California for other states, more people left than moved into the state.

California, with local births and migration from 1960 to 1997 gained 410,000 people.

SOUTH CAROLINA
1791–1799

CHERAWS DISTRICT

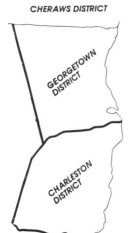

GEORGETOWN DISTRICT

CHARLESTON DISTRICT

Districts, 1800–1814

Marion 1800

Horry 1801

Williamsburg 1804

Georgetown

NORTH CAROLINA

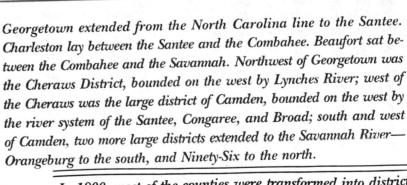

ATLANTIC OCEAN

All Saints 1767

Prince George 1721

Prince Frederick 1734

Black River

St. James Santee 1706

St. Stephens 1734

St. Philip's 1706 & St. Michael's 1751

Santee River

St. Thomas & St. Denis 1706

Christ Church 1706

St. Johns Berkeley 1708

St. James Goose Creek 1706

St. Andrews 1706

St. Matthew's 1768

St. George 1717

St. Paul's 1706

St. John's Colleton 1730

Edisto River

St. Bartholomew's 1706

Combahee River

St. Helena's 1712

Prince William 1745

Coosawhatchie River

St. Luke's 1767

St. Peter's 1747

Proprietary Counties, 1682

COMBAHEE RIVER

SAVANNAH RIVER

CRAVEN

WINYAH BAY

BERKELEY

STONO RIVER

AWENDAW CREEK

COLLETON

later GRANVILLE

ATLANTIC OCEAN

The formation of counties in South Carolina

In 1682, after the first hard years of settlement, the Proprietors ordered three counties laid out. Berkeley County, centering around Charleston, extended from the Stono River on the south to Seewee Creek (present-day Awendaw Creek) where it emptied into Bulls Bay on the north. Craven County lay north of Berkeley, and below Berkeley, Colleton extended to the Combahee River. Later, a fourth county, Granville, was laid out between the Combahee and the Savannah rivers.

Georgetown extended from the North Carolina line to the Santee. Charleston lay between the Santee and the Combahee. Beaufort sat between the Combahee and the Savannah. Northwest of Georgetown was the Cheraws District, bounded on the west by Lynches River; west of the Cheraws was the large district of Camden, bounded on the west by the river system of the Santee, Congaree, and Broad; south and west of Camden, two more large districts extended to the Savannah River— Orangeburg to the south, and Ninety-Six to the north.

In 1800, most of the counties were transformed into districts. Marion District was formed from part of Georgetown, Colleton District from part of Charleston, and Barnwell District from part of Orangeburg. Georgetown yielded Horry District in 1801 and Williamsburg District in 1804.

Throughout the colonial period, the small population and its limited legal needs kept most government, records keeping, and judicial activity confined to the municipal limits of Charleston. Parishes of the established Anglican Church served as election districts, and courts with jurisdiction over the entire colony sat in Charleston.

◄ Parishes of the Anglican Church

William Whitfield received a grant of land in Marlboro County, SC, in 1812, according to original paper with Pulaski County, GA, descendants. William Whitfield had a son, George B. Whitfield, who lived in Marlboro District, SC, until 1821. In 1823 George B. moved to Putnam County, GA. In 1826 he moved to Houston County, GA, and thence to Lowndes County, AL, where he died in 1839. Two sons: 1. Henry Hodges Whitfield 91826 GA-1886 GA) was a Judge. He was in the General Assembly from Pulaski County, GA, in 1836, 1839, and 1840. In the 1850's and later he identified with mercantile interests in the community. He married twice and had 11 children. Henry Hodges Whitfield, Jr. and Birtie Manne had two children: 1. Sarah Whitfield married Morris Lee. 2. Henry Hodges Whitfield, III, married Lois Burch. Henry and Elizabeth and seven other children survived him. 2. William S. Whitfield had a daughter who married Dr. S.W. Taylor and they had two daughters.

_____
Reference:
1. History of Pulaski County (Georgia).
2. Judge Henry Hodges Whitfield of Warren Grice. A biographical sketch, pages 439, 440.

Georgetown County, South Carolina Record.
Georgetown County subdivided and they all lived in Marion County, SC, before it was made a county. They never moved from Pee Dee town, along Pee Dee River. Georgetown District became Georgetown County, Williamsburg County, Marrion County, and Horry County.

Marion Co., SC Record. The General of the Revolutionary War at Marion District was General Francis Marion. W.W. Marion solicited supplies and materials for the Continental Army. Archival documents on the Whitfield and Whitefield claims for supplies were audited with dates 1780 to 1785.

Luke Whitefield was Luke Whitfield born about 1746 in North Carolina and died December 2, 1796 in South Carolina.

Luke Whitefield served as a captain in the St. David's Parish Militia during 1776 under Colonel George G. Powell. Yearbook, 1893. Heitman, p. 588, Council of Safety, February 21, 1774. Served in South Carolina in 1775, 1776, 1777. (See Luke Whitfield ca. 1746 NC-1796 SC). He lived in SC.

Georgetown District, SC. Study was made on George Grabiel Powell who was a Colonel and member of SC Council of Safety. Names of his daughters and marriages were obtained. There was not a daughter named Rachael Powell.

Marriages of Johnston County, NC, 1762-1868 compiled by Brent H. Holcomb, 1985 list these names of Whitfield: Bryant, JARROT, WESLEY and THEOPHILUS.

Marriages performed after publication of banns, had no bond, license, or other public record of marriage required.

SOUTH CAROLINA PROVINCIAL TROOPS 1775

Troop with Captain Luke Whitefield and George Whitefield. George Whitefield wrote a letter to his relatives at Glasgon near 96th District on July 18, 1775.

The Troop officers knew that Captain Luke Whitefield had knowledge of what the Orders were from the Council of Safety at North Carolina. At Fort Charlotte, 96th District, on July 12,1775, Major James Mason sent messenger to Captain Whitefield and the message was, "He in the name of the Council of State take possession of FORT CHARLOTTE." The arms, ammunition and store supplies had keys. Captain Luke Whitefield was without power to do this, and he acquiesced. Captain sent supplies before May 1775. George Whitefield and Louis D. St. Peirre, July 12, 1775, endorsed protest.

Captain Whitefield and his troop moved to Fort Charlotte, 96th District, SC. The return of artillery, ammunition and stores were made to Fort Charlotte, May 20, 1775. Captain Whitefield then sent to the Governor in Charles Town and he lent 500 pounds of gun powder and lent to merchants in Augusta, GA. On return of supplies there was a deficiency of 695 in weight and a few articles not returned. Captain Whitefield promised to make good. List of returns were delivered by Captain Whitefield. Report by Jas (James) Mayson, July 18, 1775, 96th District, SC.

Reference: Alexander S. Salley wrote the book South Carolina Provincial Troops.
1. George Whitefield found on pages 115, 117, 119. George Whitefield on page 8.
2. George Whitefield on p. 5.
3. Captain Luke Whitefield on pages 5, 8, 10, 11.
4. Note. Captain Luke Whitefield was Luke Whitfield (ca. 1746 NC-1796 SC). George Whitefield was a Whitefield from Georgia.

Reference:
Roster of South Caroline Patriots in the American Revolution by Bobby Gilmer Moss, Limestone College, SC. Whitefield appears on page 987. Book published in 1985. Note: Benjamin, Luke, Lewis were Whitfield brothers

---

References:
1. Heitman Year Book. Roster of Soldiers, 1782. Provincial Troops.
2. Heitman Year Book. Revolution Provincial Soldiers, published 1897.
3. Georgia Land Lottery. Land Deeds. Waynesboro, Burke County, GA. Surveyor General's Office, State Archives Atlanta, GA. Books 1786 KKK p. 431. 1789 SSS p. 198. 1796 year YYYY p. 130. 1815 K-5 p. 259.
4. N.S.D.A.R. Frances Jane Mitchell Sproles. National Number 771212. Filed April 5, 1996. Penelope Whitfield Number 760 97.
5 Historical Register of Officers of Continental Army During the War of the Revolution, April 1773 to December 1783.

549

APPENDIX

MISCELLANY RECORDS
California. North Carolina.

California Record. At the close of 1995 year, there were 11.9 million house units in California. 7.4 million (or 62%) were single family units, 3.9 million (33%) were multi-family units, and 600,000 (5%) were mobilehomes.

Mary C. Whitfield born Feb. 3, 1910, Pennsylvania, and died Jan. 5, 1997, at Martinez, CA. Second wife and widow of Roy Whitfield who was an immigrant from England. Roy was an electronic technician at Diablo Valley College, Pleasant Hill, CA. They lived first at Concord and then at Martinez towns. They had one son Roy Whitfield, and he had children by first marriage in Pennsylvania.

North Carolina Record. Letters of Military Resignations (6) Edmund Whitfield, Dec. 6, 1822, Major, Wayne County, NC. Appointed Dec. 24, 1817.

Letter written by Major General James' B. Whitfield, Lenoir County, July 10, 1837. Elected Colonel George Whitfield of Lenoir County, NC, to command the 26th Regiment. Former General N. Washington had resigned. On Feb. 22, 1845, George Whitfield was Brigade General 12th Regiment. James B. Whitfield died Oct. 10, 1841. He was Major General 6th Division.

Nathan Bryan Whitfield, Lenoir County, NC, April 14, 1835. Major General of 6th Division. He resigned determined to become a citizen of another state.

Reference: Abstracts of Letters of Resignations of Militia Officers In North Carolina 1779-1840. Compiled and abstracted by Timothy Kearney. Pgs. 53, 78, 83, 99.

First Land Acquisition by the Brothers. Present were Governor Eleaze Allen, Mat Rown, E. Mosely, R. Moore, W. Forbes (1), Luke Whitfield, Elvy Whitfield, Edward Outlaw, Lewis Powell, John Grady, Moses Powell and 22 other men to share in the land outlay of Henry McCulloh. At Edenton, NC, this meeting was held by Governor's Council, November 8, 1743. (2)

Reference:
(1) North Carolina Council Minutes 1746. Council Journal at Wilmington, NC, November 22, 1746. p 210.
(2) The Colonial Records of North Carolina. (Second Series), Volume VIII. "Records of the Executive Council 1735-1754." Pages 210, 403. Compiler Robert Cain. Petitioners and no land grants. Pgs 141, 181, 202, 271, 285.

Eunice Waller Whitfield (Mrs. Aldine Whitfield) died March 13, 1983. Resident of Mount Olive, North Carolina.

Continued from page 290 Missouri Chapter.

Descendants or relatives of JEFFERSON LAFAYETTE WHITFIELD (b. 1867 TN-1937 MO), resident of Eagle Creek, BENTON County, Tennessee, and STEELE, Missouri. Surnames of spouse who married a Whitfield woman in Tennessee: CURTIS, HORNER, TIPPITT, SYKES. Surnames of a spouse who married a Whitfield man in Tennessee: DOBSON, HUBBS, PRIMM, WARREN.

Surnames of spouse who married a Whitfield woman in Missouri: FLOYD, HOLLOWAY, QUINN, HENLEY, ANDREWS, DYE, THORNTON, TURNER, TSCHANNEN, WELCH.

Surnames of spouse who married a Whitfield man in Missouri: BOSTIC, GORDON, BAILEY, FRANKUM, BERRY, HUFFINE, HERR, JACOB, MATHENIA, VICKERS, WARD, WELCH, WOOTEN.

....Submitted by ILA MAE Whitfield TSCHANNEN (b. 1924-living 1998), (Mrs. KEN BECCHEL TSCHANNEN) of GOLDEN VALLEY, MINNESOTA. All generations of descendants from Jefferson L. Whitfield and LOU ELLEN MATLOCK Whitfield are written in a genealogical lineage.

Whitfield orphans in Henry County, Tennessee, between 1842 and 1849 were named Eliza, Hannah, James, John, Elizabet, Lewis, Needham, Sally, William.

BIBLIOGRAPHY

If it be true that no person has judgement better than the facts, it would seem likewise that no study of collective materials is better than its authentic sources.

This text has public government records and colonial records. It also has private records from people. References in the book cite these sources.

WHITFIELD BOOKS

Whitfield, Emma Morehead, Whitfield, Bryan, Smith and Related Families. Volume One WHITFIELD (New York, 1948).

Whitfield, Vallie Jo Fox, Whitfield History and Genealogy of Tennessee. First Edition (California, 1964). Second Edition (Michigan, 1979). Reprint of Tennessee State Library collective archival records.

Whitfield, Vallie Jo Fox, Virginia History and Whitfield Biographies. (California, 1976).

Baker, Bill R., CATCH THE VISION, (University Press of Mississippi, 1974). The Life of Henry L. Whitfield of Mississippi.

QUINCER, Sheldon B., Whitefield's Sermon Outlines (Michigan, 1956, 1967, 1971). Volume III.

DIRECTORIES

Search public telephone directories of major cities, "Report of Distribution of Surnames in the Social Security File" by H.E.W., BDF Publication #034-75, National Data Banks automotive registations. RESULTS OF HOUSE-TO-HOUSE CANVASSING FOR CROSS STREET DIRECTORIES. The International Business Machine computer project yield. The directory on living Whitfield heads of family and addresses.

Five books with historical and genealogical articles have been written and with a Whitfield Directory and published between 1983 and 1997.

BAYLEY, BERNICE, Whitfield Family Heritage, published 1983. Feature articles "History of Ethnic Origins," "The Meaning and Origin of Heraldry." Genealogical information. 1981 Whitfield Directory.

TAYLOR, SHARON. How to do genealogy and Whitfield Directory published late-1980s.

The World Book of Whitfields, published by Halbert's Company, Bath, Ohio, 1992. Feature articles: Migration Name Origin. Heraldry. How to Discover Your Ancestors. International Registry. Whitfield Directory 1992.

CALDWELL, Amy, Senior Editor, The Whitfield Family Who's Who in America. Published by Family Archive Press, Phoenix, Arizona, 1994. Feature article, Family Groups and History and Whitfield Directory.

The Whitfields In America From 1790 to 1997. Published by Halbert's Company, Bath, Ohio, 1997. Doris P. WHITFIELD. Feature artciels: The Beginnings of America. American Migration West. How to Discover Heritage. Census Enumerations. Place-names. Whitfield Directory, 1997.

INDEXES EXPLANATION NOTES

Many of the names appearing less than ten times are printed individually. However, there may be a single name with all pages where the name is found.

Searches were made for wives names but the marriage records were limited. Fire and flood and disasters had destroyed some records. Laws were developed as late as 1911 before records were made the public requirement. Before the Revolutionary War and Independence the records were property of England. Age destruct records. There are people who work to preserve records of history. The earlier censuses did not list women and children. Courthouses have burned. In 1995 there is more effort put forth to save records than before. 552

INDEXES EXPLANATION NOTES
Consolidated Index and Supplement Index

These indexes are indexes of persons. There are six thousand, nine hundred and fifty names in the book <u>Whitfield Records of United States 1620 to 1995</u>. There are 4,370 Whitfield names, 200 Whitefield names, and 2,380 other surnames allied with Whitfield and Whitefield.

The manuscript was completed May 30, 1997, with 515 pages and indexing for Standard Index was made. Each name in the index was lengthy and would have required 170 pages of Index. To reduce the number of Index pages, a Consolidated Index was made with twenty-nine pages.

Page numbers where names appear were printed in Index. The individual names to Whitfield had a long list of multiple names for there were records on 56 men named Benjamin Whitfield, 26 Bryan, 37 Charles, 159 George, 121 James, 58 Henry, 214 John, 49 Joseph, 30 Lewis, 9 Luke, 31 Matthew, 14 Mathew, 28 Reuben, 30 Richard, 89 Robert, 19 Samuel, 107 Thomas, 105 William.

The most popular male Whitfield first name was John with 214 names. Then 159 men named George, 121 men named James, 107 named Thomas, and 105 William. These large lists were reduced names with all pages where name appeared in text. Also was noted 26 Bryan Whitfields, 37 Charles, 58 Henry, 49 Joseph, 30 Lewis, 9 Luke, 31 Matthew, 14 Mathew, 28 Reuben, 30 Richard, 89 Robert. All these men with surname of Whitfield.

An example how indexing was done with reduction of listing on name William so many time. For a Standard Index William would have been listed 105 times. Consolidation chose printing of William seventy times. There are seventeen first names William Whitfield and fifty-three William who have a second name, easier to identify. Reader must read the pages of William Whitfield records to locate a person; and state postal initial is used to help with William and the residences.

A reader or researcher on a particular William Whitfield will have to read William and record on numbered pages to locate a specific William Whitfield in a state. The book has 850 records for persons which is broken by type-spacing or reference. The Index print sample means the name William Whitfield is printed one time and the state and page numbers are where a William is found.

Example: Indexing was WILLIAM (IL)-196-197 (KY)-208-212 (LA)-218 (MI)-227. This means there are William Whitfields in a state postal in a chapter of book and the page or pages... IL is Illinois for Chapter of book and one person named William appears on two pages 196 and 197. ...KY is Kentucky for Chapter of book and page 208 has three men named William Whitfield. William (1688 -1770)is repeated and two William, Sr. and Jr. appear on one page. There are five men named William Whitfield in the Kentucky chapter..... LA is postal abbreviation for Louisiana. Two named William Whitfield on Census. William (1743-1817). So there are three men named William on LA page 218.... MI for Michigan state. One William on 1850 census of Michigan.... In indexing the word

William is used for IL, KY, LA, MI. Four states with nine men named William Whitfield. Appears in Consolidated Index.

Once a name has been found in the Consolidated Index on indexing line or a collective of pages where a person like William Whitfield (1688-1770) has page numbers grouped, then it is time to turn to the Supplement Index to see if this name has been extended in Appendix or added to end of a page in another chapter other than resident of the person.

Supplement Index was over records collected from June 1996 to December 1997. Many of these records were a study on Whitfield and Whitefield of South Carolina. There are eight pages with supplement Index.

There are thirty-seven pages for the two indexes known here as Consolidated Index and Supplement Index. There are very few pages with heading <u>Miscellany Records</u> and were received late and did not get into an Index. They are pages 547 to 554.

RULES: 1. All persons names are listed in alphabetical order. 2. All page numbers where names appear in book are printed. 3. Women appear with first name under the surname and the married spouse surname is in parenthesis. 4. ____ with surname means the first name is unknown. 5. Index has single surnames and page numbers lead to all other surnames in this Index.

Surnames pertain to Related Families. In-laws, neighbors in deeds, associated people and contributors of both private and public sources. The book has a very interesting and rare listing of surnames and makes records useful for other surnames and searchers. There are Indian tribes names. There are 35 Williams, 16 Winstead all blood kinships, 15 Ruledge, all different persons, 18 Taylor, 22 Smith, 13 Manning. These are mostly single surnames. Some surnames do not carry forth for a hundred years, and this is due to females who married and produced females.

One hundred seventy-three Whitefield names in Consolidated Index. 14 George, 8 John, 7 Thomas, 14 William and 7 Elizabeth. Whitefield was in only a few states: Georgia state, Person County, North Carolina, Tennessee state. The few named Whitefield in other states were migratory people. Whitefield is sometimes used for Whitfield because of the easier pronunciation of the spelling. Pronouncing Whitfield (Witfield) can be uncertain.

Women are different for they have maiden names from the father. A birth name is a blood relationship and fits into a pedigree lineage. Women have married surnames of husbands and they are in-law names. A blood line can be from the father or mother for a lineage. Many names are used in maternal lineages.

Female names appear under Whitfield and if it is a married woman, her maiden name may be spelled out if it is known. In the Index wives are listed under Whitfield. The most popular female name is Mary (231 times in index), 110 named Sarah, 97 named Elizabeth, 80 Martha names, 52 Nancy names, 34 Margaret names. There are 19 Catharine, 21 Frances, 13 Hester, 16 Jane, 26 Julia, 22 Lucy, 23 Rebecca, 15 Rachel, 3 Rachael, 10 Sallie, 23 Sally, 23 Susan, 17 Virginia, and 20 Ann, 12 Anna, 15 Annie. These appear in the Consolidated Index.

CONSOLIDATED INDEX

CONSOLIDATED INDEX

CONSOLIDATED INDEX

CONSOLIDATED INDEX

CONSOLIDATED INDEX

CONSOLIDATED INDEX

CONSOLIDATED INDEX

CONSOLIDATED INDEX

WHITFIELD

Alexander - 67-81-88-167-
191-349-350-386
Alfred - 69-95-294-322-417-
451-453-459-460-461
Alford - 458-460
Alice - 58-59-65-74-76-164-
238-240-332-334-371-453-
460-474-502-507
Allen (AR) 70-71-72-75-76-
81-85-91-457
Allen - 42-58-67-88-144-
162-173-198-461-487-488-
489
Allen - 353-354-356-357
Allis - 292-371
Almiler (Paradise) - 168-169
Almira Augusta - 224
Alston - 235-240
Alvirah M. - 224
Alvis Freeman - 330
Amanda - 47-266-267
Amanda Lou - 256-260-271
Amarillus (Jones) - 328
Amarylis - 332
Amelia - 43-45-46-192-231-
236-238-327-411
America - 259-271-272
Amons - 357
Amy L. Blackburn - 125-
128-471
Amme Keyes - 211-212
Ana Juaris - 140
Andrew - 72-76-81-167-176-
186-188-240-327
Andrew Jackson - 101-103-
112-123
Angela Forte - 394
Angeline - 451-458
Ann - 160-319-326-366-381-
384-478
Ann (Alexander) - 495
Ann Claudia - 503
Ann Clevenger - 397
Ann E. Rickey - 235
Ann Forgeson (Dunn) - 197-
305-306-307-308-309-318
Ann Marie - 227

WHITFIELD

Ann Nicholas Hill - 236
Ann (Powell) - 170
Ann (Smethwick) - 327-384
Ann Staten - 186
Ann Williams - 414
Anna - 292-356-357-361-496
Anna Belle - 142-259-338-
432
Anna - 47-87-89-162-240-
336-415
Anne - 23-185-187-221-236-
404-415-478-492
Annie - 87-89-172-173-391-
465
Annie A. Benton - 222-502
Annie Beatrice - 336
Annie Belle South - 238
Annie E. - 172-173-238
Annie Eliza Morehead - 328-
499
Annie Kate - 238
Annie Lorain - 125-128
Annie Mae - 408
Annie Matilda (Rierdon) -
186
Annie Porch - 280
Annis (Bird) - 329
Ansel - 457
Ansella - 42
Ansil - 42-69-417
Anthony - 201-202-357
Anthony Dyer - 187-237-406
Antinelda - 176
Appley - 173
A.R. - 47
Araminta - 458
Archibald - 353-354-355-363
Archibald Griffin - 321-326
Arie Baker - 430
Aribella Williams - 329
Argil C. - 502-507
Arimetta - 458
Armanda - 172
Armin - 487
Arnold - 336-337-338-353-
354-355
Arpha C. Dyer - 261

WHITFIELD

Artemisia - 344-347-387
Arthur - 69-144-235-244-
245-260-299-415-416-417-
431-489
Artis Odell - 267
Asa - 72-76-92-190-195
Ashbury - 294
Aslet - 53
Ataline Eahly - 328
Atkins - 512
Atkinson - 478-485-486
Attrice Cobb - 337
Audie - 207
Audry - 272
Augusta - 371
Augustin - 140
Augustine - 478
Augustus - 58-60-138-140-
178-211-371
Ava Platts - 110-111
A.W. - 357

B

Barbara - 40-92-133-134-
135-151-327-371-377-384-
465-471
Barnett - 206
Barney - 151-245
Barthena A. - 190
Barthia - 22-24-397
Basil Phifer - 83
Batlemore - 357
Benjamin - 502
Benjamin - 504-506-508-
509-510
Benjamin - 506
Benjamin - 502-506-509-
512
Benjamin - (AL)-39-42-187
(CA)-133-134-135 (FL)-
160-163 (LA)-218
Benjamin - (AR) (NC)-70-
96-99-100-101-102-103-
110-112-120-122-141-196-
197
Benjamin - (GA)-144-160-

Page 562

CONSOLIDATED INDEX

WHITFIELD

163-165-166-167-174-176-
186-187-190-195-381-404-
405-406
Benjamin - (MS)-234-235-
236-239-250-251-266
Benjamin - (MS)-250-251-
255-258-260-263-264-265-
267-341-342-343-347-387-
449
Benjamin - (NC)-258-263-
264-265-266-267-269-328-
339-340-341-342-343-344-
345-346-353-354-387-449
Bejnamin - (NC)-311-315-
319-320-321-323-324-362-
363-365-377-416-417-465
Benjamin - (NC)-327-350-
352-353-355-357-384-495
Benjamin - (RI)-401 (SC)-
402-407
Benjamin - (TN)-431-451-
459-460
Benjamin - (VA)-478-479-
488-489-492
Benjamin Griffin - 321-326
Benjamin Jasper - 336-337
Benjamin Walter - 104-105-
108-209-110-111-113-121
Beatrice - 297-337
Belinda - 460
Belle - 470
Belva J. Wiggins - 125-128
Belvia Long - 119
Bennett Kilroy - 486-504-
509-510
Bernice Sanders - 92
Bertha - 45-119
Bertie L. Manne - 178
Berry - 166-179-323-325-
357
Bessie - 58-59-83-439
Bessie Winifred - 55-218-
236-242
Betsey - 292-377
Betsy - 187-190-329-369-
404
Bettie - 356-361-496

WHITFIELD

Betty - 40-42-91-94-237-
434-478-479-492
Betty (Sturdivant) - 418-428-
447
Beulah (Jones) - 125
Beverley - 160
B.H. - 207-357-461-503
Bill - 503
Billy - 92-272
Birdie - 109-279-282-284-
290
Birtha - 87-89
Bithey - 489
Blackledge - 65
Blake - 97-116-122
Blake Sedgley - 72-82-83
Blanch Garvin - 109
Blanche - 336-338
Blanchard Kearney - 218-
219-220-240-26
Boaz - 39-66
Bobby Cleo - 92
Bolling - 177-186
Brad R. - 242
Bray - 166
Brenda Phifer - 248
Bret - 357
Bryan - (AL)-41-57-238 (FL)
162-163-164 (IL)-196-197-
430 (KY)-207-208-212-214
(NJ)-292
Bryan - (GA)-167-169-176-
188-386
Bryan - (GA)-170-171-172-
406
Bryan - (NC)-233-330-336-
353-355-372-380
Bryan - (NC)-350-351-352-
356-369
Bryan - (TN)-379-414-415-
438-451-452-460
Bryan Watkins - 57-58-60-
211-212
Bryant - (GA)-166-185-188-
206
Bryant - (NC)-354-356-357-
446

WHITFIELD

Bryant - 196-206
B.T. - 357
Bud - 148
Bula May - 279-282-284-290
Burton - 357
Buster - 408
B.V. - 160-163
B.W. - 210-299
Bynum - 42

C

C. - 65-272-460
Caddie B. Powell - 338
Calladona A. Woodcock - 83
Calons - 42
Calvin - 42-83-325
Canaela - 458
Candies Kuhn - 393
Caney - 336
Care - 242
Carla - 338
Carlie Letton - 270-279-282-
283-291
Carl Dean - 72-91-93
Carlton - 408
Carol B. Simpson - 91-93
Caroline - 39-57-66-187-
237-246-406-407-447
Carolyn - 380-439
Carre Anding - 503
Carrie - 109-113-161-209-
215-261-336-469
Carter - 196-197-453-460
Cartie Seltton - 430
Cary - 338
Casey - 76
Catey - 478-485
Catharine - 231-368-458
Catharine Faulk - 192-193
Catharine Dansby - 200-425-
437
Catharine Diggs Hart - 59
Catharine E. (Williams) -
235-379-415
Catharine McDonald - 235
Catharine Ogilvie - 297

CONSOLIDATED INDEX

WHITFIELD

Dorothy Sheaffe - 152-153-157-159
Dorson - 486
Dorthea Evelyn Shuffield - 106
Dove - 60-62
Dovie M. - 89
Doyle - 383
Drew Fitzhugh - 240
Drewsey (Bunn) - 320-326
Drucilla - 488
Drury - 402-407
Druscilla - 407
Duke - 160
Duncan - 251-415
Dundenah - 470
Dwight - 125-127-465-471

E
E. - 173-207-400-453-460-461-463
Eady - 479
Earl - 109-160
Easter - 324
E. B. - 133-134-135
Edatha C. - 457
Egar - 51-119-225-243
Edith - 39-52-55-56-58-59-235-238-245
Edith Jones - 168-328-365-382
Edmond - 235-238-469
Edmund - 235-236-251-252-353
Edna - 87-89-109-238
Edward - 19-22-25-89-209-226-272-292-294-295-357-460-499-508
Edwin - 161-236-240-242-355-457
Edwin - 272-347-350-353-466-567
Edy - 323-324-357
Effa - 458
Effie McCoy - 260
E. H. - 458

WHITFIELD

Eil (Eley) - 191
Eine - 478
E. J. - 460
Ela - 160
Elbert Foster - 119
Eldrige - 357
Eleanor - 52-59-328-338
Elette - 173
Eley - 191
Eli - 67-69-73-74-85-88-95-122-173-191-356-376-417-457-488
Elias - 357-397-398-473-487
Elijah - 191-402-478-489-509
Elisabeth - 315-499
Elisah - 354-356-357-365-453-478-486-488-504-505-507-509-510-512
Eliz - 23-394
Eliza - 23-25-392-458-460
Eliza Ann Felton - 115-116-117-119
Eliza Bell Hatley - 430
Eliza Fledmeak - 74
Eliza (Hays) - 329
Eliza (Hardian) - 327
Eliza (Ledbetter) - 263-266-272
Eliza Nolen - 280
Eliza Nolan - 419
Eliza Richardson - 280
Eliza Stephenson - 329
Elizabeth - 40-57 (AR)-67-88-94-97-101-102-123 (GA)-165-173-179-185 (KY)-212 (MS)-237 (NC) 305-306-307-320-325-326-331-333-334-335-351-353-354-355-356-362-369-370-376-377-392
Elizabeth - (PA)-401 (SC)-402-407 (TN)-453-457-458-460 (TX)-499 (VA)-478-479-487-488
Elizabeth Ann - 503
Elizabeth Ann Kemp - 115-

WHITFIELD

117-119-129
Elizabeth Avis - 327-384
Elizabeth Augusta - 297
Elizabeth Birdwell - 101-102-416
Elizabeth Borden - 401
Elizabeth Bryan - 187
Elizabeth Cooper - 297
Elizabeth Dillinham - 209-215
Elizabeth (Crenshaw) - 509
Elizabeth Denny Dixon - 224
Elizabeth Eason - 417
Elizabeth Easty - 69
Elizabeth Fuller - 330
Elizabeth (Goode) - 187-267-406
Elizabeth Goodman - 40-161-186-187-197-208-212-219-233-240-302-360-368-369-371-373-374-377-414-431-438-450-474
Elizabeth H. - 73-82-161-236
Elizabeth Herrod - 70-96-99-101-102-103-110-112-141-323-416-465
Elizabeth Hively (Yeary) - 81-82-83-95
Elizabeth Jones - 371-379-488
Elizaeth Louise Louge - 438
Elizabeth Lynn - 93
Elizabeth (Marshall) - 330
Elizabeth Matilda (Perryman) - 187
Elizabeth (Metcalf) - 414
Elizabeth Monford - 199
Elizabeth (Montfort) - 333
Elizabeth (Nelson) - 344-347-349-387
Elizabeth (Outlaw) - 328-368-372
Elizabeth (Perry) - 430
Elizabeth Pipkin - 178
Elizabeth C. Ramay - 117
Elizabeth Ryder - 16
Elizabeth (Smith) - 41-438

CONSOLIDATED INDEX

WHITFIELD

Elizabeth (Sturdivant) - 418-447-478-495-499
Elizabeth (Taylor) (Beck) - 197
Elizabeth (Thomas) - 101-103-112-123
Elizabeth Tomlinson - 418-428-499
Elizabeth Wallace - 195
Elizabeth Watkins - 55
Elizabeth (Welch) - 263-266
Elizabeth Wilkerson - 330
Ella - 151-162-186-235-238-336-337-415
Ellen - 113-168-169-292-330-357-380
Elliott Temple - 235
Ellis - 109-113
Elma L. (Duke) - 51
Elsie - 54-465
Ellsworth - 151
Elvina - 357
Emaline - 461
Emanuel - 353-354-357
Emeline - 292-488
Emer Francis - 224
Emily - 47-104-108-109-110-111-113-114-116-172-238-246-263-266-267-458
Emma - 169-173-235-245-337-338-458-460
Emma Morehead - 233-239-498
Emma Williams - 43-45-51-52-192
Emmeline - 499
Emmett - 195
E. P. - 462
E. R. - 406
Ercell Hayes - 438
Ersell - 431
E. S. 166-363
Essex - 392
Essie - 177-186
Estella - 178-236-297
Esther - 415-465-479
Esther Josephine - 298-513

WHITFIELD

Esther (Skinner) - 272
Esther Tennessee - 124-127
Esther Witherspoon Friarson - 65
Ethel - 51-54-133-134-135-245
Etta - 463
Eugene - 83-160-177-186-237-338-443-457
Eugenia - 329-332-408-409-443-460-489-492-496
Eugenie M. Butler - 185
Eula June (Cantley) - 394-395
Euna Mae Price - 248
Eunice - 383-408
Eura Briggance - 281
Eva - 60-133-134-135-178-235-338-462
Evelene - 52
Eveline - 329-356-361-492-496
Evelyn - 57-163
Everitt - 172
Evie E. (Raines) - 261
Exum Philip - 384-474
Ezma - 443

F

Faiford - 357
Famos - 357
Fannie E. (Fitzgerald) - 177
Fanny - 70-103-297-323-392-416-479-497-499
Farrel C. - 106-128
Faye Jessen - 92
F. Drannon - 83
F. E. - 384
Federick - 257
Felicia - 272
Felix - 206-420-457
Felix - 419-420-447-451-457
Ferebe (Persell) - 327-384
F. Eugene - 497
F. G. - 461
Finis - 72-76-92-98-99-104-

WHITFIELD

105-106-110-111
Fitzhugh Ails - 238
F. L. - 207
Flora - 81-116-235-394-469
Florence - 212-240-457
Floyd - 104-108-109-113-114-404
F. M. - 460
Foscue Bryan - 160
Foster - 281
Frances - 53-61-76-82-133-134-135-148-161-179-211-243-244-252-332-345-356-380-407-473-479-485-489-499
Francis - 133-134-135-161-218-236-242-245-246-292-330-356-418-428-447-457-479-489
Frank - 63-161-236-357-460
Franklin - 97-116-122-328-355-356-363
Fred - 151-502-503
Freda Evelyn - 206
Fredrick - 22-173-227-229-231-299-398
Freeda Faye (Powell) - 106-128
Frieson - 245

G

G. - 147-172-461
Gaius - 56-57-59
Garland Quinche - 235-236
Garrison - 488-489
Gary - 148-356-394-395
Gelene Thomas - 92
Gene I. - 133-134-135
General - 357
Geneva - 147
Genevieve Bryan - 248
Genie - 148
Genjamin - 406
Geogania - 355
George - 22-25 (AL)-39-42-60-65-66 (AR)-70-71-77

CONSOLIDATED INDEX

WHITFIELD

(CA)-141-149-151 (FL)
160-163-164 (GA)-165-
167-176-178-186-187-188-
190 (KY)-206 (MD)-224
(MS)-235-236-237-251-
252 (NJ)-292 (NY)-294-
295-296
George (NC)-327-338-356-
381-384-237 (PA)-400-401
(SC)-401-402-404-406-407
(TN)-414-451-453-457-
458-460 (TX)-465-469
(VA)-479-485-486-487-488-
497-504-508-509
George - 351-352-353-354-
355-356-357
George A. P. - 47
George Ann (Kembo) - 192
George B. - 178-179-227-
294-297-387-458
George Benjamin - 344-346-
347
George C. - 357
George Dibrell - 437-474
George Edward - 224
George F. - 227-356
George Hendry - 239
George Herman - 72-92
George Hillman - 236-239
George J. - 133-134-135
George Monroe - 280-281
George M. T. - 172-173
George Nathan - 57
George Neville - 416-443
George O. - 147-510
George S. - 294
George T. - 23
George T. - 462-463-489
George Talbat - 162
George Thomas - 505
George V. - 324
George W. - 42-166-218-
255-327-328-354-368
George Washington - (AR)-
74 (LA)-218 (MS)-248-
259-260
George Washington - 419-

WHITFIELD

437-453-462-463-466-470
George Washington - 505-
510
George William - 59-178
Georgia - 246
Georgia Ann (Kembro) - 43-
45
Georgia H. Brown - 177-186
Georgia R. (Anderson) - 17
Georgia Seago - 248
Georiana - 489-499
Georgianna Whitehurst -
344-345-346-387
Grace (Duncan) - 236
Grace Fonville - 59
Grace Naomi - 92
Grace Valentine Falk - 416-
431
Gracie Alma - 76
Grady - 272
Guilford Griffin - 321-326-
354-355
Gus - 280
G. W. - 335-356
Gerald - 272
Gertrude Jean Baker - 211
Gilbert - 18-19-22-26-380-
479-489
Gibson - 409
Giles - 489
Gladys Fern (Estes) - 72-91
Gladys (Moore) - 502-503
Golden - 279-282-288-290
Gordon - 461
G. P. - 462
Grace - 59-92-236-239-416-
431
Gracie Alma - 76
Grady - 272
Guilford Griffin - 321-326-
354-355
Gus - 280
G. W. - 335-356

H _____
H. - 453-461

WHITFIELD

Hamilton W. - 295
Hampton - 65-187
Hana - 356
Hannable Jewell - 209-215
Hannah - 39-66-179-357-
443-457-479-511
Hansel Kytle - 408
Hardy - 162-236-309-311-
315-322
Hardy Griffin - 321-324-325-
326-352-362-363-279
Harker - 144
Harkless - 357
Harlen Dewayne - 179
Harold - 92-160-299-473-
489
Harriet - 179-197-237-329-
357-415-421-430
Harrison - (TN)-415-418-
419-420-421-422-424-428-
434-443-446-447-449-450-
451-459
Harrison II. - (TX)-419-420-
422-428-434-447-451-460-
463-467-479
Harry - 435
Harvey - 89-91-453-460
Hatch - 234-251-353
Hasty - 328
Hattie Marie Counts - 98-99-
105-110-111
Hattie - 338-383-434
Hartwell - 377
Haynes - 209-479
Haywood - 353-356
Hazard - 355
Healey (Porter) (Jarnagin) -
70-71-72-73-77-84-85
Helen - 238-240-360
Helena - 402-437-474
Henery Alvan - 144
Henreta - 357
Henrietta - 238-357
Henry - 20-22-23-24
Henry - (AL)-42-59-61

WHITFIELD

Henry - (AR)-67-88-117
Henry - (CT)-152-153-155-157-157-158
Henry - (GA)-168-178-187-195
Henry - (KY)-206-212
Henry - (MA)-225
Henry - (MI)-231
Henry - (MS)-237-238-240-249-267-280
Henry - (NY)-297-299
Henry - (NC)-324-328-338-254-355-356-357-372
Henry - (OK)-394-396
Henry - (PA)-397-400
Henry - (SC)-406-408
Henry - (TN)-414-419-434-435-437-448-451-453-458-459-460
Henry - 461-463-474-486-488-489-496-497
Henry Allen - 231
Henry Buchanon - 187-195-237-406
Henry C. - 117-394-396-414
Henry D. - 297-299
Henry E. - 324-448-497
Henry G. - 356
Henry H. - 168-178-355-463
Henry Jones - 59-61
Henry Leo - 338
Henry Lewis - 237-240-249
Henry Lewis - 267-357
Henry Massey - 238
Henry Montague - 238
Henry - Santon - 206
Henry W. - 280-435-451-453
Henry W. - 437-460-461-463
Hepsiba Hatch - 377
Herbert Terra - 415-479
Herman - 212
Hermon Wesley - 279-282-290-430
Herri - 328
Herring - 357
Herron Thompson - 72-76-77-85-91-93-94

WHITFIELD

Herschel - 382
Hervey - 415-443
Hery - 460
Hester - 197-208-212-214-245-374-377
Hester - 408-415-430-512
Hester (Grady) - 328-368-372-374
Hester McKeel - 431
Hesther - 479
Hexy H. Winston - 328
Hicksy - 355
Hinds - 323
Hiram - 357
H. Leland - 144-398
Holliday - 486
Holloway - 295
Horatio Staten - 185-404-406
Houston - 109
Howard - 299
Hubert - 473
Hugh H. - 416-431
Hunter - 240
Hyman Johnson - 328
Hyrus Bury - 166

I

Ida - 53-54-210-246-294-297
Inez - 294-299
Iola May Vaughn - 447
Iolause St. Louisa - 240
Irene - 226-238-240-252
Isaac - 133-134-135-319-324-326-461
Isaac - 329-353-354-356-357-362
Isabella - 133-134-135-218-291-329
Isabelle - 25
Isadore Buffaloe - 235
Isah - 461
Isham - 186-236-479
Isaiah J. - 228-229-231
Israel (Ezaral) - 309-311-315-321-322-363-377
Ivey - 319-321-326-386-480-

WHITFIELD

485-511
Irving Lorenzo - 74
Ivy E. - 166

J

J. - 168-170-177-207-332-356-461-462
Jack - 84-147-357-418-428-441-447-480-486
Jack - 418-419-420-421-428-447
Jackson - 85-357
Jacky Ann - 325
Jacob - 186-299-319-324-326-352-357-362-363-366-377-461-480
Jacobur M. - 439
James - 25 (AL)-55-57-58-59
James - (AR)-89-91
James - (CA)-144-145-147
James - (CT)-152-153-155-156-157-158
James - (FL)-162
James K. - 57-453-460
James L. - 499
James M. - 87-89-239-434-435-451-453-457-459-460-498-499
James Matthew - 104-105-110-111-113
James Monroe - 419-437-463-466
James N. - 357
James P. - 299-510
James Raymond - 431
James Roe - 92
James - (GA)-165-167-185-186-187-188-195
James - (IL)-198
James - (KY)-206-212
James - (LA)-221
James - (MD)-224
James - (MI)-227-231
James - (MS)-236-237-250-251-252
James - (NY)-294-295-299

CONSOLIDATED INDEX

CONSOLIDATED INDEX

WHITFIELD

Margaret Murrell Hackney - 209-215
Margaret N. Henry - 329
Margaret Outlaw - 195
Margaret R. - 163
Margaret (Violett) - 345-347
Margaret Williams - 360
Margaret Winnifred - 337
Margett - 356
Margie Brandon - 238
Margie Brown - 124-127-128-465
Margueritc Gueliesse - 149
Maria - 358-487
Maria C. Breedlove - 177
Mariah - 231-358-487
Marianna Bryan - 59
Marie - 25-198
Marie Stuart - 92
Marie Whitaker - 185
Marie Yvonne Mouton - 218-220
Marina Robbins (Alexander) - 235
Marina Serina McCloud - 71-74-75
Marinda - 454
Marinda - 460
Marion - 249-257
Marion Anderson - 462
Marion Francis - 179
Marion Wiley - 185
Marjorie - 502
Mars - 355
Martha - (AL)-42-47 (AR)-76 (GA)-165-167-169-172-174-187-190-195 (MS)-235
Martha - (NC)-336-337-353-358 (SC)-402-407
Martha - (TN)-431-442-452-454-457-458-459-460
Martha - (AL)-42-47 (AR)-76 (GA)-165-167-169-172-174-187-190-195 (MS)-235 (NC)-336-337-353-358
Martha - (SC)-402-407 (TN)-431-442-452-454-457-458-

WHITFIELD

460
Martha - (TX)-473-487-488-489 (VA)-512
Martha A. - 427-438-454-460
Martha A. Travis - 422-463-466
Martha Ann - 47-172-458
Martha Ann (Charter) - 419-423-424
Martha Ann Marilda Lankford - 257-258-259-261-269-271-272
Martha Ann Snider - 470
Martha Ann (Stallings) - 329
Martha Ann (Williams) - 329
Martha Cofield - 328-361-496
Martha E. - 355
Martha Ella (Watkins) - 259
Martha Eliza - 280
Martha Elizabeth (Eley) - 510
Martha Elizer (Murray) - 280
Martha F. Cagle - 116-469
Martha (Glesson) - 330-384
Martha ("Mattie") H. Bishop - 240
Martha Hathaway - 344-347
Martha Hicks - 47-180
Martha (Hobbs) - 4-447-499
Martha Ida (Powell) - 338
Martha J. - 454
Martha Jane - 499
Martha Jane Allman - 502-507
Martha Jane (Hardy) - 43-48-50-192
Martha Jones Walton - 187
Martha Langkford - 248
Martha L. Cunningham - 281
Martha M. - 185
Martha M. - 406
Martha Matilda - 321-326
Martha Patsey (Milburn) - 327-384
Martha S. - 420-457
Martha (Walker) - 329

WHITFIELD

Martha Whitfield (Whitfield) - 499-509
Martin - 141-206-207
Martin Luther - 35-347
Mary - 22-23 (AL)-39-53-57-66 (AR)-70-82-95-120 (CA)-134-135-147-149 (CT)-153-154-159
Mary - (IL)-196-197 (KY)-212 (MI)-227 (MS)-239-263-266 (MO)-281
Mary - (NC)-305-306-307
Mary - (NC)-309-315-316-317-318-320-322-326-334-363-366-376-377
Mary - (NC)-335-336-360
Mary - (NC)-353-354-355-358
Mary - (NC)-369-372-397
Mary - (RI)-401 (SC)-402 (TN)-415-416-439-452-454-458-460
Mary - (TX)-465 (VA)-481-482-485-487-489-495-496-499-512
Mary A. - 454-460-487
Mary A. ("Polly") - 67-69-85-88-122-179-325-417
Mary Adeline Hicks (Kembro) - 43-44-45-46-180-192
Mary Alice Foscue - 40-59
Mary Allcock - 327
Mary Ann - (AL)-54-56 (AR)-86 (MO)-280 (SC)-407
Mary Ann Brown - 164
Mary Ann (Brown) - 245
Mary Ann Brown - 327
Mary Ann (Bryan) - 327
Mary Ann Fitzhugh - 240
Mary Ann (Gibson) - 409
Mary Ann Hargrove - 505-509-510
Mary Ann (Holmes) - 236-242
Mary Ann Sutton - 328
Mary Taylor - 329
Mary Anne - 238-419-492
Mary Anne (Criddle) (Avery)

WHITFIELD

WHITFIELD

WHITFIELD

WHITFIELD

WHITFIELD

WHITFIELD

N

WHITFIELD

Rosabelle Frances - 218-219-382
Rosal - 87-89
Rose A. - 356
Roselee - 89
Row - 406
Roy - 383-415
Roy E. - 160
Roy F. B. - 345-347
Roy R. - 134-135-149
Roy R. - 147-148-149
Roy Williams - 148-149
Rozelle (Daniel) - 431-441
Ruebin - 362-363
Ruben - (AL)-47 (AR)-112-118-121-122-123-127 (GA)-172-185 (NC)-350 (TX)-461
Ruben Henry - 168-174
Ruben Henry - 192-193
Ruben Willis - 121-124-127-128
Rubin - 352-358
Rubin - 464
Rubin L. - 87-89
Ruby - (AL)-53 (AR)-109 (NC)-338-368
Ruby Arien Beights - 267
Ruby Lee Avery - 46
Ruby Lee (Bynum) - 87-89
Ruby Van - 96-98-107-416
Ruby Wilson Trammell - 162
Rudy Sill - 173
Ruth - 20
Ruth - 437-474
Ruth - 483
Ruth Ferguson - 221
Ruth J. Talley - 394
Ruth Mae McClellan - 92
Ruth Speight (Dunn) - 336

S

S. - 460-461
S. B. - (FL)-160-163 (MS)-245
S. D. - 411
Sadie - 437-474

WHITFIELD

Sallie - (TN)-422 (VA)-483
Sallie Atkinson - 238
Sallie (Bass) - (TN)-420 (TX)-467
Sallie Bourne - 414
Sallie Dillahunty - 419-426
Sallie (Oliver) Hurst - 377
Sallie Perryman - 186
Sallie Vick Stevens -
Sally - (AR)-69 (NC)-358-372 (TN)-417-455-460 (VA)-482-483-499
Sally Ann - 235
Sally Ann (Coggin) - 329
Sally Boon - 504
Sally F. - 355
Sally (Francisco) - 281
Sally Howell - 499-509
Sally Johnston - 327
Sally M. - 457
Sally Martin Ayres - 237
Sally Sarah McKenny - 87-89
Sally (Sarah) (Revell) - 499-509-510-512
Sally Slade - 327-384
Sally Warren - 330
Sally Watkins - 369
Saloma - 132-134
Sampson - (GA)-167-174-176 (OH)-392 (VA)-486
Samuel - 25 (AL)-53 (GA)-167-170-173-174-188-195
Samuel - (MS)-238 (NY)-294-296 (NC)-358 (RI)-401 (VA)-483-496
Samuel Benning - 260
Samuel Bradshaw - 499-512
Samuel C. - 407
Samuel G. - (NC)-361 (VA)-496
Samuel H. - 354
Sanford - 53
Sarah - 15-25 (AL)-42 (GA)-178-185-187 (KY)-212 (MI)-231 (MS)-233
Sarah - (NC)-315-319-326-331-361-363-366-369

WHITFIELD

Sarah - (OK)-394 (SC)-402 (TN)-416-439-454-455-458-460
Sarah - (TX)-46-470 (VA)-491-496-499-500-512
Sarah - 169-170-172
Sarah - 353-356-358
Sarah A. - (CA)-132-134-135 (GA)-173 (NY)-395 (TN)-427-457 (VA)-489-500
Sarah Ann Primore - 141-142-432-463
Sarah Ann Sullivan - 407
Sarah Antoimette Smith - 234
Sarah (Arnett) - 328
Sarah Bennett - 328
Sarah Beth - 93
Sarah (Bourne) - 414
Sarah Burge - 246
Sarah ("Sallie") Bryan (White) - 237
Sarah (Bryant) - 57
Sarah Bryant - 319-326
Sarah C. - (NC)-358 (TN)-458 (VA)-496
Sarah C. (Eley) - 510
Sarah C. (McPhail) (Nichols) - 419-423-424-427-435
Sarah Collier - 414
Sarah Cornelia - 414
Sarah Derenda Byurd - 179
Sarah B. Dibrell - 200-201-202-419-425-437-474
Sarah Dillahunty - 280
Sarah E. - (NC)-393 (VA)-499
Sarah E. Robinson - 263-266
Sarah Elizabeth - (AL)-55 (GA)-178 (OK)-394
Sarah Elizabeth (Crone) - 104-105-110-111-112-113
Sarah Elizabeth Gable - 267
Sarah Elizabeth (Pallet) - 141-143-432
Sarah Elizabeth Phillips - 234
Sarah Elizabeth Wooten - 384
Sarah Estelle (Saley) - 186
Sarah Ellen Robertson - 236

CONSOLIDATED INDEX

WHITFIELD

Sarah Francis Paralee Lackey
- 81
Sarah (Graves) - 245
Sarah Hatch Cmsry - 377
Sarah Haughton (Holmes) - 63
Sarah (Higginson) - 152-153-
159
Sarah Hughes (Jones) - 238
Sarah Hunter Bond - 419-437-
470
Sarah J. - (TX)-463 (VA)-502-
508
Sarah (Jackson) - 185
Sarah Jane - 54
Sarah Jane Cate - 179
Sarah Jones - 499
Sarah Katherine - 238
Sarah Kirkham - 294
Sarah L. - 458
Sarah M. Berry - 435-447
Sarah M. Blackmon - 170-
179-192
Sarah McCarty - 243
Sarah Pierce - 330
Sarah Prigmore - 101-141-
142-432-463
S. (Mrs.) - 22-26
Sarah R. (Bullock) - 177
Sarah Ramus (Rollins) (Gray)
- 101
Sarah (Revell) - 492
Sarah (Rogers) - 172
Sarah Saunders - 504
Sarah Stanford - 47
Sarah (Trigg) - 414
Sarah (Turnipseed) - 187
Sarah Virginia - 280
Sarah Wall - 414
Sarah Watkins - 40-55
Sarah (Weaver) - 333
Sarah Whitley - 329
Sarra - 53
Savanna (Wheeler) - 47
Scott - 461
Scott Harris - 93
S. E. - (KY)-208 (MS)-245
(NC)-356

WHITFIELD

Seaborn Britt - 243-244-245-
246-248
Seaborn Merritt Joseph ("S.
M. Joe") - 245-247
Sebron C. - 245-246
Serena ("Seanea") - 207-208-
214
Serena A. - 67
Seward - 132-134-135
Seymore - 483-485-499-509
Sharack - 392
Sharlott - 460
Sharon (Jones) (Parker) - 465-
471
Sharpee - 485
Sharper - 392
Shellman - (AL)-47 (GA)-
172-195
Shepard - 358
Shirley McPhaul - 186
Sidney Gooding - 327
Sidney N. - 132-134-135
Sidy (Outlaw) - 328
Silas - (AL)-53 (GA)-172-173
(TN)-458 (VA)-487
Silas D. H. - 461
Silas Dillahunty - 280
Silas W. - 408
Silvester - 402
Silvia - 167-174-176
Simon - 295
Simpson - 166
S. M. - 455-460
Smith - 461
Smith C. - 420-457
Smith O. - 427
S. N. - 400
Solomon - 310-315-319-324-
350-358-366
Solomon - 482-485-486-487
Solomon - 499
Solomon - 507
Sookey (Susan) - 317-326
Sophronia - 67-88
Sophronia M. Coon - 419-
420-428-434-452-460-467
Sophronia (Sanders) - 76

WHITFIELD

Sory Stinnett - 210
S. T. - 461
Stacey - 338-368
Starkey - 338-368
Stella - 439
Stella (Roebuck) - 368
Stephen - 489
Stevens - 297
Strather Ray - 210
Stuart E. - 227
Sue Honeaa - 54
Sue Trammell - 398-473
Susan - (MS)-263-266-267
(NC)-354-355-356-358
Susan - (TN)-455-457-458-
460 (TX)-461-473
Susan - (VA)- 483-486-489-
499-507
Susan A. - 337-507-461
Susan Adaline (Bunting) - 338
Susan Agusta - 45-192
Susan B. - 299
Susan (Fort) - 414
Susan M. (Howe) -
Susan Matilda Croom - 235-
236
Susan (Snookey) - 326
Susan Viola Stockstill - 246
Susanna - 22-25 (PA)-397-398
Susanna Brown - 228
Susanna (Churchill) - 229-231
Susanna Shurley - (GA)-179
(NC)-360
Susanna Wilkinson - 258-263-
264-265-266-267-269-341-
342-349-387-449
Susanna Williams - 507
Susannah Bradshaw - 502-505
Susannah Minshew - 330-384
Susannah (Smith) - (GA)-185
(SC)-406
Susanne Demoss Oliphant -
437
Susie - 514
Susie Egerton Cameron - 163
Susie Hix - (AR)-125-127
(TX)-465-471

WHITFIELD

Susie Juanita (Haycock) - 336-337
Susie Northsteen - 394
S. W. - 97-116
Sylvia Marie Sodders - 416-431
Syntha - 454-460

T

T. - 179
Tadd D. 245
Talbert - 97-116-122
Tabitha (Whitaker) - 329
Tabitha - 354-355
Tabitha - 452-460
Tabitha - 487
Talmadge - 272
Tamer - 338
T. B. - 160
Tempa - 487
Temperance - 69-417
Temperance - 336
Temperance Manning - 265-328-344-345-346-355-356-387
Temperance Jones - 331-334-335
Tenada - 459
Tennessee (Ivie) - 76
Teresia Fonveille - 327-384
Terry, Mrs. - 272
Texie Bell - 54
T. F. Faircloth - 328
T. H. - 461
Thad Rack - 392
Thelma Eunice Knight - 416-431
Theodore - 207-235-236-345-347-356
Theodore - 239-499
Theodore Marshall - 224-233-389-498-499
Theodosia (Clagett) - 419-423-424
Theope - 328
Theophilus - 329-354-355-358

WHITFIELD

Theophlulas - 336
Theresa Fornville - 40
Thomas - (CT)-152-153-154-159 (GA)-166-167-176-188-190 (ID)-196 (MI)-228 (NY)-294-299 (NC)-306-330-354-355-356-358-386
Thomas - (OK)-393 (RI)-401 (SC)-401-403-404-405 (TN)-415-422-428-430-452-458-460 (TX)-462-463-465-470 (VA)-483-484-485-487-489-491-493-499-500-510-511
Thomas - 305-306-307-309-318-483-492
Thomas - 149-275-418-419-420-421-424-425-426-428-441-443-447-484-486-490-493-495-508
Thomas - 305-306-307-308-309-483
Thomas - 94-97-179-302-306-308-309-310-311-312-314-315-316-317-318-319-320-322-326-334-364-376-377-469-491
Thomas - 94-97-310-311-315-318-319-323-350-363-376
Thomas - 419-420-428-435-447
Thomas Allen - 382
Thomas Andrews - 83
Thomas Ashley - 344-345-346-347
Thomas B. - 415
Thomas Branon - 165
Thomas C. - 455-460
Thomas Chesterfield - 443
Thomas Cleveland - 278-436-448-455-460
Thomas D. J. - 461
Thomas E. - 188
Thomas H. - 420
Thomas Holmes - 60
Thomas J. - 196-455-461
Thomas Japheth - 222-502-

WHITFIELD

505-507
Thomas Jefferson - 186
Thomas Jefferson- 187
Thomas Jefferson - 149-275-280-426-436-447-448-449-455
Thomas Jefferson - 149-275-280-419-426-447-448-449-451-455-466
Thomas K. - 457
Thomas L. - (TN)-422 (TX)-467
Thomas McCleland - 235
Thomas Nice - 230-231
Thomas Pickett - 63-186
Thomas R. - 511
Thomas Revell - 509
Thomas Revell - 510
Thomas Sledge - 439
Thomas W. - (MI)-227 (TN)-435-455-460 (TX)-466
Thomas Wesley - 278-279-282
Thomas William - 380
Thomas Woodbridge - 225
Thomas Y. - 450-451-457
Thomas Yough - 69-417
T. J. - 458-460
Timothy - (KY)-212 (NC)-372
Tina - (GA)-179 (NC)-325-358
Tinsly - 402
T. L. - 177
Tobias - 21
Toby -
Tom - 160
Tony - 160
Travis - (MS)-272 (NC)-329 (TN)-457
Trim - 358
Truman - 147
Truman Arthur - 179
Tucker - 167-191
Turner - 358
Turner Watkins - 234
T. V. - 452
T. W. - 461

WHITFIELD

T. W. - 462

V

Valentine - 358
Valerie Elaine Vaughn - 93
Vallie Jo Fox - 1-95-123-131-
145-146-147-148-149-150-
316- -- -382-411-412-427-
436-437-441-444-447-493-
498-502-504
Vanna Lasinana - 404-407
Varsh - 407
Vassena - 160
Veatrice (Thornton) - 426
Velma - 151
Velma Marie (Britton) - 368
Vera Woods - 260
Verta Lee - 240
Vickie Faye Hill - 107
Victoria O. Meins - 186-236
Vina - 323
Viney - 450-451
Viney - 485
Viney Adline - 105-110-111
Vinney - 461
Viola (Spencer) - 345-347
Virgil - 358
Virginia - (AL)-65 (TN)-455-
460 (VA)-489-499
Virginia (Braidwood) - 238
Virginia C. Thally - 329
Virginia C. (Cliffe) - 419-424-
435
Virginia C. (Wade) - 335
Virginia Dare (Bento) - 336-
337-338
Virginia Dibrell - 60-65
Virginia Lenora Goodwin - 63
Virginia (Parker) - 470
Virginia Pope - 382
Virginia (Quinn) - 426-430-
434
Virginia Ray (Johnson) - 196-
209-214-215
Viola (Bullock) - 344-347
Vivian Gale Brewer - 441

WHITFIELD

Vivean Oneeda (Beebe) - 106-
128
V. L. - 160
Vohilion Carolinus - 240

W

W. - 358-393
W. A. - 160-163-218
Wade - 59-65-147
Walter - 227-248-262-294-
358-470
Wannie (Schmidt) - 109
Washington - 358
Watson - 489
W. C. - 272-497
W. E. - 358-461
Wendy A. - 338-368
Wesley - 330-484
Westley - 358
W. H. - 358-455
Whitmale - 101-103-112-123
Wilbert J. - 132-134-135
Wiley - 326
Wiley - 352-358
Wiley - 362
Wiley S. - 196
Wiley William - 97-115-116-
117
Wilkins - 149-200-273-275-
415-418-420-423-424-425-
426-428-437-439-447-450-
451-452-457-484-495
Wilkins - 452-458-461
Wilkins Cliffe - 447
Wilkins C. - 447
Wilkinson - 484-485-486
Wilkinson - 508-510-511
Will Roger - 209
Will White - 249
Willet M. - 132-134-135
Willey - 326
Willey (Baines) - 323-329
Willfreds A. Michell - 247
William - 18-19-21-22-23-25
William - (AL)-40-41-42

WHITFIELD

(AR)-40-41-42-74-88-95-
101-103-112-120
William - (CA)-132-134-135-
141-142-144 (FL)-160-163-
164-174-179-185-187-188-
191-195
William - (IL)-196-197 (KY)-
208-212 (LA)-218 (MI)-227

William - (MS)-234-239-244-
250-251-252 (MO)-280-281
(NH)-292 (NY)-294-295-299
William - (NC)-233-301-320-
326-335
William - (NC)-302-368-369-
370-374
William - (NC)-311-315-317-
320-334-335
William - (NC)-323-324-326
William - (NC)-325-327-328-
329
William - (NC)-218-368-369-
374-377-380-438
William - (NC)-300-330-331-
333-328
William - (NC)-350-352-353-
354-355-356
William - (NC)-358-360-362-
363-365
William - (NC)-377-378-386
William - (NC)-41-55-96-98-
99-106-107-128-160-161-
186-187-197-208-212-219-
233-240-246-302-360-368-
369-370-371-373-374-414-
431-438-450-474
William - (VA)-473-494-513
William A. - 172-235-252-
330-256-360
William Airey - 238
William Alexander - 218-219-
220
William Andrew - 394-395
William Anthony - 338-368
William ("Joseph") Aultman
-247
William B. - 67-88-356-378

WHITFIELD

WHITFIELD

WHITFIELD

Y

Z

SURNAMES *(continued)*

W

CONSOLIDATED INDEX

SURNAME

SUPPLEMENT INDEX

SURNAME

SURNAME

SUPPLEMENT INDEX

SUPPLEMENT INDEX

SUPPLEMENT INDEX

WHITFIELD

Ralph - 205
Ralph Wilson - 460
Rebecca - 462
Rebecca - 523
Rebecca Bonnell - 181
Rebecca Jane (Newman) - 206
Rebecca (Lazarus) - 526
Rebecca Williams - 506
Rebekah - 520
Reuben - 359
Reuben - 365
Reuben - 544
Reuben - 241
Rubin - 96
Rhoda - 527
Richard - 526
Robert - XIX (19)-XXI (22)
Robert - 241-544
Robert - 515
Robert - 526
Robert - 526
Robert Asbury - 368-391
Robert Edward - 147-216-
  438-449-460
Robert Latham - 368
Robert Lue - 391
Robert Wilson - 492
Rosa Johnson - 503
Roy - 147
Roy R. - 216
Rozelle (Daniel) - 460
Ruben - 116
Ruby - 368
Rueben - 467

S

Salle - 460
Sallie (Bass) - 420
Sallie J. - 359
Sally - 359
Samson - 181
Samuel - 488
Samuel - 522
Samuel - 492
Samuel C. - 407-530
Sarah - 126

WHITFIELD

Sarah - 107-241-544
Sarah - 359-460
Sarah B. Dibrell - 86
Sarah Bryan - 177
Sarah (Bryan) - 544
Sarah Catherine (Durbin) -
  206
Sarah F. - 359
Sarah (Herring) - 532
Silas - 192-460
Sophronia Conn - 462
Solomon - 359
Stacey - 368
Starkey - 368
Stella (Roe Buck) - 368
Sterling - 107
Sterling T. - 107-241
Susanna De Moss Oliphant -
  87
Susan M. (Howe) - 252
Susan Mariam (McCabe) -
  514
Susan Marian - 503

T

Tabithy - 359
Tara Jean - 460
Terecy - 322-405-474-523-
  527-540
Thedore - 513
Theodore Marshall - 374-533
Thomas - 126
Thomas - 181
Thomas - 358
Thomas - 359
Thomas - 462
Tomas - 527
Thomas - 527
Thomas - 527
Thomas - 533
Thomas Cleveland -4 60
Thomas De - XXII (22)
Thomas Japeth - 503
Thomas Jefferson - 460
Thomas Jordon - 261-527
Thomas Tinsley - 195

WHITFIELD

Tina - 359
Trim - 359
Tcker - 107-241
Turner - 359

U

V

Valentine - 359
Vallie Jo Fox - 147-216-287-
  449-515
Vanna Lasina - 53
Velma Marie (Britton) - 368
Virgil - 359

W

Walter - 359
Wanie R. - 96-106
Washington - 359
W.B. - 359
Weldon Jasper - 391
Wnde Gail - 391
Wendy A. - 368
Wesley T. - 503
Wesley T. - 514
Westley - 359
W.H. - 359
Whitfield - 342-516
Whitmon - 127
W.L. - 359
Wilkins - 87-460
William - 90
William - 357
William - 359
William - 322-352
William - 314-334-344-383-
  531-532-533-536-537-538-
  539
William - 206-374-476-525-
  530-531-532-536-537
William - 322-405-519-523-
  528-541
William - 460
William - 362
William - 506

SUPPLEMENT INDEX

WHITFIELD

SURNAMES (Continued)

W

Y

```
WHITFIELD

AND

WHITEFIELD
```

NOTES